W9-AFX-326

New Challenges for Defense Planning

Rethinking How Much Is Enough

Edited by Paul K. Davis

RAND

The writing of this book was sponsored by RAND using its own research funds.

Library of Congress Cataloging in Publication Data

New challenges for defense planning : rethinking how much is enough
/ edited by Paul K. Davis.
    p.   cm.
"RAND Corporation–supported research."
"MR-400-RC."
Includes bibliographical references.
ISBN 0-8330-1527-3
    1. Military planning—United States. 2. United States—Military
policy. 3. World politics—1989–   I. Davis, Paul K., 1943–
II. RAND.
U153.N48   1994
355´.03—dc20   94-9770
                                           CIP

RAND is a nonprofit institution that seeks to improve public policy through
research and analysis. RAND's publications do not necessarily reflect the
opinions or policies of its research sponsors.

Cover design: Peter Soriano
Published 1994 by RAND
1700 Main Street, P.O. Box 2138, Santa Monica, CA 90407-2138
To order RAND documents or to obtain additional information, contact
Distribution Services: Telephone: (310) 451-7002; Fax: (310) 451-6915;
Internet: order@rand.org.

PREFACE

This book contains 23 papers describing RAND studies of defense planning issues for the post–Cold War era. The rethinking of defense planning will go on for some years, but many of the ideas and conclusions presented here will continue to be quite germane. Some of the work discussed has already been influential, either in helping policymakers to shape the terms of debate or in providing information that contributed to choices made under uncertainty. While I have made no attempt to develop a monolithic "RAND view" on the many challenges defense planners face, readers will see in this collection themes and methodologies characteristic of RAND's recent defense-planning work. I hope these will be of interest to a broad class of individuals in government, military service, universities, and industry. My intention has been to seek papers that are problem-focused and interesting, that describe enough of the research and analytic reasoning to convey a sense of how the studies were conducted, and that should be useful for some years, despite also being topical.

Most of the research underlying the papers in this book was accomplished in RAND's three national-security federally funded research and development centers (FFRDCs): Project AIR FORCE, the Arroyo Center, and the National Defense Research Institute (NDRI), which are sponsored by the Air Force, the Army, and the Office of the Secretary of Defense and the Joint Staff, respectively. The book itself was organized in RAND's Defense and Technology Planning Department and was made possible with substantial corporate funds and through the auspices of the RAND Graduate School of Policy Studies. RAND's national-security divisions also contributed research-support funds to cover some of the administrative expenses.

Paul K. Davis
Corporate Research Manager
Defense and Technology Planning

CONTENTS

ACKNOWLEDGMENTS

Producing a book like this depends on a great deal of cooperation and effort by many people. First, of course, I thank the authors for their contributions and responsiveness. Many colleagues were kind enough to review individual chapters, often on a short deadline. David Kassing reviewed many of the more difficult chapters, including my own, and helped tighten numerous arguments. Paul Bracken, David Chu, and Glenn Kent made useful suggestions on the whole as well as on some of the parts. I also thank RAND's Publications Department, especially Nikki Shacklett and Janet DeLand, with whom I worked closely, for their prodigious, patient, and responsive efforts in editing, formatting, and managing the complex process of producing a long multiauthor book in an effort in which everything was nonstandard. Janis Lane put in countless arduous hours at the computer doing the composition and page layout. Joyce Peterson, a communications analyst, read many of the chapters, identified what made them difficult to understand, and suggested improvements. Ingred Globig helped prepare some of the final manuscript material and kept the office running while I was buried in completing the book. And, finally, I thank my wife Joyce for her patience and support.

Part One

Introduction

Chapter 1

INTRODUCTION

Paul K. Davis

The end of the Cold War is requiring a profound and ongoing reassessment of defense planning. For the first time in decades, we are starting afresh on fundamental issues affecting the basic character and size of our military capabilities. These issues involve not only the classic question of "How much is enough?" but also questions about objectives; the *range* of capabilities we might need, given the changes in warfare and diversity of potential adversaries; and—more important than ever   how best to use the funds available for defense.

Addressing these questions is especially challenging: Planning accomplished now will determine capabilities for the first decade of the next century, but we assuredly do not know what the world will then be like. It is possible, of course, that U.S. military concerns will still revolve around major regional contingencies involving Iraq and North Korea, but that seems unlikely. We could instead see an approximation of the New World Order, a series of "Bosnias" and numerous states disintegrating into chaos, serious troubles around the periphery of a more conservative Russia, emergence of new military powers such as China or Japan, or some combination of the above.

These emerging questions and uncertainties are a boon for those involved in defense planning, because starting afresh is interesting and challenging. This book describes how a number of RAND analysts have been addressing the basic questions. The book is unusually broad, although not comprehensive. Each chapter is an independent essay, but with considerable cross referencing of ideas and arguments. The essays are somewhat personal, because they deal not only what the authors have learned from research and analysis, but with their "sense" of the issues. The intention, then, is to convey to readers what a number of senior RAND analysts currently see as the nature, state, and challenges of defense planning.

DIFFICULT QUESTIONS

These are some of the questions the book addresses:

- What kind(s) of world and what kind of scenarios should the United States plan for? What grand strategy should it adopt, and how should this affect defense planning?

- What approach should be taken to deterrence, including deterrence of aggression against weak states in whose security the United States has interests—but not "vital" interests?

- What are the implications for U.S. strategy and defense planning of proliferating nuclear, biological, and chemical weapons, and of delivery systems such as ballistic missiles?

- What special challenges do peacemaking requirements pose?

- How low can the defense budget go? Do we still have to maintain sizable forces and modernize them in a world with no other superpowers and no current threats comparable to the former Soviet Union or even the pre–Desert Storm Iraq?

- What kinds of re-engineering should the defense department consider? Because of technological change, is it time to substantially reconfigure our forces and rework doctrine? Should roles and missions be reconsidered?

- How should we think about tradeoffs between active forces and reserve forces, between force structure and modernization, between combat forces and support structure, and between variable-cost items such as force structure and "fixed-cost" items such as infrastructure?

- Is it time to rethink the *process* of defense planning because assumptions, methods, and images rooted in the Cold War are still so embedded in the very fabric of the Planning, Programming, and Budgeting System (PPBS)?

RECURRING THEMES

As the authors address these questions, a number of recurrent themes echo from chapter to chapter. This is not coincidental, because those themes have become increasingly important in a great deal of RAND work. The most prominent of the themes are the following:

Planning Under Uncertainty. The central challenge for the Department of Defense is planning under uncertainty. In building the defense program, the United States should discard the traditional focus on one or a few sharply defined scenarios in favor of a many-scenario approach (indeed, a "scenario-space approach") that puts a premium on assuring future strategic and operational adaptiveness. This would require radical changes in mind-set and process, including a focus on capabilities for generic operations and missions potentially important in *many* contexts.

Dealing with Proliferation. A profound challenge for military planning is the proliferation of weapons of mass destruction (WMD) and related delivery systems. This challenge can no longer be left to foreign policy because of the extent of proliferation that is already happening. The United States will need theater-level tactical ballistic-missile defenses, a range of counterforce options to deny launch of such weapons, and operations plans recognizing that such defenses will be imperfect and that U.S. forces may need to operate after being attacked with chemical, biological, or even nuclear weapons.

Deterring Regional Aggression. A continuing strategic challenge is conventional deterrence, which has historically proved very difficult—except when related to the most obviously vital national interests. The United States and its many regional allies must enhance the credibility of conventional deterrence in other cases (e.g., threats against Poland or the Baltic states, or in a "next Bosnia") by facing and clarifying interests that in the past have not always been apparent until they were threatened, and by developing credible political, military, and economic strategies for *punishing* aggressors when we cannot, realistically, stop the aggression militarily.

Capabilities-Based Planning. Planning should focus on capabilities. It should look at how quickly various types of capability can be increased for a particular spending increment. Such planning is much better suited for encouraging diversity and adaptiveness than is "requirements-based" or "threat-based" planning, where attention dwells on meeting estimated needs for a few precisely defined threat scenarios.

Competing Well and Leveraging Strengths. To maximize effectiveness as budgets and force levels are reduced, the United States should make choices that preserve and exploit its areas of superiority, notably airpower, worldwide naval presence, strategic mobility, command and control (and the related potential for information dominance), forced-entry capabilities, and the exceptional quality of our systems and military personnel.

Reducing the Discipline Gap. Because the defense program now has so much less slack than in previous decades, the United States needs to be as realistic as possible in developing the defense program and to maintain "discipline" when implementing it. This means full funding of outyear programs and more success in implementing cuts in unproductive activities. Failures here will have a disproportionately large effect on combat capabilities because of the increasing fraction of the "fixed-cost" part of the defense program.

Re-engineering. The Department of Defense should plan an across-the-board effort to rethink and re-engineer combat forces, support forces, infrastructure, and the processes by which decisions are made about all of them. This will mean redesigning "divisions, doctrine, and depots" (and Air Force and Navy analogs), as well as the PPBS itself. These efforts must reflect the profound technological changes occurring in military systems and warfare, and the role of information dominance. The military-technical revolution is real.

Peacekeeping and Peacemaking. The Department of Defense should pay increasing attention to the special challenges—for doctrine, force structure, training, and strategy—of multinational peacekeeping and, especially, peace-making operations.

Looking to the Next Century. Increasingly, defense planning should focus on next-century contexts: These will include nations aspiring to superpower status and other adversaries who have adapted their strategies to avoid U.S. strengths. Related to this, the United States must consider its military power as an important instrument for *shaping the future environment*—for example, by maintaining capability and presence to avoid creating power vacuums, co-operating in multinational efforts to promote regional stability, or developing capabilities to trump those that might be available to would-be superpowers.

STRUCTURE OF THE BOOK

Without elaborating, let me now sketch briefly the structure of the book and the remaining individual chapters, which can be read in any order depending on the reader's interests.

Principles for Defense Planning

Part Two of the book deals with principles for defense planning. My chapter, "Planning Under Uncertainty Then and Now: Paradigms Lost and Paradigms Emerging," is an overview of much that follows. It reviews the classic methods of defense planning introduced during the McNamara era (1961–1968) and the transitional changes introduced by Secretaries Cheney and Aspin as the Cold War faded into history. It then lays out a set of propositions and principles to guide our approach in the next decade, including suggestions about how to re-engineer the Department of Defense itself. As the title of the book suggests, a continuing theme is the need to allocate resources wisely amidst a great deal of uncertainty, and in the context of competing demands for the marginal federal dollar.

The next chapter, "Objective-Based Planning," written by Glenn Kent and William Simons, sketches an influential framework (sometimes called "strategies to tasks") that has been used extensively by and in work for the Air Force, Army, Joint Staff, and CINCs. The theme is deceptively simple—there should be a coherent and visible set of relationships all the way from national military strategy down to operational objectives, tasks, and force-employment concepts for accomplishing them. Kent and Simons also describe a constructive relationship that should be created among the various types of civilian and military planners.

This relationship is reflected as well in the chapter that follows, "Institution-alizing Planning for Adaptiveness," in which I summarize and extend work done for the Joint Staff. In this chapter I propose radical measures to transform the way much defense planning is conducted. Taken together, these measures would significantly integrate strategic, program, and operations planning—both conceptually and to ensure that related civilian and military cultures are intermingled through planned rotations and exercises. The approach would modify many elements of the PPBS to encourage more use of campaign analyses (for diverse contingencies) and multiple measures of effectiveness relevant to wartime and peacetime mission accomplishment. Noting how easily the Gulf War could have been a disaster if Saddam Hussein had not paused in Kuwait, the chapter calls for the United States to develop the capability (including command-staff capability) for responding *quickly* and adaptively in times of crisis, rather than depending on on-the-shelf war plans or on having months to rethink the situation before combat occurs.

The last chapter in Part Two draws on a considerable body of historical research. "The Discipline Gap and Other Reasons for Humility and Realism in Defense Planning," by Kevin Lewis, argues that the defense program is now very tight and that further budget cuts would probably result in far greater reductions in fighting capability than is usually appreciated. This thesis is based on observing consistent historical differences between what is planned and what eventually transpires, differences traceable to a systematic "discipline gap"—i.e., a gap between what analysis tells us is a wise allocation of resources and what emerges as the result of political compromises, organizational inertia, and other factors that hamper implementation of early plans.

Planning at the Strategic Level

Part Three deals with planning and reasoning about the nature of future conflict, the nature and feasibility of deterrent strategies, the new military missions of the post–Cold War era, and arms control. My chapter on "Protecting the Great Transition" describes a 1991 RAND grand-strategy study to bring out a wide range of provocative options and issues. It illustrates generic methods for thinking seriously about "environment-shaping" and "hedging" strategies. Richard Kugler, in "Nonstandard Contingencies for Defense Planning," discusses the use of planning scenarios and the plausibility of many nonstandard contingencies that should be taken seriously in developing our plans. Kugler notes that today's uncertainty is *strategic* in nature, not merely one of operations and tactics, and he argues for an unprecedented degree of strategic flexibility that would allow the United States to expand or contract its military forces, and to channel them in different directions, depending on how events play out in the next decade. He also urges that development of the defense program concern itself more with "generic mission-based planning" than with specific scenarios.

The next chapter reinforces concern about nonstandard scenarios. In "Improving Deterrence in the Post–Cold War Era: Some Theory and Implications for Defense Planning," I summarize work on the potential reasoning (both strategic and psychological) of aggressors and the implications of that reasoning for deterrent strategy. Inconsistency is a central problem: Nations undercut deterrence by refusing in peacetime to recognize interests that are not direct and compelling, but then discover too late for deterrence to work that they have to confront aggression that has taken place. The chapter argues for a more expansive understanding of interests in peacetime (including contingency planning for difficult scenarios) and, in times of crisis, the willingness to take prompt and unequivocal measures that some may consider provocative or dangerous. That recommendation is in sharp conflict with the doctrine of overwhelming force, because rapid deployment of overwhelming force is often impossible.

The chapter that follows is a change of pace. Jennifer Taw and Bruce Hoffman provide a survey on "Operations Other Than War," drawing lessons (both cheerful and sobering) from a number of case histories, including Bangladesh, Panama, and Somalia. Their chapter helps us visualize how very different some of the new missions and operations really are, and how easily an operation with achievable mission objectives can slip into becoming an operation destined for failure.

Part Three wraps up with two chapters dealing with ballistic missiles. In "Priorities for Ballistic Missile Defense," Russ Shaver reviews the history of missile defense from the 1950s, explaining the conflicting strategic, economic, and technological considerations that have always proved troublesome in this domain. He makes the case that interest in national-level BMD will inevitably rise again (perhaps soon, because of proliferation) and that the DoD must therefore continue to establish an appropriate R&D base. He also discusses the pressing need for theater-level BMD to protect U.S. projection forces and friendly countries in crisis. Finally, in "Future U.S. and Russian Nuclear Forces: Applying Traditional Analysis Methods in an Era of Cooperation," Dean Wilkening describes how strategic analysis can still be very useful even though the United States and Russia are monumentally uninterested in a strategic arms competition. There are practical problems to be dealt with, such as how to size the offensive and defensive forces so that new strains will not be *created* and so that even if new military crises arise between the United States and Russia, they will be less dangerous than they might otherwise be. Wilkening also touches on the potential implications of deeper reductions in a START II agreement, with and without ballistic-missile defense.

Planning at the Operational or Campaign Level

Part Four of the book describes studies and analysis with an operational flavor. Fred Frostic and Chris Bowie introduce this with "Conventional Campaign Analysis of Major Regional Conflicts," which paints with a broad brush the "campaign perspective" of joint and combined warfare that plays a central role in planning for major regional contingencies.

The next chapter, "The Use of Long-Range Bombers in a Changing World," by Glenn Buchan, describes how systems analysis has evolved to address the kinds of strategic and programmatic issues now important, including assessments of when stealth technology pays its way. The chapter highlights the critical but underappreciated role that long-range bombers now have in U.S. military strategy for conventional conflict, especially early in conflict.

The next chapter looks at a rather different kind of problem, the military challenges faced by one of the newly independent states of Eastern Europe. This is of considerable interest, because it deals with the more generic issue of how weak states can defend themselves, with and without some assistance. Their security is a matter of concern to the United States, but is not a "directly vital" national interest. In "A First Look at Defense Options for Poland," Charles Kelley, Daniel Fox, and Barry Wilson consider a variety of military strategies that Poland might employ in establishing a significant, although not robust, defense against a hypothetical future Russian threat.

In "Not Merely Planning for the Last War," Bruce Bennett, Sam Gardiner, and Daniel Fox describe a research project to understand the kinds of creative political-military strategies that could be used against the United States by opponents who have learned the lessons of the Gulf War, including lessons about U.S. airpower. They caution that the United States should be concerned about aggression involving fast-moving campaigns, campaigns with limited objectives, and campaigns in confused political-military contexts. They also discuss the problems created by weapons of mass destruction and ballistic-missile threats.

In "Extended Counterforce Options for Coping With Tactical Ballistic Missiles," Richard Mesic examines the system problem of dealing with tactical ballistic missiles (TBMs) and the potential leverage of strategies and systems that would attack those weapons before launch or in the boost phase of flight. The technical and operational problems involved are substantial, but the analysis leads inexorably to the conclusion that such options are critical.

The last chapter of Part Four is another change of pace. "Military Issues in International Operations," by Margaret Harrell and Robert Howe, gives an introductory survey of how international operations such as peacekeeping and peacemaking create demands for changes in training, equipping, controlling, and operating the U.S. Army.

Building the Defense Program

Part Five shifts attention to the building of the defense program, deliberately juxtaposing chapters on subjects as diverse as aircraft modernization and rethinking the mix and character of active and reserve Army forces. William Stanley's chapter, "Assessing the Affordability of Fighter Aircraft Force Modernization," is a virtual primer on the continuing problem of dealing realistically with procurement in defense plans when procurement cycles occur on longer time scales than the defense plans. He explains the methods that can and must be used to spread the cost of the next procurement cycle over time if modernization is to be affordable.

Ted Harshberger and Russ Shaver, in "Modernizing Airpower Projection Capabilities: Looking to Get More Out of Less," give an integrated picture of what path the Air Force's and Navy's airpower modernization should probably take over the next two decades. They draw on a great deal of RAND analysis, but they stress the role of subjective judgments and the need to revisit those judgments over time as, for example, better information becomes available about the costs of future systems such as the F-22.

Following these two chapters on modernization and weapon-system affordability, the next chapter deals with force-structure issues. "Assessing the Structure and Mix of Active and Reserve Army Forces," by Bernard Rostker, Bruce Don, and Kenneth Watman, summarizes a congressionally mandated RAND study exploring alternative ways to configure, train, and use the Army National Guard forces in a "total-force" approach.

Forces, of course, are useful only if they can be deployed to where they are needed. David Kassing's chapter, "Strategic Mobility in the Post–Cold War Era," reviews strategic mobility programs and issues, including lessons learned from the Gulf War. It ends with an emphasis on the need for the DoD to take more of a fort-to-foxhole approach in its management of strategic mobility and the need for much better decision-support systems to ensure efficient and adaptive uses of our mobility systems in times of crisis.

Next, we have a chapter dealing with the important area of logistics, which is often given short shrift in public discussion of defense planning, despite its military significance and enormous impact on the DoD budget. "Reinventing the DoD Logistics System for the Post–Cold War Era," by Rick Eden, John Dumond, John Folkeson, John Halliday, and Nancy Moore, is an overview of much recent RAND work to rethink fundamentals of logistics for the Air Force, Army, Joint Staff, and OSD, drawing heavily on the last decade's experiences from American industry, which has been taking radical measures to improve productivity. The authors stress that order-of-magnitude improvements can be achieved in the effectiveness of some DoD logistics systems.

Part Five ends with a chapter dealing explicitly with economic issues. In "Defining a Balanced Investment Program for Coping with Tactical Ballistic Missiles," Richard Mesic describes the kinds of insights parametric cost-effectiveness analysis can provide at the outset of a process that may take a decade or more, insights about what kinds of systems might plausibly be both effective and affordable if the requisite technological capabilities could be developed. The general methods used in this chapter have broad application to defense planning in an era of difficult choices and economic pressures.

With this background, then, Part Two opens with a broad discussion of principles for defense planning.

Part Two

Principles for Defense Planning

Chapter 2

PLANNING UNDER UNCERTAINTY THEN AND NOW: PARADIGMS LOST AND PARADIGMS EMERGING

Paul K. Davis

Planning under uncertainty has long been a theme of secretaries of defense, but the principles and analytic methods for planning under uncertainty should now change radically, especially since planning around two specific major regional contingencies (MRCs)—one in Korea and one in the Persian Gulf—no longer makes sense and will probably not long be sustainable. This paper reviews classic planning and important transitional changes introduced by Secretaries Cheney and Aspin. It then offers controversial propositions about what should come next. The paper argues for basing planning on objectives of environment shaping, deterrence (including deterrence of aggression against nonvital interests), timely and adaptive crisis response, and long-term strategic flexibility. It stresses "capability-based planning" and chunky marginal-analysis methods as a replacement for "requirements-based planning," which is overfocused on particular threats, scenarios, and measures of capability. The paper reviews the current program and concludes that—so long as major combat formations and support structure are organized as they are today—the overall force structure and budget recommended by the Clinton administration in 1993 are about right. However, it is in fact time to rethink fundamentally how to size and configure our major formations and support structures. How large need they be and for what next-century missions should they be designed? How can they cope with chemical and biological weapons? What mix of active and reserve forces should we use for the new era's range of wartime and peacetime missions? How much and what kind of support structure and infrastructure is needed? The traditional question of "How much is enough?" should be replaced by "What kinds of capabilities will be needed for the full range of plausible missions, and what mix is it prudent to buy when there are competing national demands for public-good dollars?" The United States now has the luxury of being able to buy less "catastrophic" insurance, but needs to have more explicitly "comprehensive" insurance at a good price. Much of the next decade's challenge will be to find ways to have that coverage at a reasonable price tag. This will require a good deal more re-engineering of the posture than has been attempted so far.

INTRODUCTION

It is a cliché that defense planning in the post–Cold War era must change fundamentally to reflect the new geostrategic context. There are, however, many misconceptions about what has and has not changed. In particular, it is by no means only in the post–Cold War era that the Department of Defense has recognized the need to plan under enormous uncertainty and to build defense capabilities flexible enough to cope with unforeseeable future contingencies. To the contrary, this has been a recurring theme for over three decades. What has changed, and what is still changing, is *how* the DoD does so—e.g., how it goes about establishing, assessing, and justifying defense programs and postures. Part of this is addressing the perennial question, "How much is enough?" (Enthoven and Smith, 1971). Another part is assuring appropriate operations planning and the ability to adapt quickly in crisis (Davis, 1994b).

This paper begins by reviewing Cold War defense-planning concepts and strategy, along with their successes and failures. It goes on to describe the substantial transitional changes introduced by Secretaries Cheney and Aspin. It then contrasts current concepts and strategy with what may be needed in the near future. The result is to contrast the "paradigms lost"—i.e., the paradigms that no longer serve us well—with the new ones that have emerged and others that are still taking shape.

THE CLASSIC (COLD WAR) DEFENSE-PLANNING APPROACH

Origins

The defense-planning approach that can now be considered "classic" was developed under Secretary Robert McNamara in the early 1960s.[1] McNamara recognized the challenges of doing organized planning under uncertainty, notably the need for defense programs to provide capabilities that would eventually be used in unforeseen contingencies. By the end of 1961 (after the Berlin crisis) it seemed clear that general war with the Soviet Union was unlikely, although deterring Soviet expansion remained critical. Indeed, a large study conducted for McNamara in 1961 identified 16 theaters in which the United States had military commitments, in 11 of which U.S. forces might be needed. The Soviets were involved in only some of these contingencies.

How does one plan against so many possibilities? And even if one has developed a concept for what is needed (i.e., for establishing "How much is enough?"), how does one explain and justify that concept—to the Congress and, ultimately, the general public? This was what McNamara had to address.

---

[1]See Kaufmann (1982, 1986, 1992), McNamara (1968a,b), and Davis and Finch (1993: chap. 2 and apps. A and B).

The Grand Concept

The approach the DoD took from those early days in the 1960s until recently can be described abstractly as follows, with some secretaries giving more or less emphasis to particular items:

1. *Overall force structure (and the size of the defense program) was based and justified in terms of the most stressing identifiable threat scenarios.* In the early 1960s, these were the Soviet threat (primarily to Central Europe), the Chinese/North Korean threat, and a lesser contingency such as one involving Cuba or Southeast Asia (nominally, a "2-1/2 war strategy"). Through most of the 1980s, the emphasis was on a global war with the Soviet Union, with Europe's Central Region and Iran as the principal land theaters.

2. *The analytic "requirements" for total force structure were derived for important, credible, defensively oriented, high-minded, and affordable military objectives—notably, deterring aggression against our allies and other pivotal nations.* Thus, the objective was to hold or restore the border in our defense, e.g., of West Germany and South Korea.[2] Or, at least, to deny the enemy confidence of victory.

3. *Since the nuclear deterrent was the paramount instrument for avoiding general war with the Soviet Union, certain cost-cutting risks were accepted in defining the "requirements" for conventional ground and air forces.* In particular, air and ground forces were sized for successful initial conventional defense under bad, but not worst-case, assumptions. For example, it was assumed that NATO would mobilize cohesively and fight effectively, thereby not needing a large operational reserve. Requirements were based largely on a short war, with relatively little planning for long wars or counteroffensives, both of which would have been expensive.

And, particularly important for maintaining diversity and coping with uncertainty:

4. *Having sized overall structure largely in terms of the most stressing threat, the original idea was then to "fill in" by acquiring specialized capabilities that might be needed for other scenarios,[3] and to establish a strategic reserve suitable*

---

[2]U.S. operations planning was not always defensive. For example, in 1962 and 1963 the United States planned and exercised for a possible invasion of Castro's Cuba. Khrushchev had some basis for claiming success in the Missile Crisis, since the United States agreed not to invade Cuba (Garthoff, 1989; Reeves, 1993).

[3]A confusing point here was that secretaries of defense often spoke of the total force structure determined by the most stressing requirements as being adequate to deal with "lesser included cases." While this did not logically exclude the "filling in" mentioned here, it did rather undercut its perceived priority.

for varied contingencies worldwide along with adequate strategic mobility forces (airlift, sealift, and prepositioning ships).[4] McNamara's Office of Systems Analysis worked to formulate this elaborate program, but the war in Vietnam and other factors reduced its funding. It was not until the Carter and Reagan years, under Secretaries Brown and Weinberger, that the DoD was more successful in this regard.

5. *Given defense programs consistent with the overall force structure justified in this way, the Secretary of Defense then charged the military services, the Joint Chiefs of Staff, and the various CINCs with preparing operationally not only for the principal threat scenarios (those used to justify overall force structure), but also for a wide range of smaller contingencies.* These exhortations were common over three decades of secretaries. Under Schlesinger and Cheney, they were further supported by having multiple planning scenarios (one each for a number of different theaters).

Figure 1 summarizes the grand concept schematically. For good reason it does not look much like traditional depictions of the Planning, Programming, and Budgeting System (PPBS). The shaded items were typically informal processes, relatively invisible except within portions of the Office of the Secretary of Defense (OSD) and the Joint Staff.[5] In particular, it was not always appreciated from outside the DoD (or even from many portions within it) that the planning scenarios were carefully chosen to balance a range of considerations, including the money available for defense.[6] Secretaries of defense are expected to argue for a higher DoD budget, but they are also members of the President's cabinet with broad national responsibilities. Ultimately, planning defense capabilities under uncertainty is deciding on how much insurance to buy against unlikely but plausible events. There is no rigorous and objective means for judging how much insurance is enough when there are competing demands for

---

[4]McNamara created the Strike Command (U.S. STRICOM) in 1961 for the contingency-oriented reserve in the United States. He proposed extensive procurement of airlift and sealift, including fast-deployment logistics ships (FDLs) analogous to the maritime prepositioning ships of the current era. The C-5 and C-141 programs proceeded, but were significantly underfunded; Congress never procured the FDLs. STRICOM proved ineffective, in part because of conflicts with the services over roles and missions as then defined (see Powell, 1993:xi and Peters, 1993:12), and in part because Vietnam created demands for many of the forces; STRICOM was disbanded in 1971.

[5]I was led to make these "offline" processes explicit as the result of a discussion of mutual experiences with Deborah Christie, then in OSD's office of Program Analysis and Evaluation.

[6]See Builder (1993) for a less charitable discussion of the traditional planning approach. See Builder and Dewar (forthcoming) for discussion of different planning methods.

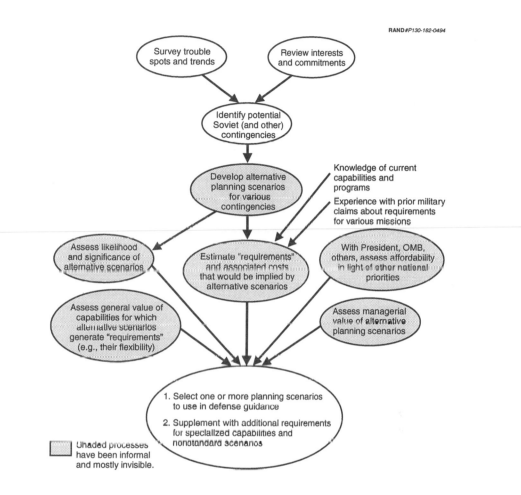

RAND #P130-182-0494

Figure 1—Traditional Approach to Choosing Planning Scenarios

the same public money. As a result, subjective considerations can and should enter the problem.

Figure 1 also suggests that part of choosing defense planning scenarios is assessing their utility for managing the department as a whole (e.g., for assuring that the services' programmed combat and support-force capabilities have a rational relationship to one another by requiring all of them to be able to meet the requirements of a common scenario). Also, the choice of scenarios reflects judgments about whether they will be useful in creating "requirements" leading to capabilities desired for reasons going beyond details of the specific scenario. For example, if procuring more strategic airlift is important in many contingencies, the standard planning scenario should stress airlift capabilities. Or, if one wants to assure having some amphibious-assault capability, then one can build an associated operation into that scenario, even if doing so is less than entirely natural.

Given the choice of planning scenarios by OSD, classic defense planning has *allowed* for a systematic process—seldom as neat as pictured here, to say the least—of translating the scenarios' challenges into operational objectives, operational strategies, mission requirements, defense programs, and other actions. As the process proceeds and as risks, costs, and constraints become clearer, there are often adjustments as suggested in Figure 2. Thus, the overall process is iterative (consistent with resource-programming techniques introduced by McNamara). To be sure, much vitriol is spilled when iterations occur (e.g., with accusations, sometimes valid, that the government is rationalizing inadequate capabilities), but they reflect the prioritizations that occur in a democratic process.

Some of this may seem bizarre to those who believe that planning should proceed top down from "objectives" through "requirements" to programs and budgets, but the reality is that decisionmakers must avoid establishing objectives or "requirements" that they cannot meet because of other economic demands. It is not accidental that DoD has never claimed (even in the days of the nominal "2-1/2-war strategy") an objective of being able to fight and win two major regional conflicts starting at precisely the same time—even though adversaries might plausibly orchestrate their aggressions. The implication of this objective might be a "requirement" to *double* the airlift and sealift fleets. *Off line*, then, and quite informally, judgments have been made that the price of that particular insurance is too high.

Analytic Paradigms and Methods for Standard Contingencies

OSD's Analytic Methods. Given the grand concept, how did DoD actually develop the various conventional-force requirements? As is so often the case, the devil was in the details and there was a great deal of cleverness, art form, and strategic judgment used—above and beyond that associated with the offline processes of Figure 1. In practice, the methods focused heavily on "standard" contingencies, notably defense of the Central Region. A new OSD or Joint Staff analyst learning the trade in the 1970s or 1980s would have been told something like the following about that problem (OSD, 1979a, Thomson, 1988):[7]

---

[7]Analysis of non-NATO contingencies was less well developed until the late 1970s. Also, in considering Chinese contingencies, such as an invasion of Taiwan or South Korea, there was more reliance on the nuclear deterrent, although this may or may not have made sense.

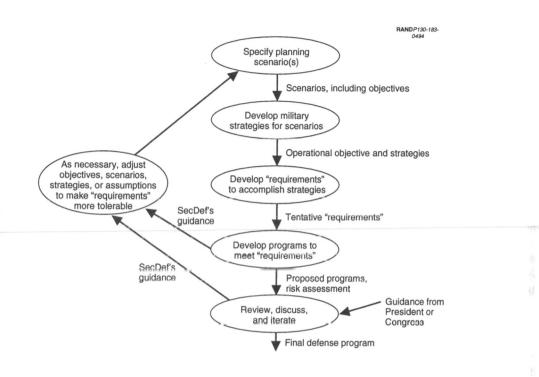

Figure 2—An Iterative View of Classic Planning

- *Focus primarily on ground forces,* since war will be determined largely by armored combat on the ground. Air forces are important, even critical, but should not be counted upon to compensate for other problems.

- *The key is to develop "build-up curves" for the Warsaw Pact threat in a variety of scenarios.* As part of this, *characterize ground-force capabilities in armored-division equivalents* (ADEs), which account for gross differences among divisions in quantity and quality of combat equipment. *Assume equal quality of personnel,* even between active forces and reserve-component forces, but assume reserve-component forces cannot be deployed until after a training time consistent with their national doctrine.

- From among the possible scenarios, *pick a planning scenario that severely stresses NATO in ways that can be redressed with feasible and affordable defense programs.* Recognize that choosing a defense planning scenario is one of DoD's principal functions and that the choice must balance a number of strategic and budgetary considerations.

- *Use analytic rules of thumb,* rooted in more detailed war gaming and analysis, *to establish NATO force requirements.* Typically, this means requiring that the theater-level force ratio be no worse than about 1.5:1 and that NATO ground forces be dense enough so that a given division need not defend a frontage greater than about 25 km.[8]

- Compare projected capabilities with "requirements," *identify the shortfalls, and define defense programs to remedy them* (Figure 3). For ground forces, this could mean, e.g.: (a) increasing NATO's active armies, (b) improving reserve-component readiness, (c) prepositioning equipment in Europe, (d) modernizing divisions, (e) increasing operational reserves in NATO's Northern Army Group, or (f) reducing the threat through arms control (CFE).

- Since we lack a simple and credible method for defining Air Force "requirements," scale the number of Air Force wings more or less in proportion with the number of ground-force divisions to maintain a subjectively reasonable balance. Also, maintain a rough balance with Pact air forces, after making some allowances for differences in structure and quality. In addition, assure the ability to attack target sets effectively (an alternative sizing method) and identify specialized requirements such as those for close air support, as provided by the A-10 program championed by OSD. Consider

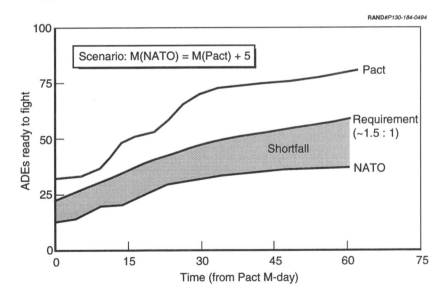

Figure 3—Illustrative Requirements Analysis from the Cold War

---

[8]For discussion see Davis (1990), Kugler (1991), and Biddle, Gray, Kaufman, DeRiggi, and Barnett (1991).

ways to use air forces to reduce pressure on ground forces, but don't count heavily on this.[9]

- *Size the Navy for control of the sea lanes* and provide peacetime presence with carrier battle groups (CBO, 1977).

- *Provide munitions and support adequate for at least 30 days of war* (achieved), and preferably 90 days (never achieved for high-quality munitions).

Despite a great deal of bottom-up work on such matters, there was no analogously algorithmic approach to defining requirements for support structure or infrastructure. There were, however, occasional pressures on the services to increase tooth-to-tail ratio (e.g., by limiting the division "slice," including support, to 48,000 personnel).

Other Analytic Methods for Standard Contingencies. Not all analysis followed this simple pattern, of course. Some civilian analysts went on to compute attrition and movement versus time using Lanchester-like equations and simple movement equations (e.g., Epstein, 1990, and Kaufmann, 1992), usually treating air forces as a source of additional firepower. Other analysts argued that this dynamic treatment added little (e.g., Biddle, 1988, and Mearsheimer's article in Miller, 1990). T. N. Dupuy developed a method sensitive to qualitative factors such as national fighting effectiveness as well as more standard factors (Dupuy, 1979). Still others such as Richard Kugler added to the dynamic approach a feature highlighting NATO's problem of maintaining an adequate force-to-space ratio as battle continued.[10]

Organizations such as the Joint Staff, the services, RAND, and IDA also did a great deal of work with computer simulations accounting for terrain, defensive preparations, various possible effects of airpower, maneuver, and, in some cases, other factors. In particular, RAND work reflected the differing fighting quality of armies highlighted by Dupuy and the special non-Lanchestrian nature of operational-level breakthroughs due to forward defenses with poor force-to-space ratios (Davis, 1988a, appendix), the lower effectiveness of reserve-component forces with minimal refresher training (Davis, 1988b), the need to adjust force "scores" to reflect the combat situation (Allen, 1992), and

---

[9]This may seem to have been unduly pessimistic, but the Pact had far more aircraft than NATO and an extraordinarily dense air-defense system; also, the Air Force was perceived as not fully committed to supporting ground forces, and air forces had proven less effective than expected in the Yom Kippur War and Vietnam. Further, the Air Force had to win an air-superiority campaign before it could turn to the ground war in mass. Finally, there was relatively little experience as yet with precision-guided munitions.

[10]See Miller (1990) for relevant articles from *International Security* by John Mearsheimer, Joshua Epstein, Barry Posen, Eliot Cohen, and others. See also Davis (1988a, 1988b, and 1990).

likely or "optimal" force-employment adaptations by theater commanders. The results often illuminated a host of problems invisible to the cruder analysis—particularly problems related to operational strategies, force employment, and arms control (Davis, 1988a,b; Kugler, 1991; Hillestad and Watman, 1992).

Paradigms and Methods for Nonstandard Contingencies

Throughout most of the Cold War there was little in the way of paradigms or methods to guide defense planning for nonstandard contingencies (i.e., contingencies other than the specific DoD planning scenarios). There were many individual studies, but no general and widely understood methodology.[11] The studies often worked at a level of abstraction such as buildup curves, without operational details.[12]

Let us now review some of the DoD's efforts to plan for flexibility. Whether or not there was a general methodology, how did DoD do? The answer is mixed.

CHRONOLOGY OF COLD WAR EFFORTS TO ASSURE FLEXIBILITY

Good Ideas but Failed Efforts in the 1960s and 1970s

Despite the grand concept and the intentions of McNamara and his successors, the United States was not very successful during the 1960s and 1970s in building defense capabilities (or flexible operations plans) for diverse contingencies—i.e., in "filling in" as discussed in items 4 and 5 of the grand concept. Except for the Vietnam period, during which the United States eventually developed a vast array of specialized units and logistical capabilities, the preponderance of effort focused on "the principal threat," that of a Warsaw Pact invasion of Western Europe and possible broader war.

---

[11]Late in the Cold War, RAND developed such a methodology and the related RAND Strategy Assessment System (RSAS) under the sponsorship of OSD's Director of Net Assessment, Andrew Marshall. It emphasizes analytic war gaming and multi-scenario analysis (see, e.g., Davis, 1988a and citations in Bennett, Gardiner, and Fox, 1994).

[12]On a personal level, it was troublesome, in the period 1979–1981 when I worked in OSD on programs for what has become USCENTCOM, that program analysis for Southwest Asian scenarios had to be twisted into forms recognizable to a community familiar primarily with NATO-oriented analysis, when the *real* analysis of my office depended so heavily on a joint-campaign style of thinking and region-specific details.

What went wrong? The most important causes of failure were probably these:

- Congress rejected critical elements of McNamara's proposed defense program, which it saw as having the potential to make the United States into a global policeman.

- The Vietnam War sucked up enormous energies and left no enthusiasm for optional contingencies that might be unpleasant.

- The military departments never bought into the concept of planning seriously for uncertainty, instead preferring to focus on the principal threat, plus particular crises as they arose.

- The Secretary of Defense and OSD focused too exclusively on strategic and programmatic planning, paying too little attention to operations planning and capabilities (Davis and Finch, 1993). This was exacerbated by the level of analysis, which tended to stop with numbers of divisions and the like without considering adequately the many other capabilities and prepara tions necessary to fight specific wars, even lesser contingencies.

The failure of the military organizations to explicitly buy into planning for uncertainty was particularly important. When resource decisions had to be made, when choices had to be made about training orientation, or when individuals thought about career-enhancing assignments and focuses, the tilt was toward Europe's Central Region or, before 1969, Vietnam. Important exceptions here were the Navy, Marines, and Special Forces (de-emphasized after Vietnam).

Secretary James Schlesinger recognized the narrowness of de facto planning and exhorted a broader view by employing multiple planning scenarios similar to the Illustrative Planning Scenarios (IPS) used under Secretary Cheney seventeen years later. These included a variety of large and small regional conflicts. Again, however, the exhortations were not effective.

To illustrate the pervasiveness of the focus on Central Europe and global war, consider that as of the late 1970s, the United States had woefully inadequate strategic mobility, only very light Marine units, no mountain infantry, minimal ability to provide purified water to expeditionary units in places such as Saudi Arabia or Iran, helicopters that were highly vulnerable to desert dust, and very little capability aside from Marine amphibious units to land equipment "over the shore" where access to high-capacity ports was unavailable.

An Exceptional Period and Hints of a New Paradigm: Creation of the Rapid Deployment Force, 1979–1983

Much changed in the late 1970s and early 1980s, and some of what transpired is a paradigm for what defense planning should be like in the years ahead. It very much represented planning under uncertainty in the sense we mean it today. Ironically, some of that experience has been forgotten because the Reagan administration dwelled so heavily on the global Soviet threat.

With Vietnam in the past, President Carter's National Security Council raised the issue of "regional contingencies," notably possible threats to Persian Gulf oil. An OSD study overseen by Paul D. Wolfowitz identified a variety of possible Persian Gulf and Middle Eastern contingencies—including, prominently, an Iraqi threat to Kuwait, an Iran-Iraq war, and a Soviet invasion of Iran (OSD, 1979b). The study proposed programs to provide broad capabilities for the region, without focusing on a single threat or scenario. Reflecting the views of the entire study team, I noted prominently in the report that in the case of Southwest Asia no one could tell with confidence who would be the enemy of whom ten years hence. The study's approach, then, was very much in the spirit of what we find necessary in the 1990s. Rather than identifying firm "requirements," it sought to increase "capabilities," without taking too seriously notions about precisely how they would be employed or precisely how much would be needed (threat projections were extremely uncertain, and scenario details dominated the problem).

In any case, hedging programs motivated by the study and subsequent analysis were initiated late in 1979 (Komer, 1984:17), although there was a great deal of controversy about the Iraqi scenario. Few remember this now, but these first programs were oriented more toward generic threats (e.g., Iraq) than toward the threat of a Soviet invasion. The programs included maritime prepositioning for new partially "heavied" Marine brigades, airlift improvements, and base-related efforts (DoD, 1992:D-29; Davis, 1982).

After the Soviets invaded Afghanistan in December 1979, concerns about the region increased greatly. Secretary Harold Brown and Under Secretary Robert Komer quickly initiated a substantial program (Davis, 1982), which was expanded under Secretary Caspar Weinberger and his deputy Frank Carlucci, who succeeded Weinberger as secretary. The program sought to build capabilities for deterring, and perhaps defending, in the Persian Gulf. Part of this involved developing the Rapid Deployment Joint Task Force (RDJTF), later the U.S. Central Command (USCENTCOM). This program was by far the most important effort during the Cold War to build capabilities for contingencies other than full-scale war with the Soviet Union in Europe. It proved its value in Desert Shield and Desert Storm.

The RDJTF/CENTCOM program and related strategy were controversial within the military and in some of the public debate (e.g., Record, 1981). Some strategists believed that any war with the Soviets would become global, in which case the United States would not realistically be able to defend in the Persian Gulf region. Others quarreled about roles-and-missions issues (e.g., about whether the Marines should have the lead role). Others resisted efforts for Southwest Asia because they believed the real prize was Western Europe, where the balance was allegedly so fragile that even the relatively small commitment of forces envisioned for SWA would endanger NATO. The battle within the Pentagon was won by those of us who believed that deterring (or even, perhaps, defeating) a Soviet invasion of the Persian Gulf region was feasible because of the distances and logistical hardships the Soviets would face in attempting to reach the oil-rich regions of southern Iran and the Arabian peninsula, and also because the U.S. deterrent would be credible because of the West's dependence on the region (OSD, 1979b; Brown, 1981; Davis, 1982; Ross, 1981; and Epstein, 1981), especially if Iranian resistance were significant and coordinated to some degree with U.S. applications of airpower (Levine, 1985). We also believed that failure to lay plans for defense in Iran could be a disastrous policy that might weaken Saudi resolve and encourage Soviet aggression ("negative environment shaping").[13] Finally (recall Figure 1), we believed that the capabilities sought were desirable for any of many possible contingencies, including eventual Iraqi or other scenarios.

Despite controversy, then, the RDJTF became a reality. Ironically, and despite lip service to diversity, detailed military planning by the Joint Chiefs, the RDJTF, and services soon focused almost exclusively on the Soviet threat to Iran—virtually ignoring others such as the Iraqi threat to Kuwait.[14] Thus, even the RDJTF initiative was not a full triumph of DoD planning for uncertainty: it produced superb material *capabilities*, but not the operational flexibility for quick and adaptive response. Finally, in 1989, Under Secretary Paul Wolfowitz recommended and the Secretary and Chairman directed changing the focus to regional threats, notably Iraq (DoD, 1992:D-4).

The Anomalous 1980s and the Image of a Global Monolithic Threat

Although programs for the RDJTF/CENTCOM continued and expanded in the Reagan administration, strategic planning moved away from Secretary Brown's regional orientation (primarily but not exclusively against Soviet threats) to an emphasis on a potential global war with the Soviet Union. There emerged an image of a global and monolithic threat. This came about because, by the late 1970s and early 1980s, the Soviet Union appeared to have developed capability for aggression in several theaters (Central, Northern, and

---

[13]There are parallels when one considers deterring a future Russian invasion of Ukraine or the Baltic states, which do not *directly* affect vital U.S. interests. See also Davis (1994a).

[14]Levine (1985:20) documents this and notes some of the reasons, which included an intelligence scare in August 1980 suggesting that the Soviets had raised readiness of their forces north of Iran and were contemplating invasion.

Southern Europe, Southwest Asia, and the Far East) and U.S. planning had to consider the *possibility* of more-or-less simultaneous wars in Southwest Asia and Western Europe.

In dealing with this, Secretary Weinberger (1981) (influenced by Under Secretary for Policy Fred Iklé and Assistant Secretary "Bing" West) stated that if the Soviet Union went to war in one region, the United States might escalate "horizontally" by conducting offensives in regions of Soviet weakness. Other reports suggested that these actions might include the high seas, Soviet naval bastions, remote areas of the Soviet Union such as the Kamchatka peninsula, and Soviet allies or proxy states such as Cuba or South Yemen. In the new dominant image, then, this would be a war fought for cosmic objectives with few constraints, a war that might even escalate into general nuclear conflict. Superficially, at least, there was little thought given to the myriad of complications that bedevil political and military leaders in more "normal" wars, which may have limited objectives, recalcitrant allies, and painful compromises to bring war to a close. Indeed, many participants believed deterrence was enhanced by emphasizing the all-or-nothing character of war should it occur.[15] Some of our European allies were very reluctant to stress conventional defenses, because they believed that mutual fear of nuclear war was the crux of deterrence and security. This was a continuing source of tension, because U.S. defense secretaries championed conventional defense and deemed it feasible and preferable to a single-minded dependence on a dubious extended nuclear deterrence (Kugler, 1993a:160).

Was There Serious Planning Under Uncertainty: Was the Cup Half Full or Half Empty?

Despite shortcomings here and there, it can reasonably be argued that the classic planning methods worked well for the United States from 1961 through 1988 or so. In particular, NATO developed and maintained a fair conventional defense supplemented by the nuclear deterrent. And in the 1980s, the United States developed the capability to fight a global conventional war if necessary. Further, U.S. force structure was large and diverse enough so that the United States was able to respond to lesser contingencies along the way— this despite the fact that defense programs seldom turned out as planned and

---

[15]Behind the scenes, many policymakers recognized that wars might be limited and not at all ideal. Secretary Brown and Under Secretary Komer issued planning guidance for contingency planning, which specified best-estimate assumptions on sensitive matters to be used in operations planning. Such guidance was revived under Secretary Cheney. Also, throughout the 1980s, OSD's Director of Net Assessment, Andrew Marshall, sponsored political-military war games exploring subjects such as multitheater conflict, horizontal escalation, and war termination.

wars seldom turned out to look much like the planning scenarios (Lewis, 1994).

The report card looks poorer when we go beyond total force structure and ask how well the United States was prepared *operationally* for the range of contingencies that *might* have occurred. In fact, there were many gaps in specialized capabilities and little in-depth operations planning for complex nonstandard contingencies. Further, presidents and defense secretaries were sometimes very dissatisfied with operations plans' rigidity and failure to deal adequately with political and strategic constraints.[16] Crisis-action teams were well respected, but could deal effectively only with smaller crises.

Ultimately, despite efforts to plan for flexibility, the monolithic-threat-and-ideal-war paradigm dominated military planning for four decades. Many secretaries of defense and strategists attempted to take planning under uncertainty seriously, but it was always an uphill struggle, seldom took center stage, and was easily supplanted by a "business-as-usual" approach with single-scenario focus. As of August 1990, planning revolved around a particular standard Iraqi scenario that posited significant strategic warning time and U.S. deployment well before D-day. Despite the glorious success of Desert Shield and Desert Storm, the United States should be under no illusions: it was unprepared operationally for this most likely of all the "lesser contingencies." In particular, it was unprepared militarily and politically to act *quickly* in a nonstandard contingency (Davis and Arquilla, 1991). On the other hand, the physical capabilities that had been procured, and the quality of the forces themselves, were excellent. Further, by historical standards, response *had* been prompt. The cup was both half full and half empty.

With this background on classical defense planning, let us now consider where we are today and where we are or should be going. That is, let us now consider how we move toward a new approach to defense planning—discarding the old ideas that no longer serve us well, retaining but updating others, and introducing new ones.

TOWARD A NEW APPROACH TO DEFENSE PLANNING: SOME CONVENTIONAL AND UNCONVENTIONAL PROPOSITIONS

The first observation to make is probably this: that while some analysts have always argued we *should* do so,[17] we are now in an era in which the DoD *must* plan for a wide range of distinctly nonideal, nonstandard wars, wars that

---

[16]Kennedy's frustrations on this score are well documented (e.g., Reeves, 1993).

[17]See Iklé and Wohlstetter (1988), Hoffman and Rowen (1988), Davis (1988a), Wohlstetter et al. (1979), Winnefeld and Shlapak (1990), and Gorman (1988).

are messy in numerous dimensions (Cohen, 1984 and Hosmer, 1987) and involve us with uncertain allies, uncertain and conflicting objectives, and political constraints such as avoiding American casualties (and even, perhaps, excessive opponent casualties). Military leaders will understandably continue to argue that U.S. armed forces should be employed in war only when the nation has first established clear objectives and the determination to accomplish them (see Summers (1984) for sentiments embraced by an entire generation of officers), but the reality will often not be so ideal.

In discussing how the United States is and should be moving toward a new era of planning under uncertainty, it may be useful to deal with unabashedly subjective propositions, propositions about what has been accomplished already and about what constitutes the most important unfinished business. Whether or not the reader agrees with all the propositions, they may still be provocative and help clarify issues. Eight such propositions follow. The first three will displease critics of the DoD and label me as too mainstream, but the rest may alter this impression.

Proposition One

Higher-level U.S. military strategy and policy are now generally sound (for the next decade).

In many respects, the Department of Defense adapted quickly and well to the end of the Cold War. In 1990, indeed just as the crisis in the Gulf began, President Bush and Secretary Cheney preemptively proposed substantial reductions in the DoD budget before Congress could impose them (Nunn, 1990), and did so with a strategic rationale that fully recognized that the world had changed. The Joint Staff under General Colin Powell played a lead role in much of the strategic thinking, and there has been remarkable civil-military cooperation throughout the transition period.

In the first year of the Clinton administration, Secretary Les Aspin conducted a major Bottom-Up Review (BUR) of defense planning (Aspin, 1993). In many respects it corroborated or built from the "Base Force" posture developed under Cheney and Powell, but it called for modest additional cuts and laid out a more substantial and explicit foundation.

The changes in strategy and policy that took place under Secretaries Cheney and Aspin were, then, far-reaching. Key features of change included:[18]

---

[18]See Cheney (1993a,b), Aspin (1993, 1994), Powell (1992), and Bush (1992, 1993). For a more critical assessment, see Kaufmann (1992). Indeed, many observers—and participants in Pentagon planning—believed that Cheney and Powell were unreasonably fixed on the Base Force as being a minimum and stubborn about not fac-

- *Redefining U.S. national security interests and objectives.* In the wake of the Cold War, the United States had to rethink fundamentals. It did so and produced authoritative statements on the subject.[19]

- *The Russians as just another plausible regional threat.* Starting with Cheney and Powell, the Soviet and Russian threats have been reduced to the same status as other regional threats (my own view is that Aspin went too far on this, barely mentioning Russian threats, even though eventual Russian moves against Ukraine, Eastern Europe, or the Baltic states are very much plausible).

- *The concept of environment shaping.* The United States is now concerned at least as much with environment shaping (e.g., encouraging regional stability or peaceful change, and reducing incentives for other nations to seek superpower status) as with more traditional military missions. Consistent with that, Cheney and Aspin reaffirmed the need for significant U.S. forward presence in critical regions worldwide because of the unique opportunities and responsibilities the nation now has *and* because it is so strongly in the U.S. interest to avoid the kinds of regional instabilities that might ensue if power vacuums arose—e.g., a military competition among Japan, China, and Korea in the Far East, or various worrisome possibilities in Europe.[20] One aspect of environment-shaping strategy is DoD's appreciation of the fundamental importance to U.S. security of the newly independent nations of Eastern Europe and the former Soviet Union being successful in their democratization and economic growth.

- *Reducing insurance coverage.* There was a clear decision to reduce catastrophic insurance against reemergence of a powerful and aggressive Russia or some other global superpower. Rather than maintain all the existing force structure for such an eventuality, the United States has chosen to depend on having strategic warning measured in years and the ability to reconstitute military capabilities when and if needed. DoD also concluded that we can slow the pace of modernization now that the Russian military is in disarray.

---

ing up to its being seriously underfunded. Others take the view that they were merely playing a high-stakes political game in which they could not afford to show slippage for fear of seeing the DoD budget go into free fall.

[19]It is interesting that McNamara's posture statements were not organized around interests and objectives; the requirement to have authoritative statements on such matters came with the Goldwater-Nichols legislation.

[20]This has been a continuing theme of RAND work since 1988. See Davis (1989), Winnefeld, Pollack, et al. (1992), Winnefeld (1992), and Levin and Bracken (1994). Similar ideas are reflected in Kugler (1993b). For brief treatments, see Davis (1994d) and Kugler (1994). See also Slocombe (1991) for a short but especially cogent treatment of such issues.

- *Major coverage reductions, but at deliberate speed.* One of Cheney's and Aspin's principal accomplishments will be their defining a *measured* program to cut back the defense budget substantially over the course of a decade, thereby avoiding many of the severe dislocations seen in previous buildups and cutbacks. This was accomplished prudently by first reducing force structure (variable-cost items) while protecting the infrastructure that would have allowed a reversal of course and, subsequent to the dissolution of the Soviet Union, more emphasis on reducing "fixed-cost" structure. Readiness is being maintained (Perry, 1994).

- *Coalitions, not unilateral action.* With some notable lapses (e.g., the absence of much discussion of the subject in the BUR), DoD continues to emphasize the critical role of NATO and other coalitions, rejecting any image of the United States as a unilateral world policeman.

- *Fighting to win.* The United States now plans to *win* any wars it enters, which may require decisive counteroffensive operations while minimizing casualties. This is a drastic departure from the classic emphasis on holding or restoring the border or, in Europe, having a conventional defense adequate merely to supplement the nuclear deterrent.

- *More realism in threat assessment.* DoD is increasingly willing to assume that the adversary in most plausible contingencies will have substantially less capable weapon systems, command-and-control systems, and personnel than the United States.

- *First steps in adaptive operations planning.* At the operations-planning level, DoD is now requiring military commanders to prepare for a broader range of situations and *adaptive planning.* (See Chapter Three of Davis and Finch (1993) for discussion of the Joint Staff's progress on this front.)

- *First steps toward building-block forces.* DoD is now using conceptual building-block forces for major and lesser regional contingencies (MRCs and LRCs), each building block with its own types of capability.[21]

- *The shadow of WMD.* Increasingly, DoD has emphasized the problems of proliferation of both weapons of mass destruction (WMD) and ballistic-missile technology.

- *New military missions.* DoD is increasingly sensitive to the need for the United States to participate in or lead peacekeeping or peacemaking mis-

---

[21]The MRC building block involves 4–5 Army divisions, 4–5 Marine Expeditionary Brigades (MEBs), 10 Air Force fighter wings (TFWs), 100 Air Force heavy bombers, 4–5 Navy carrier battle groups (CVBGs), and special operations forces (SOF). The LRC building block involves two Army light divisions, one MEB, 1–2 CVBGs, 1–2 composite TFWs, SOF forces, and various support units, including those for civil affairs. See Aspin (1993:10, 13).

sions. Some effort is even going into peacetime domestic uses of the military (Aspin, 1994).

- *Extensive lift and prepositioning plans.* The United States is planning substantial mobility forces and prepositioning abroad (Kassing, 1994; Aspin, 1994).

If high strategy and policy are reasonable, then what about the general size of the defense program? The answer depends on how much fundamental change can be made in the internals of the program and posture. Let me first assume that the changes will be evolutionary and that the Department of Defense will have to manage diligently and creatively even to buy the posture it is planning. Proposition Two follows in that context.

Proposition Two

The BUR force is not unreasonable in cost and is about right in number of major combat formations.

There are several ways to think about how much force structure and defense budget are enough. None are individually persuasive, and some at first blush appear anti-intellectual. The fact is, however, that there is no way to determine rigorously how much is enough. As a result, strategic planners often find it useful to view their problem from many perspectives, including a historical perspective that ignores changes in technology and international politics. When I do this, I conclude that the BUR force structure is about right—for the next ten years—in number of major formations, even though DoD's appearing to base its rationale on two *specific* more-or-less simultaneous MRCs is unfortunate and likely to cause trouble when North Korea fades from the scene. The reader may reach different conclusions from the same data.

Let us consider in turn measures of how much we are spending (input), how much we are spending as a percentage of the GDP (the defense burden), numbers of major formations (intermediate output), and the sufficiency of that structure as measured by force comparisons and analysis of warfighting capabilities (output).

Defense Expenditures Versus Time. The obvious first measure is budget versus time. In the wake of the Cold War we might reasonably demand that defense cost a great deal less, perhaps about what it did before the buildup for the Korean War. However, since the United States was in terrible shape militarily at that point (Kugler, 1993a:33), it would be reasonable to argue that the budget should be *significantly* higher than in 1950, although much less than the peak during the buildup for the war. *A priori,* I think of FY51 as a reasonable peg point.[22] Figure 4 shows the history and projected history of defense outlays. We see that the budget projected for FY99 will be about 10 percent higher than in FY51, but lower than at any time since then. Since unit costs of military equipment and personnel have gone up substantially in real terms for decades, I find it remarkable that the projected defense budget will be so close to that of FY51. Apparently, efficiencies and a reduction in capital stock have compensated for higher unit costs.

The Defense Burden. Figure 5 measures the burden of U.S. defense expenditures (i.e., outlays as a fraction of GDP). We note that the U.S. defense burden is already at pre–Cold War levels and dropping. It follows from Figures 4 and 5, coupled with the premise that the United States had too small a defense establishment in FY50, that the defense program is affordable and not obviously too expensive in absolute terms, although there should be opportunities for cost savings as discussed below. Whether a dollar on the margin is better spent on defense or domestic programs is another issue.

But what about *needs?* Do we need as much capability as we are planning?

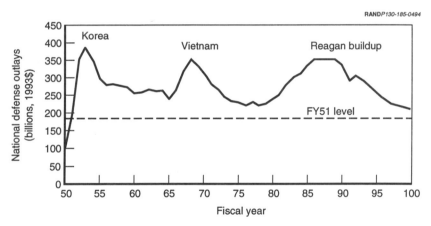

SOURCE: Calculated from data in OMB (1994).

Figure 4—Defense Outlays Versus Time in 1993 Dollars

---

[22]Others argue that FY50 is a better peg point, because the FY51 budget included significant war expenditures. Still others argue that even FY50's expenditures are too high a base, because the general threat is going down (Morrison, Tsipis, and Wiesner, 1994).

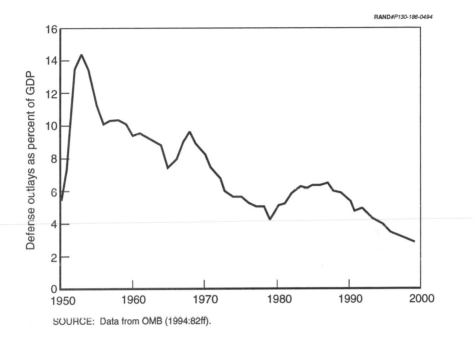

RAND#P130-186-0494

SOURCE: Data from OMB (1994:82ff).

Figure 5—The Defense Burden Versus Time

Major Formations Versus Time. One crude but useful measure of military capability is the number of major formations—e.g., divisions, carrier battle groups, and air wings. Figure 6, adapted from Lewis (1989), arrays the number of Army divisions versus time. We see that even the Base Force of 12 division equivalents would be smaller than any Army force since World War II. On a historical basis, then, the even smaller BUR force of 10 active divisions does not seem excessive. Similar arguments can be made for the Air Force, Navy, and Marines.

Another way to assess the number of major formations is by arraying them in terms of mission. Figure 7 does this for Army forces using a format adapted from Rostker, Don, and Watman (1994), which allows us to see how both active- and reserve-component forces fit into the overall set of missions. Figure 7 represents *one* possible interpretation of how the BUR force will be implemented (details have not yet been released by DoD). Although reasonable people can and do disagree (Kaufmann, 1992), the structure does not seem excessive to me. Considering the importance ascribed to environment shaping and forward presence, our forces in Europe and Korea will be marginal. Any-

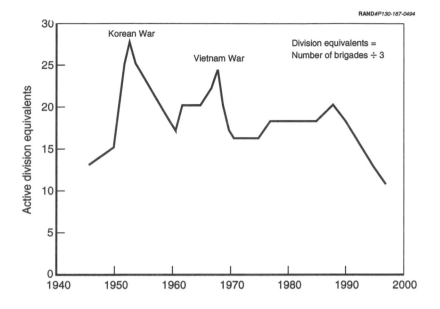

Figure 6—Historical Level of the Active Army in Division Equivalents
(Brigades divided by 3)

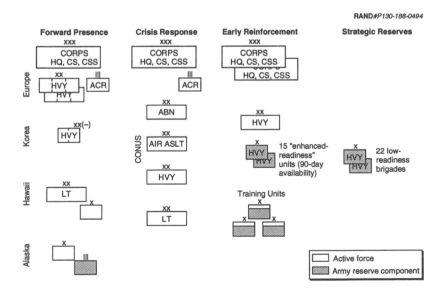

Figure 7—Depiction of Possible Army Force Structure Versus Mission

thing smaller might reduce U.S. clout significantly (e.g., if the United States could no longer claim to have the basis for a "capable corps" in Europe, that might affect the role and influence of the U.S. commander there). It could surely undercut environment shaping for Eastern Europe and the former Soviet Union by indicating a U.S. strategic withdrawal.

The BUR building block for MRCs, shown in Figure 7 in the crisis-response column, includes 4–5 Army divisions, which is significantly less than what was committed in Korea, Vietnam, and the Gulf War (Kugler, 1994; Lewis, 1994). The early-reinforcement forces appear reasonable to deter or fight in a second contingency *or*, significantly, to reinforce a single major contingency in which airpower did not prove quite as magically powerful as it did in Desert Storm. The strategic reserves (almost entirely National Guard forces) are smaller than those of many other countries, and some such forces are needed for domestic missions as well as for reinforcements in a long war. The training units are essential if the United States is to have the capability to train reserves efficiently (Rostker, Don, and Watman, 1994).

Force Comparisons. While "bean counting methods" are appropriately in low repute because technological factors, fighting effectiveness of the personnel, and logistics can all have such large effects (Levin, 1988), it is nonetheless relevant to ask whether the planned U.S. force levels will be large or small compared with those of other significant countries, both allies and potential adversaries.[23] As a rough cut at this, Figure 8 shows total active military personnel and active ground-force personnel for each of a number of nations in 1992, along with the planned levels of the BUR building block for MRCs. We see that the building block is comparable to or smaller than the likely force levels of China, Iraq, Iran, North Korea, Russia, Syria, and Vietnam. Comparisons of active ground-force personnel make the BUR seem even smaller, since the United States has an unusually large Navy and Air Force. The size of the Chinese and Russian armies should give us pause, especially when we contemplate the environment-shaping objective mentioned earlier. Including reserve forces would make U.S. capabilities appear smaller.[24]

---

[23]Another way to look at sufficiency is to ask whether the United States could tilt the balance decisively when foreign states such as North and South Korea are in competition or conflict. Such a discussion is beyond the scope of this paper, because answers depend on specialized capabilities, asymmetries of capability, and scenario details.

[24]To be sure, U.S. forces would be qualitatively superior in most or all instances, which would mitigate the numbers problem. However, minimizing casualties often requires highly favorable force ratios, and many types of conflict require large numbers of personnel, not mere firepower and technological virtuosity.

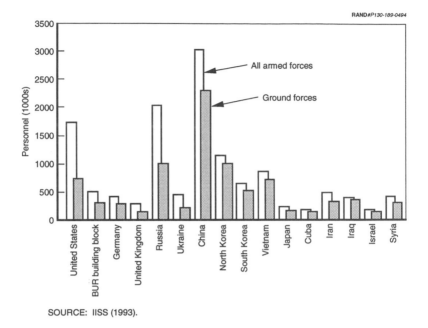

SOURCE: IISS (1993).

Figure 8—Force Comparisons (Active-duty personnel)

Can Allies Compensate? DoD's skeptics, when shown such comparisons, invariably complain about the need to consider allies. However, while allies can greatly reduce ground-force requirements in some contingencies, they cannot in others: e.g., the allies may be late in a fast-moving crisis, ineffective, or already severely weakened from war. The United States should vigorously seek allies, but cannot always count on them.

Fighting two more-or-less simultaneous MRCs. The bean-count comparison dealt with personnel levels. But what about warfighting? According to the BUR report, 10 active divisions and 6 reserve-component divisions are adequate for the two standard MRCs. That is consistent with prior RAND analysis (Bowie, Frostic, et al., 1993). Indeed, one can imagine air-force-favorable versions of the two MRCs in which the United States could devastate the adversaries with an even smaller force.[25]   The question, however, is why we should expect the adversaries to fight again in a manner of our convenience

---

[25]As pointed out by Taibl and Kosiak (1993) and Conetta and Knight (1993), neither administration analysis nor the RAND analysis described in *The New Calculus* (Bowie, Frostic, et al., 1993) "proves" the need for the force levels used in a replay of Desert Storm. Nor, however, do they claim to do so.

(Bennett, Gardiner, and Fox, 1994). When one looks seriously at this issue, it is not clear how many divisions might be needed even to fight *one* MRC successfully, but it could well be a good deal more than a BUR building block. While I am troubled by the excessive emphasis given to the Iraqi and Korean scenarios currently (no one should believe that the two-MRC objective would go away if merely North Korea ceased to be a threat), a two-MRC objective seems sensible. My own view is that

- The force structure should be adequate to decisively defeat an opponent in one MRC and either to deter a second (mostly with airpower) or to limit the second aggressor's gains and then reverse the aggressor later (Davis, 1994d). Anything less strikes me as inappropriate, since aggressors would have a free ride if we were tied down with our single MRC.

Overall, then, I conclude that the BUR force is clearly not excessive and may even be too small if we insist on a win-win posture rather than one sized for win-deter/win-hold-win.

If, then, high strategy, policy, the size of the defense program, and the number of major formations appear to be reasonable, what more needs to be done? In fact a great deal, for at least three reasons. First, it is at least possible that a re-engineering of the Defense Department, much like American industry has been undergoing, would allow further cuts in the defense budget, which would be welcome given our many domestic needs. Second, because of current underfunding, it will be a major struggle merely to buy the BUR force posture, a struggle requiring a great deal of efficiency and tough choices that have not yet been identified. The third reason is that DoD has only begun to think about how to prepare for next-century challenges, including from nations that may develop capabilities tailored to counter our own and to exploit our weaknesses (Bracken, 1993). The next proposition fits with all of these.

Proposition Three

We should rethink the size, composition, and operations of major formations, increasing efficiency and introducing next-century doctrines.

As a preface here, it is useful to recognize that a great deal of thinking about "requirements" stems from use of "markers." For example, an Army officer contemplating operations may view a map, identify lines of communication and key cities, and see the need for "a division here, here, here, and there, with at least a division or two in reserve" (a judgment sometimes dictated as much by geography as by the size of the enemy force). These judgments reflect the doctrinal capabilities of the markers (divisions, in this case), which depend on number of maneuver units, support units, and command-staff capabilities.

Only seldom is that reasoning sensitive to the precise size of the division or its constituent units. If the various functions could be accomplished with fewer people or in different ways, so be it, but the task requires the functions associated currently with a division. But this raises questions such as:

- Could the division be smaller? For example, do we still need as many tanks per platoon given the increased range and lethality of our tanks and modern battlefield surveillance?

- Could independent combined-arms brigades fulfill some of the tasks now performed by divisions?

- Would modern information technology and maneuver of long-range fires allow a new command structure with fewer layers?

Navy and Air Force officers have similar questions to ask regarding the nature of their markers (primarily carrier battle groups and tactical fighter wings) and commands. Does a carrier battle group in the late 1990s have to be the same as one of the 1980s? Also, when could helicopter carriers or cruisers be substituted for aircraft carriers? How large should Air Force squadrons and wings be, and how much can be done with composite wings (already a consideration) and other changes?

There are also important questions about the reserve-component formations and their relationships to active forces. For example:

- Why must the ratio of active and reserve-component Army divisions be so high?

- Why have Israel and Germany, but not the United States, been able to depend on high-readiness reserve-component combat divisions?

- If the root problem is that the regular Army has no faith in the fighting capability of the National Guard, then is *drastic* reorganization needed despite the political problems involved? (With more effective reserves we could reduce the number of active divisions further.) Or should we deemphasize entirely the combat role of the National Guard?

- If we maintain the number of active units now planned, then on what basis do we decide requirements for reserve-component readiness? What is the rationale for requiring deployability of 15 National Guard brigades in 90 days? (RAND work suggests that such a goal is highly unrealistic without additional unprogrammed training units and increased strategic lift.)

In any case, defense planning should shift from concerns about force structure in the large to concerns about configuration, diversity, and wholly new operational concepts exploiting technology and, where achievable, information dominance. We should be rethinking the nature, composition, and functions of major formations from scratch, looking to the 21st century rather than the past for an image of what is needed.[26]   The services all have thinkers and innovators working on these matters, but pressures from the Secretary of Defense will be needed if they are to be valued and heeded. Change does not come easily, but is needed as the next proposition asserts.

Proposition Four

The U.S. force structure is poorly configured for wars other than replays of Desert Storm.

If the United States reviews its major formations, it may soon conclude, as did an Army-sponsored study by colleagues James Quinlivan and Fred Frostic, that current U.S. forces are poorly configured for many possible future contingencies (Frostic and Bowie, 1994).   For example, it can be argued that the Army has a shortage of *mobile* light divisions (or, within heavy divisions, of infantry battalions) appropriate for operations in urban, jungle, or mountain environments.   There are also shortages of specialized early-available support units such as military police and language experts (Taw and Hoffman, 1994; Winnefeld and Shlapak, 1990).   Given the increased importance of peacemaking/peacekeeping operations and the likelihood of other contingencies to which airborne and air assault forces would be best suited (e.g., for forced-entry operations in difficult versions of the standard MRCs, as discussed in Davis, 1994b), it seems that the priority being given to heavy units—the very forces for which Air Forces can most nearly substitute on the margin—may be overdone.   Traditional straight-leg infantry has only a very limited role, but more lethal and mobile infantry, in combined-arms groupings, appears to be quite valuable.

It may be, of course, that the solution here is to have the Marines be the specialists in modern light infantry operations (along with the 82nd Airborne and 101st Air-Mobile Air-Assault divisions), reducing further their emphasis on amphibious operations, but playing up vertical envelopment.   This would require more support structure and mobility.

Another example of what this proposition involves relates to weapons of mass destruction, especially chemical and biological weapons, which must be

---

[26]This will mean worrying about Third World countries having more sophisticated weapons, including WMD and ballistic missiles, and about how would-be superpowers might be configuring their forces in the next century and how we could continue to trump their efforts through, e.g., exploiting our advantages in the collection and effective use of information.   For a provocative article on thinking beyond the next five to ten years, see Bracken (1993).   See also Bennett, Gardiner, and Fox (1994).

viewed as a very serious and plausible threat. U.S. operations in Desert Shield and Desert Storm involved high concentrations of combat forces, support forces, and ammunition. Are such concentrations acceptable for the future? If not, what implications does this have for the size and character of our major formations, and the doctrine they follow? Similar questions arise if merely we impute to next-century adversaries modern cluster munitions and delivery mechanisms.

Let me now turn to issues of program and budget.

Proposition Five

The "natural" processes of budget making over the next few years will leave the United States with much less capability than currently expected unless drastic reforms occur.

Another reason for re-engineering comes from cost concerns. Colleague Kevin Lewis (Lewis, 1994) makes a persuasive case that the process of cutting back force structure is far more complex and insidious than is generally appreciated (see also Zakheim and Ranney, 1993).

- The currently projected force structure is significantly underfunded (by perhaps $50 billion or so over six years).

- The effects of that and any additional cuts will be worse than proportional to the dollar amounts: capability versus dollars spent is a distinctly nonlinear function because of R&D, infrastructure, and overhead costs.

- The services will tend to hold on to remaining structure, but doing so may severely hurt modernization and readiness (although DoD is attempting to avoid this, as discussed in Perry, 1994). They may also fail to make adequately drastic cutbacks in support by redesigning systems; instead, they may scale down an inappropriate structure or shift more capability into the reserves, including capabilities that might be badly needed early in crisis.

- At any budget level, expenditures will inevitably be distinctly nonoptimal because of managerial mistakes and constraints imposed by Congress causing the overhead fraction to increase. The force purchased with a given expenditure may be the force analysts would have expected from an expenditure 20 percent less. This is my statement of what Lewis calls "the discipline gap."[27]

---

[27]In 1992, RAND held an internal defense-planning workshop at which we discussed what cuts could be made to the then-sancrosant Base Force. Our analysis of MRCs suggested that the United States could reasonably reduce to a force structure that translated into a 1997 budget of about $200 billion (in 1993 dollars). However, after a sobering discussion of the historical record in implementing programs, we concluded

Figure 9 summarizes some of the problems with an influence diagram in which a positive arrow linking two items means that an increase in the first item tends to increase the second; a negative arrow means that an increase in the first tends to decrease the second or that a decrease in the first tends to increase the second. One message of the figure is that the various influences reinforce each other. For example, as domestic needs increase (top of figure), the defense budget decreases, but this puts more items at risk (e.g., bases) (not shown), which causes the Congress to impose more constraints than in an easy-money environment, which increases the discipline-gap problems, which results in a higher overhead factor. That reduces actual capability (e.g., requiring even more cutbacks in the number of bombers procured and an increase in their unit cost, which is seen as an overrun) and—in the low-threat environment—DoD is criticized for its mismanagement and the defense budget comes under more pressure rather than less.

Against this background of needs and humility about the ability of defense planning to achieve its objectives, what approach should be taken in making the difficult choices that underlie the defense program?

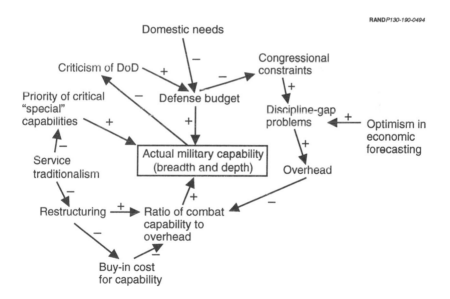

RAND P130-190-0494

Figure 9—Influences Adversely Affecting U.S. Military Capabilities

---

that the force structure we were treating as marginally acceptable would cost more like $230 billion because of the discipline gap and subtle modernization-related underfunding in the Base Force budget. We may have been optimistic.

Proposition Six

DoD should identify a broad range of important operational objectives and then emphasize "capabilities-based planning."

Despite the manifold uncertainties about the precise contingencies that will emerge, the United States should clearly plan capabilities permitting it to fight effectively in Southwest Asia, Korea, and Eastern Europe. To deal with uncertainty, however, DoD should—for each region—identify the substantially different *generic military campaigns* that might be necessary and, for each campaign, identify associated operational objectives and tasks. It should then go about building the best mix of capabilities for the range of objectives and tasks. Because of the varied nature of the possible campaigns, and because there are other important claimants for the marginal federal dollar, the focus should be on what is sometimes called "capabilities planning," as distinct from "requirements planning." In capabilities planning, one seeks to identify the mix of force elements and systems that maximizes capability for different levels of the budget, and to keep track of how rapidly needed capability is rising with additional expenditures. Since significant reforms with big payoffs often require a buy-in expense, this analysis should be based on "chunky marginal analysis." That is, the question is not how best to spend the marginal dollar, but the marginal billion or ten billion dollars.

Another key feature of capabilities analysis is that it strongly encourages measuring the value of additional expenditures with multiple measures of effectiveness (e.g., measures recognizing substantially different contingencies or contingency details, problems of sustainability and all-weather suppression of air defenses, and the potential need for vertical envelopment and armored offensives). By contrast, "requirements analysis" is structured around finding the least-cost way to accomplish a particular set of requirements (e.g., executing a particular time-phased deployment list with particular required delivery times) and may yield a force mix that is ill suited to other cases. Further, the language of requirements analysis is inappropriate except when the "requirements" are truly required.[28] When planning against uncertain potential threats of uncertain capability in uncertain contingencies, it is wise to keep track of how much one is paying to decrease risk.

Figure 10 illustrates the point for a notional relationship between the number of ground-force divisions and expenditures. At low expenditure levels we are buying into the problem with R&D and the development of production

---

[28]A good analyst can in theory reach the same conclusions with either a requirements-based or a capabilities-based approach. In practice, however, the former is often inferior because people take "requirements" too seriously.

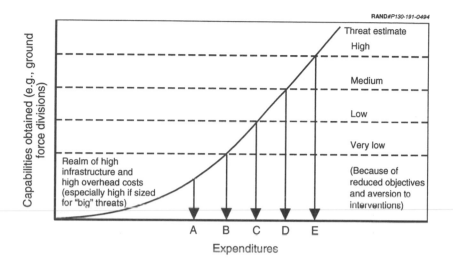

Figure 10—Capabilities, "Requirements," and Budgets

capabilities. A budget level at point A would be economically inefficient. If we had a narrow concept of national interests and saw little direct threat to those interests, the threat we might see would be very low (e.g., corresponding to a budget at point B). However, if we had a more expansive concept of national interest—as have a long series of administrations—then the issue would be to assess the likely threats to be met by our postulated ground-force capabilities. In the current world, there are enormous uncertainties about who and how capable that threat might be, as illustrated by points C, D, and E. If the consequences of being wrong were catastrophic, then we would have to consider point E a "requirement" and pay the price. If the consequences would merely be serious but not catastrophic, we might decide to stop at points B or C, depending on what other claims existed for the marginal budget dollar. That is, we would be chary of buying excessive insurance.

An alternative way of viewing the problem is to fold together notions of how large and capable the threats might be, the likelihood of different threat magnitudes, and the risks of being wrong. The result is a kind of utility function for additional expenditures as indicated in Figure 11 (see the solid curve with its postulated band of uncertainty, reflecting doubts about the various likelihoods and consequences). In this case, Figure 11 shows notionally the perceived overall value of the defense program as a function of its size, indicating the size of the program at its peak, at the Base Force level, and at the BUR force level. Figure 11 suggests that the plot of perceived value versus expenditures is highly nonlinear. At the high end, it incorporates what economists refer to as diminishing returns. In the realm of interest, and in looking at reductions rather than increases in budget, it reflects the notion that when the defense program is reduced, fixed-cost elements of the system are a larger share of the total, forcing greater-than-proportional cuts in combat capability. Figure 11 also reflects schematically the implicit conclusion of the Bush and Clinton administrations that further cuts in the defense budget would result in rapid and important declines in capabilities. The crux of the debate with those who advocate much larger cuts is indicated—in a somewhat exaggerated way—by the "alternative" assumption curve, which could reflect the belief that current capabilities are more than we really need (for a mix of reasons involving judgments about national interests and objectives, and about the likelihood and severity of various possible contingencies) and the belief that further reductions in budget would lead to more-or-less proportional cuts in fighting capability (i.e., cutting the budget by 20 percent would reduce divisions, wings, and carrier battle groups by about 20 percent).

There is no basis currently for any claims of rigor about what curves are "right," but my own judgment, affected strongly by concerns about current underfunding and the discipline gap, is that the BUR program is at the edge of prudence—i.e., that further cuts would have serious negative consequences.

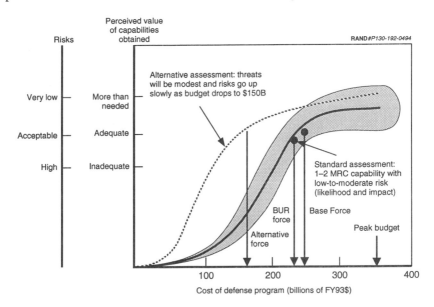

Figure 11—Value of Defense Capability Versus Size of Defense Budget

It is possible, of course, that we could find dramatically effective new ways to exploit technology and reorganize combat forces, support forces, and infrastructure; that we could eliminate all but "essential" infrastructure; and so on. If so, the curve of value versus expenditure would drop off more gently with further cuts. But, the current program is already known to be underfunded, and we will have to work very hard merely to make the BUR force a reality.

To summarize, taking the heavy curve in Figure 11 as our basis of reality, we surely don't want to spend so little as to be on the buy-in portion of the curve; nor do we want to be spending to buy the very expensive insurance at the top end, where the curve is flattening; instead, we want to be working at or a bit above the knee—i.e., at the outset of the realm of "diminishing returns." This is an old concept among economists and systems analysts, but it was seldom applied when threat "requirements" were taken literally.

Against this background, I offer the following proposition about the basics of the defense planning system.

Proposition Seven

The PPBS system—and its conceptual underpinning—need to be substantially reworked and revitalized.

The conceptual and managerial system for building the defense program has changed little for decades. We have not yet seen a major study on "reform of the PPBS," even though the mind-set of the current PPBS does a poor job of reflecting some of the new strategic and policy concepts. In this regard, consider the following:

- Nearly all quantitative discussion of the Bottom-Up Review and its implications has focused on traditional *requirements-based planning*—and for two highly specific major regional contingencies at that. Analysis has had little to say about how one accomplishes the missions of environment shaping, deterring "difficult" aggressors (e.g., a future Russia threatening Ukraine or the Baltic states), or peacemaking and peacekeeping.[29] Nor has there been much discussion of nonstandard scenarios.

- Although DoD now uses multiple scenarios, it has only one scenario per theater, despite the fact that a real scenario in a given theater could take a variety of forms. As an example here, consider that decisions on the active-reserve mix (and the nature and readiness of our reserve force) were driven by specific standard-scenario assumptions, even though the Korean problem

---

[29]Some exceptions here are Winnefeld, Pollack, et al. (1992), Martin, Cockell, Kraus, and Weaver (1993), Davis (1994a), Taw and Hoffman (1994), Harrell and Howe (1994), and Lewis (1993).

is likely to disappear before long and conclusions about what makes sense in the mix are sensitively dependent on details of scenario (Rostker, Don, and Watman, 1994).

- There has been relatively little work in recent times to define optimal mixes of forces—i.e., studies making difficult tradeoffs.

- The current PPBS has become comfortable with existing organizational structures and has not effectively stimulated consideration of radically force configurations. There has been little re-engineering as yet.

- There is little in the PPBS system itself to underwrite, much less enforce, the concept of planning for adaptiveness or the desired attributes of robustness and flexibility (Davis, 1994b). Nor is there much to encourage an explicit objectives-to-tasks approach (Kent and Simons, 1994).

- There is little in the institutional mind-set of the PPBS to value nontraditional uses of the military ranging from peacemaking/peacekeeping abroad to nation building and various types of activity in the United States itself. Given the desire to maintain a larger active military than is likely to be needed for warfare, would we not be giving higher weight to such nontraditional missions, despite the traditional reluctance of the U.S. military on such matters? (See also Davis, 1994d.)

- The PPBS has no agreed basis for how to analyze how-much-is-enough questions with respect to support structure and infrastructure—even though, increasingly, that is where the money is (Eden, Dumond, Folkeson, Halliday, and Moore, 1994).[30]

- The PPBS is so institutionalized and complex that it significantly increases defense programming costs by rewarding certain management skills (like inside deal-making) and not rewarding other initiatives that hold much promise for efficiency, like outsourcing and partnering alliances with the private sector in R&D.

So far, I have dealt with issues of defense posture and the process of developing that structure. In thinking about re-engineering, however, we should also consider *operational* capabilities for rapid and flexible action. Based on the close call in the Gulf War (what if Saddam had continued to roll into Saudi Arabia?) and the likelihood that future opponents will have learned from the experience (Davis, 1994b; Bennett, Gardiner, and Fox, 1994), a new attitude about speediness is needed.

---

[30]This is not entirely fair, since DoD is attempting to reform acquisition and defense management (Cheney, 1993:30; Aspin 1994; Perry, 1994).

Proposition Eight

Operations planning should be reformed to assure capability for extremely rapid force employment and adaptation.

The Joint Staff has made great progress in improving the extent to which the United States can adapt to circumstances in contingencies. The days in which planners took the monolithic operations plan literally are now past us. However, as described at length elsewhere, there is much more to be accomplished, and there is reason to doubt that it will be accomplished without strong leadership from the Secretary of Defense and a more general institutionalization, through exercises and doctrine, of assuring the capability for *rapid* adaptive planning and execution in crisis (Davis and Finch, 1993; Davis, 1994b).

Taken together, the last five propositions suggest rather dramatic reforms.

TOWARD A NEW GRAND CONCEPT OF DEFENSE PLANNING

If one accepts most of the propositions, what is the new grand concept toward which we should be heading? With some trepidation, since this essay is a *starting* point for analysis rather than the conclusions of a careful study, I believe major elements of that grand scheme should be as follows:

1. *Establish important, credible, high-minded, and affordable objectives.* These should be to help preserve international peace through environment shaping; to deter strategically significant aggression (which includes aggression indirectly affecting our interests); if deterrence fails, to decisively defeat the enemy with tolerable casualties or, in other cases, to punish the aggressor to deter future aggression; and to posture ourselves flexibly so that, in the next century, we can adapt either to a more peaceful world or the emergence of major new threats (Kugler, 1994).

2. *Plan for adaptiveness.* Establish overall force structure and the size of the defense program in terms of how to pursue these objectives effectively and efficiently, using chunky marginal-cost methods and multiscenario, multidimensional capabilities analysis rather than the traditional "requirements" analysis, and emphasizing planning for adaptiveness (Davis, 1994b) rather than planning around specific scenarios.

3. *Be conservative in single-MRC analysis.* Be relatively conservative in assessing how much is enough for conventional forces in a single MRC, be-

cause: (a) the United States would want to minimize casualties in any conflict and (b) deterrence will depend on conventional capabilities. In particular, size air and ground forces for successful conventional-defense campaigns under worse-than-expected conditions.

4. *Expand concepts of deterrence.* Recognizing that we cannot deter certain types of faraway aggression by defending weak states that are not directly vital to our interests, plan specifically to deter aggression by being capable and willing to severely *punish* aggressors through air strikes, naval blockades, and general economic measures. Where appropriate, assist the defended nations in building *nonoffensive defenses* (NOD) that would greatly raise the price of invasion. Think through U.S. and allied ability to use punishment methods against nations with weapons of mass destruction.

5. *Exploit the airpower card.* Assure that the United States can apply airpower early in crisis and can readily establish air supremacy in all theaters of interest. The U.S. advantage in airpower is extremely important and should be fully exploited. As a minimum, U.S. airpower greatly constrains the potential strategies of our adversaries.

6. *Prepare for nonstandard contingencies.* Build capabilities to cope with nonstandard scenarios that would require early U.S. forced-entry operations and other specialized and demanding operations.

7. *Re-engineer formations and doctrines.* Because of the changing nature of likely adversaries and wars, change the structure of major formations with an eye toward reducing personnel and assuring capabilities suitable for diverse scenarios in next-century contexts. Consider especially scenarios in which airpower and armored forces have reduced effectiveness.

8. *Plan on sustained peacekeeping and peacemaking operations.* Reconfigure the posture, including the active-reserve mix, to permit sustained peacekeeping and peacemaking operations in an international context, without endangering U.S. capability to fight and decisively win a quick-breaking major regional contingency.

9. *Be ready to cope with weapons of mass destruction.* Assume weapons of mass destruction will be a major factor in future regional contingencies, and that the United States must be prepared to deter use, defend against, operate forces in the presence of, and respond to use of such weapons in ways effective from the perspective of our allies as well as ourselves. That is, even standard MRC scenarios should be scenarios with a strong WMD shadow, and potential WMD use (Millot, Molander, and Wilson, 1993). Particularly worrisome here are chemical and biological weapons.

10. *Overhaul the operations-planning process to emphasize planning for adaptiveness.* Seek an adaptive planning system that could, within hours or a few days, generate appropriate and executable operations plans for rapid deployment and employment of forces in real-world crises with numer-

ous elements of surprise or complication. Assure the quality of the system with frequent no-notice testing in stressful challenge scenarios developed by the Office of the Secretary, and by in-depth follow-up (Davis, 1994b).

11. *Review and either improve or reduce the strategic reserve.* Maintain and improve capabilities for a strategic reserve (reforming the Army National Guard if necessary) suitable for a wide range of contingencies worldwide. Provide strategic mobility forces so that the reserve can be used effectively, but be wary of "requirements" based on the timelines of particular scenarios. Reconsider the whole range of flexible-readiness options for reserve-component forces (e.g., Nunn, 1990). If high-quality combat reserve capabilities emerge, reconsider the number of active-component ground-force divisions.

SUMMARY USING THE INSURANCE METAPHOR

If defining the defense program is indeed something like buying insurance, then how far can the metaphor be pushed? Rational purchase of insurance involves worrying about both coverage against *catastrophic* events and *comprehensive* coverage against a broad array of lesser possibilities. In the new era of defense, we can afford to set lower limits on our catastrophic insurance (and demand lower premiums), because the likelihood of anything catastrophic is small and the worst plausible war would be much less catastrophic than it used to be. At the same time, we need to pay close attention to whether we are buying *comprehensive* insurance, because some of the protections we had previously as a spin-off from our catastrophic insurance (i.e., the ability to cope with a diversity of unplanned contingencies) may disappear as we reduce our premiums. And, finally, we need to use creative approaches to organization and to the exploitation of technology to see whether we can reduce the price of maintaining high-quality comprehensive insurance. But such "better management" will require a level of innovation and reform in the Department of Defense that has not been witnessed in several decades. It can be an exciting time for defense planning.

ACKNOWLEDGMENTS

Paul Bracken, Mike Hix, David Kassing, and Richard Kugler all provided very useful reviews. David Chu, Fred Frostic, David Gompert, Glenn Kent, and Kevin Lewis made numerous informal comments that also helped. None of these colleagues, however, are responsible for the final results.

BIBLIOGRAPHY

Allen, Patrick (1992), *Situational Force Scoring: Accounting for Combined Arms Effects in Aggregate Combat Models*, RAND, Santa Monica, CA.

Aspin, Les (1993), *The Bottom-Up Review*, Department of Defense, Washington, D.C.

———— (1994), *Annual Report to the President and Congress*, Department of Defense, Washington, D.C.

Bennett, Bruce W., Sam Gardiner, and Daniel B. Fox (1994), "Not Merely Planning for the Last War," in Davis (1994c).

Biddle, Stephen D. (1988), "The European Conventional Balance," *Survival*, March/April.

Biddle, Stephen D., David Gray, Stuart Kaufman, Dennis DeRiggi, and D. Sean Barnett (1991), *Defense at Low Force Levels: The Effect of Force to Space Ratios on Conventional Combat Dynamics*, Institute for Defense Analyses, P-2380, August.

Bowie, Christopher, Fred Frostic, Kevin N. Lewis, John Lund, David Ochmanek, and Philip Propper (1993), *The New Calculus: Analyzing Airpower's Changing Role in Joint Theater Campaigns*, RAND, Santa Monica, CA.

Bracken, Paul (1993), "The Military After Next," *Washington Quarterly*, Vol. 16, No. 4.

Brown, Harold (1981), *Department of Defense Annual Report Fiscal Year 1982*.

———— (1983), *Thinking About National Security: Defense and Foreign Policy in a Dangerous World*, Westview Press, Boulder, CO.

Builder, Carl (1993), *Military Planning Today: Calculus or Charade*, RAND, Santa Monica, CA.

Builder, Carl and James Dewar (1994), "A Time for Planning? If Not Now, When?" to be published in *Parameters*.

Bush, President George (1992, 1993), *National Security Strategy of the United States*, The White House, January.

Cheney, Dick (1993a), *Defense Strategy for the 1990s: The Regional Defense Strategy*, January 1993. (Said to be very similar to the official Defense Planning Guidance, which is classified).

———— (1993b), *Annual Report of the Secretary of Defense to the President and the Congress (for FY 94)*, Department of Defense, U.S. Government Printing Office, Washington, D.C.

Cohen, Eliot A. (1984), "Constraints on America's Conduct of Small Wars," *International Security*, Vol. 9, No. 2.

Conetta, Carl, and Charles Knight (1993), *RAND's New Calculus and the Impasse of US Defense Restructuring*, Project on Defense Alternatives Briefing Report 4, Commonwealth Institute, Cambridge, MA.

Congressional Budget Office (CBO) (1977), *Planning U.S. General Purpose Forces: Overview*, Washington, D.C.

Davis, Paul K. (1982), *Observations on the Rapid Deployment Joint Task Force: Origins, Direction, and Mission*, RAND, Santa Monica, CA.

———— (1988a), *The Role of Uncertainty in Assessing the NATO/Pact Central Region Balance*, RAND, Santa Monica, CA. Available also in General Accounting Office, *NATO-Warsaw Pact Conventional Force Balance*, GAO/NSIAD-89-23B.

———— (1988b), *Toward a Conceptual Framework for Operational Arms Control in Europe's Central Region*, RAND, Santa Monica, CA.

———— (1989), *National Security in an Era of Uncertainty*, RAND, Santa Monica, CA.

———— (1990), "Prospects for Military Stability in a Deep-Cuts Regime," in Ian Cuthbertson and Peter Volten (eds.), *The Guns Fall Silent: The End of the Cold War and the Future of Conventional Disarmament*, Institute for East-West Security Studies, New York. A similar article, "Central Region Stability at Low Force Levels," appears in Reiner Huber (ed.), *Military Stability*, Nomos Verlagsges-ellschaft, Baden-Baden, 1990. Available also from RAND.

———— (1994a), "Improving Deterrence in the Post–Cold War Era: Some Theory and Implications for Defense Planning," in Davis (1994c).

———— (1994b), "Institutionalizing Planning for Adaptiveness," in Davis (1994c).

———— (ed.)(1994c), *New Challenges for Defense Planning: Rethinking How Much Is Enough*, RAND, Santa Monica, CA.

———— (1994d), "Protecting the Great Transition," in Davis (1994c).

Davis, Paul K., and John Arquilla (1991), *Deterring or Coercing Opponents in Crisis: Lessons from the War With Saddam Hussein*, RAND, Santa Monica, CA.

Davis, Paul K., and Lou Finch (1993), *Defense Planning for the Post–Cold War Era: Giving Meaning to Flexibility, Adaptiveness, and Robustness of Capability*, RAND, Santa Monica, CA.

Department of Defense (DoD) (1992), *Conduct of the Persian Gulf War*, Washington, D.C.

Dupuy, Trevor N. (1979), *Numbers, Prediction, and War*, Bobbs Merrill, Indianapolis, IN.

Eden, Rick, John Dumond, John Folkeson, John Halliday, and Nancy Moore, "Reinventing the DoD Logistics System for the Post–Cold War Era," in Davis (1994c).

Enthoven, Alain, and K. Wayne Smith (1971), *How Much Is Enough: Shaping the Defense Program, 1961–1969*, Harper and Row, New York.

Epstein, Joshua M. (1981), "Soviet Vulnerabilities in Iran and the RDF Deterrent," *International Security*, Vol. 6, No. 2.

———— (1990), *Conventional Force Reductions: A Dynamic Assessment*, The Brookings Institution, Washington, D.C.

Frostic, Fred, and Christopher J. Bowie (1994), "Conventional Campaign Analysis of Major Regional Conflicts," in Davis (1994c).

Garthoff, Raymond L. (1989), *Reflections on the Cuban Missile Crisis* (rev. ed.), The Brookings Institution, Washington, D.C.

Gorman, Paul (1988), *Commitment to Freedom: Security Assistance as a U.S. Policy Instrument in the Third World*, and *Supporting U.S. Strategy for Third World Conflict*, both submitted to the Commission on Integrated Long-Term Strategy, U.S. Government Printing Office, Washington, D.C.

Harrell, Margaret Cecchine, and Robert Howe, "Military Issues in Multinational Operations," in Davis (1994c).

Hillestad, Richard, and Kenneth Watman (1991), *Integrating Conventional Arms Control and Force Enhancements in NATO*, RAND, Santa Monica, CA.

Hoffman, Fred S., and Henry S. Rowen (1988), *The Future of Containment: America's Options for Defending Its Interests on the Soviet Periphery*, a report of the Offense-Defense Working Group of the Commission on Integrated Long-Term Strategy, Department of Defense, U.S. Government Printing Office, Washington, D.C.

Hosmer, Stephen T. (1987), *Constraints on U.S. Strategy in Third World Conflicts*, Crane Russak, New York.

Iklé, Fred C., and Albert Wohlstetter (1988), *Discriminate Deterrence: Report from the Commission on Long-Term Integrated Strategy*, Department of Defense, Washington, D.C.

International Institute of Strategic Studies (IISS)(1993), *Military Balance, 1993–1994*, London.

Joint Staff (1992), *1992 Joint Net Assessment*, Joint Chiefs of Staff, Washington, D.C.

Kassing, David (1994), "Strategic Mobility in the Post–Cold War Era," in Davis (1994c).

Kaufmann, William W. (1982), *Planning Conventional Forces, 1950–1980*, The Brookings Institution, Washington, D.C.

——— (1986), *A Reasonable Defense*, The Brookings Institution, Washington, D.C.

——— (1992), *Assessing the Base Force: How Much Is Too Much?* The Brookings Institution, Washington, D.C.

Kent, Glenn A., and William E. Simons (1994), "Objective-Based Planning," in Davis (1994c).

Komer, Robert W. (1984), *Maritime Strategy or Coalition Defense*, Abt Books, Cambridge, MA.

Kugler, Richard L. (1991), *NATO's Future Conventional Defense Strategy in Central Europe: Theater Employment Doctrine for the Post–Cold War Era*, RAND, Santa Monica, CA.

——— (1993a), *Commitment to Purpose: How Alliance Partership Won the Cold War*, RAND, Santa Monica, CA.

——— (1993b), *U.S. Military Strategy and Force Posture for the 21st Century: Capabilities and Requirements*, RAND, Santa Monica, CA.

——— (1994), "Nonstandard Contingencies for Defense Planning," in Davis (1994c).

Kugler, Richard, Ronald Asmus, and Stephen Larabee (1993), "Building a New NATO," *Foreign Affairs*, Fall.

Levin, Carl (1988), *Beyond the Bean Count: Realistically Assessing the Conventional Military Balance in Europe*, U.S. Congress, Senate Armed Services Subcommittee on Conventional Forces and Alliance Defense.

Levin, Norman D., and Paul Bracken (forthcoming), *Preparing for the 21st Century: The U.S. Military Role in a Changing Asia*, RAND, Santa Monica, CA.

Levine, Robert (1985), *Flying in the Face of Uncertainty: Alternative Plans and Postures for Interdiction in Southwest Asia*, RAND, Santa Monica, CA. A Ph.D. dissertation done for the RAND Graduate School of Policy Studies.

Lewis, Kevin (1989), *Historical U.S. Force Structure Trends: A Primer*, RAND, Santa Monica, CA.

———— (1994), "The Discipline Gap and Other Reasons for Humility and Realism in Defense Planning," in Davis (1994c).

Lewis, William H. (ed.) (1993), *Military Implications of United Nations Peacekeeping Operations*, National Defense University, McNair Paper Seventeen.

Martin, James J., William A. Cockell, George F. Kraus, and Gregory J. Weaver (1993), *Asian Security Challenges: Planning in the Face of Strategic Uncertainties*, Science Applications International Corp., San Diego, CA.

McNamara, Robert S. (1968a), *The Fiscal Year 1969–1973 Defense Program and the 1969 Defense Budget*, Department of Defense, Washington, D.C.

———— (1968b), *Essence of Security: Reflections in Office*, Harper and Row, New York.

Miller, Steven E., and Sean M. Lynn-Jones (eds.) (1990), *Conventional Forces and American Defense Policy: An International Security Reader*, MIT Press, Cambridge, MA.

Millot, Marc Dean, Roger Molander, and Peter A. Wilson (1993), *"The Day After . . ." Study: Nuclear Proliferation in the Post–Cold War World*, 3 vols., RAND, Santa Monica, CA.

Morrison, Philip, Kosta Tsipis, and Jerome Wiesner (1994), "The Future of American Defense," *Scientific American*, February.

National Defense Research Institute (1992), *Assessing the Structure and Mix of Future Active and Reserve Forces: Final Report to the Secretary of Defense*, National Defense Research Institute (NDRI), RAND, Santa Monica, CA. The project leader on this effort was Bernard Rostker.

Nunn, Sam (1990), *Nunn 1990: A New Military Strategy*, Center for Strategic and International Studies, Washington, D.C., Vol. XII, No. 5 in the Significant Issues Series.

Office of Management and Budget (OMB) (1994), *Budget of the United States Government, Historical Tables, Fiscal Year 1995*, U.S. Government Printing Office, Washington, D.C.

Office of the Secretary of Defense (OSD) (1979a), *NATO Center Region Military Balance Study, 1978–1984*, authored by Richard Kugler in the Office of the Assistant Secretary for Program Analysis and Evaluation. (Declassified)

———— (1979b), *Capabilities for Limited Contingencies in the Persian Gulf*, Office of the Assistant Secretary for Program Analysis and Evaluation. The study leader and summary author was Paul K. Davis, working under the general direction of Paul D. Wolfowitz. Other contributors were Frank Tapparo, Dennis Ross, Kenneth Holtel, John Tillson, Geoffrey Kemp, Linton Wells, and Bill Davies. (Declassified)

Perry, William J. (1994), *Department of Defense Fiscal Year 1995 Budget*, a briefing, Department of Defense, February 7.

Peters, John E. (1993), *The U.S. Military: Ready for the New World Order?* Greenwood Press, Westport, CT.

Powell, General Colin (1992), *National Military Strategy of the United States.*

———— (1993), *Roles, Missions, and Functions of the Armed Forces of the United States*, Joint Chiefs of Staff, Pentagon, Washington, D.C.

Record, Jeffrey (1981), "The RDF: Is the Pentagon Kidding?" *The Washington Quarterly*, Vol. 4, No. 3.

Reeves, Richard (1993), *President Kennedy: Profile of Power*, Simon and Schuster, New York.

Ross, Dennis (1981), "Considering Soviet Threats to the Persian Gulf," *International Security*, Vol. 6, No. 2.

Rostker, Bernard D., Bruce W. Don, and Kenneth Watman (1994), "Assessing the Structure and Mix of Future Active and Reserve Army Forces," in Davis (1994c).

Slocombe, Walter (1991), "The Role of the United States in International Security After the Cold War," in *New Dimensions in International Security*, Institute for International Strategic Studies, Adelphi Papers, Winter 1991/1992, London.

Steinbruner, John (ed.) (1989), *Restructuring American Foreign Policy*, The Brookings Institution, Washington, D.C.

Summers, Harry (1984), *On Strategy: A Critical Analysis of the Vietnam War*, Dell, New York.

Taibl, Paul, and Steven Kosiak (1993), *An Affordable Long-Term Defense*, Defense Budget Project, Washington, D.C.

Taw, Jennifer Morrison, and Bruce Hoffman (1994), "Operations Other Than War," in Davis (1994c).

Thaler, David (1993), *Strategies to Tasks: A Framework for Linking Means to Ends*, RAND, Santa Monica, CA.

Thomson, James A. (1988), *An Unfavorable Situation: NATO and the Conventional Balance*, RAND, Santa Monica, CA.

Weinberger, Caspar (1981), *Annual Report to the Congress, FY 1982*, Department of Defense.

Winnefeld, James A. (1992), *The Post–Cold War Force-Sizing Debate: Paradigms, Metaphors, and Disconnects*, RAND, Santa Monica, CA.

Winnefeld, James A., Jonathan D. Pollack, Kevin N. Lewis, Lynn D. Pullen, John Y. Schrader, and Michael D. Swaine (1992), *A New Strategy and Fewer Forces: The Pacific Dimension*, RAND, Santa Monica, CA.

Winnefeld, James A., and David Shlapak (1990), *The Challenge of Future Nonstandard Contingencies: Implications for Strategy, Planning, Crisis Management, and Forces*, 2 vols., RAND, Santa Monica, CA.

Wohlstetter, Albert, et al. (1979), *Interests and Power in the Persian Gulf: Summary and Overview,* Pan Heuristics, Draft.

Zakheim, Dov S., and Jeffrey M. Ranney (1993), "Matching Defense Strategies to Resources: Challenges for the Clinton Administration," *International Security,* Vol. 18, No. 1.

Chapter 3

OBJECTIVE-BASED PLANNING

Glenn A. Kent and William E. Simons

There is a continuing need in the planning and development of military capabilities for a clearer sense of direction and linkage to national interests. This need has been reflected in public law, through the Goldwater-Nichols Act of 1986, which mandates that the national interests and objectives of the United States be made explicit in annual executive branch reports to the Congress. This paper elaborates on a concept for such planning. The concept centers on a subordination of objectives whereby outlining a plan for attaining stated goals at one level of organization defines objectives to be achieved at subordinate levels of implementation. It describes a process by which one may proceed coherently from stated national security objectives, to national military objectives, to regional campaign objectives, to operational objectives, and finally to military tasks. The process provides a clear audit trail from top to bottom, gives clear meaning to plans of action (strategies) formulated at each level, and offers a certain stability for our national security planning, year by year and era by era. The concept sets the stage for a process of allocating national defense resources to best effect and could be applied to the DoD's Planning, Programming and Budgeting System (PPBS).

INTRODUCTION

The first step in defense planning is to define a clear sense of direction that can be followed consistently and thus set the stage for providing the most relevant military capabilities within the constraints imposed. The challenge is to link the processes of developing and acquiring military equipment, and of organizing, training and equipping forces, more closely to recognized national security objectives.

Fundamental to any improvement is a disciplined way of thinking. This discipline is needed in two respects: a reliable management framework and a consistent lexicon for describing important elements of the framework. The management framework must include a number of key functions:

- Articulating projected campaign and operational objectives.
- Identifying critical deficiencies.

- Formulating new concepts to alleviate deficiencies and to achieve projected objectives to the maximum extent possible.
- Deciding which concepts to implement.
- Initiating and completing programs to implement the agreed-upon concepts.

To be effective, the framework must encourage consideration of *alternative* campaign plans, *alternative* concepts to alleviate deficiencies, and *alternative* programs to implement a given concept. Indeed, a strength of the approach is in avoiding using the term "requirement" to give inappropriate blessing to what is in fact only one proposed mechanism for accomplishing an objective.

This paper addresses the need for and the fundamental process underlying an objective-based approach to defense planning. Much of it is excerpted from a larger RAND report (Kent and Simons, 1991), which includes also a detailed development of the management framework referred to above. The present paper deals mainly with the initial element of that framework, namely how and why a hierarchy of objectives—security objectives, campaign objectives, and operational objectives—should be articulated. It begins by reviewing the statutory basis for objective-based planning and clarifying the frequently cited "need for a clearer national strategy." It follows by recommending a process to move from a statement of those hierarchical objectives to corrective action.

GOLDWATER-NICHOLS LEGISLATION

In October 1986, the Congress acted to give the force of public law to several procedures it believed important for improved defense planning. Some of these had been recommended by the earlier Packard Commission (the "Blue Ribbon Commission on Defense Management," commissioned in July 1985). With respect to the linkage of defense planning to strategic objectives, the Department of Defense Reorganization Act (Goldwater-Nichols) requires the President to submit an annual report on the national security strategy of the United States to the Congress. The law stipulates that this report include a discussion of at least the following:

- Worldwide interests and objectives of the nation that are vital to national security.
- Foreign policy, worldwide commitments, and national defense capabilities necessary to deter aggression and implement national strategy.
- Proposed short-term and long-term uses of the political, economic, military, and other elements of national power to achieve U.S. objectives.
- Adequacy of U.S. capabilities to carry out national strategy and the balance among all elements of national power in this regard.

Further, Goldwater-Nichols mandates that the annual report to Congress by the Secretary of Defense will henceforth reflect—in certain stipulated areas—the content of the President's national security strategy report. The stipulated points include a justification for the major U.S. military missions during the following fiscal year, together with an explanation of the relationship of the military force structure to those missions.[1]

The intent of Goldwater-Nichols with regard to defense planning is also indicated in its requirement of a one-time series (in 1987) of DoD management reports. Among other requirements, these reports were intended to provide Secretary of Defense, Chairman of the Joint Chiefs of Staff, service secretary, and independent contractor views on whether:

- DoD organization ensures that strategic planning and contingency planning are linked to, and derived from, national security strategy, policies, and objectives.

- DoD's Planning, Programming, and Budgeting System (PPBS) ensures that strategic planning is consistent with national security strategy, policies, and objectives.[2]

President Bush continued the review process, and a number of changes in process were introduced (Cheney, 1989). Nonetheless, much remains to be accomplished if the coherence called for by the Goldwater-Nichols act is to be achieved.

STRATEGY OR OBJECTIVES?

Most laments about the alleged lack of rationality in the current defense-planning process center around the observation that the United States lacks an explicit post–Cold War strategy at the national security and national military planning levels.

A strategy is a plan for using available resources to achieve specified objectives.[3] In a sense, such plans do exist at the levels mentioned. They exist in the form of budgets. However, these spending plans usually lack a coherent audit trail showing how allocating resources in this manner achieves recognized national security objectives. Or, if an audit trail is evident, the allocation may not be what the critic would prefer. So part of the defense-planning problem

---

[1] Public Law 99-433, *Department of Defense Reorganization Act of 1986*, October 1, 1986, Sec. 603.

[2] Public Law 99-433, Sec. 109.

[3] This is a paraphrase of the definition given in the *Joint Dictionary of Military Terminology*, JFM 1-2.

centers on the perception that public budget statements do not reflect an underlying rationale for the allocation of resources reflected in the documents.

Objective-based planning reflects the fundamental relationship between strategy and objectives: *Outlining a plan (strategy) to attain stated goals at one level of organization simultaneously defines objectives to be achieved at the next-lower level of implementation.* Thus, plans for one of the executive departments, e.g., the Department of Defense, identify objectives appropriate for each major division and functional agency. An important advantage afforded by attention to this pattern of subordinate objectives, rather than by a series of elaborate strategy papers, is its utility in supplying a clear audit trail from the highest level of policy articulation down through successive levels of administration.

HIERARCHY OF OBJECTIVES RELATING TO DEFENSE PLANNING

The hierarchy of defense-planning objectives—from national security objectives, derived from the mandate to protect our fundamental goals, down to specific military tasks—is depicted in Figure 1.[4] Plans of action are defined at each level in response to perceptions of the threat and the strategic environment. Strategists at the national security level identify national security objectives. Planners at the national military level identify national military objectives and regional campaign objectives. Regional commanders and regional planners define operational objectives in campaign plans and identify specific military tasks to be accomplished in a concept of employment. Feedback (see slender arrows in Figure 1) enables plans to be modified in reaction to changing operational and fiscal constraints and the changing threat.

Against this background, we now provide specific illustrative examples for the elements of the hierarchy. They do not, however, represent an exhaustive or definitive catalogue of U.S. national security objectives.

Fundamental Goals to Maintain

Fundamental goals are defined by the Constitution of the United States. They include physical safety for our citizens, independence for the nation, and

---

[4]In Figure 1, the dark, heavier arrows depict formal directives from higher authority; the shaded arrows depict less direct, but significant, influences; the slender arrows depict feedback from subordinate organizations. To be sure, there are sometimes conflicts among objectives and instances in which objectives are inherently ambiguous to some degree. There are also a variety of constraints affecting the processes to which Figure 1 applies. Despite these complications, a great deal can be accomplished in this framework.

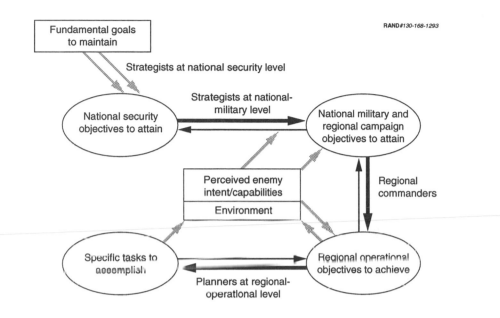

RAND#130-168-1293

Figure 1—Hierarchy of Objectives Relating to Defense Planning

a democratic way of life. They are enduring and unchanging. There is no feedback loop. These fundamental goals are to be maintained regardless of the threat and at all costs.

National Security Objectives to Attain

National security objectives are derived in response to threats to our fundamental goals. They are established at the level of the National Security Council (NSC). For example, the presence of many Soviet divisions on the inter-German border after World War II, coupled with the actions and statements of Soviet leaders, caused strategists at the national security level to define (among others) the following national security objectives:

- Prevent the Soviet Union from dominating Western Europe.
- Deter the Soviets from launching a large military campaign to overwhelm Western Europe.
- Prevent such a campaign from being successful if launched.

In the new era, our urgent attention is focused on other regions—especially Southwest Asia and Northeast Asia. The policies of rogue leaders in these areas threaten our vital interests.

Strategists at the national security level have defined our national security objectives, a *few* of which we mention here, as follows:[5]

With regard to Southwest Asia:

• Defend the sovereignty, independence, and territorial integrity of our partners in the region. Assure access to oil from the region.

• Deter recourse to war, terrorism, and subversion, and enforce UN Security Council resolutions.

• Successfully counter military aggression, if it occurs.

With regard to Northeast Asia:

• Preclude any single power or consortium of states from attempting to dominate the region.

• Deter aggression by North Korea or defeat it should deterrence fail.

• Preserve the U.S.-Japanese security linkage.

National Military Objectives and Campaign Objectives to Attain

Whereas national *security* objectives embrace all instruments of national power, i.e., political, economic, and military, national *military* objectives state those objectives to be achieved—at least in part—through the use of military resources. The national security objectives defined above prompt planners (strategists) at the level of the Secretary of Defense and the Chairman of the Joint Chiefs of Staff (the principal military adviser) to adjust and refine subordinate objectives.[6]

To illustrate, we continue the example of national security objectives for Northeast Asia. These objectives include assuring the security of South Korea and improving the current situation between North and South Korea. Implied by this is the need for a robust defense of South Korea in the event of invasion

---

[5]See Bush (1993) and Cheney (1993). The latter is more candid and comprehensive in matters relevant to defense planning.

[6]We deal here only with military objectives potentially requiring the use of military forces in combat. There are other important objectives such as environment-shaping (arguably a means rather than an end), deterrence (related to but not identical with having warfighting capabilities), effective crisis response, peacekeeping, and peacemaking. Many of these are discussed in Davis (1994b).

by the North. Indeed, should war occur, *the central regional campaign objective would be to conduct a successful forward defense of South Korea.* This would be important because the capital city, Seoul, and much of South Korea's wealth is located close to the border.

Although we shall not elaborate here, the operational objectives, subordinate to stated campaign objectives, are often phased. For example, in the first phase of a campaign to defend South Korea, the United States would have an operational objective of successful rapid reinforcement of South Korean and U.S. capabilities in Korea in time to avoid collapse of the defenses.

The framing of military objectives for a particular region reflects the defensive capabilities of our local allies as well as the military capabilities of potential opponents who threaten our national interests and security objectives for that region. For example, even for a region as important to U.S. interests as Northeast Asia, preparations to conduct a successful forward defense would not be accorded the status of a U.S. national military objective unless it was perceived that the region was threatened by an opponent with the capability of carrying out an effective invasion or a damaging attack against local defenses. Thus, as the perceived intent and capabilities of potential enemies and our allies change, the relevance of a given U.S. national military objective for a particular region can intensify or fade. That relevance is also affected by such variables as economic and political conditions.

Regional Operational Objectives to Achieve

Once the Secretary of Defense and the Chairman of the Joint Chiefs of Staff (CJCS) have defined desired campaign outcomes, regional commanders must orchestrate the preliminary deployments and the employment of many different force elements made available to them. This level of planning has become known as *operational art.*[7] In the course of these preparations, a number of different regional operational objectives are identified and pursued. These are stated in the campaign plan. Achieving these operational objectives, according to the campaign plan, attains the outcomes already stated.

---

[7]The concept of military operational art as a distinct planning realm connecting strategy with military tactics was developed in the German General Staff and taught in the Kriegsakademie in the period just prior to World War I. It was adopted and elaborated upon by the theoreticians and staff colleges of the Red Army in the interwar period and incorporated in Soviet military science. The general concept was embraced by the U. S. Army in the 1970s and 1980s and is reflected prominently in its AirLand Battle doctrine.

The following list contains some probable operational objectives subordinate to the regional campaign objective of "conduct a successful forward defense of South Korea."[8]

- Halt invading armies short of Seoul.
- Gain air superiority:
    - Suppress generation of enemy air sorties.
    - Defeat enemy air attacks.
    - Defeat enemy air defenses.
- Provide command and control of force elements.
- Disrupt enemy's command and control—especially, disengage leadership from control of deployed forces.
- Evict and destroy enemy armies once halted:
    - Interdict enemy ground forces.
    - Provide close support to friendly ground force elements.
- Prevent or defend against use of weapons of mass destruction.

Some of these objectives are more central than others. For example, halting invading armies short of Seoul is a central operational objective, while gaining air superiority is a supporting objective to which suppressing generation of enemy air sorties is itself subordinate. As we noted above, the weight of effort among operational objectives may also be phased. Attaining air superiority might be a prerequisite for the phase of the campaign that would "evict and destroy" enemy forces.

Specific Military Tasks to Accomplish

The next subordinate level of planning objectives differentiates among the major tasks that must be completed to achieve a stated regional operational objective. Needed here are statements of what different force elements in the region might actually do, so that collectively the desired operational objective is achieved. In our illustrative example, we further disaggregate the operational objective "provide command and control of force elements," and list the separate tasks subordinate to that objective:

---

[8]We say "probable" because it would be possible, of course, to develop a different campaign plan, depending on the political-military context. Planning under uncertainty involves defining rich enough military campaigns for planning purposes so that the capabilities needed for a wide range of circumstances are generated and refined. Much can be built into individual campaigns when one appreciates the need for flexibility, but alternative campaign concepts are also necessary (Davis, 1994b).

- Conduct surveillance of the target areas and related support structures.
- Assess target data collected by sensor systems.
- Define target structure and individual characteristics.
- Allocate available resources among selected missions to implement theater concept of employment.
- Allocate specific targets among designated force elements.
- Select flight routes, tactics, and ordnance for specific targets.

A further illustration is provided by the operational objective "suppress generation of enemy air sorties." The separate tasks subordinate to that objective are as follows:

- Crater runways.
- Mine operating surfaces.
- Disrupt/damage airbase infrastructure.
- Damage aircraft in open.
- Damage aircraft in shelters.
- "Pin down" takeoffs.

As shown above, several different tasks may be undertaken in pursuit of the same operational objective. The operational commander and the planner are confronted with the problem of allocating the appropriate weight of effort to each task relative to the others, depending in part upon the opportunity costs of using available force elements to accomplish one task rather than others and to achieve the stated operational objective rather than others.

Military tasks are defined as theater commanders refine their *concept of employment* of the resources they expect to have at their disposal in pursuing specified operational objectives. These concepts of employment indicate the probable allocation of effort among tasks: where, how frequently, and for what scope and duration force elements will be applied to the accomplishment of the various tasks.

THE PROPER ORGANIZING THEME—OBJECTIVES OR CONFLICTS?

In defense planning, to focus on "conflicts" (threat-based planning) invites attention to forecasts of enemy actions. Will the Soviets launch a major offensive against NATO? Will the leader of Iraq attempt to take over some country (or countries) rich in oil? Since we cannot know the answer to these questions, we are left to lament, in the context of "conflicts" as our organizing theme, that we must plan in the face of great uncertainty.

To focus on objectives creates a much different construction. Although we do not know, with any certainty at all, what a potential enemy intends to do, we do know what we do not want the enemy to do: We do not want him to dominate a region in which our vital national interests would be threatened. Thus, a focus on objectives invites attention to what steps might be taken—political, economic, or military in nature—to shape the political environment in that region and to deter or dissuade an enemy leader in a particular region from engaging in activities (including military aggression) that impact on our vital interests. At the same time, we must ensure that we have the military capability to counter military aggression should it occur.

Said another way, we should focus on objectives in organizing our thoughts. This approach is quite distinct from a focus on "conflicts" as the organizing theme. Objectives are enduring. Whether or not there will indeed be an actual conflict in some region is not knowable and is a subordinate issue. In the final analysis, the outcome we seek is to attain our stated objectives in the absence of conflict. Thus, objective-based planning (according to a hierarchy of objectives) is both more relevant and more enduring.

RELATING THE HIERARCHY OF OBJECTIVES TO ACTIVITIES

Establishing a relationship between the hierarchy of objectives and various activities to enhance military capabilities is crucial if we are to have a coherent approach. Figure 2 describes such a relationship.

Six Activities for Enhancing Military Capabilities

The DoD engages in six interrelated activities:

- *Worriers* identify deficiencies and missions in need of special and increased emphasis, make "Mission Need Statements," and direct action be taken to explore new concepts. This is done in the presence of campaign and operational objectives defined and stated by regional commanders and statements of operational requirements by those commanders.

- *Technologists* identify promising technologies and direct that technology aggregates that have possible application to stated operational requirements be matured.

- *Conceivers* engage in concept development—formulating, defining, evaluating, and finally demonstrating new operational concepts for accomplishing tasks and new concepts for employment to achieve operational objectives.

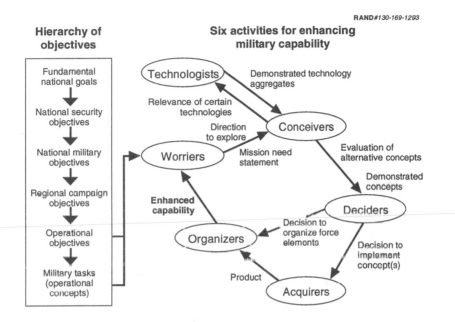

Figure 2—Hierarchy of Objectives and Activities for Enhancing Military Capability

This activity is central and is conducted in the presence of the Mission Need Statement and existing and emerging technology.

- *Acquirers* conduct programs for developing and acquiring new systems to implement selected operational concepts.

- *Deciders* decide about the allocation of resources. This activity (part of the PPBS) overlies all other activities except the first.

DISCUSSION: WHY DOES ANY OF THIS MATTER?

The top-down framework we describe here may seem unexceptional, and even obvious. However, decades of experience have indicated that making this framework or something like it into a reality is difficult and generally not practiced. In addition to its value in establishing a better understanding between Congress and the Department of Defense as defense budgets are approved, the framework can be a powerful unifying device for the national security community. It can help the many players in the executive branch (all the way from national-level strategists down to the military forces preparing to accomplish specific tasks in combat) to see how they and their responsibilities relate to one another. Further, it can mitigate natural organizational processes that interfere with sound planning. These inhibiting and confusing practices include:

- Establishing and then maintaining and enforcing "requirements" at the wrong level of detail, as in establishing "requirements" (which are actually performance specifications) for particular weapon systems rather than for accomplishing military tasks and achieving operational objectives. In actuality, these tasks might be accomplished and the objectives achieved in any of several ways, with different methods being appropriate in different circumstances (e.g., as a function of enemy capabilities and strategy and of costs associated with alternative concepts).

- Establishing parochial mind-sets that undercut joint (and combined) operations to accomplish higher-level objectives.

- Overfocusing on some tasks and objectives while failing to address others that would be critical to the outcomes in overall campaigns.

In recent years this general framework (often and unfortunately misnamed the "strategies-to-tasks" approach) has been developed and applied successfully in a number of RAND studies for the Air Force, CINCs, and Joint Staff. Figure 2 is a literal description of how RAND has organized and conducted some of its work (e.g., work sponsored and participated in by the Commander in Chief of the Strategic Command).

Much of the work has been in the context of rethinking how to accomplish both acquisition and the front-end work (e.g., creatively identifying operational concepts to accomplish tasks and achieve operational objectives, including efforts to exploit existing and emerging technology and other U.S. strengths) that should precede acquisition (Kent and Thaler, 1993). Some has been in the context of improving the effectiveness of CINCs' participation in the PPBS process (Lewis and Roll, 1993) and improving the coherence of Cost and Operational Effectiveness Analyses (COEAs). In practice, the framework and its embellishments have been succeeding in the marketplace.

SUMMARY AND IMPLICATIONS

We have shown how one can go coherently from stated national security objectives, to national military objectives, to regional campaign objectives, to operational objectives, to military tasks. There is a clear audit trail from top to bottom. Since we have subordinated from the top down, we can also integrate upward. For example, force elements acting in concert accomplish tasks that in the aggregate form the regional commander's concept of employment to achieve stated operational objectives. Achieving operational objectives according to the commander's campaign plan provides the means for attaining the stated campaign and military objectives for that region.

This hierarchy of objectives is at the very core of defense planning and offers real advantages. First, by specifying the ends to be *sought* at each level of planning, this approach provides clearer meaning to the strategies being formulated. Second, it provides a certain stability to our national security policies, year by year and era by era; the relative priorities among objectives and their specific character may change, especially at the national security and national military levels, but the essential elements provide a general continuity for the nation's defense effort. Third, when applied as a basis for constructing the DoD's Planning, Programming, and Budgeting System, it sets the stage for an allocation of national defense resources to best effect.

BIBLIOGRAPHY

Bush, George (1993), *National Security Strategy of the United States*, The White House, Washington, D.C.

Cheney, Dick (1989), *Defense Management Report to the President*, Department of Defense, Washington, D.C.

———— (1993), *Defense Strategy for the 1990s: The Regional Defense Strategy*, Department of Defense, Washington, D.C., January.

Davis, Paul K. (ed.) (1994a), *New Challenges for Defense Planning: Rethinking How Much Is Enough*, RAND, Santa Monica, CA.

———— (1994b), "Planning Under Uncertainty Then and Now: Paradigms Lost and Paradigms Emerging," in Davis (1994a).

Kent, Glenn A., and William Simons (1991), *A Framework for Enhancing Operational Capabilities*, RAND, Santa Monica, CA.

Kent, Glenn, and David E. Thaler (1993), *A New Concept for Streamlining Up-Front Planning*, RAND, Santa Monica, CA.

Lewis, Leslie, and Robert Roll (1993), *Strategies to Tasks: A Methodology for Resource Allocation and Management*, RAND, Santa Monica, CA.

Pollack, Jonathan, and James A. Winnefeld (1990), *U.S. Strategic Alternatives in a Changing Pacific*, RAND, Santa Monica, CA.

Chapter 4

INSTITUTIONALIZING PLANNING FOR ADAPTIVENESS

Paul K. Davis

This paper proposes ways to improve the adaptiveness of U.S. military capabilities for the post–Cold War world. In the process, it proposes to integrate the currently distinct activities of strategic planning, program planning, and operations planning. Doing so would require new concepts and methods, and major institutional changes. The paper argues four main points: (a) strategic and program planning should adopt methods of analysis with an operational perspective, i.e., a campaign perspective, that highlights issues in actually employing forces effectively in diverse contingencies demanding different combat forces, support forces, and concepts of operation; (b) in its strategic and program planning, DoD should discard the traditional emphasis on meeting "requirements" for one or a few detailed defense-planning scenarios in favor of an approach that recognizes the enormous range of plausible scenarios (even within a given theater) and then allocates resources efficiently to increase the region of "scenario space" for which capabilities would be adequate; (c) DoD should organize operations planning around rapid and adaptive crisis planning, rather than dependence on monolithic "on-the-shelf" plans, and should be able to develop executable, strategically appropriate, and context-specific plans within days; and (d) to assure such capabilities, DoD should restructure its operations-planning system around building-block methods and frequent exercising monitored by a Readiness Inspector reporting to the Secretary of Defense.

BACKGROUND

In mid-1990 the Joint Staff's Director for Strategy and Plans asked RAND to conduct a study that would help define and communicate a new approach to defense planning emphasizing adaptiveness and realism in anticipating "nonstandard" contingencies—i.e., contingencies very different in detail from the standard defense planning scenarios that have dominated DoD planning for decades (Davis, 1994c). The request, by General George (Lee) Butler, was due to prior RAND work on planning under uncertainty (Davis, 1988, 1989; Winnefeld and Shlapak, 1990).

Before work had actually begun, Iraq invaded Kuwait in a prototypical example of a nonstandard scenario. Early project work focused on ideas for dealing with the crisis and learning how to build alternative models of opponent reasoning to assist in strategy development (Davis and Arquilla, 1991a,b; Davis, 1994a). Subsequently, attention turned to the conceptual and organizational issues involved in making planning for adaptiveness (adaptive planning, for short) a reality. The Joint Staff was already making important changes in operations planning, but more far-reaching changes appeared desirable. Further, the problem involved not only operations planning, but also strategic and program planning. Comprehensive change would need the imprimatur of the Secretary of Defense. The challenge, then, was to develop the philosophy of adaptive planning, to identify methods for turning that philosophy into something practical and analytic, and to suggest ways to address the realities of organizational inertia. This paper briefly summarizes and extends the principal themes and conclusions of that study, which is documented in more detail elsewhere (Davis and Finch, 1993).[1] These themes and conclusions are radical, calling for fundamental changes in the way defense planning is conducted. In the sections that follow I first discuss the problem itself, that is, the ways in which DoD planning has been ill suited for adaptiveness; I then identify components of organizational reform and discuss each of them at some length. Finally, I discuss some of the obstacles to reform and how they might be circumvented.

BASIS FOR CONCERN: RIGID PLANNING

Rigidity? Hasn't the DoD Always Been Adaptive?

As a preface to stating the problem that motivated the study, it is worth emphasizing that the U.S. military has often proven remarkably adaptive. Most of its officers are highly competitive, well educated, and innovative. The services are also rightfully proud of their noncommissioned officers, who set a tone for their units and determine success or failure. Indeed, in the last fifteen years, the United States has enjoyed having military personnel generally of exceptionally high quality, and that quality is reflected every day in grass-roots adaptiveness. If there is a problem, then, it is not in our personnel.

What about our organizations, then? Here the story is mixed. On the one hand, the Department of Defense has adapted exceptionally well to many challenges over the years. Examples include the buildup for the Korean War, the logistics system established for Vietnam, the specialized units developed for

---

[1] I had two principal colleagues in the study: Lou Finch, who co-authored the study while at RAND before taking a senior position in the Office of the Secretary of Defense, and Paul Bracken of Yale University, who worked as a RAND consultant, particularly on organizational learning.

Vietnam, the development of the Rapid Deployment Force, and the doctrinal shift toward more operational-level aggressiveness (e.g., the AirLand Battle). The United States has also fielded the best systems in the world. When wars have arisen, plans have gone out the window as necessary and new ones have been developed (e.g., as in the Gulf War, which found the United States putting together a massive counteroffensive operation exploiting airpower in a way never before seen in warfare). And at the level of small-scale ad hoc crises, the U.S. military has generally done well (e.g., in Libya, Grenada, Panama, and Somalia). What, then, is the problem? Does a problem even exist?

One Challenge Is Achieving *Speedy* Adaptiveness

Having stated what the problem is *not*, let me now turn to what I believe the problem really is. The essence of the argument is as follows:

- In its strategic, program, and operations planning for large-scale conflicts (major regional contingencies or MRCs), the DoD continues to *create* rigidity that could be exceedingly dangerous early in such a conflict.

- That is, the United States is not well prepared for *speedy* adaptive planning early in large-scale crises or conflicts (i.e., adaptations made within hours or days rather than months and years).

- The United States has been lucky so far. Our adversaries have given us considerable time in which to ponder, react, and adapt. We cannot expect such a luxury in the future, especially since would-be aggressors drawing lessons from the Gulf War will surely conclude that a preferred strategy for dealing with the United States is to act quickly and decisively (see, e.g., Bennett, Gardiner, and Fox, 1994).

- The threat of *fait accompli* situations will be even more worrisome against adversaries with weapons of mass destruction (WMD), because dislodging them from their ill-gotten gains will be a more dicey proposition, both politically and militarily. In political-science terms, we should prefer to make deterrence work, because compellence—never easy—may become more difficult than ever (Millot, Molander, and Wilson, 1993; Watman and Wilkening, forthcoming).

- Deterrence is notoriously difficult, but an essential ingredient in success is often firm action early in crisis, even if that action is militarily (and politically) risky. Crises that could be quelled by such early action can quickly become disasters otherwise.[2]

---

[2]Without in any way underestimating the difficulty of *taking* the requisite actions, I would argue (Davis, 1994a) that Saddam Hussein's invasion of Kuwait and Serbia's aggression in the former Yugoslavia could both have been prevented by firm military and other actions early in crisis.

The Rigidity of Detailed Strategic, Program, and Operations Planning

Is it true that U.S. planning for large-scale conflicts has been rigid? After all, conventional wisdom in some circles has it that Cold War defense planning was well developed and sophisticated, although changes are now necessary to deal with diverse and vaguely defined current or potential threats. In fact, there were many serious deficiencies. Much Cold War planning could have been described with adjectives such as rigid, unrealistic, monolithic, and stereotyped. This was true despite the expressed desire of successive secretaries of defense for flexibility.

Consider, for example, the extraordinary emphasis placed on developing a single operations plan for the defense of Western Europe. This plan (and the mostly similar scenario used for programmatic work) depended on dozens of crucial assumptions that were treated as good predictions, despite everyone's knowing better. Although military leaders surely thought about wartime adaptations, they were unable to develop them in detail, much less exercise them. As a second example, consider the 1990 Gulf crisis. Prior planning assumed: considerable actionable warning; a series of partial alerts, mobilizations, and deployments; and a particular sense of what was and was not to be defended. Not surprisingly, the assumptions were wrong (indeed, the United States did not even begin deployment until D+4!). Had Saddam Hussein continued into Saudi Arabia without delay, the United States would have had an extremely difficult time countering the invasion—not only because of the distances involved and political constraints, but also because it was ill prepared to make major changes in large-scale operations rapidly. There had been inadequate discussions with political leaders about alternative military objectives and strategies (e.g., defending Kuwait rather than Saudi Arabia), there were few preliminary measures taken in response to strategic warning, the military planning system was too slow in adapting, there were major misunderstandings about what could realistically be done by a deploying CINC and his staff, the on-the-shelf plan was sketchy, and adaptations made by the CINC could not be accommodated gracefully by the command-and-control system.

An Organizational Obstacle: The Deliberate Planning System

Despite important recent reforms in U.S. military planning,[3] the current system is unlikely to meet the challenge posed above because much of it is still

---

[3]The Joint Staff's new guidance to CINCs requires them to consider multiple scenarios and to develop plans with some built-in flexibility, somewhat akin to that of

structured around so-called "deliberate planning." The system includes many features likely to undercut capability for rapid adaptive planning in large and complex contingencies that cannot be handled effectively by the excellent crisis-action teams that now exist. To be sure, the deliberate planning system includes many critical functions that must be retained (e.g., developing and testing procedures, databases, and planning factors), but even the improved version of deliberate planning is fundamentally flawed. In particular, deliberate planning:

- Produces a few detailed plans (albeit with significant flexibility within those plans) rather than refining an adaptive planning *process* able to deal quickly with challenges not foreseen in the preplanned options.

- Has no routinized *testing* of plans or adaptive planning for nonstandard situations. (It is analogous to a football team building playbooks and options without the benefit of stressful practice and games to test, refine, and broaden the options.)

- Has no success standards relating directly to crisis planning (e.g., rapid adaptiveness and flexibility for the President).

- Does not include many of the participants that would be most significant in crisis and does not go far enough in laying the framework for coordinating political, economic, and military instruments (which coordination would be an NSC function).

- Relies on communications, obsolete data-processing systems, expertise, and other supporting tools that are inappropriate for crisis operations.

- Discourages planners from dealing often enough and well with scenario variants that are decidedly nonstandard.

To elaborate on this last item, consider the importance of thinking through scenarios currently deemed improbable (until they happen) or "unacceptable" (e.g., scenarios presupposing a type of U.S. military involvement currently believed to be undesirable). Ideally, planners should routinely be working through nonstandard scenarios that are objectively plausible and important, whether or not they are pleasant to contemplate (Kugler, 1994). For example, it is entirely appropriate for DoD to study in detail possible strategies for deterring a Russian reinvasion of Lithuania or Ukraine, including strategies focused on deterrence through threat of punishment rather than capability to defeat an invasion. Similarly, DoD should be constantly studying—*long before they become salient*—potential strategies for contingencies as unpopular as limited

---

football teams, which have options triggered by "audibles" before the snap. For discussion, see Davis and Finch (1993:53ff).

military intervention in the former Yugoslavia under various coalitional arrangements and with various distinctly limited objectives.[4]

Philosophical Obstacles to Speedy Adaptiveness: Desires for Clear Objectives, Political Consensus, and Decisive Force

One obstacle to planning for *prompt* adaptiveness is the U.S. military's understandable antipathy toward ad hoc operations undertaken without careful consideration of potential consequences and development of both political consensus and determination. Still another obstacle is the military's desire to go into any conflict with overwhelming force so that casualties can be minimized and objectives achieved decisively. Under General Colin Powell, this emphasis on decisive force became a key element of military doctrine.

Unfortunately, there is a tension between, on the one hand, a reasoned and deliberate approach that avoids risks to tripwire forces[5] and eventually produces overwhelming force, and, on the other hand, the need in many crises for prompt and politically decisive actions. For example, the invasion of Kuwait would probably have been averted if the United States had been willing and invited to deploy a small tripwire force directly into Kuwait (Davis and Arquilla, 1991a), backed up by tactical air forces in Saudi Arabia. Instead, for a variety of reasons that included attitudes of regional states, the United States attempted to show resolve with the most timid of military actions, which was probably a counterdeterrent. Significantly, the use of militarily insignificant and potentially counterproductive "signals," rather than the dispatch of more substantial military forces into harm's way, is a psychologically natural approach that nations continue to use in attempts at deterrence. U.S. Flexible Deterrent Options (FDOs) may have these problems (Davis, 1994a).

---

[4]A major problem here is that leaks can cause a political brouhaha, as occured in 1991 when DoD was criticized for having a defend-Lithuania scenario. Some prominent members of Congress worried that DoD was getting out ahead of national policy and seeing vital interests, and threats to those interests, where neither existed. The greater danger is that the United States will fail to think seriously about politically troublesome contingencies until after they occur and it becomes clear that U.S. interests are greater than they previously appeared to be (Davis, 1994a).

[5]These risks should not be underestimated. Army officers all remember the disaster of Task Force Smith at the outset of the Korean War. Fortunately, the United States today has the option to insert small, lethal, and mobile forces, with survivability enhanced by supporting tactical and long-range air forces. In some cases, precision-strike capabilities from standoff positions can be substituted for classic tripwires. In other cases, however, tripwire forces on the ground may be needed. The risk to them must be weighed, in each case individually, against the potential for avoiding a much larger and bloodier conflict.

A Final Problem: Planning for Adaptiveness in an Era of Tight Budgets

So far, I have emphasized speedy adaptiveness in crisis. But there is another problem. While it is true that the U.S. military has been remarkably adaptive in past crises and wars over a time scale of months and years, much of that has been possible only because it had a massive military establishment. Equipment in short supply could be borrowed from other units, capabilities believed only by a minority to be important could be procured and protected, and mass could compensate for specialized capabilities (Lewis, 1994). We will not have such luxury in the years ahead. Instead, the pressure will be to eliminate all but the most critical of capabilities, which in turn will translate into eliminating capabilities (e.g., light infantry) that are less prestigious but critical in some circumstances (Davis, 1994c). Unless the planning system changes so as to highlight the existence of "holes," the scaling-down process will seriously hurt U.S. military adaptiveness.

TOWARD A NEW APPROACH TO EMPHASIZE ADAPTIVENESS

Under the assumption that one is convinced that the United States badly needs to improve its planning for adaptiveness, what steps should be taken? RAND's study for the Joint Staff (Davis and Finch, 1993) recommended an approach with four key elements of reform. Taken together, they would be revolutionary. They were: (a) reconceptualizing planning to more seriously confront the issue of uncertainty, building heavily on recent Joint Staff initiatives; (b) building-block planning for rapid plan development and adaptation; (c) revising organizational relationships to better integrate work on strategy, programs, and current operational planning; and (d) constant exercising of the system's capabilities.[6] Let us now consider each of these in turn.

PLANNING UNDER UNCERTAINTY: A NEW WAY TO CONCEPTUALIZE THE PROBLEM

The preeminent challenge of U.S. defense planning is dealing with uncertainty (Davis, 1994c). It is this challenge that leads to requests for adaptive-

---

[6]Some officers to whom the study was briefed believed that major reforms were well underway and that operations planning, at least, had already become sufficiently adaptive. We were unconvinced, and concluded that the organizational changes underway were insufficiently radical; further, even those changes might slip into history as normal organizational processes reassert themselves (see Davis and Finch, 1993:102).

ness.   There are literally hundreds of critical factors that determine what constitutes an appropriate military strategy in time of crisis or conflict.   How does one take all of these into account in planning?   And how is this different in the cases of strategic, program, and operations planning?

Discarding the Illustrative-Scenario Approach

In our study we concluded that the first step should be to reject categorically, once and forever, the longstanding approach of focusing on one or a few standard scenarios.   Planning would still use scenarios, and there would still exist analytical baseline cases, which are essential for guidance and analysis, but the baseline cases would no longer form the centerpiece of planning (and would include cases very different from current planning scenarios).   So long as standard scenarios are the centerpiece, and despite protestations to the contrary, many peacetime planners will come to treat them as predictive and will develop mental attitudes, analytical constructs, and procedures making *rapid* adaptation in crisis difficult.   Empirically, we know that calling the scenarios "illustrative" has never solved this problem, because organizations yearn for concreteness and the "test cases" become "the" cases. This is especially so with respect to organizational processes, routines, and measures of effectiveness.[7]

---

[7]This recommendation may seem unreasonable to some readers who, like me, have actually done program planning. Defense-planning scenarios have been exceptionally valuable for managing the Department of Defense (e.g., by establishing a common yardstick by which competing programs can be measured and by simplifying the task of coordinating the efforts of four military services with respect to both combat and support capabilities). Further, such scenarios have been a major tool in selling the defense program to Congress.   Experienced individuals such as Les Aspin and William Kaufmann have argued that selling uncertainty doesn't work and that DoD must focus on one or more specific and plausible contingencies (Kaufmann, 1992:27).   My response here is twofold. First, as discussed later in the paper, analytical baseline cases would continue to exist under the new approach. There would be more of them, but this would improve the quality of defense management and should not overload the system given an appropriate choice of people to oversee analysis in DoD and the services. Second, the ability to "sell" the defense program with "requirements" for two specific MRCs is probably not sustainable in any case (Davis, 1994c). DoD and Congress will need to learn how to do more candid assessments of what and how much is needed. For much more extensive discussion of the scenario issues, see Kugler (1994); for another critical view of standard scenarios, see Builder (1993).

The Scenario-Space Methodology

The next step is to conceptualize the planning problem as one of dealing with a large "space" of plausible scenarios. This does not mean simply having one scenario for each of many geographical regions. Instead, each currently standard scenario for a given geographical region (e.g., North Korea's invasion of South Korea) should be considered merely one point in a large space of possible scenarios. This scenario space can be thought of as having six aggregate dimensions, as indicated in Figure 1, with a single scenario being just one point in that many-dimensional space.[8]

Note that in this perspective almost nothing is "fixed." There is a willingness to face up to what is truly massive uncertainty. For example, we often do not know within a factor of two how effective various enemy and allied forces would be in combat, even though we understand their weapon holdings and order of battle. Nor do we even know, in advance, what political-military objectives will be established, because those will depend on details of the situation. Even the "military science" is riddled with uncertainties, as should be evident to those who recall the dramatically different before-the-fact estimates of likely U.S. casualties in the counteroffensive that began against Iraq early in 1991. The point here is this:

- Uncertainty is not a mere nuisance requiring a bit of sensitivity analysis; it is a dominant characteristic of serious planning.

Single-scenario analysis makes no sense at all, except for its managerial advantages in peacetime.

Obviously, the United States cannot reasonably seek military capabilities assuring success in all scenarios. However, defense planners should know "the envelope," i.e., know what portions of scenario space the United States could now and should in the future be able to deal with effectively—perhaps assuming a bit of luck. This concept of scenario space and the coverage envelope of a particular U.S. force may be useful to defense planning in several ways.

Pushing Back the Envelope as an Objective. Instead of focusing on meeting "requirements" for standard scenarios, defense programs could focus on improving capabilities for entire *regions* of scenario space. Figure 2 illustrates this for a broad class of scenarios described by the items under "Case"

---

[8]This breakdown is intended to be practical, not merely conceptual. My colleagues and I have used it to characterize scenarios and to design multiscenario analyses involving many hundreds of variations. Such broad exploratory analyses, which are still quite unusual, are often exceptionally informative. See Davis (1988), Bankes (1992), and, for at least brief mention, Rostker, Don, and Watman (1994).

RAND#130-157-0394

1. *Political-military setting* (e.g., origin of crisis; alliances; broad interests; and timing of warning, alerts, mobilization, deployment, etc.)
2. *Operational objectives and strategies* (for the U.S., opponents, allies, and third countries)
3. *Forces and other instruments of power* (e.g., orders of battle, structure of units)
4. *Weapon-system and individual-force capabilities* (e.g., accuracy of precision munitions, the movement rate of armored units, efficiency of command-control systems, and the qualitative effectiveness of officers and men resulting from training, morale, and other factors)
5. *Geographic and other aspects of environment* (e.g., weather, terrain, transportation networks, and port facilities)
6. *The processes that govern military operations, including combat* (e.g., the equations describing the phenomena of combat and movement)

Figure 1—Dimensions of Scenario Space

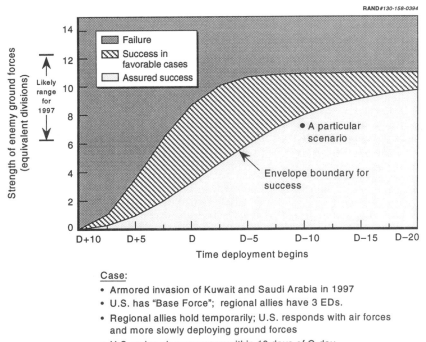

Case:
- Armored invasion of Kuwait and Saudi Arabia in 1997
- U.S. has "Base Force"; regional allies have 3 EDs.
- Regional allies hold temporarily; U.S. responds with air forces and more slowly deploying ground forces
- U.S. gains air supremacy within 10 days of C-day

Figure 2—Notional Objectives Expressed in Scenario-Space Terms

(war with Iraq, revisited). Within this context, the x and y axes represent two of the most important scenario variables, the time available before D-day and the size of the enemy threat. The diagram then expresses notional objectives as follows: we want the capability to deal with *all* the scenarios in the light region inside the "envelope boundary for assured success." We also want the capability to deal successfully—given favorable circumstances with respect to other scenario variables (e.g., weather and allied cooperation)—with all the scenarios in the region with slashes. By contrast, we do not seek the capability to deal successfully with the scenarios in the dark region, except perhaps in instances in which all other factors are highly favorable. Note that objectives are expressed in terms of a *region* in scenario space, not a particular point scenario.

Figure 3 is a discretized representation of similar notional objectives (or what some might call requirements), but with some additional nuances treated. Here again, "light" means that the requirement is for success without demanding much luck; slashes mean that the requirement is for success in instances in which circumstances are favorable; and dark indicates cases that are too hard (or too expensive) to deal with rapidly. We would need to consider them also, but with different kinds of strategies, such as a lengthy campaign to reenter the region.

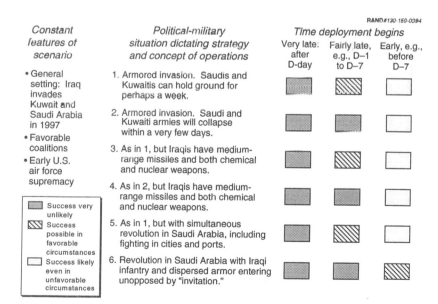

Figure 3—An Illustrative Scenario-Space Display of Objectives

Figures 2 and 3 assume that we know our objectives, but in reality cost is always a factor, whether explicitly or implicitly (Davis, 1994c). Figure 4 illustrates how one can use this type of scenario-space display to appreciate program choices. It shows capabilities as a function of programs with different costs. Note that Figure 4 includes information about six different scenarios varying in effective enemy force level and the deployment time available to the United States before D-day.

Classes of Scenario and Generic Campaigns

Dealing with the enormity of scenario space would be nearly impossible if it were not for the fact that large regions of scenario space would involve similar military activities. To implement the scenario-space approach it will be necessary, for each region, to identify such classes of scenario and, for each such class, to define generic concepts of operations or, to use a shorter phrase, generic campaigns. Being able to conduct such campaigns then becomes the objective around which systematic military planning can take place. Figure 5 indicates schematically how this differs from past practice.

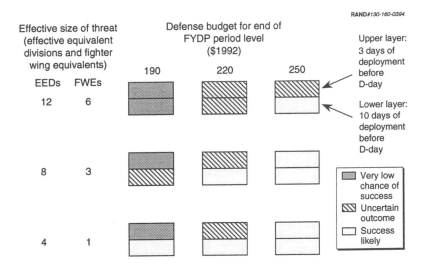

Figure 4—An Illustrative Display of Projected Capability as a Function of Threat, Reaction Time, and Budget Level

RAND#130-161-0394

1980s	Current	Proposed
One scenario for global war with Soviet Union. Requirements to be able to prevail militarily in the scenario.	One scenario for regional wars in each of Southwest Asia, Korea, plus some discussion of "generic" scenarios at a very high level of abstraction. For each specific scenario, requirements to be able to prevail militarily.	For each region of concern, a set of campaign classes, each with its own generic concept of operations. For each class of campaigns, extensive exploration of scenario and campaign variations and an effort to "push back the envelope" on the scenario-space region that can be handled.

Figure 5— Proposed Replacement of the Single-Scenario Approach

To illustrate the concept of classes of campaigns, consider again the example of a new war in the Persian Gulf (a reader finding this example "old" may want to think about the same issues for Korea or a war in Eastern Europe). Consider next that the time available for deployment before D-day is impossible to know in advance. Clearly, however, this variable is very important, as suggested earlier in Figures 2 and 3. Some cases are "impossible," but suppose we distinguish between the class of cases in which there is at least enough time to deploy so that the U.S. forces are in place before major losses of territory and bases occur, and the class of cases in which by the time U.S. forces arrive there are significant but not catastrophic problems at key bases and, perhaps, in the capital cities of our allies (e.g., due to an internal revolution fomented by Iraq in coordination with the invasion). In the former case, the premium would be on armored forces and airpower; in the latter case, the premium would be, initially, on forced-entry capability and airpower.

Figures 6 and 7 now illustrate schematically how different the concepts of operations would be for these two classes. That is, the *campaigns* would be very different.

How many classes of scenario are there? That is a subject for research that has not yet been accomplished. Clearly, there are more than two. To continue the Southwest Asian example, there is a class of scenarios in which the United States would have to fight its way back onto the northeastern side of the Arabian peninsula over a period of many months. Perhaps there are many more. However, my experience to date suggests that distinguishing among a few classes (for each "broad" scenario such as a new invasion by Iraq) goes a long way in laying bare the full range of needs, assuming extensive exploration of variations around a baseline case for each class.

RAND#130-162-0394

D-day   D+7   D+10   D+60

Time (weeks)

	D-day	D+7	D+10	D+60
Regional allies (target of aggression)	Conduct holding operations to protect key areas	(Continue as capable)		
Strategic bombers	Blunt armored attacks	Attack air bases, C3I and armies		
Special Operations forces	Secure key points; provide recon.; etc.		Conduct diverse support operations	
Ground-based air defenses	Defend key air and sea ports	Plus defend important areas	Plus defend theater air space	
Light infantry	Defend key air and sea ports	Defend other key points		
Air defense aircraft	Defend key areas	Attack enemy air forces		
Surveillance and battle-management aircraft	Support defensive operations	Support counter-air operations		
Fighter aircraft for air-to-ground missions		Conduct SEAD operations	Attack LOCs and ground forces	
Fighters and bombers for "strategic" bombing			Attack air bases and C3I	
Armored forces (including MPS Marines)			Defend key areas (MPS)	Conduct counteroffensive (Army and Marines)
Support forces	Support defensive operations			Support counteroffensive

Figure 6—Concept of Operations for Adequate-Warning Situation

RAND#130-163-0394

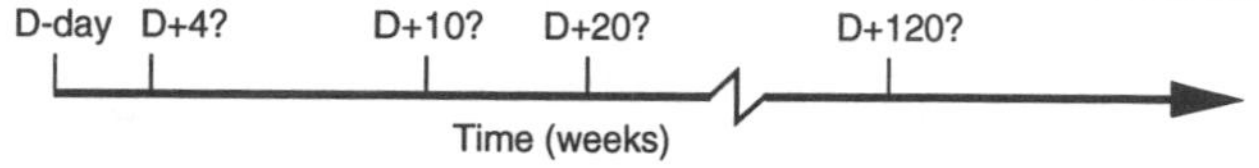

D-day D+4?   D+10?   D+20?   D+120?

Time (weeks)

	D-day / D+4?	D+10? / D+20?	D+120?
Regional allies (target of aggression)	Do best possible to survive coup de main tactics and internal revolution	Retake and secure key areas. Reestablish control. Reestablish armed forces, C3I, etc.	Participate in counter-offensive
Strategic bombers	Attack enemy's homeland for compellence?		
Special Operations forces	Support and conduct assault operations		Conduct diverse support operations
Ground-based air defenses		Defend key air and sea ports / Plus defend important areas	Plus defend theater air space
Light infantry	Assault and capture, then defend, key air and sea ports Protect allied leadership, C3I, etc.	Defend other key points Retake and secure some key urban areas. Reestablish friendly government. Conduct infantry operations in difficult terrain	
Air defense aircraft (Air Force and Navy)	Provide air cover for deploying forces	Attack enemy air forces	
Surveillance and battle-management aircraft	Support defensive operations	Support counter-air operations	
Fighter aircraft for air-to-ground missions	Support operations as feasible from available bases and carriers	SEAD Attack LOCs and ground forces where possible	
Fighters and bombers for "strategic" bombing	Support operations as feasible from available bases and carriers		
Armored forces (Army and MPS Marines with significant armor)		Defend key areas (MPS units)	Conduct counter-offensive (primarily Army)
Support forces	Support defensive operations		Support counter-offensive

Figure 7—Concept of Operations for Forced-Entry Situation

Taking such a multiscenario analysis approach has many effects on one's thinking. It highlights the *possible* need for capabilities that are unnecessary in standard cases, or for having those capabilities available much earlier than normally assumed. It also illustrates dramatically how sensitive contingency outcomes can be to details of operational strategy and, significantly, to the adaptiveness of the strategies followed. And, finally, it gives those participating in such work an excellent sense for how military strategy could be adapted in a wide range of circumstances—i.e., it builds the expertise needed for at-the-time adaptations. In peacetime analysis, this amounts to developing the expertise needed to put together substantially different strategies and scenarios in a matter of hours rather than months.[9]

NEW OPERATIONS PLANNING: AT-THE-TIME PLAN DEVELOPMENT USING BUILDING-BLOCK METHODS

If one buys into the general concept of taking uncertainty seriously, and of using scenario-space methods to discuss it, how does one go about the practicalities of operations planning?

To military officers experienced in crisis action, the approach needed for planning military operations under uncertainty is fairly obvious: refine the skills and processes needed to create plans at the time of the crisis or conflict, without pretending to be able to anticipate the details in advance. Doing so involves thinking through many versions of a class of crises, identifying actions that could be taken and forces that could be used, and thinking of them as "building blocks" to be assembled appropriately when the time comes. This is indeed what good officers do already when they can; it is quite natural to competitive and adaptive American officers. The deliberate planning system, however, is poorly structured to exploit these talents and attitudes, even with the new changes, and the crisis action system is not designed for large-scale operations. As a result, the United States today would have great difficulty

---

[9]Techniques for defining and experimenting with realistically adaptive military strategies in theater-level war games and simulations were highly developed in the late 1980s in RAND research sponsored by Andrew Marshall, the Director of Net Assessment in the Office of the Secretary of Defense. See, e.g., Davis and Howe (1990). Adaptive logic of an algorithmic "optimizing" character is included in RAND's TACSAGE model and an emerging simulation system (TLC), both designed by colleague Richard Hillestad. By and large, however, most military simulations still depend on scripted strategies and tend to deemphasize the critical importance of adaptive logic.

adapting quickly to a subtle, complex, and fast-breaking *major* regional contingency that departed substantially from in-going assumptions.[10]

Key to achieving this type of adaptive-planning capability is a great deal of practice, experimentation, and learning. This would include war gaming and exercises, no-notice testing to produce realistic and executable plans, and participation of civil leaders who would formulate policy in a crisis—and who often might make decisions that military leaders might not like, because of a variety of political constraints, and because of different strategic judgments. The criterion for success would not be the richness or efficiency of plans for dealing with standard scenarios well known in advance, but rather the ability to produce quickly viable plans covering the range of political-military objectives that a President might want to consider.

The vision, then, recommends a new approach to operations planning (Figure 8) that would deal with organization, methods, training and exercising, and decision-support tools. It would:

- Eliminate the deliberate-planning system (although retaining many of its functions, which are critical in laying the building-block groundwork for any kind of operations) and greatly extend the crisis-action-planning system.

- Develop in moderate detail, for each of a number of geographical regions, multiple "analytic baseline" plans for points in scenario space representative of different classes of scenario, with each class being characterized by a significantly different concept of operations.

- Allocate levels of effort so that baseline plans are only starting points, with most effort being directed toward exercising rapid-planning capabilities for variants from the baselines. Criteria for exercise success would be executability of plans, political-military appropriateness of the options, and robustness of plans with respect to plausible opponent actions and random events.

- As part of the testing of the rapid-planning system, evaluate and refine building-block operations and force modules, as well as ways to compensate when building blocks don't quite work.

- Exploit new decision-support technologies for planning and for planning, conducting, and evaluating exercises, including distributed interactive simulation and distributed war gaming.

---

[10]It is likely that the most difficult adaptations would be those in which basic assumptions about military objectives, allies, or mobilization proved wrong. One example might be if the President decided to attempt to deter or counter an imminent invasion of a nation, the independence of which was not, in itself, a "vital" national interest.

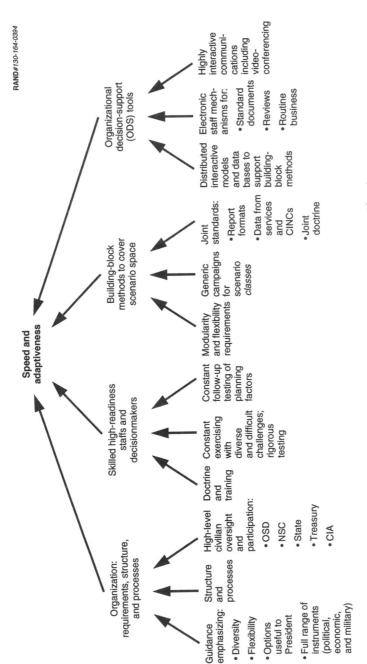

Figure 8—Components of an Overall Approach to Operations Planning

NEW DEFENSE PLANNING RELATIONSHIPS: INTEGRATING STRATEGIC, PROGRAM, AND OPERATIONAL PLANNING

Overall Approach: Creating a Common Framework

So far, I have focused mostly on operations planning, but the study also sought ways in which the *methods* of strategic, programmatic, and operations planning could be better integrated (without losing track of the distinctions among them, which stem from their different purposes and time scales). Figure 9 summarizes the approach. It starts (left branch) by recognizing a need for *national*-level planning guidance to assure integration of political, economic, and military instruments of contingency operations. DoD would take the lead in staffing and developing the appropriate interagency operations, but the NSC would guide the effort. A second key element is establishing a common intellectual framework, which needs to reflect an "operational perspective." That is, all types of planners should have the objective of producing effective capabilities for real-world operations in crisis, which means that thinking in terms of capabilities for successful military campaigns should be central. With this in mind, the third component involves methods of analysis focused on scenario-space concepts, generic campaigns and generic concepts of operations, and multiscenario analysis exploiting modern simulation technology over many thousands of cases, not handfuls.[11]

Given the challenge of this idea and the range of skills needed, how might it be accomplished? If the deliberate-planning process is eliminated in favor of a new process focused on developing the capability for rapid adaptive planning at the time of crisis, then personnel in this system would spend some time developing detailed baseline plans, a great deal of time performing sensitivity analysis and problem exploration, and considerable time training or exercising crisis-planning capabilities under realistic conditions.

In our study we recommended that:

- Operations planners should rotate among assignments involving near-term operations planning and operations-planning-style assessment of possible future capabilities that might be included in the defense program.

- The latter assessments should be conducted in an activity sponsored by the Secretary and Chairman jointly. It should involve both the military planners and civilian analysts from OSD and, in some instances, other agen-

---

[11]In this integrated approach, the emphasis in program planning should be on *capabilities analysis and marginal analysis*, since there are enormous uncertainties about effective threat levels and scenario details and we cannot afford to buy unlimited insurance. Further, marginal-analysis methods should be used to determine how much of a capability it is sensible to have, given competing priorities within a fixed budget.

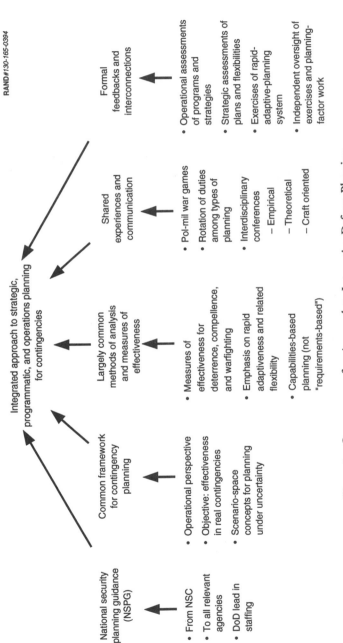

Figure 9—Components of an Approach to Integrating Defense Planning

cies.[12]   It should be managed by the Joint Staff so that activities could readily involve appropriate personnel from the CINC staffs, using methods, software, and equipment relevant to crisis-action planning where appropriate.   Some of these activities might be supported or supplemented by federally funded research and development center (FFRDC) efforts.

- The Joint Staff should consider defining documents to be produced routinely from this activity to be part of the Joint Strategic Planning System, PPBS, and DoD participation in the postulated NSC-level activity on cross-agency contingency planning.   Alternatively, it might define a process that would identify each year key reports to be developed over the next two years.[13]

- In organizing particular activities, the Joint Staff should consider adopting a task-force framework suggested in Figure 10   (adapted from Kent and Simons, 1991).[14]

The framework of Figure 10 employs teams of people that break down as shown into worriers, conceivers, technologists, and so on.   The "conceivers" are people such as operations planners, who are able to solve military problems identified by the "worriers" (e.g., analysts and mid-to-long-range planners from the services, Joint Staff, CINCs, OSD's Office of Net Assessment, and FFRDCs) by constructing notional campaign plans (concepts of operations) that would employ capabilities proposed by the "technologists."   Such concepts would be evaluated with analysis and gaming (including, perhaps, complex distributed war gaming).   Where they proved attractive, they would be picked up by those who build and manage programs, and eventually by the operators

---

[12]Some readers with long memories will note similarities to the concept of an in-government Strategic Assessment Center proposed a decade ago. See Davis and Winnefeld (1983) for discussion of those ideas, including government intentions at the time.   What emerged was an analytic war gaming system (the RAND Strategy Assessment System or RSAS), which is used extensively in the war colleges and for quite a number of studies. The more sophisticated studies, however, have been conducted by RAND (for a variety of OSD, Joint Staff, and service sponsors), rather than in the government itself.

[13]The studies at issue here might range widely in character and might include items that were somewhat comparable to such older documents as the annexes of the Joint Strategic Planning Document (JSPD), the Strategic Mobility Requirements Study (SMRS), the reports on Total Force Capabilities Analysis (TFCA), the Congressionally Mandated Mobility Study (CMMS), and various regional studies done in OSD (PA&E).

[14]This framework is quite powerful and is being proposed by our colleague Glenn Kent as an organizing principle for restructuring the way in which the DoD approaches both R&D and acquisition.

RAND#130-166-0394

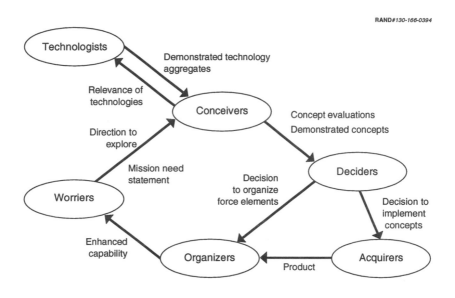

Figure 10—A Proposed Process for Cooperation

who would use them. From the start, however, the activity would include representatives of all types of planning.

In this approach there would be a ubiquitous role for analysts in defense planning, as indicated in Figure 11, which may at first glance look like a standard top-down planning diagram. Upon inspection, however, note that analysis plays a pivotal role at all stages. Indeed, even the initial top-down guidance must (or at least should) follow initial analysis to decompose the scenario space problem into workable pieces of greater and lesser importance. In my image of post–Cold War defense planning, there should be a great deal more multiscenario analysis and a great deal less in the way of arbitrary or semiarbitrary "requirements" and point scenarios. In this vision, then, the information flowing from one type of planner to another is rich, sophisticated, and framed to deal well with uncertainties of all kinds. Analysts are essential in making that information transfer work.

Given a particular class of campaigns, it is possible to systematically identify the operational tasks that must be (or at least may need to be) performed, thereby working from an operational-level concept to challenges that must be met by properly orchestrated tactical operations and systems. Competing methods for accomplishing the same tasks can and should be identified and

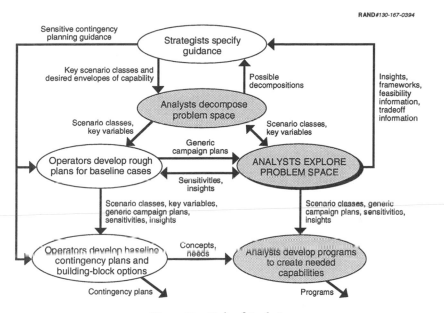

Figure 11—Role of Analysis

evaluated. The "requirements" (or, better, the objectives) are the ability to do the various tasks, not the need to buy a particular weapon system.[15]

Shared Experience and Feedbacks

We have discussed the first three components of Figure 9. The fourth component of the approach is to assure that the various types of planners have shared experiences by rotating across boundaries in their assignments, by participating in war games and other exercises, and by having some common professional outlets.

Finally (rightmost branch of Figure 9), the approach involves a series of formal feedbacks and interconnections:

- Strategic planners (NSC, OSD, CJCS, State) would formulate broad guidance about desired current and future capabilities using scenario-space con-

_____

[15]See Kent and Simons (1991) and Thaler (1993) for detailed description of the "strategies-to-tasks" methodology developed by colleague Glenn Kent and applied widely within the Air Force as a means for clarifying thought and assuring that alternative ways to accomplish essential missions are considered. Kent now prefers the methodology to be called objectives-based planning because it proceeds from operational objectives downward.

cepts. Guidance would specify key *regions* in scenario space and suggest pol-icy-relevant criteria for testing capabilities (e.g., conditions for the use of force, war termination objectives, acceptable costs in casualties and fiscal re-sources, timeliness of planning response, and the range of options available to the President).

- Operations planners, when not doing field duty, would rotate between two kinds of assignments: (a) near-term operations planning, and (b) similar work conducted in support of mid- and longer-term studies related to strategies and programs. They would use closely similar methods and tools. Results would be fed back to strategic planners and program analysts to give insights about what was feasible with different degrees of risk and depen-dence on special circumstances, and what capabilities appeared to be most and least important.

- Program planners would conduct additional analyses and would then for-mulate and assess programmatic options. Initial option assessment and nar-rowing would be conducted by the program planners themselves. Their products might again be fed to operational planners for evaluation.

- For this process to work effectively, it would probably require neutral over-sight. Given that power relationships among participating institutions could be strongly affected, there would seem to be inherent pressures on this process to bias testing and reporting to serve institutional interests. Therefore, creation of a "Readiness Inspector" reporting to the Secretary of Defense and Chairman should be considered.

- Finally, the product of this process (including uncertainty analysis), might, after suitably removing diplomatically sensitive material, be used before Congress as the evidentiary basis for the President's budget and programs. Conceivably, a very few senior congressional representatives might also use-fully participate in parts of the testing process itself, given the substantial role Congress plays in determining the circumstances under which military force would be used.

ORGANIZATIONAL CHANGES FOR IMPROVED DEFENSE PLANNING

Many changes will be needed if the vision is accepted. With the exception of the new Readiness Inspector for defense planning, no existing institutions would be created or eliminated, but changes in what planning organizations do and how they do it would require bold initiatives. The most important changes (consistent with Figure 9) are as follows.

The NSC and its staff should:

- Formulate and coordinate the requisite interagency studies, implementing directives, and legislative requests.

- Provide strategic policy guidance.
- Actively participate in exercises to test operational planning.

The Secretary of Defense and his staff should:

- Overhaul the Planning, Programming, and Budgeting System (PPBS) to make it responsive to the objectives of the approach. This would include changing standard measures of effectiveness used in reviewing defense-program options and educating OSD officials with respect to the kinds of challenges faced by operations planners.
- Direct appropriate high-level participation in crisis planning exercises and tests of the crisis-planning system.
- Assure that the operational planning system is able to produce executable plans with options appropriate for presentation to the President.
- With the Chairman, use a newly created "Readiness Inspector" for defense planning to provide an independent assessment of the testing methods and results.

The Chairman of the Joint Chiefs of Staff should:

- Develop a permanent staff of war planners to work with CINC staffs in honing the skills and processes needed for the new system. The Joint Staff participants should think of themselves as "strategic assemblers" rather than mere coordinators.
- Put into place the technology to facilitate close teamwork between the Joint Staff and CINC staffs. This would include extensive model-supported videoconferencing—for staffs, not just for commanders.
- Develop highly interactive and user-friendly computer models and databases for effective building-block planning. This decision-support system would be very different in nature from the JOPES system, which reflects the "data-processing mentality" of an earlier generation of technology and a different part of the technical community than that responsible for, e.g., the success-ful DART interface.
- Institute a program of command-post exercises to assure effectiveness in rapid planning. This program would include no-notice test exercises with only rudimentary prior knowledge of the crisis to be focused upon, and with realistically complex changes of political-military ground rules occur-ring in the course of the exercise. Follow-up studies should determine the degree to which plans developed in the exercises could, in fact, have been executed.
- Become an active but cautious and analytically critical early user of both distributed interactive simulation (DIS) and associated war gaming on the one hand, and highly interactive analytic war gaming models on the other.

- Develop information requirements to assist rapid adaptive planning (e.g., requirements for services and CINCs to define a wide variety of standard support packages for ground, air, and naval units operating in different circumstances of terrain, potential opposition, mission, and time criticality).

The War Colleges should, even if it means sacrificing other courses:

- Revise curricula to introduce basic concepts of planning under uncertainty and adaptive planning, and provide officers with personalized computer tools to experiment with adaptive planning (e.g., microcomputer war games with intelligent opponents and allies, and with random factors affecting decisions and operations).

- Devote more curriculum attention to realistic assessment of opponent capabilities and opponent reasoning, with an eye toward refining officer capability to understand tradeoffs between the virtues of timely actions for deterrence and delayed actions with more substantial forces.

CONCLUSIONS

In summary, a major RAND study of contingency planning concluded that the United States was ill prepared for the kind of rapidly adaptive planning that might be critical in a large-scale crisis (i.e., a major regional crisis rather than something smaller that could be dealt with by the normal crisis-action process). Further, it concluded that the problems went far beyond operations planning, which has already been significantly improved through the efforts of General Powell particularly. The problems involve the longstanding disconnect among strategic, program, and operations planners, which has led to an overall system that does not value, much less assure, rapid adaptiveness of military capability. In the years ahead, as the United States scales down its military forces substantially, much of the adaptiveness that it has enjoyed as a by-product of a massive overall defense establishment may be lost. This makes it even more desirable that the defense planning be reformed to institutionalize planning for adaptiveness as an end in itself. The measures I have proposed would surely be radical in some respects, but in many respects they would seem only natural to American military officers, who prize and thrive on adaptiveness when the system allows it. Whether the Department of Defense will undertake such changes is not yet clear. Let us hope that the United States does not have to suffer a minor disaster (e.g., a crisis in which it was unable to adapt quickly enough to avoid a substantial loss) before it commits to the kinds of reform I have described here.

BIBLIOGRAPHY

Bankes, Steven C. (1992), *Exploratory Modeling and the Use of Simulation for Policy Analysis*, RAND, Santa Monica, CA.

Bennett, Bruce W., Sam Gardiner, and Daniel B. Fox (1994), "Not Merely Planning for the Last War," in Davis (1994b).

Builder, Carl (1993), *Military Planning Today: Calculus or Charade?* RAND, Santa Monica, CA.

Davis, Paul K. (1988), *The Role of Uncertainty in Assessing the NATO/Pact Central Region Balance*, RAND, Santa Monica, CA. Available also in General Accounting Office, *NATO-Warsaw Pact Conventional Force Balance*, GAO/NSIAD-89-23B.

—— (1989), *National Security Planning in an Era of Uncertainty*, RAND, Santa Monica, CA.

—— (1994a), "Improving Deterrence in the Post–Cold War Era: Some Theory and Implications for Defense Planning," in Davis (1994b).

—— (ed.) (1994b), *New Challenges for Defense Planning: Rethinking How Much Is Enough*, RAND, Santa Monica, CA.

—— (1994c), "Planning Under Uncertainty Then and Now: Paradigms Lost and Paradigms Emerging," in Davis (1994b).

Davis, Paul K., and John Arquilla (1991a), *Deterring or Coercing Opponents in Crisis: Lessons from the War with Saddam Hussein*, RAND, Santa Monica, CA.

—— (1991b), *Thinking About Opponent Behavior in Crisis and Conflict: A Generic Model for Analysis and Group Discussion*, RAND, Santa Monica, CA.

Davis, Paul K., and Lou Finch (1993), *Defense Planning for the Post–Cold War Era: Giving Meaning to Flexibility, Adaptiveness, and Robustness of Capability*, RAND, Santa Monica, CA.

Davis, Paul K., and Robert Howe (1990), *Representing Operational Strategies and Command-Control in the RAND Strategy Assessment System (RSAS)*, RAND, Santa Monica, CA. Published also in the proceedings of the Symposium on C³ in Combat Models and Games sponsored by the NATO Defense Research Group and held June 6–7, 1990, at NATO headquarters.

Davis, Paul K., and James K. Winnefeld (1983), *The RAND Strategy Assessment Center: An Overview and Interim Conclusions About Utility and Development Options*, RAND, Santa Monica, CA.

Kaufmann, William W. (1992), *Assessing the Base Force: How Much Is Too Much?* The Brookings Institution, Washington, D.C.

Kent, Glenn A., and David E. Thaler (1992), "The Military Departments and Up-Front Planning: Strengthening Their Role as Integrators," unpublished RAND briefing, December.

Kent, Glenn and William E. Simons (1991), *A Framework for Enhancing Operational Capabilities*, RAND, Santa Monica, CA.

Kugler, Richard (1994), "Nonstandard Contingencies for Defense Planning," in Davis (1994b).

Lewis, Kevin (1994), "The Discipline Gap and Other Reasons for Humility and Realism in Defense Planning," in Davis (1994b).

Millot, Marc Dean, Roger Molander, and Peter Wilson (1993), "*The Day After...*": *Nuclear Proliferation in the Post–Cold War World*, 3 vols., RAND, Santa Monica, CA.

Rostker, Bernard, Bruce Don, and Kenneth Watman (1994), "Assessing the Structure and Mix of Future Active and Reserve Army Forces," in Davis (1994b).

Watman, Kenneth, and Dean Wilkening (forthcoming), *U.S. Regional Deterrence Strategy*, RAND, Santa Monica, CA.

Winnefeld, James A., and David Shlapak (1990), *The Challenge of Future Nonstandard Contingencies: Implications for Strategy, Planning, Crisis Management, and Forces*, 2 vols., RAND, Santa Monica, CA.

Thaler, David E. (1993), *Strategies to Tasks: A Framework for Linking Means and Ends*, RAND, Santa Monica, CA.

Chapter 5

THE DISCIPLINE GAP AND OTHER REASONS FOR HUMILITY AND REALISM IN DEFENSE PLANNING

Kevin N. Lewis

The DoD budget is being reduced to levels unprecedented in modern experience. The plan for doing so is relatively specific and "tight" in that it will demand a good deal of pain and leave the United States without much slack in its force structure: to avoid problems, it will be necessary to execute plans with great fidelity. As this paper demonstrates, however, the empirical history of DoD budgets over more than 40 years should encourage great humility on the part of planners. Not only could the actual program turn out to be significantly different from the plan, it almost certainly will turn out differently, in part because of a chronic and probably inevitable "discipline-gap" problem that makes it impossible to manage resources as efficiently as planners anticipate. Further, as funds are diverted to suboptimal uses (e.g., maintaining unneeded bases or imbalanced reserve components), U.S. fighting capabilities will erode even faster because of the nonlinear effects of treating too much overhead and infrastructure as "fixed." Consequently, programmed cuts may be dangerously deep—especially since historical experience indicates that we may be underestimating the true requirements for major regional and other contingencies. To mitigate such risks, defense planning should focus on the internals of DoD's budget rather than its top line: major restructuring of resource allocation patterns could yield significant savings. In any case, the history of our defense budget and posture shows strong evidence of organizational inertia in suspiciously constant allocations of budget among services and types of systems within services, all of which suggests that such rethinking, however difficult, is long overdue.

INTRODUCTION

The United States military establishment faces the most dramatic challenges since those confronted after World War II. Justifiably, planners and policymakers have attributed the need to reassess and revamp our defense posture and budgets to the devolution of the classical Soviet bloc military threat, but that explanation for the wrenching changes we now contemplate and debate tells only half the story. More subtle factors have also been at work. Evaluation of long-term trends—particularly of how we have allocated our national resources to national security and competing enterprises—suggests that what we had come to accept as a "baseline" Cold War posture would not have been indefinitely sustainable in any case. Thus, the dramatic world changes forcing defense cutbacks are also requiring us to come to grips with issues that have long been suppressed or dealt with piecemeal.

The purpose of this essay, then, is to provide an overview historical analysis of these issues so that we can better understand the real issues that confront us now.[1] To be sure, looking at the record of the last 40 years may be misleading, since it is possible that the future will be very different. However, there is reason to believe that the underlying causes for much of what I shall be describing are still very much at work. Thus, defense planners ignore the lessons of history at their peril.

Even at an overview level, we can draw some important conclusions from certain large-scale historical indicators:

- Based on our experience, it is a good bet that the defense posture we are planning to build and the one we will wind up building are probably going to be very different things.

- Historically, the budget has followed a characteristic but unpredictable *cyclical* boom-erode pattern that is partially tied to external events, but which has also come to be a self-replicating consequence of historical choices. This has considerable import for the future because our *de facto* "strategy" for modernization has been to rely on periodic budget booms. Now, however, no such boom appears on the horizon, and problems of block obsolescence will emerge early in the next century.

- There has been a steady convergent trend in budgets and posture: that is, the overall U.S. defense program has come to be quite structurally "patterned" in terms of the activities underwritten and the division of budget resources. Some of these features will inevitably be retained for good reason, but others merit serious review. The signs of costly organizational inertia are striking.

- As a result of political influences, externally generated demands, and organizational inertia, even if we had an agreed long-range defense program, the odds of seeing it through to fruition would be poor. For instance, we should expect to see nontrivial funding diverted to economically inefficient activities. This effect, which I call the *discipline gap* in planning, can have serious consequences. Historically, budgets and force levels were large enough to tolerate such inefficiencies. In the future, our vastly leaner posture and budget will tolerate them less well.

- The debate over future plans and strategies has been closely tied to the "front end" (combat-force portion) of the defense posture, but such force

---

[1] The material in this paper is based on continuing internally sponsored RAND research on budget analysis. My book on the subject is in preparation.

structure accounts for a decreasing part of our defense budgets. Overhead—ranging from operational support for our major force elements to what we would call "true overhead and infrastructure" such as health care, basing structure, and administration—accounts for an ever larger share of the total budget. We need to get a better grip on such overhead activities, and though everyone agrees with this, there are some major conceptual and technical challenges involved.

- Over the course of the Cold War, we planned routinely for certain canonical major conflicts with the USSR and its allies (Davis, 1994b; Kugler, 1994). Instead, we found ourselves fighting other conflicts akin to what are now called major regional contingencies (MRCs). The historical record indicates that *we consistently underestimated or misestimated the true requirements of these other contingencies.* We coped, because we had a large and diverse posture generated by our planning for the Soviet threat; but now, because we will have smaller force reserves, our estimates of the requirements for MRCs must be correct. Unfortunately, there is reason to believe the traditional optimism about requirements continues.

All of this is highly germane to the present day because, on the one hand, the Clinton plan as described in the Bottom-Up Review (BUR) (Aspin, 1993) is deliberately "tight," by which I mean that the planned force structure is considered to be adequate, but with very little slack.[2] Because the Clinton plan is so tight, because history tells us that there will be significant differences between plans and actual programs due to congressional action and other factors, and because of the difficulty in reducing the "overhead" dimensions of our program, there is reason for concern. To summarize:

- History suggests that we may be underestimating the forces we will find it necessary to send to contingencies (or that will be tied down in various missions) and, at the same time, seriously overestimating the capabilities we will generate with our defense programs.

With this introduction, the paper proceeds as follows. First, I give an overview of the DoD budget over time, pointing out a number of lessons that can be learned from it. I then draw implications for current defense planning.

---

[2]Many authors have argued for deeper defense cuts, but the Bush and Clinton administrations came up with remarkably similar results, and President Clinton, in his State of the Union address, made clear his intention to avoid further cuts in defense. Office of Management and Budget director Leon Panetta discussed the tightness of the budget in "Match of Bottom-Up Forces, Dollars is a 'Tight One,'" *Defense Week*, 8 February 1994, p. 1. See also Kugler (1993) for discussion of why the planned posture appears lean and why more severe problems are likely late in the decade and early in the next century.

HISTORY OF THE DoD BUDGET AND PROGRAM

Overview of Defense Spending

No other metric provides as useful a starting place for considering our defense planning experiences as the budget, but there are, alas, few analytic avenues more complex, winding, and, often, obscure. The reasons for this are basic flaws in what many consider the ideal planning model of the Cold War. Some of these flaws are that: (1) we are unlikely in peacetime to spend everything that prudent professional planners would consider necessary for "high-confidence" defense; (2) in any event, our programs turn out to produce much less than our plans envisioned; (3) it takes more time than expected to institute even agreed-upon changes; and, as a result, (4) the ultimate and most important choices we must make every year have to do with concerns that are elementally judgmental and more tactical than strategic.

Consider now a topline view of our budget history, as shown in Figure 1.[3] Analysis of the details of this trace does much to explain the history of our Cold War experience.

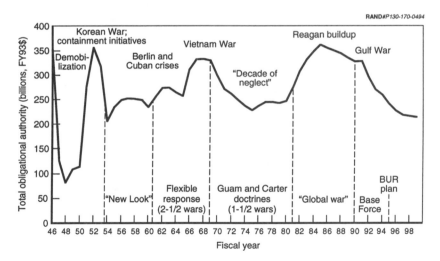

Figure 1—History of DoD's Total Obligational Authority

---

[3]The data here are for the 051 account, direct DoD-authority. This omits certain non-Defense national security budget items, mainly spending by the AEC/DOE on nuclear weapons.

Probably the most significant feature of the data in Figure 1 is the *cyclical nature* of the DoD total topline value, which is given here as total obligational authority (TOA) in FY93 dollars.[4] We see, first, a rapid demobilization following World War II followed by an equally abrupt upward movement in the budget occasioned by numerous dramatic events occurring around 1950, the most important of which was the outbreak of the Korean War.[5] Following that period of emergency response, the budget begins to drift downwards as a result of the Eisenhower administration's "New Look" (or "Massive Retaliation") strategy, which sought to use atomic weapons and other technologies to avoid the need for large and costly conventional forces to match the hordes of troops thought to be available to a unified Communist military juggernaut. Over time, the Eisenhower budget principle (known as the "Iron Law") led to a gradual erosion in both defense budgets and the posture.[6]

But doubts about the wisdom of heavy nuclear reliance as well as the impossibility of conventional defense with existing forces led to the formal adoption and implementation in the early 1960s of "Flexible Response." This approach put on line a reasonably good combination of military capabilities of all types, which permitted the United States and its coalition partners to respond to potential aggression at an appropriate level (Kaufmann, 1982). In implementing this strategy, significant improvements in general-purpose capabilities were launched. These were made possible not only by some additional funding in the early 1960s, but also by the restructuring of various elements of the overall defense posture. As this restructuring proceeded, however, requirements for the conflict in Southeast Asia began to claim an ever larger slice of the total budget. After 1969, with the adoption of the Guam Doctrine and Vietnamization, war-related budget elements declined steadily.

---

[4]TOA is an accounting concept unique to the Department of Defense: in most years it is very similar to the Budget Authority metric used in some documents, with the exception that TOA represents the value of all authority required to underwrite the defense program regardless of origins.

[5]In addition to war requirements, however, the budget spike in the early 1950s reflects steps to implement the inchoate concept of containment. At the same time that units were rushed to Korea, for instance, four additional divisions were mobilized for deployment to Europe, and there was a dramatic acceleration in many modernization programs, including those strategic offensive and defensive forces required under the "New Look" policy.

[6]Eisenhower's Iron Law (a sort of predecessor of Gramm-Rudman) simply required that the sum of defense and nondefense programs be equal to total federal income. As the 1950s went on there was a major drawdown in many posture elements, although many of the forces concerned were "junk posture" for reasons of obsolescence or lack of readiness.

In the early-to-mid 1970s, we again see a steady process of budgetary erosion.[7] Attention in planning then refocused on general conventional deterrence, particularly in Europe, but constant-dollar budgets resided in a historically low trough throughout the balance of the 1970s. (The reader will recall that during this time, defense spending was strongly affected by general U.S. economic woes.) The overall result has been described by some as a "decade of neglect."[8] A third major "boom" in defense budgets occurred in the early 1980s, which reflected a powerful (if transitory) popular perception that the U.S.-Soviet military balance had deteriorated to a dangerous degree.[9] This perception was fueled by such shocks as the Teheran embassy takeover, the Soviet invasion of Afghanistan, and the Desert One fiasco. The result included remarkable gains in defense spending during the early years of the Reagan administration. Between FY80 and FY83, DoD TOA rose by 34 percent; subsequently, momentum continued to push authorizations to historically unprecedented levels until FY85, when DoD budgets reached an all-time post–Cold War peak of $362 billion in FY93 dollars (an increase above FY80 levels of 46 percent).

Once the budget reached that zenith, the historically typical process of erosion set in again. Given the political and economic climate of the time, it seemed highly likely that the downward part of the "boost-glide" pattern of defense budgets had kicked in, even though proposed DoD long-term plans continued to call for real increases until the FY89 budget (Lewis, 1990). To complete this brief account, note the effects on the budget of the remarkable developments transpiring between the mid-1980s and the present. Given that the defense budget had already entered a downward trajectory, it was inevitable

---

[7]This erosion of resource levels was, as we shall see, linked to a decline in many major force elements (both those generated for the Southeast Asian conflict and for some continuing ones). Reasons other than budget requirements account for some of these reductions, however. Among these were the arrival at the end of their scheduled service lives of a great block of World War II–vintage ships, and force reductions and restructuring undertaken in light of the shift to an all-volunteer force and the reorganization of the reserve components.

[8]Some of the economic factors besetting defense planners during this time included severe inflation problems and rapid increases in the cost of some readiness accounts. It should be noted that some have disputed the term "decade of neglect," arguing that in light of global requirements, the situation at the time was not so severe as has been made out subsequently. See Robert Komer, "What Decade of Neglect?" *International Security,* Fall 1985.

[9]A report detailing a series of polls conducted by the Chicago Council on Foreign Relations (Reilly, 1987) indicated most clearly an abrupt—but highly short-lived— spike of national support for increased defense spending. For an account of the politics and certain other influences surrounding this odd moment in defense planning history, see Stockman (1986).

that the spectacular events of the late 1980s (including, one after the other, the cessation of Soviet depredations in Afghanistan and Nicaragua, the fall of the Berlin Wall and the collapse of the Warsaw Pact, and, finally, the fragmentation of the USSR itself) would combine with popular concerns about alternative domestic priorities to keep the defense budget line heading south. Not even the equally remarkable episodes of Desert Shield and Desert Storm and the coup attempt in Russia could deflect spending trends. As the Cold War approached its end, the key questions became how much further spending should fall and what size establishment the U.S. military should maintain.

Each and every development influencing the evolution of the DoD budget as a whole was, essentially, a "one-shot" affair. Indeed, many developments would have seemed preposterous to planners had they been sketched out before the fact. Certain consistent patterns nonetheless emerge from Figure 1. Most significant is the fact that the defense budget has been cyclical. Periodic budget booms—which, big or small, tend to be "event-driven" and are therefore unplanned and often specially focused—come along occasionally and push budgets up substantially. Thereafter, we find a typical extended period of gradual real-budget erosion—until another cycle kicks in. Figure 2 summarizes certain aspects of this history.

We see from Figure 2 that while the values of the defense budget over the entire period 1948–1993 ranged from $82 billion to $362 billion (Figure 1),

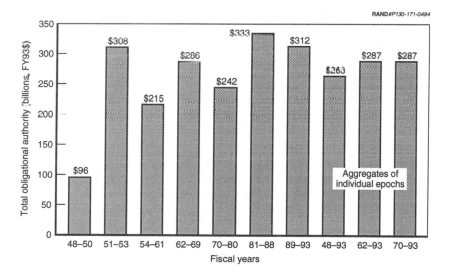

Figure 2—Average TOA Budgets for Different Year Groups

the budget generally oscillated more modestly around an average value of about $263 billion over the whole period in question. If we look at more modern data only, we see that average DoD TOA is the same for two intervals (FY62–93 and FY70–93).

Another way to consider the historical movement of the DoD topline is to look at year-to-year real growth rates as shown in the first line of Table 1. The average TOA growth rates in the various periods fluctuated from –3.5 percent up to 7 percent. If we exclude exceptional years with growth rates exceeding 5 percent, we get what in some respects is a better picture of (modal) normality (the last line of the table). Here we see that, with the exception of the early 1980s, the average growth in all periods was negative, with the overall average between FY56 and FY93 being a negative 2.1 percent. In viewing the history of the Cold War defense budget, then, we are seeing neither constancy nor anything like an unlimited "race to oblivion." Instead, we see a cyclic fluctuation around a reasonably intermediate mean, with most periods in fact being periods of slow *erosion* of the budget after short booms.

The DoD's Share of the Pie Over Time

No overview of budget history would be complete without making certain points about what the "burden" of the defense budget has and has not been. Figure 3 shows defense spending and employment as a component of various

Table 1

Summary of Trends in Annual Real Budget Change Over Time, FY56–93

	Annual Average Real Rate of Change During Epoch					
	FY56–61	FY62–69	FY70–79	FY80–85	FY86–93	FY56–93
TOA	+1.5%	+3.6%	–2.6%	+7.0%	–3.5%	+0.7%
Number of FYs of real TOA growth	3 of 6	4 of 8	2 of 10	6 of 6	1 of 8	16 of 38
FYs wherein real TOA growth > 5%	2 of 6	3 of 8	0 of 10	4 of 6	0 of 8	9 of 38
Average TOA growth rate, excluding FYs > 5%	–1.4%	–1.3%	–2.6%	+2.9%	–3.5%	–2.1%

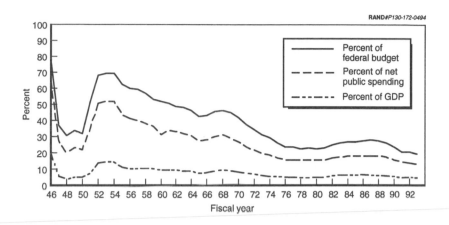

Figure 3—DoD Shares of Various Economic Aggregates Versus Time

larger national accounts.[10]   Here we see national defense spending as the following: a share of the federal budget as a whole, a fraction of net public spending, and a percentage of total gross domestic product (GDP).

Depending on what index we are using, we see that between the Korean and early "Massive Retaliation" period and the present, national defense falls by at least half of its proportional value, and sometimes by much more.   The particularly substantial decline in national defense as a fraction of the federal budget and of net public spending reflects the dramatic growth over the past three decades or so in nondefense accounts, and especially in entitlements (Lewis, 1990).

Because so much of the total growth in federal budgets has taken the form of entitlements, national defense represents the lion's share of the total that is defined as being "relatively controllable"—i.e., not tied to legislative requirements such as automatic inflation adjustment.   This has meant, of course, that when deficit control becomes an issue, national defense reductions become particularly interesting to those seeking outlay cuts.   Under the Clinton administration plan, the downward trend in defense as a share of the total federal or national effort is expected to continue.

The bottom line here is that while national defense has generally fluctuated within a particular envelope during the Cold War, the growth of government in general has driven it steadily downward as a component of the economy and of the total public sector effort overall.   Comparing these numbers to those in Figure 1, we might form the impression that the question "What can we afford

---

[10]Note that, unlike Figure 1, this chart is based on outlays, not authority, and it uses the broader "050" definition of national defense.

to spend on defense?" may not be very meaningful. The issue in defense budgeting is not really one of ability—we can and have spent what at the time the political consensus thought fit for security—but rather one of will. That is, administrations generally tend to try to hold the line on defense cuts. However, the overall process includes enough adjustments so that the net result in most years is modest real decline. But when explicit exogenous circumstances have so demanded, or when perceptions of threat or an ailing military balance prevailed, the nation has ponied up whatever resources were needed.

Not only does historical experience tend to dilute the significance of the question of whether we can afford a given level of defense spending,[11] it also casts some doubts on the image of top-down planning as laid out in some of the models of how defense planning should work (i.e., models that assume we decide objectives and strategy, build a sensible multiyear program and budget, and then implement it). How much we spend on defense is a function of two things above all others: the existing size of the defense establishment, and the political context in which an annual budget is formalized. Further, as we shall see, the majority of the defense budget does *not* go into direct-combatant accounts. When we ask the question "How much is enough?" we are implicitly talking about capabilities—how many forces, of what kinds, configured and employed in what ways, etc.—might be required to meet the contingencies that we may face. But, depending on how one does the accounting, only something like 20–35 percent or so of the total budget *directly* supports those combat forces that figure so much in our public debate. Put in an admittedly extreme way, it would be possible to zero out all components of our defense posture actually able to engage potential enemies and still have a defense budget well over $100 or even $150 billion a year (depending on how this absurdity were to be managed). Before continuing with this point, however, let us briefly touch on a few last points about the defense budget as a total entity.

Planning "Failures": The Gap Between Projected and Actual Outcomes

Let us now begin to examine the empirical evidence for the assertions made at the outset of the paper. Let us look first for evidence of how well official plans have fared—i.e., how closely actual programs and spending approxi-

---

[11]Nor can it be said that defense should somehow be fingered automatically and singularly for any larger economic woes. For instance, in recent years, national defense spending has been accused of responsibility in the growth of federal deficits—yet these deficits can be laid more to the automatic nature of entitlements growth, debt service, and income reductions than to defense. After all, in recent years, the deficit has tended to increase regardless of whether defense spending is growing or declining.

mated expectations. What we find is that, almost universally, budget plans have postulated modest rates of year-to-year changes and, except for some recent years, upward changes. When we compare the plans that have been sent to Congress each year as required by law with the actual experience in the subsequent program period (i.e., what Congress authorized), we see a rather startlingly dramatic disconnect. What happens has routinely not been what was "expected" to happen.

This is apparent in Figure 4, which compares the gap between the projected total value (in constant dollars) of historical five-year defense plans (FYDPs) and the value of the total DoD budgets for those five years as they actually played out for those years for which all data are available. A negative value in this portrayal means that the total defense budget for a given five-year period fell short of what had been forecast for these five years in a given plan. A positive value means that more TOA was available than had been expected at one time. Many factors account for the great variation in the "fates" of each plan; some are somewhat technical in nature (e.g., part of some of the variation is explained by errors in economic forecasts), but the bulk of the gap results from the effects of the larger political process. For instance, plans in the mid-1970s proposed a gradual rebuilding of defense, an expectation that was not realized in actual experience. But the consequences of the "unplanned" dramatic buildup of the early and mid-1980s led to a trove of unexpected resources. Ignoring the inevitable process of cyclicality, budgets for the mid-1980s continued for a while to anticipate significant real growth, even as the DoD topline began to head south—thus the gap between plans and expectations began to shift in the other direction. The real point of Figure 4 is that our planning process as a whole does not seem very clairvoyant, to say the least. Programs have turned out quite differently than planned. This has been true at the microscopic level also. Tables 2 and 3 illustrate this with Air Force systems, but similar data exist for the Navy and Army. As we see in the two tables, actual procurements of bombers and fighter-attack aircraft have sometimes been greatly different from those planned. In other periods, the discrepancies have been in the other direction, with procurement greatly exceeding original plans (e.g., when the Air Force procured 1985 F-16s through FY92 rather than the total of 650 planned as of FY76).

Four Lessons from History

Four lessons lurk in the data about DoD topline budget histories. First, there will usually be steady pressures tending to produce a mild erosion in DoD's budget, even under rather routine circumstances. Second, while many administrations have developed plans calling for a steady-state budget (or slow

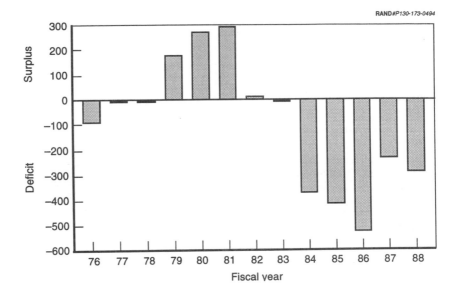

Figure 4—Failures of the Five-Year Defense Plan

Table 2

The Fate of Major Force Modernization Plans for Bombers

Bomber Program	Planned Procurement	Projected or Actual IOC[a]	Actual Procurement[b]
B-52G/H	295	Late 1950s	295
B-58	290	Late 1950s	86
B-70	225	Early 1960s	0
FB-11	263	Late 1960s	76
B-1	241	Late 1970s	0
B-1B/B-2	232	Mid 1980s	120

[a]IOC is "initial operational capability."

[b]Actual procurement excludes prototypes and test models.

but steady growth), the eventual budgets have been quite different. Seen in this context, we must doubt the validity of the Clinton administration's projected force posture as described in the BUR (Aspin, 1993), which forecasts a fairly steady rate of decline and, presumably, the ultimate stabilization of the budget at some future point (see also Kugler, 1993).

Table 3

FY70 Projected Versus Actual USAF Fighter-Attack Posture:
Combat Forces in Tactical Wing Equivalents

	Plan FY62	Actual FY70
Long-range attack	17.8	3.3
Air superiority	1.0	1.3
Multirole fighters	6.6	25.2
Attack	0.0	1.9
Total tactical air force	25.4	31.7
Tactical photo-recce	6.1	7.3
Air defense fighters	15.6	8.1
Grand total	47.1	47.1

The third lesson will become clearer in what follows and is related to the failures to implement steady-state or steady-change budget plans; it is that historical events such as real or perceived crises cause various initiatives that produce self-perpetuating budget requirements. This is especially true in our major end-item procurement accounts. During years of budget plenty, we might, for instance, procure large numbers of fighter planes. But these systems will subsequently reach the end of their service lives at the same time, producing a requirement for a major investment initiative to prevent block inventory obsolescence. On the other side of the coin, during periods of relative austerity we may defer procurement of all kinds of systems, from major front-line weapons to trucks and radios. We employ a great many techniques to keep systems of all types running if they cannot be replaced on an ideal timetable, but there are always limits to this approach. Eventually, we must make good on our deferred investment (usually during the "next" budget boom)—at which time we are often made to pay for our deferral decision when we must procure items at less-than-ideal production rates.

The last of the four lessons is that defense budget totals are by no means the outcome of anything approximating an orderly process of planning based on commitments, requirements, threats, or contingencies.

A general warning begins to emerge from even the most cursory analysis of this pertinent history. At first glance, it appears that the Clinton administration's plan (and that of its predecessor) is underfunded, has little slack, and is unlikely to produce the kinds of minimum capabilities sought by its underlying strategy unless we enjoy a historically unprecedented level of discipline and control. Further, if our plans about *what* capabilities are required are wrong, the resulting situation becomes that much more precarious.

OBSERVATIONS ON THE INTERNAL STRUCTURE OF THE DEFENSE BUDGET

So far we have seen that the history of the defense budget has been complex. Equally complex has been the allocation of resources *within* the defense budget. There are particular unique dynamics within the defense budget that have some implications for our future planning efforts. After all, the specific decisions we make about development efforts, operational tempos, acquisition, personnel policies, etc., reflect in the most tangible way the interplay between contemporary management concerns and the perceptions of those involved in internal budget allocation of the priorities, risks, and so on that should most strongly influence our choices. Internal DoD budget allocation, in short, is where "the rubber meets the road" in defense policy, though the topic, for a variety of reasons, is often neglected by students of strategy and defense planning.

A full analysis of internal DoD budget allocation issues and trends could fill an encyclopedia, so I will limit my remarks here to a few of the more salient matters of interest to defense planners. I will comment on:

- The general tendency toward stability (or convergence) in budget accounts over time.
- The emphasis on investment (and especially procurement) during upward movements of the DoD topline.
- Shifts in the representation, within the budget, among "functional accounts." There has been a gradual shift away from the "front end" of our force structure toward (1) what we might call a combat "support" account (consisting of capabilities that support or contribute to the activities of "front end" forces) and (2) more traditionally defined "overhead" such as health care, quality of life, and maintenance of physical infrastructure.

Convergence Within Major Budget Accounts

To illustrate what I mean by "convergence," Figure 5 shows the percentage of TOA allocated to the various military services over time (the difference between the sum of the shares and 100 percent is due to expenditures on defensewide and OSD/OJCS activities such as military retired pay).[12] In

---

[12]The data given in this chart are based on total service toplines as a share of DoD TOA. It should be noted that over the period in question, there are, however, some shifts in the way that certain overhead accounting is done (among other things) that have introduced certain biases into this figure. For instance, as of FY84, retired pay for military personnel was moved out of a DoD-wide overhead account into the budgets of the services. Most of the adjustments in question involve such shifts; but a few involve

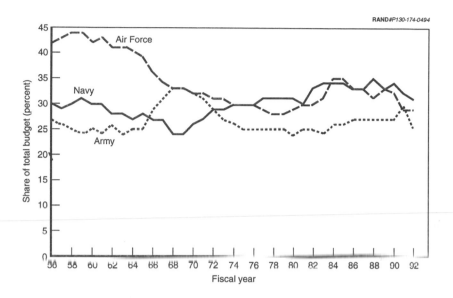

RAND#P130-174-0494

Figure 5—Stability of Service Budget Shares

studying Figure 5, we can, for instance, see a decline in the Air Force share of the budget in the early years as the defense establishment moved away from a strategic-oriented "Massive Retaliation" posture and toward one better config- ured for the doctrine of "Flexible Response" with a significant component of initial conventional defense. During the Vietnam years, the Army share grew somewhat because that service expanded its personnel needs and, to a lesser ex- tent, because it pursued ABM capability.

What is interesting about this chart is how the relative service shares fall into a fairly consistent ratio over time. Given the many major developments transpiring over this historical epoch, the result is surprising. Indeed, the sta- bility is even projected into the future under the Clinton plan. The same sorts of consistency can be seen in other major accounts (when adjusted for particu- lar developments, accounting changes, etc.). We are entitled to ask why the force toward stability (i.e., toward convergence) in budget shares should be so strong. On its face, Figure 5 would seem to be very strong evidence of organi- zational inertia rather than optimal planning, since about 1970.

---

the movement of funds from service accounts to centralized ones. The amounts in- volved are not that large relative to the total quantities in question, but they are signifi- cant enough to explain some movement in the lines in Figure 5. For our purposes, however, it suffices to note that the effects produced are systematic—they affect all the services proportionally—even while certain longitudinal inconsistencies result.

The phenomenon also occurs at the level of force structure, as Figure 6 indicates for a large-scale metric, major force elements of the Army, Navy, and Air Force and as Figure 7 indicates for a more refined indicator, i.e., inventory representation of different types of Air Force aircraft. In these and other cases, the degree of convergence since about 1970 is significant. We could draw any number of charts at all levels of detail and would find that a surprising number match this convergent pattern: a result we might not suspect in light of the size of shifts in budgets, requirements, etc. over the periods of interest.

There is, of course, no single and fully satisfactory answer for the convergence phenomenon in either budget shares or force structure. A student of bureaucratic politics might argue that relatively constant service shares reflect the outcome of a continuing tight competition among services and their supporters in Congress. Another explanation flows from the inertial properties of the budget. The DoD budget is so complex, and supports so many continuing activities, that major shifts in emphasis are hard to accomplish in the short run and then sustain—*unless some major, defensewide realignment of basic planning principles has been undertaken* (as was the case with the shift from a nuclear-

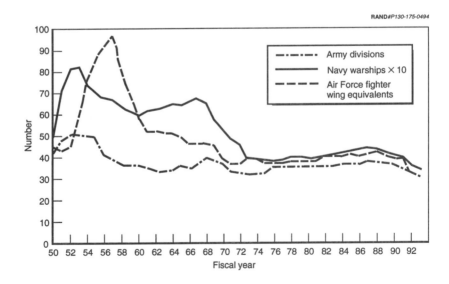

Figure 6—Convergence of U.S. Force Structure Over Time

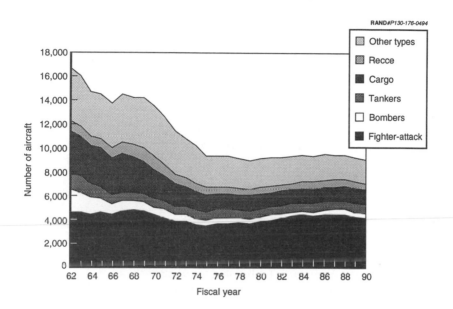

Figure 7—Evolution of Air Force Inventory (Active/Reserve total active inventory)

oriented posture to a flexible response posture in the early 1960s).[13] It is possible, of course, that the near-constant shares are the best allocation. That would seem to be remarkably fortuitous, however.

Whatever the reasons for approximate stability in major service shares (and stability within service budgets as indicated by Figure 7), the key point for our purpose is that these stabilities exist.[14] Such relative constants bespeak a pattern, and we would be wise to presume that the patterns will endure unless overwhelming evidence to the contrary can be brought forth (e.g., decisions

---

[13]Relevant here is the fact that the annual "defense budget debate" has really addressed only a fairly modest percentage of the total defense budget. That is, if one is committed to a posture of a given size, and to given levels of support and infrastructure, and when one takes into account the consequences of decisions already made, program momentum, etc., the total financial consequence of all DoD and congressional decisions in any one year will be relatively small compared to the size of the budget that rolls along in predictable fashion. Long-term stability of budget shares simply means that the cumulative net effects of these marginal decisions zero out.

[14]Note that the approximate stability I refer to here is for the part of the budget not taken up by nonservice DoD budget elements. The sum of the service shares in Figure 6 has shrunk over time as DoD-wide activities have increased.

explicitly and substantially changing the shares). In fact, the Bush and Clinton administrations have not obviously made any such large-scale shifts.

Topline DoD Budget Cycles and Internal Budget Mixes

A second major finding of an analysis of internal DoD budget trends relates to the cyclical property of budget toplines discussed above. If so many aspects of the internal DoD budget tend to stay relatively constant over time, then what happens inside the budget when one of the relatively few major budget booms takes place? The answer to this question is complicated greatly by the unique traits of each of the major buildup and falloff cycles. But one feature underlies the cyclical topline pattern over the entire historical interval examined, and it has major consequences for our future planning. That feature involves what we might term episodic surges of investment funding, especially spending for development and procurement of major weapon end-items, during major budget buildups. To be sure, some buildups are associated with combat actions, and so a considerable amount of any buildup might go for war-related consumption or the operational and personnel costs of increased force structure. But in every case, we typically see a surge in procurement during a major budget buildup; and when the buildup ends, we typically see that procurement falls off the fastest.

Figure 8 plots, using constant-dollar TOA data, procurement and "all other" accounts for the last two buildups (i.e., the period FY62–FY92), showing each as a fraction of the respective value in 1975, the bottoming-out point for DoD's TOA after the post-Vietnam drawdown. We see, from both the rates of increase in these ratios and their absolute size, that procurement is far more volatile than the balance of the DoD budget as the budget grows and contracts. That is, when the budget rises, procurement tends to grow faster than anything else, and when it falls off after a buildup, procurement is, relatively speaking, the big loser.

This phenomenon of procurement volatility is of particular note at the present time when we consider two factors: the duration and amount of procurement spending programmed over the current planning cycle. We can easily see that there is a historical tendency to do a relatively great amount of weapons buying during buildup periods. We then "live off" that investment until the next procurement upswing, at which point we attempt to refresh as much of the inventory as possible. This tendency arose initially as a consequence of circumstance (e.g., no one planned the Korean War or its associated buildup), but once we became enmeshed in this cyclical pattern, it became institutionalized. Since we have made a lot of purchases all at once, it follows that a lot of our inventory items may reach the end of their service lifetimes

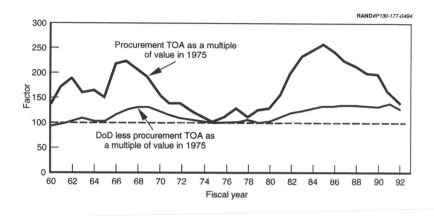

Figure 8—Procurement Volatility

simultaneously, creating a requirement for another major procurement initiative.[15] In the past, historical events have provided the necessary boom.

To illustrate how this boom-erode cycle works at the micro level, let me simplify greatly a complex distinction between those force elements that constitute what I call the "core" of a service's force structure and those that I shall call "noncore" force elements. They are noncore because we have procured them mainly during discrete intervals during which there was a pressing need: they would not necessarily have been acquired otherwise. The concept of noncore procurement is best explained anecdotally. For the Air Force, one component of core posture has been a diverse array of fighter-attack aircraft. Plans for future procurement, and ongoing development efforts, continually program initiatives for the modernization of these forces no matter what the status of budget levels may be. But periodically, demands for the acquisition of ancillary posture elements (the noncore elements) have arisen.

For instance, the requirements of the air war in Vietnam produced a brand new demand for various kinds of specialized combat and combat support aircraft.[16] These forces were expeditiously acquired: often, they were put on line by unconventional means.[17] The total special operations and air rescue force

---

[15]There are, obviously, exceptions to this rule—we do buy weapons for some force elements during periods of relative budget austerity.

[16]Including combat search and rescue, psychological operations forces, various sensor and targeting systems, defense suppression forces, aerial gunships, and so on.

[17]Consider, for instance, the modification of several types of transports for gunships and other exotic purposes, the reactivation of retired A-1s for service with the U.S. and Vietnamese air forces in combat roles, and the Air Force's adaptation of some Navy helicopters for analogous usage.

in Southeast Asia grew to enormous size: around 1969, the Air Force fielded more than 400 SOF/Air Rescues and Recovery-type aircraft in theater. After the war, many of these types were retired, but others were retained or gave rise to more modern successors. Thus, such types of aircraft (which are in the force today in such forms as the AC-130 or HH-60) fall into the category of noncore force structure because their entry into the posture was brought about not as a result of routine posture-planning activities but of some other influence. The reason that I introduce the notion of noncore procurement is that the entry (and modernization) of this type of force structure is associated with major budget buildups. This is so for two main reasons: (1) the budget buildup is associated with some actual contingency that gives rise to specific "real world" requirements for such capabilities; and (2) the budget buildup provides enough funding so that options beyond rehabilitation and modernization of core posture can be entertained.

The importance of these noncore force and budget intervals to our total posture can be illustrated by considering the case of various Navy combatant ships. There is no arguing the question that both surface combatants and submarines should be considered "core" Navy fleet posture elements. On the other hand, some people might note that the Navy has tended to pay relatively less attention to certain other types of ships, such as amphibious-lift or mine-warfare vessels. Figure 9 shows the total numbers of each type for various historical intervals associated with periods of relative budget plenty or austerity.[18]

Consider now the significance for future budget planning. Two things in particular are strongly suggested by these data: (1) that by projecting a continuing decline out through the entirety of the planning period, the Clinton administration's plan departs substantially from historical trends insofar as investment cycles are concerned; and (2) that the notion of a continuing stable budget profile extending beyond the end of the current planning period—a pattern the administration's plan seems to imply—is probably not feasible (barring an abandonment of current U.S. strategic concepts and, most likely, our status as a global military superpower)(see also Kugler, 1993). Let us consider each point briefly.

---

[18]This figure omits craft, boats, military assistance procurement, certain experimental types, and conversions. The large numbers of noncore-type ships procured in the last two bars in the chart can be attributed to the acquisition then of various small mine-warfare ships that had slipped from their procurement schedules earlier in the decade on account of various programmatic and technical problems (such as the outright failure of the *Cardinal* class).

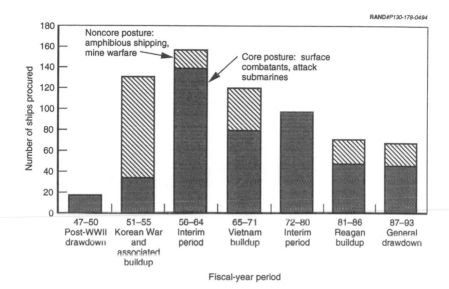

Figure 9—Acquisition of Core Versus Noncore Force Structure: The Case of Navy
General-Purpose-Forces Ships

First, it is interesting to note that even as the Berlin Wall fell, and even as
Desert Shield and Storm unfolded, the defense budget not only continued to
decline, it did so more or less "on schedule." We noted above that when DoD
budgets fall, procurement is hit particularly hard. Figure 10 shows the declines
of total DoD budget and procurement for both the post-Vietnam builddown
and the present one. Each expenditure is shown, not in absolute terms, but as
a percentage of its level in the highest year of each budget buildup. It is interesting to note that, compared with the post-Vietnam builddown, the current
one has been more gradual.[19] This fact we owe to a constellation of political
developments. In particular, the concept of the Base Force (in concert with the
"Rose Garden" budget agreement) played an essential role in preventing the
defense drawdown from becoming a rout during the Bush years.[20] However

_____

[19]The starting point for the recent decline was appreciably higher than earlier (see
Figure 1). Furthermore, unlike the case for the Vietnam-related budget bulge, we did
not in the 1980s experience the massive diversion of materiel (whether by consumption
in combat operations or in the form of military assistance handouts). On the other
hand, the force structure and materiel items financed by the 1980s buildup are generally
more expensive on a unit basis.

[20]Senior defense leaders from several administrations deserve the great thanks of the
American people for their clever and determined efforts in preventing the gradual draw-

that may be, in contrast to the post-Vietnam decline, which turned around in FY75, the current drawdown is expected to endure through the end of the century (for a total duration through FY99 of an unprecedented 14 years). By that time, authority will have fallen well through the nadir of the post-Vietnam decline in both real and proportional terms.

As we saw in Figure 8, intervals of extended restrained investment between upward procurement cycles have never remained so low for so long as current plans envision. To some degree, the effects of this extended period of

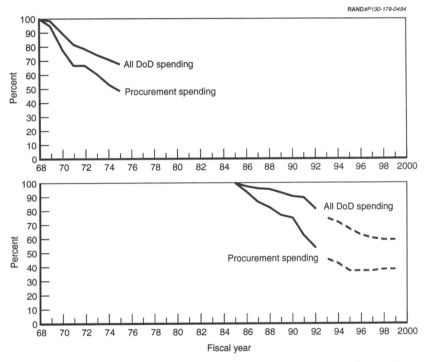

NOTE: All figures are TOA figures, in constant dollars, divided by base-year figures, either 1968 or 1985.

Figure 10—Drawdown Rates After Vietnam and After the Cold War

down following FY85 from becoming a chaotic unravelling. Secretaries Carlucci and Aspin did their parts; special mention is due Secretary Cheney. If it served no other purpose, the "Base Force" concept, laid out originally under the guidance of JCS Chairman Colin Powell, also played a key role in making sure that the ongoing build-down stayed orderly.

"disinvestment" are mitigated by the fact that the remaining force structure is planned to be smaller. This fact allows us to postpone some modernization initiatives and to pursue others in less grand scale. The specifics of future modernization and replacement problems vary on a case-by-case basis (Stanley, 1994), but it is possible to produce detailed estimates of future capitalization needs by determining what equipment needs a smaller force would have (given that we would presumably have discarded older systems when possible) for selected assumptions about the service life of remaining force constituents, options for life extension, etc. Even for a smaller posture, most such analyses show some demand for some kind of procurement effort to parallel (albeit on a more modest and hopefully better-managed basis) the previous procurement cycle for that kind of system. Almost all of these procurement/replacement "requirements" lie after the last year in the current plan, FY99, some just after it (Kugler, 1993). Major problems potentially lurk, of course, when several major replacement demands stack up on top of each other. These problems will also be complicated if any new investment requirements (say, in the form of a theater antimissile system) are added to the replacement program for our mainline posture. Further aggravating the situation will be the fact that the unit prices of our major force components are increasing (in line with their increased performance and capabilities, the requirements placed upon them, reduced production quantities, etc.).

This brings us to the second problem cited above, namely the notion that the budget somehow could fall to some point or other (according to the Clinton plan, something in the vicinity of $220 billion) and then reside there more or less indefinitely. History doesn't support this interpretation. Nor do the numbers (i.e., the numbers indicating systems that must eventually be replaced as they become obsolescent). It will be imperative at some future point to make one of two decisions: either approve a new cycle of upward defense budget movement with a special emphasis on recapitalizing our forces, or accept a marked reduction in our force structure and a shift in our basic strategy to go with it. Since we are already at what the administration has called a "minimum" force level for a baseline global power strategy, that would seem to imply that we would at that point have to abandon any pretense of remaining a classic global superpower. Further, the longer we postpone that decision, the more "catch-up ball" we will have to play—and the more of that game we play, the more inefficiencies we will court in our production programs. It would be better to smooth out the amplitudes of the cyclical investment curves (Stanley, 1994). And the longer we must await increased investment spending, the more trouble we will experience as we struggle to keep an ever more elderly posture functional in both operationally and logistically meaningful ways. On top of this, we must remember that not only investment accounts but other budget components will be increasing in real terms on a unit basis. There is no reason to suspect, in other words, that health, retirement, quality of life, and other personnel and operational costs will somehow lag inflation rather than exceed it as they have done in the past. This will place further pressures on any future effort to fund a core posture.[21]

In short, the notion of the budget somehow coming to rest at some steady-state level flies in the face of our historical experience. We are, as we look to the years and even decades ahead, the prisoners of our past choices.

Historical Assessment of Functional Budget Categories.

As a last piece of our look at the internal DoD budget over time, let us examine what may be, from a managerial point of view, the most important issue we may face over the short run: balancing properly the future defense establishment among what I here describe as *functional* categories.[22] By "functional," I have in mind a distinction among major budget components according to the role they play with respect to the fielding of major operational combat capabilities. Policymakers have always been interested in this topic under a variety of guises. For instance, concern has often been expressed about the "tooth-to-tail ratio" within the defense establishment as a whole—whether we might be spending too much on the "tail" (i.e., the supporting structure and infrastructure upon which the defense effort as a whole relies) and too little on the "tooth" (the actual front-end combat capabilities). The issue has gained particular currency over the past few years as force structure levels have repeatedly been cut to meet budget targets. Fearing that cuts beyond minimal levels of necessary capability might occur, particular emphasis has been placed on the reduction of a number of infrastructure and overhead accounts—for instance, the closure of bases no longer required given the new strategic context and a smaller overall posture.

One unfortunate aspect of the recent cuts and plans developed has been that our understanding about just how to go about thinning down "overhead" in general is not well informed by solid analytic methods and other assessments. Another problem derives from the politics of certain overhead reductions. Issues surrounding, say, the closure of certain installations or the standing down of certain reserve activities are well known to any seasoned defense man-

---

[21]Secretary Perry has stressed the importance of basic R&D initiatives: presumably by the end of the decade some of these will have moved along to the point that they will generate options for major investment if we are to exploit any gains made.

[22]I mean "functional" only in a general sense. While some elements of the DoD program fit logically into one category or another, others are harder to assign. I have used one allocation methodology; others would yield different absolute numbers, but for sensible categorizations, the overall trends would be similar.

ager to be among the most sensitive possible, given the resistance of many political constituencies to such efficiency measures. An additional problem has to
do with the technical aspects of these economy initiatives themselves. For instance, closing a certain military base might actually involve more costs than
savings in the short run, on account of various factors (e.g., the environmental
restoration of the base, the provision of assistance to the local affected economy, etc.).

A final—and perhaps the most important—problem with going after
"overhead" (however one elects to define that) has to do with the nonlinear nature of the relationship between the purpose of that overhead and its size. We
can relatively easily adjust many front-end force elements on the margin: reduce the number of aircraft assigned to our tactical squadrons, trim personnel
in battalions (or cut battalions from divisions), etc. But downsizing infrastructure often involves some precarious step-function and other discontinuous
phenomena. To take a deliberately extreme case, consider, for instance, the
Global Positioning System (GPS) navigational satellite system. This resource,
an undeniably important part of our defense overhead (both literally and figuratively), can function only with a minimum constellation of satellites in place:
we cannot trim the system by 10 percent (say) without undermining the capabilities of the whole program. Such complex relationships between the "inputs"
and "outputs" of many overhead elements are common, and they represent a
real problem for planners charged with trimming budgets to meet year-to-year
outlay targets.

As a result of these difficulties—both in understanding the problem and in
implementing solutions—and because the DoD has traditionally tied its justification for military forces to specific (and now waning) military threats, the
force structure itself has been the primary target in budget cuts to date.
Indeed, for unclear reasons, a kind of direct relationship between budgets and
force structures seems to exist in the minds of many. Because of this targeting
of force structure in successive rounds of budget cuts so far, we see disproportionately large reductions in the "tooth" parts of our posture compared with
the relative drop in budget levels proposed.

To illustrate this, Table 4 and Figure 11 show how the number of Marine
fighting units (battalions and squadrons) drops as a function of reductions in
personnel. The figures are for three different proposed budget levels (and have
not yet been updated for the results of the BUR). It is hard to break out specific budget figures for the Marines as an integrated force, since the Navy procures many items used by the Marines and provides some personnel support to
Marine formations, but Marine personnel is a fair surrogate for budget, and we
see that combat structure is dropping twice as fast as personnel (and roughly
twice as fast as dollars).

Table 4

Consequences for Fighting Units of Cuts in Marine Budget

	FY89	FY92	FY95 (planned)[a]
Force element			
Total personnel	197,000	188,000	159,000
Rifle battalions	27	24	16
Fighter-attack squadrons	28	23	17+3[b]
Decline (percent) from 1989 baseline			
Personnel		5	19
Battalions		11	41
Squadrons		12	39 (29)[c]

[a]USMC end-strength subsequently revised upward by BUR to 171,000.

[b]Three squadrons programmed under BUR as "dual" squadrons.

[c]Including dual squadrons.

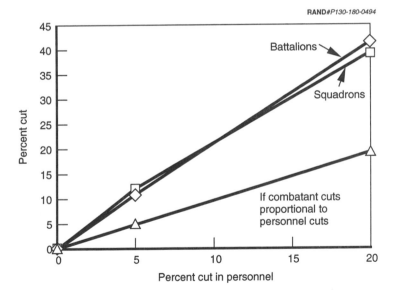

Figure 11—Combat Capability Decreases Twice as Fast as Personnel Levels
(Proxy for budget levels)

The reasons for this peculiar relationship are tied to several factors, one of which is the nature of the Marine personnel infrastructure base. Given hard-to-cut baseline requirements for a training base and other functions (e.g., providing embassy and ship security details, headquarters staffs, etc.), cuts can only be taken from active combat units themselves. Similar charts could be drawn for other elements of other services. The ultimate result of such a process, of course, is the absurd situation in which the United States maintains a given basing structure, communications and intelligence system, headquarters and training bases, and a whole array of other support assets—but has in hand no usable combat forces.

Defining infrastructure—never mind assessing its payoff—is a complex and tricky task. We are confronted with a basic problem about the difference between what we have traditionally defined as the "combatant" part of our posture and the nature of what is left over. But not all relative growth in "overhead" in general is necessarily bad: one very favorable outcome of our years of experience and technical developments has been our ability to devise a series of support assets, "force multipliers," and other capabilities that we might not tally in our "bean count" assessments of the military balance but which without doubt enhance in an immediate way the ability of our "shooters" to do their jobs in operational settings. For example, one of the major accomplishments of the U.S. Air Force in the years between Vietnam and Desert Storm has been the development of numerous electronic warfare systems, control, targeting, and intelligence systems, defense suppression capabilities, and the like, all of which enabled allied air power in the Gulf War to score enormous successes against Iraqi forces with unbelievably low attrition. Similarly, our abilities to transport major force elements rapidly by air or sea, to refuel an entire range of aircraft in flight, to surveil and communicate on a global and an instantaneous basis, etc., are without any doubt the capabilities that make the United States a true military superpower. Sometimes, the tail does seem to wag the dog.

But it continues to be difficult to say what tradeoffs should be considered between, say, a certain number of extra JSTARS targeting aircraft and a given number of tactical fighter-bombers. It is even harder to conceive in traditional cost-benefit terms of what we should spend on logistical support and high-quality training. What is possible, however, is to consider certain trends in our budgetary allocations among a spectrum of capabilities ranging from pure combatant elements on the one hand (wings, divisions, surface combatants, etc.) to pure infrastructure and overhead costs on the other (retired pay, health care, base maintenance, etc.). One way of conceiving of the problem divides the total defense budget into five categories, as follows:

- *Combat forces—the "teeth" of the posture.* This category includes all accounts associated with the direct operating, manning, and equipping of those force structure elements that most people think of as our basic military posture (like numbers of divisions, fighter wings, bombers, carriers, submarines, etc.) as well as certain other units (such as special operations forces, strategic defense units, antisubmarine warfare surveillance and defense forces, etc.).

- *Capabilities for supporting and sustaining combat forces.* This is a quite varied category that includes such diverse activities as logistical support, procurement of war reserve spares, the development of new technologies for possible future employment in combat weapon systems, mobility resources, and so on.

- *Defense operational infrastructure.* This collection of activities refers not so much to specific units and direct support functions as it does to command, service, and defensewide activities like communications, recruiting and training, medical and related personnel support, and the like.

- *Defense physical infrastructure.* This category consists, as the reader would suspect, of the activities normally thought of as "bases and installations"—it also includes pertinent military construction and family housing accounts, the maintenance of test and training ranges, etc.

- *Central defense management, command, and related accounts.* This is the costs of headquarters and administration, plus various other endeavors— support of diplomatic and foreign military activities, undifferentiated (basic) R&D, and other odds and ends.

This scheme is just one of the many that could be devised, but it has the virtue of having relatively few categories so that we can see rather simply the large-scale movement in and among them. Let us now turn to the results of a longitudinal investigation of the data appearing in this portrayal. But before proceeding, it is important to note that the descriptions of the composition of each category are deliberately not more precise—because the point of this discussion is not to dispute how to divide up the categories but rather to simply display the results of one research approach to assessing them. I have investigated other approaches, and the results are entirely in agreement with those I give here.

Figure 12 shows the DoD (in TOA) broken out into the preceding five categories on a percentage basis over the period FY62–92. The movement over time in each category and the interactions among them are a consequence of many factors, some of them highly complicated ones. But two factors that are particularly important are: (1) correspondence of certain phenomena in these statistics to various large-scale (topline, appropriation title, etc.) developments; and (2) certain longer-term trends. For instance, the category describing our combat forces is rather sensitive to procurement of these systems—hence this category shows an increase during the buildup of the 1980s (when many costly weapons end-items were procured). At the same time (taking into account this bulge), we note a general process of decline over time in the share represented in the budget by this category from the high 30 percent range to the high 20s

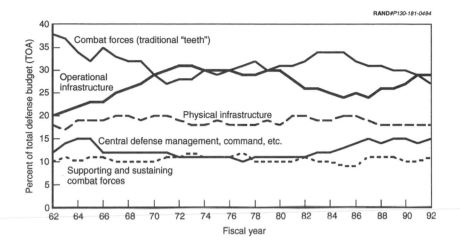

Figure 12—Breakdown By Components of TOA, FY62–FY92

during the so-called decade of neglect (a level that is reattained at the end of this period as the 1980s procurement buildup faded out).

It is worth highlighting some findings from the chart and thoughts about the Clinton program:

- Certain categories—management and command, physical infrastructure, and combat force support—tend to stay relatively constant over the course of the whole interval. These categories stay, respectively, within the following general proportional ranges: 11–15, 18–20, and 10–12 percent. Closer analysis of the data underlying this figure indicates some mixing among the constituent elements of these categories, but in general, their effects balance out over time.

- Ruling out the major procurement of weapons of the 1980s, operational support has gained over time "at the expense," if you will, of front-line combat forces.[23]

---

[23]This phenomenon reflects the drawdown and rationalization of the force structure associated with the shift to Flexible Response (influenced, of course, by Vietnam War developments).   Note that detailed analysis of the factors contributing to overall movement in the absolute or proportional constitution of these categories reflects a general process of decline in front-end "core" posture representation in the budget and corresponding gain in certain ancillary posture elements (recently, these include, for instance, special operations forces).   Of even greater significance has been the steady if not entirely regular growth as a share of the budget in communications, intelligence, and related resources.

- Because (a) very little combat system procurement is programmed for the balance of the decade, (b) force structure has declined and is programmed to decline further, and (c) there have been no corresponding reductions in certain support undertakings, we should see, through the rest of the 1990s, a considerable decline in the "tooth" part of the posture and a proportional growth in other accounts, especially those related to defense operational support.

This demonstrates several factors of note. First, the general process of patterning (in the form of "convergence") is apparent in this portrayal, as well as in others. Second, the general movement over time away from a budgetary emphasis on front-end combat units toward various supporting programs (particularly operational support) is clear from this chart, and we should expect to see this phenomenon amplified greatly as a result of the Clinton administration's plans for the future (and those of Bush's before them). Force structure has been targeted especially heavily (and, of the constituent force accounts, *procurement* of major force elements has in particular been heavily hit) for a number of reasons: these accounts are understandable to policymakers; they are often controversial; they are associated in the public eye with strategy; and so on. Third, while we may retain too many bases and other physical infrastructure, and while there is a continual drive afoot to streamline managerial and command "overhead," the greatest internal budget cost pressures are not in these categories but rather in two main areas: (a) those related to personnel costs (the same problems the domestic economy has experienced with, among other things, health care costs have hit the military just as hard);[24] and (b) those related to command, communications, intelligence, etc.[25] The significance of these findings for our consideration of our future defense prospects has not, in my view, been adequately considered. In particular, we run the risk—if budgets continue to decline and if various effects produce a year-to-year demand for continued program trimming—that we will continue to take cuts from posture and not from certain overhead accounts.

---

[24]Indeed, as of a couple of years ago, more than a sixth of the defense budget took the form of entitlements—health care, retirement benefits, support of dependents, etc.

[25]This should be apparent to anyone who has followed our recent operational experience. An inevitable "lesson learned" from every recent operation, from Urgent Fury to Just Cause and to Desert Storm, has been "the need for more and better communications and intelligence." There seems, indeed, to be an almost unlimited demand for such resources. While this demand is no doubt justified from many perspectives, there does not seem to be much corresponding concern with tradeoffs—if we take the force versus C^3I budget competition to an extreme, for instance, we wind up with a completely ineffectual but extremely well-informed spectating military posture.

ARE WE ALSO UNDERESTIMATING REQUIREMENTS?

So far in this overview I have sought to persuade the reader that there is every reason to believe we will end up with a good deal less combat capability than our current plans project. But does it matter? What are our needs? This is not the place to discuss this in any detail (see also Davis, 1994b and Kugler, 1993). Let me instead note that both the Bush and Clinton administrations came to very similar conclusions about the appropriate minimum size of the defense establishment, despite having come in with rather different attitudes on the subject. Further, current planning revolves around major regional contingencies and posits the adequacy of force levels substantially lower than those we have routinely sent to analogous contingencies in the past. As Figure 13 indicates, there has been a remarkable consistency in MRC commitments—at levels significantly above the "building block" that the BUR associates with an MRC (4–5 Army divisions, 1–2 Marine divisions, 4–5 carriers, and 10 wings). And while some cynics will say that this merely reflects organizational behavior or gamesmanship rather than needs, it did not seem at all unreasonable to General Schwarzkopf to ask for a doubling of the Desert Storm force before beginning a massive counteroffensive. While it is not provable, it seems to me

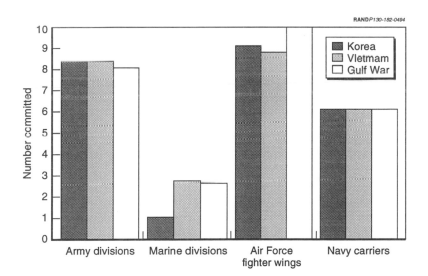

Figure 13—Forces Committed in Korea, Vietnam, and the Gulf War

plausible that the two most recent administrations have been correct and that the present defense program is moving us toward minimally adequate capabilities. If this is so, then we should be concerned, because the likelihood of the program's turning out to be as effective as the plans call for is small. Let me end, then, by again urging humility upon our defense planners. We should not be "betting the ranch" on the current plans being implemented efficiently. Instead, we should expect inefficiencies, and substantially more negative effects on capability than might be expected from these inefficiencies, because of the increasing role of "fixed-cost" overhead items. There is, in other words, a discipline gap that we should assume will not easily be reduced.

BIBLIOGRAPHY

Aspin, Les (1993), *The Bottom-Up Review*, Department of Defense, Washington, D.C.

Davis, Paul K. (ed.) (1994a), *New Challenges for Defense Planning: Rethinking How Much Is Enough*, RAND, Santa Monica, CA.

———— (1994b), "Planning Under Uncertainty Then and Now: Paradigms Lost and Paradigms Emerging," in Davis (1994a).

Kaufmann, William W. (1982), *Planning Conventional Defenses, 1950–1980*, The Brookings Institution, Washington, D.C.

Kugler, Richard (1993), *U.S. Military Strategy and Force Posture for the 21st Century: Capabilities and Requirements*, RAND, Santa Monica, CA.

———— (1994), "Nonstandard Contingencies for Defense Planning," in Davis (1994a).

Lewis, Kevin N. (1990), *National Security Spending and Budget Trends Since World War II*, RAND, Santa Monica, CA.

Reilly, John (ed.) (1987), *American Public Opinion and U.S. Foreign Policy, 1988*, The Chicago Council on Foreign Relations.

Stanley, William (1994), "Assessing the Affordability of Fighter Aircraft Force Modernization," in Davis (1994a).

Stockman, David (1986), *The Triumph of Politics: Why the Reagan Revolution Failed*, Harper and Row, New York.

Part Three

Planning at the Strategic Level

Chapter 6

PROTECTING THE GREAT TRANSITION

Paul K. Davis

This paper describes a 1991 study applying a strategic planning methodology to sketch the elements of a possible American grand strategy. It then updates the study and draws implications for American defense planning and defense analysis. The analytic methodology used may be appealing to readers even if they differ with the particular assumptions used in the paper. The paper's principal thrust is that uncertainty is a dominating characteristic of the landscape and this should be reflected in the fundamentals of any U.S. grand strategy and defense-planning framework. The first implication is that we should plan flexible and robust military capabilities for diverse contingencies, large and small, not just the contingencies now fashionable for planning. Crucial details of standard scenarios are very unlikely to be correct. Nonetheless, most likely theaters of major conflict can be identified, along with plausible objectives and strategies of protagonists. A second implication is that since the likelihood of a large-scale military threat in the next decade seems to be small, national security strategy should give unusual attention to other concerns, notably economic issues, deterring or coping with second-rate regional aggressors, peacemaking, and peacekeeping. This said, it would be dangerous to ignore the potential early in the next century for larger conflicts or future superpower rivals, because doing so might create vacuums that would make the emergence of such rivals more likely. Against this background, the paper argues that defense planning should now be centered on a combination of (a) environment-shaping, (b) deterrent, and (c) contingency-fighting needs, and that the nature of defense analysis should change substantially if it is to address these needs rather than become irrelevant. The paper suggests a number of specific implications for defense planning.

INTRODUCTION

Background

Late in 1991, at the request of senior officials of the Bush administration, RAND staff members began writing a series of short papers to inform and stimulate broad discussion of national security strategy (or "grand strategy"), which were subsequently collected and sent informally to policymakers. One of those papers (Davis, Drezner, and Hillestad, 1992), applied a RAND methodology for thinking about grand strategy in a way encouraging "divergent thinking" and provocative ideas.[1] In this paper I present and up-date some of that earlier work as a case history illustrating the methodology. I also draw subjective inferences for defense planning, highlighting deviations from tradition. Readers are invited to think about how they could use the same planning approach to come up with conclusions based on their own judgments and values.

The Methodology for Thinking Afresh About Grand Strategy

The work began with a brief exercise attempting to characterize options for U.S. national security strategy in the wake of developments in 1990 and 1991, notably the disappearance of the Soviet Union and the emergence of the Commonwealth of Independent States, which seemed unlikely to be a long-term fixture of the landscape. The methodology used had been developed specifically for planning under uncertainty, and to replace the classic approach of identifying and agreeing upon "threats," deriving "requirements" to cope with those threats, and then deriving related strategies for meeting the re-quirements. Its components were as follows:[2]

- Describe the emerging *core environment* and major uncertainties, particu-larly in the form of *scheduled uncertainties* that can be thought of as future branch points and *unscheduled uncertainties* in the form of potential *shocks* (i.e., potential developments that are quite plausible, but that would never make it onto a list of approved best-estimate threats).

- Develop a set of alternative grand strategies, referred to by "one-liner" themes for convenience, although all are multifaceted.

- For each grand strategy, develop a *core strategy*, an *environment-shaping strat-egy*, and a *hedging strategy*, thereby dealing with uncertainties as a primary matter.

---

[1] Other methods are more suitable for carefully structured top-down efforts con-necting interests, objectives, strategies, and military missions or tasks. For a description of the "strategies-to-tasks" approach, which is due largely to colleague Glenn Kent, see Kent and Simons (1991) and Thaler (1993).

[2] I first developed the methodology with RAND consultant Paul Bracken of Yale University in a study for OSD and the Joint Staff. For a subsequent summary of that work, see Davis (1989). For antecedents in business practice, see Bracken (1989). RAND has used the methods also in studies for USCENTCOM, USPACOM, and the U.S. Army (Levin, 1994).

- Compare the grand strategies in a summary framework based on *differentiating attributes* of strategy.

- Consider ways to integrate some of the strategies in comfortable ways by exploiting the willingness of the proponents of all strategies to acknowledge the need to adapt strategy over time.

Several features of this approach are particularly important. First, the approach encourages a broad view of the environment rather than one focused on one or a very few threats. Second, it encourages an attitude of *environment-shaping* rather than the more passive attitude of seeking to "react" to threats as they arise. While simple in concept, this has important implications for national security planning. Third, it specifically requires one to build a hedged strategy rather than one focused exclusively on dealing with best-estimate problems. Last, it moves from a divergent phase of developing substantially different "strategies" to a convergent phase that seeks to combine strategies intelligently, rejecting false dichotomies and false orthogonalities.[3] The approach is especially helpful for breaking out of standard mind-sets and encouraging broad and integrative thinking; it is excellent for brainstorming and group discussion. On the other hand, it tends to generate lists that include "apples and oranges" and are neither logically "tight" nor comprehensive. Thus, the approach is a *complement* to more traditional methods of strategic reasoning and analysis, but not a substitute for them.

Let me now sketch how the approach was used in our 1991 study. The first step was to characterize the environment—both the "core environment" (roughly speaking, a "canonical" view of the environment and trends, one heavily dependent on extrapolation and continuity) and the principal uncertainties of the environment.

THE ENVIRONMENT

The Core Environment

Most features of the emerging core environment were and are familiar (little has changed in the last two years). We referred to "The Great Transition"[4] (GT) to describe the structural shift that had taken place (and that may or may

---

[3]Some of these concepts were used by colleague Zalmay Khalilzad when he headed OSD's policy planning office in 1991–1992. They were adopted by Secretary Cheney, as reflected in Cheney (1992) and other official documents.

[4]The term "Great Transition" was used by Herman Kahn in *The Next Hundred Years,* (Kahn, 1976:6). See also Kahn (1979), which elaborates the arguments.

not still be proceeding) at the geostrategic level.[5]   Table 1 summarizes the environment and trends as we saw them, but includes some additions in italics that I would make today (March 1994).   The phrases "Second World" and "Third World," respectively, represent nations that are not yet "developed" but apparently capable of becoming so, and nations that are in much more trouble and with much less favorable prospects apparent.   Examples of the former are Eastern Europe, China, and parts of the former Soviet Union; examples of the latter are other parts of the former Soviet Union, much of the Mideast, and most of Africa.   We used the term "developed nations" rather than, for example, "the free world," "the Western world," or other previous terminologies.

Another aspect of core environment involves domestic constraints affecting what national security strategies are feasible.   Table 2 describes what we saw as some of the most important.   Although some can be mitigated by skillful packaging and communication of strategy, constraints will play an even more major role in future planning than in the past, primarily because of the absence of a clear-cut threat, but also because small wars are "different" (Cohen, 1984). Some of the constraints are in tension.   For example, while most act to limit U.S. military preparations and activities, the last acts in the opposite direction. In certain types of crisis, there will be strong pressures for the United States to "act like a superpower," for reasons that include perceived world responsibilities as well as the need for the President to protect our more narrow interests (e.g., our access to Persian Gulf oil or the territorial integrity of formal allies to whom we have given security guarantees).   Finally, note a problem of a different sort: There is considerable impatience that takes the form of demands that the President develop a strong vision of the future U.S. role and build a clearcut and consistent strategy.   That is asking too much, and it stems from an implicit nostalgia for the clarity of Cold War planning.   We argued, instead, for an adaptive and evolutionary strategy that would avoid overfocusing on particular threats or assumptions.

---

[5]Opinions differ on the extent of this great transition.   The most articulate optimistic appraisal is probably Fukuyama (1992).   See also Ajami (1993) and Bartley (1993), responding to the more pessimistic discussion of Huntington (1993).   For more pessimistic discussions with a structural-realist bent, see Mearsheimer (1991) and Layne (1993).   In the wake of events in Bosnia and Somalia, even those of us who believed, cautiously, in the great transition are now less sanguine than we were in 1991. Nonetheless, long-term trends may still be favorable and the United States can affect those trends through leadership.

Table 1

Highlights of the Emerging Core Geostrategic Environment

Threats
- Threat of global war almost nonexistent.
- *Threat of great-power war almost nonexistent.*
- Russian threat to Western Europe almost nonexistent. Eventual reconstitution of threat at most "plausible."
- China or Japan as eventual security threat at most "plausible."
- Greatest U.S. "threats" now economic and social, and widely seen as such.
- *Many threats to United States are diffuse, ambiguous, and not much affected by military power.*

However,
- World filled with danger spots that may require small or moderate military intervention *(e.g., Bosnia, Somalia).*
- Distinct threat of Russian coercion or reabsorption of Baltic states *or Ukraine* if conservatives replace Yeltsin.
- Many potentially unfriendly nations and combinations of nations with large armies.
- *Worrisome ethnic strife at many points.*

World political-economic environment
- Clear trend away from communism.
- Apparent trend in Second World toward liberal democracy and market economies, or at least legitimate governments and relatively unregulated capitalism.
- Trends in Third World less clear-cut; strong strands of fundamentalist Islamic thinking. In some areas, continued calls for "order" and "a strong hand."
- Many sources of instability throughout Third World and parts of Second World.
- *Emergence of large trading blocs.*
- *Very strong growth in several Asian countries.*
- Economic decisions increasingly made by triad of United States, Japan, and European Community through institutions such as G-7, IMF, and even NATO.
- *Overall environment still a mix of rich and very poor countries.*

U.S. security role in world
- United States no longer dominant in Europe; may become minor player soon, or be invited out.
- United States clearly primary worldwide, with no plausible competitor for the role visible.
- United States constrained to act mostly in coalitions, while remaining able to act quickly and unilaterally in some cases.
- U.S. sense of own role still evolving.

NOTE: Items in italics added in January 1994.

Table 2

Constraints Affecting Strategy Development

- Downward trend of defense expenditures, coupled with diminished sense of threat.
- Aversion to significant U.S. casualties in military actions.
- Instantaneous press coverage, resulting in the need for convincing case to act at all and the need to conclude visible actions rather quickly.
- General concerns about U.S. economic outlook limiting support for external military activities and forward deployments.
- Political obstacles to major changes in reserve-component structure or to depending on the draft for response to strategic warning.
- Obstacles to redirecting the use of the military in peacetime to domestic purposes (e.g., the military cannot be perceived as taking jobs away in teaching, construction, and other areas).
- Moral constraints on use of military (e.g., avoiding civilian casualities).
- Political imperative, at time of crisis, to "behave like a superpower."

Uncertainties as a Central Feature of the Environment

An early conclusion of our 1989 efforts, repeated in the 1991 ministudy, was that the most important feature of the environment from the perspective of planners is the *dominance* of uncertainty. Most striking is the fact that we do not even know who or what will constitute the most serious future threats (see also Kugler, 1994). This is in stark constrast to the situation over the last four decades. We are in an era in which we are military enemies of almost no one to start with, but during which we will unquestionably find ourselves, from time to time, in confrontation—either diplomatic, economic, or military—with a variety of nations. Which nations will be our partners and which will be our opponents will vary with issue and circumstance. We are in a period of multidimensional *competition,* which in some respects is a better way to view our problem than focusing on one or two specific military threats.[6]

A key element of the planning approach, and one that encourages group discussion of a sort that breaks away from traditional conventional wisdom, is recognizing that uncertainties fall into several different classes.

Some uncertainties can be represented as crudely scheduled branches in time. That is, some issues are already on the table, issues that may be resolved in ways we cannot predict now with confidence, but for which we know generally the possible outcomes. Table 3 indicates the ones we identified at the

---

[6]This theme has been pursued also by OSD's Director of Net Assessment, Andrew Marshall, by Daniel Goure, David Andre, and others. See, e.g., Andre (1991).

Table 3

Major Uncertainties with Potential Branch Points

- What will be the political, economic, and military futures of the former Soviet Union: *Russia, Ukraine, the Baltic states . . . ?*
- Regional instabilities: Will the Arabian peninsula settle down politically, or will antimonarchy forces become stronger? If the latter, which type of forces?
- New large threats: Will China become aggressive? Will Japan remilitarize and become a military competitor? Will the Koreas unite peacefully?
- *Will the North Korean nuclear program destabilize East Asia and undercut U.S. counterproliferation efforts generally?*
- *Will Israel and the Palestinians be successful in their efforts to reach a peace agreement?*
- *Will NATO expand its membership and charter to deal with Eastern Europe?* (Asmus, Kugler, and Larrabee, 1993; Harries, 1993)
- Proliferation: Will potential proliferators see more or fewer incentives? Will the scientists and technicians of the former Soviet Union be a major factor in proliferation?
- Terrorism: Will there be a new wave of terrorism stemming from the Middle East? How will this affect interest in ballistic missile defense?
- Drugs: Will the international drug problem require offensive military actions?
- Economic threats: Will the real or perceived economic threat lead to trade wars and other aspects of political-economic warfare?

---

time, plus, in italics, those that I would add today. Some of the principal changes are that even Russia's stability is in question; Israel and the Palestinians are attempting to reach a peace accord; and North Korea's nuclear program looms as a major threat to stability (Bracken, 1993a, and Khalilzad, Davis, and Shulsky, 1993). Perhaps there will be some "resolution" of the Bosnian conflict, although not one that will or should endure.

A rather different type of uncertainty involves possible *shocks*—events that will come as a surprise when they happen (i.e., we will be completely or partly unprepared for them, even if we have previously recognized them as possibilities) and that will have a significant impact. These are the stuff of crises. *Further, they are a crucial factor in prudent defense planning, which must not be captive to the "best-estimate" mentality of the day.*[7] Table 4 summarizes some of the many shocks possible in the years ahead, with a few new items added in

---

[7]Events in the Soviet Union and Russia since 1989 illustrate well how appropriate the emphasis on uncertainty was in the 1989 study and the 1991 follow-up described here. Political dynamics are to a substantial degree inherently unpredictable during a period of structural change. Such changes are continuing as 1993 draws to a close.

Table 4

Potential Shocks

Regional
- Former Soviet Union *(and Russia)* has civil wars, starvation, dissemination and loss of control of nuclear weapons.
- Cuba collapses: accommodates to United States or has civil war.
- India and Pakistan go to war; nuclear weapons used.
- Islamic or other anti-Western revolution occurs in Saudi Arabia.
- Saddam Hussein regains influence; agents foment coup in Saudi Arabia.
- Sendero Luminoso wins in Peru and exports its revolution *(now unlikely)*.
- North Korea launches last-ditch invasion *(or implodes with subsequent chaos and violence)*.
- *North Korea disappears from the scene, eliminating one of the two major regional contingencies around which DoD force-planning has been regrettably but nominally structured and reopening the debate, "How much is enough?"*
- Russia invades or coerces Baltic states.
- Russian invades or coerces Poland *or Ukraine.*
- United States is asked to leave Europe; NATO dissolves.
- Transition of Hong Kong turns violent.
- Renewed civil war occurs in Cambodia.
- Japan, observing North Korea or for other reasons, decides to develop nuclear weapons.
- United States is asked to leave Korea and Japan.
- United States suffers a deep depression.
- Germany becomes a troublesome and more militant actor.
- Mexico has economic collapse with explosion of emigration.
- *Peacemaking or peacekeeping operations evolve into wars (e.g., in Bosnia).*

Cross-regional
- Terrorists actually use or threaten use of nuclear, chemical, or biological weapons.
- Terrorists use or threaten use of ballistic missiles; alternatively they use or threaten use of *cruise missiles* or *satchel nuclear bombs* (these would have very different effects on interest in ballistic missile defense).
- Japanese exercise an "economic weapon" (e.g., backing away from U.S. securities) in response to U.S. pressures.
- Islamic fundamentalism accelerates suddenly (e.g., in Iran, the southern republics of the former Soviet Union, Egypt, and/or Turkey).

---

italics. Humility is appropriate in thinking about such shocks, because the past record of governments in anticipating and preparing for them has been dismal.[8] Doing somewhat better in this regard in the future should be a major

---

[8]In a spring 1990 application of the strategic planning methodology to Southwest Asia for General Schwartzkopf, then Commander in Chief of USCENTCOM, I listed as mere examples of previous shocks: the Korean War (1950), the Yom Kippur War

priority.[9] This probably means recognizing better the broad range of possible shocks and improving the ability to adapt quickly when shocks occur, rather than improving the quality of strategic warning.

Of the new (italicized) items in the list of potential shocks, the most interesting may be the postulated disappearance of North Korea. If the North Korean threat vanished, then the entire argument about "How much is enough?" would have to be reopened. The DoD would either have to identify a new major regional contingency (MRC) for planning (with no good alternative now visible) or rationalize its force structure without requiring nominal capability for two specific concurrent regional conflicts. This change of paradigm would be difficult to make and sell, but would be desirable in many respects (Davis, 1994b,d).

BASIC THEMES FOR ALTERNATIVE GRAND STRATEGIES

The Concept of Guiding Themes

Having described the environment, the next step was to develop some alternative grand strategies. A bona fide grand strategy must be multifaceted, addressing all the components of strategy in enough detail to establish directions and priorities (see also Davis, 1989). However, it is useful to distinguish among primitive grand strategies by identifying the themes that would be their central feature. If one strategy's theme is to rebuild America, that does *not* imply an isolationist foreign policy akin to that of the 1920s and 1930s, but it *does* imply a heavy priority on domestic issues.

The principal factors appearing in the themes we used related to: (a) the degree to which the United States seeks actively to protect and perhaps extend the Great Transition; (b) the degree to which the United States seeks to take the leadership position in world security affairs; and (c) the balance between

---

(1973), the fall of the Shah of Iran (1979), the taking of hostages by the Ayatollah Khomeini (1979), and the Soviet invasion of Afghanistan (1979). My colleague Zalmay Khalilzad and I also discussed how even variants of "standard" planning scenarios can be shocks and noted how difficult real contingencies involving an Iraqi threat to Kuwait could be because of the ambiguity likely about intentions. In that same project we later conducted a contingency planning game in July 1990, which included working through a crisis that turned out to be almost identical to the shock a month later, when Saddam Hussein invaded Kuwait. The point is not that we were prescient, because we did not *expect* an invasion either (although considering it quite possible), but rather that what later appear as "shocks" can often be anticipated if we move beyond the tyranny of the best estimate.

[9]A different but related strategic-planning method asks participants to identify fundamental *assumptions* which, if violated, would seriously invalidate their baseline strategic plans. This approach is described in Dewar, Builder, Hix, and Levin (1993).

emphasis on domestic issues and external security (and, therefore, the allocation of resources between domestic and defense spending).

Alternative Themes

We next developed a baseline strategy and three relatively "pure" grand strategies, which were deemed to be largely orthogonal (i.e., mutually independent). We subsequently compared them more carefully and constructed hybrids.[10]

A Projection of Then-Current Strategy (Creatively Adaptive "Muddling Along" as a Leader?). It was difficult to characterize the current U.S. grand strategy as of late 1991, but it seemed that it had involved timely and creative adaptation rather than proactive planning. U.S. leadership had been strong and effective, but often reluctant. Except for certain speeches shortly after Saddam Hussein invaded Kuwait, President Bush had seemed rather conservative in his expectations about the world and in his judgments about what could be accomplished. And while the President's defense program called for impressive across-the-board cuts over the next five years, the changes in the defense program were rather straightforward reactions to an unequivocally reduced threat. There had been little refocusing on the economy and social problems (which some believe cost President Bush the election in 1992) and, many claimed, no strategy to guide details of the military drawdown. As of late 1993, similar criticisms were being made about the Clinton administration, despite Secretary Aspin's having concluded his "Bottom-Up Review" (Aspin, 1993).

Protecting the Great Transition. This strategy put top priority on the set of foreign-affairs and defense measures necessary to consolidate the Great Transition. It was concerned about assuring the long-term security of Eastern Europe (and even the Baltic states, despite the extreme difficulty of protecting them militarily) and avoiding the reemergence of a major military threat from Russia. Although proponents fully recognized the difficulties in protecting either Eastern Europe (including Ukraine) or the Baltic states militarily, they were even more sensitive to the vacuum created by having a whole belt of newly independent but militarily weak states emerge. These have become buffer states.[11] Further, proponents believed that for the foreseeable future,

---

[10]More recently, RAND conducted under Army sponsorship a somewhat similar study using the methodology I describe here. In this more extensive and careful work, the alternative grand strategies were characterized in classic terms: realism, multilateral security, democratic internationalism, and strategic independence. See Levin (1994).

[11]Proponents saw Saddam Hussein's invasion of Kuwait as a failure of deterrence caused, in large part, by the ambiguity of U.S. interests and the absence of security

deterrence of any Russian adventures against these states (e.g., under a conservative successor to Yeltsin) should not be hard with a combination of political, economic, and military measures, including prior planning and clarification of Western interests. In the short run, at least, this strategy implied vigorous U.S. leadership, albeit in cooperation with appropriate allies. Proponents disagreed about the appropriate long-run U.S. role, with some believing in a partial handover of security responsibilities to regional states and collective-security organizations such as the UN and Western Economic Union. In general, proponents of this option believed that the Great Transition was more fragile than sometimes recognized: they argued that the debacle in Yugoslavia (evident even in late 1991) should give us pause; future problems between Russia and its neighbors were distinctly plausible.

Protecting and Extending the Great Transition. This strategy went farther than the previous one in that it reflected a belief in the universal values of liberal democracy and the universal effectiveness of market economies. Further, it reflected the belief that U.S. national interests will be served as more nations embrace these values. This strategy argued for the developed nations and international organizations (definitely not the United States acting in isolation) to take a broad range of educational, humanitarian, political, economic, and military measures to encourage extension of the Great Transition to other nations worldwide. Proponents of this strategy would, by and large, favor liberalization even when it came into conflict with other near-term interests. For example, proponents would cautiously encourage liberalization of the Arabian Peninsula nations (at least in the sense of assuring legitimacy of governments), even though that would mean difficulties for the current monarchies. Proponents would seek prompt and effective collective actions against murderous dictators and other enemies of Great Transition values, although they would select their instruments carefully, and did not think of the strategy as propagating a narrow-minded "ideology" or a particular way of achieving the universal values.[12] It did not involve the missionary zeal or level of hubris the United States was sometimes accused of in the 1950s; it was also more patient.

---

guarantees. They believed such ambiguities should be avoided with respect to Eastern Europe. See Davis and Arquilla (1991).

[12]It is undeniably difficult to define where support of universal values slips into zealously propagating an ideology. One example involves requiring that governments derive their legitimacy from the consent of the governed, but without specifying how that legitimacy is demonstrated. Thus, "one man, one vote" is a good deal less "fundamental" than the requirement of legitimacy. Religious freedom is arguably fundamental, but that does not necessarily imply that there cannot be an official state religion. And so on. These are inherently complex matters, but it is striking to note how many values have been adopted by the UN because of their being far more than mere "Western" values.

Nonetheless, it was confident in the ultimate validity of universals, and consistent with that, it pursued "human rights agendas" actively.

National Renewal. This strategy put utmost emphasis on revitalizing America: rebuilding the nation's physical and intellectual infrastructure, addressing a broad range of social problems, and encouraging a high level of international competitiveness. It saw the defense budget as the obvious source of funds for these efforts, and was willing to bet on there being no near-term military threat that would require a large military structure. Proponents thought in terms of reducing the defense budget by 50 percent rather than 25 percent in real terms over the five-year period (see Kaufmann and Steinbruner (1991) for one such budget). Proponents were by no means isolationists, however. They expected the United States to be strongly involved in many aspects of foreign affairs, but they placed top priority on improving economic conditions (establishing a level playing field, avoiding being locked out of the European market, etc.). Proponents saw threats, but the threats they saw were economic. Proponents of this strategy did not believe the United States should be distracted by efforts to establish a new world order, or even to extend arms control (although they would accept as moderately useful some further arms-control efforts, especially reciprocal unilateral efforts accelerating reductions of defense spending).

CORE, ENVIRONMENT-SHAPING, AND HEDGING STRATEGIES

Given grand-strategy themes, the next step was to force proponents to separately define core, environment-shaping, and hedging strategies (Table 5), and in the process of doing so to describe political, economic, military, and perhaps other components. Having done that, we reorganized the results to compare the alternative grand strategies along a number of dimensions (Table 6).

Upon comparing the strategies, it became clear that there were false dichotomies among them. Why, for example, was it assumed that the United States cannot renew itself economically *and*, at the same time, protect and perhaps even help to extend the Great Transition? The U.S. defense budget was already slated to drop substantially in real terms over the next few years. Further, the defense burden (defense budget as a fraction of GDP) had been dropping for some time and would soon be the lowest that it had been in many decades. And, finally, the cost of accomplishing worldwide security missions would now be lower than in the past, because there were no major threats, the United States had many natural allies, and it had qualitative military dominance in most cases (although it might lack important forward-based infrastructure). This did *not* appear to be a time when we needed to back away from a security role because of concerns about overreach.[13] Instead, we could hope to do as much or more with a good deal less.

Another troubling aspect of the initial strategies was that they accepted the traditional U.S. view that U.S. military forces should be focused almost exclusively on deterrence and warfighting roles (except for occasional humanitarian operations). Why? Do we not have other problems to which military forces are well suited (e.g., by virtue of their discipline, organizational skills, mobility, and diversity of capabilities), and given the need to maintain a significant force structure (greater than needed for "best estimate" military challenges) for environment-shaping and hedging, should we not consider how best to use some of that force structure in peaceful missions?[14] It is worth noting that the U.S. Army has arguably been the greatest "democratizing agent" of the 20th century as the result of its role in postwar Japan and Germany, and perhaps in the Philippines in the 1930s.

With this and other such items in mind, we constructed a hybrid option called "Renew and Extend Cautiously." By this we meant that the United States would indeed focus on renewing America, but would simultaneously take on the task (with a variety of suitable coalitions and forums) of protecting the Great Transition and, where practical, extending it. To be sure, this strategy would be very cautious about involving the United States in military activities abroad, especially activities that might plausibly be a drain on resources, but it would be proactive in looking for low-risk opportunities to encourage further good trends. Even more important, it would be proactive in developing security arrangements to deter aggression against the newly independent states of Eastern Europe. Since neither these activities nor the most plausible ad hoc military contingencies would require many combat forces (e.g., no more than 3–7 divisions and/or 6–7 wings of air forces), this strategy would establish a new set of missions on which a significant number of regular forces would focus in peacetime, although retaining a secondary combat mission as well. These would include large-scale efforts to improve domestic physical infrastructure (e.g., roads, bridges, and perhaps even urban core areas), to address major environmental problems, and, overseas, to participate in humanitarian activities to eradicate certain diseases and assist development.[15] We recognized

---

[13]This conclusion differs sharply from those of historian Paul Kennedy and various structural realists (e.g., Layne, 1993).

[14]Implicit here is the fact that my colleagues and I rejected the usual threat-based approach of "deriving" force structure "requirements," because we did not find any of the particular accepted threats to be sufficiently compelling and stressing to justify the force structure we believed was desirable for broader reasons.

[15]One of the obstacles to such a strategy would be the perception by commercial contractors that they rather than the military should be doing the various jobs (e.g., rebuilding highways). It is plausible, however, that a package deal could be struck in

that this was highly controversial, but we believed it should be looked at seriously: the military could do a uniquely good job, and the problems are of very high priority nationally. We also thought that the symbolic value of such an initiative might be as great as its economic value in that period of gloom (late 1991). Such a strategy would be drastically different from current strategy and had little precedent in recent American practices (especially in its use of the military), but it made sense to us.

Tables 5 and 6 summarize the resulting comparison among the original four options and the hybrid.

CONCLUSIONS OF THE 1991 STUDY

The principal purpose of exercises such as the one we conducted in 1991 was to provide a sense of possible direction and some *alternative* constructs. We also believed that we could give some conclusions—not about precise directions, but about general guidelines, including new concepts to be looked at *seriously.* The summary conclusions of this quick-look study were as follows:

Broad Strategy

- Overall national strategy needs to shift substantially toward renewal of America and posturing America for a fierce multidecade global economic competition and improvement in the quality of life for its own sake.

- National strategy should also include a national security strategy maintaining U.S. leadership in global security affairs; it should protect and even extend, opportunistically and selectively, the "Great Transition" in the general direction of liberal democracy and market economies. The United States has a historic opportunity and responsibility, but one that can be discharged only in cooperation with other developed countries and international organizations, not as a matter of imperial will.

- Significantly, in seeking to protect and extend the Great Transition, the United States and its allies can *proceed adaptively*—taking opportunities, but backing away, without apology, when the price is too high. This is a long-term strategy, not a plan for completing development of a new world order in the next decade.

---

which the jobs would be shared between the commercial and military sectors. So long as the net effect was to add jobs, such a package might be possible. Given the scope of the challenges available, that seems plausible. Importantly, we believe the investment is desirable.

Table 5

Comparison of Simple Options with a Hybrid Option

	1. Timely Adaptation (Current)	2. Protect GT	3. Extend GT	4. Renew America	5. Renew and Extend Cautiously
Core strategy	Encourage liberalization of former Soviet Union and E. Europe.	Encourage liberalization of former Soviet Union and E. Europe.	All items of Option 2.	Reduce security burden although "encouraging" further good trends worldwide.	Protect and extend GT, but choose extension cases very cautiously.
	Pursue Middle East peace and, as minimum, establish U.S. position as honest broker.	Protect newly independent states via collective security arrangements (e.g., CSCE).	Encourage liberalization worldwide through multiple measures, including human-rights agenda in UN.	Refocus resources to domestic agenda of renewing infrastructure and increasing competitiveness.	Emphasize domestic agenda. Establish major domestic renewal role for military. Reduce base force somewhat, especially active ground units.
	Lead developed nations in international security.			Minimize foreign aid. Let Europeans and others fund E. Europe and CIS	Lead developed nations in broad approach to security.

Table 5—continued

	1. Timely Adaptation (Current)	2. Protect GT	3. Extend GT	4. Renew America	5. Renew and Extend Cautiously
	Go slow on economic aid.			Reduce force structure and reduce presence (e.g., 50%, not 20%).	Use military to improve domestic infrastructure and worldwide environment.
	Maintain "base force" and forward presence.			Grant leadership roles to regional states or groups (e.g., WEU).	
Environment-shaping strategy	Maintain benevolent forward presence to enhance regional security and U.S. influence.	Invest in economic development of E. Europe and former USSR (possible "Marshall Plan").	Be visbily prepared, with allies, for selective political, economic, and even military intervention.	Invest in infrastructure. Actively seek "level playing field" in foreign trade.	Greatly increase humanitarian use of military. Rejuvenate and liberalize security assistance.
	Take unilateral nuclear reductions; eliminate most TNF; seek central control of former USSR's weapons.	Be prepared, with allies, for pol-econ-mil intervention to protect E. Europe. Thus, deter.			

Table 5—continued

	1. Timely Adaptation (Current)	2. Protect GT	3. Extend GT	4. Renew America	5. Renew and Extend Cautiously
Hedging strategy	Base force larger than likely contingencies. Create reconstitution base (undefined).	Maintain a base force and forward presence. Base force larger than likely contingencies. Reconstitution base. Maintain plans and capability for unilateral action in vital areas.	In Mideast, be willing to grant international security guarantees. Reduce dependence on undemocratic states (e.g., Saudi Arabia).	Identify potential tactics of economic warfare by Japanese and others. Reduce vulnerability. Depend on reconstitution for military hedging.	Maintain benevolent forward presence and leadership. Prepare for economic warfare. Reduce vulnerability. Reduce dependence on undemocratic states. Develop high-readiness reserves.

Table 6

Comparisons by Attribute

Strategy Attribute	Creative Adaptation	Protect GT	Extend GT	Renew America	Renew and Extend Cautiously
POLITICAL					
Preeminent objective	Maintain stability in vital regions. Adapt to encourage good trends.	Also, protect GT	Also, extend GT and move toward a new world order	Revitalize America, while reducing security burden.	Revitalize America *and* protect GT
U.S. role in international security	Lead cooperatively, reactively, and adaptively.	Lead proactively	Lead proactively	Lead very selectively, on foreign trade issues. "Pass" on optional security issues.	Cooperative and selectively proactive leader
Protect GT?	Ambiguous in advance. Strong in response.	Strong, proactive	Strong, proactive	Very cautious but perhaps strong in response.	Strong, proactive
Extend GT?	Very cautious	Cautious	Strong, proactive, but fairly selective	Encouragement only	Strong, proactive, but selective
Approach to nonproliferation	Adaptive	Adaptive	Proactive, even interventionist	Adaptive	Proactive, even interventionist, but with emphasis on resolving root security problems also

Table 6—continued

Strategy Attribute	Creative Adaptation	Protect GT	Extend GT	Renew America	Renew and Extend Cautiously
Pol-econ interventionism?	Ad hoc and very cautious	Strong to protect GT only	Very willing, in collective setting	Opposed	Very willing in collective setting
Attitude toward UN and other collective-security organizations.	Arm's-length except to use	Supportive, but not subordinating	Supportive and sometimes with U.S. subordinated	Opposed except for standard humanitarian activities	Expansive and supportive, but with attitude of "using" and "leading." Variant: hand off in time
ECONOMIC					
International economic policy	Ambiguous	?	?	Insist on level playing field; apply sanctions if necessary	Insist on level playing field, but depend more on economic revitalization[a]
Federal role in competitiveness?	Modest, via cooperation on regulations, etc.	?	?	Substantial; some industrial policy	Moderate. Negotiations focused
Foreign aid to former USSR, E. Europe	Modest	"Marshall Plan"	"Marshall Plan" and others (e.g., Mideast)	Minimal	"Marshall Plan" and others. Allies to pay most.
Foreign aid to basket cases	Modest	Modest	Moderate, via UN	Minimal	Minimal

Table 6—continued

Strategy Attribute	Creative Adaptation	Protect GT	Extend GT	Renew America	Renew and Extend Cautiously
MILITARY					
Military interventionism?	Ad hoc and very cautious	Willing but very selective	Willing but selective	Opposed	Willing but selective
Force structure (army divs. in active/reserve/cadre)	12/4/2	10/6/2	10/6/2	7/4/?	8/4/6 if reserve reform possible
Approach to planning	Multiple operation plans	Building blocks	Building blocks	?	Building blocks
Humanitarian use of military	Modest	Modest	Moderate	?	Major
Use of military to improve domestic infrastructure	No	No	No	No	Major
Use of military for environmental problems	No	No	No	No	Yes
Optional hybrid national service (mil/domestic)	No	No	No	No	Yes
Structure of NSC	As now	As now	As now	As now	Strengthen economic component
Domestic NSC?	No	No	No	No	Yes

aThe "level playing field" issue has great significance politically, but achieving it fully is less important economically than getting our internal macroeconomic house in order.

- It is possible to do both of the above (renewal and global security): *The dichotomy between seeking a new world order and attending to our domestic problems is false.* It is false because our economic health is fundamentally intertwined with international affairs; because we do *not* need to be over-stretched economically as the result of our worldwide security activities; and because actions on the one do not contradict actions on the other. It will be necessary, however, to clarify the linkage between national security (broadly construed) and domestic well-being.[16]

Political and Economic Strategy

- Investments in Eastern Europe, countries of the former Soviet Union, and other nations potentially ready for the Great Transition should be seen as national security investments, not as "foreign aid." Their main purpose is to increase the likelihood that current liberalizing movements will be irreversible.

- *The United States, Western Europe, and UN should take special pains to protect the new Independence of the Baltic states and Eastern Europe.* Although a Russian threat to either seems remote today, that situation could reverse quickly if conservative elements replaced Yeltsin. Furthermore, clarifying interests and establishing security guarantees now, however unpopular in some political circles, would fill the vacuum that might otherwise lead to trouble some years hence. Further, Russia would today cooperate in establishing such guarantees.

- The United States should be cautiously proactive in protecting and even extending the Great Transition. It should be ready, in cooperation with appropriate allies and international organizations, to intervene in support of movements in states seeking to make the transition, but only if the situation warrants it and the price is acceptable. Most interventions should be political and economic, but should be planned as carefully as military operations—for effect, not cosmetics. West European (and UN) failure to intervene effectively in what was Yugoslavia has been a prime example of how *not* to do things.

- The United States and its developed-nation allies should be vigorous in deterring or reversing dangerous proliferation. However, this will often require efforts to resolve underlying security problems, which in turn may require developing multinational guarantees for affected countries (e.g., Israel, Pakistan, and even North Korea). The alternative is learning to live in a world with more proliferation.

- The peacemaking effort in the Mideast should continue. In addition to security guarantees for Europe, a satisfactory solution may require significant

---

[16]The reader may remember that at the time of the study the alleged overextension of the United States was being widely discussed, due principally to the book on the subject by historian Paul Kennedy.

changes in the nature of Jordan. We should anticipate a substantial price tag to make the solution attractive. Whether the oil-rich Arab states can be persuaded to fund this is unclear. Also, even if peace can be achieved, the economic and social prospects of the region appear dismal without fundamental changes.

- Because of profound cultural differences, which even obscure the universality of some human rights principles, encouraging extension of the Great Transition to Middle Eastern states should be done with the greatest of care and in a language comfortable to the nations involved and through institutions they trust. Finding ways to accomplish this deserves considerable research, since the antipathy toward "Western ways" is deep and broad. We cannot afford to have the Islamic world forever poor and hostile toward the West, and the Islamic world cannot succeed without adopting many of our values and habits, but we must avoid "helping" them in ways they would consider to be threatening.

- The United States should remain involved in diverse formal and informal coalitions, but these will need to adapt to circumstances (e.g., as NATO is attempting to do). Which nations will be our allies and adversaries will vary with issue and instance on political, economic, and military matters.

Military Strategy

- The defense program should be revisited, even though the President's program in 1990–1991 already anticipated many of the world changes and took many of the scaling-down measures that are needed.

- In contemplating tradeoffs among air, ground, and sea-based forces, *the United States should plan to be able to conduct and win one major regional contingency and, more or less simultaneously, to be able to deter a second major regional contingency in circumstances where that can be accomplished with substantial air forces* and allied ground forces supporting the regional states in distress (e.g., Baltic or Eastern European states under pressure from Russia, or South Korea under pressure from North Korea). There should be no requirement to be able to commit substantial U.S. ground forces in a second, concurrent, major regional contingency. Should deterrence fail in such a second regional contingency, the full U.S. response might be delayed for months.

- *Defense planning should be based on building-block missions, capabilities, plans, and organizations.* The mind-sets associated with rigid planning should be eliminated, which will require major reorganizational changes to deemphasize traditional "deliberate planning" procedures and encourage development of teams skilled in adaptive planning. The United States must plan to operate with ad hoc allies, but must be prepared to operate early and unilaterally in some contingencies. Building-block planning will require basic changes in the strategic planning system, including the form of OSD guidance to the Joint Staff and the form of Joint Staff guidance to the services. (See Davis, 1994b.) Despite the success of Desert Shield and Desert Storm, U.S. military planning is *not* well suited for contingencies arising quickly.

- Analytical agonizing over the precise size of the new base force for the military is inappropriate. Qualitative judgments are adequate and inevitable. *The new base force should be substantial* (e.g., 10, 6, and 2 active, reserve-component, and active-cadre army divisions, or something similar with a smaller fraction of active units), not because of major current threats, but because of (1) the size of numerous other national armies; (2) the need to deter other nations from seeing a military vacuum and filling it; (3) the need to avoid rearmament of Japan, which might result from a drastic downsizing of American forces; and (4) the need to be able to intervene in force (e.g., with 3–7 divisions) anywhere worldwide, while maintaining a comparable force in reserves (important not only as a hedge against simultaneous crises, but to provide a training base for reservists and to reduce the risks of and therefore increase the credibility of threatening a military intervention). Thus, the size of the new base force should be justified by a combination of environment-shaping (e.g., not creating vacuums) and hedging.

- In fine-tuning the new base force, serious effort should be given to developing high-quality army reserve units capable of effective employment within 120–180 days of call-up that would permit a reduction of active army divisions to approximately 6–7. Similar but smaller reductions should be possible for the other services.

- Even more important than the precise size of the revised base force is maintaining the vigor and quality of specialized high-leverage support activities, such as the C^3I infrastructure, work on advanced concepts of organization and doctrine, investment in the R&D necessary to maintain unequivocal technological superiority, and the National Training Center. As a strategy, we should be willing to trade *variable-cost* components for quality in such support and to have our allies provide most of the manpower.

- To maximize peacetime effectiveness of the force structure sized for environment-shaping and hedging rather than probable threats, the military services need to be tasked with substantial missions for peaceful activities, missions involving perhaps 10 percent of the defense program and military units and requiring many new specialty billets for high-quality officers as part of their normal career development.

- The option should be created for volunteers to join a special national-service program that would provide a combination of military training, education, and participation in peaceful military applications in the United States or abroad. This would provide upward mobility options in some ways comparable to those that have traditionally been provided by the U.S. military.

- Peaceful uses of the military should be based on "thinking big" and should include, in cooperation with private contractors who would otherwise claim they had been improperly deprived of opportunities:

  — Massive reworking of physical infrastructure such as roads, bridges, and ports.

  — Cleaning up environmental hazards.

  — Cleaning up and developing lowest-level infrastructure for major cities in distress.

  — Eradicating selected diseases in target countries.

  The principal focus should be on domestic infrastructure, not foreign assistance, especially since foreign-assistance efforts can be counterproductive unless the host governments are reform minded. Importantly, peaceful applications of the military cannot succeed on a large scale without enthusiastic public support that changes institutional perceptions of what is valued.

- Vigorous, broad, and innovative R&D, including prototyping experiments with military units as well as weapon systems, should be seen as a powerful and relatively inexpensive environment-shaping deterrent, as well as the ultimate hedge against reversals in world events. The United States should outclass all competitors with respect to the quality of its weapons, forces, and doctrine. In the event of conflict, achieving success with very few casualties will be a goal. We should pay for this base of R&D and high-technology forces with reduced force structure and readiness of selected units (while maintaining high readiness for key units). In our work with coalitions, we should provide the high-tech leverage and planning skills, while regional states provide, e.g., most of the ground forces.

- In contemplating reconstitution needs, we should be increasingly more concerned with being able to mobilize new forces with best-in-the-world capabilities in the year 2005 than with being able to mobilize 1990-era armored forces in the year 1995.

CRITIQUE AND AN UPDATE

How do the results look today, in March 1994? My answer is, "Not bad, considering the study was done very quickly" (see Levin (1994) for a more recent and extensive effort). Indeed, it looks very much like what has evolved as national policy in many respects. As the result of his Bottom-Up Review, Secretary Aspin has announced (Aspin, 1993) a new force structure and defense plan that is only slightly below the Bush administration's base force and that is very much consistent with the force structure of the 1991 study (but no cause-effect relationships should be assumed). There are some important differences between now and 1991, however:

- The Western nations have done a disastrously poor job in dealing with the former Yugoslavia, and there is still no clear national policy on what should be done now. Indeed, there is no agreement even on what should, in retrospect, have been done at the beginning of the crisis—before "ethnic cleansing" became a household word and a embarrassment for all mankind. While no one argued that the developed world had to succeed with each challenge to the new order, this failure was highly visible and came very soon.

- There is still relatively little strategic appreciation for the importance of developing security arrangements to protect the newly independent states such as Ukraine, Poland, and the Baltic states, and for doing so *now* rather than later, in five or fifteen years, when crises arise (see also Davis, 1994a). There are, however, some interesting proposals being discussed, particularly proposals that would allow for the expansion of NATO to include those threatened states—and Russia as well. The criterion for entry into "the club" would include acceptance of the club's standards of behavior [17]

- As noted above, Secretary Aspin has announced a new force structure and defense plan that is only slightly below the Bush administration's base force and that is very much consistent with the force structure of the 1991 study except, importantly, in emphasizing active forces rather than enhancement of reserve forces. I still believe more could be done with the reserves (see also Rostker, Don, and Watman, 1994).

- There has been little progress in tasking the services to take on major peacetime roles of the sort proposed. There has, however, been a string of peacekeeping/peacemaking activities that have sorely stressed some of our force structure, particularly support forces that are primarily based in the reserves.

- The expansion of Asian capitalism has proven even more important than was thought earlier. Chinese economic growth, coupled with the severity and duration of the Japanese recession, imply dynamics in the region that were not adequately anticipated in 1991.

IMPLICATIONS FOR DEFENSE PLANNING AND DEFENSE ANALYSIS

Higher-Level Defense-Planning Objectives

Grand strategy is inherently rather abstract. What implications does it have for defense planning at a more detailed level? It seems to me that there are many important ones. First, as Table 7 suggests,[18] defense planning should

---

[17]This is controversial; see Khalilzad (1993), Asmus, Kugler, and Larrabee (1993), and Harries (1993).

[18]This table is adapted slightly from Winnefeld (1992). See also Kugler (1994).

Table 7

Regional Breakdown of Higher-Level Defense-Planning Objectives

	East Asia	Europe	Middle East	Elsewhere
Environment-shaping (long term)	Creating conditions where no single power is seen as military hegemon	Creating conditions where no single power is seen as military hegemon	Demonstrating that access to resources is vital U.S. interest	Precluding rise of major military power
	Making arms races unnecessary	Making arms races unnecessary	Demonstrating that U.S. and Arab security interests are not irreconcilable	Improving security climate
	Encouraging orderly change	Encouraging orderly change		
Deterring threats (near and midterm)	Korea, SLOCs, Russia, and rest of CIS	Russia and rest of CIS	Iraq, Iran, Libya, SLOCs	Protecting U.S. citizens, property
Responding to contingencies (near term)	Korea	Residual Europe, Libya	Aggression in Gulf, against Israel, U.S. citizens	Drug traffic, counter-subversion, counter-terrorism

focus less on meeting the demands of precisely defined but highly questionable planning scenarios for major regional contingencies and more on "softer" requirements. Note the emphasis on (a) environment-shaping, (b) deterring threats, and (c) responding to contingencies.

Contrasts Between Classic Planning and New-Look Planning

Despite uncertainty, it is possible to draw some contrasts between classic defense planning and the planning suitable for the post–Cold War era consistent with the kinds of grand strategy the United States appears to be pursuing and the strategy recommended here. Table 8 (adapted from Davis and Finch, 1993) summarizes differences in emphasis. The number of bullets in each category indicates impressionistically the relative emphasis of the various

Table 8

Contrast Between Old and New Emphases

Subject	Cold War	Post–Cold War
Great-power deterrence	•••	•
Strategic equivalence (nuclear and conventional)	•••	•
Nuclear crisis stability	••	•
Great-power arms-race stability	•••	
Alliance solidarity	•••	••
Superpower arms control	•••	•
Regional stability	•••	••
Nuclear proliferation and counterproliferation	•	•••
Ballistic-missile, chemical, and biological-weapon proliferation	•	•••
Regional-power deterrence	•	•••
Regional military stability and related environment-shaping	•	•••
Regional arms control		••
Discouraging new military great powers and related environment-shaping		••
Coalitional intervention in support of new world order concepts		•••(?)
Crisis management and rapid decisionmaking	••	•••
Reactions to or preemption of terrorists and third countries with weapons of mass destruction	•	•••
Ability quickly to create and operate militarily with ad hoc coalitions	•	•••
Realistic war objectives	•	•••
Concern about casualties	•	•••
Concern about achieving national consensus before action	•	•••
Fiscal restraint	••	•••

topics.   It suggests a shift away from great-power deterrence, strategic equivalence, and the like toward more emphasis on regional issues and regional environment-shaping.   There *may* be more coalitional intervention in the Third World, but that remains to be seen and may depend on events in Somalia and the former Yugoslavia over the first months of 1994.   The table also indicates much more explicit concern about realistic war objectives, minimizing casualties, ground-roots support for military action, and—above all, perhaps—fiscal restraint.

Special Challenges for Defense Analysis

It follows, I believe, that analysis for defense planning should give particular emphasis in the years ahead to:

- Measures of how easy or difficult it would be for nations to become miltary superpowers, and what the United States could do to make those steps less attractive (e.g., by consistently identifying trump cards (see also Bracken, 1993b).

- Theater ballistic-missile defense systems with the potential to be used for continental ballistic missile defense as well.

- Ways to assist newly independent nations such as Ukraine and the Baltic states in establishing a reasonable degree of deterrence-based security despite being bordered by a far more powerful neighbor. This could include trans-ferring or selling highly effective defensive weapons or developing deterrents based on the ability to punish aggressors, probably through the use of preci-sion bombing.

- Weapons and tactics effective in peacemaking and peacekeeping operations.

- Rapid adaptive planning and rapid force deployment for major regional contingencies that unfold in very "nonstandard" ways (see also Davis and Finch, 1993, Davis, 1994b, and Kugler, 1994).

- Creative ways to employ the active force structure in peacetime so as to jus-tify its size.

ACKNOWLEDGMENT

I would like to acknowledge the collaboration of Paul Bracken in develop-ing the methods discussed here and of Richard Hillestad and Stephen Drezner as co-authors of the 1991 study. Jonathan Pollack, Paul Bracken, and Stephen Drezner provided useful review comments on the current paper.

BIBLIOGRAPHY

Ajami, Fouad (1993), "The Summoning," *Foreign Affairs*, Vol. 72, No. 4.

Andre, David J. (1991), *Competitive Strategies in the Changing Security Environment*, Vols. I and II, Science Applications Incorporated (SAIC), McLean, VA.

Asmus, Ronald D., Richard L. Kugler, and F. Stephen Larrabee (1993), "Building a New NATO," *Foreign Affairs*, Vol. 72, No. 4.

Aspin, Les (1993), *The Bottom-Up Review*, Department of Defense, Washington, D.C.

Bartley, Robert L. (1993), "The Case for Optimism," *Foreign Affairs*, Vol. 72, No. 4.

Bracken, Paul (1989), *Strategic Planning for National Security: Lessons from Business Experience*, RAND, Santa Monica, CA.

—— (1993a), "Nuclear Weapons and State Survival in North Korea," *Survival*, Vol. 35, No. 3.

—— (1993b), "The Military After Next," *Washington Quarterly*, Autumn.

Cheney, Dick (1992), *The Regional Defense Strategy*, Department of Defense.

Cohen, Eliot A. (1984), "Constraints on America's Conduct of Small Wars," *International Security*, Vol. 9, No. 2.

Davis, Paul K. (1989), *National Security in an Era of Uncertainty*, RAND, Santa Monica, CA.

—— (1994a), "Improving Deterrence in the Post–Cold War Era: Some Theory and Implications for Defense Planning," in Davis (1994c).

—— (1994b), "Institutionalizing Planning for Adaptiveness," in Davis (1994c).

—— (ed.) (1994c), *New Challenges for Defense Planning: Rethinking How Much Is Enough*, RAND, Santa Monica, CA.

—— (1994d), "Planning Under Uncertainty Then and Now: Paradigms Lost and Paradigms Emerging," in Davis (1994c).

Davis, Paul K., and John Arquilla (1991), *Deterring or Coercing Opponents in Crisis: Lessons from the War with Saddam Hussein*, RAND, Santa Monica, CA.

Davis, Paul K., Stephen M. Drezner, and Richard J. Hillestad (1992), "Protecting the Great Transition and More," unpublished RAND research.

Davis, Paul K., and Lou Finch (1993), *Defense Planning for the Post–Cold War Era: Giving New Meaning to Flexibility, Adaptiveness, and Robustness of Capability*, RAND, Santa Monica, CA.

Dewar, James A., Carl H. Builder, William M. Hix, and Morlie N. Levin (1993), *Assumption-Based Planning: A Planning Tool for Very Uncertain Times*, RAND, Santa Monica, CA.

Fukuyama, Francis (1992), *The End of History and the Last Man*, Free Press, New York.

Harries, Owen (1993), "The Collapse of the West," *Foreign Affairs*, Vol. 72, No. 4.

Huntington, Samuel P. (1993), "The Clash of Civilizations," *Foreign Affairs*, Vol. 72, No. 3.

Kahn, Herman (1976), *The Next Hundred Years*, William Morrow and Co., New York.

———— (1979), "The Economic Present and Future," *The Futurist*, June.

Kaufmann, William W., and John D. Steinbruner (1991), *Decisions for Defense: Prospects for a New Order,* The Brookings Institution, Washington, D.C.

Kent, Glenn A., and William E. Simons (1991), *A Framework for Enhancing Operational Capabilities,* RAND, Santa Monica, CA.

Khalilzad, Zalmay (1993), *Extending The Western Alliance to East Central Europe: A New Strategy for NATO,* RAND, Santa Monica, CA.

Khalilzad, Zalmay, Paul K. Davis, and Abram Shulsky (1993), *Stopping the North Korean Nuclear Program,* RAND, Santa Monica, CA.

Kugler, Richard L. (1994), "Nonstandard Contingencies for Defense Planning," in Davis (1994c).

Layne, Christopher (1993), "The Unipolar Illusion: Why New Great Powers Will Rise," *International Security,* Vol. 17, No. 4.

Levin, Norm (ed.), with Graham Fuller, Ian Lesser, Benjamin Schwarz, and Kenneth Watman (1994), *Prisms and Policy: U.S. Security Strategy After the Cold War,* RAND, Santa Monica, CA.

Lynn-Jones, Sean M. (ed.) (1991), *The Cold War and After: Prospects for Peace: An International Security Reader,* MIT Press, Cambridge, MA.

Mearsheimer, John (1991), "Back to the Future: Instability in Europe After the Cold War," in Lynn-Jones (1991).

Nye, Joseph S. (1990), *Bound to Lead: The Changing Nature of American Power,* Basic Books, New York.

Powell, General Colin L. (1991), *National Military Strategy,* Department of Defense, U.S. Government Printing Office, Washington, D.C.

Rostker, Bernard, Bruce Don, and Kenneth Watman (1994), *Assessing the Structure and Mix of Future Active and Reserve Forces: Final Report to the Secretary of Defense,* RAND, Santa Monica, CA.

Thaler, David E. (1993), *Strategies to Tasks: A Framework for Linking Means and Ends,* RAND, Santa Monica, CA.

Winnefeld, James A. (1992), *The Post–Cold War Force-Sizing Debate: Paradigms, Metaphors, and Disconnects,* RAND, Santa Monica, CA.

NONSTANDARD CONTINGENCIES FOR DEFENSE PLANNING

Richard L. Kugler

During the Cold War, U.S. defense planning was conducted primarily on the basis of a few canonical scenarios used to define force structures capable of handling other conflicts as well. This practice is now being carried forth into the post–Cold War era with adoption of canonical scenarios for major regional contingencies (MRCs) in the Persian Gulf and Korea. This paper argues that while canonical scenarios should continue to be used, they should be supplemented by serious analysis of nonstandard scenarios involving different versions of the standard conflicts and different conflicts altogether. In some cases, such nonstandard scenarios could not be handled by U.S. forces sized and designed to fight the more canonical scenarios. The paper develops this thesis by first examining the inability of the canonical MRCs to reflect the complex trends underway in international security affairs. It then defines a number of plausible and stressful nonstandard scenarios, ranging from small conflicts, to major conventional wars, to regional nuclear crises. It concludes with a call for major changes in the ways U.S. force planning is conducted, including replacement of "contingency-based" planning with generic "mission-based" planning. These changes aim at producing greater intellectual breadth, an adaptive planning process, and a more flexible force posture.

INTRODUCTION

A new era of international security affairs is dawning, and the United States faces a difficult challenge in planning its future conventional defense strategy and forces. This paper addresses one central aspect of this challenge: the need to be prepared not only for a few canonical cases, but also for a wide range of *nonstandard* contingencies[1]—i.e., conflicts that are significantly different in political and military terms from the limited set of usual (canonical) scenarios largely used to guide defense planning. The nonstandard conflicts are

---

[1] This need is a major theme of Davis and Finch (1993) and Winnefeld and Shlapak (1990); Davis (1994a) summarizes major elements of the thesis and proposes fundamental changes in strategic, programmatic, and operations-oriented defense planning.

important because many of them are plausible and they might not be lesser included cases—i.e., the United States might not be able to manage them with the force structure and strategies derived from focusing on canonical scenarios.

The idea that the United States needs to be prepared for nonstandard conflicts is not new. In recent years, the Joint Staff and CINCs have increased the adaptiveness of operations planning, and the Secretary of Defense has exhorted the entire Department of Defense to prepare for diverse contingencies.[2] Nonetheless, the Joint Staff's conversion to adaptive operations planning is not yet complete, and more generally, the staffs of the Department of Defense continue to rely heavily on canonical scenarios, especially for program development, but also for assessment of readiness and many other functions. Nonstandard conflicts are too often regarded as side excursions—i.e., as of marginal importance or as mere lesser included cases.

The attractiveness of canonical scenarios is due to their specificity and the value of having standard cases against which, for example, to measure alternative program options. A canonical scenario helps impart intellectual focus to defense planning by specifying—in place, time, and features—an important future wartime conflict that might actually be encountered.[3] It typically includes a single-point estimate of adversary and allied force levels, mobilization and reinforcement times and rates, strategy and doctrine on both sides, and other key data. Owing to these details, canonical scenarios provide concrete information that can help inform decisions about force requirements and program priorities. The core purpose of these scenarios is to empower the defense effort, not imprison it. But using them in a straightjacket way can purchase indepth focus on a few events at the expense of grasping a wider set of challenges.

Canonical scenarios first rose to prominence during the Cold War, and although they had a constructive impact, they also left behind a mixed legacy. The canonical scenarios of the Cold War have now been cast aside, but new ones have replaced them. Acting on the strategy goal of being prepared for two roughly concurrent major regional contingencies (MRCs), the Pentagon is now employing MRCs in Southwest Asia and Korea as its primary basis for strategic

---

[2]Aspin (1993) specifically notes that the canonical scenarios of the Bottom-Up Review (BUR) are *illustrative* only, and that the wars actually fought are often very different from the ones used for planning. Powell (1991) also stresses the role of uncertainty. The challenge, however, is translating such exhortations into capabilities.

[3]Another virtue of the canonical scenarios is that they help to establish a credible *rationale* for U.S. defense policy and programs. Whereas future conflicts in diverse locations are "invisible," today's MRCs are "visible" and therefore "believable." A sense of proportion is needed, however, for the future should not be discounted because of its being unforeseeable (Winnefeld, 1992).

planning. The Persian Gulf scenario involves a repeat Iraqi invasion of Kuwait and Saudi Arabia, launched by a force of 20 divisions and 750 combat aircraft. The Korea scenario envisions a North Korean attack on South Korea, one employing 35 divisions and 800 combat aircraft. These MRCs are being supplemented by several lesser regional conflicts (LRCs), similar to that of Operation Just Cause, when U.S. forces intervened in Panama. Because LRCs impose only modest demands, the two MRCs seem destined to play the dominant role in future defense decisionmaking. To a degree, they will help shape operational doctrine for employing U.S. military power on the basis of decisive force. Equally important, they will help shape plans for building a new force posture (see Aspin, 1993 and Powell, 1991).

This paper accepts and expands upon the thesis that planning for nonstandard conflicts needs to be moved to center stage. The goal should be military plans and planning capabilities that are readily adaptive and a force posture that can perform a broad range of missions in ever-changing situations (Davis and Finch, 1993; Davis, 1994a). These demands cannot be met if defense planning wears intellectual blinders.

To explore the issue of canonical versus nonstandard scenarios, the paper proceeds as follows. First, it surveys the international security environment and demonstrates that it makes no sense for the United States to base planning on the canonical scenarios. Second, it notes that the current MRCs do not even necessarily establish appropriate force-posture goals. Third, it describes with a broad brush a diversity of plausible nonstandard scenarios that should be considered. Finally, it draws some conclusions for defense planning, arguing for an emphasis on generic *mission-based planning methods* that could support an adaptive planning process and a more flexible force posture.

TRENDS IN THE INTERNATIONAL CONTEXT AND U.S. MILITARY MISSIONS

Regional wars of the type identified by the canonical MRCs are probably the largest plausible military conflicts for the relatively near future. Since the threat of a global hegemon has passed into history and is unlikely to reappear, worldwide war, as encountered in World War II and prepared for during the Cold War, should no longer animate U.S. defense policy. Iraq and North Korea are highly plausible aggressors against vital U.S. interests. The issue is not whether planning should highlight these two threats, but whether the specific canonical scenarios dealing with them are a sufficient basis for gauging military needs for the full spectrum of situations that might lie ahead. The real military contingencies the United States will face may turn out to be very different scenarios involving Iraq or North Korea,[4] or they may involve altogether different adversaries, theaters, and military and political environments.

The stage can best be set for analyzing this issue by first evaluating trends now underway in international security affairs. If future wars erupt, they will occur as a result of international political dynamics. The trends at work today suggest that the future may offer greater turbulence than was commonly anticipated in the months following the Cold War's abrupt end.[5]

The End of History or Its Rebirth?

As of 1990–1991, popular academic fashion in some quarters held that the end of the Cold War meant not only the disappearance of a rival global hegemon, but also the end of all forms of major military conflict. Several trends were cited: the alleged worldwide triumph of liberal democracy, which was to bring a taming influence to diplomacy; growing economic interdependence; ready access to resources through open trade; the settlement of territorial disputes; the decline of aggressive ideologies; the withering of the nation-state; and the growing power of multilateral institutions. This thesis held that the conflicts of the future would be small-scale affairs that could be handled with only moderate doses of military power. Requirements for these small conflicts presumably could be met through multinational cooperation among the liberal democracies, thereby obviating any need for a powerful U.S. defense establishment.

This optimistic thesis drew inspiration from two books, Francis Fukuyama's *The End of History and the Last Man* and Samuel Huntington's *The Third Wave.* Both were misinterpreted when they appeared. Although they celebrated the triumph of democracy and free markets over Bolshevik communism and command economies, neither predicted permanent global peace anytime soon. Fukuyama's book was more an analysis of political philosophy, including Hegel's long-neglected importance, than a new theory of international politics. Its key point was that the ideological conflict between democracy and totalitarianism has now been settled in ways that allow for the rebirth of 19th century optimism, which had become a casualty of 20th century pessimism.

---

[4]Davis and Finch (1993) emphasize that it is an error to assume that "multiscenario planning" or "planning for nonstandard scenarios" is adequately accomplished by considering one scenario each for a diversity of theaters and adversaries. Instead, one should consider the vast diversity of plausible scenarios involving the canonical threats (currently, Iraq and North Korea)—e.g., scenarios with nonstandard assumptions about warning, political alliances, and military objectives.

[5]For elaboration of many of these points, see Kugler (1993), a strategic-planning study conducted for the Joint Staff, one with a relatively long time horizon.

Yet it was far from blind to the stresses ahead in the coming decades. Huntington's book argued that democracy, originally located in Western Europe and North America, is spreading outward, especially in Latin America. But it also noted that democracy now covers only about one-half of the globe, that reversals might be experienced, and that democracy is not yet well installed in many regional hotbeds of future conflict.

The sobering events of 1992 and 1993 underscore that if the presence of liberal democracy increases the prospects for harmony, then its absence weakens these prospects. Moreover, the thesis that democratic states do not wage war against each other merits scrutiny. The 19th century shows many examples of democratizing nations in conflict. For example, Britain and France both *became* democracies during this century but spent most of this period in rivalry with each other, and often came close to blows. Indeed, democracy's emergence across Europe was feared as a harbinger of war because it brought nationalism, populism, and mass mobilization in its wake. Also, the United States—democracy's shining light—collapsed into a bitter civil war. The Western democracies joined together in alliance when totalitarianism appeared on the scene in the 20th century. But this development, an exercise in *realpolitik* as well as common values, is no guarantee of global tranquility in regions outside the Western alliance now that totalitarianism is fading.

Because democracy stresses human rights and the peaceful settlement of disputes, it helps buffer against the propensity to go to war. But volumes of textbooks argue that interstate conflict is caused by many factors that can overpower common ideology. This particularly is the case when the tenets of liberal democracy stop at a nation's borders. Democracy helps ensure that the decision for war is made not only by executive institutions, but by parliaments and the mass public as well. Yet parliaments and mass publics have a long history of being as warlike as kings and presidents, often more so. Popular opinion can pressure even unwilling governments to go to war; conversely, governing elites can choose war in the face of domestic dissent if they conclude that the national interest requires that step. Democracy is no impenetrable barrier to warfare among nations that hate each other for reasons that go beyond similarities or differences in governmental structures. After all, the slaughter in the Balkans has not been caused by a dispute over political ideology.

Recent trends suggest that the collapse of European communism is being accompanied in many places not only by democracy and capitalism, but also by a growing emphasis on national self-determination, as opposed to cooperation with other nations. In Europe, not only has the Yalta agreement of 1945 collapsed, but so also has the Versailles peace order created after World War I. The effect has been to wipe away the Soviet empire and the system of multinational states that was established in the 1920s to stabilize ethnic conflict and rampant nationalism in east central Europe, the Balkans, and the Caucasus.

Coming in the wake is a host of new nations that define their identities in exclusionary terms, along with muddled borders, many citizens residing abroad, and the reawakening of long-suppressed animosities. Already, Europe has become one of the globe's most violent regions. When these developments are fully manifest, the result might be even greater turmoil and violence (Asmus, Kugler, and Larrabee, 1993). What applies to Europe may also apply elsewhere around the globe, where severe strains require no similar collapse of Versailles and Yalta to unleash them.

If the events in Bosnia have not provided adequate refutation to the thesis of global harmony, the emerging academic literature has called its postulates into question and offered a vision whose sobriety approaches outright pessimism. A good example is the landmark article, "The Clash of Civilizations" (Huntington, 1993), which partly repudiates the earlier optimism of *The Third Wave*. Huntington now forecasts a gloomy world in which the dominant cultures will clash on a global scale, possibly bringing about a plummet into enduring rivalry over the very basics of human life. He foresees a clash in Europe between the Christian West and the Slavic culture led by Russia. In the Middle East, Islam will clash with its old nemesis, infidel Europe. Elsewhere, he asserts, conflicts among Islam, Hinduism, Confucianism, and the Japanese culture will produce a widespread strife that may overpower efforts to fashion order.

Zbigniew Brzezinski (1993) refrains from pessimism this deep, but he foresees a chaotic future marked by sharp conflicts among nations in key regions, abetted by moral weakness in the West itself. The historian John Lukacs (1993) forecasts that communism in Europe will be replaced not by democracy, but by the return of atavistic ethno-nationalism and militaristic fascism. Paul Kennedy (1993) argues that the key fault line will not be in Europe, but between the modern West and the Third World. He points to the Middle East and other regions where an ongoing population explosion will interact with deepening poverty to produce deep hostility to the West. As for the idea that the Western allies will remain cohesive, Jeffrey Garten (1993) worries that the United States, Japan, and Germany will fall into political conflict over dominance of the global economy. In their chilling book, George Friedman and Meredith Lebard (1991) go beyond forecasts of U.S.-Japanese economic rivalry to predict a replay of World War II in the Pacific.

To be sure, these predictions should not be accepted uncritically. They may represent the tendency of the academic literature to conform to Hegel's model of dialectical idealism. The original thesis of optimism is now giving way to an antithesis of pessimism, which might be replaced by a synthesis. Even so, this gloomy literature contains enough penetrating arguments to suggest that even if the future will not be one of pure Hobbesian realism, it will fall far short of Wilsonian idealism.

The Rise of Multipolarity

As many have noted, the stable bipolarity of the Cold War is giving way to a modern version of multipolarity. Despite the ever-present danger of U.S.-Soviet confrontation, the bipolar era proved to be remarkably stable. This outcome was brought about by nuclear deterrence, by a conventional balance of power, and by political equilibrium because both sides already controlled the areas that were important to them. Multipolarity replaces this stability with new and untested global dynamics that, if not carefully managed, can produce chronic tension, conflict, and war.[6]

Multipolarity is not unstable if the global system is homogeneous (i.e., nations do not harbor incompatible agendas) and a stable balance of power exists. But instability has often been the outcome, owing to deep-seated heterogeneity that produces political-economic tensions. In this situation, the strong have opportunity to prey on the weak undeterred by fear that a collective response will be mounted. Fear of aggression, in turn, can give rise to policies aimed at self-defense that come across as threatening to others. The quest for unilateral security translates into paranoid insecurity for all, further eroding stability. This, at least, was the case during periods when multipolarity was at its height (Aron, 1966).

Owing largely to the status of the United States as a superpower and the Western alliance system, the future system will be far from purely multipolar. Yet interstate anarchy will be a core feature, for the nation-state is not going away. The number of nations is increasing, amidst a host of internal and external constraints that deny governments confidence in their capacity to shape their own destinies. Although the impulse to cooperate is growing in some areas, it is declining in others. The United Nations and other institutions are already showing a weak capacity to impose the norms of international law in today's more multipolar conditions. Much will depend upon whether these collective security bodies acquire greater power and the ability to use it effectively or suffer the fate of the League of Nations.

A bright future for collective cooperation is far from ensured, for the global trends at work today are pulling in the direction of fragmentation. In addition to the chaos brought about by the collapse of the Soviet empire and the Warsaw Pact, the Western alliance system is weakening as many of its members turn inward to deal with long-neglected domestic problems. The world economy is struggling, and even if a collapse into protectionism and mercantilism is not foreordained, the once-bright future of cooperative free trade is uncertain. Equally important, immoderate ideologies are making a comeback. This is the

---

[6]For discussions of these matters, see articles by Mearsheimer and others in Lynn-Jones (1991); see also Layne (1993).

case in Europe, where resurgent nationalism threatens democratic reforms and peaceful resolution of disputes, but it also applies elsewhere, most notably in the Middle East. There and elsewhere, endemic poverty coupled with population explosion threatens to produce anti-status-quo ideologies and deep anger toward the Western democracies.

If these negative trends spin out of control, the result could be a witches' brew of 19th century politics, 20th century passions, and 21st century technology. Even if the worst fails to occur, the future may offer widespread turbulence, along with violence and war, at least until democracy and free-market prosperity finally triumph sometime in the distant future. The Persian Gulf and Korea will remain zones of conflict, but the dangers ahead are far from limited to these two regions. Because the future international system will be unstable in important ways, the dangers are global. They will manifest themselves in many different spots, in ways that include, but go beyond, the threat of renewed regional aggression by Iraq and North Korea.

The Proliferation of Military Power

While it is clearly difficult to forecast the future in the currently turbulent international system, one thing can be said: warfare will remain an important instrument of statecraft. A growing number of nations will have the capacity to conduct aggression on their own; Iraq and North Korea are only two among many nations in this category. Moreover, the feasibility of aggression multiplies many times over when alliance formation is considered. Fear of encountering U.S. military opposition will remain a potent deterrent, but as the Persian Gulf war shows, aggressors can misinterpret the signals coming from Washington. Moreover, the U.S. deterrent will remain potent only if American military power remains strong and can be projected to the locations of conflicts.

In response to the political tensions now emerging in the international system, the spread of nuclear weapons and other instruments of mass destruction seems likely to accelerate in future years. Ukraine has been quite ambivalent about yielding the large nuclear arsenal bequeathed by the collapse of the Soviet Union (although a breakthrough was achieved early in 1994), and Iraq and North Korea have been resisting international efforts to dismantle or stop their nuclear weapon programs. Other nations doubtless have similar programs and may escape international sanctions in ways that allow them to succeed. The disturbing case of South Africa shows how a modern nation, even one under international scrutiny, can cross the nuclear threshold. Because delivery systems must be created, more is involved than assembling nuclear devices, but even so, modern industry is giving many nations the assets to become nuclear powers. If proliferation is to be prevented, this goal will not be accomplished because supply is cut off, but because demand is controlled. In the final analysis, most nations in possession of modern industrial technology can build nuclear weapons. If they remain members of the nonnuclear club, it will be for reasons of their own political choice, not because nuclearization is physically impossible. Demand is best reduced by ensuring security, but the coming multipolar era is making many nations feel insecure. This applies not only to status-quo nations, but also to nations whose dissatisfaction may lead them to act like rogue elephants.

Behind the scenes, modern conventional weapons are also proliferating. This development alone promises to alter the face of warfare and the requirements facing U.S. defense planning. Notwithstanding the collapse of the Warsaw Pact, Europe remains an armed camp, with many nations capable of inflicting immense violence on each other. This is the case in the former USSR, but it also is true in east central Europe and the Balkans, a region of great security dilemmas and simmering ethnic hatreds. The Middle East and Persian Gulf also remain armed camps, and many nations there, including several that embrace Islamic ideology, have embarked upon efforts to bolster their arsenals. Animating this effort is the realization that, given Iraq's disastrous defeat, modern defense establishments will be needed if these nations are to stand up to Western-equipped forces.

In Asia, the end of the Cold War has been accompanied by a little-noticed but startling development. Virtually all nations have launched efforts to build stronger military establishments. These efforts owe to growing economic strength, but they also reflect deep-seated worry that the new era will be turbulent. North Korea remains a military threat, but China, benefiting from a decade of sustained economic growth and favorable prospects, has launched a sweeping program of military reform. What lies ahead remains to be seen, but China, long an inward-looking nation, may acquire an impressive capability for power projection.

In response to fear of North Korea and China, South Korea and Japan continue to strengthen their forces. Indeed, Japan today has one of the world's largest military budgets. Owing to its mutual security treaty with the United States, Japan's defense posture is focused on protection of the homeland and nearby sea lanes. Regional economic and security dynamics, however, could lead it in the direction of acquiring forces for power projection. The effects are not confined to Northeast Asia. Several Southeast Asian nations are all taking advantage of growing economic strength to bolster their military power. Indonesia, Malaysia, and Singapore are acquiring better military assets, not only to protect their homelands, but also to project forces abroad. Meanwhile, India and Pakistan both possess formidable conventional defense postures that are being slowly modernized. Even absent further nuclear proliferation, South

Asia and Southeast Asia both will house plenty of conventional firepower for major conflicts.

The outcome could be stability if all these nations act in ways that counter-balance each other. But for mathematical reasons alone, balance will be hard to achieve, owing to large differences in national military power and the un-stable dynamics of coalition formation. This would be the case even if partici-pating nations are joined together in a global pact in search of military balance. Equilibrium will be doubly difficult to achieve because, apart from the Western alliance system, collective security is in short supply, and many nations will be seeking a margin of advantage over each other.

The looming prospect of major military imbalances amidst a more multi-polar system makes the likelihood of tensions all the greater. This prospect fur-ther suggests that future conflicts may take quite different forms than antici-pated by DoD's current MRCs for the Persian Gulf and Korea. These two MRCs will need to be guarded against as a central focus of U.S. defense plan-ning. But any literal and mechanical application of them as the sole focus might result in blindness to the much larger spectrum of very different conflicts that could lie ahead.

Peacetime Purposes of U.S. Military Power

Because these political-military trends do not augur well for enduring global tranquility, they confront the United States with the challenge of figuring out what is implied for its foreign policy and defense plans—not only for war, but for peacetime as well. Facing major domestic problems and a troubled but ambiguous external setting, the United States is now struggling with the dilemma of deciding how to strike a satisfactory balance between assertive global leadership and selective restraint. Exacerbating this dilemma is a diffi-cult policy tradeoff. Over the long term, the United States will be unable to exert global leadership if it fails to restore its economic health. Domestic re-covery will be hard to achieve if weighty international burdens must be carried during the time this effort is pursued. Yet if the United States casts aside these burdens in some wholesale way, the result could be a free-fall collapse into in-ternational turbulence that makes recovery impossible. Prospects for a coop-erative world economy—a precondition for U.S. recovery—might be lost. Beyond this, an expensive military rearmament might become necessary, thereby draining scarce resources away from domestic investment.

The task of striking an appropriate policy balance is complicated by the sin-gular American historical experience with foreign policy. Because the United

States arrived on the world scene only in the 20th century, it has no backlog of involvement in dealing with multipolar politics reminiscent of the 19th century. It is seasoned only in pursuing confrontational politics with totalitarian hegemons and in managing tightly knit security alliances to deal with these hegemons. As a result, it is now hard-pressed to develop the policies and grass-roots attitudes needed for a multipolar era of fluid, ever-shifting relations with other nations. Also, it suffers from confusion in defining its own interests in a more Palmerstonian era in which its global involvements are growing. There will be fewer permanent friends or enemies, and enduring interests will play an influential role in shaping the policies of all nations.

Throughout the Cold War, the United States was able to reconcile realism and idealism because confrontation with communism allowed it to pursue global power politics on behalf of moralist principles. The coming era of greater multipolarity threatens to deprive the United States of this luxury in ways that will compel adoption of a new synthesis, one that runs against the grain of traditional American thinking. Because the threat of totalitarian hegemonism has been vanquished, pursuit of a global victory for democracy is the only beckoning moral crusade. Yet the future seems destined to be far too complex to allow this crusade to be the only principle to govern U.S. policy. Indeed, democracy is unlikely to flourish unless security can first be guaranteed. International stability amidst multipolar fluidity will have to be pursued. This goal will be achievable only if the core principles of realism are respected: legitimacy, equilibrium, respect for national interests, and a stable balance of military power.

A critical distinction must be made, however, between a "balance of power" *policy* and a policy that includes recognition of the need for a balance of military power. The former harks back to the days of 19th century imperial conduct, when nations blindly pursued their own interests, thought in "blood and iron" terms, viewed politics as a "zero sum" game, exploited other nations, and intimidated potential opponents by manipulating multipolar rivalries. The latter policy aims for a healthy synthesis of realism and idealism. It recognizes the centrality of national interests, but in acknowledging the common good, it also pursues democracy and cooperative security. It prefers multilateralism, but will behave unilaterally when necessary. It strives for a military balance of power partly in response to realism's dictates, but also because this balance is needed if idealism's goals are to be attained.

American military power must remain engaged abroad, for this power will be key to preserving a stable military balance in many vital regions. Its potential can best be realized through alliance relationships and other multilateral institutions, but these organizations will be weak unless they are undergirded by

U.S. commitments. Military power can support enduring commitments to allies, promote cooperation with new friends, and discourage misbehavior by potential adversaries. These functions will have to be performed in regions where aggression might be mounted by medium-sized states, but they will have to be performed in ensuring stability among the great powers as well. Today Germany and Russia are not in conflict, and neither are Japan and China. Long-run stability among these ancient rivals, however, may continue to depend to some degree on the presence of U.S. forces.

If this larger strategic agenda is to animate U.S. foreign policy, the very paradigm of planning for MRCs in a narrow military way may miss the most fundamental point. This will be the case if these MRCs have been forged on the assumption that the international system is stable to the point where U.S. military power can now be viewed as a sword in a sheath, to be hauled out only when wartime threats emerge and regional military crusades must be launched. To the extent this assumption is being employed, it is being rendered invalid by international trends. A broader conception of the purposes of U.S. military power is needed.

Current U.S. defense policy is not bereft of larger purposes, but the difference between today's situation and that of the Cold War is stark. During the Cold War, DoD's canonical scenarios were embedded in a sophisticated framework of global security policy. Notwithstanding the official attention being paid to other dangers—failures in nuclear deterrence, democratic reforms, and economic recovery (Aspin, 1993)—the current MRCs stand outside any similarly elaborate framework for the new era. At a minimum, heavy reliance is still being placed on Cold War precepts. The key task is not really to fine-tune plans for MRCs, but rather to craft a policy and strategy that lays down innovative precepts governing the peacetime use of military power in a very different era of international politics.

The challenge of carrying out this peacetime mission will be demanding because the foundations of U.S. military strategy are changing, as are U.S. capabilities. During the Cold War, the United States carried out this mission through the vehicle of large overseas deployments backed by sizable forces in CONUS. In the era ahead, overseas deployments will be far smaller: present plans call for only about 100,000 troops each in Europe and Asia, and only a modest presence in the Persian Gulf. This situation will necessitate greater reliance on power projection from CONUS, but the drawdowns underway will leave smaller forces for this purpose. Crafting an image of credible peacetime strength will be one of the most important requirements confronting future U.S. defense planning. Being prepared for canonical MRCs is only one part of the solution. Nonetheless, it is an important part. Let us now consider the related requirements.

DO THE CANONICAL MRCs ESTABLISH APPROPRIATE FORCE NEEDS?

Even if international affairs are turbulent and many conflicts are possible, it can be argued that focusing on the canonical MRCs in planning the defense posture is still justified. At issue is whether doing so would provide the requisite flexibility. Involved here are not only the enemies and theaters to be engaged, but also the kinds of U.S. responses to be mounted, and the size and mix of the combat posture needed to mount them.

Force Requirements for Persian Gulf and Korean Conflicts

A strength of the two canonical MRC scenarios for Southwest Asia and Korea is that they call for strong U.S. military forces, thereby barring any wholesale disarmament. They do so by postulating short warning and roughly concurrent enemy attacks aimed at overrunning Kuwait/Saudi Arabia and South Korea. Sizable mobility forces—airlift and sealift—would be needed to deploy large U.S. forces to these theaters fast enough to save the day. Once these forces arrived, the situations in both theaters would mandate a stylized U.S. military response as envisioned by the Decisive Force doctrine (Powell, 1991). In the Persian Gulf, large combat operations would be conducted in order to stop the enemy attack and then launch a sweeping counterattack, akin to Desert Storm, to eject the enemy, destroy his forces, and attain political objectives. In Korea, U.S. and South Korean forces initially would have to mount a stiff defense to block the North Korean advance. They then would have to launch a counteroffensive to restore the border, destroy enemy formations, and achieve related goals. Following success in both theaters, most U.S. forces would withdraw, leaving behind postures as required for peacetime conditions (see also Frostic and Bowie, 1994).

The amount of U.S. forces required for these MRC scenarios is a matter of debate, but the Defense Department's Bottom-Up Review (BUR) tabled an MRC "building block" of 4–5 active Army divisions, 4–5 Marine brigades, 10 USAF fighter wings, 100 USAF heavy bombers, 4–5 Navy carrier battle groups, and special operations forces (Aspin, 1993). This posture, DoD asserted, will be adequate to deal with either MRC. As a hedge, the BUR announced a program to increase the readiness of 15 Army Reserve Component (RC) brigades so that they will be deployable after only 90 days of training (although lift capabilities may be inadequate to exploit this readiness). The Pentagon thus implied that, if both MRCs are to be fought concurrently, about 10 Army divisions, 3 Marine divisions, 20 USAF fighter wings, and 10 carriers will be needed, backed up by the high-readiness Army RC brigades.

This total accounts for all BUR forces except 20 Army low-readiness RC brigades and 1 Navy carrier. Thus, the BUR concluded that while reducing the Bush administration's Base Force by about 15 percent was acceptable, further cuts should be rejected as unsafe (Aspin, 1993:27–31).

Is this theory of requirements anything more than an ex post facto justification for decisions taken on other grounds? Critics may levy this accusation, but the DoD's MRC "building block" approach serves as a good tool for orientation. One problem, however, is that it does not resolve the debate, because "requirements" for these MRCs are not reducible to single-point estimates. As we shall see in the section on nonstandard contingencies, there is a big difference between the *names* of the MRCs (Persian Gulf and Korea) and the scenario details, and those details greatly affect "requirements." The size of the future adversary force is now a variable, not a constant, as is the type of military operation that U.S. forces will be called upon to conduct.

Are Persian Gulf Contingency Requirements Underestimated? Anticipating some of the discussion of nonstandard cases, note that the DoD building block may actually *underestimate* force needs for the Persian Gulf MRC. A recent RAND analysis (Bowie, Frostic, et al., 1993), entitled "The New Calculus," concluded that a DoD building block could defeat an Iraqi thrust southward, but was careful to point out that many battlefield dynamics would have to work in favor of U.S. forces. Rapidly deploying USAF units would need modern munitions that will be available only in future years. Air bases in Saudi Arabia already would have to stocked with enough fuel, munitions, and supplies to permit immediate full-scale air operations. The "new calculus" assumed an Iraqi ground threat of 20 divisions, ten of which were lightly equipped motorized infantry units, and readily suppressible Iraqi air defenses. It further assumed that the Iraqi advance would proceed at less than lightning speed, thereby allowing USAF units time to deploy, and that Iraq would fail to suppress U.S. air bases. Under these conditions, USAF/USN air operations were accurately assessed as enabling a successful counterattack by only 4–6 Army/Marine divisions, provided these divisions could be deployed fast enough to carry out the task. But do these assumptions reflect the future?

We shall consider alternative versions of the Iraqi scenario later, but even the BUR noted that additional forces might have to be sent to compensate for possible failures in the initial defense, to mount a decisive counteroffensive, or to accomplish more ambitious war objectives. The report did not call for more air or naval forces, but it did suggest that two additional Army divisions might be needed, thereby raising the Persian Gulf ground force from 5–6 divisions to 7–9 divisions. This is an important caveat, for it elevates potential U.S. force needs far closer to what was used in Desert Storm (17 coalition divisions, roughly 10 of them American), and to what was deployed in Korea and Vietnam: wars where airpower could not play a dominant role.

Are Korean Contingencies Overstated?   If the BUR potentially understates Persian Gulf requirements, it may overestimate force requirements for the Korea MRC.   North Korea today enjoys a roughly 1.5:1 quantity edge over U.S./South Korean forces in combat units and hardware.   However, the U.S./South Korean defense posture benefits from prepared positions, rugged terrain, and knowable axes of advance.   The chief risk is not that U.S./South Korean forces will be defeated, but that Seoul will be lost in the early fighting.   Thus, in the likely event that South Korean forces acquit themselves well, a U.S. force of only 2–3 divisions, 8–10 fighter wings, and 2–3 carriers might be adequate (but additional forces could be needed if early events do not go well or for a counteroffensive).   Thus, the BUR may understate needs for Iraq and inflate needs in Korea in ways that cancel each other out, thereby yielding an overall estimate that is on target.   If so, marginal reductions in the Base Force, as discussed in the BUR, will not compromise a two-MRC strategy provided U.S. forces are well prepared, but further reductions could invalidate this strategy.

Force and Posture Needs for Other Conflicts

We have seen, then, that the total force requirements derived from the two canonical MRC scenarios appear roughly right, but with significant uncertainties.   Another issue, however, is whether these two MRCs are an appropriate canonical basis for planning military strategy and posturing those forces we maintain.

On the positive side, the two MRCs compel the United States to maintain a sizable force structure, big mobility forces, and well-developed deployment plans.   Further, they mandate diversity in that the Persian Gulf MRC calls for heavy armored/mechanized units, whereas the Korea MRC mandates lighter infantry, airmobile, and artillery formations.   For both theaters, the required campaign plans demand joint and combined operations, and both defensive and offensive actions.   Modern doctrine would have to be employed in both cases, anchored on a coordinated combination of firepower and maneuver carried out by forces that are armed with high-technology weapons, ready, well trained, well led, and fully supported.

Surface appearances suggest then, that if U.S. forces can deal with these two MRCs, they should be capable of responding to a broad range of challenges, including very different situations.   Yet this is not automatically the case, because the proverbial "lesser included case" sometimes turns out to be neither lesser nor included.   History shows plenty of cases in which military forces that were well prepared for one type of conflict experienced reversals when war came wearing different clothes.   If the U.S. experiences in Korea and Vietnam do not illustrate this point, then the brutal lesson learned by France in May 1940 should do so. At the time, the French army was regarded as the world's best, but it had spent twenty years preparing for a canonical scenario of its own: a repeat of World War I. When the German army crafted a nonstandard scenario through attack by blitzkrieg, the French army proved incapable of reacting, and was swept off the battlefield in one month.

One risk is that in preparing a choreographed response for the two canonical MRCs, U.S. forces might be hard-pressed to shift course if events in these two conflicts mandate a different response. Another, and possibly even greater, risk is that war might break out elsewhere: in an entirely different place, against a different enemy, and requiring very different U.S. deployment and campaign plans. If confronted by nonstandard challenges, could U.S. forces deploy fast enough and then carry out the operational campaigns needed for success? Perhaps so, but in the final analysis, the answer can be known only if nonstandard situations are studied.

The need for deep thought and a long view is manifest because uncertainty inhibits our ability to foresee which nations will appear on the scene as enemies. What *can* be said is that Iraq and North Korea are not destined to be our only military rivals. Politics can and often does change faster than U.S. military forces are altered. Today's enemies can be tomorrow's friends, but the converse also is true for nations whose internal politics or external interests can produce a sudden about-face. After all, Iran was once deemed a permanent friend, but almost overnight it became an implacable enemy when Ayatollah Khomeini arrived.

New adversaries can build imposing military forces that permit more ambitious operations than might be feasible today. Force improvement cannot occur overnight; the act of building modern forces that can compete with Western troops and weapons is costly and time-consuming. But especially if outside assistance is provided, buildups can take place, and perhaps faster than is commonly expected. After all, Germany in the 1930s went from being disarmed to becoming the world's strongest military power in only six years. Much will depend upon the resources, skill, and determination of future adversaries. Nations formerly regarded as military lightweights can achieve at least middleweight status, and perhaps more, in the space of several years. In the interim, their efforts can be observed, but the act of discerning their intentions and ultimate ambitions often is not easily accomplished. This especially is the case for nations whose original agenda is unthreatening but becomes menacing only after military power is built.

Different physical circumstances thus might be encountered that do not offer favorable terrain, a well-developed military infrastructure, prepositioned assets, host nation support, and allied military contributions. Owing to their unique features, Saudi Arabia and South Korea are relatively easy to defend once U.S. forces have been deployed. Other countries might be harder to protect, and even difficult to reach with sizable U.S. forces—doubly so if the timelines of war do not permit the six-month U.S. buildup that was possible in the Persian Gulf.

Future conflicts might be waged in response to political dynamics that are very different from those postulated by these two MRCs. Whereas these MRCs postulate aggressive enemy attacks aimed at conquering friendly nations, other conflicts might witness aggression aimed at different goals: e.g., seizure of nearby urban areas, destruction of lives and property, or imposition of a new government. One example is a civil war in Saudi Arabia aided by Iraq and Iran. The goal would not be the physical conquest of Saudi Arabia, but rather a takeover of its government. Coalition political dynamics also could be quite different. Whereas these two MRCs postulate the support of many friendly governments, other conflicts might witness neutrality or even opposition. Moreover, U.S. goals might be something other than the rapid destruction of invading enemy forces and restoration of allied borders. These dynamics could call for military operations quite dissimilar from those planned for the two canonical MRCs.

Future conflicts might be waged against adversaries that pose quite different military threats than mountable by Iraq and North Korea. Some adversaries might be less well armed, but others may (eventually) field larger and better-equipped forces. These forces might also be better trained and led, and guided by modern doctrines equivalent to that of Western forces. Whereas Iraq and North Korea today pose primarily ground threats, future adversaries might deploy strong air and naval forces that will have to be engaged. Indeed, some conflicts might be fought in the air and at sea, with little ground combat. Equally troublesome, some adversaries might arrive on the battlefield with nuclear forces and other weapons of mass destruction that could be employed against U.S. forces.

Another issue is whether these two MRCs adequately cover the problem of simultaneity. They presume that at the time of their occurrence, no other conflicts will be in progress. But what if a peacekeeping operation is underway at the same time that tensions rise in both the Persian Gulf and Korea? A peacekeeping operation could consume 1–2 U.S. divisions and therefore stretch thin the BUR's posture. Or what if an even larger conflict takes place, one that demands more U.S. forces? At issue here is the degree of insurance to be sought from the U.S. military posture. Perhaps the likelihood of three simultaneous conflicts is too low to be taken seriously, or at least not high enough to merit the extra budgetary cost of buying additional forces. Yet the prospect of a peacekeeping mission is not easily dismissed, for during 1993, the United States found itself conducting one peacekeeping operation in Somalia and preparing for another one in Bosnia. To the extent that similar requirements arise in the future, the simultaneity problem might not be solved by deploying only enough forces to carry out two MRCs.

To pull things together here, consider that the great advantage of the Cold War for planning was that conflicts were relatively predictable. The focal points of potential aggression could be pinpointed, and entire areas could be discounted. Enemy threats were knowable, as were allied contributions. U.S. goals, strategy, and campaign plans could be decided upon in advance. The need to plan for global conflict ensured that three principal theaters—Europe, the Persian Gulf, and Northeast Asia—were covered. For these reasons, the Department of Defense enjoyed confidence that canonical scenarios left it prepared for other circumstances and sufficiently flexible to adjust to the unexpected. These advantages seem destined to be lost in the new era in which uncertainty abounds.

This important change magnifies the risks of relying on a small set of canonical scenarios. For example, the two MRCs in vogue today do not even consider Europe as a potential site of major regional war. What if this assumption proves invalid? What if major operations must be launched well east of NATO's borders in Europe, or in Central Asia, or anywhere in Asia aside from Korea, or anywhere in the Middle East/Southwest Asia apart from Saudi Arabia? Will the United States be able to respond flexibly if it plans only on the basis of these scenarios? The troublesome answers to these questions illuminate the case for paying careful attention to other scenarios that, while "nonstandard," might be altogether too real. Let us now identify some specific nonstandard scenarios.

NONSTANDARD SCENARIOS FOR THE FUTURE

Any attempt to speculate about specific nonstandard scenarios is a hazardous enterprise, one vulnerable to charges of implausibility and worry-warting. Nevertheless, this section offers a few possibilities. The following analysis is intended to be illustrative. What it offers is an opportunity to break out of current plans by imagining different conflicts that, in one way or another, might be feasible—if not now, then within, say, a decade. The analysis speculates only about future military conflict in the critical theaters of Europe, the Middle East and Persian Gulf, and Asia. It ignores entire regions that could become focal points of conflict: South and Central Asia, sub-Saharan Africa, and Latin America. But coverage of the selected theaters is sufficient to illuminate the central point: the need for broad intellectual horizons, and for flexibility and adaptiveness, in U.S. defense planning.

Conventional Conflicts

Nonstandard Conflicts in Europe. Because Europe does not even play in current MRC planning, this theater is a good place to start. Absent war with Russia, small powers in east central Europe and the Balkans are unlikely to band together to create the large enemy force needed for any single conflict to qualify as an MRC. Yet if regional strains intensify, conflicts far larger than LRCs are possible, for the nine nations there will deploy a total of 60–70 heavy combat divisions and 2500 combat aircraft. Apart perhaps from Serbia, no other nation there qualifies today as an adversary of the United States, but many harbor profound animosity for each other. The possibilities for confrontation are multiple, and if U.S./NATO forces are drawn in, the result could be a new form of warfare: something between an MRC and an LRC.

Although peacekeeping in east central Europe or the Balkans is the mission most likely to be performed by Western forces, a situation might arise in this region in which major peacemaking/enforcement operations, or even large combat interventions, must be mounted. In the case of concurrent conflicts, overall requirements could be for as many as 10–12 divisions and 650–800 combat aircraft. The NATO allies could contribute heavily, but even so, U.S. contributions might be as high as 2–4 divisions, 150–300 combat aircraft, and naval forces. This is less than an MRC requirement, but sizable nonetheless.

The complex politics of the situations to be encountered create many different possibilities for the employment of U.S. forces in a NATO operation. U.S. forces might be used to keep the peace in Bosnia, to pressure Serbia, to protect Romania's borders, to quell imperial conduct by Hungary, or to defend Poland against Ukraine. U.S. forces might help bring stability to the Baltics, the Caucasus, or south central Asia. All of these situations could require military operations very different from the neat and clean script followed in Desert Storm. Indeed, politics and diplomacy likely would dominate military strategy. Even if forces were initially committed on behalf of clear policy goals, these goals might change in response to new conditions, thereby causing military strategy to shift, perhaps several times over. If so, the prospect would be for a very messy relationship between politics and war.

The coming years might witness NATO's expansion to include new members in east central Europe and elsewhere. The Partnership for Peace proposal will offer Article 4 guarantees to participating nations, and it holds out the possibility of NATO membership for some. Obvious candidates are Poland, the Czech Republic, and Hungary. This development would extend combined NATO planning eastward. Along with West European forces, U.S. forces would have to acquire the capacity to deploy to these new nations and to defend their borders. The outcome could be a new era of NATO military strategy. If all of this were accomplished well, it would be seen as a step *toward* rather than against Russia (Asmus, Kugler, and Larrabee, 1993:37). In time, assuming further democratization and development, Russia itself might join NATO.

If democracy failed in Russia and that nation returned to imperial conduct, the prospect of war with it could again have to be factored into U.S. defense planning. This conflict would be an MRC and beyond, for Russia would probably field an army of 50 divisions and equivalent air forces, at least half of which could be committed. The size of the adversary force could increase further if other Commonwealth nations joined the fray. The need to deal with an imposing enemy force would be far from the only troublesome issue confronting U.S. defense planning, for weighty political issues would enter the calculus. For example, where would the war be fought, in Poland, or Ukraine, or the Baltics? What political goals would be pursued? What would be the overall diplomatic context? The answers would have profound implications for force planning, and multiple answers could drive planning in many different directions.

Indeed, war in Poland alone could be fought in many different ways. Western forces might be committed early, or in the middle of an impending crisis, or late, after fighting had already begun. The politics of this intervention could be clear or very muddy, marked by uncertainty about the goals and calculations of many different participants. NATO might respond as a unified alliance through its integrated command, but alternatively, an ad hoc operation, with only a few nations participating, might have to be launched outside the integrated command. If NATO itself had fallen apart, the intervention might have to be mounted on the fly, with only Germany providing an infrastructure and forces. Bases and reception facilities might be available in Poland, but they might instead have been overrun by Russian forces (Kugler, 1992a).

Western forces might be called upon to defend Warsaw and the Bug River, to halt a Russian drive midway through Poland, to launch a counterattack from western Poland aimed at restoring that country's borders, or even to march into Belarus. The operation might be launched with air forces alone, with large air forces and some ground units, or with large ground formations. The ground campaign might take the form of a linear defense, a defensive maneuver battle, a flanking counterattack, a sweeping counteroffensive, or all of these in sequence. The war might be over quickly, or drag on for weeks and months. The possibilities here are endless, and many are quite different from Desert Storm.

Nonstandard Contingencies Involving Iraq. If regional tensions intensified in the Persian Gulf, an equally wide range of possibilities might have to be addressed. For the near future, small-scale operations will remain the order of the day, e.g., enforcement of the no-fly zone over Iraq coupled with antiproliferation and humanitarian missions. In the midterm and more distant future, a wide variety of MRCs are possible, some like Desert Storm, some others quite different.

An important issue here is whether Iraq would attack with a force as ill-prepared and a political approach as ham-handed as in 1990. As discussed in Bennett, Gardiner, and Fox (1994), there are many possible ways in which Saddam Hussein might hope to improve his prospects for success. For example, a repeat Iraqi invasion might take the form of naked aggression, but it might be mounted amidst complex political conditions such as a domestic upheaval in Saudi Arabia in which a revolutionary movement seized power and called for Iraqi help. An Iraqi invasion might again stop at Saudi Arabia's borders, but equally likely it could press beyond and aim at overrunning that nation. An Iraqi drive into Saudi Arabia might move slowly, but might unfold at high speed. The United States might respond quickly, but in contrast to Desert Shield, it might react sluggishly.

Sensitivity analyses of nonstandard versions of the Iraqi scenario need to assess how requirements would be affected by a stronger and faster-moving Iraqi attack, or if U.S. air operations were much less effective than postulated by the DoD "building block." At issue also is the adequacy of a ground posture that, even counting allied forces, would still leave U.S./allied forces outnumbered by 2 or 3 to 1 and fighting on open terrain that invites mobile operations by both sides. Despite the superiority of U.S. weapon systems, some defense planners might assess this deficiency as too great for a confident defense against a capable opponent if U.S. airpower is anything less than truly dominant. To be sure, U.S. airpower could inflict enough damage on an exposed Iraqi army to lower U.S. ground requirements if given 2–3 weeks to operate before the ground battle begins. But what would happen if the next war does not permit a lengthy preparatory air campaign?

The nature of the U.S./allied ground defense campaign also could have a bearing on the adequacy of the planned force. In the unlikely event that a forward linear defense is mounted, a U.S. posture of only 5–6 divisions (along with 3 allied divisions) would be affected by force-to-space relationships and thereby could be hard-pressed to form an adequate line to contain an Iraqi thrust. Much would depend upon the Iraqi army's ability to move off existing roads and advance across the open terrain. In the more likely event of a mobile defense, force requirements could be elevated by the need to perform pinning maneuvers, frontal assaults, and flanking operations. Mobile defense is far from a cure-all if the enemy is skilled at maneuver (Kugler, 1992b), and the need for adequate forces is all the greater when counteroffensives are conducted. These reasons were influential in shaping requirements for Desert Storm (17 coalition divisions, 10 of them American).

For all these reasons, the range of military possibilities in defending Saudi Arabia alone is quite wide. U.S. forces might again be granted time to build up imposing defenses on Kuwait's border, but they also might have to land in Saudi Arabia amidst an onrush of attacking Iraqi formations. At the outer extreme, U.S. forces might have to launch an invasion of a Saudi Arabia already fully occupied by Iraq. U.S. offensive operations might stop once Saudi and Kuwaiti borders have been restored, but this time they might be followed by an invasion of Iraq aimed at toppling its government. These cases would require substantially different forces and concepts of operations (Davis and Finch, 1993:74–75).

Other Nonstandard Scenarios in the Greater Middle East. Iraq might not be the only adversary nation encountered in the Persian Gulf. Indeed, Iran is now improving its forces under a still-zealous regime, and might transform itself into a well-armed enemy intent on imperial conduct. How would Iran react to another U.S. intervention aimed at inflicting military defeat on Iraq? Would it remain neutral, or might it try to foul the intervention, perhaps by using its air and naval forces to block the Straits of Hormuz and the Persian Gulf? If Iran did insert itself in these ways, U.S. force operations would need to change dramatically away from the Desert Shield/Storm model. Indeed, how would a war with Iran alone unfold? In all likelihood, it would be an air and sea war, with U.S. operations mounted heavily from Saudi Arabia and other Gulf sheikdoms. But it might include a forced U.S. landing on Iranian soil followed by a major campaign into that nation.

Future conflicts in the greater Middle East are also not limited to the Persian Gulf. For example, Israel might be attacked in ways calling for larger U.S. interventions than in the past. Although force commitments probably would not be large for defending Israel, they could be larger if Turkey were to be attacked by a coalition of radical Arab partners: e.g., Syria and Iraq. In this case, large U.S. air and naval forces, with major logistical support, would be needed by Turkey. If the Turkish army proved unable to stop the advance and restore lost territory, sizable U.S. and NATO ground forces might have to be committed. In this event, a military operation akin to Desert Storm could be mounted, but the geographical and logistical conditions would be quite different.

What will happen if Islamic fundamentalism sweeps over the Middle East and North Africa, in ways producing a united coalition of radical Arab governments all angry at the West? The idea that another Muslim invasion of Europe could be launched—akin to that faced by Charles Martel at Tours—is far-fetched. Yet, jihad can be conducted in other ways. In addition to spawning terrorism across Europe, Arab nations might assemble the air, missile, and naval forces needed to contest the Western powers for control of the Mediterranean, the Suez Canal, and the Red Sea. The result could be a long-running saga of air and naval clashes that would entangle not only West European forces, but also U.S. forces. This conflict would not be an MRC, but to U.S. forces it might seem that way, and current MRC plans would provide few solutions.

Nonstandard Contingencies in Asia. Similar judgments apply to future security affairs and conventional military conflict in Asia. In Korea, a canonical MRC could unfold in many different ways, each having different implications for U.S. forces and defense plans. In the optimistic case, a powerful North Korean attack might run into a stone wall when encountering the South Korean army, its prepared defense positions, and the mountainous terrain straddling the border. In this event, North Korean forces might make little headway while suffering high losses, and their drive might stall after making little, if any, progress. With the South Korean army providing the primary vehicle for containing this unsuccessful attack, only limited U.S. military assistance would be needed: C^3I, tactical air, naval, and logistic support.

A wide spectrum of pessimistic Korea scenarios are equally plausible, however (Bennett, 1993). North Korean forces might threaten to punch through South Korean defenses and seize Seoul. Alternatively, they might actually capture Seoul and surrounding territory. A worse outcome is that the South Korean army might be left too battered to counterattack and recapture Seoul. Even worse, the South Korean army might unravel, thereby leaving all of the Korean peninsula open to North Korean aggression, as happened in 1950.

Each of these pessimistic scenarios imparts a different meaning to U.S. force requirements and defense plans. In the least threatening case, not only USAF forces, but also some U.S. ground units would have to be used to help contain breakthroughs and shore up South Korean defenses near the border. If Seoul were to be lost, larger U.S. ground and air forces would have to be committed to recapture the capital city, restore South Korean borders, and destroy enemy forces—all the more so if South Korean forces themselves were left too depleted to lead the counterattack. In the extreme case of a complete South Korean collapse, quite large U.S. forces might be compelled to launch a large amphibious attack as a forerunner to a sustained drive up the peninsula.

If these possibilities help illuminate the situations that might be encountered in Korea today, future planning might have to undergo a fundamental reorientation if Korea reunifies. Perhaps U.S. forces would withdraw entirely, and the need to plan for any war in Korea would disappear. Alternatively, the U.S.–South Korean military alliance might be redefined to deal with new security challenges after unification. What would these challenges be? The U.S. perspective might focus on the threat to Korea's northern borders posed by an assault from China or Russia. By contrast, the Korean perspective might call for defense preparations against a potential threat from Japan—a key U.S. *ally* in Asia. Alternatively, a reformed U.S.–South Korean alliance might play a regional role in Asia.

Future U.S. defense planning also will need to take into account the many other political-military changes now sweeping over Asia. For the past 20 years, the threat of war with China has not been taken seriously in U.S. defense planning. But China is now undergoing a military buildup, and if that nation were to embark on an imperial course in an atmosphere of mounting political confrontation, an entirely different situation could unfold. Exactly how would a renewed Chinese military threat be manifested? Although traditional examples are threats to Korea, Taiwan, and Southeast Asia, the new era might prove to be untraditional. China might pose a mounting nuclear missile threat to Japan; indeed, if relations with Russia were also to sour, Japan might find itself besieged by new threats from both countries. Another possibility is that China might develop the larger and better-equipped navy that would allow for maritime power projection into the western Pacific. In this event, naval combat might prove to be a core feature of new U.S. defense planning in Asia.

The possibilities would magnify many times over if Japan were to follow the course of expanding its maritime power projection capabilities. Especially in this event, major-power naval rivalry might spread outward from Northeast Asia by expanding into Southeast Asia, the Strait of Malacca, the Spratly Islands, and eventually linking to the turbulent situation in South Asia. Along with distantly deployed naval forces could come networks of new military bases across the region for projecting air and ground power. Inevitably, the Southeast Asian nations would be affected, and new security alliances would form, perhaps in ways destabilizing to the entire region. None of these outcomes are foreordained or even probable, but with Asia changing so rapidly in such profound ways, they are not beyond the realm of the possible.

The new challenges posed to U.S. military forces would necessitate major changes in the entire American defense planning framework for Asia. All the more so if political change were also to bring about a major withering of the security alliances that have provided U.S. forces with invaluable military installations for so many years. Already, U.S. bases in the Philippines have been lost, compelling a difficult search for other alternatives. What would happen if the U.S.-Japanese security alliance were terminated, and if the U.S.-South Korean alliance suffered the same fate? Loss of military bases in these countries could compel a wholesale change in U.S. military strategy for Asia. Provided disengagement was rejected, the United States presumably would be compelled to rebuild its old bases on islands in the Pacific. Even so, it would be left with a military strategy of distant power projection and expeditionary operations.

Regional Nuclear Scenarios

Because these global scenarios deal only with conventional war, the looming prospect of regional nuclear crises adds yet another dimension to the upheavals potentially ahead for U.S. planning. How would the United States act in regional nuclear crises in the Persian Gulf and Korea? Although the answer is not obvious, current plans might have to be radically altered, for any mechanical deployment of large U.S. forces might serve only to supply a target-rich environment to enemy forces. For both MRCs, new plans would have to be crafted, plans capable of dealing with conventional and nuclear threats (Millot, Molander, and Wilson, 1993).

Beyond these two regions, nuclear crises might appear elsewhere, and the possibilities are mind-numbing. The United States might find itself facing a nuclear confrontation between Russia and Ukraine that would threaten all of Europe. Another possibility (less detailed than a "scenario") is a tactical nuclear standoff between nations in east central Europe or the Balkans that had managed to get their hands on these weapons. A third is a nuclear crisis in the Middle East or North Africa. A fourth is a crisis in South Asia pitting India against Pakistan, or one that spreads to Central Asia in ways entangling Russia and China. A fifth encompasses many subcases in Asia that do not originate in Korea. A sixth is even bleaker, for it would fundamentally alter the global security system: Japan and Germany, pressured by mounting insecurity and diminished confidence in U.S. deterrent coverage, might themselves decide to develop nuclear forces.

Even if the threat of destabilizing actions by Japan, Germany, and other responsible nations is discounted, the need to prepare for regional nuclear crises caused by rogue states is growing. To the extent that U.S. combat operations might be undertaken, the prospect of regional nuclear crises will resurrect concerns of the past. During the Cold War, defense planning in Europe viewed conventional and tactical nuclear operations as interconnected. This interconnection would have to be recaptured in new plans, since the old concepts of flexible response, graduated escalation, and massive retaliation no longer apply.

Summary of Contingencies

Table 1 displays the various contingencies discussed here. It is by no means comprehensive, but it illustrates a spectrum of events.

Table 1

Potential Future Contingencies Involving U.S. Military Forces

---

Conventional Contingencies in Europe
- Peacekeeping or peace enforcement and crisis management in east central Europe, the Balkans, and the former USSR
- Medium-sized warfare in east central Europe and the Balkans
- Defense of new NATO members, and cooperation with other partners
- MRC versus Russia in Poland
    — At Bug, Vistula, or western Poland
    — Linear defense, mobile defense, or counteroffensive

Conventional Contingencies in Persian Gulf and Middle East
- MRC in Saudi Arabia and Kuwait
    — Forward defense
    — Intervention after Saudi Arabia is partly overrun
    — Reinvasion after Saudi Arabia is conquered
- Civil conflicts exploited by outside powers
- War with Iran
- Defense of Israel
- Defense of Turkey
- Conflict in North Africa and Mediterranean
- Conflict in the Caucasus

Conventional Contingencies in Asia
- MRC in Korea
    — Defense of border
    — Recapture of Seoul
    — Reinvasion of conquered South Korea
- Defense of unified Korea
- Defense of Japan
- Defense of Taiwan
- Maritime conflict with China
- Maritime conflict in Southeast Asia
- Intervention in South Asia

Regional Nuclear Crises
- In Europe
- In Asia
- In Middle East/Persian Gulf

IMPLICATIONS FOR U.S. DEFENSE PLANNING

Changing Needs, Changing Requirements, and Flexibility

The need for national military preparedness stems from reasons far more fundamental than the transient mechanics of contingency analysis. Because the United States will remain a superpower with overseas interests to protect, it will need strong military forces to underwrite its purposes in peace, crisis, and war. Specific adversaries will come and go, but the requirement for military power will remain—a product of enduring geostrategic realities. What is required now is a true strategic concept, one portraying the rich set of premises and postulates that are the appropriate foundation for the U.S. defense posture and budget. During the Cold War, the United States was blessed with a coherent strategic concept; today it needs one for the post–Cold War era. Once this strategic concept is fashioned, canonical scenarios can be retired to the more limited roles for which they are suited.

If one thing is obvious, it is that defense planning will need to be quite dynamic. The days are gone when the Department of Defense could erect an elaborate analytical framework that would endure untouched for many years. Because static thinking will no longer be feasible, basic military strategy may have to be uprooted every few years, and specific plans might have to be altered more often yet. Therefore, the emphasis should not be on reestablishing a timeless edifice of plans for the new era, but rather on creating an energetic planning process that is capable of handling regular upheaval.

To the extent that scenario analysis continues to be employed, the emerging military environment is rendering invalid many of the nostrums that animated defense planning during the Cold War. The challenge will be to construct a new planning framework that casts out old invalid thinking but avoids misinterpreting the new era. Desert Storm overturned many of the analytical approaches that derived from the old NATO–Warsaw Pact confrontation in Central Europe (Davis, 1994c). These include the practices of valuing quantity over quality, of discounting differences in readiness and modernization when there are large disparities in mass, of assessing ground requirements in terms of a fixed ratio in comparison to enemy forces, and of striving for a predetermined mix of ground, air, and naval forces. Yet if these old practices are no longer appropriate, Desert Storm itself was a unique war in many ways, owing to the many advantages enjoyed by U.S. forces (Record, 1993). The challenge will be to assess future conflicts on their own merits, and to anticipate a broad range of possibilities (Davis and Finch, 1993; Davis, 1994a).

The need to prepare for the twists and turns of events has special implications for DoD's operations plans (OPLANS), which determine how forces are deployed, and for CINC campaign plans, which determine how forces are to be employed on the battlefield. In the past, these plans often offered only one fixed blueprint for operations. In the future, as the Joint Staff and CINCs are aware, these plans need to be modular, and based on building blocks capable of being rapidly adjusted to handle different situations. Modularity can be achieved only if scenario analysis examines a broad spectrum of events and determines the alternative responses that might have to be mounted. Analysis of individual contingencies should employ, e.g., decision tree analysis—composed of multiple branch points—to determine the alternative paths that military operations might have to take in any single conflict.

Planning for Generic Missions

Future uncertainty is so great that U.S. defense policy might be well advised to shift away from threat-based planning to mission-based planning. For all its quantitative appeal, threat-based planning is an unreliable instrument for dealing with a change-filled era. If the Israeli-Arab dispute is settled and Korea reunifies, today's canonical MRCs could disappear overnight. But this development would not remove the need to be prepared for major regional wars, which might occur in different places for different reasons. What is needed is a planning mechanism that enables the United States to be prepared for these and other conflicts, wherever they might occur.

Under the new approach contemplated here, defense plans would not focus on specific threats posed by specific nations as the final arbiter of decisions. Rather, it would identify the generic military missions that will need to be performed in order to deal with many different threats. The U.S. force posture and defense program would then be designed to perform these missions. In this approach, canonical scenarios would still be employed, but not in an exclusive sense. Rather, planning would consider several categories of scenarios for determining the multiple military missions that might have to be performed in many different situations (Kugler, 1992a).

Table 2 illustrates eleven different categories of contingencies that should be taken into account in force planning. Because all these categories may be encountered in three or more theaters, and in several different forms, the number of permutations is quite large. Mathematics alone suggests that a narrow planning framework of only two canonical MRCs might fail to address all of these permutations; even inclusion of a few LRCs might not solve the problem. Common sense says likewise.

Each of these classes of contingency imposes unique requirements for missions to be performed by U.S. forces. "Peacetime stability/presence" refers to the role that U.S. forces, especially those deployed overseas, will play in reassuring friends, dissuading adversaries, and otherwise guiding the international system toward stability. "Humanitarian assistance" refers to the delivery of food and other supplies needed in regions suffering devastation from war or natural causes. "Peacekeeping" refers to the mission of deploying forces in noncombat missions to help maintain an existing agreement. The missions required for "counterterrorism and hostage rescue" are obvious from the titles, and the missions imposed by "lesser regional contingencies" have been discussed above. "Crisis management and resolution" refers to the use of forces to exert politi-

Table 2

Types of Future Contingencies Requiring
Commitment of U.S. Forces

1. Peacetime stability/presence
2. Humanitarian assistance and peacekeeping
3. Counterterrorism and hostage rescue
4. Lesser regional contingencies (LRCs)
5. Crisis management and resolution
6. Peacemaking and peace enforcement
7. Medium-sized regional contingencies
8. Canonical MRCs
9. Nonstandard MRCs
10. Greater-than-expected MRCs
11. Regional nuclear conflict

cal-military pressure on adversaries for the purpose of achieving U.S. goals in a
confrontational situation short of full-scale war. "Peacemaking and peace enforcement" refer to the use of force in combat missions to either transform an
existing conflict into peace, or to ensure that an existing accord continues to be
carried out.

Whereas these first six categories deal with the use of military forces in the
gray area between war and peace, the final five categories deal with military
missions in wartime settings. "Medium-sized regional contingencies" refers to
conflicts that fall between LRCs and MRCs. Whereas the category of
"canonical MRCs" refers to the Persian Gulf and Korean scenarios now employed in DoD planning, "nonstandard MRCs" refers to either major variants
of those scenarios or entirely different conflicts of similar magnitude.
"Greater-than-expected MRCs" refers to potential conflicts in which stronger
enemy forces are employed than projected in typical MRC planning. At the
outer extreme are potential "regional nuclear conflicts" that escalate beyond
conventional fighting.

In the coming years, U.S. forces will be required to perform many of these
missions. The canonical MRCs offer the promise of enabling the U.S. posture
to wage a repeat of the Persian Gulf war while deterring aggression in Korea.
But will this posture be able to perform the peacetime mission of undergirding
international stability? Will its forces be able to conduct the small-scale but
important missions of humanitarian assistance, peacekeeping, counterterrorism, and hostage rescue? Will it be capable of performing in lesser regional
contingencies? How about the thorny operations that might have to be conducted under the rubric of crisis management and resolution, peacemaking,
and peace enforcement? What about a medium-sized wartime contingency in

east central Europe or the Balkans, far away from existing bases and infrastructure? What about a truly nonstandard MRC: a major naval tussle with China in Asia? What about a greater-than-expected MRC that involves a major war with the Russian army fought in Poland, the Baltics, or Ukraine? And what about a regional nuclear conflict in any of three different theaters?

If sufficient forces are available to deal with the two canonical MRCs, in all likelihood the U.S. posture will provide enough combat forces—in overall size—to address any single nonstandard conflict in the other categories. The real problem is that for many of these nonstandard contingencies, specific capabilities might be lacking because they are not mandated by the canonical MRCs. For example, peacekeeping can require specialized training and equipment that is quite different from that needed for major warfighting. Crisis management/resolution, peacemaking, and peace enforcement normally require combat forces similar to those needed for warfighting, but they normally mandate employment doctrines very different from Decisive Force. A medium-sized regional contingency in east central Europe or the Balkans might require logistic support forces larger than, and quite different from, the support forces needed for the Persian Gulf and Korea. A regional nuclear contingency might require specialized forms of C^3I and air-strike operations quite different from that needed for a canonical MRC. These are but a few examples of how unique capabilities might be needed for nonstandard contingencies, but they illustrate the basic point.

Perhaps force sizing will continue being based on the two canonical MRCs, but the act of developing military plans and future-looking programs should be guided by a much broader framework. In essence, planning should begin by taking a careful look at all eleven categories. For each category, potential contingencies in all three theaters should be considered. In each case, the robustness of solutions should be tested by examining significant deviations from expected norms. The resulting analyses should be used to gauge the adequacy of force plans and programs. The goal should be a robust and flexible military posture that can perform many different kinds of operations, aided by deployment/employment plans and military doctrines that are sufficiently adaptive to respond to the situations at hand.

Analyses of this sort admittedly would complicate the defense planning process. The goal of planning, however, is comprehensiveness, not simplicity. The drawback of a few canonical scenarios is that they buy detailed appraisals of a few major events at the expense of roughly accurate assessments of a far larger class of conflicts that might actually occur. They thus help give the Department of Defense penetrating vision for expected conflicts, but may leave it largely blind to the surprises created by the unexpected. The outcome of considering nonstandard scenarios would be greater confidence that the

Defense Department will not be flying blind in a coming international era seemingly destined to create a fog of confusion of its own.

BIBLIOGRAPHY

Aron, Raymond (1966), *Peace and War: A Theory of International Relations*, Doubleday and Company, Garden City, NY.

Asmus, Ronald D., Richard L. Kugler, and F. Stephen Larrabee (1993), "Building a New NATO," *Foreign Affairs*, Vol. 72, No. 4.

Aspin, Les (1993), *The Bottom-Up Review*, Department of Defense, Washington, D.C.

Bennett, Bruce (1993), *Global 92 Analysis of Prospective Korean Conflicts in 2002*, RAND, Santa Monica, CA.

Bennett, Bruce, Samuel Gardiner, and Daniel Fox (1994), "Not Merely Planning for the Last War," in Davis (1994b).

Bowie, Christopher, Fred Frostic, Kevin Lewis, John Lund, David Ochmanek, and Philip Propper (1993), *The New Calculus: Analyzing Airpower's Changing Role in Joint Theater Campaigns*, RAND, Santa Monica, CA.

Brzezinski, Zbigniew (1993), *Out of Control: Global Turmoil on the Eve of the 21st Century*, Robert Stewart, New York.

Davis, Paul K. (1994a), "Institutionalizing Planning for Adaptiveness," in Davis (1994b).

——— (ed.) (1994b), *New Challenges for Defense Planning: Rethinking How Much Is Enough*, RAND, Santa Monica, CA.

——— (1994c), "Planning Under Uncertainty Then and Now: Paradigms Lost and Paradigms Emerging," in Davis (1994b).

Davis, Paul K., and Lou Finch (1993), *Defense Planning for the Post–Cold War Era: Giving Meaning to Flexibility, Adaptiveness, and Robustness of Capability*, RAND, Santa Monica, CA.

Friedman, George, and Meredith Lebard (1991), *The Coming War with Japan*, St. Martin's Press, New York.

Frostic, Fred, and Christopher Bowie (1994), "Conventional Campaign Analysis of Major Regional Conflicts," in Davis (1994b).

Fukuyama, Francis (1992), *The End of History and the Last Man*, Free Press, New York.

Garten, Jeffrey E. (1993), *A Cold Peace: America, Japan, Germany, and the Struggle for Supremacy*, Twentieth Century Fund, New York.

Huntington, Samuel P. (1991), *The Third Wave: Democratization in the Late Twentieth Century*, University of Oklahoma Press, Norman.

——— (1993), "The Clash of Civilizations," *Foreign Affairs*, Vol. 72, No. 3.

Kennedy, Paul (1993), *Preparing for the Twenty-First Century*, Random House, New York.

Kugler, Richard L. (1992a), *NATO Military Strategy for the Post–Cold War Era: Issues and Options*, RAND, Santa Monica, CA.

———— (1992b), *NATO's Future Conventional Defense Strategy in Central Europe: Theater Employment Doctrine for the Post–Cold War Era*, RAND, Santa Monica, CA.

———— (1993), *U.S. Military Strategy and Force Posture for the 21st Century: Capabilities and Requirements*, RAND, Santa Monica, CA.

Layne, Christopher (1993), "The Unipolar Illusion: Why New Great Powers Will Rise," *International Security*, Vol. 17, No. 4.

Lukacs, John (1993), *The End of the Twentieth Century and the End of the Modern Age*, Ticknor and Fields, New York.

Lynn-Jones, Sean M. (ed.) (1991), *The Cold War and After: Prospects for Peace: An International Security Reader*, MIT Press, Cambridge, MA.

Millot, Marc Dean, Roger Mollander, and Peter A. Wilson (1993), "*The Day After . . .*" *Study: Nuclear Proliferation in the Post–Cold War World*, 3 vols., RAND, Santa Monica, CA.

Powell, General Colin L. (1991), *National Military Strategy*, Department of Defense, U.S. Government Printing Office, Washington, D.C.

Record, Jeffrey (1993), *Hollow Victory: A Contrary View of the Gulf War*, Brassey's (U.S.), Washington, D.C.

Winnefeld, James A. (1992), *The Post–Cold War Force-Sizing Debate: Paradigms, Metaphors, and Disconnects*, RAND, Santa Monica, CA.

Winnefeld, James A., and David Shlapak (1990), *The Challenge of Future Non-Standard Contingencies: Implications for Strategy, Planning, Crisis Management, and Forces*, RAND, Santa Monica, CA.

Chapter 8

IMPROVING DETERRENCE IN THE POST–COLD WAR ERA: SOME THEORY AND IMPLICATIONS FOR DEFENSE PLANNING

Paul K. Davis

This paper describes an interdisciplinary theory for conventional deterrence of regional aggressors in post–Cold War crises. A basic assumption is that the opponent is attempting to make rational decisions by comparing options on the basis of their prospective payoffs (as viewed in the opponent's personalized and context-sensitive scheme of values) in what he judges to be the most likely, most favorable, and worst cases. Despite attempting to be "rational," the opponent is quite likely to make errors of judgment and assessment because of uncertainties, misperceptions, and a variety of standard psychological phenomena such as ignoring altogether risks below some threshold of perceived likelihood. At the same time, the nation attempting to deter aggression is also likely to make serious mistakes, which include underestimating how unacceptable the aggression would be once it happened and being unwilling to take effective deterrent actions early because of the political costs of doing so and rationalizations about why the agression won't occur. The theory has been applied to analyze why deterrence of Saddam Hussein failed and whether it would have been possible to deter him with different actions. It has also been applied to some much earlier historical cases. After discussing those applications, the paper examines the generic challenge of avoiding future aggression against weak states such as Kuwait, Saudi Arabia, Poland, Lithuania, and Ukraine. It ends by noting significant implications for defense analysis, intelligence assessments, and the process of crisis deliberation.

INTRODUCTION

Conventional deterrence is difficult. *Extended* conventional deterrence, where one nation attempts to influence the actions of a second nation concerning a third, is even more difficult. Further, it is poorly understood, perhaps because during the Cold War so much theoretical attention in the West was focused on the very special case of deterring invasion of NATO by the Warsaw

This paper draws on a chapter in Huber and Avenhaus (1993). It also benefited from reviews by Kenneth Watman and Paul Bracken and comments by John Arquilla.

Pact. That problem was special because: (a) the requirement to defend was widely accepted; (b) the threat appeared to be real, massive, and monolithic; (c) large military forces were stationed close to each other and maintained at high levels of readiness; (d) nuclear weapons played a central role; and (e) the opposing sides knew a great deal about each other's strategic thinking and military culture. The situation is quite different when we contemplate deterring the kinds of aggression that seem most likely in the next decade or so. Iraq's invasion of Kuwait was a massive failure of deterrence. It can be argued that the United States did not *try* seriously to deter the invasion, and that Saddam's invasion was therefore less a failure of deterrence than a U.S. failure to recognize and appreciate national interests in advance. However, the evidence is that the United States *did* try, ineffectually, to deter invasion, as evidenced by the President's message to Saddam, the ineffective warning provided by Ambassador Glaspie, and an ill-conceived naval exercise to indicate U.S. concerns. The ongoing war in the former Yugoslavia and its despicable "ethnic cleansing" activities are more recent examples of failure and a setback for those hoping for something approaching a "new world order." It is not difficult to identify many other potential trouble spots for the years ahead. It follows, then, that we should be interested in a theory of deterrence so that the future can be better than the recent past.

ASSUMPTIONS

There are many ways to approach the issue of deterrence. These include: statistical analysis of political, military, and economic factors present in historical crises (Huth and Russett, 1990); attempting to generalize from anecdotal accounts in the biographies and autobiographies of participants in crisis (Khrushchev, 1990; Garthoff, 1989); applications of game theory (Schelling, 1980; Dixit and Nalebuff, 1991); military stability analysis (Huber, 1990; Huber and Avenhaus, 1993); applications of classic balance-of-power theory (Walt, 1987); observations from history (Payne, 1992); and other theories (e.g., George and Smoke, 1974; George, 1991; Watman and Wilkening, forthcoming).[1] All of these approaches have much to offer, but the one I have been pursuing focuses on an aspect of the problem that has been largely neglected: understanding and attempting to influence the *reasoning* of the potential aggressor (who may not think of himself as an aggressor). Thus, I am concerned with human perceptions, arguments, and logic—all of them affected by psychological considerations. However, I am concerned less with making

---

[1] See Arquilla (1992) for discussion of diverse approaches to understanding aggression and deterrence. It includes a good bibliography of both classic and current writings.

mere observations about psychological factors in crisis than with describing such reasoning *analytically*—i.e., with building models of reasoning that can be used not only to improve insights retrospectively, but also to guide strategy *prospectively*.[2]

In attempting to describe reasoning analytically, one could structure the problem in any of several ways. My approach assumes *limited rationality* and *universal classes of reasoning patterns*.

By "limited rationality" I mean that the relevant leaders: (a) attempt to relate means to ends (i.e., their decisions and actions have purpose); (b) consider a range of options; and (c) evaluate those options in terms of likely outcome, most favorable outcome, and worst-case outcome. Thus, the leaders *attempt* to be rational and even take uncertainty into account. However, their decisions may be flawed for a wide range of reasons that include incomplete or incorrect information, the mental frames through which information is viewed, anxieties, extreme dissatisfaction with the status quo, oversimplified and sometimes highly erroneous mental models of the other protagonists, and other factors. Perceptions may even shift wildly during a fast-moving crisis. Further, leaders have very different attitudes about risk taking.

It is controversial to assume rationality, but while it is surely possible for a national leader to be a lunatic making random decisions, there are few examples of that in history, despite references to "crazy states" in some of the literature.[3] Most of the national leaders who have sometimes been described as irrational (e.g., Adolph Hitler, Joseph Stalin, the Ayatollah Khomeini, and Saddam Hussein) were quite rational in the sense defined above. Some of them suffered from severe psychological problems and exhibited bizarre and abhorrent behavior, but their most strategically significant decisions can be understood in terms of their objectives and perceptions. It is also important to recognize that *all* of us are subject to making a wide variety of perceptual and reasoning errors, but we do not consider ourselves irrational. "Limited rationality" allows for a wide variety of such cognitive "errors."[4]

---

[2]For a more detailed discussion, see work with my colleague John Arquilla in Davis and Arquilla (1991a,b) and Arquilla and Davis (1992). These studies were sponsored by the Joint Staff. They contain citations to relevant literature in psychology, political science, international relations, and economics, including citations to work on the origins of flawed reasoning in crisis by Robert Jervis, Robert Axelrod, Alexander George, Daniel Kahnemann, Amos Tversky, and others. Shafer and Pearl (1990) is a good compilation of classic articles on uncertain reasoning.

[3]See, e.g., Jablonsky (1991). Despite framing his work in terms of "crazy states," Jablonsky also recognizes (e.g., Chapter 2) that there can be much that is rational about crazy-state behavior, if merely we understand its perspective.

[4]There are many examples associated with terms such as *framing, anchoring, attributional inference,* and *group think* (Davis and Arquilla, 1991b). Humans sometimes

The second assumption is that it is useful to structure the theory around universally observable types of reasoning rather than culture-specific concepts such as the so-called "Arab, Oriental, Latin, or Western minds." To be sure, cultural factors can have profound effects that must be reflected in any application of theory, but the approach I describe has such factors entering along the way in context-dependent ways rather than as part of basic structure. My principal reason for the assumption is that the relevant behaviors of historical leaders can be found in all cultures, albeit with different frequencies. For example, the Arab world has produced Anwar Sadat and Saddam Hussein, and the Western world has produced George Bush and Adolph Hitler.

MODELING OPPONENTS AND THEIR ASSESSMENT OF OPTIONS

Assessment of Options

Let me next describe a way that many aggressors may, *in effect*, have reasoned about their options in the past and how many others may do so in the future. To repeat, they are attempting to make rational decisions. They are considering options and are also examining likely and possible consequences of those options, as suggested in Table 1. The format here is that for each option the reasoner estimates the likely outcome, most favorable outcome, and worst-case outcome. He then makes an overall assessment of the option based on these estimates. Each outcome is characterized by a value in the set {very bad, bad, marginal, good, very good}.[5]

---

take greater risks than a decision theorist would consider warranted when they perceive their current circumstances to be intolerable, and are often exceedingly risk averse when they are comfortable with their current and projected circumstances (this is described by so-called "prospect theory" in the literature). Humans are often reluctant to part with possessions, even when offered more for them than their apparent economic worth. Humans also depend heavily on seeing and exploiting patterns, which sometimes leads to technically unsound judgments when they see the "wrong" pattern (e.g., when they misconstrue the intentions of other people). Humans are often overconfident in their estimates of risk. These behaviors are based in biology and are not easily corrected by mere education. Further, many of them stem from heuristic reasoning processes that are quite useful on average and probably confer survival advantages on the species. A premise of my work is that these individual-level behaviors exist also at the level of nations, especially when decisions are dominated by individuals or cohesive like-minded groups.

[5]To be sure, humans seldom reason in so linear and reductionist a manner in the course of their decisionmaking process. Ideas arise and are considered; competing ideas arise; some ideas are forgotten, others are championed; organizational and group-dynamic considerations dictate how options are presented and when; procedural methods may or may not exist to enhance "rationality"; and so on. However, the assumption

Table 1

Generic Decision-Table Format for Assessing Options

Option	Likely Outcome	Most Favorable Outcome	Worst-Case Outcome	Assessment
Option 1				
Option n				

This basic structure is generic, but estimates of the various outcomes depend sensitively on perceptions and values. To understand how a potential opponent might reach individual judgments about, e.g., the worst-case outcome (would it be very bad, bad, marginal, good, or very good?), we need:

- Alternative mental images of the opponent,

- An understanding of what factors are most likely to affect the opponent's reasoning, and

- A way to go systematically from the image and factors to estimates of the opponents' various judgments.[6]

Alternative Images of the Opponent

Developing *alternative* images is crucial as an antidote to some of the problems associated with the normal focus on best-estimate thinking (Davis and Arquilla, 1991b). To develop alternative "images" of the opponent's reasoning, my colleagues and I have used a combination of essay writing, attribute lists, influence diagrams, and cognitive maps. In one image, for example, the opponent may be pragmatic and incrementalist; in another, he may be exceedingly ambitious and frustrated; in yet a third, he may feel cornered, surrounded by enemies, and desperate.

Figure 1 shows contrasting "cognitive maps" (closely related to what others call "influence diagrams") used in a study of Saddam Hussein (Davis and Arquilla, 1991a). They represent schematically two very different images of

here is that, at the end of the day, the decisionmaker is either literally or *effectively* comparing options by considering the array of judgments shown in the table. The decisionmaker may or may not be aware that he is consciously going across all the options and considering upsides, downsides, and so on, but the search for a "best" decision encourages doing so.

[6]This approach stems from earlier research modeling decisions in nuclear crisis. See, e.g., Davis (1987).

Saddam's perceptions about the economic situation in mid-1990. The convention in such diagrams is that when an arrow connects two items, an increase or improvement in the first leads to an increase or improvement in the second, unless there is a negative sign, in which case an increase or improvement in the first leads to a decrease or worsening in the second. Negative signs are usually used to indicate a troublesome influence. For example, at the bottom of Figure 1a, we see that an increase in U.S. trade sanctions would *worsen* Iraq's economic status.

Figure 1a represents the cause-effect relationships emphasized in the intelligence community's "best-estimate" understanding of Saddam prior to the invasion. Figure 1b represents an alternative image that could readily have been formulated and disseminated at the time, except for the pressures to focus on a single best estimate. It includes some very important additional factors, factors such as Saddam's perception that his problems were the direct result of Iraq being squeezed deliberately by his enemies (the United States, Kuwait, and Saudi Arabia among them). It also highlights the connection between his eco-

RAND#130-91-0194

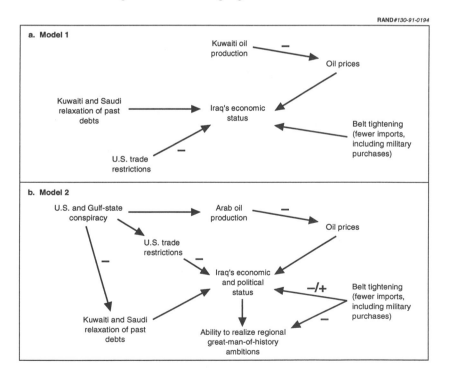

Figure 1—Saddam's Image of the 1990 Economic Situation: Two Models

nomic travails and his grandiose ambitions. Note that while nearly all the experts would have agreed on all the factors in either diagram being "significant," the dominant mental image (Figure 1a) was one in which some of the factors weren't given much emotional weight. The purpose of the diagrams is merely to highlight differences of perspective, in this case differences in perspective about how Saddam might be viewing the world. We used a number of such diagram pairs in depicting our two images or models of Saddam Hussein. Although we started our work after the invasion and therefore had no trouble constructing a model to explain it, our models proved both insightful and predictive for Saddam's subsequent behavior through February 1991 (i.e., his failure to pull out of Kuwait in the kind of compromise American strategists feared).

Table 2 illustrates a different method for clarifying distinctions between images of the opponent, one based on an attribute list. Again using the example from our study of Saddam Hussein, model 1 is painted as being essentially pragmatic and relatively risk averse. Model 2 is more ambition driven and risk accepting.

Identifying the Factors Affecting Judgments and Decisions

Suppose we have used methods such as the cognitive maps, attribute lists, and other devices to develop strong alternative mental images of the opponent—i.e., suppose we have reached the point of being able to say, in a discussion, "No, no, that's not the way model 1 would look at the situation. Where he's coming from is . . . and what he would be concerned about is. . . . Model 2 might reason the way you're talking, but not model 1!" What next? The next step is identifying the factors (i.e., variables) most likely to contribute to the opponent's judgments, notably judgments about the likely, best-case, and worst-case outcomes of various options. It is not very useful to attempt this in abstract terms, because so much of what seems to matter is exquisitely context dependent. My approach is to brainstorm the problem with an interdisciplinary mix of regional experts and strategists, to identify key factors in concrete "natural" language (e.g., Saddam Hussein's assessment of President Bush's resolve), and to develop *hierarchies* of such factors (or variables). This reflects the observation that people make their most reasoned judgments on the basis of only a few "high-level" variables, but these variables, in turn, sometimes reflect many subordinate judgments about "lower-level variables" (Davis, 1987).

To illustrate this, consider how Saddam Hussein may, in mid-1990, have assessed his worst-case outcome (i.e., his "risks") for an option in which he invades Kuwait. Is the worst-case outcome (risks) very bad, bad, marginal, good,

Table 2

Comparing Attributes of Models 1 and 2 of Saddam Hussein

Attribute	Model 1	Model 2
Ruthless, power-focused; emphasizes *realpolitik*	••	••
Ambitious	••	••
"Responsive"; seeks easy opportunistic gains	••	•
Impatiently goal seeking; likely to seek initiative	•	••
Strategically aggressive with nonincremental attitudes		••
Contemptuous of other Arab leaders	•	••
Contemptuous of U.S. will and staying power		••
Financially strapped and frustrated	••	••
Capable of reversing himself strategically; flexible (not suicidal)	••	••
Clever and calculating (not hip-shooter)	••	•
Pragmatic and once-burned, now cautious	••	
Still risk taking in some situations	•	••
Grandiosely ambitious	•	••
Paranoid tendencies with some basis	•	••
Concerned about reputation and legitimacy in Arab and Islamic worlds	••	
Concerned only about being respected for his power		••
Sensitive to *potential* U.S. power not immediately present	••	•

or very good? Well, in the summer of 1990 as Saddam Hussein contemplated this matter, it is likely that he considered the risks to be due to two principal possibilities: the possibility that the United States would defend Kuwait directly and immediately (i.e., that war would begin when he crossed the border) and the possibility that even though the United States didn't defend Kuwait itself, it would deploy forces into Saudi Arabia and change the balance of power in the region (both militarily and, through sanctions, economically). We don't *know* that Saddam thought about the problem this way, but it is likely that however he expressed the issues, these possibilities were on his mind explicitly or implicitly. To assess risks, then, he would be concerned about the likelihood of each of these possibilities and the consequences. The consequences of an immediate war with the United States would obviously be very bad, but the likelihood of that (i.e., the likelihood of the United States defending Kuwait) probably did not appear large. The United States was more likely to deploy into Saudi Arabia, although the Saudis *probably* wouldn't permit it, but even if such a deployment and related sanctions occurred, it is likely that Saddam judged the likely consequences to be tolerable: the Saudis would tire of the U.S. presence, other regional states would deplore it, and economic sanctions would probably not last longer than six months or so.

Figure 2 illustrates how we characterized Saddam's likely risk assessment hierarchically when he contemplated the particular option of conquering Kuwait. For example, the figure suggests that Saddam would have seen larger risks if there had been strong and credible political warning of U.S. intervention, warning evidenced by strong and credible diplomatic messages along with other indications of resolve by President Bush and Congress. Saddam would also have seen higher risks if there were reason to believe that the United States considered Kuwait to be a vital national interest. Indicators of that might have been a defense agreement, the presence in Kuwait of U.S. forces, or "objective" considerations such as the expectation that Iraq would cut off Kuwaiti oil to the West. Diagrams such as Figure 2 can be worked out in group discussions, and then embellished with subsequent analysis.

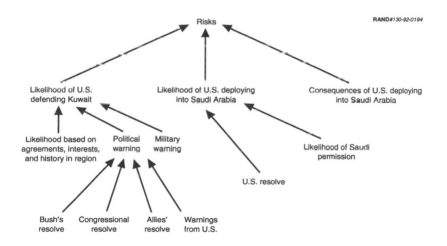

Figure 2—Possible Map of Saddam's Assessment of Risk Before Invading

Estimating the Opponent's Judgments and Decisions

Given alternative images of the opponent and an understanding of likely options and major variables or factors, it is possible to estimate how the opponent might reason in a wide variety of circumstances—not merely today's circumstances, but those that might exist tomorrow or next year. For each image of the opponent, we can develop what I call judgment tables and decision tables.[7] Judgment tables represent how the opponent might look at each of several factors and reach an overall judgment about, say, the most-likely or worst-case outcome of a given option. A decision table is similar, but relates specifically to evaluating the options in a common format.

Table 3 illustrates a judgment table for model 2 of Saddam Hussein evaluating risks of a conquer-Kuwait option in mid-1990 consistent with the factors identified in Figure 2. Note that Table 3 covers a wide variety of possible world situations. The line indicated in bold letters shows the situation that Saddam probably believed best characterized reality in mid-1990, with the result that he probably considered risks to be marginal rather than bad or very bad.

Table 4 now shows a decision table for model 2 of Saddam Hussein evaluating strategic options in late July 1990. Its net assessment for the conquer-Kuwait option is very good. (By contrast, model 1's assessment was very bad.)

Where do the judgments and decisions (i.e., the values in the last columns of Tables 3 and 4) come from? The answer is that they are subjective estimates made by analysts who have studied the alternative images and tried to "get inside their minds." However, there is a great deal of logic connecting the elements of the image (e.g., the cognitive maps and attribute lists) with the individual judgments. Indeed, some of this can be treated mathematically to improve "rigor." It is also possible to build artificial intelligence models to formalize the logic.

To illustrate one way to express the "combining logic" mathematically, consider the following formula calculating the net assessment of an option (Davis and Arquilla, 1991a, app. A):

$$N = R\{aL + bM + cW\}/\{a + b + c\} . \tag{1}$$

---

[7]Collectively, these and some additional lines of code can constitute a complete *formal* model of the opponent's reasoning. Indeed, one can construct computerized artificial intelligence models. The price of the formality, rigor, and completeness is very high, however. Models of this sort developed to better understand possible nuclear crisis decisionmaking (Davis, 1987) involved roughly 15,000 lines of code for each of two models of the Soviet Union and United States. Even these were not complete.

Table 3

Model 2's Late-July Risk Assessment for the Conquer-Kuwait Option

Likelihood of U.S. Defending Kuwait	Likelihood of U.S. Deploying into Saudi Arabia	Consequences of U.S. Deploying into Saudi Arabia	Attitudes in Arab World About Invasion (Attitudes Toward Iraq)	Risks[a]
Low	High	Very bad	—	Very high
Low	Marginal	Very bad	Bad	High
Low	Marginal	Very bad	Marginal or good	High
Low	Low	Very bad	Bad	Low
Low	Low	Very bad	Marginal or good	Low
Low	High	Bad	Bad	High
Low	High	Bad	Marginal or good	High
Low	**Marginal**	**Bad**	**Bad or marginal**	**Marginal**
Low	Marginal	Bad	Good	Marginal
Low	**Low**	**Bad**	**Bad**	**Low**
Low	**Low**	**Bad**	**Marginal or good**	**Low**
Low	High	Marginal	Bad	Marginal
Low	High	Marginal	Marginal or good	Marginal
Low	Marginal	Marginal	Bad	Low
Low	Marginal	Marginal	Marginal or good	Low
Low	**Low**	**Marginal**	**Bad**	**Very low**
Low	Low	Marginal	Marginal or good	Very low
Low	—	Good or very good	—	[Not plausible]
Marginal	—	—	—	High or very high
High	—	—	—	Very high

[a]Values of variables: Likelihood . . . : {high, marginal, low}; Consequences . . . : {very bad, bad, marginal, good, very good}; Attitudes . . . : {bad, mixed, good}; Risks . . . : {very high, high, marginal, low, very low}.

Here N is the net assessment of an option; L, M, and W represent the likely outcome, most-favorable outcome, and worst-case outcome; R is a rounding operator; and a, b, and c are weighting factors. If reasoning itself is qualitative, then the formula can be used by first mapping the qualitative values into numbers (e.g., very bad $\rightarrow$ −2, bad $\rightarrow$ −1, . . .), computing the net assessment numerically, and then remapping the result back into qualitative values. This approach creates a preference order for the options.

One model's logic might correspond to $a = 1$, $b = 2$, $c = 1$, and $R = R^u$, where R^u corresponds to rounding up (e.g., 1.5 becomes 2, −1.5 becomes −1, etc.). The rounding operator is necessary because if reasoning includes discrete concepts such as very good and good, then outcomes may sometimes be "in be-

Table 4

Model 2's Assessment of Saddam's Options, Late July 1990

Option	Current Status	Likely Prospects	Risks (Worst-Case Prospects)	Opportunity (Best-Case Prospects)	Net Assessment of Option
1. Coerce Kuwait	Very bad	Bad	Very high	Marginal	Bad
2. Occupy part of Kuwait	Very bad	Marginal	Very high	Good	Marginal
3. Conquer all Kuwait	**Very bad**	**Very good**	**Marginal**	**Very good**	**Very good**
4. Invade Kuwait and Saudi Arabia	Very bad	Very bad	Very high	Very good	Bad

tween." This type of reasoning would give most weight to the likely outcome and lesser weights to the most-favorable and worst-case outcomes. On the margin, the reasoning would lean toward optimism.

It is useful to postulate several types of reasoning that differ primarily in attitudes toward risk, and that they assume a higher willingness to take risks when the current and projected situations are deemed to be very bad, and a reduced willingness to take risks when the current situation and prospects are deemed to be reasonably good. This reflects the well-established (and intuitively familiar) psychological phenomenon described in "prospect theory," developed largely through the work of Daniel Kahneman and Amos Tversky.[8] Psychologically, the reasoning styles might better be characterized as having a predisposition to "go for it" or "take no chance," depending on perceptions about the goodness of the current situation and current trends. Another point I have emphasized in my own work is the role of thresholds: below some level of perceived probability, risk is treated as zero, despite the consequences of the

---

[8]Kahneman and Tversky (see their work and others' in Shafer and Pearl, 1990) have based most of their work on empirical testing of individuals. In this work I am claiming that a similar prospect-theory phenomenon occurs at the level of *national* decisions, which are not usually the result of a single individual making choices unilaterally. As noted by colleague Kenneth Watman, there is interesting theoretical and empirical work to be done in testing the claim. In any case, I mention the Kahneman-Tversky work not as "proof" of the approach, but rather as providing some corroborating evidence.

risk. That is, not only do we often underestimate risks, we often go farther and ignore those we have judged "low." The reverse also happens: we sometimes rule out options because we see them as involving a level of risk beyond some threshold of acceptability.[9]

The point here is that we can not only construct formal models to reflect best-estimate notions about how the opponent is and may in the future be reasoning, we can also construct alternative models to reflect fundamental uncertainties about the nature of that reasoning. The principal question, of course, is whether we have to consider an infinite number of such alternative models. The answer appears to be no. Indeed, having two or at most three models appears to go a very long way, especially since one can also do sensitivity analysis within a given model. This is crucial, because it means that the technique, which is surely good for getting groups to confront uncertainty and be more humble about any "best estimate," should also be workable in practice. Formal intelligence estimates and high-level meetings should be able to cope with two, or conceivably three, very different perspectives on how the opponent may be thinking.

FACTORS TENDING TO INCREASE RISK TAKING

Since risk-taking propensity is such an important issue in determining aggression, it is worthwhile to review major factors tending to increase willingness to assume risk (see Figure 3). Starting at the top and moving clockwise, we see first the previously mentioned role of the current situation. The next factor is the degree to which the decisionmaker can make decisions unilaterally, without broad discussion that might mitigate perceptions and introduce new considerations. The next factor is ambition. This is often underestimated in thinking about adversaries in crisis and conflict. Status-quo powers fairly comfortable with their own circumstances are especially likely to underestimate others' ambitions. So it is that Saddam Hussein was erroneously assumed to be "pragmatic" and to be merely looking for a way to improve Iraq's economic situation "somewhat," when in fact he had grandiose goals. Similarly, the United States applied incrementalist compellence logic to Ho Chi Minh, when he was an idealist revolutionary. Other factors include opportunities for reaching important goals, the abstractness of risk factors (the more abstract the risk factor, the more it may be underestimated by someone who is yearning for

---

[9]Such thresholds, coupled with a grasping-at-straws phenomenon, were crucial in earlier studies using Soviet and U.S. models to understand possible escalation and de-escalation in nuclear crises. See, e.g., Davis (1992).

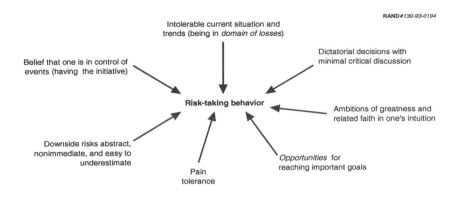

RAND#130-93-0194

Figure 3—Factors Contributing to Risk-Taking Behavior

action),[10] pain tolerance, and the degree to which the protagonist believes he is in control of events and therefore able to "make his own luck." All of these factors should be familiar to us from everyday life supplemented by a knowledge of history.

It should perhaps be obvious that in applying the theory described above, one considers the presence or absence of the factors in Figure 3 when estimating how a given type of decisionmaker might judge the worst-case outcome of a given option. One also uses these factors in judging which reasoning models to employ (e.g., in choosing parameter values a, b, and c, and rounding rules of equation 1, to correspond to more or less risk aversion).

A GENERIC SITUATION ENCOURAGING AGGRESSION

Let me now sketch how the theory applies to real-world problems of defense planning and foreign policy. To do so, let me first describe, using a decision table, a remarkably generic situation to be avoided, one in which aggression is possible and deterrence is difficult. Table 5 is the decision table that we do not want potential aggressors to have in mind. That is, we want to avoid situations in which, when the potential aggressors consider options, they end up reasoning as shown in Table 5.

---

[10]See Arquilla (1992) for examples of how aggressors have often underestimated the power and will of maritime powers and naval forces.

Table 5

Dangerous Assessments Encouraging Aggression

Option	Likely Outcome	Best-Case Outcome	Worst-Case Outcome	Assessment
1. Continue peaceful policies	Very bad	Bad	Very bad	Very bad
2. Coerce target	Bad or marginal	Marginal	Very bad	Bad
3. Take limited military action for limited gains (e.g., conquer a portion of target's country)	Marginal or good	Good or very good	Bad or marginal	Marginal or good
4. Invade, conquer target country	Very good	Very good	Bad or marginal	Marginal or good

The salient features of this somewhat generic dangerous situation are:[11]

- The perception that the current situation is very bad (implicit in the conclusion that a continuation of peaceful policies would have a very bad likely outcome).

- The perception that continuing current or other peaceful policies will not improve the situation.

- The perception that mere coercion may have a payoff, but not much, and might make things worse (e.g., by strengthening the coalition of hostile interests and by causing the potential target of aggression to increase its defenses).

- The perception that military action is likely to pay off, may pay off handsomely, and involves risks that are not outrageous and perhaps only marginal.

Importantly, national leaders have their own standards in evaluating "current situation" and the outcomes of various options. These often differ substantially from the standards that leaders of other nations might expect. As suggested above, it is easy to underestimate ambitions (and emotions) of adver-

---

[11]This discussion overlaps with classic expositions on the causes of war (e.g., Blainey, 1983 and Howard, 1984).

saries by assuming that they will behave "pragmatically" or "reasonably," by which is meant being satisfied with only marginal improvements in their situation. See Arquilla and Davis (1992), Payne (1992), and Arquilla (1992) for historical cases in which deterrence "should" have worked as judged by relative power, but did not.

It is also a profound mistake to believe that adversaries necessarily reason in a way that decision theorists would describe as attempting to maximize expected utility. In my view, exceedingly ambitious goal-driven people often behave so as to maximize the likelihood of success, which is quite different psychologically from maximizing expected utility. That is, utility theory is a poor way to represent such reasoning even though one can look at behavior and infer effective utility functions.

DANGEROUS POLITICAL-MILITARY CONTEXTS

Having discussed briefly how the reasoning of potential aggressors may be characterized analytically, and having described in that framework the kind of situation that breeds aggression, let us now consider what kinds of political-military context would cause a potential aggressor to reach the conclusions suggested in Table 5, even when there is the material potential for deterrence.

Figure 4 indicates schematically one such context. Here one country is considering aggression against a target country and another country or group of countries are potential protectors. The potential aggressor, the potential protectors, and the target all have allies or potential allies. They also have *images*, or *perceptions*, of how all the other actors reason and behave. Even this complex set of interactions is incomplete, because each country has an image of itself that may or may not be correct, and each ally has an image of all the actors and itself. Further, each actor may have an image of how each other actor views each other actor, and so on recursively to infinity. It is often adequate, however, to simplify to the level of detail indicated.

If the potential protectors regard the target country as "vital national interests," then they will ordinarily communicate that view to the potential aggressor, who will then take that into account in making decisions. If deterrence fails, it may then be because of an unstable *military* balance (see relevant discussion in Huber, 1990 and Huber and Avenhaus, 1993). The case I am most interested in, however, is the one in which the potential protectors are materially capable but ambivalent. They are not clear in their own minds about how important the security of the target country is to them. It may be, for example, that one of the target's regional neighbors is a vital interest and that the target itself is a buffer between the potential aggressor and those interests, but is not

RAND#130-94-0194

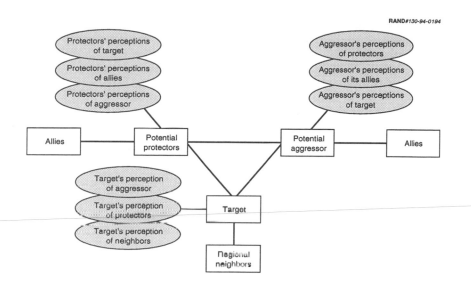

Figure 4—An Illustrative Crisis Context

itself important (and perhaps may not even be friendly). Or it may be that what happens to the "unimportant" target country could somehow affect events in their own countries (e.g., through the spread of revolution, the disparaging of new-world-order concepts, or the enhanced reputation and stature of the aggressor, who is attempting to foment revolution in their own countries), but the relationship seems abstract.

Will deterrence work? Not easily. Consider that not only is the potential protector ambivalent, it must also have cooperation from the target and its own allies in order to do anything. Indeed, it is worse than that, because the protector is often a democracy with internal political processes. Even if its executive branch believes in protecting the target, it may well be that the legislative branch and public do not. Even the military may be unwilling to get itself embroiled. And, because the executive branch is aware of these reluctances, it may be self-deterred.

So let us now suppose that the potential aggressor looks at the situation. It may observe that the protector is doing little, that there are internal political divisions within the protector's country, that some of the protector's allies are unwilling to participate, and so on. It sees the risks associated with its aggression as being low or at least tolerable, thereby creating one of the principal features of the situation in Table 2.

Or consider the target country. It may see the lack of cohesion, will, and support in the protector country and its allies. It may also see lack of support and cohesion in its own regional neighbors. One thing it does know, however, is that making the potential aggressor mad could bring serious trouble. Under these circumstances, how hard should the target country even work to request assistance from the protector? If the request becomes known (which is likely) and fails, which is very possible, the result may be to decrease rather than increase its security.

It is presumably evident that this illustrative case corresponds to specific instances in history and prospective history. In the case of Iraq threatening Kuwait, the situation obtained almost precisely (Davis and Arquilla, 1991a). Before August 2, 1990, the United States had no policy or internal political consensus about whether Kuwait was a vital interest worth protecting; Kuwait and Saudi Arabia did not believe Iraq would invade, but when they thought about it they questioned the reliability of the United States as a protector. Saudi Arabia felt that it did not want to further enrage Iraq. Saddam Hussein looked for indicators of Western resolve and saw nothing to cause him much worry: no military buildup, only equivocal warnings, no indications that Saudi Arabia would permit the United States to come to Kuwait's aid even if it chose to do so, and no evidence that Kuwait was even considered vital.

But the case of Kuwait was not unique. Consider now the situation in Europe where both Western Europe and Russia have at one time or another viewed Eastern Europe as a buffer. One might naively assume that both would consider the security of Eastern Europe to be very important, but it is hardly surprising that, in peacetime, little is being done to create that security. Would it be so surprising if at some point in the future a crisis arose between parts of the former Soviet Union and parts of Eastern Europe—or between Russia and other parts of the former Soviet Union such as Ukraine? Would it be surprising if military action occurred and that *after that action occurred*, observer nations decided that their own stakes were higher than they had previously realized? Consider here the case of Yugoslavia. Originally, it was not seen as a "vital national interest" of any of the NATO nations, or of Russia. But after seeing what has happened, with a level of willful and brutal aggression against civilians that has not been witnessed in Europe for decades, many in those nations wish they had acted firmly at the outset of crisis. It is now too late for deterrence, and compellence is proving as difficult as always.

In reality, there are numerous examples of potential future crises that fit the picture sketched here (Table 6). The generic features of the crises considered here are:

- The stakes are likely not appreciated beforehand by the potential protector and its critical allies;

Table 6

Possible Challenge Cases in the 1990s

Target	Aggressor	Potential Protector	Potentially Critical Regional States
Kuwait	Iraq	U.S.	Saudi Arabia, Iran
Saudi Arabia	Iraq	U.S.	Egypt, Oman, UAE, Iran,...
Poland	Russia	Germany, U.S.	Rest of NATO
Baltic states	Russia	NATO	Other states of the former Soviet Union
Hong Kong	China	U.S.	Japan, South Korea, Russia

- There is reluctance to believe that the aggressor will take military action of a sort that will prove unacceptable;
- There is widespread failure to communicate candidly about the situation and options beforehand;
- There are major perceived domestic-political and alliance-related *costs* to attempting deterrence; and
- The potential aggressor perceives weakness and lack of either cohesion or will.

In addition, the potential aggressor may feel *compelled* to action by strategically adverse trends and may be overconfident because of recent payoffs for decisive action or recent failures of its adversaries to take actions when they should have done so.[12]

THE SPECIAL PROBLEMS CAUSED BY PROLIFERATION

Although I shall not dwell on these issues here, the proliferation of weapons of mass destruction (and delivery systems for those weapons) makes deterrence and compellence even more difficult, as becomes evident when one "games

---

[12]The tendency toward overconfidence in human reasoning is well documented in the empirical literature and should be familiar from military history. Conquerors and other successful risk takers often come to believe that they are lucky or even invincible. There is a fine line between that poor judgment and the more correct one that vigorous and decisive people often "make their own luck" or the one that in warfare it is important to achieve and maintain the initiative.

out" various crises using the methods I have described only briefly here.[13] For example, if Saddam Hussein had had survivable operational nuclear or biological weapons, and if there had been reason to believe he would use them, it is less than obvious that Kuwait would exist today. This subject deserves far more attention than is possible here, but two observations are especially salient based on work to date:[14]

- The United States is more likely to intervene to deter an invasion by an aggressor armed with weapons of mass destruction than it is to intervene to roll back an invasion that has already occurred. Thus, early crisis response is more critical than ever before (Davis and Finch, 1993).

- It is highly desirable that the United States possess credible options to respond with chemical and nuclear weapons to attacks on U.S. forces or allies with weapons of mass destruction. In some cases at least, it does not seem likely that conventional attacks with precision-guided munitions would have comparable deterrent or compellent value.

IMPROVING APPROACHES TO DETERRENCE AND COMPELLENCE

Having described situations and reasoning patterns that undermine stability and efforts to deter aggression, it is now natural to suggest improvements of approach that would help avoid these situations and patterns.

Elevating the Recognized Importance of Indirect Threats and Buffer States. A challenge for statesmen is to recognize, and to persuade their governments to recognize, that many indirect threats to security are threats to "vital national interests." This is difficult, because it is not even intuitively obvious. The challenge will increase as those who grew up during the 1920s and 1930s retire from the political scene and new figures take their place, figures who will not have the same memories about appeasement.

I have seen related issues in my own graduate-level classes in the United States, and in discussions elsewhere involving serious mid-career military officers, when the people in question think about what is and ought to be the

---

[13]See Millot, Molander, and Wilson (1993) for discussion of an extensive set of exploratory games conducted on such matters. These, the "Day After" games, were designed primarily to get analysts and policymakers to think seriously about the consequences of proliferation for future crises and the consequences for U.S. defense planning.

[14]A study (Watman and Wilkening, forthcoming) discusses these and other issues in more detail. It makes important distinctions between the effects of weapons of mass destruction on the U.S. willingness to intervene and its likely war aims given that it does intervene.

President's national security strategy. Such discussion often begins by reviewing what are considered to be fundamental values and enduring interests. It is common for arguments to break out almost immediately, because there are disagreements about whether the security of allies and other nations is a fundamental interest of the United States. It seems evident that the security of other nations is important, but is not a "vital" interest.[15] If so, however, the tendency is to conclude that any strategy to maintain that security should be "political" and "tentative," without creating obligations that might lead to war. That undercuts deterrence. Statesmen have understood this problem and overcome it in many instances, most notably by developing treaties such as those that bind the United States to its NATO allies and Japan, even though the treaties create obligations that could lead to war, and even to nuclear war. Statesmen have been much less successful, however, in dealing with threats less monolithic and less menacing than that of the Soviet Union during the Cold War.

Recognizing Uncertainty in Assessing Intentions of Potential Aggressors. As argued elsewhere (Davis and Arquilla, 1991a,b), there is a chronic tendency for governments to focus unduly on "best estimate" assessments of what potential aggressors are up to, even though there is a long history of the best estimates having substantially overestimated or underestimated threats. The tendency to focus on the best estimate, and to filter information through the lens of that estimate long after the contrary evidence is strong, is typical of human reasoning in general. It can, however, be mitigated by changing the *processes* by which governments study potential crises in advance and the processes by which they write national estimates and conduct crisis deliberations. In particular, I recommend requiring staff agencies to develop, maintain, and treat seriously alternative models of other-country reasoning, and to have national-security staffs develop strategies that hedge against the less popular of the models proving to be correct. Despite cynical claims to the contrary about the inability of top-level political leaders to deal with complexity, discussing such hedged strategies should be quite feasible at the highest levels (e.g., in the U.S. National Security Council). Is there really any reason to believe that presidents, prime ministers, cabinet members, congressional and parliamentary leaders, and four-star generals cannot deal with uncertainty and hedging requirements?

Reducing the Costs of Hedging. I am confident that political and military leaders can do better in thinking about uncertainty and the need to hedge. For

---

[15]A major problem here is semantic. People read the phrase "vital national interest" and interpret it literally, when a better interpretation might be "an interest over which the nation would go to war, whether or not doing so would be required for the nation's survival." That is, "vital" interests are often not, in practice, "vital."

this thinking to be fruitful, however, it is also necessary that it be easier for them to take actions consistent with their analyses. Currently, it is extremely difficult for statesmen to take actions to underwrite deterrence or to make compellence effective in crisis. Until events reach some point of clarification, many of the very steps that are most needed are considered—by other policymakers, elements of the news media, and the man in the street—as potentially provocative and very dangerous. Consider a President contemplating vigorous military, economic, and political actions to avert aggression (including internal aggressions such as that occurring in the former Yugoslavia). He must worry about tomorrow's headlines, which may claim he is recklessly leading the United States into war, or recklessly committing the nation to be "policeman of the world," even in portions of the world where other countries should be providing police functions. These costs of action are real, tangible, and certain, whereas the actions themselves may be in the name of "hedging" against "possible" intentions by other countries, intentions that may in fact be much more benign.[16]

What can be done to reduce the costs? I see several generic approaches:

- Create political obligations and doctrines that compel actions (e.g., security agreements committing the United States to the protection of other nations).

- Have top aides (including relevant generals), and subsequently policymakers, "play" through the political-military crises when there is strategic warning of crisis, so as to sensitize them to the need for early actions to reinforce deterrence if the crisis worsens. Use modern technology such as videoconferencing to assure participation by all appropriate people.

- Have them do so in cooperation with allies and other organs of government so that necessary political alliances will form quickly in the event of crisis.

- Prepare in advance for how to explain necessary actions to the public.

All of this would require governments to do a far better job than their predecessors in reacting to strategic warning, which almost always precedes serious crises.

Preparing for Early Intervention. The best time to deter an opponent is before events go too far. Doing so may require only a moderate application of power (political, military, and economic), because the tactical objective is to change perceptions about stakes—i.e., to demonstrate unequivocally one's commitment to protect interests. This, unfortunately, runs directly counter to military conservatism, which agonizes about the risks posed to military forces

---

[16]The critical role of hedging costs was clarified for me in discussions with colleague Arnold Horelick.

that may be sent as political signals, and which objects deeply to intervention that precedes clear expressions of national objectives and the development of a political consensus assuring support for what will be necessary. The concept of a tripwire force is anathema to many military officers, and the notion of piecemeal commitment of military forces before developing political and moral support from the nation as a whole is even more so (Summers, 1984). Currently, the U.S. military emphasizes the importance of "overwhelming force" and de-emphasizes early actions beyond mere signaling of a sort that does not greatly endanger U.S. forces. My own recommendations here (for the United States and NATO in particular) are to develop rapidly deployable forces that are far more lethal and mobile (and hence survivable) than traditional initial projection forces such as the 82nd Airborne Division. Such forces might include a mix of tactical air forces with modern munitions and highly mobile ground forces such as the 101st Air Mobile/Air Assault Division (augmented with additional attack helicopter units), or armored cavalry regiments. Such forces could be put in harm's way early, so as to demonstrate commitment and protect politically important boundaries or locations. They could also provide a formidable defensive challenge and hope to do so while surviving. This is especially plausible because of the likelihood that the United States would have or quickly gain air supremacy, after which time an attacking armored force would be extremely vulnerable to airpower.

Let me end this item on a sober note by observing that it is the height of folly to establish tripwires without having the will and capability to respond massively to attacks on such a force. Tripwires can be, and often have been, tripped. The nation has moral obligations to any of its military personnel that it places in jeopardy.

Paying Attention to Theory When Developing Plans of Action. Perhaps the most remarkable feature of the deterrence concepts discussed here is how readily some of them are accepted in casual conversation and consistently overlooked or rejected in practice. Let me mention a few examples here (Davis and Finch, 1993):

- The doctrine of overwhelming force is widely accepted, but is antithetical to timely deterrence.

- The flexible deterrent options (FDOs) developed by the Joint Staff in recent years are excellent in name, but may be counterproductive in practice if the options are seen as evidence of timidity by the aggressor or our allies. Examples of such timid actions in crisis include: (a) President Carter's 1979 deployment to Saudi Arabia of *unarmed* tactical aircraft, intended to show support for Saudi Arabia during a period of turbulence after the fall of the

Shah;[17] and (b) the late-July 1990 exercise in the Persian Gulf involving naval forces and KC-135s, intended to be a signal to Saddam of U.S. support for the United Arab Emirates and Kuwait.[18]

- Nations consistently attempt deterrence and compellence with threats of gradually escalated political and economic sanctions, only seldom backed up with military options. Gradualism is seldom effective and threats that are not backed up with military power are often not taken seriously by the most dangerous types of aggressor.

A New Emphasis on "Punishment Options." The cold reality is that the United States and its allies are not likely to be able or willing to defend many of the weak states that may, in the decade or two ahead, be the subject of coercion or invasion. Kuwait was a close call; the Balkans were a failure; Ukraine and the Baltic states are far away and isolated; Hong Kong is far away and isolated; and so on. My own view is that the United States and its principal allies should move toward deterrent strategies that would focus on severe and immediate political, economic, and military punishment of aggressor states.[19] The image here should be one of both attacking the aggressor from the air and sea to charge him a high price, and following up with political and economic isolation. Would it be possible for the major nations to arrive at such an approach? Is it conceivable that it might achieve some status of legitimacy in the United Nations over time? Could such a deterrent strategy be used against a nuclear-armed country such as Russia? As I have attempted to demonstrate, deterrence is exceedingly difficult to accomplish. We need deterrent strategies that are better than those nations have used historically. This, it seems to me, is a profound issue, because the alternative to a new strategy may be a continuation of history.

---

[17]See Woodward (1991:240) for a description of how counterproductive Prince Bandar felt that deployment had been, causing the Saudis to worry about American "guts."

[18]Not only was the exercise militarily meaningless and very ambiguous as a signal, it was approached timidly because even this action was considered by some (including the UAE and other Arab states) as provocative. As General Powell later noted, the exercise got Saddam's attention, but didn't scare him; it did scare our allies.

[19]Richard Haas sharpened this point in my mind by emphasizing strenuously that the key to a punishment strategy is deliberately *not* establishing compellent objectives. It is within our power to punish, and even to do so severely. It is often not within our power to successfully compel the behavior we seek. The credible threat of punishment, however, might well deter the action in the first place; the exercise of punishment might deter those who would copy the actions of a "successful" aggressor.

BIBLIOGRAPHY

Arquilla, John (1992), *Dubious Battles: Aggression, Defeat, and the International System*, Crane-Russak, Washington.

Arquilla, John, and Paul K. Davis (1992), *Extended Deterrence, Compellence, and the "Old World Order,"* RAND, Santa Monica, CA.

Blainey, Geoffrey (1983), *The Causes of War*, Free Press, New York.

Davis, Paul K. (1987), "A New Analytic Technique for the Study of Deterrence, Escalation Control, and War Termination," in Stephen Cimbala (ed.), *Artificial Intelligence and National Security*, Lexington Books, D. C. Heath and Co., Lexington, MA.

——— (1992), "Behavioral Factors in Terminating Superpower War," in Stephen J. Cimbala and Sidney R. Waldman (eds.), *Controlling and Ending Conflict: Issues Before and After the Cold War*, Greenwood Press, New York.

——— (ed.) (1994), *New Challenges for Defense Planning: Rethinking How Much Is Enough*, RAND, Santa Monica, CA.

Davis, Paul K., and John Arquilla (1991a), *Deterring or Coercing Opponents in Crisis: Lessons from the War with Saddam Hussein*, RAND, Santa Monica, CA.

——— (1991b), *Thinking About Opponent Behavior in Crisis and Conflict: A Generic Model for Analysis and Group Discussion*, RAND, Santa Monica, CA.

Davis, Paul K., and Lou Finch (1993), *Defense Planning for the Post–Cold War Era: Giving Meaning to Flexibility, Adaptiveness, and Robustness of Capability*, RAND, Santa Monica, CA.

Dixit, Avinash K., and Barry J. Naleduff (1991), *Thinking Strategically: The Competitive Edge in Business, Politics, and Everyday Life*, W. W. Norton and Co., New York.

Garthoff, Raymond L. (1989), *Reflections on the Cuban Missile Crisis*, rev. ed., The Brookings Institution, Washington, D.C.

George, Alexander (ed.) (1991), *Avoiding War: Problems of Crisis Management*, Westview Press, Boulder, CO.

George, Alexander, and Richard Smoke (1974), *Deterrence in American Foreign Policy*, Cornell University Press, New York.

Howard, Michael (1984), *The Causes of War*, 2d ed., Harvard University Press, Cambridge, MA.

Huber, Reiner K. (ed.) (1990), *Military Stability: Prerequisites and Analysis Requirements for Conventional Stability in Europe*, NOMOS Verlagsgesellschaft, Baden-Baden.

Huber, Reiner K., and Rudolf Avenhaus (eds.) (1993), *International Stability in a Multipolar World*, NOMOS Verlagsgesellschaft, Baden-Baden.

Huth, Paul K., and Bruce Russett (1990), "Testing Deterrence Theory: Rigor Makes a Difference," *World Politics*, Vol. 42, pp. 466–501.

Jablonsky, David (1991), *Strategic Rationality Is Not Enough: Hitler and the Concept of Crazy States*, Strategic Studies Institute, U.S. Army War College, Carlisle Barracks, PA.

Khrushchev, Nikita (1990), *Khrushchev Remembers: The Glasnost Tapes*, edited by Jerrold Schecter with Vyacheslav Luchkov, Little Brown and Co., Boston.

Millot, Marc Dean, Roger Molander, and Peter Wilson (1993), *"The Day After . . ." Study: Nuclear Proliferation in the Post–Cold War World*, 3 vols., RAND, Santa Monica, CA.

Payne, Keith B. (1992), *Deterrence and the Lessons From History*, National Institute for Public Policy, Washington, D.C.

Schelling, Thomas C. (1980), *The Strategy of Conflict*, Harvard University Press, Cambridge, MA.

Shafer, Glenn, and Judea Pearl (eds.) (1990), *Uncertain Reasoning*, Morgan Kaufman Publishers, San Mateo, CA.

Summers, Harry (1984), *On Strategy: A Critical Analysis of the Vietnam War*, Dell, New York.

Walt, Stephen M. (1987), *The Origins of Alliances*, Cornell University Press, Ithaca, NY.

Watman, Kenneth, and Dean Wilkening, with John Arquilla and Brian Nichiporuk (forthcoming), *U.S. Regional Deterrence Strategy* RAND, Santa Monica, CA.

Woodward, Robert (1991), *The Commanders*, Simon and Schuster, New York.

Chapter 9

OPERATIONS OTHER THAN WAR

Jennifer Morrison Taw and Bruce Hoffman

Unprecedented population growth, urbanization, and population displacement will not only lead to conflict in the developing world, but will change the nature of conflict. This has strategic, operational, and tactical implications for U.S. military forces that may become involved in such conflicts. Case studies of U.S. operations ranging from direct intervention to peacekeeping to disaster relief yield many practical lessons for U.S. forces operating in the more urban, heavily populated, and politically constrained conflict environments likely to predominate in the developing world. Examinations of U.S. efforts in Panama, Lebanon, Somalia, and Bangladesh also reveal that the operations most likely to succeed are those conducted in a stable operational environment (whether peace or war), where the United States has clear-cut political and military objectives. This was true in both Panama and Bangladesh, despite the fact that one was a combat operation and the other a noncombat effort. In Lebanon and Somalia, on the other hand, the political and military objectives were less clear and the operational environment was fluid. In both instances, U.S. forces were deployed to accomplish a humanitarian mission— for which they were carefully selected, prepared, and equipped—only to find themselves in a more threatening situation and taking a more aggressive stance. U.S. military planners will have to better prepare U.S. forces for future such efforts, where shifting operational environments and changing political goals will require concomitant shifts in military objectives, missions, and capabilities.

INTRODUCTION

For more than 40 years the U.S. military concentrated its attention, energy, and resources primarily on defending Western Europe from Soviet aggression and, in turn, on preparing for total victory through the application of decisive force against the Warsaw Pact. Even when U.S. strategists and planners were forced to shift their focus to Korea in the 1950s and Indochina in the 1960s, the American military's fundamental operational imperatives and basic approach to warfighting remained unchanged.

Although the U.S. military's primary mission remains to fight and win the nation's wars, the increasing salience of military operations other than war (OOTW) in the years since the Cold War's end have imposed additional, and in some cases new, missions and responsibilities. Operations other than war include peacekeeping (PKO), peace enforcement (PE), counterinsurgency (COIN)/insurgency, counternarcotics (CN), counterterrorism (CT), noncombatant evacuation operations (NEO), arms control, support to domestic civilian authorities, humanitarian assistance (HA) and disaster relief (DR), security assistance (including training), nation assistance (including civic action), shows of force, and attacks and raids (U.S. Army, 1993). In retrospect, planning and mission preparation during the Cold War appears almost straightforward compared to the complex variations of the OOTW missions of the new era. Such missions will often be conducted within a highly fluid operational continuum: ebbing and flowing between peace and conflict, combat and noncombat operations, and conventional and nonconventional activities.

OOTW, moreover, are likely to occur in parts of the world where the United States has traditionally had few critical interests, areas that therefore have received little attention or interest from the American military (recent OOTW conducted in the Kurdish enclave in northern Iraq, in Somalia, and in Bangladesh bear out this point). The global nature of new post–Cold War political pressures will possibly increase demand for OOTW missions such as disaster relief, humanitarian assistance and/or support, peacekeeping, etc.—with the attendant likelihood that the U.S. military will be called upon to deploy to unfamiliar and, in many cases, physically demanding corners of the globe.

Within the context of the intensive population growth, migration, and urbanization now unfolding throughout the developing world, this paper focuses on how these emerging OOTW missions will affect strategic, operational, and tactical planning for future conflicts (limited conventional combat or nonconventional combat operations such as insurgency), noncombat missions (humanitarian assistance and disaster relief), and peacekeeping and peace enforcement operations.

THE CHANGING NATURE OF CONFLICT

Although the overall worldwide population growth rate is slowing, the populations of 37 of the world's most populous countries—which are all located in less-developed parts of the globe (i.e., the nonindustrialized regions of Asia, Africa, Latin America, and the Middle East as well as certain parts of Central Europe and the southern regions of the former Soviet Union)—are continuing to grow by more than 3 percent annually (*The Economist*, 1990).[1]

---

[1] The projected world population of eight billion in 2020 will double the population of 1976 and quadruple that of 1930. By comparison, it took from the dawn of time until 1830 for the world to acquire just one billion people. See Green (1989:2).

Between 1990 and 2025, the fastest population growth will occur in the world's least-developed countries, which will experience a 143 percent increase in population. In the rest of the developing world, the population will grow by 75 percent over that same period, while the developed regions will have only a 12 percent increase. Thus, the countries with the greatest population growth are already among the world's poorest, least developed, and most economically deficient.[2]

Admittedly, problems of population growth, poverty, and hunger are not new to the less-developed world and have been throughout history the fulcrum for war, revolution, and subversion. But what sets today's developments apart are the monumental urbanization and mass migration processes that are together transforming the less-developed societies from predominantly agrarian to urban.[3] As rapidly as these countries' populations are growing, their urban populations are increasing at more than twice that rate (Rogers, 1982:1 and Yeung and Belisle, 1988:99).

For the first time in history, more people today live in cities in the developing world than in the industrialized world.[4] By the turn of the century, 264 of the world's 414 cities with a million or more people will be located in the less-developed parts of the globe.[5] Africa, the world's poorest continent, alone will have more than 50 of these cities (compared to only 19 in 1980 and just 6 in 1950),[6] and by 2025 it will have an urban population three times that of North America (Camp, 1990:1). The number of million-plus cities in Asia will double by the turn of the century from 81 to 160 (McAuslan, 1985:127),

---

[2]Within the next decade, at least 65 countries (including 30 of Africa's 51 countries) will be completely dependent on food imports. Africa, for example, currently holds 28 of the world's 42 poorest countries and will experience a threefold population increase within the next 35 years. See *The Economist* (1990) and Crossette (1990).

[3]By the year 2000, for example, half the world's population will be urban—compared with 30 percent today and just 17 percent in 1950. See Rogers and Williamson (1982:1) and Rogers (1982:466, 486); see also McAuslan (1985:127). Although slightly different figures are cited, the same general pattern is identified in Yeung and Belisle (1988:99).

[4]Although demographic change and population growth have long been staples of fertility, health, economic, and sociological studies, their effects on international politics or their potential as catalysts for intranational and transnational conflict have not been scrutinized to the same degree. Exceptions are Chourchi (1983, 1974) and Sarkesian (1989).

[5]Rogers and Williamson (1982:1). Some 58 of the world's largest metropolitan areas, for example, are now located in developing countries. See Camp (1990:1).

[6]McAuslan (1985:127). Indeed, by 2025, Africa will have 36 cities of four million or more residents, with an average of nine million, more than greater London today. By contrast, 40 years ago, no African city between Johannesburg and Cairo had even one million inhabitants (*The Economist*, 1990).

and although less dramatic urban growth rates are projected for Latin America, by the year 2000 more than three-quarters of its population will live in urban areas (compared to 50 percent today), representing the highest proportion of urban dwellers on any continent (McAuslan, 1985:129; Regional Conflict Working Group, 1988:12; and Yeung and Belisle, 1988:100). Moreover, as fast as cities in the developing world are growing, the slums and shantytowns are growing twice as fast, thereby contributing to the uncontrolled geographical—as well as numerical—expansion of these urban centers.

Finally, the implications of population displacement go beyond the problems of urbanization. Refugees (who migrate across international borders) and internally displaced persons (who migrate within their own countries) frequently relocate without even a minimal amount of clothing, food, and shelter to places where, without assistance, they could not survive. They may carry diseases, expand existing or create new slums and shantytowns, and exacerbate racial, religious, and ethnic prejudices. They drain the local or national host government's limited resources for social services, infrastructural development, and policing, often creating resentment that can lead to violence. Unsurprisingly, perhaps, the world's poorest countries typically experience the heaviest flows of displaced persons. For instance, the average number of displaced people (including refugees and internally displaced people) for countries with a low per-capita gross domestic product (GDP) is 465,000, in contrast to the 222,000 mean for high per-capita GDP countries.

The Demographics of Future Conflict

The massive expansion of both the population and geographical dimensions of the developing world's urban centers will have a profound effect on both conventional and unconventional conflict. On the one hand, this radiating urbanization process—consuming increasingly large tracts of a country's territory and inevitably encompassing key lines of communication, transportation nodes, and road and rail links—will make it difficult in conventional warfare for ground forces to bypass or maneuver around cities as they have traditionally attempted and as warfighting doctrine mostly stresses. On the other hand, the proliferation of weapons—including small arms, machine guns, rocket-propelled grenades (RPGs), and plastic explosives, as well as weapons of mass destruction—throughout the developing world will facilitate the growth of insurgency and heighten the potential for other forms of political violence.

Conventional MOUT (Military Operations on Urban Terrain). Most traditional warfighting doctrine has stressed the desirability of avoiding combat in cities. As urban warfare is often intensive, protracted, and conducted among a surrounding civilian population, emphasis has long been given to avoiding urban areas whenever possible.[7]   However, combatants have a natural attraction to centers of political and economic activity as a means of controlling populations at large.   In addition, the massive urbanization described above not only increases the probability of urban warfare by sheer chance, but has related consequences that can themselves lead to conflict, including dissatisfaction that grows as city infrastructures prove increasingly incapable of supporting rapid influxes of people.

Because of the historical emphasis on avoiding urban combat, the U.S. military has not stressed MOUT in its doctrine, training, or equipping, and its capabilities for conventional operations on urban terrain are thus arguably inadequate to operate in this new threat environment.   Furthermore, military MOUT capabilities that do exist emphasize the U.S. advantage in massive firepower.   Little doctrine or training is therefore relevant to combat in the developing world's heavily populated urban areas, where strict rules of engagement are likely to limit the utility of a firepower advantage.   In this environment, the need for combined arms, artillery, snipers, and armor is paramount.   Tanks and armored personnel carriers, for example, can be invaluable in MOUT—provided they are defended by dismounted infantrymen.   Similarly, artillery can provide direct-fire support or be used more for psychological effect (see McLaurin et al., 1987).

Unconventional MOUT (Insurgency).   Urbanization in the developing world will also fundamentally alter the nature of insurgency.   As rural populations, uprooted by poverty, hunger, and conflict, continue to migrate to the cities, the guerrilla forces dependent upon them for food, information, concealment, and support will have no choice but to follow, adjusting their strategies and tactics along the way.   Thus, the future killing grounds of the developing world will not be the impenetrable forests or remote mountain areas where guerrilla wars have traditionally been fought, but increasingly the crowded slums in and around the less-developed world's burgeoning urban centers, whose residents will become inextricably enmeshed in insurgent-government conflict.

These conflicts will differ from the ultimately unsuccessful urban insurgencies conducted in Argentina, Bolivia, and Brazil in the 1960s, insofar as a variety of hospitable conditions enables today's guerrillas to better adapt their rural insurgency strategy to an urban environment.   Urban guerrillas have the same benefits and advantages that they enjoyed in rural areas: control over territory, the allegiance (whether voluntary or coerced) of a considerable part of a country's population, inaccessibility to security forces, and a reasonably secure base for operations around the heart of the government and its administrative and

---

[7]See, for example, O'Connell (1992); Dewar (1992); McLaurin, Jureidini, McDonald, and Sellers (1987); and Mahan (1983).

commercial infrastructure. They also have more opportunities for media coverage and international attention that would be unobtainable in isolated jungles or mountains.

Because of their warren-like alleys and unpaved roads, the slums have become as impregnable to security forces as a rural insurgent's jungle or forest base. The police are unable to enter these areas, much less control them. Urban insurgents in Lima today and in San Salvador during the late 1980s, for example, have been able to seize control of defined geographic areas in the band of slums and shantytowns ringing those cities, sometimes establishing shadow goverments that exercise a crude form of sovereignty and provide public services or scarce commodities while repulsing government efforts to reassert control over these so-called "liberated zones." The insurgents thus pursue a deliberate strategy to sever the government's authority over its urban centers and thereby weaken both its resolve to govern and its support from the people, the aim being to eventually take power, first in the cities and then in the rest of the country.

This phenomenon is no longer restricted to Latin America. As other regions of the less-developed world begin to sustain the high rates of urbanization that occurred in Latin America two or more decades ago, they too are experiencing the same—arguably inevitable—rise of urban insurgency. The renewed insurgency in Angola, for example, has been fought in and for that country's urban centers. The most vicious combat has taken place in the resource-rich cities of Huambo, Uige, Menongue, Kuito, and Luanda. Using a strategy of capturing some urban areas while bottling up government forces within others, the rebel organization UNITA has now effectively deprived the government of control in three-quarters of the country. Similarly, insurgents in Liberia have focused their efforts in the capital city of Monrovia, while guerrillas in Sierra Leone have battled the government repeatedly for the diamond-mining hub, Koidu. Shiite rebels in Afghanistan have brought their conflict with government troops into the heart of Kabul.

Even if insurgents choose not to base their operations in urban areas, they can nonetheless take advantage of urbanization. Rural-based insurgencies are finding cities increasingly attractive and lucrative targets. Whereas cities were once the culmination of a revolution, with the new proliferation of urban areas—and the inability of governments to defend them all—cities have become relatively simple targets that yield high dividends for low cost. Insurgent groups can disrupt energy and telecommunications facilities, draw international attention, demonstrate the government's inability to protect its people, and recruit from among the disaffected population. Thus, even the insurgencies that remain based in rural areas can take advantage of urbanization by increasing their reliance on urban terrorism.

Likely Impact on Military Operations Other Than War

Most MOUT operations in the post–Cold War era, however, are likely to be conducted in the "gray world" of OOTW, where the operational environment can be highly fluid and able to shift quickly from peace to conflict. The environment may also require the full range of OOTW missions, including peacekeeping, peace enforcement, disaster relief, and humanitarian assistance as well as counterinsurgency, counterterrorism, noncombatant evacuation, and nonproliferation operations. The problem for many U.S. military forces is that they are well versed in the missions at either end of the OOTW operational continuum—with skills in urban combat honed through conventional MOUT courses on the one hand and familiarity with disaster relief and humanitarian assistance on the other—but they are hampered by inexperience with the OOTW tasks falling somewhere in between, such as crowd control, riot duty, and other activities more akin to police work.

For example, traditional MOUT training has only recently—if at all—included any of the preceding tasks in the context of those activities doctrinally associated with OOTW, such as nation assistance, combating terrorism, peacekeeping operations, peace enforcement, support to domestic civil authorities, or counterinsurgency. Nor has that training typically been linked to noncombat missions or oriented to close cooperation with the variety of civilian government agencies or nongovernment humanitarian and relief organizations likely to be present in the OOTW environment.

Also, given the relatively small size of most typical OOTW deployments, units tasked with these missions (a light infantry unit, for example) may find themselves performing tasks and executing responsibilities that would otherwise fall to various special operations forces (such as Special Forces, Civil Affairs, and Psychological Operations personnel) or support units (such as Military Police) if sufficient personnel from such units are not available. Accordingly, given the dynamic operational environment inherent in most OOTW deployments, U.S. military forces will need to be trained to perform tasks across the OOTW operational continuum, including those usually performed by special or other support units.

Greater attention in both doctrine and training therefore needs to be paid to MOUT operations in the OOTW operational environment. Account must be taken of operations in densely populated, built-up areas; restrictive and specially imposed ROE (rules of engagement); responsibilities more akin to police than to traditional military operations; and work relationships with civilian government agencies and nongovernment humanitarian assistance and relief organizations. Moreover, while considerable attention is already given to training American light infantry in some specialized tasks such as MOUT, disaster relief, and noncombatant evacuation operations, the scope should be still broader. Light infantrymen in OOTW environments will be working with or taking on the responsibilities of Special Forces, Civil Affairs, Psychological Operations, and Military Police units, and should receive the requisite cross training or joint training. Finally, units designated for, or likely to be tasked with, OOTW need to be ready to make the best use of limited assets and specialized equipment in dynamic conflictual environments and also to function effectively without such assets and equipment if need be.

Although urban insurgent activities are usually restricted to sabotage, sniping, barricades, roadblocks, and terrorist or criminal acts, such activities cannot be easily checked, since counterinsurgent options in cities are severely circumscribed. In most cases it would be counterproductive to use massive firepower, indirect fire, or airpower in urban environments, given the difficulty of avoiding civilian casualties. Indeed, insurgents can deliberately conceal themselves within the population, trading the concealment of the jungle for the anonymity of crowds, emerging only to attack.

Given that urbanization and population growth in most developing countries are creating conditions that can lead to internal conflicts, U.S. forces likely to become involved (i.e., light infantry, SOF, MPs, etc.) should be schooled in the political and military requirements of successful OOTW.[8] They should be prepared to respond with appropriate measures in both the cities and the countryside. This will require a diversity of capabilities, as well as an appreciation for the causes of internal conflict and the political requirements for resolving it.

Urban OOTW requires a unique combination of the doctrine, training, and equipment appropriate for military operations on urban terrain, counterterrorism, and traditional counterinsurgency operations. On the one hand, troops must be prepared for the kind of urban offensive that took place in San Salvador in 1989, which required conventional combat skills tempered by stringent rules of engagement. On the other hand, effective use of intelligence, civic action, psychological operations (PSYOP), and population protection could perhaps prevent urban insurgency from developing to the point it did in San Salvador. Such activities must be supported by appropriate doctrine, training, and command-and-control arrangements, and must be undertaken in support of a broader political and legislative effort.

As they learn the specialized skills required by each environment (urban and rural), forces must also be trained to treat the civilian population with respect, so as to prevent popular alienation and to improve the conditions for gathering human intelligence. They may also have to coordinate police and military responsibilities with the civilian government's political countermeasures, if any, as well as efforts by other agencies.

---

[8]Hoffman and Taw (1991, 1992); Hoffman, Taw, and Arnold (1991); Mockaitis (1990); Beckett and Pimlott (1985); Paget (1967); and Thompson (1979).

These general observations concerning future requirements for American armed forces, given the massive population flows and urbanization unfolding throughout the world, are brought into sharp focus by the four case studies that follow. These case studies of past U.S. military OOTW illuminate through specific examples the critical operational requirements already created by these demographic changes. They also shed light on the range of capabilities and further adjustments in doctrine, training and equipment that the U.S. military will need to perform well in a highly fluid future operational environment.

THE CHANGING NATURE OF MILITARY MISSIONS: INVITATION VERSUS INTERVENTION

As discussed above, conflicts such as that in Somalia—characterized by humanitarian components, urban and rural combat, refugee movements, fractionated social structures, dilapidated or destroyed infrastructures, and fragile or nonexistent governments—are increasingly likely in the developing world, where exponential population growth, unprecedented rates of urbanization, and massive migration flows combine to create a volatile situation where governments cannot meet the needs of their people. Even when conflict does not arise, the marginal survival of a country's populace in such circumstances can easily be threatened by natural disaster, unexpected immigration flows, or even shifts in the international economy.

Where and when the United States will provide assistance or intervene is difficult to predict. U.S. interests in pursuing the drug war, for example, have brought U.S. military forces into Colombia, where they are currently involved in humanitarian assistance efforts. Concerns about migration flows led to the foreshortened deployment of U.S. armed forces to Haiti in 1993. Relations with Europe predicated sending U.S. troops to Macedonia as peacekeepers. And U.S. soldiers remain part of the multinational force (MNF) in the Sinai. Although the United States will probably proceed cautiously before involving itself in further conflicts or humanitarian crises in the developing world, the recently released Draft Presidential Directive does not preclude deploying U.S. forces for future unilateral or coalitional operations other than war.

The U.S. military must therefore be prepared for any such future operations other than war. Even though U.S. military doctrine, training, and equipment for these operations remain nascent, their development slowed by greater attention to (and funding for) more traditional conventional military requirements, lessons from similar operations in the past can help guide future efforts.

In the following pages, we will examine the lessons learned from the failed U.S. peacekeeping operation in Lebanon, the humanitarian assistance efforts in

Somalia, the direct intervention in Panama in 1989, and the disaster relief operation in Bangladesh. Lessons gleaned from these various OOTW can serve as guideposts in developing doctrine, training, and equipment for future efforts.

Peacekeeping and Mission Shifts: Lebanon and Somalia

Although some would argue that U.S. peacekeeping in Lebanon failed and U.S. humanitarian assistance in Somalia succeeded, the two efforts yield similar lessons for future operations. They were both multinational efforts; both evolved, respectively, from simple, well-meaning peacekeeping and humanitarian assistance to something more aggressive, costly, and far less neutral; and both took place in complex political environments riven with territorial claims and power struggles between longstanding factional rivals. Moreover, in both Beirut and Mogadishu, urbanization, population growth, and population migration compounded, and to some extent caused, the conflicts that arose and clearly affected the nature of the conflicts as they unfolded.

In Lebanon, for example, the conflict was based in and around Beirut, where Palestine Liberation Organization (PLO) fighters had set up operations specifically to take advantage of a more defensible—and hence offensively frustrating—urban environment. The migration of Palestinians into Lebanon and the establishment of refugee camps were causes of concern for both the Lebanese government and the Israelis, who worried that the PLO could operate freely out of the camps. The peacekeeping forces in Lebanon functioned in an almost entirely urban environment, dealt daily with issues related to the refugee camps and the Palestinians' migration, and thus found themselves in the middle of a volatile, densely populated operational environment.

Similarly in Somalia, cities became the hub of the confrontation between the country's rival warlords. Relief supplies were blocked and militiamen from the various contending factions controlled the streets from their "technicals" (trucks and jeeps mounted with machine guns). Thus, when the U.S. Marines first arrived in Somalia in December 1992, they had to stabilize the urban areas first before moving into the countryside. Throughout the American and UN operations, tensions and violence remained most prevalent in the cities, especially Mogadishu. Additionally, the peacekeepers conducted operations in heavily populated areas and helped control the flow of Somali refugees out of country, and they were involved in repatriating Somalis back into the country from neighboring states.

Lebanon.[9] U.S. military forces were deployed to Beirut alongside French, Italian, and, eventually, British troops between 1982 and 1984 as part of the First and Second Multinational Forces (MNF 1 and MNF 2). MNF 1 was a peacekeeping force, intended on one hand to prevent the Israeli Defense Force (IDF) and Christian Lebanese militia from further attacks against Palestinians in Lebanon, while on the other to supervise the withdrawal of the PLO from Beirut to Syria by sea and land. These efforts were meant to satisfy the competing demands of the Israelis, the Palestinians, the predominantly Christian Maronite government in Lebanon, Moslem militias, and the Syrians. Although MNF 1 apparently succeeded in its efforts—nearly two weeks ahead of its own four-week deadline—tensions quickly resurfaced upon the coalition's withdrawal. Syria allegedly sanctioned the September 14, 1982, assassination of Lebanese President Bashir Gemayel; the IDF entered West Beirut where Palestinian and other Moslem civilians lived; and the Christian Phalange militia, with alleged Israeli complicity and on the premise of ousting hidden PLO guerrillas, entered the Palestinian refugee camps in Sabra and Shatila, massacring hundreds of noncombatants.

The MNF coalition members hastily returned to Lebanon as MNF 2, with more and heavier military forces, although they were far outnumbered by the Sunni, Shiite, and Druze militiamen in the capital, and the Syrian and Israeli armies stationed around Beirut. MNF 2's mission remained peacekeeping. It established a presence and interposed itself between the warring parties. Yet the peacekeeping efforts were never completely neutral: the Lebanese Armed Forces (LAF) were involved with every aspect of the coalition effort, while contact with the Moslem militias and other contending factions involvement was far less institutionalized.

As the security situation in Lebanon continued to deteriorate, the MNF 2 coalition itself splintered. The Americans and the French committed themselves to support LAF attempts to restore and maintain order, thus unwittingly becoming partisan players in the conflict. Meanwhile, their relations with the Israelis and the Moslems continued to worsen. By contrast, the British and the Italians strove to remain more evenhanded in their dealings with the government and the Moslem militias, remaining effectively neutral and avoiding the complications and violence that were to follow.

Not surprisingly, the U.S. and French troops became inextricably identified with the Lebanese government, and were targeted in a series of deadly attacks by Moslem factions, beginning with the April 18, 1983, bombing of the American Embassy—which claimed 17 American and more than 40 Lebanese

---

[9]This section is in large part derived from research conducted by John Schmeidel, a RAND consultant.

lives—and culminating with the October 23, 1983, bombings of the French MNF encampment and American Marine barracks, which, in total, left three hundred dead. Four months later, the British, Italian, and American members of the MNF withdrew their forces from Lebanon. A month later, the French followed suit.

A number of lessons can be gleaned from MNF 2's experiences in Lebanon. The three most important issues relate specifically to multinational peacekeeping: neutrality among peacekeepers, the clarity and practicability of the mission, and the nature of the coalition arrangement.

MNF 2's rapid establishment precluded careful prior arrangements with the various parties to avoid the semblance or substance of bias: when the coalition included the LAF in the peacekeeping efforts, it relinquished neutrality from the outset.   Subsequent American and French decisions to support the Maronite government and military only exacerbated an existing problem. Without neutrality, the peacekeepers lost all legitimacy, and simply became participants in the conflict.

MNF 2's mission, too, was unclear. Even the force structure demonstrated the general confusion about MNF 2's objectives: although the heavy forces sent into the country were too aggressively oriented for peacekeeping, they were numerically insufficient to make a viable show of force against the welter of militia factions and massed troops either within or surrounding the city. Once the forces were in the country, MNF 2's mission changed quickly, but without official acknowledgment, from peacekeeping to a combination of counterinsurgency, nation assistance, and security assistance, with the coalition forces acting in support of the Christian government and armed forces. Indeed, U.S. Marine and Army units actually trained elite LAF units into a quick-reaction force. This shift in mission left U.S. forces in a precarious position: prepared and equipped for peacekeeping, they nonetheless became participants in the conflict, with all the attendant risks and none of the requisite planning or preparations.

On a more positive note, the multinational arrangement—in which each national contingent operated in parallel, within discrete and contiguous zones of responsibility, and with informal liaison between the forces—worked remarkably well. Though MNF 2's contingents did not always provide a united front, their efforts were not plagued by the language difficulties, political considerations, and logistical confusion that have affected similar UN operations.

Other, more general, tactical and operational lessons emerged from MNF 2, applicable to future OOTW activities. U.S. command and control (C^2), for example, was deeply stratified, leading to slow decisionmaking. In contrast, the British, French, and Italians established direct, real-time radio links with their cabinets and defense ministries back home, substantially speeding the decisionmaking process.

Another lesson involved the rules of engagement (ROE) followed by U.S. forces in MNF 2, which failed to evolve, much less keep pace, with the growing threat in Lebanon, leaving the Marines in Beirut insufficiently armed or ready for the hostilities that eventually engulfed them.

Also, the Marine Amphibious Units that provided troops for the U.S. contingent in MNF 2 did not have enough intelligence personnel, including translators. Moreover, the information gathered was not efficiently or effectively shared between the various U.S. agencies, nor passed in a timely manner to the tactical commanders on the ground in Beirut.

Finally, U.S. forces in Lebanon could have benefited from adopting some proven British tactics for peacetime operations on urban terrain: cooperating directly with civilian police and civil administrators in urban combat areas; deliberately using patrolling as a means of gathering intelligence by observation and contacts; and educating soldiers in ground-level negotiation skills and sensitizing them to the civilian population they would be interacting with.

Each of these operational and tactical lessons has applicability beyond multinational operations or peacekeeping. Future U.S. involvement in OOTW activities would therefore benefit from a close examination of the C^2, force structure, training, ROE, and intelligence efforts in MNF 2.

Somalia. U.S. involvement in Somalia began in 1992 as a strictly humanitarian effort. Operation Provide Relief (OPR) was a small, predominantly Air Force operation for lifting food and other assistance into the war-torn country from neighboring Kenya. While the United States conducted these aid lifts, the United Nations began its own peacekeeping efforts in Somalia (UNOSOM). Few countries signed on with the UN, although Pakistan sent 500 troops to serve as peacekeepers.

It soon became clear that the American and UN efforts were having little effect in ameliorating either the hunger or the conflict endemic to the country. Assistance packages were continually stolen, aid workers were harassed, and starvation in certain areas persisted. In December 1992, therefore, the United States launched a coalition effort under the operational control (OPCON) of the U.S.-led United Task Force (UNITAF). The U.S. component of the coalition effort was known as Operation Restore Hope (ORH). The mission of ORH, and UNITAF more generally, remained humanitarian, although with a larger security component than OPR had: secure ports and food distribution points, provide open and free passage of relief supplies, ensure security for relief convoys and operations, and otherwise assist the United Nations and non-government organizations (NGOs) in providing humanitarian relief under UN auspices (Freeman, Lampert, and Mims, 1993:64).

From the outset, a date was set for transferring control of the coalition forces from the United States to the UN, which would then consolidate, expand, and maintain security in Somalia to allow the process of humanitarian assistance, economic assistance, and political reconciliation to proceed.[10] On May 4, 1993, the transfer of control took place, and UNOSOM II superseded both UNOSOM I and UNITAF.

Although U.S. forces were supposed to withdraw following the transfer of control to UNOSOM II, a number of U.S. support units nonetheless remained in Somalia under UN operational control. Elements of the U.S. Army 10th Mountain Division (Light Infantry) also remained in the country, reorganized as a Quick Reaction Force (QRF) under the operational control of the U.S. Commander-in-Chief, Central Command (CINCCENT) (with a few narrowly defined exceptions, where they fell under the operational control of the UN Force Commander). These U.S. efforts during UNOSOM II are known as Operation Continue Hope.

Under the United Nations, the mission in Somalia continued to shift from humanitarian assistance to security. Tensions between the followers of Somali warlord Mohammed Farah Aideed and UN forces quickly increased, culminating in the June 5, 1993, ambush of a Pakistani convoy in Mogadishu, during which Aideed militiamen killed 24 Pakistani soldiers. Tensions continued unabated, and a month later the UN issued a call for the arrest of General Aideed. U.S. Rangers and other elite special forces arrived in Somalia in August and, on September 22, captured Osman Ato, Aideed's chief financier. Less than two weeks later, on October 3, 18 Americans were killed and 84 wounded when an attempt to capture more of Aideed's top officials went tragically awry.[11]

Reevaluation of American policy in Somalia began immediately. Four days after the incident, President Clinton canceled the hunt for Aideed and his followers, ordered the deployment of 1700 additional Army troops to Somalia and the offshore emplacement of two amphibious groups with 3600 Marines, and set a March 31, 1994, deadline for the complete withdrawal of U.S. forces from Somalia.

The patchwork of military efforts in Somalia yields valuable lessons for future OOTW. In particular, the lessons relating specifically to multinational peacekeeping closely parallel and reinforce those from Lebanon. For example, problems arose in Somalia regarding neutrality in peacekeeping and the clarity and practicability of the mission. Furthermore, whereas coalition arrangement in Lebanon was relatively effective and practicable, the arrangements in Somalia were much more problematic, providing a useful contrast for analysis.

UNOSOM II lost all semblance of neutrality when the UN criminalized Aideed and called for his capture. At that point, the UN forces simply became another faction in the conflict, just as U.S. and French forces had in Lebanon ten years before. Even though they continued to maintain the pretense of

---

[10]UNOSOM II briefing, 1993.

[11]For more discussion of the failed raid, see Atkinson (1994a,b).

neutrality, the UN forces were now unquestionably a faction in the conflict and thus became perceived as legitimate targets for Aideed's militia. Yet those forces had been deployed for only a limited security mission, and were neither prepared nor equipped for a more aggressive stance. As in Lebanon, the forces in Somalia thus found themselves in a dangerous and frustrating situation: their ROE remained limited, they were armed and equipped for peacekeeping, but the Somali militias clearly considered them opposition forces.

This dilemma was exacerbated by the changing mission over the course of operations in Somalia. However, although the mission was said to "creep"— and did to some extent during ORH at the operational level, when bored U.S. forces began to conduct limited nation assistance and civic action in nearby villages—the mission shift was in fact far more deliberate than that at the strategic level. The political intent to adjust the mission over time from strict humanitarian support to more security tasks and greater nation assistance activities existed from the moment the decision was made (prior to ORH) to conduct—under UNOSOM II—a broader security and nation assistance operation in the interests of political reconciliation and eventual Somali elections.[12] The political intent, however, remained garbed in the language of peace operations, and was never translated into explicit military requirements or plans. Thus, as mentioned above, UNOSOM II forces were still ostensibly in Somalia to conduct peacekeeping operations, and were equipped, staffed, and prepared for that mission rather than the more aggressive one that emerged.

In addition, the coalition arrangements in Somalia actually exacerbated and were accentuated by the problems with neutrality and mission shift. Under both UNITAF and UNOSOM II, coalition forces yielded their operational control to a central command, led by the United States and United Nations, respectively. Although the forces cooperated effectively under UNITAF, their mission was far clearer and less controversial than it would be under UNOSOM II. During UNOSOM II, as operations became more dangerous and the mission more controversial, coalition forces increasingly began to turn to their national commands for guidance rather than to the UN, and they frequently refused or demanded revisions to UN orders. Lacking adequate contingency plans for such situations, planned UN operations thus often had to be canceled or postponed. Also, as the preferences and concerns of different national contingents surfaced in response to the mission changes, any semblance of a united UN front vanished.

Other operational and tactical problems surfaced during ORH and UNOSOM II. Communications problems between the contingents, owing to

---

[12]At one point, the United Nations actually planned to end UNOSOM II in March 1995 with general elections in Somalia ("Somalia Pullout Date Set," *The New York Times*, September 23, 1993).

incompatible equipment and language differences, slowed planning and made combined operations more difficult and dangerous. Widely divergent doctrine, training, and general practices frequently meant that combined operations had to be geared to the lowest capability rather than the highest. U.S. forces could not use tear gas in riot control, for example, until the United States donated gas masks to the UN for distribution to other coalition members in Somalia; also, although the United States uses air support in its ground operations, many of its coalition partners in Somalia were unfamiliar with such operations, limiting its utility and use. Coalition members also developed different relations with the Somalis, who learned to distinguish between contingents and respond accordingly. The June 5 attack, for instance, deliberately targeted the Pakistanis, one of the most aggressive national contingents.

U.S.-specific lessons emerged from Somalia as well: human intelligence (HUMINT) was insufficient prior to ORH and was difficult to cultivate given the dearth of U.S. military or intelligence personnel proficient in Somali languages or knowledgeable about the Somali culture. The rapid development of links with Somali scholars in the United States and Somalia would have been helpful. Maps, too, were outdated and depicted Somalia's vast expanses at useless scales for urban combat. Too few special operations forces, especially Civil Affairs and Psychological Operations personnel, were sent to Somalia. Uniformed troops therefore had to take up the slack and perform civil affairs duties. There were also far too few liaison officers to interact with the various nongovernment organizations, local civilians, and other national contingents in Somalia, so uniformed personnel were tasked with that responsibility as well. Had hostilities broken out under UNITAF, there clearly would not have been sufficient surplus personnel to perform these tasks, as the fire support and other support personnel temporarily assigned to such duties would immediately have had to resume their primary responsibilities. In the future, accordingly, similar operations will need to be staffed with greater numbers of liaison and SOF personnel. Finally, the U.S. military would have benefited from better and more standardized rules for command and control of U.S. forces in coalition activities. Had the lines of command and control been clearer in Somalia, for example, the October 3 debacle with the Rangers might have been avoided. As it was, because separate chains of command and control had been established for the Rangers and the QRF, the QRF was not aware it might be needed to support the Rangers' operation and was therefore unavailable when the contingency arose.[13]

Again, as in the case of Lebanon, the practical lessons learned in Somalia have relevance beyond multinational peacekeeping operations to a range of fu-

---

[13]From interviews with 10th Mountain Division (Light Infantry) personnel deployed home from Somalia, Fort Drum, August 1993.

ture OOTW activity. Where the lessons are redundant, their validity is reinforced; valuable lessons can also be drawn, however, when different approaches to the same objective yielded different results, as in the case of C² or coalitional arrangements.

Intervention: Operation Just Cause in Panama

The U.S. operation in Panama provides a useful comparison to the operations in Lebanon and Somalia, insofar as the military objectives were clearly established from the outset and (despite rhetoric to the contrary) closely matched the Bush administration's political goals. The mission was clear, and success would be easily recognizable. The emphasis in the operation was on a traditional U.S. military strength: firepower. And although some operations other than war were planned for the postcombat phase of the operation, they were not emphasized in either planning or preparation. Nonetheless, the conflict in Panama shared characteristics with the conflicts in Lebanon and Somalia insofar as the operations conducted there were almost entirely urban and undertaken in heavily populated areas. Indeed, because the U.S. objectives included decapitating the Panamanian Defense Force (PDF), capturing Panamanian leader Manuel Noriega, and preserving the country's infrastructure, operations were necessarily conducted on urban terrain, where the PDF was based and where most of the country's key infrastructure is located. Issues of refugee flow and presence were also important in Panama City, where the U.S. forces had to control population movement and limit civilian casualties. Thus, in Panama, as in Lebanon and Somalia, population growth, migration, and urbanization were each critical factors in shaping the nature of the conflict.

The U.S. intervention in Panama, Operation Just Cause (OJC), followed more than a year of increasing animosity between the United States and Noriega. When U.S. forces finally invaded the small country, their mission was to protect American lives, assist the democratically elected government that Noriega had denied power to, seize and arrest Noriega (who had been indicted in the United States for drug trafficking), and defend the integrity of U.S. rights under the Panama Canal treaties.[14] The United States achieved all these objectives: the PDF was dismantled after the attack and neutralized; during the operation, U.S. forces swore in the Endara government, whose victory in the May 1989 election had been annulled by Noriega; Noriega himself was eventually caught, brought to the United States, tried, and imprisoned; and

---

[14]From excerpts of a speech by U.S. Secretary of State James Baker, December 20, 1989, reported in *Latin American Weekly Report*, WR-90-1, 1990, p. 2.

U.S. concerns about control over the Panama Canal reverting in the year 2000 to an unsavory Panamanian government were arguably allayed.

Operation Just Cause was strictly a unilateral intervention to pursue American political and strategic objectives, and it had only a limited pretense of humanitarian objectives. Yet the operation could almost be considered fortuitous, in that it afforded the United States the opportunity to conduct OOTW under extremely advantageous circumstances. The errors and miscues that did take place were to be expected: OJC represented a significant departure from both the conventional battlefield warfare that U.S. forces have trained for since the end of World War II and the unconventional jungle operations of the Vietnam War. Indeed, it was most similar to the U.S. stability and peace operations in the Dominican Republic (1965–1966) and Grenada (1983).

OJC was nonetheless unique: planning and operations were fully integrated across all four services; much of the operation was conducted on urban terrain; a large number (the largest number since Vietnam, but surpassed during Desert Shield) of U.S.-based forces were rapidly deployed; special operations forces played a highly visible and critical role in the operation; rules of engagement were uncommonly restrictive; soldiers were expected to apply minimum use of force; indirect fire and aerial bombing were limited; surgical strikes were necessary; and the *preservation* and defense of infrastructure and public utilities were key objectives.

These characteristics are also common to recent OOTW in Somalia, Bosnia, Iraq (among the Kurds), and Bangladesh. At the same time, however, OJC was also simpler than subsequent military operations other than war in Kuwait, Iraq, Bangladesh, Bosnia, and Somalia. Because it was a unilateral effort, no coalition issues or problems complicated or slowed U.S. operations. The communications, logistics, planning, and command-and-control issues that arise in multinational operations never surfaced during OJC. Nor did the United States have to coordinate its efforts with nongovernment organizations (NGOs) or humanitarian relief organizations (HROs). As recent events attest, future U.S. OOTW operations are unlikely to be unilateral, and as much as they will benefit from both coalition and NGO/HRO support, Desert Storm and Somalia demonstrate that U.S. forces will also have to adjust training and doctrine to accommodate such cooperation.

Moreover, in Operation Just Cause, U.S. armed forces outnumbered the PDF by more than two to one. The Panamanian military was also a known quantity to its American counterparts, who had trained it and were consequently well versed in its doctrine, skills, and capabilities. Nor did the U.S. military face angry crowds, violent uprisings, or even passive popular resistance: the people of Panama welcomed the Americans and provided little, if any, support to the PDF. Communication with both the public and the PDF was not a problem, because many members of the U.S. military speak Spanish as a first or second language. Finally, tension between the United States and Panama had escalated for more than a year, allowing sufficient time for planning and practicing an operation such as Just Cause. Each of these factors contributed to the ease and speed with which the PDF was defeated and U.S. military objectives met.

Despite all these unique advantages, OJC offers a number of wider, practical lessons for application in current and future OOTW. One very good example involves postcombat stability operations and the role of civilian agencies in OOTW. Planning was conducted separately for conventional offensive operations, special operations, and stability and civil-military operations. This led to problems during OJC as it transitioned from the combat phase to posthostilities stability operations, when insufficient numbers of Civil Affairs personnel were available to assume responsibility in the operation's wake. There was also very little civilian input into planning the stability phase of OJC. Yet because military planners were not always aware of what civilian agencies could realistically be expected to step in and do (especially with little advance notice), both military personnel and civilians were overwhelmed with actual postcombat requirements. Coordination and cooperation between the military and civilian agencies requires improvement for OOTW in which civilians may be expected to assume responsibility for such diverse tasks as assisting with the demobilization of militaries, reestablishing or building infrastructure, setting up or reconfiguring judiciaries or electoral systems, and assisting in the procurement and distribution of humanitarian aid.

OJC also demonstrated that U.S. military training in military operations on urban terrain was inadequate and that more units needed to include MOUT in their mission essential task lists (METLs). Intelligence also was a problem: electronic intelligence, though essential in conventional battlefield warfare, is often irrelevant in OOTW, and must be supplemented by human intelligence. The military and CIA must therefore develop arrangements allowing greater military access to the civilian intelligence community's HUMINT. Efforts to streamline intelligence in joint operations also must not overlook unit-specific needs and therefore should take particular care to maximize use of special operations forces by employing them in the specialized tasks for which they are trained. Equipment was another issue, as OJC clearly demonstrated the special requirements of MOUT. Advancements in technology applicable to OOTW have been made since 1989, but the military's priority in research and development remains conventional weaponry and materiel.

Perhaps the most interesting thing about OJC in the context of OOTW, however, is that it demonstrates the value of a clear and sustainable mission (especially in contrast to operations in Lebanon and Somalia), while at the same time illustrating precisely the shortfalls in the U.S. military's ability to plan or prepare for operations other than war. On the one hand, Operation Just Cause was an unqualified success: the planning, C^2, force structure, equipment, and logistics were ideal for the operation, and all of the mission objectives were met. On the other hand, planning for the postcombat phase was deemphasized and underfunded, with no civilian input, creating problems in the transition from combat to stability operations and only partial success in reconstruction and stability efforts. Clearly, this has implications for operations in fluid environments, where the need to adapt U.S. efforts swiftly to changes from combat to noncombat (or vice versa) might be required.

Disaster Relief and Humanitarian Assistance: Operation Sea Angel in Bangladesh[15]

To complete the circle of comparisons, a case study of a pure and simple noncombat effort—in this case, disaster relief—is extremely useful. At one end of the scale is OJC: a straightforward conventional military intervention, with some characteristics of OOTW. In the middle lie MNF 2 and the operations in Somalia: fluid operations with shifting missions, each of which began as a purely humanitarian effort but—in the face of conflict and changing political goals—became much more aggressive and complicated operations. And finally, Operation Sea Angel (OSA) in Bangladesh lies at the other end: a straightforward humanitarian OOTW in a benign and stable environment. Again, however, the demographic trends that shaped the crises in Lebanon, Somalia, and Panama also affected OSA. Indeed, the government's inability to respond adequately in the aftermath of a natural disaster was due in large part to the country's limited resources and relatively huge population.

When Cyclone Marian struck Bangladesh on April 29–30, 1991, much of the country's infrastructure was destroyed or damaged. Transportation became nearly impossible, ships sank and blocked the port, water supplies were disrupted, millions were left homeless, over a million cattle died, and crops on tens of thousands of acres were completely wiped out. The fledgling civilian government was young, inexperienced, poor, and yet had to avoid any appearance of weakness or incompetence.

The United States responded within 10 days with practical emergency assistance and short-term recovery operations. A U.S. Contingency Joint Task Force (CJTF) was established to run OSA. The bulk of the U.S. force in Bangladesh was from Amphibious Group 3 and the 5th Marine Expeditionary Brigade (5th MEB), supplemented by Army and Air Force elements (in

---

[15]For a more detailed discussion of OSA, see McCarthy (1994:4–6), from which this section is heavily drawn.

particular, a special operations forces Damage Assistance Relief Team—DART—from Okinawa).

The operation was not unilateral: British, French, Japanese, and Pakistani units acceded their own operational control to the CJTF, and Indian and Chinese forces, while not officially OPCON to the CJTF, nonetheless worked closely with the task force to deliver aid. The CJTF also cooperated effectively with the nongovernment organizations in Bangladesh, providing them with transportation and communication assets and acting as a liaison between them and the government of Bangladesh (with which they had longstanding poor relations). The NGOs, in return, helped identify the regions in greatest need, procured supplies, ran reconstruction programs, and generally operated efficiently and competently in providing a full range of assistance.

CJTF's mission in Bangladesh was to provide command, control, and coordination in support of humanitarian assistance efforts in the country. U.S. forces helped distribute food, water, and medicine, conducted area assessments, established secure communications between outlying areas, and offered limited medical assistance.

Operation Sea Angel is unique among the cases discussed in this paper, insofar as it began and in fact concluded as a purely humanitarian mission. Yet in other aspects, it is very similar to other OOTW: it was a joint U.S. operation with heavy SOF involvement; it was a multinational effort; and nongovernment organizations played a large role in the disaster relief effort.

Nonetheless, the differences, not the similarities, between OSA and other OOTW determined the success of the operation. Three factors in particular warrant discussion: the disaster relief efforts took place in a benign environment; the government of Bangladesh was intentionally left in charge, and transition of the operation to the government began three weeks after the start of OSA, exactly as planned; and neither mission creep nor mission shift took place.

Perhaps the most important factor in the operation's quick success was the absence of conflict. U.S. forces were able to work with the Bangladesh government, rather than trying to function in either a vacuum or an anarchical situation like Somalia's. Accordingly, they faced no threat, and did not have to worry about force protection, combat, or rules of engagement. The populace was supportive of the U.S. efforts and extremely cooperative. The nongovernment organizations, for the most part, were also supportive and cooperative—in direct contrast to the often problematical military-NGO relations in Somalia, where NGOs were critical of the military's role and actions in the country. With no controversy or concern about threats or mission objectives, national contingents were readily prepared to accede their operational control to the U.S. task force, thus simplifying command and control and coordination. Finally, the U.S. forces were in Bangladesh simply to clean up after a

244 New Challenges for Defense Planning

natural disaster; they were not involved at all in the politics of the country, and their limited disaster-relief activities were unlikely to spark political controversy.

A second and perhaps equally important factor in the success of OSA was that U.S. forces in Bangladesh very deliberately did not exceed their mandate, difficult as it sometimes was for troops to limit their assistance in the face of the country's overwhelming poverty and need. Offshore basing, for example, allowed a minimum U.S. "presence" in the country, thus helping the government to retain relatively greater visibility in the relief operations.[16] Restoration of the country's infrastructure was not part of the mission, nor was nation assistance or civic action; these were left to the Bangladesh government and the NGOs. Where construction or reconstruction took place, things were built back to previous standards, not to U.S. standards. And throughout the operation, Lieutenant General Stackpole, the CJTF commander, made a point of not overstating what U.S. forces would do, so as to maintain realistic expectations among the Bengalis, who would have to assume full responsibility for operations once the Americans withdrew. OSA is thus a positive example of how careful definition of, and adherence to, a mission can facilitate an operation. U.S. forces could easily have become embroiled in trying to provide nation assistance to Bangladesh, but they carefully limited their involvement to disaster relief from the outset.

Other lessons for application in future OOTW can be drawn from Operation Sea Angel. For example, the concept of a two-tiered command-and-control system was implemented during the operation for the first time, and worked extremely well. Under the two-tiered system, built around existing commanders and their staff, the chain of command (especially at the higher levels) was clearly defined, and Lieutenant General Stackpole was able to add or delete units fairly rapidly. Coordination and cooperation between the military and local government officials and NGOs was also a critical factor in the success of the operation and depended, in part, on the military's self-imposed limitations. Each agency worked to its comparative strength, and the military, far from interfering, coordinated its own activities to complement those of the other agencies.

Of course, OSA had its problems. Resupply lines were established late, and many parts requested simply never arrived in the country. Some of the units involved in the operation did not have standard operating procedures (SOPs) for disaster relief/humanitarian assistance and therefore failed to anticipate some logistical and communications problems. Participating aviation units, for example, did not develop load plans and lists of equipment and personnel until

---

[16]Sea basing also helped U.S. forces avoid problems related to health risks, lack of infrastructure, and force protection.

the day the unit received its alert notification. Intelligence and maps, as in other OOTW, were insufficient and inadequate in OSA. Finally, communications were a significant problem throughout the operation, with links required between CINCPAC (Hawaii), ships anchored offshore, two major regional airfields, the Main and Forward task force headquarters, helicopter landing zone teams, NGOs, and the DARTs. Satellite and SOF communications networks were helpful, but they quickly became overloaded. The situation improved only after the 4th Combat Communications Group arrived on May 16. Even then, air-to-ground communications remained problematic, because Marine aircraft did not have a VHF (AM) radio, which many foreign countries, including Bangladesh, use for aircraft control. Nor was all USMC and Navy communications equipment compatible, further exacerbating the problem.

Summary

Each of the brief case studies above—representing peace operations, direct intervention, and disaster relief—demonstrates the U.S. military's lack of familiarity with OOTW in general and OOTW requirements more specifically. The cases also provide practical tactical and operational lessons applicable to the range of OOTW missions. These lessons can help the U.S. military in its nascent efforts to adapt doctrine, training, equipping, and planning to take these requirements into account.

However, it is perhaps more instructive to note how these cases demonstrate the distinction between straightforward operations conducted in easily identifiable operational environments and more flexible operations conducted in fluid situations with the potential to shift from peace to conflict with little warning. Although OJC and OSA were respectively straightforward combat and noncombat operations, they both benefited from well-articulated political and military goals and objectives—which translated into clear and steadfast missions—that were carried out in well-defined and easily gauged operational environments: Panama was clearly conflictual[17] and Bangladesh was clearly benign. In contrast, the operations in Lebanon and Somalia both began as humanitarian efforts, but the missions could not be as clearly defined in the absence of straightforward political objectives or stable operational environments. Moreover, political rhetoric was often inconsonant with the actual political

---

[17]It is true that the operational environment in Panama was not typically conventional. Yet, strict ROEs and concerns about collateral damage notwithstanding, planners knew that U.S. forces needed to be able to defend themselves and their mission, and could plan accordingly. In other words, planners knew the threats posed by the environment for which they had to equip and prepare the forces.

goals—but rhetoric nonetheless still often drives military planning. Planners, accordingly, could not adequately select, prepare, or equip forces for operations. In both cases, forces found themselves in much more threatening situations than they anticipated.

This distinction has implications for every aspect of planning for future U.S. military involvement in operations other than war, from C^2 to intelligence efforts to force mix. Military planners already know how to prepare for either end of the OOTW continuum—OJC and OSA—but they must nonetheless reevaluate planning and preparation for less clear-cut efforts in the changeable OOTW operational environment that is often neither strictly peace nor strictly war.

CONCLUSION AND RECOMMENDATIONS

The United States is seeking to adapt to the "new world order" and to move from a national strategy of containment to one of collective engagement (i.e., involving the world community in such transnational issues as the environment, drug enforcement, economic development, democratization, humanitarian relief, and conflict resolution). The changing landscape of population distribution throughout the less-developed world and the likely urban cynosure of future conflict in these regions may require changes in U.S. military training, doctrine, and equipment.

The history of U.S. and multinational military efforts in peacekeeping, peace enforcement, urban operations, disaster relief, humanitarian assistance, humanitarian intervention, and urban warfare seems to show that although the United States is capable of succeeding in some operations other than war, most such operations suit neither its culture nor its military.

The United States seems best able to involve itself in operations other than war when those operations have clearly defined goals and endpoints, can be relatively quickly achieved, are likely to have limited loss of American soldiers' lives, and are not intended to resolve any longstanding social, political, or economic issues. For example, the U.S. military has proven adept at disaster relief, as Operation Sea Angel in Bangladesh has shown. Disaster relief requires no combat or warfighting equipment, and it is carried out by light forces focused on extensive communication and cooperation with local civilian officials and humanitarian organizations. The United States has also proven itself very capable at direct intervention, the form of conventional warfighting that it is most likely to undertake in the less-developed world in the post–Cold War period. Direct intervention requires not just combat but massive firepower and maximum force, extensive planning and coordination, a mix of heavy and light forces, warfighting materiel, rapid deployment, signal and human intelligence, force protection, and a myriad of other requirements.

However, U.S. forces are not ideally prepared to operate in the gray area between these two extremes, i.e., more urban, less conventional conflict environments. If ever they are called upon to do so, their mission must be based on a solid understanding of the conflict environment and it must be clearly defined and delimited from the outset. Otherwise, U.S. forces may be sent to resolve a simple problem and become engaged in the treacherous causes underlying it. This was true in Beirut in 1983, and it was equally true in Somalia in 1992. Moreover, strictly defined and limited missions are of great importance given the U.S. public's reluctance to become militarily involved in operations other than war unless they directly affect U.S. interests, pose little or no threat to U.S. soldiers, are of short duration, and are relatively easily achieved. Peace enforcement, peacekeeping, humanitarian intervention, and urban counterinsurgency are thus questionable missions for U.S. forces

Faced with similar dilemmas in the past, the United Nations learned how to sidestep overwhelming, longstanding problems while helping resolve conflicts. Peacekeeping evolved precisely because it allowed this kind of flexibility. UN forces did not have to engage combatants to quell them—indeed, they avoided such direct involvement. Yet this solution requires that peacekeepers accept long-term, perhaps indefinite, operations (such as on Cyprus since 1964), which is an unpalatable option for U.S. forces. The one time UN peacekeepers did become actively involved in the conflict around them (the 1960 operation in the Congo), they were immediately considered a faction and their mission ended disastrously—much like the U.S. mission in Beirut 20 years later.

Although both the U.S. public and the U.S. military are reluctant to participate in OOTW, such involvement may be unavoidable. The demographic pressures in the developing world will inevitably lead to conflicts, some of which can threaten U.S. interests. Although the United States may avoid future humanitarian interventions, other concerns may well motivate U.S. involvement. Massive population flows into the United States from beleaguered countries, conflict within or between countries with nuclear weapons or other weapons of mass destruction, or increased control of a country by drug traffickers could be sufficient cause for U.S. participation in urban, unconventional conflict.

BIBLIOGRAPHY

Atkinson, Rick (1994a), "Night of a Thousand Casualties," *Washington Post*, January 31.

———— (1994b), "The Raid That Went Awry," *Washington Post*, January 30.

Beckett, Ian, and John Pimlott (eds.) (1985), *Armed Forces and Modern Counter-Insurgency*, St. Martin's Press, New York.

Camp, Sharon (1990), *Cities: Life in the World's 100 Largest Metropolitan Areas*, Population Crisis Committee, Washington, D.C.

Chourchi, Nazli (1974), *Population Dynamics and International Violence: Propositions, Insights and Evidence*, Lexington Books, Lexington, MA.

———— (1983), *Population and Conflict: New Dimension of Population Dynamics*, United Nations Fund for Population Activities, Policy Development Studies Number 8, New York.

Cowell, Alan (1990), "Water Rights: Plenty of Mud to Sling," *The New York Times*, February 7.

Crossette, Barbara (1990), "The 42 Poorest Nations Plan a Campaign for Help," *The New York Times*, February 12.

Dewar, Colonel Michael (1992), *War in the Streets: The Story of Urban Combat from Calais to Khafji*, David & Charles, Newton Abott, Devon. Distributed by Defense Technical Information Center, Cameron Station, Alexandria, VA.

The Economist (1990), "Squeezing in the Next Five Billion," January 20.

Foreign Report (1989), "Terrorism and Water in Turkey," No. 2086, November 2.

———— (1990), "Quaddafi Takes to Water," No. 2097, February 1.

Freeman, Waldo D., Robert B. Lampert, and Jason D. Mims (1993), "Operation Restore Hope: A U.S. CENTCOM Perspective," *Military Review*, September.

Green, Marshall (1989), *Population Pressures: Threat to Democracy*, Population Crisis Committee, Washington, D.C.

Haberman, Clyde (1990), "Dam Is Watering Hope of New Fertile Crescent," *The New York Times*, March 30.

Hoffman, Bruce, and Jennifer Morrison Taw (1991), *Defense Policy and Low-Intensity Conflict: The Development of Britain's "Small Wars" Doctrine During the 1950s*, RAND, Santa Monica, CA.

———— (1992), *A Strategic Framework for Countering Terrorism and Insurgency*, RAND, Santa Monica, CA.

Hoffman, Bruce, Jennifer M. Taw, and David Arnold (1991), *Lessons for Contemporary Counterinsurgencies: The Rhodesian Experience*, RAND, Santa Monica, CA.

Latimer, John C. (1985), *Considerations for Operations on Urban Terrain by Light Forces*, Command and General Staff College, Fort Leavenworth, KS. Distributed by Defense Technical Information Center, Cameron Station, Alexandria, VA.

Mahan, John J. (1983), *MOUT: The Quiet Imperative*, U.S. Army War College, Carlisle Barracks, PA.   Distributed by Defense Technical Information Center, Cameron Station, Alexandria, VA.

McAuslan, Patrick (1985), *Urban Land and Shelter for the Poor*, International Institute for Environment and Development, London.

McCarthy, Paul A. (1994), *Operation Sea Angel: A Case Study*, RAND, Santa Monica, CA.

McLaurin, R.D., Paul A. Jureidini, David S. McDonald, and Kurt J. Sellers (1987), *Modern Experience in City Combat*, U.S. Army Human Engineering Laboratory, Aberdeen Proving Ground, MD.   Distributed by Defense Technical Information Center, Cameron Station, Alexandria, VA.

Mockaitis, Thomas R. (1990), *British Counterinsurgency, 1919–1960*, St. Martin's Press, New York.

O'Connell, Lieutenant Commander James W. (1992), *Is the United States Prepared to Conduct Military Operations on Urbanized Terrain?* Naval War College, Newport, RI.   Distributed by Defense Technical Information Center, Cameron Station, Alexandria, VA.

Paget, Julian (1967), *Counter-Insurgency Campaigning*, Faber & Faber, London.

Regional Conflict Working Group (1988), *Supporting U.S. Strategy for Third World Conflict*, report submitted to the Commission on Integrated Long-Term Strategy, the Pentagon, Washington, D.C.

Reiss, David W., et al. (1983), *Survey of Current Doctrine, Training, and Special Considerations for Military Operations on Urbanized Terrain (MOUT)*,   U.S. Army Research Institute for the Behavioral and Social Sciences, Fort Benning, GA.   Distributed by Defense Technical Information Center, Cameron Station, Alexandria, VA.

Richards, Charles (1990), "Conflict Over Water Threatens Near East," *The Independent*, London, November 10.

Rogers, Andrei (1982), "Sources of Urban Population Growth and Urbanization, 1950–2000:   A Demographic Accounting," in Rogers and Williamson (eds.), *Urbanization and Development in the Third World*, University of Chicago Press, Chicago.

Rogers, Andrei, and Jeffrey G. Williamson (1982), "Migration, Urbanization, and Third World Development: An Overview," in Rogers and Williamson (eds.), *Urbanization and Development in the Third World*, University of Chicago Press, Chicago.

Sarkesian, Sam C. (1989), "The Demographic Component of Strategy," *Survival*, International Institute for Strategic Studies, London.

Thompson, Sir Robert G. K. (1979), "Regular Armies and Insurgency," in Haycock (ed.), *Regular Armies and Insurgencies*, Croom Helm, London.

U.S. Army (1993), *Operations*, Army Field Manual, Washington, D.C.

Yeung, Yue-man, and Francois Belisle (1988), "Third World Urban Development: Agency Responses with Particular Reference to IDRC," in David Drakakis-Smith (ed.), *Urbanisation in the Developing World*, Routledge, London.

Chapter 10

PRIORITIES FOR BALLISTIC MISSILE DEFENSE

Russ Shaver

This paper discusses how the United States may wish to approach programs for ballistic missile defenses during the next ten years. It starts by summarizing the history of strategic defense, particularly ballistic missile defense (BMD). It then turns to the changing international situation, with special emphasis on the proliferation of weapons of mass destruction and ballistic missile systems. These threats are cause for serious concern—for U.S. troops that might be employed overseas and for friendly nations neighbored by threatening countries. The paper next discusses options for theater ballistic missile defense (TMD). It emphasizes the importance of pressing forward with development of such defenses as well as their limits. The paper then turns to defense of the United States and what would be required to protect the country against a variety of threats such as unauthorized attacks from Russia or other major nuclear states, or from small numbers of ballistic missiles launched from Third World countries. In contemplating national (and global) missile defenses as something that might eventually be deployed cooperatively, the paper considers implications for nuclear stability in the context of START treaties. Finally, the paper expands the discussion and addresses the central underlying issue: What role should ballistic missile defenses have in our overall national security strategy? Because the answer appears to be that "it depends on how the world develops," the paper ends by suggesting a series of programmatic and other actions that would establish TMD-related priorities in the near term, but provide important hedges for the mid and long term that would permit future national and global missile defenses.

INTRODUCTION

Early in the Clinton administration, as part of reductions in DoD's budget, it was decided to reduce the funding available for ballistic missile defense (BMD) from the planned expenditure of $39 billion over a five-year period to $18 billion. This very sharp reduction has important implications for the future of BMD, raising questions about the appropriate balance across the various goals that Congress set for BMD in the Missile Defense Act of 1991.[1] The

---

[1] The MDA mandated a program that would (1) assure early deployment of a limited national military defense that would be highly effective but consistent with the

question of priorities was addressed in Secretary Aspin's Bottom-Up Review (BUR). While the BUR essentially codified the priorities already in place, placing first priority on theater missile defense (TMD), with national missile defense (NMD) a distant second, the funding tied to these priorities was far from balanced. The result was a TMD budget still two-thirds of that planned by the Bush administration, but a budget for NMD only one-fifth of its previously planned amount. Other activities, e.g., various technology efforts, were similarly affected.

Ironically, this shift in program balance and funding levels comes after a decade of prodigious BMD-related research and development focused primarily on NMD, i.e., on protection of the United States. This decade of research appears to have placed the United States in the position of having the technical capability to field an effective defense against sizable, albeit limited, ballistic missile attacks.[2] While the shift toward focusing the research on TMD began several years before the Clinton administration took office, and was well in place in January 1993, the effort on NMD was at that time still substantial, with planned initial deployment dates within about a decade. At BUR support levels, it is no longer clear when an initial limited NMD might be deployed.

The focus on TMD is certainly justified by current international events. And it is difficult to argue that budget priorities for DoD don't demand sharply reduced budgets for BMD in general. Is the issue therefore resolved? A central thesis of this paper is that interest in (and even demand for) NMD may well increase in the future as the result of events that seem very hypothetical today. It follows then that DoD's BMD programs should strike a balance between focusing budgetary support on obvious near-term priorities (TMD rather than NMD) while maintaining and creating executable options for national-level defenses when their need becomes obvious. This paper seeks to explain what analysis can say about how to proceed.[3]

Let me begin by defining and distinguishing more carefully among three types of ballistic missile defense:

ABM treaty (a difficult feat); (2) maintain strategic stability; (3) develop a highly effective theater missile defense (TMD) system as quickly as possible to protect U.S. forward-deployed forces and U.S. friends and allies; and (4) give space-based defenses (notably including the Brilliant Pebbles concept) low priority (DoD, 1992).

[2]Not all of the skeptics, the author included, believe that BMD technology has reached the point where defense can handle sophisticated, albeit small, attacks.

[3]The material discussed in this paper comes from a variety of sources. I greatly appreciate the cooperation and support of Mike Miller, Susan Everingham, Herb Hoover, and Richard Mesic. And I owe a special debt of gratitude to Ambassador Henry Cooper for his review. While I am solely responsible for the contents of this paper, many of the good ideas and original analysis came from them, and I am in their debt.

- *Theater missile defense* (TMD) seeks to defend against short- and intermediate-range missile threats such as those that may be faced by U.S. projection forces and by friendly nations.[4] The options for TMD consist presently of THAAD (an advanced high-altitude terminal-defense system) and an enhanced version of Patriot, which will act as an augmentation to and underlay of THAAD.[5] One of the current debates is the extent to which activities focused almost exclusively on target-area defense should be augmented by boost-phase defenses (seeking to kill theater ballistic missiles (TBMs) while they are in powered flight) or counterforce attacks (seeking to kill TBMs or their transporter/erector/launchers (TELs) on the ground before launch).

- *National missile defense* (NMD) seeks to defend the United States against missiles of all ranges, including intercontinental. The current system concept for NMD involves one or more ground-based radar (GBR) sites, one or more ground-based interceptor (GBI) sites, and other long-range surveillance sensors (including the possibility of new acquisition radars at current BMEWS sites). The GBI are nonnuclear hit-to-kill missiles that engage targets before reentry into the atmosphere.

- *Global missile defense* (GMD) seeks to provide a comprehensive ballistic missile defense, not only for the United States, but also for its allies and selected other countries as appropriate.[6] The GMD initial-system concept currently consists of hit-to-kill space-based interceptors (Brilliant Pebbles or BP), aided by space-based sensors.[7] Later variants might include space-based beam weapons (e.g., lasers) and/or designators to aid midcourse tracking and discrimination as well as to affect kills. Global missile defense would be an overlay to theater- and national-level missile defense systems.

The paper discusses all of these, as well as how the United States may wish to build programs to develop and, in some cases, to deploy them. The paper proceeds as follows. It provides historical background and then discusses the many implications for BMD of the changed security environment, especially the need to defend U.S. projection forces and allied nations in various regions. The paper then discusses TMD, NMD, and space-based missile defense (SBMD) issues in successive sections, touching on issues of feasibility, need, and other matters. After this survey, the paper reviews some of the most trou-

---

[4]TMD should concern itself with cruise missile threats as well as ballistic missile threats, but attention has centered so far on the latter. I will discuss the former only briefly in this paper, despite its importance.

[5]Another system, CORPSAM, would augment TMD with a low-altitude defense layer, but the CORPSAM program has been deferred (Aspin, 1993).

[6]GMD usually is a surrogate for space-based BMD. We will use it in this context.

[7]Space-based sensors can support all defense deployments and should not be categorized as part of GMD.

blesome issues and dilemmas in attempting to define a sensible long-term approach to BMD. The paper ends with some personal observations and recommendations.

BACKGROUND

The advent of nuclear weapons changed U.S. security in a fundamental way. In his 1948 *Foreign Affairs* article, Bernard Brodie captured the fears of future U.S. presidents when he wrote the following:

> It is now three years since an explosion over Hiroshima revealed to the world that man had been given the means of destroying himself. Eight atomic bombs have now been detonated . . . and each was in itself a sufficient warning that the promise of eventual benefits resulting from the peacetime use of atomic energy must count as nothing compared to the awful menace of the bomb itself. The good things of earth cannot be enjoyed by dead men, nor can societies which have lost the entire material fabric of their civilization survive as integrated organisms (Brodie, 1948).

As Brodie warned, nuclear weapons have put the survival of civilizations at stake. Faced with the awful consequences of nuclear weapon employment, all presidents from Truman until today have sought the means to provide at least some protection for the United States. Political and budgetary support for strategic defenses have waxed and waned over the years, depending on attitudes, DoD budgets, etc. However, the underlying rationale for strategic defense never wavered: *Provide protection for the United States, its people, and its institutions in the face of foreign nuclear capabilities over which it has no direct control.* Debates about strategic defenses, and more particularly ballistic missile defenses, and their relevance to nuclear deterrence and national survival should be viewed in this context.

Strategic Defenses Before Ballistic Missiles

In 1950 the Soviet Union detonated its first atomic bomb, and the race between strategic offensive and defensive forces commenced. In response to first the threat and then the fact of USSR possession of nuclear weapons, Presidents Truman and Eisenhower undertook extensive active and passive strategic defensive measures.[8] Because the only delivery vehicles available were aircraft, the United States (and similarly the Soviet Union) heavily invested in strategic air

---

[8]York (1970) estimated that by 1970 the United States had spent about $30 billion on air defenses and the Soviets about $75 billion. In today's dollars, the figures would be roughly $90 billion and $225 billion.

defenses. While by no means leakproof, the U.S. air defenses nonetheless provided some confidence that a Soviet bomber attack would not totally devastate the United States, nor disarm it to a degree that would threaten its ability to carry out a devastating retaliatory blow. Further, the air defense system was thought to be capable of handling a partially damaged and poorly coordinated Soviet attack of the sort that might follow a preemptive strike by the massive U.S. bomber force, perhaps in the context of Soviet preparations for nuclear attack on the United States following an attack on Western Europe.[9] This preemptive capability, in turn, underwrote the U.S. policy of extended deterrence (i.e., U.S. deterrence of a Warsaw Pact invasion of Western Europe by threatening a retaliatory nuclear attack on Warsaw Pact forces and possibly the Soviet homeland as well). The 1950s was an era of U.S. strategic nuclear superiority in militarily meaningful terms, and U.S. strategic defenses played a central role.

More broadly, the U.S. strategy for protecting the country evolved during this period into a combination of three approaches: (1) first and foremost, *punishment-oriented deterrence*, through threats of massive retaliation; (2) *prevention-related deterrence* (or counterforce capability), through the credible threat of a substantial damage-limiting preemptive first strike; and (3) *direct defense*, through a combination of "passive" measures such as civil defenses and aircraft shelters and "active" defenses in the form of multilayered air defenses.

None of these were believed to be infallible. Nor were they viewed as satisfactory to protect the United States against future threats from other countries that might acquire nuclear weapons. Thus, in addition to being a decade that fostered major expenditures on strategic air defenses, the 1950s saw continuing efforts toward controlling the spread of nuclear weapons and limiting global access to technologies that could hasten both that spread and the development of ever-more-difficult-to-counter nuclear delivery systems. Policymakers continued to hope, however wistfully, that the security of the United States could be kept under U.S. control. While nuclear war might be awesomely destructive, it was not unreasonable—if controversial—to argue that with appropriate

---

[9]The commander of the Strategic Air Command (SAC), General Curtis LeMay, once shocked Robert Sprague, deputy head of the Gaither Commission, by explaining his (LeMay's personal) preemption planning: "If I see that the Russians are amassing their planes for an attack, I'm going to knock the [expletive] out of them before they take off the ground" (Kaplan, 1983:134). At that time, in the mid-1950s, SAC had an extensive fleet of long-range and overseas aircraft constantly observing the Soviet Union to provide strategic warning. There were routine penetrations of Soviet airspace. Ironically, had the Soviet Union been able to accomplish a risky surprise attack, SAC's forces would also have been exceedingly vulnerable. That was the essence of the famous RAND "basing study" (Wohlstetter, Rowen, Hoffman, and Lutz, 1954). For a good history of this era, see Kaplan (1983).

strategy and preparations, the United States might *survive* a nuclear war (see, e.g., Kahn, 1960). That policymakers thought similarly was evident from the major efforts of that era in civil defense programs.

The Introduction of ICBMs and the Need for BMD

The introduction of large numbers of ICBMs into the Soviet weapon inventory in the early 1960s began to change all this dramatically, as had been anticipated by the Gaither Commission in 1957. Air defenses would no longer suffice, and early U.S. efforts to transform existing surface-to-air antiaircraft missile systems (SAMs) into crude BMD systems were unsuccessful.[10] The strategy choices facing the Kennedy administration included (a) developing more effective BMD systems, (b) developing an effective first-strike counterforce capability against both missile and bomber threats, or (c) forgoing serious hope of defending the United States well against large-scale attack. All of these possibilities had strong proponents. It is important to note, however, that the original primary objective of strategic defense remained protection of the United States—not deterrence or some notion about military balances. That was the "natural" objective, in contrast to what came later.

This natural objective still underlies interest in BMD today. To be sure, other uses for BMD have been suggested, emphasized by strategic analysts, and even pursued for some years—e.g., protecting Minuteman missiles against a Soviet counterforce attack, protecting U.S. national leadership, and protecting bases and troops in the field from attacks by short-range tactical ballistic missiles. None of those rationales, however, has had the staying power or continued persuasiveness regarding core issues. In the 1960s, 1970s, and again in the 1980s, BMD systems were proposed and even planned for other purposes, but the rationale was not convincing once people concluded that BMD could not accomplish its potentially unique mission of directly defending core values. Minuteman missiles could be protected in other ways and at less cost (or done away with in favor of more survivable systems). So also could the leadership be defended in other ways. But the devastating effects of nuclear weaponry on population centers could not be denied without actively preventing the weapon from detonating over the target.

---

[10]The lack of an effective BMD also raised serious questions about the vulnerability of the air defenses themselves. Without protection from ICBM attack, the air defense command-and-control network was highly vulnerable to even small attack sizes. This fact alone led Robert McNamara to cease large expenditures on existing air defense systems and initiate new programs (e.g., AWACS) that might better deal with this situation. Consequently, funds for air defense dropped sharply in the 1960s.

Damage-Limitation Studies

With the introduction of Soviet ICBMs and SLBMs in the early 1960s, the United States had to rethink its nuclear strategy. Because the population was no longer protected even if the United States initiated a preemptive attack, damage limitation as originally conceived (and initially supported by the Kennedy administration)[11] was no longer workable. To recapture some degree of population protection, Secretary of Defense Robert McNamara put forward in his famous Ann Arbor speech of June 1962 the novel strategy of city avoidance, i.e., in case of a nuclear war, each superpower would pledge not to target the cities of the other. This strategy died quickly when the Soviet leadership rejected the notion out of hand.[12] Faced with mounting costs to maintain some semblence of damage limitation, McNamara directed the Office of the Director, Defense Research and Engineering (DDR&E) in early 1964 to undertake a comprehensive reexamination of the feasibility of preserving damage limitation capabilities over the long term. Colonel Glenn Kent (then in DDR&E) prepared a seminal report on damage limitation that examined counterforce, BMD, and passive defense options for various survival criteria (Kent, 1964). At the direction of McNamara, this study examined the following questions:

- For any proposed level of expenditures on "damage limiting" forces, what is the "optimum" allocation of the total among the various means that contribute to this function: (1) civil defense; (2) terminal ballistic missile defense and terminal bomber defense; (3) area bomber defense; (4) strategic offensive forces; and (5) defense against Soviet missile-carrying submarines?

- What are the possibilities available with regard to limiting damage to the United States and its allies? For example, what is the "percent surviving" in the United States as a function of the total expenditures on damage limiting for various contingencies?

---

[11]Early in his administration, President Kennedy was faced with a serious crisis over the future of Berlin. The prospects of nuclear war were all too real, as was the vulnerability of the United States to Soviet nuclear attack. Kennedy took damage limitation seriously, urging Americans to become prepared through civil defense measures, and he sharply augmented DoD's budget (with added money for civil defense). See Reeves (1993).

[12]The Soviet leadership was also interested in damage limitation, but their nuclear systems did not have the requisite capabilities (in either accuracy or numbers) to seriously threaten the U.S. nuclear arsenal, and they too were having difficulty in developing an effective ABM defense. Thus, they saw McNamara's initiative as a U.S. attempt to regain strategic superiority.

Figure 1, drawn from that report, shows the extent to which the U.S. population could be protected as a function of the ratio of U.S./Soviet costs to reduce/impose this level of damage. Two curves are shown: one in which the United States executes a successful first strike, the other in which the Soviets strike first. The calculations behind these curves assume optimum choices for the United States, i.e., the best mixture of counterforce, active defenses, and passive defenses. The Soviet responses were confined to simple ICBM proliferation; more stressful responsive threats (e.g., MIRVing of the ICBMs) would have made the curves significantly worse for the United States. Even under the optimistic assumptions of a U.S. first strike and a mundane Soviet responsive threat, the figure shows that the Soviet Union could insure holding at risk at least 20 million Americans by spending only one dollar for every three spent on U.S. damage limiting systems. If the United States sought even fewer casualties, the ratio would have been even higher. According to Kaplan (1983), these charts confirmed McNamara's fear that achieving meaningful levels of damage

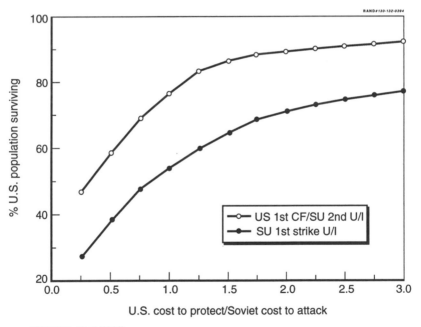

SOURCE: Kent (1964).

Figure 1—Cost/Exchange Ratios as a Function of Population Survival

limiting was impossible, and trying to do so would lock the United States into a very unfavorable and unwinnable arms race (see also DoD, 1965).[13]

Reluctantly but inexorably, U.S. defense policy shifted away from notions of damage limitation and toward an explicit and nearly complete emphasis on deterrence. That emphasis held throughout the remainder of the 1960s and 1970s, although the strategy for accomplishing deterrence matured—going far beyond assured destruction and toward the assured-retaliation capability of denying the Soviet Union (or any other attacker) the ability to achieve its war aims (mainly believed to be expanding its control over Europe and Asia). Thus, U.S. nuclear targeting strategy increasingly embraced a comprehensive set of military targets, both "strategic" and "general purpose" (e.g., armies, navies, air forces, and their vast infrastructure), as well as the "political control structure" consisting of Communist Party leadership installations.[14]

Early U.S. Ballistic Missile Defenses

Active BMD was the big loser in Kent's study. Nonetheless, proponents of active BMD did not abandon their fight. Many arguments were put forward for BMD's utility. These included responding tit-for-tat to the Soviet deployment of a BMD system around Moscow, defending against light attacks (e.g., from what was described as an emerging Chinese threat), defending U.S. strategic offensive forces, and hedging against a possibly much more extensive Soviet deployment of BMD systems. Also, some believed that NATO's policy of graduated escalation, and especially its reliance on nuclear escalation, lacked credibility because of the growth in Warsaw Pact capabilities; BMD, as a means to protect the United States against limited Soviet attacks, could strengthen that credibility. As for capability, technology had advanced from attempts to adapt air defense systems to the much more advanced systems (e.g., the Spartan and Sprint missiles and a family of phased-array radars) that might indeed enable defenses to successfully defend the United States against limited and technically unsophisticated attack. These arguments did not convince Robert McNamara, but President Johnson, apparently for domestic political

---

[13]Although not part of Kent's study, these curves are sensitive to the absolute size of the threat, smaller being better in terms of limiting damage at specific cost/exchange ratios. And they are very sensitive to defense performance.

[14]For a good review of this approach to deterrence, under the rubric of the *countervailing strategy*, see Slocombe (1981). In practice, U.S. targeting policy under the Reagan administration was substantially consistent with that developed under the Carter administration, which in turn drew heavily on conclusions from Ford administration studies. For discussion of continuity, see Nolan (1989).

reasons, decided in 1968 to deploy the Sentinel system at a small number of sites around the periphery of the United States.

Soon upon taking office, President Nixon decided to cancel the Sentinel system and to deploy instead a less expensive Soviet-oriented "new system" called Safeguard that would focus on defending U.S. Minuteman silos. In fact, Safeguard used the same hardware as Sentinel, but the change in mission and cost was important because Nixon saw ABM strictly as a bargaining chip to be used in attempting to gain control over the development of Soviet strategic *offensive* systems. In his evaluation of SALT's Summit I, he had this to say:

> The ABM treaty stopped what inevitably would have become a defensive arms race, with untold billions of dollars being spent on each side for more ABM coverage. The other major effect of the ABM treaty was to make permanent the concept of deterrence through "mutual terror". . . Each side therefore had an ultimate interest in preventing a war that could only be mutually destructive (Nixon, 1978:618).

Most analysts judged the planned Safeguard deployment for defense of ICBMs to be technically plausible and at least a modest addition to U.S. deterrent potential.[15] It was also viewed as stabilizing (and thus acceptable to many of the earlier ABM opponents).[16] However, the ABM treaty, signed in 1972, confined Safeguard deployments to a single site selected to be at Grand Forks and limited both countries to defensive interceptor numbers not to exceed 100. Safeguard became operational in 1973 and was decommissioned almost instantly on grounds of operational cost and effectiveness. The sole vestige of this deployment, a long-range acquisition radar, still exists at Grand Forks.

Note that arguments for BMD slipped from full protection of the country, to protection of the population against only small attacks, to protection of only our retaliatory forces to augment deterrence, and finally to bargaining leverage for banning ABM altogether. By the late 1970s, a balance of nuclear capabilities was commonly accepted as a stable and desirable state for nuclear forces. While heated debates continued between those who supported a nuclear deterrent based on mutual assured destruction (MAD) and those who argued for an array of city-sparing nuclear targeting options,[17] countrywide BMD was, at

---

[15]The proponents of BMD also viewed its deployment as necessary to maintain the scientific and engineering personnel who had been attracted to ABM research in the 1960s, as well as a potential precursor to a countrywide deployment. In this there are many parallels between then and now.

[16]In fact, Safeguard augmented U.S. retaliation capabilities only marginally and thus would have made little difference if disabled.

[17]In reality, the SIOP (Single Integrated Operations Plan) offered a wide array of options from which the President and his advisers could choose. These debates had more to do with basic national strategy than with nuclear employment planning.

best, placed on the back burner.[18]   Indeed, at one point in the 1970s, the Congress actually enjoined DoD and the Army from pursuing BMD technology that might contribute to broad-area BMD, i.e., population protection.

The Issue Is Reopened: The Star Wars Speech

On March 23, 1983, President Reagan reopened the BMD debate.[19]   In his famous Star Wars speech, Reagan called on the technical community to examine prospects for making (nuclear-armed) ballistic missiles "impotent and obsolete," in conjunction with a call for deep reductions in nuclear forces.   In strategic terms, he brought into question the efficacy of any long-term strategy of reliance on mutual assured destruction.   The result was substantial ferment, with the debate tending to fall along ideological, and often partisan, lines. This was unfortunate, because the questions Reagan was raising deserved to be asked and answered.   Interestingly, some of the original negotiators of the ABM treaty agreed and were by no means hostile to reopening the question of BMD, even if it meant changing the treaty.   They were, however, skeptical about whether BMD was more attractive than it had been in 1972.

After a comprehensive study of the technical factors that might make a comprehensive defense possible (the so-called Fletcher Report), the Strategic Defense Initiative Organization (SDIO) was formed to pursue the more promising technological opportunities.   SDIO reported directly to the Secretary of Defense and lasted until 1993, when it was disbanded by the Clinton administration.   During its ten-year existence, it spent something in excess of $30 billion (then-year dollars), perhaps half of which was over and above what would have otherwise been spent in a less centralized and focused set of service programs.   Interestingly, during this ten years, history was repeated.   As in the 1960s, initial enthusiasm revolved around population defense, but scientific and technical experts concluded once again that this was not yet in the cards.   Slowly, the focus of BMD under the Star Wars program was shifted, almost inexorably, toward defense of the deterrent force and protecting population against a variety of vaguely defined light attacks.   Then, in

---

[18]Many opponents of MAD as policy based some of their arguments on the immorality of attacking innocent civilians.   The Catholic bishops heatedly debated the morality of assured destruction, almost (but not quite) confronting the Reagan administration in the early 1980s (van Voorst, 1983).   Questions were raised about the legality of nuclear attacks against civilians (Builder and Graubard, 1982), and even supporters of the existing policy toward nuclear deterrence felt the need to address its ethics (Nye, 1986).   These ethical and logical issues were used by the proponents of BMD in trying to make the case to reopen debates on nuclear strategy.

[19]For discussion of the history of Star Wars, see Nolan (1989) and Shultz (1993).

1991, it shifted toward defense against theater ballistic missiles (TBM), a shift that was codified by the Bottom-Up Review.[20]

Current State of Missile Defense Technology

Given all the development effort on BMD, where do we stand technologically? As of late 1993, most defense analysts would agree to the following:

- Technology has advanced sufficiently so that *limited defenses against nuclear-armed ballistic missiles are both feasible and affordable.* While studies suggest that the offense can still claim some cost-exchange edge over the defense, that advantage has been reduced.[21]

- Comprehensive ballistic missile defenses, i.e., those that would protect the entire United States to a degree that would satisfy President Reagan's aim of making ballistic missiles "impotent and obsolete," are still unachievable within realistic budgets against large and sophisticated attacks (i.e., attacks that might come from Russia or a future superpower). Even so, the estimated acquisition costs for such a defense have fallen from estimates as high as $1 trillion to $100 billion or less.

- Defenses against a large attack of air-breathing nuclear delivery systems (bombers and cruise missiles) might cost as much again as comparably capable BMD deployments. Without balanced defenses against all delivery means, comprehensive countrywide protection would not exist, thereby casting into serious question the value of the expenditures.[22]

These conclusions may seem to argue against continued pursuit of ballistic missile defenses, but there is more to the story, as I shall now discuss.

---

[20]See Carter and Schwartz (1984), Hoffman et al. (1984), Office of Technology Assessment (1986), and Department of Defense (1992, 1993) for broad discussion of BMD issues, 1983–1993.

[21]By the late 1980s the exchange ratio was three or less, at which point it was approaching the ratio of the U.S./USSR GNPs, making it possible for BMD proponents to argue that the United States could win an offense-defense race even if the ratio was adverse—especially since the Soviet defense burden was already strangling the economy. With technology now on the horizon (e.g., Brilliant Eyes and Brilliant Pebbles), even lower ratios are at least plausible, except that the attacker could "open a new front" by increasing the emphasis on cruise missiles.

[22]Some advocates of BMD have argued that, as "slow flyers," air-breathing delivery vehicles do not pose a risk to nuclear stability. However, the grass-roots interest in defenses that arose after President Reagan's speech was concerned with protection, not marginally improving some theoretical notion of stability. Reagan was calling for making nuclear weapons "impotent and obsolete," not merely "slow." Further, if improving stability were the issue, there were many other less-expensive ways to proceed (i.e., increasing the survivability of offensive forces).

THE NEW INTERNATIONAL CONTEXT FOR BMD

With this brief background of BMD history, we must now consider the drastically new political-military context before thinking about appropriate direction for BMD programs. The most important elements of the new context for BMD appear to be (1) proliferation of weapons of mass destruction and ballistic missiles, (2) the START process and the opportunity it provides for cooperative U.S.-Russian efforts to draw down offensive forces and perhaps cooperate on defenses, and (3) the many fundamental uncertainties about the more distant future of international relationships. Let me discuss each of these in turn.

Proliferation-Related Challenges

There is no question that the feared proliferation of weapons of mass destruction (WMD), coupled with the ongoing proliferation of ballistic missiles and the technology associated with them, forms the primary motivation for current TMD efforts (TMD because, in the near term at least, the proliferation will probably not involve missiles that could strike the United States). Table 1 (based mostly on data from Systems Planning Corporation (1992) collates information on which countries are pursuing WMD and ballistic missiles. The data are sobering.

Desert Storm made it crystal clear that even conventionally armed TBMs could significantly affect U.S. national security interests as well as military capabilities. Without discounting the tragic loss of U.S. service personnel at the barracks near Dhahran, it must be said that the direct *military* consequences of the Scud attacks against targets in Saudi Arabia and Israel were insignificant. But the political impacts were large, leading to a massive and sustained effort to locate and suppress TBMs and their TELs.

Armed with nuclear weapons, future TBMs could well alter the outcome of future confrontations. A RAND study dealing with the consequences of confronting a nuclear-armed adversary (Molander and Wilson, 1993; Millot, Molander, and Wilson, 1993) reported the following results after a series of political-military contingency games:

- Many participants questioned whether U.S. national interests were truly at stake, suggesting American nonparticipation (or, to put it differently, evidence that the United States might well be deterred from intervening).[23]

---

[23]When asked to state the most important lesson from Desert Storm and the Gulf War, India's defense minister reportedly said that it was not to go to war with the

Table 1

Countries Pursuing Ballistic Missiles or Weapons of Mass Destruction

	Missile Producer	Missile Possessor	Space Launcher	Nuclear Program	Nuclear R&D	Chemical Weapons	Bio-Weapons
Afghanistan		X					
Argentina	X	X	X		X		X
Brazil	X	X	X		X		X
Burma						X	
Chile	X	X	X			X	
China	X	X	X	X	X	X	X
Egypt	X	X			X	X	
India	X	X	X	X	X	X	X
Iran	X	X			X	X	X
Iraq	X	X	X	X	X	X	X
Israel	X	X	X	X	X	X	
Japan			X		X		
Libya	X	X			X	X	X
North Korea	X	X			X	X	X
Pakistan	X	X	X	X	X	X	
Saudi Arabia		X			X		
South Africa	X	X				X	X
South Korea					X	X	X
Syria		X			X	X	X
Taiwan	X	X			X	X	X
Vietnam		X				X	
Yemen		X					

- Many participants seriously doubted the support of key allies in the contingencies.
- Rather generally, there was a call for restructuring power projection forces, to include greatly enhanced counterforce and active defense capability against TBMs, in order to prevent significant U.S. casualties.

This suggests that U.S. willingness to use its military capabilities to protect its interests and those of its allies would be significantly affected by nuclear proliferation. TMD can be only a partial answer because it can provide neither absolute protection nor complete coverage against all threats. Although this paper deals almost exclusively with defending against use, we should realize that a wide range of counters to TBMs are probably needed, including (1) dissuading possession, (2) deterring use, (3) devaluing threat of use, and (4) defending against use (BMD and passive measures).

United States unless armed with nuclear weapons. This lesson is almost certainly appreciated by most Third World countries.

START II and Implications for BMD

If proliferation offers challenges, U.S.-Russian nuclear arms agreements offer opportunities. Starting about a decade ago with the treaty to eliminate intermediate-range ballistic missiles, strategic arms agreements have progressed to START II (see Wilkening, 1994), which will limit the total number of strategic weapons per side to between 3000 and 3500, about one-third of those that exist today. Figure 2 depicts one plausible set of force levels in the year 2002 when the treaty comes into full force (Gershwin, 1993).

The following points are especially relevant to BMD issues:

- The Russian ballistic missile threat under START II will be sharply reduced, to roughly 2200 reentry vehicles (RVs) total (substantially fewer on alert).

- As a consequence, BMD systems would face much smaller nominal threats, be they launched by accident or deliberately, e.g.:

  - 2000 RVs from an all-out attack of fully alerted forces.
  - 100 RVs from an unauthorized attack by a "mad submarine commander," and numbers much smaller from ICBM fields.
  - 10 RVs or less from accidental attacks.[24]

  These latter two are small in size (smaller than, e.g., the Chinese arsenal and possible new threats from Third World countries).

It is also worth noting that many of the residual missiles under START II will either be deMIRVed variants of current missiles, or will otherwise have fewer RVs than they are capable of carrying. This means that either side could relatively quickly expand its offensive forces if it so desired. This could improve confidence during a coordinated deployment of defenses, because if one side sought to achieve unilateral advantage, the other could respond by deploying more weapons. On the other hand, it means that a defense sized against nominal levels could quickly find itself too small in the case of "breakout." In today's world, breakout scenarios seem much less plausible than only a half-dozen years ago, but the world could change again.

---

[24]Some policymakers are considering trying speeding up START II's full implementation date or negotiating with the Russians (and other nuclear states of the former USSR) for de-alerting or other measures that might take off active status those parts of the nuclear force that are scheduled for elimination because of START II. If such agreements can be reached, threat reductions could occur earlier, to the apparent benefit of both the United States and the former Soviet states. See Wilkening (1994).

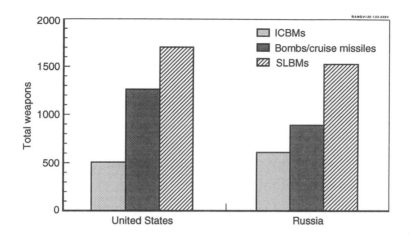

Figure 2—Illustrative SALT II Force Postures

More generally, it is important to note that with the United States and Russia working cooperatively, and with advances in technology, it is plausible that coordinated actions on reducing nuclear inventories and building countrywide defenses could create a situation in which President Reagan's goal of "impotent and obsolete" might at least be approximated. Additional technical "miracles" might still be needed, but at least a number of the technical challenges have been met. What is plausible (i.e., not impossible) now is that the United States and Russia could cooperatively shape their offensive and defensive forces so that nuclear weapons would play an increasingly negligible role in U.S.-Russian affairs, even if the two countries became adversaries again. The proverbial nuclear genie would not be "back in the bottle," but (mixing metaphors) the sword of Damocles would not be hanging so conspicuously over our heads as during the Cold War. Further, both nations would have defenses against accidents and from modest Third World threats.

Uncertainties: Political Stability of Russia and Other Issues

All of this is fine, but it depends on the current positive relationship between the United States and the states of the former Soviet Union. That positive relationship, however, is not immutable. The leaderships of those states face difficult problems, including friction between Russia and Ukraine and the growing popularity of leaders arguing for a recovery of empire. While it is difficult to imagine that even a new leadership in Russia would revert to a full-scale military competition with the United States, it is quite imaginable that a new regime might see the nuclear arms agreements as biased toward the United States, causing it to back away from them. It is also possible that the international situation could come apart if a future Russian government began aggressively seeking to recover the territories of its "empire" (the Baltic states, Belarus, Ukraine, etc.). The truth is that more generally *we do not know what the world will look like twenty years hence* (some would say even five years is a stretch). Where will the conflicts occur? Will nuclear or other WMD have been used? And so on. Reminding us of what could happen, Japan recently announced (and subsequently recanted) that it would seriously reconsider its commitment to the nuclear nonproliferation treaty if it can be proved that North Korea possesses nuclear weapons.

Against the backdrop of this changed international environment and uncertainties about the future, let me now discuss in turn issues and options for theater missile defense, national missile defense, and space-based missile defense (TMD, NMD, and SBMD).

THEATER BALLISTIC MISSILE DEFENSE (TMD): PROTECTING U.S. PROJECTION FORCES AND ALLIES

Any approach to TMD should depend on the targets to be defended, the size and character of the threat, the technical feasibility of the defense options, and a host of other factors.

Likely Targets for Enemy TBMs

What must be defended? On the one hand, U.S. opponents might target a variety of military sites (e.g., airfields and seaports) to discourage or prevent U.S. force projection into a theater of operations, as well as to disrupt force employment once the forces were deployed. To the extent U.S. power projection capabilities are at risk, these sites must be protected.   In addition, Congress has already mandated that an important objective of TMD must be to protect forward-deployed U.S. forces.

However, protecting U.S. forces is only part of the problem. Protecting our friends and allies adds a complex and sometimes subtle political dimension to the TMD problem, as we saw in the Persian Gulf war. It is also easy to imagine a situation where a neighboring country of the aggressor—i.e., a country "under the gun" of its TBMs—would believe that even a U.S.-favorable war outcome would not deter the aggressor from "getting even" after the war was over and U.S. forces withdrew. Under such circumstances would it cooperate with the United States and the country being invaded? Would the protection of U.S. TMD change the equation? Aside from fundamental humanitarian reasons, these questions strongly imply that protection for our friends and allies is also needed. Congress has also mandated that this be a central objective of our TMD developments.

The potential need to defend allied territories creates substantial coverage challenges for TMD. Indeed, much of the concern about the proliferation of ballistic missile technology has to do with likely increases in TBM range, which would dramatically increase the number of politically interesting targets within reach of an adversary. Missiles expected to have ranges of 1000 km or longer (e.g., North Korea's No Dong I and Iraq's Al-Abbas) are particularly worrisome. Figure 3 illustrates what extended-range missiles might threaten if deployed in Iraq and Libya. Given the large size of the areas to be protected, defense will be neither easy nor inexpensive.

Types and Numbers of Threat Weapons

The challenge posed to defense systems also depends significantly on the type of warhead employed and the size of the TBM threat. Table 2 provides some crude estimates, for each of several weapon types, of the area of effect against a standard military target such as an airfield with personnel in the open (see Gold and Welch, 1993). Nuclear and biological weapons have *very* large areas of effect and therefore stand above the others. By contrast, the large-area disruptive effects of chemical weapons can be substantially mitigated, assuming adequate protective suits and facilities at the base under attack. However, the persistence of these weapons is cause for concern, and the importance of chemical attacks against airports and seaports of entry should not be minimized. Unless decontamination equipment were available and successfully used, chemical attacks with persistent chemicals could close critical ports and airfields for a considerable time. Table 2 also indicates rough numbers for the inventory of threat weapons. There could be hundreds or thousands of conventional TBMs akin to Frog and Scud missiles, but the number armed with WMDs will be much less.

Feasible Goals for TMD Systems

Given the potential lethality of nuclear and biological weapons, it is natural to seek a TMD goal of near-zero leakage for small TBM attacks. Whether such a goal is practical is debatable (especially for attacks in which small num-

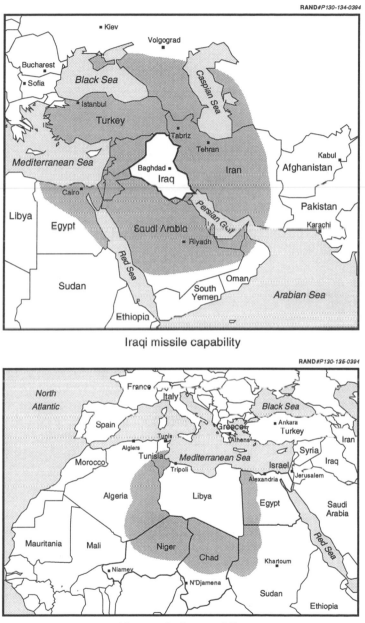

Iraqi missile capability

Libyan missile capability

Figure 3—Target Coverage for Extended-Range TBMs

Table 2

Comparative Effects of Different WMD

Warhead Type	Difficulty in Obtaining	Likely Numbers	Submunitions	Affected Warhead Area (square miles)	
				No Passive Defenses	Passive Defenses
Conventional (500 kg)	None	Many 100s	Maybe	10^3	10^2
Chemical (500 kg)	Some	10 to 100s	Yes	10^6	10^2–10^5
Biological (240 kg)	Some	1 to 10s	Yes	10^9	10^6–10^8
Nuclear (20 kT)	Substantial	A few	No	10^7	10^5–10^7

NOTES:

1. Single Scud ballistic missile attack versus airfield.

2. Affected area calculation assumes disabling of more than 50 percent of personnel.

3. Protection against chemical attack assumes MOP 5 suits and masks.

4. Protection against biological weapons assumes no inoculations.

5. Protection against nuclear weapons assumes facilities normally found on foreign airfields.

bers of WMD-armed TBMs are mixed in with and indistinguishable from a larger number of conventionally armed TBMs) but it is not mathematically unrealistic.[25] It might also be possible to achieve small leakage against somewhat larger numbers of ballistic missiles with chemical warheads—at least at selected sites, if the attacker did not know which sites were being preferentially defended or how successful his previous attacks had been.

The situation is quite different for a conventionally armed TBM threat (i.e., ballistic missiles armed with conventional explosives rather than WMD). In many cases, passive defense measures are adequate by themselves because TBMs have relatively small payloads and poor accuracies, and many targets (e.g., airfields) are tough to destroy. Even heavy and persistent allied bombing attacks against Iraqi airfields did not close those bases, despite the use in some cases of special runway-busting munitions. This outcome was consistent with numerous past studies (by RAND and others) predicting that air bases would

---

[25]Straightforward math offers the following insight. Assuming a shoot-look-shoot terminal defense capability (or, equivalently, a two-layer defense), zero leakage against a 10-RV attack can be achieved with greater than 90 percent confidence if the interceptor's single-shot kill probability is 0.9. While 0.9 is high, it falls within the design goals for many defensive systems and cannot be ruled out technically.

be hard to close and would be readily repairable except when attacked by the best of runway-busting munitions under circumstances maximizing munition effectiveness.[26]

While there is no similar wealth of vulnerability analysis of ports, army bases and the like, a simple consideration of the effects radius versus the area of such targets tells us that with the exception of, e.g., large cranes and gantries, most of these targets are not critically vulnerable to conventionally armed TBMs.

Terminal/Midcourse Defenses: The Canonical Approach and Its Limitations

In theory there are many approaches to TMD, many of them complementary. The current DoD program, however, focuses on systems to destroy the incoming weapons in the terminal or late-midcourse portions of their flight. Plans call for upgrading the Patriot and for developing and deploying the THAAD system (Aspin, 1993). Both Patriot and THAAD would be ground-based Army systems. These defenses are achievable in the relatively near term and would form an essential element of any longer-term U.S. TMD strategy. However, a good deal of RAND analysis, much of it led by colleague David Vaughan, indicates that such terminal/midcourse defenses, if forced to operate on their own, are likely to be inadequate against difficult threats. Among the most important limitations are the following:

- *Unspectacular single-shot kill probabilities (SSPKs).* It has long been custom-ary for studies of defense systems to postulate SSPKs on the order of 0.7, 0.8, or even 0.9. But the experience with Patriot in Desert Storm and sub-sequent analysis raises significant questions about what can be achieved and how confidently one should accept assertions about system effectiveness. Recent analyses suggest that Patriot's success in Desert Storm was no greater than 50 percent and perhaps much smaller.[27]

- *Availability.* Although THAAD is being designed to be easily deployed into the theater of operations, that deployment may not happen until after the

---

[26]Because these problems were well known to the Americans and British, the attacks had other goals. In particular, precision strikes against shelters probably destroyed many Iraqi aircraft and helped to motivate the flight of Iraqi aircraft to Iran.

[27]Although the Army reported immediately after the war that Patriot had achieved 45 hits in 47 engagements within its defended areas over Israel and Saudi Arabia, subse-quent analysis (Postol, 1991) suggested that the number of successful engagements was very small. Israeli reports, during the war and in late 1993, supported that view (see es-pecially Atkinson, 1993:277–278).

conflict has begun.[28]   If no other defensive capability existed, the enemy could use the unchallenged TBM threat to (1) coerce regional countries not to allow U.S. entry, (2) compel the threatened country to sue for peace (especially if WMD were involved), and (3) deny suitable ports and airfields to U.S. power projection forces.

- *Coverage.* As discussed above, the United States may need to defend allied countries in the general region.   Systems like Patriot and the baseline, ground-based THAAD may not have the requisite coverage areas to cope with extended-range TBMs.[29]

- *Collateral damage.* Again, the data from Desert Storm are illuminating. Spent boosters, maldirected interceptors, and even damaged warheads can still cause significant damage (Postol, 1991).   In the case of WMD, the mere release of the weapon products is cause for serious concern, even if the weapons do not hit their intended targets.

- *Sensitivity to details of threat, including fractionation.* Even if a BMD system has a very high SSPK against simple targets (e.g., a single warhead to be engaged well within the atmosphere), it may do poorly against actual attacks in which the targets are rather different technically than anticipated.[30] Further, the early release of bomblets or chemical canisters, as suggested in Postol (1991), would cause serious problems for any terminal-phase system (see also Mesic, 1994a, Larsen and Kent, 1994, and Canavan, 1993).

Acting on their own, terminal and late-midcourse defenses also suffer from a number of problems: battlespace constraints, which limit their shoot-look-shoot opportunities and their ability to achieve very low leakage rates even with relatively high SSPKs; limited coverage per site, suggesting either a very large deployment for full regional area coverage or leaving some targets undefended; uncertain lethality against some targets, such as chemical warheads detonated high in the atmosphere; and compatibility with the existing ABM treaty

---

[28]There are a variety of reasons why this is likely to be true. Perhaps the most important is the enemy's interest in starting the war prior to that deployment, i.e., the political and military value of its TBMs would be greatest in this case and the initiative for the start of the war rests with the enemy.

[29]The Bottom-Up Review recognized this problem and that of early availability; it called for continued development of a ship-based midcourse intercept capability, called the sea-based upper tier, which could be deployed on station prior to conflict outbreak (Aspin, 1993).

[30]For example, Iraq's Al-Hussein missile broke into pieces during reentry. This unintended countermeasure confused the Patriot's tracking algorithms and caused it in some cases to lock on to false targets. A second problem was that the Patriot fuze's timing mechanism was set for slower incoming objects (e.g., shorter-range missiles), thereby causing late detonation. Deliberate countermeasures could be even more troublesome. Whether such failures can be avoided in THAAD and other terminal defense systems remains uncertain.

(although the Russians may well agree to changes). And, not least, THAAD and Patriot will require very significant funding before their full developments are finished after the turn of the century.

None of the above suggests that THAAD and Patriot aren't essential constituents of a robust TMD system. However, it does suggest that the United States needs to consider additional options for TMD, augmenting terminal/midcourse defenses based on Patriot and THAAD.

Counterforce, Counterbattery, and Boost-Phase Options

In examining complementary TMD options, RAND work has focused on concepts of operations that can be implemented and has suggested two imperatives: (a) the need for *timely* active defense with the potential for substantial geographic *coverage*, and (b) the need to address *complex targets* (e.g., targets amid debris or protected by countermeasures) *that must be destroyed, not merely diverted.*

Timely Active Defenses With Significant Coverage. Active defenses need to be in place early in crisis to protect regional allies, deploying U.S. forces, and critical infrastructure. The approaches to accomplishing this that have been proposed most often are as follows, with the first two being the most relevant in the near term, and the ones being most seriously considered by the DoD.

- *Ship-based terminal or midcourse defense systems* using either a variant of THAAD or the Standard missile with a LEAP upper stage.[31] Deployed on Aegis cruisers, the system would use an upgrade to the SPY-1 radar for target acquisition and tracking. To be effective, the cruiser would need to be deployed near the country being attacked, limiting the defended area or potentially placing the ship in harm's way.[32] Nonetheless, ship-based defenses have great strategic and operational advantages, particularly sustainability.

- *Airborne midcourse interceptors* using SRAM as a booster and LEAP as the upper stage. The missile could be carried by several aircraft, including most bombers and the F-15E.[33] Its sensor support still needs to be determined,

---

[31]THAAD operates early in the terminal phase or late in midcourse. LEAP provides more midcourse capability; it is a missile and homing kill vehicle that has been under development by SDIO for several years. LEAP is also being considered as an upper stage for other ground-based defense interceptors and for SRAM in an airborne mode.

[32]Among the weapon systems that have been widely proliferated into Third World inventories are antiship cruise missiles and various forms of antiship mines. These could constrain Navy operations and the area defended.

[33]If required, bombers can operate from bases (including those in CONUS) well outside the theater in question. Buchan (1994b) describes RAND's recent work on the potential employment of long-range bombers in major regional conflicts. This mission

with options including the use of Cobra Ball aircraft, forward-deployed ground-based radars, and space-based sensors. To be effective, the weapon platform would have to be somewhere between the target and the launch point. Depending on the extent of early air defenses, this might or might not place the aircraft in danger. Maintaining such operations during crisis would be very expensive.

- *Space-based kinetic-kill vehicles (KKVs) (Brilliant Pebbles).* Brilliant Pebbles also would be predominantly an exoatmospheric interceptor, with the same limitations as LEAP.

- *Proliferated TMDs in threatened nations.* Still another option would be to deploy TMDs in all the countries likely to be threatened. Although there are competitors such as the Israelis, Russians, and Europeans, the United States is technically well placed to build and sell such systems to its friends and allies.

Addressing Complex Targets and the Need to Destroy Them Early. The above options provide capabilities that partially hedge against potential countermeasures, but they do not engage the threat until well past burnout; thus, they are still sensitive to many of the problems that afflict THAAD. The following capabilities would help a great deal (Larsen and Kent, 1994, and Mesic, 1994a):

- *A boost-phase intercept capability.* Various combinations of platforms and interceptors are under consideration, all of which would exploit the immediate detectability of a TBM's rocket plume. Most require overflight of enemy territory to be effective, raising questions about their availability early in conflict. Lasers and hypervelocity interceptors might not require overflight, but they are not feasible in the near term.

- *A capability to locate, identify, and kill the TBM or its TEL on the ground* (called *counterforce*). A variety of concepts of operations that might enable this capability are under consideration, but high-confidence approaches remain elusive.[34]

Obviously, killing TBMs while still on the ground would be a highly attractive capability, were it operationally feasible and affordable. However, as one might expect, the most attractive options are usually the most difficult to acquire. Figure 4 is a simple matrix showing relative difficulty in obtaining the capability versus relative attractiveness in having the capability. At the top of the attractiveness and difficulty axes is counterforce. Next in attractiveness and difficulty is boost-phase kill, and then terminal or midcourse kills. The last

---

would simply add to the list of important capabilities that bombers bring to conventional conflicts in short-warning situations.

[34]There are no confirmed cases of successful Scud hunts in Desert Storm.

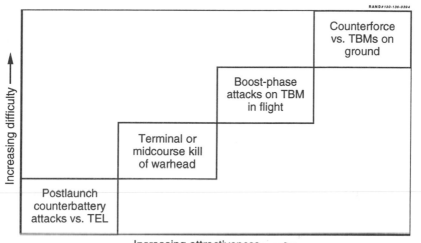

RAND#130-136-0394

Increasing difficulty →

Counterforce
vs. TBMs on
ground

Boost-phase
attacks on TBM
in flight

Terminal or
midcourse kill
of warhead

Postlaunch
counterbattery
attacks vs. TEL

Increasing attractiveness ──►

Figure 4—Ranking the Attractiveness and Difficulty of TMD Options

item is killing the TEL after the missile has been launched. Without its missile, the TEL may not appear to be a very attractive target, but if there are multiple reload missiles per TEL, destroying one would limit the number of TBMs launched subsequently.

Unfortunately, none of the approaches provides by itself a robust capability. Table 3 summarizes attractiveness for the various systems along a number of dimensions. A "+" indicates major strength for the option, a "–" indicates a negative impact, and a "0" lies somewhere in between. This table reflects my judgments; the reader should feel free to substitute his or her own.

Whether or not one agrees with the pluses and minuses of Table 3, it remains true that no single approach is likely to simultaneously provide high kill probabilities and robustness to countermeasures or other technical or scenario-related uncertainties. A combination of approaches is therefore needed in the long run, one that would, among other things, provide substantial layering of the defenses.

Having surveyed TMD issues, let us now turn again to NMD and then to global missile defense.

NATIONAL MISSILE DEFENSE

The Bottom-Up Review (Aspin, 1993) has decisively put NMD developments onto the back burner of DoD priorities. Nevertheless, NMD remains

Table 3

Strengths and Weaknesses of TMD Options

	Counter-force	Boost-Phase Intercept	Midcourse or Terminal Area Intercept	Postlaunch Counter-battery
Available				
Relocatable precrisis	0^a	0	$+^b$	0^a
Rapidly deployable	+	+	–/0	+
Exportable	–	–	+	0
Effective				
Detectable	–	+	+	0
Lethality	0	+	–	0
Insensitive to intel. data	–	+	–	0
Insensitive to responsive threats	–	+	–	+
Limits collateral damage	+	+	–	0
Provides good BDA	0	+	–	0
Synergistic	+	+	0	+
Cost				
Large coverage	+	+	0	0
Subject to attrition	–	–	+	–
Multiple mission potential	+	–	+	+
Available BM/C^{3}I	0	0	+	0
Acceptance				
In DoD plan	0	–	+	–
Operationally sound	–	0	+	0
Overall comments	Technically risky; Potential unclear^c	Relies on control of air; opportunity cost may be large	Best near-term option; important as underlay; not robust re responsive threat	Uncertain value; couples with boost-phase and counter-force

^{a}Depends on availability of friendly bases in neighborhood of threatening country.

^{b}Assumes shipborne or airborne midcourse defenses.

^{c}Depends inherently on "finder's" success in hider versus finder competition. Fiscal and operational costs of a high-confidence solution would be extremely high unless finder's ability to successfully search for and locate TBMs in large areas is very high.

an issue within DoD and Congress. After all, what is the long-term logic of defending abroad, but not at home? The near-term goal of NMD would, presumably, be to protect the entire U.S. population against an accidental or unauthorized attack from one of the states of the former Soviet Union (e.g.,

Russia), and from other adversarial states or terrorist groups that might develop ballistic missile threats to the United States. This goal will not easily be met. And in meeting it, the United States will have to face additional problems such as renegotiating the ABM treaty.

The ABM treaty limits ABM deployments to no more than 100 interceptors and related tracking radars at a single site. This section first examines the capability of a treaty-limited NMD, assuming that Grand Forks continues to be the U.S. site. Then it considers noncompliant deployments, where ground-based radars (GBRs) and ground-based interceptors (GBIs) could be located elsewhere.

Treaty-Limited Deployments at Grand Forks

The capability of an SBM interceptor launched from a particular site to intercept a warhead aimed at a specific target in the United States rests on a number of important variables. Among the most important are:

- The energy of the GBI (i.e., its "delta-V"), which translates into range and altitude versus time.

- The acquisition and target tracking sensor coverage (obviously, the earlier the detection of the RV, the earlier the interceptor can be launched and the greater the coverage).

- The command-and-control decision time.

- The defense system track-handling capability, including numbers and accuracy of the track.

- The midcourse target-discrimination capability.

The capabilities of single-site deployments are also sensitive to the launch location of the ICBM (or SLBM) in relationship to the intended targets. Figure 5 shows this by indicating the coverage of a typical GBI site if located at Grand Forks.[35] The coverage represents the area that is protected against an attack from *any* point in Russia. Thus, a single site at Grand Forks can in principle *guarantee* that 55 percent of CONUS (the contiguous states, not including Alaska or Hawaii) is protected against an attack from Russia, regardless of the location of the ICBM launch.[36] For any specific launch location of the ICBM, however, the actual fraction of CONUS protected would be

---

[35]Most of the figures in this section are derived from earlier RAND work by Michael Miller, Herbert Hoover, and Susan Everingham.

[36]These calculations are representative of, but not identical to, the estimated performance of current Ballistic Missile Defense Organization GBI concepts.

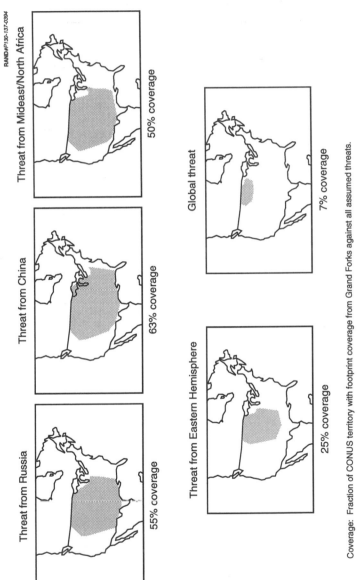

RAND#P130-137-0394

Threat from Mideast/North Africa

50% coverage

Threat from China

63% coverage

Threat from Russia

55% coverage

Global threat

7% coverage

Threat from Eastern Hemisphere

25% coverage

Coverage: Fraction of CONUS territory with footprint coverage from Grand Forks against all assumed threats.

Figure 5—CONUS Territory Coverage By Treaty-Compliant GBI System

substantially higher. For example, most of the east coast of the United States would be protected against attacks from central or eastern Russia, while much of the west coast would be protected from attacks from launches near Moscow. Thus, the coverage area shown is the "worst case" coverage in terms of launch location.

Not surprisingly, as the geographical extent of the combined ICBM threats increases, the coverage worsens. In the limit, threats that can come from any direction—as would be approximately true for Russian SSBNs if they reestablished patrols off the coasts of the United States—pose the most serious coverage problem. It is intuitively obvious that attacks from the south or from close to the United States cannot be engaged by a single GBI site in North Dakota. Furthermore, and also fairly obviously, a GBI site at Grand Forks cannot provide protection for either Hawaii or Alaska. *If the entire United States is to be protected, or if threats take on a global character, restricting U.S. BMD to the strictures of the ABM treaty cannot be permitted.*

CONUS territorial coverage (or its equivalent in fraction of CONUS population protected[37]) is but one measure of defense performance. A second major consideration is leakage. Even assuming small attacks, achieving low leakage rates is likely only if adequate battlespace exists for shoot-look-shoot opportunities.[38] Imposing a requirement for shoot-look-shoot opportunities sharply reduces the coverage of any particular BMD site. As a result, a single site at Grand Forks provides coverage and shoot-look-shoot opportunities only for that part of CONUS lying between the Appalachian and Rocky Mountains. The majority of the population that lives near the two coasts gets neither.[39]

---

[37]Because the population of CONUS is more heavily concentrated near the coasts, the fraction of area coverage does not map directly into population coverage. This is an important factor for single-site deployments, but gets less important if additional GBI sites are deployed.

[38]Shoot-look-shoot (SLS) assumes that one or more GBIs are launched against an RV and engage at some specified distance from the launch site (the first "shoot"). After that engagement, a determination is made as to the success of the first engagement (the "look"). If success is doubtful, then a second launch of one or more GBIs would occur. This second launch is possible only if there is sufficient "battlespace" for the first shoot and look opportunity to occur before the RV passes through the engagement envelope of the GBI site. Single look-shoot capabilities are usually judged inadequate for high kill probabilities because of the belief that high single-shot kill probabilities are technically difficult to achieve, and multiple salvo shots may not be adequate (because of correlated error sources) to raise the single-shot kill probability to levels needed for very low leakage rates against multiple RV attacks.

[39]Typical calculations from prior RAND research estimate that the 55 percent coverage of CONUS from a Russian attack yields population coverage of less than 40 percent. Whether SLS will be sufficient to achieve the desired high kill probabilities rests on other factors (e.g., multiple shots may still have correlated error sources).

Extending CONUS Coverage

One relatively cost-effective way to improve both the area coverage and the shoot-look-shoot opportunities is to augment the sensor support to the GBR. Figure 6 shows how both percentage of CONUS coverage and the shoot-look-shoot capabilities increase for various BMD system sensor enhancements. Three enhancement options are shown: (1) placing additional GBR sites around the periphery of CONUS, (2) adding to this option radar upgrades to existing BMEWS sites in Greenland and England, and (3) deploying a space-based target acquisition and tracking system (one such option would be Brilliant Eyes). All three options are arguable violations of the ABM treaty, but because Russia has its own motivation for wanting extended sensor-coverage capabilities, it might not challenge these enhancements seriously and might entertain treaty changes more generally.

Particularly attractive on grounds such as cost-effectiveness would be a space-based targeting system. The Bottom-Up Review recommended continued development of a long-wavelength infrared (LWIR) sensing satellite system (e.g., Brilliant Eyes (BE) or a less expensive theater version) that could do the needed job nicely.[40] BE would track an RV early in its midcourse flight, permitting GBI commitment before the RV comes over the horizon. This early-launch opportunity substantially increases coverage opportunities. In the extreme, it leads to calculations that show intercepts occurring over Miami by GBIs launched from Grand Forks, a feat that probably needs to be demonstrated before reasonable people would accept these calculations as realistic. The Brilliant Eyes program will almost certainly slip to have a timeline consistent with that of NMD.

Effective NMD Deployments and Implications for Stability

Figure 7 shows how CONUS defense protection improves as a function of the number (and location) of additional GBI sites deployed in CONUS (Alaska and Hawaii each require an individual GBI/GBR site for their protection). Both territorial and population coverage are displayed. Additional sites are deployed around the periphery of the country, mainly augmenting protection against attacks that might come from directions other than the north.

---

[40]BE would also help TMD, particularly against longer-ranged TBMs, and as such could be a valuable complement to defenses protecting U.S. friends and allies (see, e.g., Best and Bracken, 1993). The version needed would not need to be so "brilliant" or expensive as that envisioned for GMD (Canavan, 1993:7).

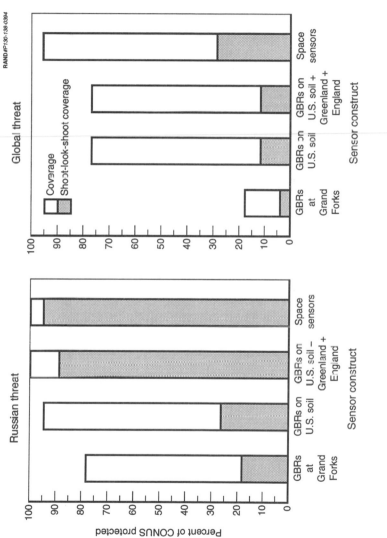

Figure 6—Providing Grand Forks GBI Deployment with Enhanced Sensor Support

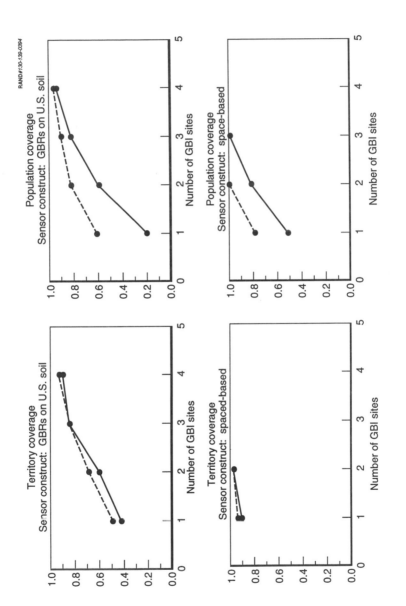

Figure 7—Multi-GBI Coverage of CONUS Territory and Population

Two cases are shown on each chart; one that assumes Grand Forks as the first site and then adds new sites in an incremented way (the solid curve), and one that allows sites to be selected optimally (the dashed curve). In all cases the fractional coverage of CONUS approaches one after a deployment of about four sites.

The effectiveness of the defense is also a function of the size of the attack, and especially so because of the ABM treaty limit on GBI deployments of 100. Figure 8 displays the total number of reliable GBIs that would need to be (optimally) deployed to successfully engage all but 3 percent of the RVs. Two attack sizes are shown, one for 50 RVs, the other for 200. The larger size exceeds the 100-RV threat that represents a nominal maximum for an unauthorized attack from a Russia compliant with START II. The indicated stockpile sizes, ranging from 800 (with only GBR sensor support on U.S. territory) to about 400 (with space-based sensors), should suffice to handle all future attacks

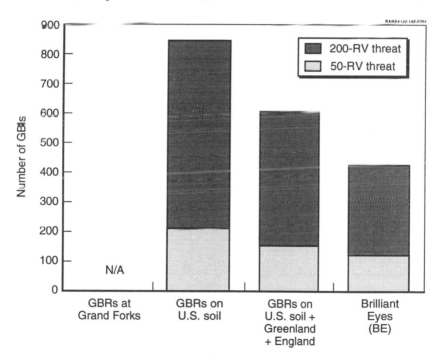

Figure 8—GBIs Required to Achieve No More Than 3 Percent Leakage

except those that might be deliberately launched from a newly hostile Russia.[41]

Of course, even 400 GBIs exceed the treaty limits. One hundred GBIs could provide low leakage protection against attack sizes of less than about 40 RVs—e.g., small accidental attacks from Russia as well as foreseeable Third World attacks from all countries except perhaps China. The treaty would still have to be altered, however, because of the need for geographical coverage.[42]

How likely is it that the Russians would accept a renegotiation of the ABM treaty, allowing GBI deployments of 400 or more? Obviously, 400 interceptors would not stop a fully alerted Russian ICBM or SLBM attack from devastating the United States, even after full implementation of the START II treaty. However, if such GBI deployments were combined with a surprise U.S. first strike against Russia's (nonalerted) nuclear forces, then it is *analytically* plausible that the follow-up Russian ballistic missile attack might be "manageable."[43] Thus, there would be the potential for first-strike instability (see also Wilkening, 1994), by which I mean that from a mathematical perspective there might be a significant incentive for conducting a first strike because if the second side attacked first, the first side would have less than a minimum retaliatory capability.[44] In some situations (i.e., with some combinations of defense capabilities), only one side would have such a first-strike incentive; in others, both would; and in still others, neither would.

---

[41]These force sizes are sensitive to the permitted maximum leakage levels. The value of 3 percent assumes low, but not zero, leakage. In a real deployment, this value would be weighed against other nuclear delivery options available to the opponent. Of course, for any given size deployment, lower leakage rates can theoretically be achieved with a given stockpile by "doubling up" on interceptor launches, salvoing two or more GBIs for each "shoot" opportunity. Thus, for most anticipated attacks, the leakage rate could be closer to zero than shown here.

[42]Because complete coverage is required, some GBIs cannot participate in engagements against threats launched from unfavorable locations. This "absentee" factor varies with interceptor capability, the sophistication of the sensor coverage, etc. For many cases, the factor is about 30 percent, i.e., about 30 percent of the GBIs are in the wrong location to engage a specific attack.

[43]"Manageable" is in the eye of the beholder. It is difficult to imagine that a U.S. president would find even a few nuclear detonations on U.S. cities acceptable under any circumstance where another option is available. To a Russian leader, however, the inability to threaten wholesale damage to the United States as a counterbalance to a similar U.S. capability may be cause for serious concern.

[44]For discussion of first-strike stability focused more on decisionmaker psychology, notably facts of desperation and fear, see Davis (1989), which disparages the purely mathematical approach to stability assessments but notes how the mathematical characterization enters the problem.

Figure 9 illustrates this using a "defense-domain plot."[45]   The discussion here is qualitative, but for more sophisticated and quantitative results see Shaver (1986), Watman and Wilkening (1986), and Kent, DeValk, and Thaler (1988).   In Figure 9, which is drawn for a particular assumed set of offensive capabilities more or less of the sort likely after START II takes effect, the abscissa and ordinant axes represent U.S. and Russian defense capabilities, respectively.   They extend from none (no capability) to perfect capability to stop all attacking weapons.[46]   Note the existence of different zones.   The

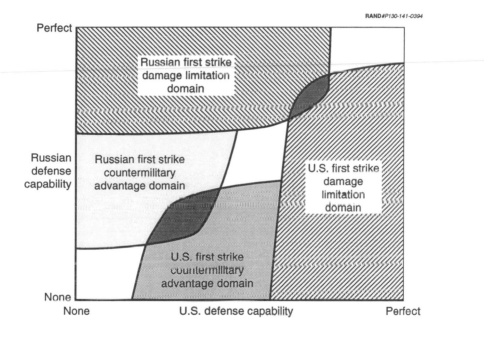

Figure 9—Conditions for Maintaining Stability

---

[45]I first used this particular graphic description for examining first-strike stability in a 1983 RAND study with James Thomson.

[46]These charts can be drawn with alternative variables for the axes.   For example, Kent, DeValk, and Thaler (1988) proposed use of a variable called "defense potential." This variable is calculated by multiplying the number of defense interceptors times their expected kill potential against the threat.   This variable has the attractive feature of allowing comparison of dissimilar offensive force postures, showing that "equal" defense deployments do not lead to balanced capabilities.   See also the later publications Kent and Thaler (1989, 1990).

shaded zones correspond to conditions where the combination of Russian and U.S. defense deployment provides to one or both sides some advantageous first-strike capabilities. In a severe crisis these advantages may be cause for instability. Instabilities are greatest wherever the zones overlap. The situation is stable in the unshaded zones, i.e., where defenses are absent or where both sides possess near-perfect defenses.

Figure 9 is merely illustrative. The actual plots depend sensitively on many details of both offensive and defensive posture, the assumed exchange scenario, and other factors, but a few general observations can be made:

- The instability regions tend to grow larger as the total size of the nuclear arsenals shrinks. Thus, START II force postures are more likely to be destabilizing with defensive deployments than those planned under START I. Further force reductions could exacerbate this situation.

- Ameliorating this is the fact that the regions shrink with reduced vulnerability of the offensive forces. Stable transition regimes are readily obtainable if both countries pay attention to insuring the invulnerability of their nuclear forces.

- The regions examined so far pertain mainly to ballistic missile forces. Bombers and air defenses interact in slightly more complicated ways, tending to further reduce the instability domains. Most mid-to-late 1980s calculations using realistic postures and planning factors for nuclear exchanges showed only small or no instability regimes, primarily because of the air breathers. It is noteworthy, however, that the air-breathing forces may have very low alert rates in the future.

So, reasonable actions to care for the survivability of the offensive forces sharply diminish instability concerns, obviously lessening any incentives for first strike while leaving ample room for both countries to deploy defenses that can provide the desired protection against Third World threats. In real-world terms, this means that U.S. defense deployments are only as destabilizing as Russian leaders are willing to allow them to be. After all, Russia controls the vulnerability of its forces to a U.S. first strike. Obviously, the United States can affect this situation by reducing its own first-strike capabilities. But a Russian commitment to higher alert rates and secure operating bastions for its SSBN fleet should mitigate if not outright eliminate any concern about U.S. GBI deployments numbering in the many hundreds.[47]

These defense domain curves also say something about the prospect of cooperative defense deployments leading toward the defense-dominant world of Present Reagan. Just being cooperative on defenses wouldn't prevent instabil-

---

[47]See Best and Bracken (1993) for an elegant discussion of n-sided stability calculations (i.e., calculations that consider many "sides" rather than merely the United States and Russia).

ity regions, but if instability regions can be avoided through careful management of both offensive and defensive deployments, then it is possible to reach the offensive-impotent region wherein neither side has lost its assured retaliation capability but each has denied to the other all options save attacking urban areas. This region would be highly stable. It is a possible target point for cooperative defensive deployments that would avoid the difficulty of finding a way for both sides to abandon their nuclear deterrence capabilities altogether.

But to what point? Defenses against Third World threats can be achieved with relatively small defense deployments, as can protection against small attacks from Russia. Stability is not an issue; the current situation of little or no defense is itself quite stable. And there is no assurance that large deployments are a positive step toward total protection from nuclear attack; at the least, covert weapon delivery capabilities would probably still exist. Moreover, defenses to reach the upper right portion of the defense domain would be extraordinarily expensive.

All of this suggests that middling defense deployments, short of those that provide meaningful damage limitings, are difficult to justify. Limited BMD deployments can be quite valuable for limiting damage from small attacks,[48] but deployments of a much larger magnitude may only be more costly and more dangerous.

GLOBAL BALLISTIC MISSILE DEFENSES

So far, we have discussed theater and national ballistic missile defenses. Let me now also discuss the kind of global missile defenses (GMD) sometimes envisioned by President Reagan a decade ago. These would not only protect the United States, but provide protection for selected nations worldwide. As a practical matter, GMD virtually implies a layer of space-based defenses, because a number of studies over the last decade have indicated that only this could provide the desired comprehensiveness and robustness to countermeasures.[49] The attractiveness of getting ballistic missiles in boost flight is obvious, but especially so when the missiles are outfitted with multiple RVs or penetration decoys. Without space-based defense overlays such as envisioned in the Brilliant Pebbles (BP) system, it would also be nearly impossible to achieve

---

[48]Among the options that merit consideration is the possibility of adapting excess Minuteman missiles as exoatmospheric interceptors. Coupling Minuteman with the LEAP vehicle and an early version of the GBR could provide the United States with a credible limited NMD system early (Cooper, 1993).

[49]While these studies strongly suggest that space-based defense would be a necessary element of a comprehensive and robust strategic defense, there remain serious questions about whether such defenses would be sufficient.

an acceptable cost-exchange ratio of U.S. defenses over Russian sophisticated offenses.

Although the Clinton administration has reduced Brilliant Pebbles and other space-based weapon concepts to at best technology status, killing any near-term prospects for GMD, it is quite possible that interest in GMD will come back in time, perhaps in the context of cooperative U.S.-Russian efforts.

To have an effective boost-phase kill potential, space-based kinetic kill (KKV) satellites (e.g., the Brilliant Pebbles system) must be in low earth orbits. This results in a significant satellite absentee factor—that is, a major fraction of the satellites are located over parts of the earth from which no missiles are being launched, and thus they cannot participate in the defense.[50] The absentee factor is sensitive to the total time that the booster is in powered flight. These times vary widely, being shorter for shorter-range missiles (e.g., TBMs) and for solid-propellant missiles. The large Russian missiles (e.g., the SS-18) have long burn times and are the most attractive targets for BPs. Figure 10 displays the potential effectiveness of deployments of BP in terms of the number of salvo-launched boosters that a constellation of orbiting BPs could intercept. Because of the absentee factor, the number of kills is small compared to the number of BPs deployed. Note also that TBMs can be intercepted, although the number of shorter-range missiles that could be handled is quite small.

Some immediate conclusions are possible. First, Brilliant Pebbles by itself does not constitute a very robust defense, at least in deployment numbers up to 2000.[51] Based on substantial RAND work by Michael Miller, Susan Everingham, and Herbert Hoover, it seems that ground-based defenses are almost certainly a more cost-effective approach to defend against limited attacks than a Brilliant Pebbles approach. The most likely future roles for space-based defenses are (1) as augmentation for ground-based defenses if defense against large and sophisticated attacks is required, and (2) as gap-fillers for both TMD

---

[50]The absentee factor is especially severe for kinetic kill vehicles, exceeding 95 percent under many circumstances. The factor is greatly reduced if these vehicles are capable of killing RVs after booster burnout. When most ICBMs were MIRVed, that MIRVing inflicted its own multiplier penalty on midcourse killers, but with START II, MIRVed ICBMs (not SLBMs) should be eliminated.

[51]Earlier studies by SDIO and others looked at BP deployments of 20,000 and larger. Even with an absentee factor of 95 percent, 20,000 BPs could theoretically engage 1000 ICBMs, even if launched nearly simultaneously. Given the small likelihood that this many boosters would be launched within a small time period, along with the fact that the remaining 19,000 BPs would still be in orbit and available for employment (unless the attacker timed its salvos to correspond with "holes" that the initial engagement created in the space-based defense), deployments of this magnitude could in theory provide a very robust strategic defense capability.

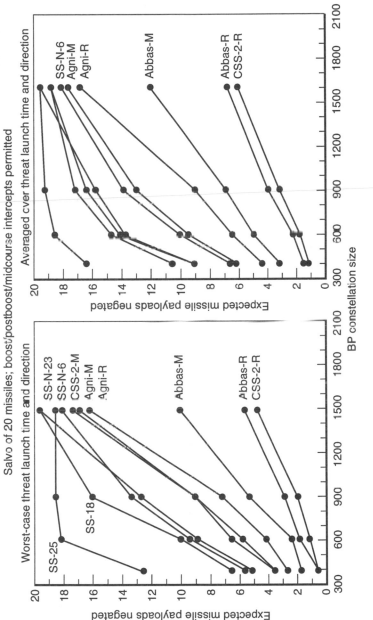

Figure 10—Impact of Constellation Size on BP Interdiction Potential

and NMD deployments where coverage gaps exist. As already discussed, one can imagine scenarios where other TMD systems either cannot or will not be in position to defend critical theater targets when needed; BP could play a (perhaps limited) role in filling this need. However, where other options exist it is doubtful that space-based systems are the most cost-effective approach to provide this coverage. Space-based *sensors* such as BE are more clearly valuable (see, e.g., Figure 8).

ISSUES, TENSIONS, AND DILEMMAS IN CONTEMPLATING THE FUTURE OF BALLISTIC MISSILE DEFENSES

Given the Bottom-Up Review, it is highly doubtful that Congress will authorize sufficient funds to support full development of both NMD and TMD systems. It is easy to anticipate that for the next few years, concern about Third World TBM threats will carry the day for TMD developments. Whether NMD will be resurrected depends on whether there are credible threats and credible ways of dealing with them.

Is There a Credible Threat Justifying National Missile Defense?

The argument *against* NMD goes something like this and depends on balancing U.S. national interests: The TBM threat is already real and growing. Especially if outfitted with weapons of mass destruction, TBMs in the hands of our adversaries clearly threaten U.S. national security interests. Furthermore, it is far from clear what will be required to deter some of our potential adversaries from executing this threat. In contrast, ICBM threats to the U.S. population and its infrastructure, while real, are diminishing. Moreover, the countries that currently possess ICBMs (and SLBMs) that could threaten the United States are judged to be deterrable. Thus, although lacking BMD, the United States is protected by its offensive retaliation forces, and strategic defenses hopefully are not needed, just as they weren't required for U.S. survival in the past.

The response to this argument, which is an argument for at least laying the base for a future NMD, starts with the assertion that even a single nuclear detonation on a U.S. city would be a disaster of unprecedented proportions for the United States. Regardless of cost-effectiveness considerations, American voters would demand an explanation as to why the United States was spending many billions on theater missile defenses to defend foreign countries but not equal or greater amounts for protection for itself. This is a question that is likely to arise even before such a detonation occurs, and reasonable answers will be required.

Ballistic missile threats against the United States can come from three sources: (1) the residual nuclear stockpile of Russia (or, conceivably, other states of the former Soviet Union), either deliberately or accidentally launched against the United States; (2) the growing but still small inventory of nuclear delivery vehicles in other nuclear states (e.g., China); or (3) a not now existing, but plausible, presence of ICBM threats from as-yet unidentified Third World countries or cross-national terrorist organizations. Because the last source of threat is likely to be the most difficult to deter, a few additional words about it are warranted.

It may be ironic, but successful U.S. counter-TBM deployments could actually *motivate* Third World development of ICBMs. Frustrated by being unable to prevent U.S. intervention, countries like Iraq may see ICBMs as an effective means to deter the United States. The technologies needed for (inaccurate) ICBMs are widely proliferated around the world, and it is to be expected that space-launch vehicles will at some time be converted for this purpose. The Indian official's observation about the main lesson from Desert Storm being "don't fight the United States unless you're armed with nuclear weapons" is a view probably shared by many Third World leaders, including Khadafi.[52] If the United States could defend regionally against TBMs possessed by antagonistic Third World nations, what would deter these nations from seeking capability against the United States itself?

How would the United States react to a Third World country that built an ICBM with an apparent nuclear weapon on top? Even if we could find the missiles (i.e., even if they were not protected by mobility, basing in caves, or whatever), would we preemptively strike the launch or storage site in hopes of destroying the threat before it could be launched? Would we do this before the onset of a crisis involving our vital national interests, or would we wait until a crisis arose? And if the President had doubts about the certainty of our capabilities to destroy the threatening missiles before their launch, would he nevertheless press ahead with plans to deploy our forces into the region of crisis? Importantly for this discussion, how would answers to these questions change if the United States possessed a limited BMD system?[53]

With or without defenses to underwrite U.S. commitments, it is hard to state how future U.S. presidents would answer these questions. But a not unreasonable speculation is that only with high-confidence defenses would they

---

[52]See Garrity (1993) for a wide variety of foreign views about the lessons of the Gulf War, including the role of nuclear weapons.

[53]When I posed some of these questions to my colleagues, the answers varied widely, ranging from "we would be absolutely deterred" to "we would turn their country into glass." Whatever the answers, one observation was common: We need to develop strategies for dealing with countries whose leaders hold different values than our own.

feel free to press forward with U.S. power projection assets, protecting our vital interests and those of our friends and allies around the globe.

Countering Other Nuclear Delivery Means

Of course, ICBMs are not the only means to threaten the United States with nuclear attack. The above list of questions applies as well to nuclear attacks delivered by aircraft or ships. If we deploy a NMD to stop a hypothetical Third World ICBM threat, what is to prevent that threat from constructing an aircraft threat, or a cruise missile threat? And if it did, would the United States be prepared to defend against it?

The answer to the last question rests in large part on the adequacy of intelligence. The United States has ample aircraft and ships to protect itself against small attacks by either airplanes or ships, so long as it knows that it is under attack and which vehicle (or collection of vehicles) constitutes the attack. Such defenses already are part of the existing military structure and come at no cost.

Not as clear-cut is whether adequate intelligence exists or will exist to the extent needed to provide U.S. decisionmakers with the needed warning to implement appropriate defensive measures. The warning must be both timely and highly credible. How this intelligence requirement can or will be met is unclear.

But Must We Live Forever Under the Threat of Nuclear Attack?

Against this background of history, new and emerging threats, and technological options, how should we think about managing the nuclear threat and the role BMD could play? Those who set long-term priorities for BMD developments should certainly address how best to manage the fact of the existence of nuclear weapons (and, increasingly, the threat of biological weapons) around the globe. Although START II promises to sharply reduce global nuclear inventories, international politics and human nature argue that abolishing nuclear warheads altogether may not be possible. Does this mean, therefore, that our children, our children's children, and their children will have to live under the constant threat of nuclear annihilation? And how do we deal with the reasonable fear that, sooner or later, some zealot or crazyman will gain access to such weapons and use them despite efforts at deterrence? Such an occurrence may be very unlikely, but events with very small probabilities happen nevertheless.

It may be useful to review the approaches available to the United States to manage this threat.

- *Active defense.* This is, of course, the principal subject of this paper. It is a subset of a more general category, denial. Denial includes direct counter-force attack as well as active defense, essentially denying to the threatening country the ability to successfully attack the United States.

- *Deterrence.* This promises the potential attacker that nothing can be gained and much will be lost by attacking the United States. It tries to influence the attacker's view of both his cost from the attack as well as his benefit from not implementing the attack.

- *Disarmament.* In its broadest sense, this seeks to deny nuclear arms to those who don't currently possess them (through the Non-Proliferation Treaty or other means) and the abandonment of nuclear weapons by countries that do have them (by international agreement, perhaps along the lines of the Baruch plan of 1946).

Active defense has the attractive feature that, to some extent, the possessor is in control of his own fate. However, as studies over the last 40 years have clearly demonstrated, it is extremely difficult and quite possibly impossible to stop all nuclear attacks by a dedicated opponent. Defenses might stop the first attack, the second, and the third, but sooner or later something is likely to get through. Thus, so long as nuclear weapons exist, active defenses need to be underwritten by deterrence, i.e., by retaining capable nuclear offensive forces.[54] This creates the burden not just to build and maintain near-leakproof defenses, but also to maintain offensive weapons that are at least as capable as any enemy's of getting to their targets. This is a far cry from the pure notion of defense dominance, where the moral dilemma of relying on nuclear retaliation would not exist.

Deterrence is hardly a sturdy reed for the indefinite future, resting as it does on the rational behavior of our opponents. But a true psychopath rarely reaches a leadership position, even in the Third World. Deterrence has worked for the past 40 years and may work for 1000 more. Who knows? But for those who would abandon it, what will replace it? Not active defense by itself, as explained above.

Deterrence also rests on the credible threat of a response that will raise the cost of the attack above its benefits as seen by the side that one is trying to de-ter (see Davis (1994a) for discussion of deterrence in the post–Cold War era). But it is far from clear just what threatened response the United States would use to deter the use of WMD against its forces in the field or against its friends

---

[54]This may seem contradictory, but it is obvious once we recognize that the country under attack must force a price on the attacker for his first attack, even if that attack is unsuccessful. Without such a price, the attacker has no incentive to stop such attacks until success is realized.

and allies. Except for direct attacks against the homeland of the United States, the credibility of U.S. nuclear use is subject to doubt.[55]

That leaves us with nuclear disarmament. The attempts to control nuclear technology and weaponry immediately after World War II were doomed to failure from the start. No country, including the United States, was ready to empower an international organization with such authority (Bundy, 1993). However, without the involvement of an international body to monitor and enforce any agreement, nuclear disarmament is most likely impossible. The process will almost certainly fall victim to power politics.

Thus, proponents of total nuclear disarmament face a serious dilemma: push for a process that the United States and other major nuclear states will almost certainly reject, or accept the likelihood of failure. Under current international circumstances it is hard to foresee conditions where total nuclear disarmament can be achieved.

Finally, there are a number of compelling reasons to believe that the spread of nuclear weapons will continue. Realistic approaches to stopping this spread are lacking. Draconian approaches, wherein some state (e.g., the United States) takes a unilateralist approach and acts to confront, deter, and if necessary disarm those states that brandish such weapons, have many flaws. Defenses will help delay the holocaust, but direct action may be needed to deny it.

"In for a Penny, in for a Pound"

All the above suggests that some combination of policies—active defense, deterrence, and (perhaps in the long term) setting the conditions for the formation of an international organization to help reduce nuclear weapon stockpiles—needs to be applied to manage the nuclear threat, hopefully leaving our children more safe and secure than we are today. Active defense can and should play an essential role, providing needed protection where deterrence fails or where the credibility of it is weak.

However, it is worth raising a question asked earlier: "How much is enough?" There is no logical stopping point for deployments of either TMD or NMD, short of near-perfect defense. Nor does there appear to be a high likelihood of turning such deployments around once started. Much like nuclear deterrence, active protection will not be abandoned easily, even if the

---

[55]Even in this case, some would question whether a U.S. president would order a nuclear attack against the offending country, especially if extensive collateral damage to that country's population was likely. Such a decision would be particularly difficult if it were felt that the country's leaders did not reflect the sentiment of its people, and that the people should not be held responsible for the actions of their leaders.

costs of maintaining it start to grow sharply. Once we are firmly down this path, there may be no turning back. Figures 11 and 12 portray two alternative outcomes associated with starting down the BMD path. One is generally favorable. The other is the opposite. Both are plausible. In either case, the world will not be the same.

FINAL OBSERVATIONS AND SUGGESTIONS

The above discussions on BMD lead to the following observations and recommendations, which are unabashedly subjective in some cases.

- The TBM and WMD threat already exists and is likely to become worse over time. It must be challenged, or U.S. global interests will be severely threatened. TMD is an important ingredient in countering that threat and deserves the priority it received in the Bottom-Up Review.

- However, the Bottom-Up Review's focus on terminal or late-midcourse defense needs to be broadened. The shortcomings of such defenses can be

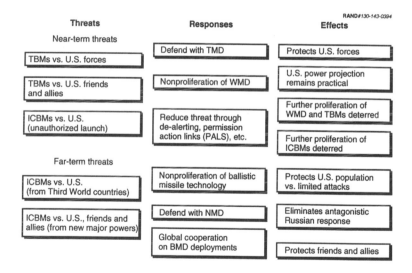

Figure 11—One Outcome of BMD Developments: U.S. Strategic Interests
Preserved and Strengthened

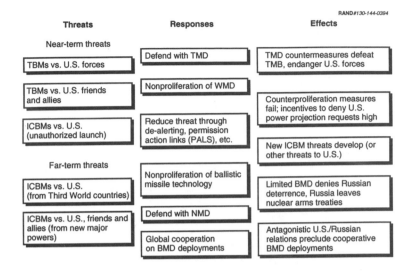

RAND#130-144-0394

Figure 12—Another Outcome of BMD Developments: U.S. Strategic Interests
Harmed with Little Protection for U.S. Population or Deployed Forces

exploited by future aggressors, greatly diminishing TMD effectiveness.
Counterforce, counterbattery, boost-phase, and early-midcourse intercept
options should all be pursued. If necessary, THAAD development should
be slowed to provide additional funds for other high-leverage counter-TBM
options.

- There are reasons to be concerned about potential unauthorized attacks em-
  anating from a turbulent Russia. However, the likelihood of such attacks is
  very small, given Russian security measures. Deliberate attacks from Russia
  and other countries (e.g., China) are also very unlikely, based on deterrence.
  On this basis, the risks associated with abandoning plans for near-term deployments of NMD are acceptable.

- However, the appearance of a Third World ICBM threat, while far from a
  certainty, could also severely threaten U.S. global interests. In this case, deterrence would work against the United States. A NMD may be a prerequisite to managing this threat. Thus, NMD developments should be kept
  on a timeline consistent with having a limited NMD deployment option
  available at the time that such a threat might appear.

- Because it provides unique capabilities, a space-based midcourse tracking
  system (e.g., Brilliant Eyes) should be developed. The timing of such a development should be paced to match threat and budget concerns.

- The importance of space-based BMD weapons rests on their ability to add important capabilities to already deployed TMD and NMD systems. It is unclear when and if these capabilities will be needed. Their current status as a technology demonstration effort seems appropriate.

These first six observations largely support current DoD policy, but they suggest a reexamination of the strategy being used to obtain robust TMD and NMD capabilities on the time scale needed. The next two suggestions cover broader issues associated with managing the long-term nuclear problem.

- Work with Russia to (a) augment the ABM treaty and (b) implement meaningful confidence and security building measures that would lower the likelihood of either accidental or unauthorized attacks from Russian soil or submarines.

- Develop a policy toward nuclear weapons that combines concerns about nuclear proliferation and both TMD and NMD deployments. That policy should address the most fundamental questions about the long-term role of nuclear weapons in U.S. national security objectives.

In conclusion, technology has offered the United States the opportunity to start down a new path—improving national security through deployment of active ballistic missile defenses—at a time when the need for BMD, at least TMD, was never clearer. However, not all of the consequences of BMD deployments are well understood. Over the next several years it will be important for U.S. policy analysts to explore these consequences, looking toward a future in which the global interests of the United States are protected and the fear of nuclear warfare is lessened.

BIBLIOGRAPHY

In addition to the references shown here, I made extensive use of current trade journals, in particular *Aviation Week and Space Technology* and *Defense Week*. Listing all the pertinent articles here would have would needlessly lengthened the bibliography.

American Institute of Astronautics and Aeronautics (1993), *Assessment of Ballistic Missile Defense Technologies*, May.

Aspin, Les (1993), *The Bottom-Up Review*, Department of Defense, Washington D.C.

Atkinson, Rick (1993), *Crusade: The Untold Story of the Persian Gulf War*, Houghton Mifflin, Boston.

Best, Mel, and Jerome Bracken (1993), *Proceedings of the Strategic Options Assessment Conference*, U.S. Strategic Command, Offutt AFB, March 9–10.

Brodie, Bernard (1948), "The Atom Bomb & Policy Maker," *Foreign Affairs*, October 27.

Buchan, Glenn C. (1994a), *U.S. Nuclear Strategy for the Post–Cold War Era*, RAND, Santa Monica, CA.

———— (1994b), "The Use of Long-Range Bombers in a Changing World: A Classical Exercise in Systems Analysis," in Davis (1994b).

Builder, Carl H., and Morlie H. Graubard (1982), *The International Law of Armed Conflict: Implications for Assured Destruction*, RAND, Santa Monica, CA.

Bundy, McGeorge (1993), *Danger and Survival: Choices About the Bomb in the First Fifty Years*, Random House, New York.

Canavan, Gregory (1993), *What Are the Best Options for Theater Missile Defense*, Washington Roundtable on Science and Public Policy, George C. Marshall Institute, Washington, D.C.

Carter, Ashton, and David N. Schwartz (eds.) (1984), *Ballistic Missile Defense*, The Brookings Institution, Washington, D.C.

Cooper, Ambassador Henry F. (1993), "Active Defense: How Can Allies and Friends and Forward-Positioned U.S. Forces Be Protected Against Nuclear Attacks," presented at the Conference on Counter-Proliferation—Deterring Emerging Nuclear Actors, Offutt AFB, July.

Davis, Paul K. (1989), *Studying First-Strike Stability with Knowledge-Based Models of Human Decisionmaking*, RAND, Santa Monica, CA.

———— (1994a), "Improving Deterrence in the Post–Cold War Era: Some Theory and Implications for Defense Planning," in Davis (1994b).

———— (ed.) (1994b), *New Challenges for Defense Planning: Rethinking How Much Is Enough*, RAND, Santa Monica, CA.

Delaney, William P. (1992), "How Do We Respond to Theater Ballistic Missile Attacks?" MIT Lincoln Laboratory, February.

Department of Defense (1965), *DoD Annual Posture Report to the Congress, Fiscal Year 1966*.

———— (1991, 1992), *DoD Report to Congress on the Strategic Defense Initiative*.

———— (1993), *BMDO Boost Phase Intercept Study*.

Eisenstein, Maurice, et al. (1992), *The Army's Role in Ballistic Missile Defense: A Preliminary Review of the Prospects and Issues*, RAND, Santa Monica, CA.

Garrity, Patrick J. (1993), *Why the Gulf War Still Matters: Foreign Perspectives on the War and the Future of International Security*, Report No. 16, Center for National Security Studies, Los Alamos National Laboratory.

Gershwin, Lawrence K. (1993), "Threats to U.S. Interests from Ballistic Missile-Delivered Weapons of Mass Destruction During the Next Ten to Twenty Years," presented at the Conference on Counter-Proliferation—Deterring Emerging Nuclear Actors, Offutt AFB, July.

Gold, Ted, and Jasper Welch (co-chairs) (1993), *Theater Defense Architecture Study*, 3 vols., Strategic Defense Initiative Organization, January.

Hoffman, Fred, et al. (1984), *Ballistic Missile Defenses and U.S. National Security*, prepared for Future Security Strategy Study, Hearing before the Committee on Foreign Relations (Strategic Defense and Anti-Satellite Weapons), United States Senate, Senate Hearing 98-750, U.S. Government Printing Office, Washington, D.C.

Kahn, Herman (1960), *On Thermonuclear War*, Princeton University Press, Princeton, NJ.

Kaplan, Fred (1983), *Wizards of Armageddon*, Simon and Schuster, New York.

Kent, Glenn (1964), "A Summary Study of Strategic Offensive and Defensive Forces of the U.S. and U.S.S.R.," prepared for the Director of Defense Research and Engineering, Department of Defense, R&E log no. 64-4165.

Kent, Glenn A., and David E. Thaler (1989), *First-Strike Stability: A Methodology for Evaluating Strategic Forces*, RAND, Santa Monica, CA.

——— (1990), *First-Strike Stability and Strategic Defenses: Part II of a Methodology for Evaluating Strategic Forces*, RAND, Santa Monica, CA.

Kent, Glenn A., Randall J. DeValk, and David E. Thaler (1988), *A Calculus of First-Strike Stability: A Criterion for Evaluating Strategic Forces*, RAND, Santa Monica, CA.

Larsen, Eric, and Glenn Kent (1994), *A New Methodology for Assessing Multi-Layer Missile Defense Systems*, RAND, Santa Monica, CA.

Mesic, Richard (1994a), "Defining a Balanced Investment Program for Coping with Tactical Ballistic Missiles," in Davis (1994b).

——— (1994b), "Extended-Counterforce Options for Coping with Tactical Ballistic Missiles," in Davis (1994b).

Millot, Marc Dean, Roger C. Molander, and Peter A. Wilson (1993), *The "Day After..." Study: Nuclear Proliferation in the Post–Cold War World* (summary volume), RAND, Santa Monica, CA.

Molander, Roger C., and Peter A. Wilson (1993), *The Nuclear Asymptote: On Containing Nuclear Proliferation*, RAND, Santa Monica, CA.

Nixon, Richard N. (1978), *RN: The Memoirs of Richard Nixon*, Grosset and Dunlap, New York.

Nolan, Janne E. (1989), *Guardians of the Arsenal: The Politics of Nuclear Strategy*, Basic Books, New York.

Nye, Joseph S., Jr. (1986), *Nuclear Ethics*, The Free Press, New York.

Office of Technology Assessment (1986), *Strategic Defenses: Ballistic Missile Defense Technologies, Anti-Satellite Weapons, Countermeasures, and Arms Control*, Princeton University Press, Princeton, NJ.

Postol, Theodore (1991), "Lessons from the Gulf War PATRIOT Experience," *International Security*, Winter 1991/1992.

Reeves, Richard (1993), *Profile of Power*, Simon and Schuster, New York.

Roberts, Brad (ed.) (1993), *Biological Weapons: Weapons of the Future?* The Center for Strategic and International Studies, Washington, D.C.

Shaver, Russ (1986), "Le Rôle Potentiel de l'IDS pour la Défense des Objectifs Civils et/ou Militaires sur la Territoire des Etas-Unis," in Pierre Lellouche (ed.), *L'Initiative de défense stratégique et la sécurité de l'Europe*, Institut Français des Relations Internationales, Paris.

Shultz, George P. (1993), *Turmoil and Triumph: My Years as Secretary of State*, Charles Scribner's Sons, New York.

Slocombe, Walter (1981), "The Countervailing Strategy," *International Security*, Vol. 5, Spring.

Strategic Defense Initiative Organization (1993), *1993 Report to the Congress on the Strategic Defense Initiative*, January.

Systems Planning Corporation (1992), *Ballistic Missile Proliferation, An Emerging Threat*, Arlington, VA.

van Voorst, L. Bruce (1983), "The Churches and Nuclear Deterrence," *Foreign Affairs*, Spring.

Watman, Kenneth, and Dean A. Wilkening (1986), *Strategic Defenses and First-Strike Stability*, RAND, Santa Monica, CA.

Wilkening, Dean (1994), "Future U.S and Russian Nuclear Forces: Applying Traditional Analysis in an Era of Cooperation," in Davis (1994b).

Wohlstetter, Albert, Harry Rowen, Fred Hoffman, and Robert Lutz (1954), *Selection and Use of Strategic Air Bases*, RAND, Santa Monica, CA.

York, Herbert (1970), *Race to Oblivion: A Participant's View of the Arms Race*, Simon and Schuster, New York.

Chapter 11

FUTURE U.S. AND RUSSIAN NUCLEAR FORCES: APPLYING TRADITIONAL ANALYSIS METHODS IN AN ERA OF COOPERATION

Dean Wilkening

With the end of the Cold War, the perceived need for a large U.S. nuclear arsenal has virtually disappeared. Thus, U.S. policymakers must confront the question of how low the nuclear arsenal should be cut, as well as whether strategic nuclear forces should be taken off alert as a symbol of the improved political atmosphere with the former Soviet Union. At the same time, interest in a limited nationwide ballistic missile defense system has increased because of concern with possible accidental, unauthorized, or deliberate third-country ballistic missile attacks. This paper applies a classical analysis of deterrence to the evolving U.S.-Russian strategic nuclear relationship. The aim is to identify potential problems that might be created during cooperative times as force levels are reduced, alert rates drop, and ballistic missile defenses deployed, so they can be avoided if tensions resurface between these two former Cold War adversaries. In general, deterrence appears to be robust with START II force levels so long as U.S. and Russian alert rates are not reduced dramatically from their current levels. However, relatively modest nationwide ballistic missile defense deployments (on the order of 600 ground-based interceptors or more) can seriously erode Russia's deterrent when U.S. and Russian forces are on day-to-day alert. This might cause Russia to react in ways making future crises difficult to control, thereby increasing fears (or the actual risk) of inadvertent nuclear war. These reactions could include rapid force generation early in a crisis or placing Russian ballistic missiles in a launch-on-warning posture, neither of which is attractive to the United States. The Russian deterrent posture is less robust than the U.S. posture on day-to-day alert because a smaller fraction of Russia's strategic nuclear forces would survive a hypothetical counterforce attack.

INTRODUCTION

With the Cold War over, U.S. relations with the states that once comprised the republics of the Soviet Union are undergoing rapid change. As part of this

---

For a more expansive treatment of the issues addressed in this paper, see Wilkening (1994).

change, the United States and Russia are reassessing the role that nuclear weapons play in their respective national security strategies. Under the rubric of "nuclear disengagement" the United States and Russia have called for deep cuts in their respective nuclear arsenals, as well as reductions in the peacetime readiness posture for the remaining forces.

The magnitude and speed of these reductions is obviously stunning by Cold War standards.[1] In the emerging environment, it is natural to ask what impact these and possible future cuts will have on U.S. security. Or, put another way, how should U.S. and Russian leaders go about future nuclear force reductions so as to minimize the likelihood that old problems associated with the U.S.-Soviet Cold War nuclear standoff will reappear? One problem to be avoided is that deep cuts, if taken inappropriately or too deeply, could weaken the stable deterrent relationship that has existed between the United States and the former Soviet Union for decades. This paper explores ways in which the U.S.-Russian strategic relationship can be modified in cooperative times so as to avoid such problems if the U.S.-Russian relationship once again becomes adversarial. Specifically, it analyzes the impact of deep cuts (as embodied in the START II Treaty), reduced peacetime alert postures, and limited nation-wide ballistic missile defenses (deployed to protect against accidental, unauthorized, and deliberate third-country ballistic missile attacks) on the deterrent relationship between the United States and Russia.[2]

First, it is necessary to say a word about the possibility of future conflicts (not necessarily hot wars) between the United States and Russia, because if one truly believes that conflict is impossible, then the analysis that follows is irrele-

---

[1] On July 31, 1991, the START I Treaty was signed, calling for a ceiling of 6000 accountable weapons in the U.S. and former Soviet strategic nuclear arsenals (a reduction of approximately 25–30 percent from the arsenals in existence in July 1991). Unilateral initiatives were declared by Presidents Bush and Gorbachev in the fall of 1991, reducing the tactical nuclear arsenals on each side to approximately 1600 weapons (a reduction of about 80 percent in the U.S. case) and removing all heavy bombers from heightened states of alert. On May 23, 1992, the Lisbon Protocol to the START I Treaty was signed, obliging Belarus, Kazakhstan, and Ukraine to eliminate all nuclear weapons formerly deployed or stored on their territory. And most recently, on January 17, 1993, the START II Treaty was signed, though it has yet to be ratified, further cutting U.S. and Russian strategic nuclear arsenals to between 3000 and 3500 total weapons. The START II Treaty represents the latest and deepest cut in both sides' strategic nuclear forces, reducing the U.S. strategic nuclear arsenal to its lowest point since the early 1960s and the former Soviet arsenal to its lowest point since the early 1970s.

[2] The analysis presented here could be extended in a straightforward manner to include other interesting nuclear interactions, for example, the United States and China, Russia and Great Britain or Russia and France, as well as Russia and Ukraine (assuming Ukraine remains a nuclear power despite its declaration to give up all former Soviet nuclear weapons stationed on its territory).

vant. Despite current cooperative trends between these two great powers, there are reasons to be cautious about concluding that conflicts could not occur.[3] Certainly U.S.-Russian relations have improved dramatically over the past several years. The Cold War is over. Global conflict, especially global nuclear war, is no longer a major threat. This is all for the good.

However, Russia is in the midst of a profound political and economic transformation—the outcome of which is far from predetermined. Major powers have rarely, if ever, undergone changes comparable to those currently underway in the former Soviet Union without a war or revolution. That these changes are occurring peacefully is truly remarkable, as well as highly desirable. Nevertheless, economic conditions continue to deteriorate, nationalism is on the rise, ethnic conflict is brewing, and crime is rampant.[4] Ultimately, conditions could become so desperate that social cohesion within Russia may come apart. The strong turnout for Vladimir Zhirinovsky (a neofascist leader favoring restoration and expansion of the Soviet empire) in the 1993 parliamentary elections is sobering.[5]

On the military front, the recent announcement of a new post–Cold War Russian military doctrine is some cause for concern, though most of it appears to be a straightforward extrapolation of former Soviet doctrine.[6] The new doctrine notes that the possibility of global nuclear war between Russia and the West is no longer a major threat. Instead, the emphasis is on future regional conflicts on the Russian periphery and on possible internal conflicts. The use of force (including offensive and defensive operations) is justified, according to the doctrine, to protect Russia's interests beyond her borders, e.g., to protect Russian-speaking peoples, as well as to quell domestic disturbances internally. Finally, the doctrine formally renounces the "no nuclear first use" pledge taken by previous Soviet governments, except against non-nuclear states that are not allied with a nuclear power. Consequently, in the future it is quite possible that Russia will increase its reliance on nuclear weapons to compensate for the

---

[3]Given that virtually no one predicted the end of the Cold War, it is curious that so many people predict with confidence that the current cooperative trends will not come to an end. Few people have ever predicted with great accuracy when, where, and under what circumstances great powers will come into conflict. For the foreseeable future, Russia will remain a great power with interests that may diverge from those of the United States, and it will also have interests in common.

[4]Also, some economists predict the imminent collapse of the Russian economy. See Lelyveld (1993).

[5]The misleadingly named New Democratic Party captured 24 percent of the popular vote. The next-closest contender was "Russia's Choice," the party supporting Yeltsin's reforms, with 14 percent of the vote. See Erlanger (1993) and Schmemann, (1993c).

[6]See, for example, Hiatt (1993) and Schmemann (1993a,b).

304 New Challenges for Defense Planning

weak state of its conventional military forces. In some respects, the Russian nuclear debate may come to resemble the U.S. nuclear debate during the Eisenhower administration, when such slogans as "defense on the cheap" and "more bang for the buck" reflected a greater emphasis on nuclear weapons in U.S. national security strategy to compensate for the high costs of maintaining robust conventional forces.

Under these circumstances it is premature to assert that U.S.-Russian relations could not take a significant turn for the worse, quite apart from the desire that this not occur. Such a reversal does not necessarily imply a return to Cold War tensions, if only because certain conflict scenarios seem virtually impossible today (for example, a Russian conventional invasion of Western Europe—a scenario that animated so much of the Cold War U.S. nuclear debate). However, the United States and Russia might find themselves embroiled in a future crisis (for example, over the territorial integrity of the Baltic states or Ukraine) where the underlying military balance, the strategic nuclear balance in particular, would be at least one factor influencing the dynamics of the crisis. Recognizing that nuclear weapons are less important today does not mean they are irrelevant, or that U.S. and Russian leaders should become blasé about the future of the U.S.-Russian deterrent relationship.

Therefore, though U.S. attention is focused currently on the problems associated with maintaining security and control over the vast former Soviet nuclear arsenal and nuclear weapons industrial complex, one must not forget that an enduring U.S. national security objective is to maintain a stable deterrent relationship with Russia while pursuing a foreign policy of increased cooperation on a range of issues vital to the security of both countries. In particular, U.S. foreign policy should promote political and economic reform within the former Soviet Union because, were it not for this transformation, the United States would still be embroiled in the Cold War, with its associated political/military tensions and high defense spending. Therefore, the United States should retain sufficient strategic nuclear force to deter any resurgent Russian threat, either against the United States or its allies, while avoiding threats that would undermine Russia's strategic nuclear deterrent, since this could upset U.S.-Russian political relations and encourage a military backlash within Russia.

Nuclear deterrence rests on the ability to deliver a crushing nuclear blow against an adversary, even after absorbing a massive nuclear attack. Hence, as Albert Wohlstetter pointed out over 30 years ago, deterrence rests on the ability to deliver nuclear weapons to the opponent's homeland and not on the mere existence of nuclear weapons in one's arsenal (Wohlstetter, 1959). Therefore, deterrence requires forces that can survive an opponent's counterforce first strike, operate reliably in a postattack environment, and penetrate any defenses the adversary has in place in sufficient quantity to threaten that which the adversary values most.[7]   In short, deterrence depends on the existence of a secure second-strike capability.

As a general proposition, deterrence becomes weaker as force levels drop. The question is: How low is too low? There is no simple answer to this question because it depends on whom one is trying to deter, from doing what, under what circumstances, and what U.S. threats appear credible under these circumstances. Deterring a risk-averse, status quo power that values the survival of its cities (i.e., its population, industrial base, etc.) from attacking the U.S. homeland with nuclear weapons does not require a sophisticated strategy. Deterring a revanchist regime from reconquering territory it believes is part of its homeland with a large conventional invasion would be much more difficult—especially if the U.S. commitment to the country being attacked is not highly credible.

As a corollary, the only rational incentive for a premeditated nuclear attack against a nuclear-armed adversary occurs when the attacker's counterforce capabilities and defenses are so robust that the attacker can significantly improve his chances for survival by striking first; i.e., he can destroy enough of the opponent's nuclear arsenal so that the ragged retaliatory strike cannot do significant damage to the attacker (particularly if it has to penetrate defenses). Hence, this paper analyzes the effectiveness of future U.S. or Russian damage-limiting first-strike options as both sides reduce their strategic nuclear arsenals, reduce the alert rates associated with these forces, and consider deploying limited nationwide ballistic missile defenses.

The perspective advanced in this analysis is not that a weak deterrence posture necessarily leads to deliberate nuclear attacks, but rather that it forces the strategically disadvantaged side to react in ways to redress its perceived vulnerability. This reaction may appear provocative to the other side in the midst of a crisis, thus setting off a spiral of mutual suspicion and mistrust that increases the chance for misperception and miscalculation of the opponent's intentions.[8] Though the likelihood that this spiral dynamic leads to intentional nuclear attacks may be small, unlike conventional scenarios, it will make crises more difficult to control, thereby increasing the chance of inadvertent nuclear war. Specifically, a vulnerable day-to-day alert posture does not imply that the

---

[7]Counterforce attacks are defined here to be attacks against strategic nuclear forces. In other words, they include attacks against ballistic missile submarine bases, long-range nuclear bomber bases, ICBM silos, mobile-ICBM garrisons, and possibly barrage attacks against mobile nuclear-delivery systems (e.g., submarines at sea, mobile ICBMs in the field, or bombers in flight). Attacks against strategic nuclear command-and-control systems and nuclear weapon storage and support facilities are not analyzed here, nor are attacks directed against theater or tactical nuclear forces.

[8]For a good discussion of spiral dynamics, largely drawn from historical examples of conventional conflict, see Jervis (1976).

opponent will launch a "bolt-out-of-the-blue" attack, because as a crisis develops, the vulnerable side can increase its alert rate, thereby increasing the fraction of its force that would survive a surprise attack. On the other hand, rapid force generation tends to be politically provocative because it often appears to the other side as a prelude to attack.[9] In this regard, the interesting strategic interaction is not the performance of U.S. and Russian arsenals when they are fully generated (the typical scenario for determining the overall size of the required force structure) but rather the mobilization dynamics as the United States or Russia move their forces from low to high states of alert; specifically, the extent to which either country might feel pressure to generate its forces rapidly in the early stages of a crisis, or perhaps to threaten to launch its vulnerable forces out from under an attack, because the peacetime alert posture does not provide an adequate deterrent.[10] To the extent such pressures exist, future crises may be more difficult to control. Suffice it to say that prudent planners should avoid creating relatively vulnerable U.S. or Russian strategic nuclear postures as both sides' forces are reduced. The likelihood of conflict with Russia may be small in the future, but with events this fateful, leaders should err on the side of caution.

FORCES AND ALERT RATES

Table 1 shows illustrative U.S. and Russian START II force structures. Both arsenals have been constructed to equal 3500 total weapons, despite the fact that President Yeltsin indicated in June 1992 that Russia might deploy only around 3000 strategic nuclear weapons. The larger Russian arsenal has been assumed because treaty ratification may require parity with the United States. The U.S. force structure is assumed to consist of 500 single-warhead Minuteman III ICBMs deployed in silos, 18 Trident submarines deployed with a mix of C-4 and D-5 SLBMs downloaded from 8 to 4 warheads each, and a bomber force of 114 nuclear-capable heavy bombers. The B-52H is assumed to be an air-launched cruise missile (ALCM) carrier, carrying both the

---

[9] For discussion of how psychology and perceptions could complicate a nuclear crisis, including assessment of force generation and efforts to de-escalate, see Davis and Wolf (1991).

[10] At the technical level, implementing START II will eliminate all land-based ICBMs equipped with multiple independently targeted reentry vehicles (MIRVs). This, so the argument goes, helps establish a more stable strategic nuclear balance by reducing first-strike incentives on both sides as well as each side's reliance on launch-under-attack to ensure the survival of these vulnerable forces. To the extent deterrence becomes weak in the future, the emphasis on launch-under-attack may reappear despite the elimination of land-based MIRVed ICBMs.

Table 1

Illustrative START II Forces (Weapons)

United States		Russia	
ICBMs			
Minuteman II	0	SS-18	0
Minuteman III/3 RV	0	SS-19/1 RV	105
Minuteman III/1 RV	500	SS-24	0
Peacekeeper	0	SS-25 silo	90
		SS-25 mobile	600
Subtotals	500		795[a]
SLBMs			
C-3 (Poseidon)	0	SS-N-18 (Delta III)	2 × 16 × 3
C-4 (Poseidon)	0	SS-N-20 (Typhoon)	6 × 20 × 10
C-4 (Trident)	8 × 24 × 4	SS-N-23 (Delta IV)	7 × 16 × 4
D-5 (Trident)	10 × 24 × 4		
Subtotals	1728		1744[b]
Bombers			
B-52H/ALCM-B	44 × 8	Bear-H6	24 × 6
B-52H/ACM	50 × 12	Bear-H16	36 × 16
B-1	0	Blackjack	20 × 12
B-2	20 × 16		
Subtotals	1272		960[c]
Total weapons	3500		3499

[a]The eventual number of mobile SS-25s that Russia might deploy is subject to debate, though 600 seems like a reasonable estimate. Russia may also deploy more silo-based ICBMs because they are less expensive and easier to maintain, and there are fewer problems providing adequate security and control over nuclear warheads in silos.

[b]The Russian SLBM force was constructed on the assumption that most of the Delta IIIs will be retired by the year 2003 because of their advanced age. No new SSBNs are believed to be under construction. The Typhoon is shown deployed with its full load of 10 warheads per SS-N-20 to keep the total number of warheads in the SLBM force relatively high. If the Russians download the SS-N-20, for example to six warheads each, then more Delta IIIs (i.e., SS-N-18s) could be retained. In either case, the SLBM force contains approximately the same number of warheads, though in the latter case these weapons are spread over more submarines. If all Delta IIIs are retired and the Typhoon is downloaded, then the SLBM force would contain closer to 1200 warheads and the total Russian force would be around 3000 weapons.

[c]This assumes that the Blackjacks currently deployed in Ukraine will be returned to Russia and that some Bear-H bombers will be retired, leaving a total force of 80 heavy bombers carrying around 960 nuclear weapons.

ALCM-B and advanced cruise missiles (ACMs). The B-2 is counted as a nu-clear-capable heavy bomber with a nominal load of 16 nuclear weapons.

Greater uncertainty surrounds possible Russian force structures. For the purposes of this analysis, the Russians are assumed to deploy around 800 ICBMs, 195 of which are single-warhead ICBMs (90 SS-19s downloaded from 6 warheads to 1 and 105 SS-25s deployed in former SS-18 silos) and 600 mobile SS-25s. The Russian SLBM force is assumed to consist of 15 missile-carrying submarines (SSBNs, or subsurface ballistic nuclear vessels) deployed with 264 SLBMs carrying a total of 1744 warheads. Finally, the Russian bomber force is assumed to contain around 1000 weapons. Despite uncertain-ties about the exact Russian force structure under START II, it will closely re-semble the U.S. force mix—with the exception of mobile ICBMs. Note that the Russian land-based ICBM force is quite small by former Soviet standards.

Quantitative analyses of deterrence must calculate the number of retaliatory weapons that can effectively be delivered to an opponent's homeland after ab-sorbing a nuclear first strike. In general, far fewer retaliatory weapons arrive on target than are contained in a country's strategic nuclear arsenal. Of the weapons in the total inventory, only those not in overhaul are available for re-taliation (approximately 10 percent of the delivery systems at any one time). Of the available forces, only those that survive the opponent's counterforce first strike, that operate reliably, and that penetrate defenses can threaten targets in the opponent's homeland and, hence, contribute to deterrence. The number of arriving weapons (as opposed to inventory weapons) is then compared to the number of targets one believes should be held at risk to judge the adequacy of deterrence. Table 2 provides illustrative "planning factors" that capture the aggregate character of each side's nuclear force posture on different states of alert.[11]

Of the available forces (those not in overhaul), the fraction that survive an opponent's counterforce first strike is a function of the scenario one chooses to analyze. For this analysis, we examine three different alert postures: day-to-

---

[11]It is important to note that these numbers represent averages over a given delivery system. As such, they gloss over numerous operational details that may affect the actual performance of specific systems, particularly for the bomber force. For example, the penetration probabilities for bombers and cruise missiles vary widely depending on the flight path, whether the targets attacked are located in heavily defended regions of the opponent's country or are terminally defended with sophisticated surface-to-air missiles (e.g., the SA-10), the degree of defense suppression, and, finally, assumptions one makes regarding the future modernization of the opponent's air defenses (an unlikely event for either country in the near term). The penetration probabilities shown in Table 2 reflect the fact that neither side is assumed to have highly effective air defenses in the next several decades.

Table 2

Illustrative Planning Factors

Weapon System	Availability	Prelaunch Survival			Reliability	Penetration Probability[a]
		Day-to-Day Alert	Partial Alert	Generated Alert		
United States						
ICBMs						
MM III/1 RV	0.95	0.20[b]	0.20[b]	0.20[b]	0.85	1.0
SLBMs						
C-4	0.90	0.67	0.67	1.0	0.80	1.0
D-5	0.90	0.67	0.67	1.0	0.80	1.0
Bombers						
B-52H/ALCM-B	0.90	0.00	0.33	1.0	0.85	0.70
B-52H/ACM	0.90	0.00	0.33	1.0	0.85	0.85
B-2	0.80[c]	0.00	0.33	1.0	0.85	0.95
Russia						
ICBMs						
SS-19/1 RV	0.95	0.20[d]	0.20[d]	0.20[d]	0.85	1.0
SS-25 silo	0.90	0.20[d]	0.20[d]	0.20[d]	0.85	1.0
SS-25 road	0.95	0.25	0.35	1.0	0.85	1.0

Table 2—continued

Weapon System	Availability	Prelaunch Survival				Reliability	Penetration Probability[a]
		Day-to-Day Alert	Partial Alert	Generated Alert			
SLBMs							
SS-N-18	0.85	0.25[e]	0.40[f]	1.0		0.75	1.0
SS-N-20	0.85	0.25[e]	0.40[f]	1.0		0.80	1.0
SS-N-23	0.85	0.25[e]	0.40[f]	1.0		0.80	1.0
Bombers							
Bear-H	0.90	0.00	0.00	1.0		0.85	0.90
Blackjack	0.90	0.00	0.00	1.0		0.85	0.90

SOURCE: Congressional Budget Office (1991:148).

[a]These penetration probabilities are illustrative. They do not include the presence of ballistic missile defenses. The air defenses are notional.

[b]Based on the assumption that one Russian warhead equivalent to an SS-18 attacks each U.S. ICBM silo. If U.S. ICBMs are launched out from under the attack, the survival probability is assumed to be 0.95.

[c]This availability is based on an inventory of 20 B-2 bombers.

[d]Based on the assumption that one U.S. warhead equivalent to the Peacekeeper ICBM attacks each Russian ICBM silo. If Russian ICBMs launch out from under the attack, the survival probability is assumed to be 0.95.

[e]Assuming approximately three SSBNs are at sea on day-to-day alert.

[f]Assuming approximately five SSBNs are at sea on partial alert.

day alert, partial alert, and generated alert.[12]   We also assume that launch-under-attack scenarios are possible on partial and generated alert, but are less likely on day-to-day alert unless a concerted effort is made to implement this option.

The survival probability for submarines and bombers is essentially determined by the number of submarines at sea and the number of bombers on strip alert.[13]   The United States is assumed to keep approximately 11 out of 18 SSBNs at sea on day-to-day and partial alert.   Russia is assumed to keep approximately 3 SSBNs at sea on day-to-day alert and 5 on partial alert. Moreover, for the purposes of this discussion, possible SSBN attrition due to antisubmarine warfare has not been included, bombers are assumed to receive adequate tactical warning to escape from their bases, and each side's strategic command-and-control system is assumed to survive well enough to make retaliation likely.[14]

---

[12]Day-to-day alert is the normal readiness posture of strategic nuclear forces in peacetime.   Generated alert is the readiness posture of U.S. and Russian nuclear forces on the brink of war.   An intermediate readiness level (partial alert) has been included here to represent situations where the alert rate has been increased in response to international tensions, but a full wartime footing has not been ordered.   There are numerous intermediate alert postures one could assume.   For the purposes of this analysis, the partial alert rates are taken to be roughly equivalent to the alert rates the United States and Russia maintained in peacetime during the latter stages of the Cold War—this being an alert rate that could be sustained for a prolonged period, e.g., during a crisis. One could as well define intermediate alert rates higher or lower than these values.

[13]One must distinguish between SLBM alert rate and SLBM prelaunch survival. Submarine survival is determined by the fraction at sea.   This is slightly different from the "alert rate" because submarines are not "on alert" unless they are patrolling within range of their targets and are standing by to receive instructions from the National Command Authority.   Submarines transiting to or from their alert stations may survive but are not considered to be on alert.   Similarly, submarines may be at sea on training missions but not standing by to receive instructions—in which case they too are not considered to be on alert, though they would survive attack.   The difference between the number of SSBNs at sea and the number on alert may be small, particularly with long-range SLBMs, because submarines can be on alert shortly after leaving port. Submarines in port may also be on alert if the SLBMs have sufficient range to strike their targets from port.   However, these SLBMs would not survive unless they are launched out from under the attack.

[14]These are reasonable assumptions for analyzing the basic U.S.-Russia deterrent relationship.   However, one should note that scenarios can be invented where these assumptions may not hold, e.g., an aggressive U.S. conventional antisubmarine warfare campaign that precedes the nuclear crisis, inadequate tactical warning for Russian bombers owing to gaps in their early-warning network created by the Soviet Union's dissolution, or attacks against the strategic command-and-control network that effectively prevent retaliation for some period.   These scenarios are important if one is interested in worst-case analyses.

The survival of silo-based ICBMs depends on whether they are launched out from under the attack (LUA) or whether they ride out the attack.[15] Table 2 gives the survival probability assuming silo-based ICBMs ride out an attack with one hard-target-kill warhead allocated to each silo. The survival probability is fairly low because, by assumption, the United States and Russia upgrade the accuracy and yield of their single-warhead ICBMs over the next decade to give them a high single-shot kill probability (assumed to be 0.8) against the opponent's silos. If silo-based ICBMs launch out from under the attack, their survival probability is assumed to be 0.95. Mobile ICBMs are less vulnerable than silo-based ICBMs, provided they obtain sufficient warning to disperse from their garrisons. The Russian mobile-ICBM alert rate in Table 2 assumes the majority of these systems are kept in garrison during peacetime, with a slight increase in the number out of garrison on partial alert. In addition, it has been assumed that the United States cannot localize these mobile ICBMs once they are deployed in the field.

Of the forces that survive an initial counterforce attack, the fraction that arrive on target is determined by the percentage that operate reliably (i.e., the delivery platform functions properly and the warhead detonates reliably) and by the fraction that penetrate the opponent's defenses. The impact of ballistic missile defenses is accounted for separately in this analysis. Hence, the penetration probabilities for ballistic missiles is 1.0 in Table 2. The impact of strategic air defenses is explicitly taken into account by the attrition factor associated with different airborne platforms.[16]

Multiplying these factors together for each delivery system and summing over the entire force structure gives the expected number of arriving or "effective" weapons for a given alert posture. The number of targets that can be destroyed for a given alert posture depends on how the attack is allocated.[17]

---

[15]If they are launched under attack, the survival probability is equal to the launch reliability. If not, the survival probability is determined by the accuracy, yield, and number of attacking warheads.

[16]The U.S. bomber penetration probabilities in Table 2 reflect the fact that the United States will deploy a modestly advanced bomber force by the year 2003 and that Russian strategic air defenses may be relatively weak for decades due to the loss of one-time Soviet early-warning and other air defense assets located outside Russia. The Russian bomber penetration probability has been set at 0.90 to reflect the fact that the United States has a thin strategic air defense system that could present a threat to some Bear-H and Blackjack bombers.

[17]Several operational factors not used in this analysis complicate the calculation of the number of targets each side can hold at risk. For example, cross-targeting with warheads from different delivery platforms improves the confidence with which high-priority targets can be destroyed. Cross-targeting was left out because single-warhead ICBM silos (a target often assumed to require two warheads) are assumed here to be targeted with only one warhead. There are relatively few high-priority targets other

It also depends on the probability that an arriving weapon destroys the target of interest. With the exception of ICBM silos, most targets in this analysis are soft. Hence, the probability that an arriving weapon actually destroys its intended target is assumed to be close to 1.0.[18]

Finally, some weapons may be withheld even from an all-out retaliatory response so the United States (or Russia) is not completely vulnerable to nuclear coercion by other nuclear powers in the wake of a U.S.-Russian nuclear war. The size of this secure reserve force—not to be confused with a secure second-strike capability—is debatable; however, numbers in the range of 100–500 survivable weapons seem reasonable under START II, depending among other things on the alert posture. The weapons withheld for a secure reserve force have not been subtracted from the number of "effective" weapons shown in the subsequent analysis, though it is not difficult for the reader to make the necessary adjustments.[19]

DETERRENCE WITHOUT BALLISTIC MISSILE DEFENSES

The extent to which the United States and Russia can maintain a secure second-strike capability for deterrence can be viewed pictorially by means of a "drawdown" curve. Drawdown curves are simply plots of the number of

---

than ICBM silos, so little error is introduced by ignoring this factor. Second, all weapon systems have physical constraints on their ability to deliver weapons on target— for example, range limitations and MIRVed footprint constraints (i.e., limitations on the degree to which warheads from a single MIRVed ballistic missile can be targeted against aimpoints separated by large distances). Since most ballistic missile systems under START II have been "de-MIRVed," this should present less of a problem.

[18]Under START II, relatively few hard targets remain in the United States and Russia because most ICBM silos will have been removed. To the extent that some hard targets exist, gravity bombs on heavy bombers and high-yield ICBM and SLBM warheads can achieve high damage expectancies. Therefore, the probability that a given inventory weapon can destroy a target is essentially the same as its arrival probability. The number of arriving weapons (i.e., effective weapons) is therefore equivalent to the total number of targets that can be destroyed, assuming one weapon is allocated against each target.

[19]The number of "effective" weapons withheld for a secure reserve force is determined by multiplying the number of weapons withheld of each type by their reliability and penetration probabilities given in Table 2. Subtracting the sum from the total number of effective weapons that survive in a given scenario yields the maximum number of effective weapons that are available for an immediate retaliatory strike. This difference is the size of the secure second-strike capability. Since SLBMs and mobile ICBMs will likely be the weapon of choice for the secure reserve force, reserves between 100 and 500 surviving weapons imply that approximately 80–400 effective weapons would be subtracted from the effective weapon totals, depending on the alert posture, to provide a more accurate estimate of the size of the secure second-strike capability.

weapons remaining on both sides after one side initiates a counterforce attack against the opponent's strategic nuclear forces. As such, they provide a convenient pictorial representation of the extent to which the defender's retaliatory strike is secure. Whether a given retaliatory capability is adequate for deterrence can be answered only by reference to a particular deterrence strategy for a given adversary (and its accompanying targeting doctrine). The virtue of drawdown curves is that they capture the quantitative aspects of each side's arsenal, leaving the reader to judge whether deterrence remains robust or is becoming "delicate" in a given scenario, based on his own criteria for sufficiency and other exogenous factors he believes are relevant.

The U.S. Strategic Nuclear Deterrent

Figure 1 illustrates the drawdown curve for a hypothetical Russian counterforce first strike against U.S. START II forces on day-to-day alert. The curve's initial point, in the upper right-hand corner, represents the total U.S. and Russian arsenals before the hypothetical attack begins. The slope of the curve at any point determines the marginal counterforce exchange ratio, i.e., the ratio of U.S. warheads destroyed to Russian warheads expended at this point in the attack. Hence, the slope indicates the relative attractiveness of this particular portion of the counterforce attack. The curve is plotted so that the most lucrative counterforce options occur first, the least attractive options last.

Initially, the drawdown curve is nearly vertical because a Russian attack against U.S. submarine bases (four are assumed in this analysis) and bomber bases (five are assumed on day-to-day alert) could destroy a large number of U.S. weapons off alert (i.e., U.S. SSBNs in port and nonalert bombers on the ground) with the expenditure of very few Russian weapons (three or four weapons are allocated to each base). Hence, by attacking a total of nine targets with approximately 30–40 weapons, the Russians could destroy a large fraction of the U.S. strategic nuclear arsenal, at least on day-to-day alert.

The next most lucrative counterforce option is an attack against U.S. single-warhead ICBM silos. This portion of the drawdown curve is broken into two segments. The first part represents the drawdown of the Minuteman force if one Russian weapon is targeted against each silo. The second segment represents the drawdown of the surviving Minuteman ICBMs if a second warhead is allocated to each silo.

After the attack on U.S. Minuteman silos, no attractive Russian counterforce options remain. On day-to-day alert, the entire U.S. bomber force is off alert, otherwise one might consider barrage attacks against bomber flyout corridors. Obviously, barrage attacks against mobile ICBMs are not considered because the U.S. force structure contains no mobile ICBMs. The only theoret-

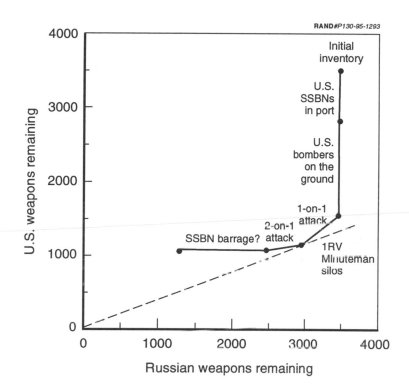

Figure 1—Russian Counterforce First Strike on Day-to-Day Alert

ical counterforce option left is a barrage attack against U.S. submarines at sea. This attack is ineffective because it has been assumed that the Russians cannot localize U.S. submarines at sea. Hence, a large number of Russian weapons would be expended with the destruction of very few U.S. weapons, i.e., the drawdown curve in Figure 1 is essentially horizontal.

The Russian counterforce attack in Figure 1 comes to an end with approximately 1200 Russian weapons remaining because these weapons—namely, bomber weapons and a few weapons associated with ballistic missiles in overhaul—cannot be used in the counterforce first strike.[20]

So far, the drawdown curve illustrates theoretical counterforce attack options. Nothing has been said about the number of weapons the Russians would actually allocate to a counterforce attack, i.e., how far down the theoretical drawdown curve they might actually proceed. Nor is it clear how many

---

[20]Bomber weapons cannot be used for counterforce attacks because it is assumed that their slow delivery provides sufficient warning for the opponent's forces to escape.

ballistic missile weapons the Russians actually have on alert (assuming their forces are also on day-to-day alert) that could participate in the counterforce attack. To determine an optimal stopping point for the counterforce attack, one must assume some objective function the Russians attempt to maximize; for example, the postattack ratio of remaining forces.[21] Using this criterion, the optimal stopping point can be found by drawing a straight line from the origin tangent to the drawdown curve (i.e., the dashed line in Figure 1). The tangent point is the optimal stopping point for this objective. This occurs after the Russians have allocated one warhead to each Minuteman silo, but before they have allocated two warheads. Therefore, single-warhead ICBM silos, though they are less attractive targets than MIRVed ICBM silos, will be attacked in a counterforce first strike. Throughout this analysis, one warhead is assumed to be allocated to each single-warhead ICBM silo. From Figure 1, one might expect intuitively that the Russians would stop after allocating one weapon against each Minuteman silo but before two weapons are allocated, since this appears to include the most attractive counterforce attack options without wasting too many weapons.

The fraction of the opponent's arsenal that must be destroyed before an attacker has an appreciable incentive to strike first is, of course, debatable. Again, the drawdown curve simply shows the number of weapons that survive, leaving it up to the reader to decide whether one side, under some circumstances, might be tempted to attack.

The classic incentive for nuclear attacks occurs when one side believes it can substantially limit damage by striking first. Whether or not one side has a significant damage-limiting counterforce capability can be determined easily using drawdown curves. The distance between the drawdown curve and the x-axis in Figure 1 indicates the size of the U.S. second-strike capability at any point along the drawdown curve. As one observes, approximately 1100 U.S. weapons survive the maximal Russian counterforce attack on day-to-day alert. Later we will see exactly how much damage this surviving force can inflict. Nevertheless, it seems clear from the figure that the U.S. deterrent is fairly robust even on day-to-day alert. If the drawdown curve came much closer to the x-axis, then the U.S. deterrent could be judged to be weak.

With this introduction, we can now use drawdown curves to display the size of the U.S. or Russian secure second strike under a wide range of possible scenarios. Figure 2 illustrates Russian counterforce attack options on day-to-day alert, partial alert, and generated alert. In the partial and generated alert scenarios, alternate drawdown curves are shown for the cases where the United

---

[21]Several authors have devised different objective functions for counterforce first strikes in an effort to determine "optimal" counterforce allocations. See, for example, Kent and Thayer (1989), Canavan (1991), Bracken (1990), and Grotte (1980).

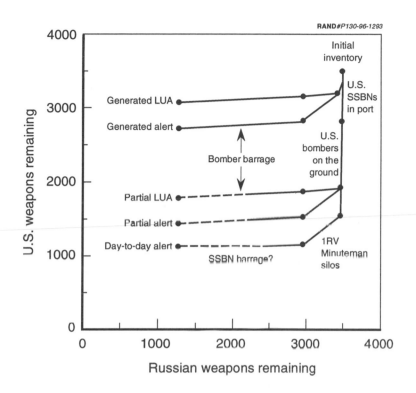

RAND#P130-96-1293

Figure 2—Russian Counterforce First-Strike Options

States launches its silo-based ICBMs out from under the attack. The solid line in each drawdown curve illustrates the number of Russian weapons that actually are available (i.e., on alert) for a counterforce first strike.[22] In the partial and generated alert scenarios, the Russian barrage attack is directed against U.S. bomber fly-out corridors because they represent more lucrative targets than U.S. SSBNs at sea—though neither barrage target is particularly attractive from the Russian perspective.

The Russian counterforce attack against the most lucrative targets, including a one-on-one attack against Minuteman silos, involves only about 530 warheads. This is a factor of six less than the number of weapons that would

---

[22]In addition to the alert forces, it has been assumed that mobile ICBMs in garrison can be generated covertly and, hence, can be used in the counterforce first strike regardless of the fraction that are actually in garrison. Note that all Russian ICBMs (mobile or silo-based) are assumed to have sufficient hard-target-kill capability to threaten U.S. ICBM silos. This may be a generous assumption. No Russian SLBMs are credited with hard-target-kill capability.

have been required for comparable attacks throughout most of the Cold War. The collateral damage associated with these attacks would, therefore, be less severe.   Whether this makes counterforce attacks more "thinkable" under START II, because they appear to be more limited or surgical in character, is debatable.   Nevertheless, one should recognize that as the number of counterforce targets shrinks, it may be easier for leaders to convince themselves that escalation can be controlled after "limited" counterforce attacks.   If ICBM silos are left out of the attack, then the Russian counterforce first strike would involve only a few tens of weapons (perhaps with another ten or so allocated against U.S. strategic C³ targets).   Hence, in the post–Cold War era it may be easier for a desperate leader to convince himself that nuclear war could remain limited, making nuclear attacks more likely.

Figure 2 shows that even under the worst-case scenario in this analysis (day-to-day alert), the United States still has over 1000 nuclear weapons that survive an all-out Russian counterforce attack.   This surviving arsenal could threaten devastating retaliation—even if this force might be insufficient to meet comprehensive U.S. targeting objectives.   The U.S. second strike thus appears to be secure under all scenarios.   On generated alert, approximately 2700 weapons would survive.   This provides enough retaliatory capability to hold at risk a wide range of Russian military, economic, and leadership targets.   Hence, on generated alert, deterrence is quite robust.   In no scenario is the United States limited to retaliation against Russian cities alone.   Eleven hundred surviving weapons provides the United States with substantial capability to threaten a large number of the most highly valued Russian military, economic, and leadership targets, though comprehensive damage cannot be accomplished simultaneously against all target categories, even if several hundred weapons are withheld for a secure reserve force.

Having weapons that survive a counterforce first strike is not the only requirement for maintaining a secure second strike.   In addition, one must have weapon systems that are reliable and that can penetrate the opponent's defenses.   Taking weapon system reliability and penetration probabilities into account, one can replot the drawdown curves in an "effective" weapon domain as shown in Figure 3.   "Effective" weapons are simply weapons that arrive on target in the opponent's homeland.   The number of effective weapons equates to the number of nuclear detonations that one side can inflict on the adversary.   If one weapon is allocated to each target, then the number of effective weapons essentially equals the number of targets that can be destroyed, assuming the probability with which an arriving nuclear weapon destroys a target is essen-

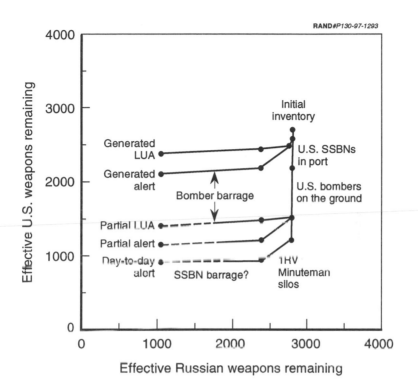

Figure 3—U.S. Secure Second Strike (effective weapons)

tially unity, which is true for most targets.[23] Hence, the effective weapon domain shows the residual retaliatory capability, at any point along the drawdown curve, measured in terms of the number of targets each side can hold at risk in the opponent's homeland (minus the number of effective weapons that would be withheld for a secure reserve force).

In Figure 3, the inventory point is at 2800 effective U.S. weapons and a comparable number of effective Russian weapons. Therefore, of the 3500 weapons in each side's inventory, only about 2800 would actually arrive on the opponent's homeland if the entire strategic nuclear inventory was used in the attack. After a Russian counterforce first strike on day-to-day alert, the residual U.S. retaliatory capability is around 900 effective weapons. U.S. forces on generated alert can hold at risk approximately 2200 targets, or around 2500

---

[23]Most targets are relatively soft. To the extent hard targets exist, each side will have sufficient hard-target-kill capability in its bomber force and prompt hard-target-kill capability in its ICBM force (and, for the United States, in its SLBM force).

targets if the United States launches its single-warhead Minuteman III ICBMs out from under the attack on generated alert.

Many people believe the essence of deterrence rests on the ability to hold at risk the opponent's population.[24]   In other words, instead of threatening to destroy a certain number of military, leadership, and/or economic targets, as implied by Figure 3, deterrence rests on the ability to target each other's cities. Put another way, when people speak of damage limitation as an incentive for striking first, it is damage to one's urban population that is to be limited. Figure 4 replots the same drawdown curves, but this time the residual retaliatory capability is measured in terms of the opponent's urban population at risk. In other words, Figure 4 translates effective weapons into urban fatalities (resulting from prompt nuclear effects alone).

Therefore, even though only 1100 U.S. weapons survive a Russian counterforce first strike on day-to-day alert (Figure 2), approximately 900 of these weapons arrive on target within Russia (Figure 3). If these weapons are targeted at major Russian urban areas, approximately 60 million people would be killed (Figure 4).[25]   Clearly, deterrence appears to be much more robust if one assumes that political leaders believe deterrence rests on the ability to

---

[24]Some people argue that as arsenals shrink, countries will tend to emphasize targeting of the opponent's cities because this creates the greatest deterrent effect with a limited nuclear arsenal. This is particularly true if a country has only a few nuclear weapons, as the United States had in 1945, or as small nuclear powers such as Pakistan, Israel, and India might have today.

[25]One should note that this calculation only includes prompt nuclear effects. No account has been made for collateral damage resulting from attacks against the opponent's counterforce targets. During the Cold War, the collateral damage associated with U.S. and Russian counterforce attacks was thought to be substantial, primarily because of the fallout created when thousands of weapons detonate over each country's ICBM silos. Under START II, counterforce attacks involve relatively few weapons by Cold War standards. As a result, the collateral damage due to fallout would be less by a factor of 5 to 10 compared to comparable attacks at the height of the Cold War. Using the calculations of Daugherty, Levy, and von Hipple, the fatalities resulting solely from the fallout created by a Russian counterforce attack against the United States would be on the order of 0.7 to 6 million deaths (the total casualties would be higher). See Daugherty, Levy, and von Hipple (1986) and Levy, von Hipple, and Daugherty (1987/88). A similar calculation for a U.S. counterforce attack against Russia produces approximately 0.8 to 2 million fatalities due to fallout alone. This is small relative to the tremendous fatalities that could be inflicted by direct attacks against each other's population. In addition, the collateral damage associated with counterforce attacks against submarine ports and bomber bases, which may be located near major urban areas, is also relatively small due to the small number of warheads used in these attacks (around 30–40) compared to Cold War attack scenarios. Hence, one can ignore these collateral effects as well, at least for the purpose of this discussion.

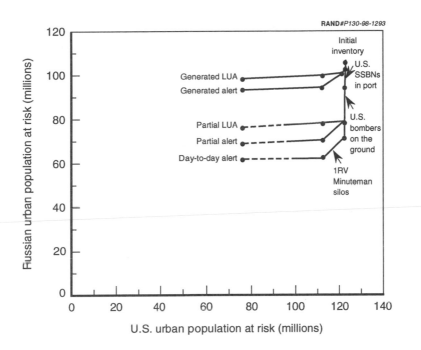

Figure 4—U.S. Secure Second Strike (population at risk)

inflict casualties on the opponent's population. Even a small surviving arsenal can do tremendous damage, as illustrated in Figure 4.

The Russian Strategic Nuclear Deterrent

So far, the discussion has focused on possible Russian incentives to strike first. We now turn to hypothetical U.S. first-strike options, particularly as they might appear to Russian leaders. Figure 5 illustrates U.S. counterforce first strikes under a range of possible scenarios. Once again, the inventory point in the upper right-hand corner represents the total U.S. and Russian arsenals prior to the attack. The most lucrative U.S. attacks are directed against Russian SSBNs in port and Russian bombers at their bases. The next most attractive option would be an attack against mobile ICBM garrisons, followed by a one-on-one attack against Russian ICBM silos. After this, no attractive counterforce options remain. In principle, the United States could allocate a second warhead against each Russian single-warhead ICBM silo, or it could conduct a barrage attack against submarines at sea or mobile ICBMs out of

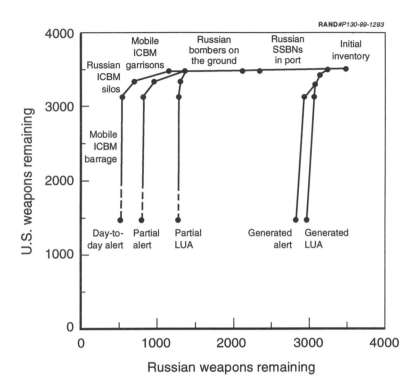

Figure 5—U.S. Counterforce First-Strike Options

garrison. The latter is illustrated in Figure 5. As one can see, this barrage attack (against mobile SS-25s out of garrison) would consume a large number of U.S. weapons and destroy very few Russian weapons (according to the assumptions used in this analysis). Hence, the likely stopping point for a U.S. counterforce first strike would be after one weapon has been allocated against each Russian single-warhead ICBM silo. This also happens to be the point at which the ratio of remaining U.S. weapons to surviving Russian weapons is at a maximum. As in Figure 2, the solid line indicates the number of weapons the United States actually has available for a counterforce attack in each scenario. Clearly, the United States has ample capability to carry out the most lucrative counterforce options.

Figures 6 and 7 illustrate the size of the Russian secure second strike measured in terms of effective Russian weapons remaining after a U.S. counterforce attack and in terms of the U.S. urban population these effective weapons could hold at risk in a retaliatory strike if Russian leaders target their retaliatory strike to maximize U.S. urban fatalities. Again, weapons withheld for a Russian se-

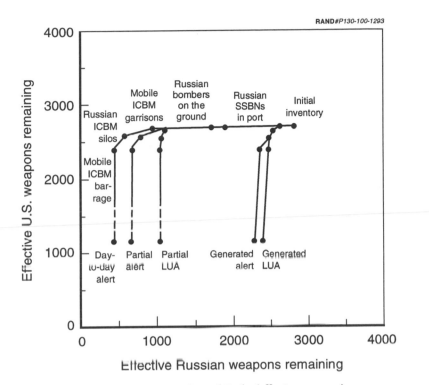

Figure 6—Russian Secure Second Strike (effective weapons)

cure reserve force should be subtracted from the numbers shown in Figure 6 to provide a more accurate representation of the maximum number of effective weapons the United States would absorb in an all-out Russian retaliatory strike.

Several interesting points emerge from this series of figures. First, a U.S. counterforce first strike against the most attractive Russian counterforce targets requires only about 350 weapons—far fewer than comparable U.S. counterforce attacks during the Cold War. Consequently, the collateral damage associated with these attacks would be relatively small when compared to comparable Cold War scenarios.[26] Hence, from the Russian perspective, U.S. counterforce attacks may become increasingly "thinkable."

---

[26]At the height of the Cold War, U.S. counterforce attacks against roughly 1500 Soviet ICBM silos would have involved around 3000 warheads fused to detonate close to the ground (thus creating significant fallout). Under START II, the comparable scenario involves only 195 U.S. weapons ground burst against 195 Russian ICBM silos. Hence, the fallout from this counterforce attack would be approximately 15 times less severe, assuming weapons of comparable yield.

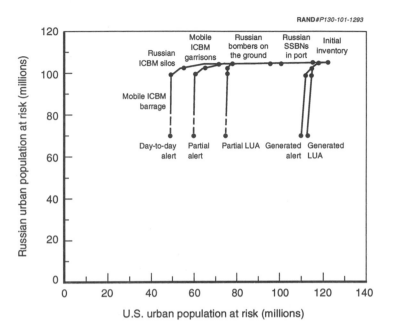

Figure 7—Russian Secure Second Strike (population at risk)

Second, on generated alert, approximately 3000 weapons would survive (Figure 5), which equates to approximately 2400 effective weapons landing on the U.S. homeland (Figure 6). In terms of countervalue damage, the lives of over 100 million Americans could be threatened (Figure 7). Hence, deterrence under these circumstances would be quite robust.

Third, at low alert rates, few Russian weapons survive by Cold War standards. In particular, on day-to-day alert, approximately 550 Russian weapons survive: about 375 weapons aboard submarines at sea, around 135 mobile ICBMs out of garrison, and about 40 silo-based ICBMs (assuming the planning factors in Table 2). All Russian bombers are assumed to be destroyed on the ground on day-to-day alert. Of these surviving weapons, approximately 450 weapons would actually operate reliably and could arrive on target within the United States (Figure 6).

Whether 450 effective weapons constitute an adequate deterrent in the minds of Russian political and military leaders cannot be answered with certainty. On paper, it seems adequate. However, these effective weapons exist on relatively few submarines at sea and a small number of mobile ICBMs out of garrison. If the Russian general staff believed the United States had a modest antisubmarine warfare (ASW) capability, or a rudimentary capability to threaten mobile ICBMs in the field, then Russian leaders might become concerned about the adequacy of this relatively small surviving arsenal. One should also recall that, though attacks against strategic nuclear command-and-control nodes have been ignored in this analysis, such fears might add to the Russian sense of vulnerability. Finally, Russia would likely withhold some weapons for a secure reserve force to deter other possible threats from China, France, Great Britain, and perhaps Ukraine (assuming Russia abides by START II even if Ukraine retains some nuclear capability). Therefore, on day-to-day alert, Russian leaders may conclude that they have only several hundred effective weapons with which to retaliate against the United States. Again, it is debatable whether Russian leaders would believe this is adequate for deterrence.

Figure 7 shows that even a relatively small surviving arsenal can do tremendous damage to U.S. cities (approximately 50 million people could be killed with 450 effective weapons). In terms of a countervalue deterrent, then, the Russian secure second strike seems adequate. Of course, for Russian leaders to derive any comfort from this, they must actually be willing to threaten U.S. cities and target their forces accordingly.

This analysis also sheds light on arms control treaties with lower ceilings or further reductions in the peacetime alert rates. Treaties that reduce the aggregate weapon total simply shift the inventory point of the drawdown curves toward the origin. The exact shape of the curves depends on the force structure and the alert rates. Without illustrating the myriad of possibilities, suffice it to say that further cuts may be reasonable if one assumes that generated alert is the only plausible planning scenario. On the other hand, further reductions in weapon inventories or alert rates may not appear attractive if one focuses on day-to-day alert scenarios. It is true that one can always strengthen deterrence by generating the force, but early force mobilization then becomes necessary for adequate deterrence. Creating a situation where one or both sides must mobilize their forces to ensure adequate deterrence may not be desirable because rapid force generation is often perceived by the other side to be provocative, especially early in a crisis.

To summarize, under START II, counterforce attacks are smaller in size and have less collateral damage compared to similar Cold War scenarios. This tends to increase the chance that leaders might believe deliberate counterforce attacks are rational instruments of policy. Nevertheless, with offensive forces constrained by START II, neither the United States nor Russia can significantly improve its chances for survival by striking first. Hence, the mutual hostage relationship that characterizes mutual deterrence will remain unless radical force reductions are implemented. This is true even when U.S. or Russian forces are on day-to-day alert, barring further reductions in the U.S., and especially Russian, peacetime alert posture.

As a secondary matter, the U.S. deterrent appears to be more robust than Russia's because the United States maintains a larger fraction of its forces on alert in peacetime. If several Russian SSBNs could be sunk by U.S. antisubmarine warfare, or if a modest number of Russian mobile ICBMs could be attacked out of garrison, then Russia's deterrent could become quite weak at low alert rates. If the United States reduced the alert rate for its SLBM force, for example by halving the number of SSBNs at sea, then it would be in much the same position as Russia. But aside from these worst-case scenarios, deterrence again appears to be quite robust under START II. This is much less true if both sides deploy limited nationwide ballistic missile defenses, as the next section will demonstrate.

THE IMPACT OF LIMITED NATIONWIDE BALLISTIC MISSILE DEFENSES

Until now, the only defenses that have been included are U.S. and Russian strategic air defenses (captured by the attrition rates associated with different aircraft in Table 2). We now add limited nationwide ballistic missile defenses (BMD).[27] For the purposes of this analysis we assume that both sides deploy ground-based BMD interceptors symmetrically. Space-based defenses are not modeled. The effect of asymmetric defense deployments can be inferred from the symmetric cases. This analysis focuses on a case where 600 ground-based interceptors are deployed on both sides, since this level of nationwide defense represents a turning point for deterrence. One should also note that theater BMD interceptors may contribute to a country's strategic BMD capability. For example, if the United States builds a large number of theater BMD interceptors and stores them in the United States, Russian leaders might fear that these theater BMD interceptors could be deployed around the continent on

----

[27]In this analysis, the defenses are assumed to be capable of "shoot-look-shoot" tactics with a maximum of four interceptors allocated to an incoming warhead. Shoot-look-shoot tactics are much more effective because the second shot(s) are directed against only those warheads that leak through the first layer of the defense. In addition, it has been assumed that all interceptors can engage the incoming attack; i.e., interceptor range limitations have been ignored. Moreover, the defenses are assumed to survive defense suppression attacks and the interceptors are assumed to be highly effective; i.e., the interceptor single-shot kill probability is assumed to be 0.8—a level of effectiveness which, in principle, could be achieved for ground-based interceptors, though a lot depends on reactions the opponent might take. These may seem like heroic assumptions for the defense; however, the point of this analysis is to examine the strategic impact of defenses, not to prejudge the question of whether such defenses could be built or whether they would be cost-effective in light of an opponent's countermeasures. If the opponent deploys effective penetration aids or develops effective tactics to suppress the defense, this would change much of the subsequent analysis.

short notice, thereby contributing substantially to the U.S. strategic BMD capability.[28]

Ballistic missile defenses affect the analysis presented earlier in two ways. First, they interfere with counterforce first strikes. This is illustrated in Figure 8 by the kink at the beginning of the drawdown curves. For example, the Russians have to expend several hundred warheads in a counterforce first strike before sufficient warheads leak through the U.S. defense to destroy nonalert submarines and bombers at their bases. After the defense is saturated, the drawdown curves appear more or less as they did without ballistic missile de-

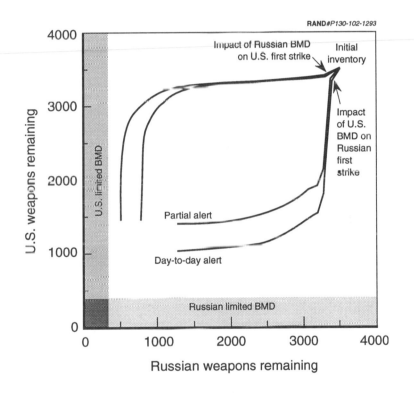

Figure 8—Notional Impact of Ballistic Missile Defenses

---

[28]See Shaver (1994) for a discussion of current and potential U.S. plans for ballistic missile defense.

fenses.[29] Second, the first-striker's defense can block a certain number of the opponent's surviving weapons, thereby reducing the number of effective weapons available for retaliation. If the surviving arsenal is relatively small, limited defenses may be able to significantly limit damage from the retaliation. This second effect is illustrated notionally by the shaded regions close to the axes. The distance between the edge of these shaded regions and the draw-down curves illustrates the number of retaliatory weapons that can penetrate the first-striker's defense; i.e., it closely approximates (apart from reliability factors) the number of effective weapons available for retaliation. If the draw-down curve moves into one of the shaded regions, then the country attacking first can significantly improve its chances for surviving a nuclear war, provided it strikes first.

U.S. Secure Second-Strike Capability

Figure 9 shows Russian counterforce first-strike options on three levels of alert assuming 600 ballistic missile interceptors are deployed on both sides. Note that it takes around 400 weapons to saturate the U.S. defense before enough leak through to destroy U.S. nonalert submarines and bombers.[30] The solid line in each drawdown curve represents the number of weapons on alert and, hence, available to conduct the counterforce first strike in each scenario.

The first point to notice in Figure 9 is that with 600 interceptors, the Russians barely have enough weapons on alert to conduct a complete counter-force attack against U.S. ICBM silos on day-to-day alert (note that the draw-down curve is still sloping downward, albeit slowly, when the Russians run out of alert weapons). Comparing this drawdown curve to the comparable curve without ballistic missile defenses (i.e., Figure 2) one observes that without de-fenses, sufficient weapons are available to attack each U.S. ICBM silo with one warhead on day-to-day alert. Hence, the first impact of a U.S. defense is to in-terfere with the Russian counterforce first strike (at low levels of alert).

---

[29]Due to the defenses, the attacker cannot determine with certainty which warheads will arrive on target. As a result, the drawdown curve cannot be neatly segmented into attacks against separate types of targets (i.e., submarine bases, bomber bases, ICBM sites, etc.). Nevertheless, comparing the general shape of the drawdown curve in Figure 8 to the cases without ballistic missile defenses, one can surmise which targets are pre-dominantly being attacked at different points along the curve.

[30]As an aside, one should note that these defenses effectively eliminate small ballistic missile attack options. In other words, "Limited Nuclear Options" using ballistic missiles, options that supposedly were included in U.S. strategy during the Cold War, would no longer be effective.

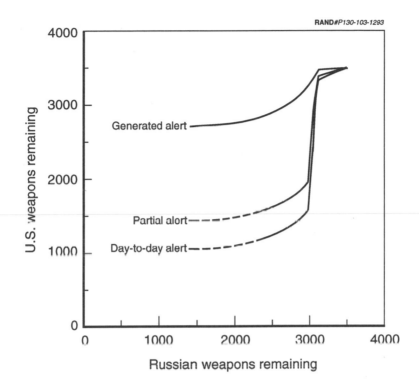

Figure 9—Russian Counterforce First-Strike Options: 600 BMD Interceptors

Therefore, defenses strengthen deterrence by making it more difficult for the Russians to accomplish a comprehensive counterforce attack at low alert levels.

It is difficult to tell exactly how many weapons the Russians might allocate to a counterforce first strike. Suffice it to say that if they wanted to reduce the U.S. arsenal to the maximum extent possible on day-to-day or partial alert, they would have to launch their entire alert force in the attack. Obviously, the Russians would not do this, because then a U.S. counterforce second strike could, in principle, disarm them, since their remaining forces would be highly vulnerable. Russian counterforce attacks thus would likely stop several hundred warheads short of the end of the solid line in Figure 9; for example, several hundred SLBMs at sea and/or mobile ICBMs out of garrison would be held in reserve.

As mentioned above, deterrence requires that weapons not only survive but operate reliably and penetrate any residual defenses. In Figure 9, the U.S. ballistic missile defense is exhausted early in the Russian counterforce first strike.

However, the Russian defense is still intact to defend against the U.S. retaliatory strike. Therefore, one must examine the drawdown curves in the *effective* weapons domain to see the true residual retaliatory capabilities after the Russian first strike. Figure 10 plots these same drawdown curves in terms of the effective weapons remaining on both sides, i.e., the number of weapons that would arrive on each country's homeland after any residual defenses are taken into account. These curves are virtually identical to the ones shown in Figure 9; however, they are shifted down because the Russian ballistic missile defense absorbs around 500 surviving U.S. warheads. Therefore, at any point along the drawdown curves in Figure 10 one can read off the residual retaliatory capability measured in arriving weapons. For example, after a Russian counterforce first strike on day-to-day alert, the United States retains the capability to deliver approximately 600 weapons against the Russian homeland (assuming the Russians withhold approximately 200 warheads). U.S. retaliatory capability on generated alert is more substantial (approximately 2000 ef-

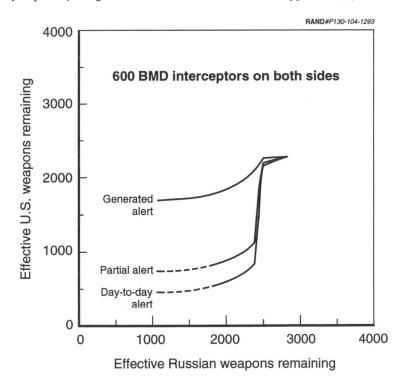

Figure 10—U.S. Secure Second Strike (effective weapons)

fective weapons). As mentioned in the previous section, these estimates do not account for weapons that are withheld as part of a U.S. secure reserve force.

If these effective weapons were targeted entirely against Russian cities, approximately 45 million fatalities would result in a day-to-day alert attack scenario, as illustrated in Figure 11. This represents an awesome countervalue retaliatory capability (assuming the United States would actually target its forces this way, contrary to past pronouncements). Hence, the U.S. secure second-strike capability appears to be fairly robust even when 600 ground-based interceptors are deployed on both sides. As the alert rate increases, this countervalue retaliatory capability becomes even more deadly.

Russian Secure Second-Strike Capability

Figure 12 illustrates U.S. counterforce first-strike options in several scenarios, assuming both sides deploy 600 ground-based interceptors. From this fig-

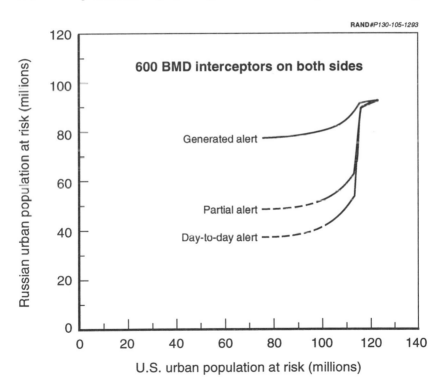

Figure 11—U.S. Secure Second Strike (population at risk)

Figure 12—U.S. Counterforce First-Strike Options: 600 BMD Interceptors

ure one can see that the United States has ample weapons available to saturate the Russian ballistic missile defense and strike at the most lucrative Russian counterforce targets. The actual number of weapons the United States would allocate to a counterforce attack is debatable. Nevertheless, if 1000 to 1400 weapons are allocated to this attack on day-to-day alert (approximately 1500 are available), Russia would be left with approximately 500 surviving weapons (for the same reasons that they had about 500 surviving weapons in Figure 5).

Again, the adequacy of deterrence can only be observed in the effective weapon domain, as illustrated in Figure 13. If virtually the entire U.S. alert force is allocated to a counterforce attack on day-to-day alert, with 600 ballistic missile defense interceptors deployed on both sides, then hypothetically only about 20 Russian weapons could penetrate the U.S. defense in retaliation. That is, of the 500 or so surviving weapons illustrated in Figure 12, only around 20 could get through the U.S. defense. This represents a better damage-limiting first-strike capability than either side ever achieved throughout the Cold War (except arguably on the U.S. side around 1960–1961). Therefore,

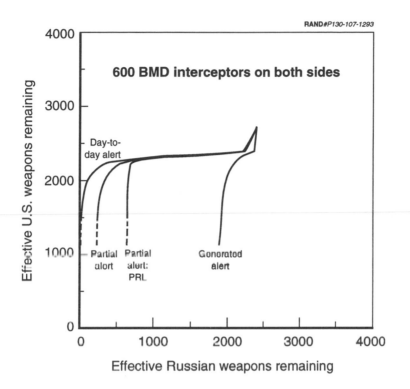

RAND#P130-107-1293

Figure 13—Russian Secure Second Strike (effective weapons)

600 ground-based interceptors (deployed on both sides) would virtually eliminate the Russian secure second strike on day-to-day alert if the United States
chose to preempt in a crisis with a massive counterforce attack. By contrast, a
Russian counterforce first strike on day-to-day alert cannot limit damage to a
comparable degree because approximately 600 effective U.S. weapons remain
after the attack (recall Figure 10).

As noted before, a relatively small number of effective weapons can cause
enormous civilian casualties if the retaliatory attack is directed against urban
areas. Figure 14 illustrates the residual Russian capability to hold at risk the
U.S. urban population when 600 BMD interceptors are deployed on both
sides.[31] Even though a U.S. counterforce attack on day-to-day alert can

---

[31]Collateral damage has again been ignored. While this was reasonable in a purely
offense-dominant nuclear balance (i.e., Figures 4 and 7), it clearly is a poor assumption
here because the number of nuclear detonations associated with U.S. and Russian
counterforce attacks has grown. Therefore, the number of fatalities shown in Figure 14

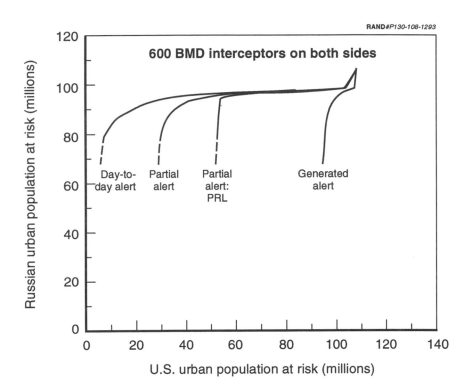

Figure 14—Russian Secure Second Strike (population at risk)

hypothetically reduce the number of effective Russian weapons to around 20, these weapons can still hold at risk on the order of 7 to 12 million American lives. While a U.S. President may believe that such large civilian casualties are sufficient to deter the United States (under most circumstances), it is doubtful that Russian leaders would feel equally confident. Hence, they would inevitably feel pressure to improve their deterrent posture, perhaps quickly.

On partial alert, the Russian secure second-strike capability equals about 250–300 effective weapons. Whether this retaliatory capability is sufficient, in the Russian leadership's mind, to deter the United States is debatable. What is not debatable is that the introduction of relatively limited defenses (i.e., 600 ground-based interceptors) begins to interfere significantly with the Russian secure second strike at low levels of alert.

should be treated as a lower bound. Collateral fatalities could add from 1 to 8 million additional fatalities.

The problems created by limited nationwide ballistic missile defenses occur first with the Russians because they have a smaller number of weapons deployed in survivable basing modes on day-to-day alert. As the defense level increases, the next scenario to encounter problems would be a U.S. counterforce first strike against Russian forces on partial alert. As defenses increase further, the U.S. secure second strike eventually becomes vulnerable to a Russian counterforce attack on day-to-day alert.[32]

Finally, one should note that on generated alert the Russian secure second strike is quite robust. If Russian forces are fully generated, they could retaliate with approximately 1900 effective weapons. The U.S. deterrent was similarly robust on generated alert (see Figure 10). Therefore, if one believes that U.S. and Russian forces will always be fully generated in a crisis, then deterrence is quite robust even in the presence of limited nationwide ballistic missile defenses. However, it is the transition from peacetime to generated alert that concerns us. Since the Russian deterrent posture at low alert rates is compromised in the presence of 600 BMD interceptors, Russian leaders have a strong incentive to react to redress this vulnerability before a crisis with the United States reaches the acute phase. This is the principal strategic problem that occurs when limited ballistic missile defenses are deployed.

Thus, at a level of around 600 ground-based interceptors deployed on both sides, one can observe two effects from limited nationwide ballistic missile defenses. First, the U.S. defense obstructs the Russian counterforce first strike, thereby strengthening the U.S. deterrent. However, the second and more pronounced effect is that a U.S. defense, in conjunction with a U.S. counterforce first strike, virtually eliminates the Russian secure second strike on day-to-day alert, thereby eroding Russia's deterrent.

Obviously, U.S. leaders are less concerned with the integrity of Russia's deterrent capability than they are with that of the United States. However, this perspective can be short-sighted because it ignores the fact that the United States and Russia are involved in a strategic interaction. Undermining Russia's deterrent will adversely affect political relations between these two countries, upsetting the current warming trend, and may stimulate another arms race as Russia attempts to shore up its deterrent. If Russia cannot afford the expense,

---

[32]As a rule, the size of the defense required to substantially interfere with an opponent's secure second strike can be determined by equating the defense potential (the number of interceptors times their single-shot kill probability or SSPK) to the number of surviving ballistic missile weapons on the opponent's side. Thus, if 500 Russian ballistic missile weapons survive a U.S. first strike, and the U.S. interceptors have an SSPK of 0.8, then the Russian secure second strike virtually disappears when the United States deploys approximately 625 interceptors, as we have seen. Using this same line of reasoning, the U.S. secure second strike would virtually disappear on day-to-day alert if Russia deployed approximately 1300 ground-based interceptors (with an SSPK of 0.8).

then it may opt for less expensive quick fixes that may be inimical to U.S. interests. Hence, as a general proposition, U.S. leaders should be concerned about Russia's deterrence capability if they wish to maintain stable relations with this former adversary.

The Russian strategic vulnerability at defense levels of 600 ground-based interceptors can easily be avoided if Russia keeps a higher fraction of its forces on alert in peacetime. However, this obvious solution may not be an option if Russia does not have the financial resources to implement it. Deploying more submarines to sea and mobile ICBMs out of garrison increases peacetime operating costs as well as maintenance costs because submarine reactors fail more frequently and mobile ICBMs experience increased problems with guidance system failures, etc. It may also affect the operational reliability of the force. In short, it is reasonable to believe that the strategic problems suggested by this analysis will come to pass.[33]   Therefore, if a crisis ever occurs between the United States and Russia in which the United States has a defense potential on the order of 500 warheads worth of intercept capability, Russia will likely feel pressure to rapidly redress its strategic vulnerability.

There are essentially three approaches the Russians might take to avoid this problem: (1) threatening to launch their vulnerable ballistic missiles out from under a U.S. counterforce attack, (2) rapidly generating their forces early in a crisis to improve their deterrent posture, or (3) limiting the size of nationwide ballistic missile defenses so the strategic problem outlined above never comes to pass.

Russian threats to launch a large fraction of their vulnerable forces (principally land-based ICBMs and perhaps some SLBMs in port) out from under a U.S. counterforce attack is perhaps the easiest way to redress this vulnerability. On day-to-day alert, this would provide approximately 600 additional surviving weapons. If Russia threatened to launch its vulnerable ICBMs under attack on day-to-day alert and target these weapons on U.S. cities, they could increase U.S. fatalities from around 10 million to approximately 40–45 million.[34] Hence, launch under attack becomes an effective means to quickly

---

[33]Another Russian concern with mobile nuclear forces has been maintaining secure control over the nuclear warheads when they are deployed off their main base. The fear of sabotage, confiscation, or accidental/unauthorized use made Soviet leaders reluctant during the Cold War to disperse too many nuclear weapons in peacetime. Instead they preferred to keep them locked up at secure storage sites under the assumption that they would receive adequate strategic warning to generate their forces. Whether this same concern will cause Russian leaders to keep most mobile nuclear forces on their bases in peacetime in the post–Cold War era remains to be seen.

[34]For a day-to-day alert–LUA scenario, the total number of retaliatory weapons is the same as in the partial alert–LUA case except that two fewer SSBNs are at sea. This reduces the number of retaliatory weapons by approximately 230, and the number of

convince the United States that it cannot improve its chances for survival by striking first.

On the other hand, implementing a launch-under-attack policy increases the chance of an accidental or unauthorized attack in the midst of a crisis, thereby increasing the likelihood of inadvertent nuclear war. This should be of particular concern to the United States given the relatively poor condition of Russia's ballistic missile early-warning network in the wake of the collapse of the former Soviet Union—though obviously this system may be improved by the time START II is finally implemented (i.e., around 2003). In addition, Russia must decide which targets to aim these LUA warheads against. If they are targeted against other U.S. military targets or urban/industrial areas, Russia could obtain substantial deterrent benefits but at the risk of losing escalation control if they actually launched these weapons against these targets.[35] Nevertheless, threatening LUA would certainly give U.S. leaders pause, particularly if they are contemplating preemptive counterforce attacks.

It is perhaps surprising that Russia may continue to rely on LUA under START II, despite the fact that the treaty eliminates MIRVed ICBMs—those weapons thought to be particularly dependent on LUA to survive. The reason is simply that limited defenses can undermine Russia's secure second strike to such a degree that it may be compelled to rely on launch under attack to deter a U.S. first strike. In other words, reliance on launch under attack should not be associated with a particular weapon type (e.g., MIRVed ICBMs); rather, it occurs when one's entire arsenal is not sufficiently survivable to provide a secure second strike. Hence, in a world with reduced offensive forces and limited ballistic missile defenses, one would expect to see an increased emphasis on launch under attack whether or not MIRVed ICBMs have been eliminated.

A second approach would be for the Russians to increase their alert rate relatively early in a crisis. Figure 13 shows that increasing the Russian alert rate from day-to-day to partial alert increases the Russian secure second strike by approximately 250–300 weapons (assuming the planning factors in Table 2). Increasing the readiness level further would provide a larger margin of security. Strategically, force generation is a stabilizing act. Politically, however, it can be

effective weapons by around 180, compared to the partial alert–LUA case. Using this information, one can interpolate between the partial alert and partial alert–LUA cases to find the approximate fatalities associated with a day-to-day alert–LUA scenario.

[35]If Russian leaders implement a LUA option, they must decide which targets to send these missiles against before the U.S. counterforce attack arrives. Sending them against U.S. counterforce targets in a tit-for-tat exchange may keep the war limited; however, most of these weapons will be wasted because few U.S. counterforce targets remain that are worth attacking after a U.S. first strike. On the other hand, if Russia sends these LUA weapons against other military targets or urban/industrial areas, it runs the risk of escalating the war.

quite provocative because it is difficult to separate offensive from defensive intent.

Increasing the alert rate may be especially provocative early in a crisis, because if one side successfully generates its forces while the other side remains at a low alert level, then the side on higher alert may have an incentive to strike first before the opponent brings its forces up to heightened states of alert. Whether first-strike incentives actually exist in this circumstance is arguable. Nevertheless, increasing the alert rate early in a crisis may send the wrong signal. When one side observes the opponent's force mobilization activities, it will feel pressure to bring its own forces rapidly up to high states of alert. Thus, the instability most likely to develop under START II with limited nationwide ballistic missile defenses is not so much first-strike instability but "mobilization instability," where both sides feel pressured to generate their strategic forces quickly as a crisis develops to strengthen their deterrent posture. This mobilization spiral does not necessarily lead to war, as has been argued was the case prior to World War I. But it will exacerbate mutual mistrust, increase misperceptions of the opponent's intent, and thereby make crises more difficult to control. Ultimately, the risk of inadvertent nuclear war increases.

Throughout the Cold War, the Russians practiced force generation less frequently than the United States. In the future, if Russian leaders believe that their day-to-day alert posture is insufficient for deterrence, they will either have to maintain a higher fraction of their force on alert in peacetime or will have to be prepared to generate their forces relatively quickly at the first signs of a crisis.[36] Moreover, the United States should expect the Russians to take these measures. U.S. leaders will have to become accustomed to viewing such actions as defensive and not as signs of offensive intent—provided the United States can match Russian mobilization rates. Once fully generated, neither side has an incentive to strike first.[37]

---

[36]Throughout the Cold War the Soviets did not increase their alert rate very often, in part because their larger arsenal provided a secure second strike even on day-to-day alert. The United States, on the other hand, used its alert rate as a form of signaling. The point to bear in mind here is that under START II, with around 600 ground-based interceptors deployed nationwide, the Russians may be forced to increase their alert rate early in a crisis in an effort to shore up their deterrent.

[37]As an aside, one should note that strategic bombers are the first force element that should be placed back on alert in a crisis. There are two reasons for this. First, bomber weapons are ineffective counterforce weapons because of their long flight time. They thus pose less threat of a surprise counterforce attack. Second, placing bomber weapons on alert increases the number of effective weapons to a greater extent than an equivalent number of ballistic missile weapons placed on alert, because bomber weapons face a less menacing defense. If either side's strategic air defense system is thought to be highly effective, this argument could be reversed—though with the U.S. and Russian strategic air defenses most likely to be in existence over the next several decades, this is not likely

A third option, which turns out to be the most attractive one under these circumstances, is to limit the size of nationwide ballistic missile defenses so they do not undermine the effectiveness of the U.S. or Russian deterrent, even on day-to-day alert. However, limiting the size of the defense may conflict with the U.S. objective of protecting against accidental, unauthorized, or deliberate third-country ballistic missile attacks. This tradeoff is discussed below.

How Much Ballistic Missile Defense Is Too Much?

Figures 15 and 16 capture the tradeoff between the level of defense required for an effective accidental launch protection system and the level that interferes with the U.S.-Russian strategic nuclear balance. Figure 15 illustrates the results of a simple model that calculates the size of the defense required to completely block an accidental, unauthorized, or third-country launch as a function of the attack size, for different levels of ground-based interceptor effectiveness (i.e., single shot kill probability).[38] The calculations shown here assume a 90 percent confidence level that *no* warheads (or objects, since some could be decoys) leak through the defense. Obviously, if one demands a higher level of confidence, more interceptors are required for a given attack size. As one can see from the figure, 100 ground-based interceptors can block (with 90 percent confidence) an attack containing up to around 60 objects, and 200 interceptors

to be the case. Hence, both countries should maintain and practice the capability to generate their bomber forces in a crisis.

[38]The defense is modeled here with a shoot-look-shoot firing doctrine using two shot opportunities, where one interceptor is assumed to engage each object in the first shot opportunity (i.e., the first "layer") and the remainder are fired in the second layer. This is close to the optimal firing doctrine for such a defense. The calculation of defense leakage is performed by using the expected number of leakers through the first layer as the input to the second layer of the defense. The binomial distribution is then calculated for the number of leakers through the second layer, assuming the shots are independent. The probability that zero objects leak through the second layer is the confidence level that the attack can be completely blocked. The errors introduced by these approximations are small compared to the factors that have been ignored in this analysis, e.g., interceptor range limitation, actual ballistic missile trajectories, etc. Nevertheless, the number of interceptors calculated using this model is probably accurate to within 10–20 percent (based on a comparison with more detailed simulations conducted at RAND by Mike Miller that include the effects of geography, interceptor range limitations, actual ballistic missile trajectories, etc.). This is certainly accurate enough for the conclusions drawn here. Finally, we have ignored factors such as the probability of establishing an initial track on a reentry vehicle, i.e., factors that are not independent between shots. If the detection probability is too small, e.g., less than 0.995, then it is not possible to achieve high confidence that no warheads will leak through the second layer of the defense. If these factors dominate the leakage rate, a different criterion than zero leakers must be selected for defense effectiveness.

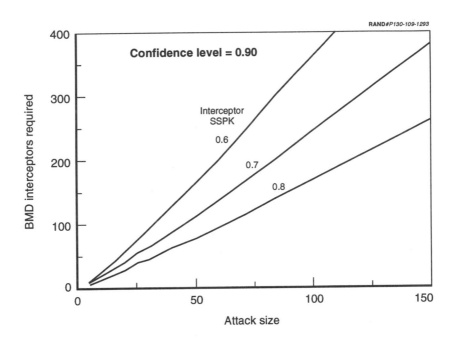

RAND#P130-109-1293

Figure 15—BMD Interceptors Required for Zero Leakage

could block an attack containing on the order of 115 objects, assuming the interceptors have a 0.8 single-shot kill probability. As the BMD interceptor effectiveness degrades, more interceptors are required to block a given attack size. For example, if the interceptors have a 0.6 single-shot kill probability, then only about 30 objects could be blocked by 100 interceptors at the 90 percent confidence level.

There is no unequivocal way to determine the size of possible accidental, unauthorized, or deliberate third-country ballistic missile attacks. However, most threats probably fall below 50–100 objects, unless one assumes a large number of decoys that cannot be discriminated by the defense.[39] Therefore,

---

[39]Most accidental Russian ICBM attacks would probably involve fewer than ten warheads, particularly after 2003, when all MIRVed ICBMs have been eliminated from the Russian arsenal—though the number of objects could be larger if decoys are deployed. Unauthorized Russian ICBM or SLBM attacks could be larger, depending on the size of the conspiracy one assumes. An unauthorized attack from a mobile SS-25 battalion could involve up to nine warheads, a single SS-18 launch control facility could launch up to 100 warheads, and a single Typhoon boat could launch 200 warheads (120 warheads if the SS-N-20 is de-MIRVed to six warheads apiece under START II).

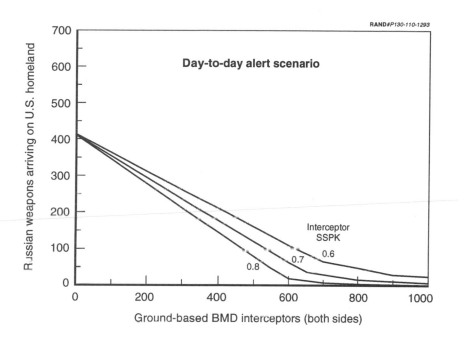

Figure 16 — Russian Secure Second Strike Versus U.S. BMD (effective weapons)

limited nationwide ballistic missile defenses on the order of 100–200 ground-based interceptors should provide sufficient protection for a wide range of accidental, unauthorized, or deliberate third-country threats, provided the interceptors are fairly effective (i.e., have a single-shot kill probability greater than 0.7).

One should note that this calculation is approximate because it ignores interceptor range limitations (i.e., it assumes each interceptor has sufficient range

---

Fortunately, highly MIRVed ICBMs will be eliminated after 2003. The "mad submarine commander" is the only scenario left that, in principle, generates large unauthorized attacks. However, this scenario should be discounted, since the Russians have recently revealed that they have Permissive Action Links on their submarines to prevent unauthorized SLBM launches. Consequently, most remaining accidental or unauthorized attacks after 2003 will likely contain fewer than 10 warheads, with perhaps as many as 50–100 objects if advanced decoys are deployed. Third countries are not likely to develop large ICBM arsenals, much less SLBMs or MIRVed ICBMs, for some time. Hence, attacks from these countries will probably involve fewer than 10 warheads. The debate about possible attack sizes will ultimately revolve around the number and types of decoys an adversary might deploy, as well as on the ability of the defense to discriminate decoys from actual warheads.

to engage any of the incoming objects), and it assumes effective warning and track information early in the ballistic missile's flight trajectory to cue the interceptors. Such an effective battle management capability requires upgrading the existing U.S. ballistic missile early warning network, possibly with space-based detection and tracking sensors such as "Brilliant Eyes." If more than a single site is required to provide coverage of the entire continental United States (due to interceptor range limitations or the lack of accurate track information early in the ballistic missile's flight), then the number of interceptors required for an effective limited nationwide defense would be larger than the numbers shown in Figure 15.[40] The exact amount depends on the number of sites, the degree of site overlap, and the extent to which one believes the attack may be focused only on one site as opposed to being spread across the entire United States (in which case, having multiple sites would not significantly increase the interceptor requirements from those given in Figure 15).

We now return to the question of how much defense is too much. From the preceding discussion, it is clear that the first strategic problem to occur under START II is the weakening of the Russian deterrent on day-to-day alert. Figure 16 plots the size of the Russian retaliation on day-to-day alert (measured in effective weapons) as a function of the number of ground-based interceptors deployed on both sides. The number of effective weapons is shown for three levels of defense effectiveness. (Until now, the size of each side's retaliation has been shown only for an interceptor SSPK of 0.8.)

This calculation assumes the United States tries to maximize its counterforce effectiveness by allocating 1400 out of the 1520 available nuclear weapons to the counterforce first strike on day-to-day alert. If 600 interceptors are deployed, the size of the Russian secure second strike drops to around 20 effective weapons (for an SSPK of 0.8), assuming none are withheld for a secure reserve force. This is the result discussed in connection with Figure 13. If more than 600 interceptors are deployed, the size of the effective Russian retaliation could be reduced, on average, to as low as 2–3 weapons. Clearly, defense deployments over 600 interceptors provide the United States with a splendid damage-limiting first-strike option on day-to-day alert—assuming the defenses can survive, that decoys can be discriminated, and that the BMD interceptors have an effectiveness close to 0.8 SSPK. If the defense effectiveness drops to 0.6, the extent to which damage can be limited drops significantly (e.g., around 110 warheads leak through a 600-interceptor defense if the SSPK is 0.6 and approximately 20 warheads leak through a 1000-interceptor defense). Thus, effective damage limitation with modest defense deployments requires high interceptor performance.

---

[40]The additional interceptors that would be required to defend Hawaii and Alaska have been ignored—something an analyst can do but not a politician.

To avoid the instability created by a U.S. damage-limiting first-strike option, the number of ground-based interceptors should be constrained to less than approximately 200 interceptors, leaving Russia with around 300 effective weapons with which to retaliate (regardless of interceptor SSPK). Note that an important assumption here is that theater BMD interceptors do not add appreciably to the strategic BMD capability—an assumption one may worry about if thousands of theater interceptors are deployed (especially in light of past debates about the strategic BMD capability of high-performance surface-to-air missiles. An ABM Treaty–constrained deployment of 100 ground-based interceptors has minimal effect on the Russian retaliatory capability. From Figure 15 one observes that 100 interceptors still provide the United States with an effective accidental launch protection system, provided the interceptor SSPK is above 0.7 and likely threats contain no more than around 50 objects.

CONCLUDING OBSERVATIONS

The United States and Russia cannot arbitrarily reduce the size of their strategic nuclear arsenals and the alert rate associated with these forces, and then deploy limited nationwide ballistic missile defenses, without eventually undermining deterrence. If U.S.-Russian relations continue to be cooperative in the future, then a robust deterrent posture between these two states may be of less concern. However, one cannot predict with certainty that crises between these former adversaries will never occur. Therefore, it behooves U.S. and Russian leaders to avoid creating, in cooperative times, a strategic nuclear deterrent posture that, in a crisis, proves to be weak. The likelihood of conflict with Russia may be small in the future, but with events this fateful, leaders should err on the side of caution.

The perspective advanced in this analysis is not that a weak day-to-day deterrent posture leads to premeditated nuclear war in peacetime, but rather that it forces the strategically disadvantaged side to react in ways to redress its perceived vulnerability. This reaction may appear provocative in a crisis and, hence, could increase the chance of misperception or miscalculation, thereby making crises more difficult to control and increasing the likelihood of inadvertent nuclear war.

With offensive forces constrained by START II, and assuming no nationwide ballistic missile defenses on either side, neither the United States nor Russia can significantly limit damage by striking first with an all-out counterforce attack. The mutual hostage relationship that characterizes mutual deterrence will remain. In particular, on generated alert—the most likely posture for U.S. and Russian forces if a crisis develops—both countries will have around 2200–2500 strategic nuclear weapons that can survive attack and pene-

344 New Challenges for Defense Planning

trate the opponent's strategic air defenses to arrive on target in the opponent's homeland. This retaliatory capability is sufficient to hold at risk a wide range of military, leadership, and economic targets even after weapons have been subtracted for a secure reserve force.

At lower alert rates, the retaliatory capability drops. For example, on day-to-day alert the United States will retain the capability to deliver up to approximately 900 weapons after absorbing a Russian counterforce first strike, assuming the United States does not reduce its SLBM alert rate. Projected Russian force postures are more vulnerable at low alert rates because relatively few Russian SLBMs are assumed to be at sea and few mobile ICBMs are assumed to be out of their garrisons when a U.S. counterforce attack arrives. Even so, approximately 450 weapons could be delivered against the United States in retaliation on day-to-day alert, unless a significant number of weapons are withheld for a Russian secure reserve force.

If one assumes that deterrence rests on the ability to inflict casualties on the opponent's population, then deterrence under START II is more robust. On day-to-day alert, the relatively small (by Cold War standards) surviving arsenals can still do tremendous damage. For example, 900 arriving U.S. weapons would be able to threaten approximately 60 million Russian fatalities (approximately 60 percent of the Russian urban population), and 450 arriving Russian weapons can threaten around 50 million U.S. fatalities (approximately 30 percent of the U.S. urban population).

Based on these observations, one might conclude that there is room for further offensive force reductions beyond the levels set by the START II Treaty, or for further reductions in U.S. or Russian peacetime alert rates. The question of further cuts depends on whether 2200–2500 effective weapons is more than is necessary to deter all plausible resurgent Russian threats (including a revanchist Russian state led by Vladimir Zhirinovsky). If one believes deterrence rests on the ability to credibly inflict societal destruction, the answer will likely be that further cuts are acceptable (desirable), possibly down to as few as 1000 strategic nuclear weapons in each side's arsenal. However, if one believes that deterrence of a resurgent Russia requires the ability to credibly threaten Russian military as well as economic assets, then reductions below START II levels are probably not possible, unless they are minor.

With respect to peacetime alert rates, again one might conclude that further reductions are possible. Certainly the U.S. peacetime alert rate seems more than adequate under START II. However, the crucial point to bear in mind is that reductions in the peacetime alert rate increase one's dependence on force generation to provide an adequate deterrent in times of U.S.-Russian tension. In principle, strategic force generation is a stabilizing act because it increases the effectiveness of each side's deterrent. Politically, however, force generation, especially if it occurs rapidly at the onset of a crisis, is frequently viewed as a provocative act. Therefore, "mobilization instabilities" may become a central feature of the future U.S.-Russian strategic nuclear interaction. Managing the dynamics associated with U.S. and Russian strategic nuclear force mobilization will become crucial for preventing future crises from spiraling out of control. This mobilization spiral does not necessarily lead to war, as some have argued was the case prior to World War I. However, it will make crises more difficult to control. Greater transparency with respect to U.S. and Russian force generation procedures might help reduce the chance for misperception. These observations are predicated on the assumption that neither the United States nor Russia deploys an appreciable limited nationwide ballistic missile defense. If such a defense is deployed, this would have a significant impact on the above observations.

Nationwide ballistic missile defenses have two competing effects. They strengthen deterrence by complicating the opponent's first strike, and they weaken the opponent's deterrent by undermining his secure second strike. Of these two effects, the second dominates at modest levels of defense.[41] In particular, with 600 ground-based interceptors deployed on both sides (space-based defenses are not considered in this analysis), the Russian retaliation on day-to-day alert could be reduced to as few as 20 arriving weapons after a U.S. counterforce attack.[42] Such a damage-limiting capability was never achieved by either side during the Cold War. Russia's deterrent is the first to become vulnerable because it has fewer weapons deployed in survivable basing modes on day-to-day alert. If one considers offensive force reductions below START II, obviously less defense would be required to limit damage to the same degree.

On generated alert, the U.S. and Russian START II deterrent forces are quite robust, even at defense levels of 600 ground-based interceptors.[43] Therefore, if one believes that U.S. and Russian forces will always be on generated alert in a crisis, then deterrence will be robust even in the presence of limited nationwide ballistic missile defenses. However, it is the transition from peacetime to generated alert that concerns us. Since deterrence at low alert rates is compromised, the Russians have a strong incentive to improve their de-

---

[41]This same critique was leveled against nationwide ballistic missile defenses in the mid-1980s. However, at that time the level of defense needed to upset the strategic balance would have been quite large. Under START II, relatively low levels of defense can undermine deterrence.

[42]This assumes highly effective ground-based interceptors, i.e., interceptors with a single-shot kill probability of 0.8 and sufficiently accurate and timely track information to allow for a shoot-look-shoot defense firing doctrine.

[43]The defense required to seriously interfere with either side's deterrent on generated alert is around 3500 ground-based interceptors—deployments that will not likely be realized in the near future.

terrent posture. Again, the point here is not that a U.S. President might be tempted to launch a surprise attack out of the blue, but rather that the Russians, realizing their strategic vulnerability, will be forced to improve their secure second-strike capability. This is the main strategic problem created in an environment characterized by low force levels (i.e., START II levels), low alert rates, and limited nationwide ballistic missile defense deployments on the order of 600 ground-based interceptors or more.

Several solutions to this problem are possible. First, Russia could simply maintain a higher fraction of its submarines at sea or mobile ICBMs out of garrison in peacetime. This is not likely to occur for reasons of cost. Second, Russia could threaten to launch its vulnerable forces out from under a U.S. counterforce attack. This is unattractive because it increases the likelihood of an accidental or unauthorized Russian missile launch in the midst of a crisis—particularly in light of the relatively poor condition of Russia's ballistic missile early-warning network in the wake of the collapse of the Soviet Union (though obviously this system may be improved by the time START II is finally implemented). This, in turn, increases the chances for inadvertent nuclear war, a situation neither country wants.

Third, the Russians could increase the alert rate associated with their strategic nuclear forces early in a crisis. From a strategic perspective, increasing the alert rate is a defensive act because it increases the fraction of the force that can survive a counterforce first strike and, hence, strengthens deterrence. However, it is also consistent with offensive intent. Force generation thus is likely to be politically provocative because it forces the United States to alert its forces fairly quickly to match the Russians. Again, one is faced with the prospect of mobilization spirals, as discussed above.

Finally, the best approach would be to limit the size of the ballistic missile defenses on both sides. If nationwide ballistic missile defenses are limited under START II to fewer than 200 ground-based interceptors deployed nationwide, deterrence would be minimally affected because the Russians would still have around 300 effective weapons with which to retaliate. A defense limited to 100 ground-based interceptors deployed nationwide, as required by the ABM Treaty, clearly would not upset the strategic nuclear balance. Note that an important assumption here is that theater ballistic missile defenses do not add appreciably to the strategic ballistic missile defense capability—an assumption one may question if highly capable theater defenses are deployed.

In addition, 100–200 highly effective ground-based interceptors should be adequate to protect against a wide range of accidental, unauthorized, or deliberate third-country ballistic missile attacks, unless one assumes that a large number of decoys cannot be discriminated by the defense. Thus, it should be possible to have a reasonably effective accidental launch protection system without undermining either the U.S. or Russian strategic nuclear deterrent—a requirement written into U.S. law by the 1991 congressional Missile Defense Act. Such a defense system may violate some elements of the ABM Treaty.[44] However, this is not necessarily inconsistent with U.S. and Russian post–Cold War security objectives.

In general, as U.S. and Russian nuclear arsenals shrink, stable deterrence will increasingly depend on maintaining a significant fraction of forces on alert, particularly if limited nationwide defenses are deployed. Reducing the number of weapons in each side's arsenal or "de-alerting" elements of the strategic nuclear force as a symbol of "nuclear disengagement" may improve political relations in peacetime; however, it can create strategic vulnerabilities that may make future crises more difficult to control. Though deterrence of a hypothetical Russian attack is not foremost in the minds of U.S. policymakers, it still behooves them to carefully weigh the implications of further reductions below START II levels, further cuts in the peacetime alert rate, and the deployment of limited ballistic missile defenses beyond several hundred ground-based interceptors before taking the next steps to reshape the U.S.-Russian strategic nuclear landscape.

BIBLIOGRAPHY

Bracken, Jerome (1990), "Stable Transitions from Mutual Assured Destruction to Mutual Assured Survival," *Canadian Journal of Information Systems and Operations Research (INFOR)*, Vol. 28, No. 1.

Canavan, Gregory (1991), *Crisis Stability Indices for Adaptive Two-Layer Defenses*, LA-11974-MS, Los Alamos National Laboratory.

Congressional Budget Office (1991), *The START Treaty and Beyond*, U.S. Government Printing Office, Washington, D.C., October.

Daugherty, William, Barbara Levy, and Frank von Hipple (1986), "The Consequences of 'Limited' Nuclear Attacks on the United States," *International Security*, Vol. 10, No. 4.

Davis, Paul K. (ed.) (1994), *New Challenges for Defense Planning: Rethinking How Much Is Enough*, RAND, Santa Monica, CA.

Davis, Paul K., and Barry Wolf (1991), "Behavioral Factors in Nuclear De-escalation," in Stephen Cimbala (ed.), *Nuclear De-escalation and War Termination*, St. Martin's Press, New York.

---

[44]Even if one assumes only 100 interceptors are deployed, the ABM Treaty would still have to be modified to allow upgrades to each country's ballistic missile early-warning network (possibly including space-based components), and it would have to be modified to allow interceptors to be deployed at more than one site.

Erlanger, Steven (1993), "Russian Nationalist Leader Offers to Cooperate in New Government," *The New York Times*, December 15, p. A1.

Grotte, Jeffery (1980), "Measuring Strategic Stability with Two-Strike Nuclear Exchange Models," *Journal of Conflict Resolution*, Vol. 24, No. 2.

Hiatt, Fred (1993), "Russia Shifts Doctrine on Military Use," *Washington Post*, November 4.

Jervis, Robert (1976), *Perceptions and Misperceptions in International Politics*, Princeton University Press, Princeton, NJ.

Kent, Glenn, and David Thayer (1989), *First-Strike Stability: A Methodology for Evaluating Strategic Forces*, RAND, Santa Monica, CA.

Lelyveld, Michael (1993), "U.S. Experts See Russia Near Economic Collapse," *Journal of Commerce*, September 14.

Levy, Barbara, Frank von Hipple, and William Daugherty (1987/88), "Civilian Casualties from 'Limited' Nuclear Attacks on the Soviet Union," *International Security*, Vol. 12, No. 3.

Schmemann, Serge (1993a), "Moscow Outlines 'Doctrine' for Its Future Military," *The New York Times*, November 3.

———— (1993b), "Russia Drops Pledge of No First Use of Atom Arms," *The New York Times*, November 4.

———— (1993c), "Russian Election Result: Shattering of New Image," *The New York Times*, December 15, p. A8.

Shaver, Russ (1994), "Priorities for Ballistic Missile Defense," in Davis (1994).

Wilkening, Dean (1994), *The Impact of START II and Limited Nationwide Ballistic Missile Defenses on Deterrence and Crisis Stability*, RAND, Santa Monica, CA.

Wohlstetter, Albert (1959), "The Delicate Balance of Terror," *Foreign Affairs*, Vol. 37, January.

Part Four

Planning at the Operational or Campaign Level

Chapter 12

CONVENTIONAL CAMPAIGN ANALYSIS OF MAJOR REGIONAL CONFLICTS

Fred Frostic and Christopher J. Bowie

In conducting future military planning, it has become increasingly important to approach many aspects of defense analysis from a "campaign perspective"—that is, one that examines the many military operations that may be necessary from the time crisis begins to the time conflict terminates, and that highlights the many capabilities that may be needed to accomplish these operations. Only this sort of approach can give visibility to the many military mission capabilities needed by U.S. forces. It is not enough that the United States have some aggregate level of armored divisions and tactical fighter wings. Indeed, the precise number of carrier battle groups appears to be less important than whether U.S. forces have the full spread of capabilities needed for deploying and employing forces in a range of diverse circumstances.[1]

Though U.S. forces will be engaged in a wide range of other activities in future years, the threat of aggression in regions where U.S. interests are involved has emerged since the end of the Cold War as the primary driver and shaper of the U.S. military posture.[2] This paper describes in some detail a "typical" military campaign of the sort RAND has used extensively in assessing capabilities, at different budget levels and under different defense programs, for responding to major regional conflicts. In the conflict analysis, this campaign must account for such diverse factors as political-military setting, geographic and environmental factors, U.S. mobility assets, the many components of a combined-arms force, and the challenge of deterring or coping with weapons of mass destruction. Such a campaign-oriented style of analysis is now a central feature of defense planning.

In future regional crises, the possible use of weapons of mass destruction could loom ominously over combat operations. The United States will need the capability both to deter and, more significantly, to prevent the use of such weapons. This will require a multidimensional approach to achieve any prospects of success. Here, we focus primarily on conventional operations.

In addition, it is likely that the United States will be engaged in a wide range of military activities besides state-to-state military conflict. These activities could include such demanding operations as counterinsurgency, combating terrorism, peace

---

[1] A useful overview of such an analytic approach can be seen in Bowie, Frostic, Lewis, Lund, Ochmanek, and Propper (1993).

[2] See Aspin (1993). For a perspective on the other types of missions that the U.S. military may be called upon to perform, see Bracken (1993) and Builder, Lempert, Lewis, Larson, and Weiner (1993).

enforcement, and providing humanitarian assistance.   They could involve large numbers of U.S. and allied forces for long periods—and the assets needed to prosecute them are not necessarily lesser included cases of major regional conflict. Clearly, adequate numbers of specialized force elements will be needed to deal with these demanding situations.

This paper, however, focuses on major regional conflicts, since the most costly defense programs and force structure decisions stem from planning for such conflicts. We begin by setting out the characteristics of regional conflicts: potential threats, warning and response, geographical and physical factors, and force characteristics. We go on to describe the three phases of regional campaigns: initial operations, combat operations, and postconflict stability operations.   Later we discuss enemy counterstrategies, and we end the paper with some observations.

CHARACTERISTICS OF REGIONAL CONFLICTS

A first step in analyzing potential major regional conflicts is to determine which countries are and which might become potential threats, what warning signs to look for, and what responses to make in order to forestall such conflicts. If warning indicators suggest the possibility of conflict, then characteristics of the region that will influence the shape of battle, such as geographic and physical factors, must be assessed. The shape of the conflict will also depend on the types of forces both sides can bring to bear and the availability of those forces over time. Below we describe each of these characteristics.

Potential Threats

Major regional conflicts (MRCs) typically involve nation-to-nation warfare (a characteristic that often distinguishes them from peacekeeping and peacemaking operations). These conflicts can pose serious threats to U.S. and allied national interests and provide the motivation for U.S. involvement. Such conflicts feature interwoven political, military, and economic objectives among all participants.

As we write this in the environment of 1994, two key theaters figure centrally in U.S. planning: Korea and Southwest Asia. In the latter theater, U.S. interests revolve primarily around maintaining unimpeded access at reasonable prices to the region's unparalleled oil resources and protecting key friendly nations. In Korea, U.S. interests involve security commitments to South Korea, Japan, and other important actors in the Pacific Rim, and the vast range of economic and political ties that have developed in that region since the end of World War II.

For a nation to constitute a serious threat to its neighbors and U.S. interests, it must possess land, air, and perhaps naval forces of adequate size, supported by a logistics base and infrastructure capable of maintaining these forces in the field. As can be seen in Figure 1, the size of the military threats facing the United States and its allies has changed dramatically from the Cold War period. The largest powers (excluding a resurgent Russia and a militant modern China) may field roughly 500,000 personnel and 10 mechanized/armored divisions (combined with an equal or greater number of infantry divisions). Typically, these ground forces are supported by air forces ranging from 500 to 1000 fighter and attack aircraft and, perhaps, a coastal navy equipped with small surface combatants and a few submarines. The exact nature of these forces, of course, will vary from case to case.

This picture could change over time. Developments in Russia and China, for example, raise the potential for regional conflicts adjacent to these regions—and the possibility for even larger-scale military operations. But because of the time needed for these nations to move to a threatening political stance, reinvest in modern military forces, and develop into a coherent military threat, the United States and its allies should have sufficient political, economic, and military warning to respond appropriately. This means that the United States must possess the ability to expand its force structure and support base should a more sizable regional or global threat reemerge.

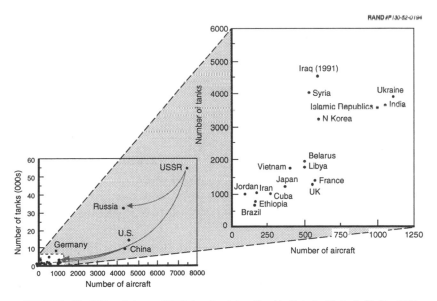

RAND #P130-52-0194

SOURCE: *The Military Balance, 1991/2*, London, International Institute for Strategic Studies, 1991.

Figure 1—Military Capabilities of Regional Powers at the Close of the Cold War

The regional threats challenging U.S. interests and threatening U.S. allies are not located adjacent to the continental United States. This adds two key characteristics to planning for regional warfare. First, U.S. forces must plan to operate in conjunction with indigenous and allied forces. This places a premium on interoperability, i.e., familiarity with doctrine and training before the onset of conflict and, perhaps, possession of the same types of equipment. Second, the bulk of U.S. military power must deploy to engage threatening regional powers. This heightens the importance of U.S. mobility forces.

Indications, Assessment, and Response

In many ways, responding to a regional conflict is a race against time. An aggressor would like to build up forces, launch an invasion, and accomplish his objectives before the United States can bring its power to bear. By attending to indications and warning signals, the United States may be able to respond with a series of preparations that significantly reduce the aggressor's chance of success—to the point where a prudent enemy planner would be deterred. Deterring aggression is most in keeping with U.S. strategy and goals, since it meets U.S. national security objectives at the least cost in blood and resources.

Precise definitions of warning and response were developed for the Cold War era. In broad terms, strategic warning was warning prior to an attack; tactical warning was warning after the start of hostilities.[3] In this new era, we believe that warning/indication categories must be redefined, and for purposes here, we have employed three broad categories: political, strategic, and tactical.

Political indications involve a broad assessment of U.S. national interests, threats to those interests, and the correct interpretation of indicators of intent for aggression.[4] In essence, the United States seeks to assess which nations might threaten its interests (as well as those of its allies) and the time at which such threats may prove credible. The indicators associated with political warning are the construction of offensive military forces, the buildup of a military infrastructure, and political actions in conflict with U.S. policy (such as support of terrorist groups, sales of weapons to hostile nations, threats against neighbors allied to the United States, claims against neighboring territory of governments friendly to the United States, attempts to undermine allied governments, and so on).

U.S. responses to political indications might be the formation of coalitions with nations that are threatened or have goals compatible with those of the

---

[3]See, for example, *Department of Defense Dictionary of Military and Associated Terms*, JCS Pub. 1-02, December 1989.

[4]Such factors play an important role in the development of formal military strategy. The latter is laid out in such documents as Powell (1992).

United States, the establishment of joint and combined training exercises, the shaping of the U.S. military posture to deal with identified potential adversaries, the construction of general campaign plans, and the development of basing facilities, prepositioning materials, and, where possible, a military support infrastructure. For example, political indications today have placed great emphasis on military planning for conflict in Southwest Asia and Korea. In the future, an emergent European or Asian continental threat might compel the United States to expand its political alliances and forces—and possibly develop and introduce new weapon systems.

Strategic indications consist of signals conveying an aggressor's intent to conduct military operations against U.S. and allied interests. This may be signaled through increasingly overt political actions (such as the announcement of grievances, territorial claims, demands for financial compensation, harassment of foreign nationals, seizure of economic assets, etc.). Such actions may be rendered more threatening by increases in military readiness (such as calling up reserve elements, increasing training, breaking out combat supplies and stocks, and stepping up surveillance and intelligence activity). The critical signal, of course, is the physical movement of combat forces into positions to conduct offensive military operations.[5]

Assessing and responding appropriately in a timely manner to indications at the strategic level has historically proven problematic for a variety of reasons. For example, apparently overt military preparations generally take place within the aggressor's territory and do not violate the sovereignty of neighboring nations. Readiness exercises can be used (and historically have been used) to camouflage overt war preparations. The problems in responding to indications become apparent in retrospective examinations of past conflicts, where strategic warning signals were often present but were overlooked or wrongly assessed. One need only review such situations as the Japanese attack on Pearl Harbor, the North Korean invasion of South Korea in 1950, the Soviet assault on Czechoslovakia in 1968, the Egyptian attack across the Suez in 1973, the Argentine invasion of the Falkland Islands in 1982, and the Iraqi invasion of Kuwait in 1990 to see examples of failures to respond to strategic indications.[6] On the other hand, successes in responding to strategic indications often have yielded deterrence—and hence may have gone unnoticed in the history books.[7]

---

[5]An important step in the process is the buildup and movement of ground forces, which require weeks or more to accomplish and are generally observable.

[6]For more on the failure of strategic warning, see the excellent discussion in Davis (1988:26–47).

[7]For example, in 1960, Israeli responses to operational warning deterred Arab forces from launching an attack.

A failure to respond to strategic indications generally occurs due to the desire not to be provocative and further inflame a crisis. Such a situation can be seen in Figure 2, which provides a brief historical synopsis of political and military events preceding the 1991 war in the Gulf. Despite continuous buildup of Iraqi forces from July 16 on, Kuwait, in order not to be provocative, reduced alert several days after initial movements of Iraqi troops, and the United States did not move ships to the Gulf until late July. In this case, the desire not to be provocative resulted in a failure to deter.

As the indications develop that an aggressor may be contemplating military operations, a series of military actions can be taken to enhance the ability to respond. These actions are comparatively inexpensive next to the cost of countering an invasion. Such actions include increasing surveillance and intelligence activities to gauge the true intent of an adversary (and send a signal of concern), enhancing the readiness of the mobility system (airlift, sealift, staging bases, and port reception units), updating mobility and operational plans, making elements of the command-and-control system operational, and preparing combat forces for mobilization and deployment.

These actions increase the ability of U.S. forces to deploy rapidly—and may serve as a deterrent to aggression. If these do not have the desired effect, the next level of action may be to deploy deterrent forces. Historically, the United States has relied on moving naval assets into position.[8] In more recent years, the deployment of airborne radar and surveillance aircraft (such as the Airborne Warning and Control System or AWACS), which can be moved into position

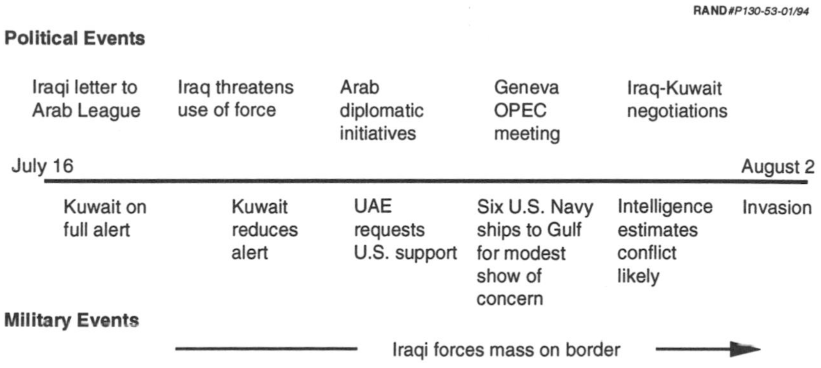

RAND#P130-53-01/94

Political Events

Iraqi letter to Arab League	Iraq threatens use of force	Arab diplomatic initiatives	Geneva OPEC meeting	Iraq-Kuwait negotiations

July 16 ─── August 2

Kuwait on full alert	Kuwait reduces alert	UAE requests U.S. support	Six U.S. Navy ships to Gulf for modest show of concern	Intelligence estimates conflict likely	Invasion

Military Events

───────────────── Iraqi forces mass on border ─────────▶

SOURCE: Department of Defense, *Conduct of the Persian Gulf War*, 1992, pp. 3–17.

Figure 2—Desert Shield Timeline

---

[8] For the U.S. Navy's perspective on this, see Department of the Navy (1993).

in a matter of hours, has emerged as an important policy tool.[9] These aircraft offer warning capabilities, increase the defensive posture of allies, and signal U.S. concern. Another step to increase U.S. capabilities to meet a regional threat is to deploy reception forces (such as personnel and equipment to unload aircraft and ships). All of this would precede the actual movement of combat forces (with the exception of naval vessels). While this is occurring, combat forces based in the United States and forward areas can be readied for deployment.

Geographical and Physical Factors

To analyze the performance of forces in major regional conflicts, the influence of key geographical and physical factors must be assessed and incorporated. These factors affect both the U.S. ability to bring sufficient forces to bear and the capability to sustain operations in an area where the United States may not have a large peacetime military presence. Political and economic pressures are combining to reduce the number of U.S. forces permanently based abroad. Accordingly, mobility and sustainment forces are emerging as an increasingly critical component of the U.S. joint force posture, and their adequacy can be assessed only when viewed from a "campaign perspective." Mobility and sustainment are greatly affected by the distance to the campaign region, the environment in that region (terrain, weather, etc.), and the military infrastructure available in the region. Each of these is discussed below.

Distance. The arrival of forces in the theater is a function of

- Their peacetime locations.
- The distance of these locations from air and sea ports of embarkation.
- The physical distance and routing forces must transit to get to the theater (either by air or sea).
- The throughput capacity of embarkation, staging, and destination bases.
- The capacity of airlift and sealift fleets.
- The types of forces being moved.

For more distant areas (such as Southwest Asia), forces deploying by air depend heavily on a system of staging bases for refueling, maintenance, and crew rest. Similarly, the arrival of forces in a theater depends on the capacity of the reception facilities (which is a function of physical assets and personnel), the

---

[9]See, for example, *Forty Five Years of Global Reach and Power: The United States Air Force and National Security, 1945–1992*, Headquarters, United States Air Force (SAF/OSX), 1992. These aircraft, along with other key elements of the command-and-control system, facilitate combat operations if they become necessary.

distance of these ports and airfields from the locus of fighting, and the transportation network found in the region.

Figure 3 provides an overview of the deployment process. In many ways, the process is a classic transportation problem in which constraints at any node as well as the capacity of the overall system affect the desired outcome—force closure. A range of sophisticated operations-simulation techniques, including linear programming, is available to provide insights into deployment capabilities.[10]

The Environment. The environment—the terrain, weather, and cultural features (e.g., cities, canals, roads, etc.) in which operations are to be conducted—has always shaped the character and outcome of campaigns and must be integrated into the analysis of regional conflict. Napoleon's and Hitler's plans for conquering Russia fell victim in part to the hostile environment (distance and winter weather). The success of Rommel's bold flanking

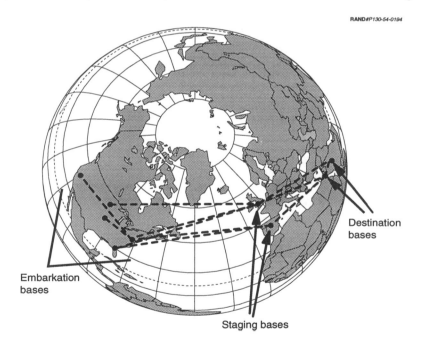

RAND#P130-54-0194

Figure 3—Deployment Schematic

---

[10]For an overview of alternative deployment strategies, see Dadant (1984). See also Kassing (1994).

maneuvers in North Africa in World War II stemmed in part from the terrain and weather. And although the environment in Southwest Asia enhanced the performance of airpower in Desert Storm, the same factor rendered airpower nearly ineffective during the opening days of the Battle of the Ardennes in World War II (Craven and Cates, 1951, chap. 19).

Weather can also have an important effect on terrain. For example, heavy rains can render fields and other areas impassable to vehicles, restrict lines of sight, and reduce the effectiveness of whole classes of weapon systems and sensors for periods of time (such as lasers, imaging infrared systems, and so on). Detailed data bases on historical weather patterns in various regions are typically employed in simulation models to simulate the effects of weather on combat. For example, if we are simulating airpower operations in a theater with a rainy season, data on average cloud ceilings, line of sight, and so on can be used to assess whether or not aircrews can sight various targets and what sorts of altitudes may be employed for effective combat operations. These considerations in turn can influence effectiveness, survivability, and aircraft combat radii.

These same considerations also play a key role in assessing ground combat performance. For example, trafficability along avenues of approach may change dramatically depending on whether the ground is sodden or frozen (as is often seen in Korean combat simulations). In fact, the construction and planning of ground campaigns often centers not just on enemy forces, but on terrain, trafficability, obstacles, and weather.

Regional Military Infrastructure. The usable military infrastructure of the region is an important factor in the conduct of modern military operations. In fact, the existing infrastructure in many ways shapes the course of a campaign.

By infrastructure we mean such things as airfields, ports, surface transportation networks, reserve stocks of fuel and storage facilities (as well as fuel distribution networks), electrical power, regional communications facilities and networks (both civil and military), and the quantity of prepositioned stocks of military equipment. Military planners and analysts must thus conduct a detailed assessment of the regional military infrastructure from two different perspectives: (1) the compatibility of U.S. and allied forces with the infrastructure in the region, and (2) the effect of the infrastructure on the enemy's ability to conduct a campaign. Understanding the infrastructure is important for determining what equipment and capabilities the United States and its allies must possess or acquire.[11]

---

[11]For additional perspectives on the influence of the regional military infrastructure upon military operations, see Bowie (1984:14–25, 44–65).

Force Characteristics

The size and composition of forces deployed to a major regional conflict are determined by a number of factors. Existing operational plans provide a useful starting point. However, consideration must be given to unique contemporary factors, such as the capabilities of allied and indigenous forces in the region, current and potential new weapon systems owned by the adversary (e.g., long-range precision attack assets and submarines), changes in the size of adversary forces and capabilities, and environmental factors.

Planning and analyzing regional conflicts involve selection of key force elements for deployment and use. These forces are drawn from all components of the U.S. military. Each situation is unique and requires forces tailored to the demands presented. For example, if indigenous forces possess sizable ground forces, the joint force commander may elect to first deploy air and naval forces to the theater. Similarly, the status of prepositioned equipment and stocks affects the commander's choice of early-arriving forces. But a core set of capabilities will prevail in a wide range of situations and over time. Let us consider the forces in the order in which a deployment in a short-warning scenario might occur: naval forces, air forces, and ground forces. In some cases, the existence of forward-based forces and differing threats and environments may change the order in which forces arrive. We will addresss these factors in greater detail below.

Naval Forces. Maritime forces offer many unique qualities. Typically, naval forces are operating around the world during periods of peacetime—and can be concentrated in areas of interest even in periods of ambiguous warning without interfering with the sovereignty of nations in the theater. These forces are assembled into task forces, often organized around an aircraft carrier. The latter provides sea-based airpower for both protection of sea lines of communication and power projection ashore.

Accompanying the carrier are a number of surface combatants and submarines. These vessels are important for projecting power ashore when equipped with sea-launched missiles, such as the Tomahawk Land Attack Missile (TLAM) and/or a modified variant of the Army Tactical Missile System (ATACMS). Additionally, the surface combatants provide protection of the fleet with air defenses. These air defenses could also be extended to provide initial ballistic missile defense over air bases, ports, lodgement areas, and the fleet when tied to spaceborne surveillance systems. To allow these forces to maintain a sustained forward presence, naval task forces are typically supported by underway replenishment groups. And accompanying the task force are submarines, minesweepers, and an array of airborne surveillance systems (such as P-3 Orions) to open and sustain sea lines of communication for the movement of sealift vessels.

The exact composition of the battle groups, location, and commitment time are important factors in analyzing the conduct of the campaign. When faced with a rapidly developing situation, there is a premium on forces available at the start of a conflict.[12]

Air Forces. Land-based airpower consists of several key elements: a set of command, control, and targeting aircraft as well as key ground facilities for surveillance and battle management; aerial refueling and airlift aircraft for mobility; and long-range bombers and fighter/attack squadrons for power projection.

Airborne targeting and control aircraft provide surveillance of the aggressor's air and ground operations and can be used to allocate and direct forces to areas of interest. These typically consist of such assets as E-3B/C airborne warning and control aircraft, the Joint Surveillance Target Attack Radar System (JSTARS), which can locate enemy ground force dispositions and movements, RC-135 aircraft for collecting electronic intelligence, and other specialized reconnaissance and surveillance assets (to include unmanned penetrating vehicles and satellites).

In terms of mobility assets, aerial refueling aircraft increase the range of operations and endurance of aircraft and have emerged as a common resource for land- and sea-based aircraft, as well as for allied aircraft. In addition, tankers serve an important role in deploying forces to the theater. Strategic airlift aircraft are necessary for the rapid movement of combat forces to the theater. Tactical airlifters are needed to move forces and supplies from arrival locations to operational areas and bases.

In terms of power projection capabilities, long-range bombers provide early attack capability (since they are relatively independent of bases in the theater of operations for the initial stages of combat). Fighter and attack squadrons must perform a range of missions such as air superiority (to include suppression of surface-based defenses) and the attack of strategic targets and enemy ground forces. As was seen in the Gulf War, the composition and capability of the land-based fighter/attack force and its arrival schedule have emerged as increasingly vital factors in analyzing the potential outcomes of the campaign, due to their enhanced lethality.

Ground Forces. Ground combat power is essential to the conduct of regional theater warfare. These forces are needed to protect key rear areas, selectively engage and channelize enemy forces (trading space for time until the situation is stabilized), continue engagements during the buildup period and thus reduce enemy forces, and finally, launch a decisive counteroffensive.

---

[12]See, for example, Perrin (1991). For a differing perspective on the relative contributions of land-based and sea-based airpower using different assumptions, see Ochmanek and Bordeaux (1993).

The early-arriving ground forces, with the exception of those possessing prepositioned equipment (such as the Marine Expeditionary Brigades) are light forces that can be transported by airlift. The personnel from armored and mechanized forces can be flown in to "marry up" with prepositioned equipment. Critical specialized combat support units, such as those equipped with ballistic missile defense batteries, armed helicopters, and long-range precision firepower, rocket and missile artillery, are also candidates for high-priority deployment via airlifters. These units should be capable of high volumes of precision firepower and tactical mobility to trade space for time.

Succeeding echelons of army forces, which come principally by sea, consist of the heavier armor and mechanized units and combat service and combat service support to sustain all elements of the joint force in the field. These succeeding echelons also constitute the forces designed to regain lost territory and secure long-term wartime objectives.

Force Availability. An important consideration in selecting forces is their availability—i.e., the time required to make them ready for deployment and operations. The times required to ready forces vary widely. For example, naval forces at sea are ready immediately. An active-component fighter squadron with a mission capability needed at the outset of a campaign and earmarked for operations in a specific theater (e.g., an F-117 unit) could be ready to deploy within hours. The same holds true for the lead brigade of the 82nd Airborne and selected elements of the 7th Transportation Group. Reserve units naturally take longer to ready for deployment. Reserve air units may not be called for several weeks to a month, and after call-up might take a week or more to prepare for deployment. And perhaps the most time-consuming is preparing a reserve-component armored (or mechanized) division for deployment—the time to prepare heavy reserve ground units may extend for months.[13]

Typically, active forces are the most ready. However, with the current structure of the U.S. military, selected reserve units will participate in operations from the outset. For example, army transportation elements and airlift and tanker crews are essential to operations from the outset of a deployment.

CONDUCTING REGIONAL CAMPAIGNS

With the available force structure, the geographic and environmental structure of the region, and the military characteristics of the enemy in mind, the planning and analysis of a regional campaign can begin. The typical starting point is to outline a reasonable set of conditions. But to explore the true di-

---

[13]For greater detail, see National Defense Research Institute, *Assessing the Structure and Mix of Future Active and Reserve Forces: Final Report to the Secretary of Defense,* RAND, Santa Monica, CA, 1992.

mensions of the "scenario space" (Davis and Finch, 1993), these conditions must be extended to ascertain the impact that key parameters can have on the capacity of enemy and allied forces.

Figure 4 provides an overview of one such study plan conducted at RAND using this approach. C-day is the time at which U.S. forces deploy. D-day is the time when armed conflict begins. Thus D = C + 5 represents the case where U.S. forces have five days to deploy to the theater before the outbreak of conflict. The plan was to vary days from the start of conflict (shown on the timeline), the mix of ground and air forces that could be applied (the two squares across the front of the box), the type of land forces used (the squares on the right side of the box), and the level of threat (the vertical squares). Each of these variables affects the rest. For example, some land force alternatives are not available until a certain number of days have passed, i.e., until they have been deployed to the region. And the effectiveness of a particular alternative depends on the level of threat. As the complexity of the figure suggests, the greater the number of variables, the greater the length of time required to conduct the analysis.

The regional conflict we use as an example begins with an aggressor invading a neighboring state with mechanized ground forces supported by infantry, air, artillery, and possibly ballistic missiles. This invasion would be opposed

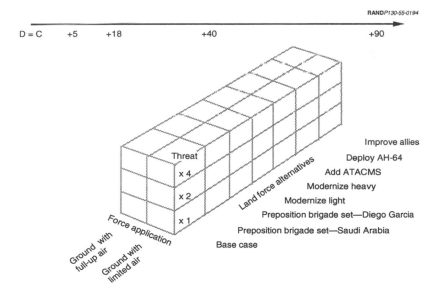

Figure 4—Project Analysis Plan for 1992 Study

first by a combination of indigenous and allied forces together with U.S. forces that are stationed in the area and/or deployed forward as the crisis develops.

When faced with an invasion, the joint force commander must establish (and prioritize) a set of objectives.[14] These typically include the following:

- To deploy sufficient forces to the theater.

- *To secure a lodgement to protect arriving forces.* Protection must be provided around key ports, airfields, along lines of communication oriented toward the battle area, in the air above the lodgement, and along air and sea lines of communication leading into the theater itself. In the past, the primary immediate threat was posed by enemy aircraft; in the future, the United States must be increasingly concerned with protecting the lodgement from cruise and ballistic missiles as well.

- *To contain the enemy's capability to conduct offensive operations.* Containing the enemy's offensive capability entails such actions as halting invading armies and establishing a sufficient degree of air superiority to deny the enemy the ability to conduct coherent air attacks (with either aircraft or missiles). Once the enemy's offensive capabilities are reduced, time becomes an ally as the joint force commander moves to bring a fuller range of combat power to bear.

- *To reduce the aggressor's capability to defend his forces and critical military resources.* This involves attacks on dug-in forces, sustained ground force engagements, continued disruption of lines of communication and supply, attrition of air and missile forces through attacks conducted at depth across his territory, denial of command-and-control capabilities and facilities, and strikes against war reserves and supporting military infrastructure.

- *To launch a decisive counteroffensive.* The purpose of the counteroffensive is to regain lost territory and seize sufficient assets to deny the enemy state the capability to repeat past aggressive actions. The counteroffensive features ground forces (supported by air assets) taking territory and seizing control of enemy forces. It also includes strategic attack operations designed to deny the enemy the capability of aggression in the future.

- *To establish postconflict stability.* This phase, while not actually part of the conflict, may involve long-term commitment of forces.

Operations to accomplish each of these objectives are described below. These operations fall into three groups: (1) precombat operations, which include deployment and establishing a lodgement; (2) combat operations, which include containing the enemy's offensive capability, reducing his defensive ca-

---

[14]The influence these objectives can have on U.S. strategy and forces can be seen in Thaler (1993). The "strategies-to-tasks" framework was originally developed and refined by Lieutenant General Glenn Kent (USAF, ret.).

pability, and launching a joint counteroffensive; and (3) postconflict stability operations.

Phase I: Initial Operations

Deployment. The time required to deploy U.S. forces is a critical element in the assessment of their combat contribution. Analyses must factor in the contributions of the joint "mobility triad": airlift, sealift, and prepositioning (both sea-based and land-based). Each element of the mobility triad offers unique advantages and disadvantages. To support U.S. national strategy requires capitalizing on each method's virtues to compensate for its limitations. Airlift forces are the fastest mobility asset, but the cargo that can be carried is limited by weight, size, and volume. Sealift provides high volume, but is much slower than airlift. The limited volume of airlift and the slow speed of sealift in turn heighten the importance of land-based and sea-based prepositioning. Land-based prepositioning is responsive, but limited in terms of flexibility. Sea-based prepositioning is slower to respond than prepositioned land-based supplies, but is much more flexible. Figure 5 provides an overview of a notional deployment to highlight the capabilities of the various mobility force elements.[15]

The amount of time afforded to the United States to deploy forces before combat begins shapes the character of planning and analysis of regional conflict. If an adversary were to provide several weeks of buildup time, the United States could deploy sufficient forces to provide a formidable defense (and an equally formidable deterrent). However, deployment of significant combat capabilities (such as land-based fighters and ground forces) during this period may be precluded by the sensitivities of regional allies and internal U.S. domestic constraints.

Though these constraints may prevent the deployment of some combat forces, important steps can be taken to improve the speed with which U.S. and allied forces can be deployed and begin conducting combat operations. Surveillance and reconnaissance assets like AWACS and JSTARS could be deployed to observe enemy movements and force dispositions. Similarly, orbits of space systems could be repositioned. And the backbone of an effective combat force—a command, control, communications, and intelligence network—

---

[15]Two major upswings in sealift delivery are shown in Figure 5. The first represents the initial arrival of sealift vessels, the second represents the movement of ships after their initial delivery back to the United States for a second loading. Generally, heavy combat forces are moved in the first cycle and a growing portion of sustainment and combat support material in subsequent sailing cycles.

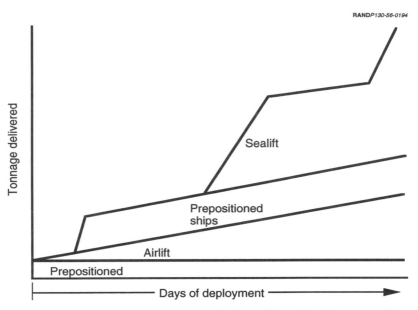

NOTE: "Prepositioned ships" includes Marine and Army unit equipment on maritime prepositioned ships.

Figure 5—Notional Deployment

could be readied and perhaps deployed. Teams for air and sea ports could be positioned forward or moved to the theater to prepare reception facilities and enroute staging bases. Airlift and sealift fleets could be brought up to higher readiness rates. And it may be possible to bring selected defensive forces into the theater (e.g., ballistic missile defense batteries and air defense aircraft). The degree to which these preparations are possible affects the theater deterrent posture and early combat capabilities.

The joint force commander's ability to achieve his objectives is governed by force availability in the theater of operations. Figure 6 provides an overview of the arrival of forces within a theater of operations and how this helps determine the timing of operations in a campaign. For approximately the first month following the decision to deploy U.S. forces, operations must be conducted with forces already stationed in the forward area, those that can utilize equipment prepositioned on ships or on land in the area of interest, and those that can be airlifted in sufficient numbers to conduct effective combat operations. During this period, U.S. forces must secure a lodgement and, if an enemy has launched offensive operations, halt and contain the incursion in conjunction with allied forces.

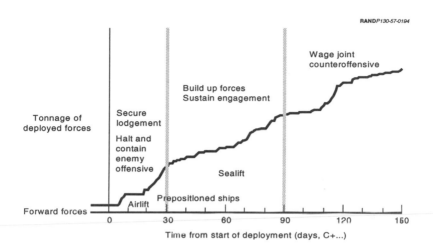

Figure 6—Force Availability Over Time

The objective in this early part of the campaign is to halt invading armies and to stop air and missile attacks in order to limit the loss of territory and key facilities. This requires a careful balancing of mobility priorities. In essence, planners must maximize the use of forces that can respond and fight quite rapidly, particularly if circumstances have prohibited the deployment of combat forces. These units include forward-based forces, forces that rely on land-based prepositioned equipment (if available), forces that are transportable by air, and forces that are supplied by maritime prepositioning assets. Setting deployment priorities for these force elements is complicated by situations where combat is deemed imminent. In such circumstances, the United States must deploy not only forces, but such critical items as adequate quantities of munitions, logistics stocks, and perhaps fuel as well. All these elements of a warfighting force compete for the limited set of mobility assets. For example, planners must decide not only whether to send a squadron of attack aircraft and their maintenance support elements, but also what level of munitions stockage must be sent for that unit.

After roughly a month, sufficient forces should be available in theater to contain the aggressor's offensive operations. Additionally, sealift begins delivering heavy land combat forces in growing numbers. While forces continue to build up, there are sufficient forces to defend, but probably not enough to go on the offensive. Additionally, the support forces needed for sustained offensive operations are arriving in the theater. Therefore, during this period, sustained operations against enemy military forces, resources, and facilities should continue in order to draw down the enemy's strength.

This period of buildup and sustained engagement continues. After several months, sufficient combat and support forces are available for joint counteroffensive operations. For these operations, forces must be positioned to support the joint force commander's scheme of maneuver and operation for the offense. Additionally, the logistics support system in the theater must be stocked for the high demands of counteroffensive operations.

In this phase, intratheater movement of personnel and supplies also assumes heightened importance. For example, arriving ground forces must be moved to positions where they can engage the enemy. Munitions need to be distributed to air bases, troops in the field, and ships at sea. These all increase the importance of intratheater movements, which are typically conducted by C-130 airlifters, trucks, and helicopters.

Establishing a Lodgement. Establishing a lodgement somewhere in the area of operations is a prerequisite for conducting military operations. The dictionary definition of a lodgement is "the action of making good a position on an enemy's ground or obtaining a foothold." Major regional conflicts require a sizable lodgement because it will be the support head for hundreds of thousands of personnel and their equipment.

The crucial objective of a lodgement is to establish an initial operating area and protect arriving forces. Ideally, the lodgement should be located far enough from the battle area to remain relatively unmolested. But even under the most benign conditions, forces must be allocated for protection of the lodgement area.

The lodgement area should include operating space for air, land, and naval forces, ports and air bases to receive forces and supplies, and for the transportation infrastructure to move ground forces to the battle area. In some situations, U.S. and allied forces may use several lodgement areas. As Figure 7 shows, the lodgement area expands over time. First, forces move into a few select ports and airheads. A port with a sizable cargo-unloading capacity is essential for handling sealift vessels. For an airlift airhead, a base with large runways, parking ramps, and fuel supplies is needed (these tend to be international airports in most nations). In selecting air bases for the deployment of combat aircraft, obviously those with developed passive defenses (i.e., shelters) would be considered first.

As additional forces arrive in theater, the lodgement expands (as Figure 7 shows) in a series of steps until it can accommodate a defensive force. Over the longer term, the lodgement provides the support for joint counteroffensive opearations.

Arriving forces may often have to depend upon indigenous forces (or navy forces adjacent to the lodgement) for protection in the first critical days. Additional protection could be airlifted in rapidly—this would include light ground forces for security and surface-to-air defenses and air superiority fight-

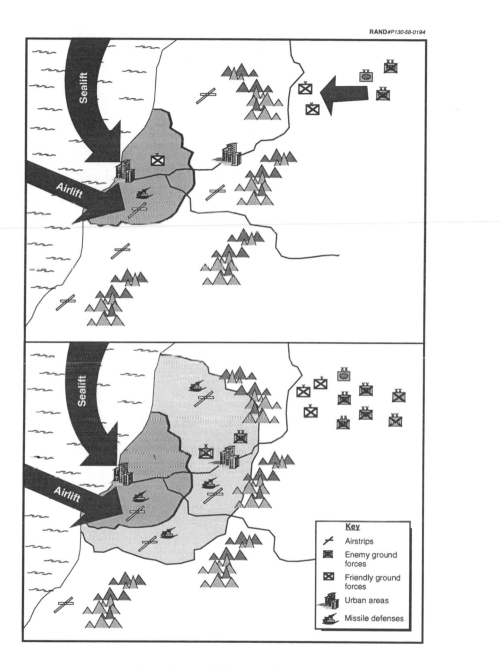

RAND#P130-58-0194

Key

⚓ Airstrips

▨ Enemy ground forces

⊠ Friendly ground forces

🏢 Urban areas

⚙ Missile defenses

Figure 7—Establishing a Lodgement

ers to protect against enemy aircraft, cruise missiles, and ballistic missiles. Ideally, the joint force commander would seek to expand the lodgement area so that forces could be dispersed to deny the enemy lucrative targets and so that adequate operating and maneuver areas are available for arriving forces.

The real campaign may not be so simple, of course (Davis and Finch, 1993). For example, the potential for contested entry must also be considered when analyzing the establishment of a lodgement. Such operations are far more complex and risky. In essence, the need to insert forces in such a manner would mean that the enemy had achieved operational surprise and had overrun the first objective areas before U.S. forces arrived—or had managed to defeat the initial U.S./allied contingent.

When faced with a contested entry, the joint force commander has two main options. The first is to establish a lodgement even farther to the rear, perhaps even beyond the range of the aggressor's offensive forces. The lodgement could even be located in an adjacent nation. Subsequent operations would aim to isolate occupying enemy forces in an interdiction campaign (thus denying them supplies), conduct direct attacks (to reduce the aggressor's forces), and launch strategic strikes (to bring home the costs of war and affect the enemy's calculus). Forces would then be built up in this rear area lodgement to advance forward to retake the initial objective area.

The second option is to make an opposed landing in the vicinity of the aggressor force, either from the sea or from the air. As seen from the landings in the Pacific during World War II and Grenada, such operations are extremely challenging to plan and execute, and they run the risks of heavy casualties. Even under these conditions, it would be desirable to have a staging base in reasonable proximity to provide air cover for the operation.

Phase II: Combat Operations

Once a relatively secure operating area has been established, the joint force commander focuses on engaging the enemy. Depending on the urgency of the situation, the friendly forces may have to be committed to combat immediately upon arrival in the theater. The joint force commander would have three phased objectives:

- Contain the enemy's capability for offensive actions.
- Reduce the enemy's defensive capability.
- Conduct joint counteroffensive operations.

Containing the Enemy's Offensive Capability. An enemy may use his land forces to invade the territory of an ally (and may complement these with irregular force operations, such as those conducted by terrorist and guerrilla bands). He may use air and missile forces to attack the opposing forces and military infrastructure. And he may perhaps employ naval forces to project power in the seas adjacent to his territory.

These offensive capabilities must be contained simultaneously through the judicious employment of leading-edge ground, sea, and air forces. Successful containment depends upon the successful establishment of a lodgement and the continued buildup of combat forces in the theater. To contain the enemy's offensive capabilities, the joint force commander would have the following objectives: halt the invading armies; gain air superiority; and conduct strategic attacks to destroy essential components of the opponent's offensive warfighting capabilities. The weight of effort devoted to each task would, of course, depend on the operational conditions in the theater. For example, if the enemy ground offensive collapsed, more attention could be given to air defense and strategic attack.

Halt the Invading Armies. Many potential aggressor nations in the world have invested heavily in ground forces. The reasons are straightforward. Relative to air and naval forces, armies are less expensive, useful for nation-building, and often essential for sustaining authoritarian regimes. In addition, they are critical for taking and holding territory in a world where territorial disputes often lie at the heart of regional conflicts.

When faced with an invading army, the United States and its allies would attempt to trade space for time. Indigenous land forces would be joined on the ground with light and prepositioned U.S./allied ground forces. The details are important when assessing the status of early defensive battle. Enemy force positions, their scheme of maneuver and avenue of attack, the lines of communication the adversary would employ to sustain the offensive, and the size and positioning of indigenous forces—all play a role in shaping the battlefield. Arriving U.S. and allied forces would join indigenous forces to conduct a retrograde covering force operation and would probably be placed to avoid the catastrophic defeat of indigenous forces early in the campaign. Simulations of these engagements can be conducted with varying degrees of fidelity to understand potential battle outcomes.[16]

As Figure 8 shows, a combination of critically positioned and tactically mobile land forces, together with land-based and sea-based airpower as needed, would first blunt the invasion and then attempt to bring it to a halt. U.S., allied, and indigenous land forces could reduce the enemy's forces and blunt the invasion by manning a series of defensive positions, sequentially withdrawing

---

[16]One useful "high-level" methodology is contained in Allen (1992). For a detailed examination of brigade-level battles combining the effects of attack helicopters and fixed-wing airpower, the JANUS model offers great utility.

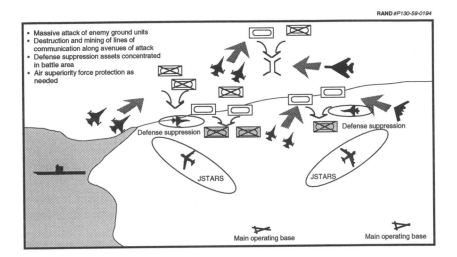

Figure 8—Halting the Invading Armies

to new positions in the rear, and engaging in counterattacks where appropriate to complicate the enemy's offensive scheme of maneuver. Such retrograde operations could use terrain and man-made obstacles such as minefields to slow the invasion and channelize the enemy.

The natural complement to the land force scheme of maneuver is the application of long-range offensive firepower. This could be provided by rocket and missile artillery (e.g., MLRS/ATACMS) as well as bombers and fighter/attack aircraft. While ground forces engage the leading elements of the enemy invading force, long-range firepower could concentrate on follow-on echelons and convoys carrying critical sustaining supplies such as food, fuel, and ammunition. Potentially, deeper attacks could be conducted against the lines of communication coinciding with the avenues of attack. Defending forces could create these chokepoints at times by attacking bridges and blocking roads and other routes.

A joint command structure and control system is essential for integrating long-range firepower with the scheme of maneuver.[17] Joint planning and employment of air and surface forces are particularly important in the early phases, since the relatively small number of arriving forces must be applied properly in order to take advantage of their synergies. For example, land forces could concentrate at the point of contact to blunt leading-edge units and cause

---

[17]See Cardwell (1992) and FM 100-5, *Operations*, Headquarters, Department of the Army, 1992.

follow-on echelons to mass. These in turn would emerge as lucrative targets for appropriately equipped airpower, which offers lethal firepower but has less persistence. Long-range rocket and missile artillery could then provide a more persistent complement to airpower. In some cases, it could also be more responsive to tactical needs.

Long-range firepower on land or aboard ships could be used to attack enemy forces deep or, when fired from rear areas, to engage enemy forces in the forward area. In some situations, long-range rocket and missile artillery and airpower could be used to cut off forward echelons from follow-on forces and supplies—thereby limiting the time over which they can sustain an attack. In addition, such isolations can assist defending ground forces in localized counteroffensives.

The effectiveness of these fires is heavily dependent upon a surveillance, reconnaissance, and battle management system to designate enemy units and support forces in the attack. Until this command-and-control system is established, the effectiveness of long-range rocket and missile artillery will be marginal. Airpower's effectiveness also depends on an effective dynamic battle management system, but not to the same extent as rocket and missile artillery, since the presence of a "man in the loop" allows combat aircraft to acquire enemy force elements and adjust delivery of firepower.

The combination of ground, sea, and air forces to halt the invading armies through attrition and maneuver could, if successful, bring the invasion to a stop. The point at which the invasion stops depends, among other things, on such factors as the attrition inflicted on the advancing force, the buildup rate of friendly forces, and the capabilities of the opposing forces. Historical norms for a successful defense involving ground forces at the level of a few divisions can be achieved at a 1:3 defense ratio, though terrain, weather, and firepower can affect the situation dramatically. In other cases, a defense may not be possible until friendly forces on the ground are equivalent to those of the invader. Air and long-range artillery also have an important impact on the outcome of battle by disrupting and reducing enemy forces. And in some cases, the increased lethality of airpower and rocket and missile artillery may make it possible to halt an invading force with a minimal ground force commitment. Figure 9 illustrates the combination of effects. When the invasion is halted, time becomes an ally of the United States and its allies.

Gain Air Superiority. Regional powers may possess means of conducting offensive operations other than ground forces. U.S. and allied forces can be threatened on the seas and on the land by aircraft, ballistic missiles, and cruise missiles. As has been consistently highlighted by history since the advent of modern airpower, air superiority—control of the air—provides strategic, operational, and tactical freedom of action while denying these advantages to the opposing side. Without control of the air, all land, sea, and air forces must at-

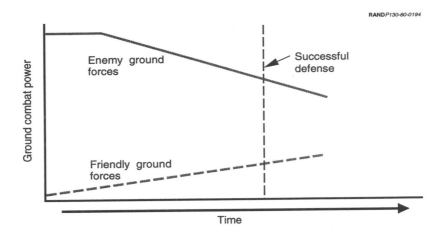

Figure 9—Halting an Invasion (Operational-level depiction)

tempt to operate exposed to air attack, something increasingly difficult to do in the face of modern airpower. As Rommel once wrote after experiencing air attack against his armored forces, "Anyone who has to fight, even with the most modern weapons, against an enemy in complete command of the air, fights like a savage against modern European forces, with the same handicaps and with the same chance of success." Simply put, denying the enemy air superiority is a prerequisite to the effective conduct of joint theater operations and would be a top priority of any joint force commander.[18]

Control of the air may be reached through several means:

- Establishing a robust air defense network (including defense against cruise and ballistic missiles).

- Suppressing enemy air defenses.

- Denying enemy aircraft the use of their own airspace.

- Destroying enemy airfield facilities, cruise and ballistic missile launch facilities, and their command-and-control network.

Ideally, these tasks should be accomplished simultaneously, but the phasing and weight of effort devoted to each task depends on the resources available

---

[18]The criticality of this mission is naturally highlighted in airpower doctrine manuals. See, for example, Air Force Manual 1-1, *Basic Aerospace Doctrine of the United States Air Force*, Airpower Research Institute, Maxwell AFB, 1990, and the British equivalent, AP-3000, *Air Power Doctrine* (2nd edition), Chief of the Air Staff, 1993. For a more popular discussion, see *Control of the Air and U.S. National Security: The Case for the F-22*, Headquarters, United States Air Force, 1991.

and the degree of threat posed by each element.   Success in one area abets efforts in the others.   For example, reduction of an enemy's air attack potential through strikes against airfields and the C^3I system reduces required effort in the air defense area.   Similarly, defense suppression efforts increase the effectiveness of strikes against airfields and a wide range of other targets.

Setting up key elements of an air and missile defense system may be possible before the outbreak of conflict.   For example, surface-to-air missile (SAM) batteries (or antiballistic missile systems) are solely defensive in nature and could be brought in to protect allied territory and signal U.S. resolve and intentions.   Prepositioning these assets or moving them during periods of crisis particularly offers benefits due to the weight of these units (and the strains their movement would place on the limited airlift force).[19]   Similarly, AWACS and other command-and-control aircraft could be deployed to watch the unfolding situation.   Finally, air superiority aircraft can be moved early and, if not present at the outset of conflict, can be deployed rapidly with small impact on the airlift flow (since their support packages and munitions are fairly light).

Figure 10 shows a concept for the establishment of a robust air and missile defense network to protect allied and arriving forces.   When analyzing the ca-

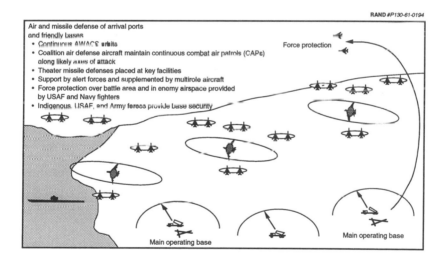

RAND #P130-81-0194

Air and missile defense of arrival ports
and friendly bases
• Continuous AWACS orbits
• Coalition air defense aircraft maintain continuous combat air patrols (CAPs)
  along likely axes of attack
• Theater missile defenses placed at key facilities
• Support by alert forces and supplemented by multirole aircraft
• Force protection over battle area and in enemy airspace provided
  by USAF and Navy fighters
• Indigenous, USAF, and Army forces provide base security

Force protection

Main operating base

Main operating base

Figure 10—Establishing an Air Defense Network

[19]For example, to move a Patriot missile battalion (which consists of one headquarters battery and six firing batteries, each of which possesses eight launchers) would require 55 C-5 sorties or 175 C-141B sorties and one C-5 sortie.   Such numbers represent commitment of half the USAF's C-5 force or almost three-fourths of the C-141B fleet.

pability of an air defense network, attention must be paid to the number of aircraft and SAMs available, the airspace to be defended, the number of avenues of approach, the ability to sustain the defense around the clock, and the capabilities and numbers of offensive adversary aircraft and missiles. Concepts for providing missile defenses are similar to air defense operations except that the time scales are much faster, ranges are longer, and space-based sensors may provide the early warning instead of airborne or surface-based radars.

Indigenous assets, if available, would provide some initial protection. These could be supplemented by fighters from forward-deployed carriers. Surface-to-air and ballistic missile defense batteries could provide missile and point defense of critical operational zones. Arriving air-to-air fighters would flesh out the defense network. Additional aircraft are needed to perform critical force protection missions (i.e., escort and fighter sweeps) and bolster the air defense network if the enemy possesses the capability to mount massed attacks.

The time required to build up a capable air defense depends on a number of factors, such as the number of air-to-air capable squadrons deployed, the capability of SAM systems, the ability of AWACS to concentrate forces in critical areas, the success of offensive counterair missions in constraining the enemy's ability to conduct massed attacks, and the qualitative superiority of U.S. and allied air-to-air forces.

While the ability to defend friendly airspace is important, offensive counterair operations, which take the fight into the enemy's territory and attack his capability at its source, are needed to gain control of the air in a theater. Offensive counterair operations involve fighter sweeps into enemy territory to engage opposing aircraft in their own airspace, and strikes against airfields, missile sites, and the command-and-control system. By doing this, friendly forces can reduce the enemy's offensive capability at its source—and continue that process through sweep and offensive counterair until the enemy is no longer capable of mounting significant offensive air threats to U.S. and allied forces. In addition, attack aircraft could attack enemy ballistic missile launchers—or, if equipped with appropriate armaments, missiles in boost phase—to reduce the number of ballistic missiles that confront terminal defenses.

Suppression of enemy surface-to-air defenses (SEAD) is also an integral part of achieving air superiority. This involves operations against SAM batteries, gun sites, radar sites, and air operation and control centers. Such operations require lethal suppression (which involves delivering ordnance against threat sites) and jamming (which temporarily denies the adversary the ability to control his forces and guide weapons, by disrupting his communications and radars). Typically, these missions are associated with dedicated aircraft systems, such as Wild Weasels. However, land- and sea-based rocket and missile artillery can play important roles, particularly against fixed targets. For example, in the Gulf War, army missile systems were employed against some elements of the Iraqi air defense network.

Conduct Strategic Attacks. Early destruction of the enemy's leadership, command-and-control assets, lines of communication, and other key warfighting capabilities can help ensure a decisive victory in war. Strategic attacks both reduce the enemy's ability to conduct war and affect his strategic and operational calculus.[20]

The planning and conduct of strategic attack operations is a complex undertaking and will have to be phased based on the availability of assets capable of mounting such operations and the competing needs to attack forces in the field. Over the short term, the objective of such attacks would be to destroy the enemy's offensive capabilities—these operations would have direct relevance for air superiority missions and the halting of the invading army. For example, by focusing on the enemy's command-and-control network, the adversary's ability to maneuver and mass forces in the field and the air, and to execute missile attacks, could be degraded. Over the medium term, such operations would be aimed at reducing defensive capabilities. As the enemy's ability to conduct immediate operations is diminished, then the priority of these attacks could further shift to striking the support structure and lines of communication needed to sustain military operations. The targets that might be attacked in this phase include arms factories, weapon storage areas, and other installations.

Portions of the bomber fleet, long-range fighter force, and standoff weapons would conduct the bulk of these attacks. This attack force would combine stealth assets; saturation with cruise missiles and decoys; and manned aircraft capable of defending themselves penetrating at low altitude protected by defense suppression and air-to-air forces. This combination of different attack assets and penetration profiles would greatly complicate an enemy's defense problem, particularly as his air defense network was suffering from the effects of offensive counterair operations.

The ability to conduct strategic attack operations has changed fundamentally with the advent of precision weapons. These weapons create opportunities and new challenges. The opportunities made available are the efficient destruction of targets and the ability to minimize collateral damage and casualties. But because aimpoints can be attacked with precision accuracy, there is a growing requirement to know where key elements of the enemy's warfighting potential are located. This in turn puts new demands on surveillance and reconnaissance systems, as well as on the interpretation of intelligence data, par-

---

[20]One of the most influential works emphasizing the importance of strategic attack operations is Warden (1989). This played an influential role in the development of the "Instant Thunder" air campaign plan for the Gulf War.

ticularly to support standoff weapons (where a person is not available to see the exact location of the target). In addition, the ability to precisely strike aimpoints without flattening entire installations in turn raises many challenges regarding bomb damage assessment. For example, a penetrating munition may leave only a small hole in the wall of a bunker, but the facility may be destroyed inside.

Enemy responses to countering a U.S. strategic air offensive may include active defenses, dispersal, camouflage, deep underground facilities, and placement of assets near or in locations where domestic or international constraints could prohibit striking (such as hospitals and schools).

Because the effects of strategic air offensive attacks may not be readily apparent for long periods and at times may have unanticipated consequences, it is difficult to assess the value of these missions, particularly during conflict.[21] For example, during Operation Desert Storm, a considerable effort was made to destroy Iraqi C^3 sites. Despite intensive targeting, communications from Baghdad to the forces in Kuwait seemed to flow unhampered. However, when the ground offensive began and forces had to maneuver, Iraqi communication requirements suddenly accelerated; the degraded system could not support the new operational tempo and collapsed.

Reduction of the Enemy's Defensive Capability. Once actions have been taken to minimize the offensive threat posed by an adversary, time becomes an ally. Two operations continue: the buildup of forces and combat support assets within the theater and, through sustained engagement, the reduction of the enemy's capability to defend. The latter involves continuing probing actions on the ground to keep the enemy off balance, sustained engagement with tube, rocket, and missile artillery across the depth of the immediate battle area, and sustained strikes by air forces against forces in the field and the supply lines that sustain them. In addition, ongoing strategic air offensive operations contribute to the overall reduction in defensive capabilities. Much as a siege in an ancient walled city did, these measures tax the enemy psychologically in addition to destroying military assets.

The overall process is illustrated in Figure 11. Continued strikes reduce the enemy's effective force capabilities while friendly forces build up in combat capability. The degree to which the enemy's defensive combat capability must be reduced is based on a number of factors. These include the size of his force posture at the time he was forced to halt his invasion, the character of the terrain, the nature of the weather, his ability to construct defensive positions, and his passive defensive capabilities, such as camouflage, deception, and dispersal. Ascertaining the status of enemy forces—and hence the point at which friendly

---

[21]For an in-depth analysis of the impact of the 1991 coalition strategic air campaign, see Keaney and Cohen (1993).

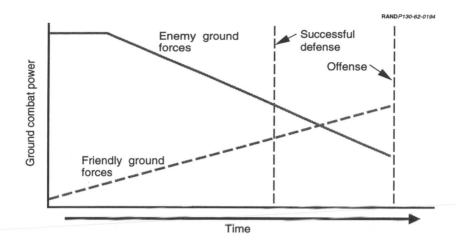

Figure 11—Reducing the Enemy's Defensive Capability (Theater-level perspective)

forces can launch a counteroffensive—depends critically on accurate intelligence. At some point (a theaterwide ratio of perhaps 2:1), the correlation of forces would permit friendly forces to launch a joint counteroffensive.

Joint Counteroffensive. The culmination of combat operations for regional conflicts involving U.S. and allied forces is a joint counteroffensive campaign to regain lost territory, seize control of the aggressor's critical warfighting assets, and neutralize opposing combat forces. While it is possible that a regional aggressor might call for a cease-fire, or cede the gains of his aggression as U.S. and allied forces build up in the theater and apply pressure through sustained engagement, a joint counteroffensive may be necessary to evict opposing forces, seize territory, and destroy enemy combat capabilities, thus creating conditions to end the conflict. The counteroffensive phase involves air, land, and sea forces in addition to logistics support for operations. Land forces typically play the predominant role in dislodging the aggressor.

The planning, timing, and determination of the forces needed for counteroffensive operations depend on many factors. Generally, a counteroffensive operation follows the defensive and sustained engagement phases described in the previous sections. Accordingly, the successes encountered in these phases, as well as ground combat force composition and deployments, shape the character of the final phase.

Each situation is unique and must be specifically laid out on the actual terrain over a defined frontage. Several quantitative relationships are available to assist in estimating the size of the ground forces needed to conduct counteroffensive operations. These relationships consider the factors shown below:

- Committed enemy force strength
- Enemy reserve force strength
- Geographical frontage
- Effective military frontage
- Friendly force disposition committed to:
  — Main attack sectors
  — Holding sectors on the front
  — Reserves

Additionally, the size and effectiveness of airpower assets in the theater help to determine the size, deployment, and composition of land forces for counteroffensive operations.

The strength of forces on either side is sometimes quantified as equivalent divisions (EDs), armored division equivalents (ADEs), division equivalents in firepower (DEFs), or division equivalents in manpower (DEMs). The relative strengths of opposing forces are generally derived from weighted averages of the units, weapons, and personnel contained in the combat forces. These factors can also be degraded, or enhanced, based upon the states of training, equipage, and sustainment.[22]

Geographical frontages depend on the size of the theater and the territorial area that enemy forces choose to contest. These frontages also reflect the positions where the battle was actually stabilized by indigenous and friendly forces. The effective military frontage is a function not only of the geographical area, but of the type of terrain as well. The category of terrain (ranging from open through mixed, rough, and closed zones) may reduce the effective frontage or, conversely, increase the frontage covered by a division up to a factor of three.

Many factors (e.g., force dispositions, terrain, obstacles, and firepower) determine what is needed for the offensive. Let us first describe calculations that apply for nations lacking the ability to maneuver long-range fires with aircraft or artillery.

Traditional Concentration for Attack. The joint force commander would have to make a number of choices affecting the size and type of the forces needed to conduct a decisive counteroffensive. The number and location of main attack axes must be determined, along with an estimate of the relative force advantage needed to break through defensive positions and contend with enemy reserves. These factors depend on the types of defenses, the terrain, and the size and location of the enemy's reserves. Finally, the joint force commander needs to decide the forces, or force ratios, to be employed in the sectors not

---

[22]See Allen (1992).

positioned along the main axes of attack. These forces will initially be called upon to defend. As breakthroughs occur and the enemy forces face the prospect of envelopment, the forces off the main attack axes may also join the forward thrust.

Figure 12 shows a notional ground force deployment prior to the joint counteroffensive. Typically, planners concentrate forces along the main thrust axes and position reserves to exploit breakthrough operations. Concentrations are generally positioned in sectors where enemy weaknesses have been identified.

A wide variety of analytical tools and methods are available to determine the forces needed to conduct offensive operations. Generally, planning for offensive operations is an iterative process, beginning with the planner's experience and coarse-grained tools to estimate the force size, composition, and disposition and then proceeding to the development of multiple courses of action. The courses of action are based on detailed map and terrain studies. Computer campaign simulations are increasingly used to evaluate the feasibility of various

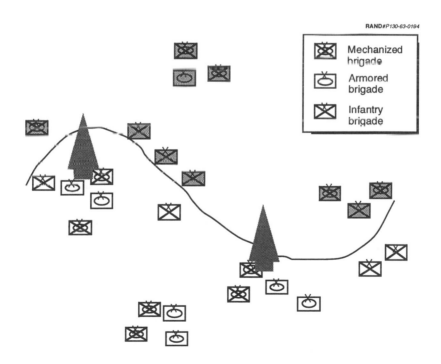

Figure 12—Ground Force Deployment for Joint Counteroffensive Operations

options. The ultimate product of the campaign analyses is a counteroffensive operations plan that details force dispositions, objectives, and the joint force commander's scheme of maneuver and fire.

Figure 13 is an example of a planning tool that can be used in determining the forces needed to launch a counteroffensive. This figure is a graphical representation of a set of equations developed for this purpose (Davis, 1989). This example represents a specific set of conditions—a nine-sector front with two main attacks selected for the main axes of attack. For this example, the commander planning the offensive has opted to accept a 2:3 disadvantage in the holding sectors (those areas where he won't immediately attack) and wishes to place a sixth of his force in reserve. The enemy has placed a third of his force in reserve as a hedge against breakthroughs along the front.

Using Figure 13 or other nomograms tailored to the anticipated operational conditions, the planners can see at the time when the theater force ratio is brought to 1.25:1 (friendly/enemy) through the buildup of friendly forces in the theater and the sustained attrition of enemy forces, the ratio of forces on the main attack sectors exceeds 5:1. This provides a margin of safety over the doctrinal ratio, as shown by the upper horizontal line on the graph, needed to break through prepared defenses in mixed terrain. If the defenses were weaker, like those characterized by deliberate defenses in flat terrain, an even more

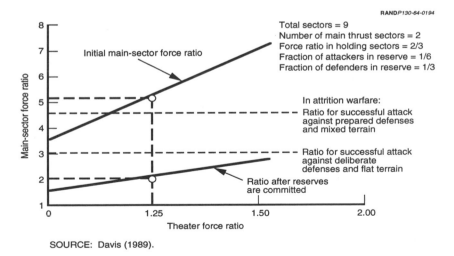

SOURCE: Davis (1989).

Figure 13—Estimating Ground Force Requirements for Joint Counteroffensive Operations

substantive margin of advantage would exist over the doctrinal norms. Further, the offensive commander would retain an advantage of 2:1 after the enemy committed his reserves.   Tools such as this aid in establishing initial force planning estimates.

Calculations such as these represent a starting point.   More refined planning estimates must be introduced to develop campaign plans for the actual terrain. These will be based on the latest intelligence estimates of enemy force strengths and dispositions.   Because enemy force strength and disposition change during the course of the early phases of the conflict, a process to assess the battle damage inflicted by friendly forces on the enemy is essential for refining campaign planning and determining when conditions are favorable for the initiation of counteroffensive operations.

The likelihood of an enemy successfully defending against counteroffensive operations is increased if the adversary can efficiently position his ground combat forces, develop strong defensive positions along the front, provide firepower to cover defensive positions, reduce allied forces, and move reserves to critical locations along the main attack axes.   These actions are made easier if the enemy is able to use surveillance assets to observe allied movements and positions.

Implications of Deep Fires.   The discussion to this point could have applied to warfare for many years past.   But the calculations are being changed by the growing capability to see deep into the enemy's territory and conduct operations with airmobile and special forces deep in enemy terrritory, and to attack enemy forces and logistics with precision and mass using airpower and standoff weapons fired from land, sea, and airborne platforms.   Similarly, if the opposing forces still possess these capabilities after the defensive and sustained engagement phases, a joint counteroffensive could be very difficult to conduct and might result in an inordinate number of casualties or failure to achieve the objectives of the counteroffensive.

The denial of surveillance assets to the enemy through strategic attack in the defensive and sustained engagement phases (as well as through deception) degrades the latter's defensive capability and, in turn, directly enhances the counteroffensive capabilities of the allied forces.   Though each campaign is unique, Figure 13 can be used to illustrate the effects.   If the enemy is unable to determine troop dispositions and movements due to the loss of surveillance assets, then defensive positions may be poorly placed.   Therefore, allied forces would have to overcome lower levels of defenses, which is similar to moving to the lower horizontal line in Figure 13.   This reduces the forces required both on the main axes of attack and in the theater overall.   Even if the joint allied commander prudently elects to conduct the counteroffensive with decisive forces to retain a safety margin, the calculation begins with a lower baseline figure.

During the sustained engagement phase, airpower, artillery, and missiles progressively reduce the enemy's combat power and supplies for sustainment. This reduces the number of ground forces needed for successful offensive operations, since the forces required are generally computed based on the relative combat power of both sides. Additionally, airpower, missiles, and deep operations conducted prior to the counteroffensive phase could be used to reduce and immobilize operational and theater reserve forces. Immobilization of reserve forces could prove to be easier to accomplish than their destruction, due to their vulnerability to attacks on fuel supplies, lines of communications between the reserves and the front-line battle area, and the vehicles needed to move reserves into position.

A counteroffensive would contain several stages, each of which has phased objectives. Both ground and air forces are integrated into a plan to achieve these objectives. The immediate goal of a counteroffensive is to breach the enemy's front-line defenses and deny remaining enemy reserves the opportunity to enter the battle. The assault on the front-line defenses is principally the mission of ground combat forces assisted by artillery and close support from helicopters and fixed-wing aircraft. The isolation of reserves from the battle area might be accomplished in the sustained engagement phase and assured as the offensive begins with deep operations and airpower. These forces should be an integral part in the joint force commander's scheme of fire and maneuver.

Objectives of the latter phases of the counteroffensive include the isolation and defeat of the enemy's front-line ground forces and destruction or neutralization of operational and theater reserves. The movement to seize territory and to fix, isolate, and destroy reserve forces throughout the battlespace may be accomplished in a series of steps, depending on the distances to be covered. The time and transportation assets needed to move supplies forward could be limiting factors, and these must enter into computations regarding rates of advance and the attainment of subsequent objectives. Calculations of logistics requirements are a critical factor in the ultimate success of combat operations. Similarly, because of the magnitude of the forces, assets, and supplies needed for offensive operations, under most situations the buildup of combat support and combat service support forces in the theater of operations is the limiting constraint on the timing of counteroffensive operations.

Airpower and deep operations with airmobile and special forces are part of the joint theater commander's plan of fire and maneuver to isolate enemy forces in the battle area. This can be accomplished through an interdiction campaign along the egress routes and direct engagement of forces beyond the range of logistically constrained offensive ground combat forces. Eventually, territory is seized and the aggressor's combat power destroyed and contained. This introduces the final phase of regional conflict.

Phase III: Postconflict Stability Operations

Winning a conflict produces a distinct set of challenges and requires different types of military forces. The demands on military forces following the successful termination of a conflict are to establish stability in the territory that has been seized, and perhaps throughout the aggressor nation, depending on the outcome of the conflict. Stability operations are defined as those necessary to establish conditions under which a legitimate government can function.

The scope of demands presented by stability operations depends on the conditions under which the conflict is terminated. The size of the territory occupied, the degree to which the population is amenable to control, the size of the population, and the extent of remaining opposition are all factors in the scope of stability operations. In addition to controlling any remaining opposition, it might also be necessary to reestablish services and infrastructure within the conquered territories. The types of forces needed for stability operations are light and mobile land forces that can accomplish police and control functions, engineers to rebuild the needed infrastructure and population support functions, and combat service support troops to provide sustainment to defeated enemy forces and the population. These forces are different from the mechanized land and airpower forces needed to conduct an offensive.

Another role of forces used in postconflict stability operations is to control and police a populace. The magnitude of the task, accordingly, is a function of the size of the population and the degree of control needed. Figure 14 illustrates the requirements posed in stability operations in the postconflict phase. The horizontal axis shows the size of the population, and the vertical axis shows the number of troops required to control it. The lines on the graph represent the level of effort required to maintain security. Because stability operations are policing activities, there are some precedents to draw upon. For example, the United States is policed at an average of two police personnel per 1000 population. Large cities in the United States are typically policed at a rate of four per 1000.

We also have several historical precedents from past military stability operations, as shown in Figure 15. The American occupation of Germany following World War II was planned to be conducted at two per 1000 population. This was a relatively easy venture, because the population accepted order. As of November 1993, Somalia was currently being policed at a level ranging from six to eight per 1000. This was a situation in which there is a higher degree of instability. In Northern Ireland, the British are faced with an unstable situation where there is a constant terrorist threat. British forces in Ulster (including the constabulary) maintain a ratio of twenty per 1000, and this presence has been maintained for years. Even higher on the scale is the Israeli policing of Gaza and the West Bank.

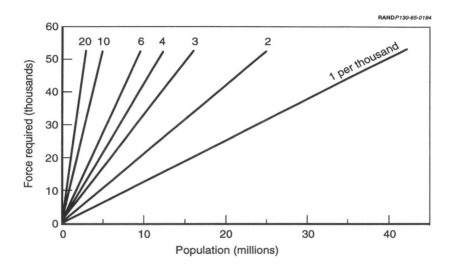

Figure 14—Relationship of Forces Needed for Stability Operations

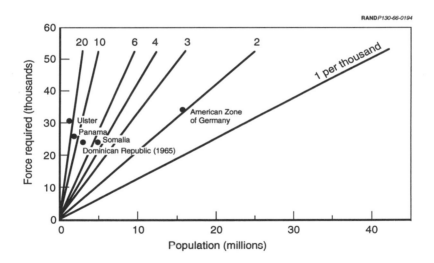

Figure 15—Historical Examples of Forces Used in Stability Operations

These historical precedents illustrate that force presence for stability operations is a function of the area, the population size, and the degree of unrest and threat present. The force requirements could be quite high and may be exacerbated in the future by population growth and by the increasing urbanization of the world. Further compounding the demand for force needs is the fact that the duration of such operations may be long.

The forces used to conduct stability operations are generally light combat forces. Combat support and combat service support forces are needed to support the light forces and perhaps supply the population. Additionally, a logistics pipeline must remain in operation to sustain stability operations.

COUNTERSTRATEGIES

This discussion of major regional conflicts has stepped through the phases of this highly stylized campaign as if it were a methodical process. Unfortunately, conflict, like all human undertakings, does not always proceed as planned. This is particularly true in wars where an opponent's nation is at stake. War is a two-sided contest; the opponent will strive to win and thwart the attainment of campaign objectives by the United States and its allies in a variety of ways. Because of this, no analysis of a major regional conflict is complete without consideration of the opponent's strategies and counterstrategies.[23]

An opponent's strategy and capabilities will vary through the course of a campaign. So will his goals. Because of the relative strength of the United States, a principal objective of any regional aggressor would probably be to avoid a direct confrontation with U.S. military forces. If a confrontation cannot be avoided, prudent aggressors will search for asymmetrical strategies and objectives that avoid pitting their forces against American/allied military strength. Finally, if U.S. and allied strength is brought to bear, regional aggressors could seek means to frustrate the accomplishment of U.S. objectives while minimizing their own losses. The choices available to potential regional aggressors are a mixture of political, economic, and military counterstrategies.

The first counterstrategy may be to delay and deter a U.S. response. As we have discussed earlier, the opening period of a regional conflict—particularly in those areas where U.S. forward presence is minimal—is critical, and success depends on the rapid deployment of sufficient forces to join indigenous military units in halting an invasion and containing the aggressor's offensive power. Therefore, a first step of a political/military strategy for a regional aggressor might be among the following:

---

[23]For a discussion of how various nations are responding to the lessons of the 1991 Gulf War, see Garrity (1993). For reactions of the Russians, see Lambeth (1992). For games attempting to suggest what future opponents will do, see Bennett, Fox, and Gardiner (1994).

- Mask intentions to threaten U.S. national interests and to conduct war on neighboring states.

- Use political and economic pressure to dissuade neighboring states to allow access to the region.

- Appeal to American and allied public opinion that U.S. involvement is unnecessary and unwise.

These actions, either individually or in combination, could delay the introduction of critical U.S. force elements into the region.

Once the commitment to deploy and use U.S. forces in a regional conflict is made and access is granted, the opponent's strategy might shift. Emphasis then could be given to the employment of forces to achieve a fait accompli or present U.S. forces with a much more difficult forced-entry scenario. Simultaneously, a regional opponent might pursue the rapid acquisition of critical areas by invasions of neighboring states and demonstrations of will and power through the destruction of key high-value assets by strategic or terrorist attack.

Delaying the deployment of U.S. forces while aggressively conducting a land invasion is another avenue open to an opponent. This might be accomplished in a twofold manner. Political pressure could continue to be used to deny access to staging losses and areas, and attacks could be conducted on key nodes of the air and sea lines of communication.

Attacks on the air and sea lines of communication could have telling effects on the rate of closure of U.S. and allied forces. The critical facilities are the following:

- The aerial ports of debarkation (APODs) or those airports where large transport aircraft can land and unload forces and cargo.

- The sea lanes that approach major ports in the region of conflict.

- Seaport facilities in the theater.

The number of such areas will of necessity be limited, and each will have some vulnerability to attack by an opponent. In the process of planning and analyzing a campaign in a major regional conflict, the potential effects of enemy interdiction of nodes in the air and sea lines of communication must be considered and measures to overcome enemy actions carefully evaluated.

An aggressive and prudent opponent might also divert a portion of his offensive capability to destroy or counter high-value U.S. assets in the early stages of the campaign. By concentrating a selected force on assets that are singularly important to the successful accomplishment of U.S. goals, an opponent might gain needed time or cut into the resolve of the U.S. public and military leaders. We have already mentioned the potential value of attacks on the nodes in the air and sea lines of communication in slowing the rate of deployment. The psychological impact of sinking a military prepositioning ship carrying munitions for aircraft or the equipment for a Marine or Army brigade could be important.[24] Similarly, an air or missile attack on an APOD filled with strategic airlift aircraft and supplies could be very damaging. Other critical U.S. force targets could be

- An aircraft carrier or other valuable ship.
- AWACS, JSTARS, or aerial refueling aircraft.
- Concentrations of U.S. force personnel or command facilities.
- A high-value stealth aircraft like the B-2.
- Operational U.S. air bases and the destruction of aircraft, fuel, and munitions.

Some of these critical target sets may be attacked with ballistic or cruise missiles. Additionally, air and terrorist attacks are relevant to some of these critical U.S. force elements. One cannot predict in advance the total effects of the enemy's destruction of key U.S. assets and people in the early days of a campaign. Such events might undermine U.S. resolve—or serve to increase it.

U.S. forces possess qualitative and quantitative advantages over most regional adversaries. If measures to dissuade the United States and its allies from intervention, or if measures to slow the rate of deployment are unsuccessful, then the picture changes for the adversary. As forces build up in the theater, the aggressor's chances for a direct military victory lessen. The strategic options for the regional aggressor lie in consolidating his gains and stalemating the situation while inflicting casualties and damage on U.S. and allied forces to increase the price of involvement.

After sufficient U.S. forces have arrived to stabilize the military situation, the enemy has a different set of options. One might be calls for cease-fires in place interspersed with dispersed, fleeting attacks. Missile and limited air attacks could also become part of an indirect strategy for a regional aggressor to consolidate his gains, sustain his forces and morale, and wear at the will of the United States and its allies.

Another option is the use of weapons of mass destruction (e.g., nuclear, chemical, and biological weapons). Such use anytime in a conflict could produce a large number of casualties among the U.S./allied forces and among the

---

[24]For example, the sinking during the Falklands War of the *Atlantic Conveyer* transport vessel, which carried almost all British transport helicopters, forced British forces to walk from the landing site to the Argentine stronghold at Port Stanley—and greatly increased the length of time needed to complete the British joint counteroffensive.

civilian population of the invaded state.   However, employment of such weapons would leave the attacker open to potential ripostes in kind.

A third option would aim at preserving enemy forces by dispersing them in an orderly fashion, moving out of the conquered territory, and reconstituting for guerrilla warfare in the aggressor's own nation where the knowledge of the terrain may favor his forces. A sustained guerrilla and terrain campaign following a regional conflict without a decisive end could be very taxing on the U.S. and allied forces' capabilities. The pressure on the U.S. ability to sustain operations in this type of warfare would be magnified if those operations had to be conducted in the aggressor's territory, and if his forces had been disengaged and dispersed early enough that his population and his forces still had a strong will to resist. This presents a situation with an indeterminate end that may be better suited to an adversary's long-term objectives than to those of the United States.

OBSERVATIONS

The discussion in this paper examines the conditions of major regional conflict in the post–Cold War era. The nature of major regional conflicts is shaped by the changed balance of military power and the reductions in U.S. overseas military presence. These factors indicate that future regional conflicts will be conducted in distinct phases, with different campaign objectives associated with each phase. The duration of the combat phase can vary with different responses by the aggressor, but it will always be bounded by the time required to deploy U.S. forces into the theater of operations.

The discussion has been presented without respect to a particular region or enemy. However, analysis and planning for regional conflict must be done with a specific opponent in a specific region, because the specific forces, facilities, and location are important. Though many now speak of the uncertainty of the post–Cold War security environment, regional threats five to ten years in the future are not uncertain. There are only two areas where potential opponents with sufficient military forces pose a threat to U.S. national interests today; these are Southwest Asia and Korea, which should serve as a focus of near-term U.S. planning efforts. While planning for the bulk of the military structure is determined in large measure by the needs established in regional conflict scenarios described in this paper, there are a number of unique force capabilities that must be determined and provided for. Examples of unique capabilities are defenses against ballistic and cruise missiles, and light infantry forces for operations in urban and jungle environments and for peace-enforcement operations.

Shaping military forces for new challenges takes a long time, owing to the lead times required to develop strategies and alliance structures appropriate for new threats and to procure sufficient numbers of new weapons and systems to support these new strategies. At present, it appears the United States will have adequate strategic, economic, and political indicators to shift its planning focus, provided an adequate level of forces is maintained to provide the bedrock for new strategic commitments. Understanding the nature, objectives, and phasing of regional conflicts, together with the range of strategies an opponent may employ, is crucial to planning these operations and deriving estimates of future required force levels and capabilities.

BIBLIOGRAPHY

Allen, Patrick (1992), *Situational Force Scoring: Accounting for Combined Arms Effects in Aggregate Combat Models*, RAND, Santa Monica, CA.

Aspin, Les (1993), *The Bottom-Up Review*, Department of Defense, September.

Bennett, Bruce W., Sam Gardiner, and Daniel B. Fox (1994), "Not Merely Planning for the Last War," in Davis (1994).

Bowie, Christopher J. (1984), *Concepts of Operations and USAF Planning for Southwest Asia*, RAND, Santa Monica, CA.

Bowie, Christopher, Fred Frostic, Kevin N. Lewis, John Lund, David Ochmanek, and Philip Propper (1993), *The New Calculus*, RAND, Santa Monica, CA.

Bracken, Paul (1993), "The Military After Next," *The Washington Quarterly*, Autumn, pp. 157–174.

Builder, Carl H., Robert Lempert, Kevin N. Lewis, Eric Larsen, and Milton Weiner (1993), *Report of a Workshop on Expanding U.S. Air Force Noncombat Mission Capabilities*, RAND, Santa Monica, CA.

Cardwell, Thomas (1992), *Airland Combat: An Organization for Joint Operations*, Air University Press, Maxwell AFB.

Craven, Wesley F., and James L. Cates (eds.) (1951), *The Army Air Forces in World War II, Volume III, Europe: Argument to V-E Day, January 1944 to May 1945*, Office of Air Force History.

Dadant, Philip (1984), *A Comparison of Methods for Improving U.S. Capabilities to Project Ground Forces to Southwest Asia in the 1990s*, RAND, Santa Monica, CA.

Davis, Paul K. (1988), *Toward a Conceptual Framework for Operational Arms Control in Europe's Central Region*, RAND, Santa Monica, CA.

———— (1989), "Central Region Stability at Low Force Levels," in Reiner Huber (ed.), *Military Stability: Prerequisites and Analysis Requirements for Conventional Stability in Europe*, Nomos Verlagsgesellschaft.

———— (ed.) (1994), *New Challenges for Defense Planning: Rethinking How Much Is Enough*, RAND, Santa Monica, CA.

Davis, Paul K., and John Arquilla (1991), *Deterring or Coercing Opponents in Crisis: Lessons from the War with Saddam Hussein*, RAND, Santa Monica, CA.

Davis, Paul K., and Lou Finch (1993), *Defense Planning for the Post–Cold War Era: Giving Meaning to Flexibility, Adaptiveness, and Robustness of Capability*, RAND, Santa Monica, CA.

Department of the Navy (1993), *From the Sea: Preparing the Naval Service for the 21st Century*.

Garrity, Patrick J. (1993), *Why the Gulf War Still Matters: Foreign Perspectives on the War and the Future of International Security*, Center for National Security Studies, Los Alamos National Laboratories.

Kassing, David (1994), *Getting Military Power to the Desert: An Annotated Briefing*, RAND, Santa Monica, CA.

Keaney, Thomas A., and Eliot A. Cohen (1993), *Gulf War Air Power Survey: Summary Report*, U. S. Government Printing Office, Washington, D.C.

Lambeth, Benjamin (1992), *Desert Storm and Its Meaning: The View from Moscow*, RAND, Santa Monica, CA.

National Defense Research Institute (1992), *Assessing the Structure and Mix of Future Active and Reserve Forces: Final Report to the Secretary of Defense*, RAND, Santa Monica, CA.

Ochmanek, David, and John Bordeaux (1993), "The Lion's Share of Power Projection," *Air Force Magazine*, June, pp. 38–43.

Perrin, David (1991), *A Comparison of Long-Range Bombers and Naval Forces*, Alexandria, VA, Center for Naval Analyses, CIM 204.90.

Powell, General Colin (1992), *National Military Strategy of the United States*, Department of Defense.

Sullivan, General Gordon, and Lieutenant Colonel James M. Dubik (1993), *Land Warfare in the 21st Century*, U.S. Army War College, Strategic Studies Institute, February.

Thaler, David (1993), *Strategies to Tasks: A Framework for Linking Means and Ends*, RAND, Santa Monica, CA.

Warden, Colonel John (1989), *The Air Campaign: Planning for Combat*, Pergamon-Brassey's, Washington, D.C.

Chapter 13

THE USE OF LONG-RANGE BOMBERS IN A CHANGING WORLD: A CLASSICAL EXERCISE IN SYSTEMS ANALYSIS

Glenn C. Buchan

In the aftermath of the Cold War, long-range bombers could play an increasingly critical role in projecting U.S. power to distant parts of the globe, particularly in the early stages of a conflict when the United States may have little military capability on the scene. Actually, the ascendance of the conventional role of long-range bombers predated the end of the Cold War, as RAND analysis at the time showed. The ability of long-range bombers to deliver massive firepower of diverse types virtually anywhere in the world in a matter of hours offers a unique capability to deal with a range of situations that might arise. Understanding that spectrum of possibilities requires a much more complex set of analytical tools and a more sophisticated overall analytic approach than the stylized sort of systems analysis employed to address nuclear issues during the Cold War. More fundamentally, new operational concepts for bombers as well as improved conventional weapons need to be developed if bombers are to achieve their full potential.

INTRODUCTION

The problems that the United States and its nominal allies are experiencing over the increasingly vexing conflicts in Bosnia and Somalia, as well as the ambiguous aftermath of the Gulf War, illustrate the difficulties that the country can expect to face in navigating the largely uncharted waters of the post–Cold War world. Defining the nature and extent of U.S. interests in the evolving world and evaluating the tools available to protect those interests are likely to remain challenges to U.S. policymakers for some time. Military forces remain among those tools that might be employed in some situations. Defining the sort of military force that can meet the country's needs in the post–Cold War world, and still be affordable in times of increasingly austere budgets, is the dominant problem facing U.S. military planners today. Choosing a bomber force and deciding how to employ it are parts of that problem.

The ability of long-range bombers to deliver large, diverse payloads virtually anywhere in the world in a matter of hours has given them a key role in U.S.

military strategy for several decades. As Figure 1 suggests, long-range bombers have long figured significantly in planning for both nuclear and conventional operations. In fact, in the aftermath of the Cold War, heavy bombers should have the easiest time of all of the strategic nuclear forces in making the transition to a largely conventional role appropriate for the "new world."

Actually, a series of RAND analyses predating the end of the Cold War showed that even then, conventional rather than nuclear requirements should dominate bomber structure decisions. However, the end of the Cold War represented an unmistakable "wake-up call." If their range-payload advantage (see Figure 2) could be exploited effectively, long-range bombers could offer unique advantages for worldwide power projection, particularly in the early phase of a distant conflict.

The analysis of heavy bomber operations has evolved as well, in the decades since operations analysis was first applied to strategic bombing in World War II.[1] During the Cold War, estimating the potential effectiveness of using long-range bombers in nuclear operations against the Soviet Union provided semi-

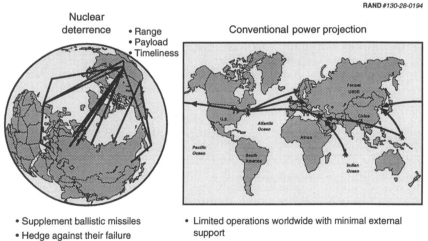

Figure 1—Long-Range Bombers Can Bring Substantial Firepower to Bear
Virtually Anywhere

---

[1] For a contemporary discussion of the early doctrinal debates on use of bombers and institutional evolution that led to the creation of the U.S. Air Force, see Brown (1992:29–67) and Sherry (1987).

RAND #130-29-0194

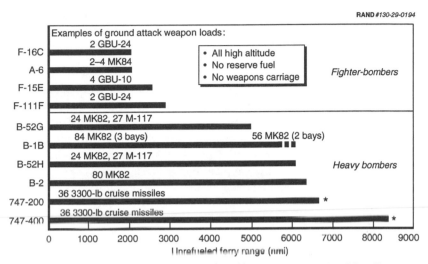

Figure 2—The Range-Payload Advantage of Heavy Bombers

nal examples of the systems analysis art.[2] Since then, both the breadth and style of bomber analysis have changed. Increasingly complex computer simulations are replacing the equations and simple computer models. Dramatic improvements in computer hardware in recent years have made such detailed models practical analytical tools and put them within reach of a much larger group of analysts. While the resulting precision has decided advantages, it also comes at a price.

An important challenge for bomber analysts is weighing those advantages and costs as they pursue the primary purpose this sort of analysis serves: to inform the choices of decisionmakers who have to worry about how bombers ought to fit into overall U.S. military strategy and what kind of bomber force the United States ought to have in the future, given all of the other competing demands for resources. Specific issues include:

- How can long-range bombers be employed most effectively? What critical roles can they play?

- How many of each type of bomber should the United States retain?

---

[2]For discussions of the use of operations analysis in World War II, see Wilson (1968:45–54), Koopman (1946), and Morse and Kimball (1987). For a personal recollection of early efforts to apply analytical methods to a bombing campaign, see Dyson (1979:19–32). See also Weapons Systems Evaluation Group (1950).

- What would the implications be of further reductions in the current bomber force?
- What additional improvements need to be made in the bomber force to make it effective in coping with future contingencies?

The purpose of this paper is to describe (1) the principal issues in employing long-range bombers and structuring a bomber force for the post–Cold War era, (2) the analytical approach that my colleagues at RAND and I have employed in analyzing bombers over the last several years,[3] and (3) some lessons learned about how such analysis has changed—for better and for worse. To those ends, this paper covers these topics: bomber analysis in a "new," uncertain world, structuring a bomber force for the new world, critical decisions for the future bomber force, and observations on the analysis process.

BOMBER ANALYSIS IN A "NEW," UNCERTAIN WORLD

Moving away from the old focus on strategic nuclear war or major conventional war with the Soviet Union and its allies requires refocusing both mindsets and analytical tools. Some things are actually easier. The intensity of the air defense environments is generally greatly reduced. Even countries with relatively high-quality defenses are less likely to have the numbers and density of air defenses of the former Soviet Union, except perhaps in very limited areas. In addition, the defenses are less likely to be effectively integrated. That makes decomposing the defenses—for example, separating SAM and airborne defenses—much easier. Similarly, the less extensive offensive forces could make analyzing traditional kinds of land combat somewhat easier than the old Warsaw Pact or even the Desert Storm cases.

On the other hand, more fundamental issues are much more difficult to deal with. For example, a much broader range of possible conflicts and scenarios must be examined. Determining the right issues and measures of effectiveness is a much less obvious task than it was in the more familiar stylized scenar-

---

[3]I want to acknowledge the contributions of numerous colleagues at RAND who have worked on the series of bomber studies that provided the "meat" for this paper. Classification restrictions prevent me from citing most of their work directly. The best I can do is thank Dave Frelinger, Jim Quinlivan, Bart Bennett, Preston Niblack, Don Stevens, Edward Harshbarger, Joel Kvitky, Dana Johnson, Joe Alt, Dave Balsillie, Myron Hura, Bob Smith, Gary Liberson, Bruce Davis, Greg Born, Ruth Berg, Karl Hoffmayer, Jim Bonomo, Ken Saunders, Dave Spencer, Mark Bolstad, Mary Chenoweth, David Novikoff, Roy Gates, Corinne Replogle, and Amanda Giarla for all of their work on bombers over the last few years at RAND. Needless to say, they are not responsible for any sins of omission or commission on my part in this paper, particularly with respect to observations on how to do bomber studies.

ios. Political nuances, alliance considerations, and other less tangible issues are likely to be more important.

In short, analyzing bomber effectiveness in the "new world" requires a lot more basic thought than repeating the old world analysis in slightly different variants. In our initial forays into this arena, we have found that a lot of trial and error is inevitable in defining the right level of detail to use in addressing various aspects of the overall problem to produce an analysis that is "good enough" to provide useful guidance to policymakers. There is still considerable room for art and judgment in addition to science. This section describes what that means in terms of the altered military picture, constructing a bomber analysis, and our analytic approach.

The Altered Military Picture

Choosing the Right Enemies and Conflicts. Figure 3 illustrates how drastically the worldwide military picture has changed following the dissolution of the Soviet Union. The figure shows the inventories of tanks and combat aircraft that various countries around the world possess. The former is one measure of a nation's capability to invade its neighbors rapidly and effectively. The latter represents a potential capability both to defend its airspace and to attack critical targets in other countries. The former Soviet Union was in a class by itself in both categories.

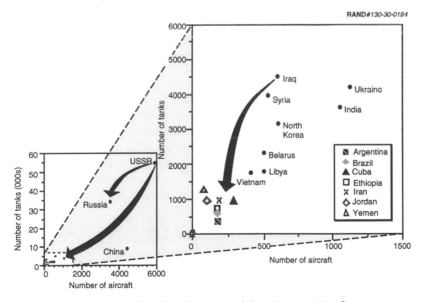

Figure 3—Worldwide Military Capabilities Remain Significant

The rest of the countries shown in Figure 3 have much smaller military establishments and are clustered near the origin on the left-hand plot. The right-hand plot shows an expanded view of the area near the origin to allow comparisons among the rest of the countries. For example, before Desert Storm, Iraq had one of the largest armored forces in the rest of the world and had a substantial air force as well. It was, in some ways, a "mini-Soviet" force relying heavily on Soviet equipment, doctrine, and training. That actually made Iraq seductive as a potential adversary for U.S. planning purposes because it seemed tailor-made for U.S. military forces that were originally designed to deal with a larger, more capable Warsaw Pact force in Europe. In fact, it was one of the few military situations in the world where old-world solutions might be applied successfully if the enemy was unwise enough to allow the United States and its regional allies the time to prepare properly. That, of course, is precisely what Saddam Hussein did, and his reward was an overwhelming military defeat.

On the other hand, using Iraq as a planning surrogate before the invasion of Kuwait was not entirely self-serving for the United States. Iraq was representative of a generic class of enemy that could both seriously threaten fundamental U.S. interests and tax its capabilities to respond:

- Iraq displayed the characteristics of a classic hegemonic power ruled by a dictator who owed much of his power to the Iraqi military.

- Even before its invasion of Kuwait, Iraq had demonstrated a willingness to use military force in its long war with Iran and its ruthless suppression of its own ethnic minorities, such as the Kurds.

- Iraq bordered on countries that were nominally allied to the United States (i.e., Saudi Arabia and Kuwait), controlled resources vital to the United States and its allies (i.e., oil), and were militarily much weaker than Iraq before the Gulf War.

- Iraq was developing nuclear weapons, as well as other types of weapons of mass destruction, and relatively long-range delivery systems that could eventually have allowed it to extend its control—directly or indirectly—over a larger share of Persian Gulf oil. Iraq would become richer in the process and control a resource vital to the West, assuring itself a "place at the table" as an important permanent player on the international scene and one potentially hostile to the United States, particularly if Saddam Hussein managed to successfully adopt the mantle of pan-Arab nationalism.

- Iraq was so far from the United States geographically that the United States would have trouble responding in a timely manner to Iraq's use of force.

For all of these reasons, a situation similar to that in Southwest Asia before the Gulf War was—and is—one generic class of conflict that is both very demanding for U.S. military forces and potentially important to U.S. interests. Forces that could deal with this sort of stressing generic scenario should also be more than adequate to deal with many less demanding situations as "lesser included" cases. *Identifying stressing cases and dominant solutions is one of the general principles in planning for an uncertain world.*

Obviously, no single scenario should be the basis for U.S. planning, particularly in such an uncertain and volatile environment. For one thing, even a legitimate-looking scenario might be dismissed by policymakers as too hard, too improbable, or too unique to be the focus of military planning. Moreover, situations are likely to be different enough so that even "lesser" cases may really *not* be lesser included cases of a major campaign such as a large-scale conflict in Southwest Asia. Accordingly, the analysis needs to be rich enough to include combinations of conditions that will stress different aspects of U.S. capability. Predicting where the U.S. equivalent of the Falklands campaign might occur is virtually impossible, particularly since even some of the more modest-looking military powers shown in Figure 3 should not be casually dismissed. For example, several countries have armored forces that include more than 1000 tanks, which is about the size of the U.S. 7th Corps that took three months to deploy to the Gulf in Desert Shield. Thus, depending on circumstances, including the political climate in the United States at the time, even minor military powers should not be taken too lightly.

The Proliferation of Advanced Air Defenses. As noted above, the intensity of air defense environments, generally, is reduced. However, conducting raids worldwide or operating in the early stages of a distant campaign when enemy air defenses are still relatively intact is likely to be increasingly difficult for bombers. Figure 4 suggests why. High-quality air defense systems—"lookdown" fighter aircraft, high-performance SAMs, airborne surveillance systems—are becoming increasingly available even in the Third World, and this proliferation is likely to accelerate in the future. In 1980, only a few countries in the Third World had any high-quality systems for air defense. These countries were generally superpower client states, and the motives of the suppliers were at least as much political as economic. Moreover, at the time, the United States and the Soviet Union could keep a relatively tight rein on their main clients, although countries like Iran had already broken away from their former patrons. A controlled situation was already becoming less controlled.

By 1990, the picture had changed considerably. First, more suppliers were in the market. Second, the suppliers, including the United States and the Soviet Union, were increasingly motivated more by economic than by political concerns: Selling fighter aircraft is a source of revenue for all, and of hard currency in particular for the former Soviet states. As a result, more and more countries are in a position to acquire high-quality air defense systems. This trend is likely to accelerate as still more suppliers get into the market, some potentially hostile countries have money (e.g., oil money), and regional security

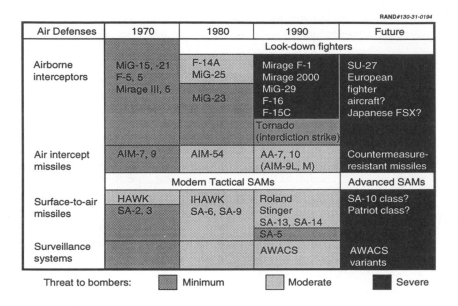

RAND#130-31-0194

Air Defenses	1970	1980	1990	Future
			Look-down fighters	
Airborne interceptors	MiG-15, -21 F-5, 5 Mirage III, 5	F-14A MiG-25 MiG-23	Mirage F-1 Mirage 2000 MiG-29 F-16 F-15C Tornado (interdiction strike)	SU-27 European fighter aircraft? Japanese FSX?
Air intercept missiles	AIM-7, 9	AIM-54	AA-7, 10 (AIM-9L, M)	Countermeasure-resistant missiles
		Modern Tactical SAMs		Advanced SAMs
Surface-to-air missiles	HAWK SA-2, 3	IHAWK SA-6, SA-9	Roland Stinger SA-13, SA-14 SA-5	SA-10 class? Patriot class?
Surveillance systems			AWACS	AWACS variants

Threat to bombers: ▨ Minimum   ▢ Moderate   ■ Severe

Figure 4—High-Quality Air Defenses Worldwide

becomes more problematical because of the perceived end of the Cold War and the disintegration of various Cold War military alliances that had maintained a measure of regional stability. The net result is that heavy bombers will have to be concerned about air defenses virtually anywhere they may need to go in the future.

Of particular concern to heavy bombers are the following:

- Modern airborne interceptors, even in small numbers, unless countered by arms or the use of stealth.

- Even small numbers of modern SAMs employed either as terminal defenses of high-value fixed targets or as mobile defenses covering invasion forces.

- Airborne surveillance systems, such as the U.S. airborne warning and control system (AWACS).

- Low-frequency early warning/ground control intercept (EW/GCI) radars in critical locations.

On the other hand, with the disappearance of the Soviet threat, life should get easier for bombers because:

- "Enroute" SAMs and other ground-based defenses should not be much of a problem unless bombers try to fly low in dangerous areas.

- Densities of air defenses do not, in general, approach those of the former Soviet Union and Warsaw Pact.

- Third World pilots are usually not well trained, and air defenses do not normally operate as efficiently and effectively as those of the West's former adversaries.

In general, small bomber forces of the future can afford very little attrition, so preparing to deal with future air defenses is crucial to planning the bomber force.

Constructing a Bomber Analysis

Over the decades that analysts have been working bomber problems, a "school solution" has emerged about how to do a bomber study. A certain number of obligatory steps and subanalyses are an intrinsic part of the standard approach. Figure 5 illustrates this process as it applies to the "old world" case of a strategic nuclear attack on the former Soviet Union. Indeed, the basic issues—basing and support of the bombers, readiness and responsiveness, range and payload capability, survivability, and effectiveness in destroying targets of interest—never really change. However, the relative importance of different pieces of the problem and the difficulty and appropriate level of detail in analyzing various aspects of bomber operations vary considerably. Moreover, our experience suggests that even when there is general agreement on the major thrust of the analysis and the issues to be addressed (admittedly, an unusually agreeable situation), there is still considerable room for argument about exactly what tools to use, how to use them, and what to make of the results. That's why the science and art of systems analysis—the critical judgment necessary to make analysis "correct," credible, and useful—remain critical even in constructing a classical bomber analysis in the old world where life was simpler.

The world of conventional operations is much less tidy; this was so even in the old world. Figure 6 illustrates some of the critical steps in the analytic process for assessing bomber operations in a spectrum of conventional campaigns and gives a sense of the overall flow of the analytical process. Even a conceptual diagram of the process is much less straightforward than in the strategic nuclear arena. The analysis is much more iterative. More choices are involved. There are more potentially competing and complementary weapon systems to consider, which in turn lead to a more complex set of alternative operational concepts and force structure options to evaluate. Also, although some analyti-

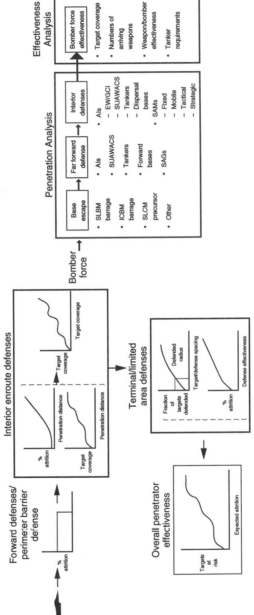

Figure 5—Steps in a Classical Bomber Analysis: Strategic Nuclear Attack on the Former Soviet Union

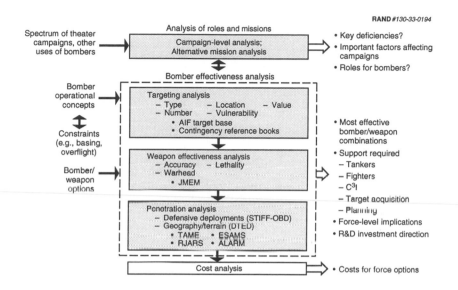

RAND #130-33-0194

Figure 6—Analyzing Bombers for Conventional Power Projection

cal tools are applicable both in the conventional and nuclear arenas, we found mismatches as well. "Force fitting" models designed for one world into the other sometimes caused massive headaches and produced analytical results of dubious value. *As the "new world" evolves, we expect this problem to increase.* Some conventional, and even nuclear, scenarios that we may have to worry about in the future are likely to be quite different from anything we have had to deal with in the past, and our thought processes and analytical methods are going to have to change accordingly.

One thing that has changed in the military systems analysis community over the last several decades is the growing number of large-scale computer simulation models employed in various phases of air campaign analysis, including the employment of bombers. In the past, really large-scale computer models were primarily used for relatively specific applications (e.g., penetration of Soviet air defenses, detailed modeling of nuclear weapons effects, design of the Single Integrated Operational Plan [SIOP]). They were employed mainly by organizations with the resources to invest in suitable computers, programmers, and analysts to develop and use them. The Advanced Penetration Model (APM) is an example of models of this genre. APM used to be the staple "official" model used by the Air Force for analyzing strategic bomber effectiveness in penetrating Soviet air defenses. "War stories" about the trials and tribulations of using APM abound in the defense community.

The revolution in computer technology over the last decade or so has caused a sea change in the way much of the defense community does analysis. The vast increases in computational capability have brought large-scale computing within the reach of a much larger segment of the defense community. As a result, modeling particular kinds of military problems (e.g., SAM engagements) in much greater detail and more routinely employing large-scale exchange models, which incorporate more refinements, have become much more practical. Accordingly, the kinds of analysis that used to be performed with simpler, more satisfying analytical models[4] now tend to be done using families of higher-fidelity, computer-intensive models.

Figure 7 shows some of the computer models that we have used in our recent bomber studies in just the penetration part of the analysis. Table 1 describes some of the features of these models, such as the required inputs and the kinds of outputs they produce, in more detail. Just sorting through the "alphabet soup" of models of various sorts can be a considerable challenge, and selecting the appropriate model for specific applications can be an art in itself

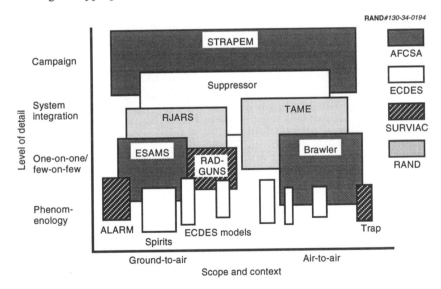

Figure 7—A Hierarchy of Penetration Models Used in RAND Bomber Analyses

---

[4]Some examples of models of this genre include Schultis (1978:1357, 1979:1431), Jacobson (1977), Cunningham (1973), and various unclassified appendixes to classified reports describing methodology for analyzing different aspects of the air defense penetration problem.

Table 1

A Taxonomy of Penetration Models

Types of Analysis	Scope	Inputs	Outputs
Phenomenology	System or subsystem characteristics that impact a particular kind of phenomenon	• Aircraft wire frame • Aircraft performance • Sensor physics • Automated logic • Countermeasures • Environment	• Detection ranges • Scenes
One-on-one	Site or combined system effects	• Aircraft performance • Weapon characteristics • Cognitive processes • Countermeasures • System tactics • Environmental effects	• Tracking distributions • Engagement envelopes • Probabilities of kill
System integration	Mission components and effects	• Platform functions and interactions • C^3I • Aggregate countermeasures • Mission tactics • Aggregate environmental effects	• Mission effectiveness • Survivability measures
Campaign	Force exchange	• Aggregated platform features • Missions/postures • Resource allocation • Force mixes • Strategies	• Force effectiveness • Impact of allocation strategies

since they differ dramatically in scope and level of detail. Even more important, wiring them together, either literally or figuratively, to produce a coherent analysis is one of the highest forms of the systems analysis art.

The models themselves vary considerably in their demands on computers and analysts. Run times on modern computers can vary from minutes to hours to days for a single case, depending on the particular models and the scope of the case being examined. More important, they typically require considerable care and feeding to employ effectively. Preparing input data for individual cases can take days even with the data largely in hand. Collecting those data can take months and may even be impossible, driving analysts to improvise and hope that they can later identify any impact on the results of less-than-ideal inputs.

Analyzing and interpreting the results of most large-scale simulation models typically requires time, effort, and experience as well. Even running the models successfully requires a certain amount of training and experience. As a practical matter, that means training and maintaining a cadre of analysts who are not only knowledgeable in substantive areas (e.g., air-to-air combat) but also able to use various community-standard models successfully. (Indeed, experience with particular computer models is becoming obligatory on résumés of military systems analysts!) Thus, there is a substantial "buy in" price in analyzing bomber operations using these sorts of tools. For example, of the two dozen or so analysts at RAND who have been involved in bomber studies in the last few years, roughly one-third have been primarily involved in the care and feeding of big computer models, and another half dozen have devoted a good deal of time to actually running the models and interpreting their results.

Actually using the models as analytical tools has drawbacks as well. There is a substantial tradeoff between investing resources in using big models and doing more thinking and "real" analysis with simpler tools. The analytical opportunity costs, in terms of the number of cases considered and overall insight into the effects of the key variables in the analysis, can be substantial when big models are employed.

Our Analytic Approach

Our approach to structuring a bomber force for the "new world" was to try to examine a wide range of conventional conflicts; identify kinds of problems, if any, that long-range bombers were particularly well suited for solving; and then use those cases as a basis for structuring a conventional bomber force robust enough to deal with a reasonable range of unpredictable future contingencies. We tried to apply the following general principles:

- Work out enough particular cases that one can *generalize from the specific.* That is, provide a spectrum of force structure options associated with a set of generic scenarios derived from considering larger numbers of specific cases to inform decisionmakers' choices about the kinds of capabilities they might want to buy and the consequences of their choices.

- *Emphasize the cases that matter.* All cases need not be worked out in equal detail. In fact, they should not be, considering the time and effort involved in analyzing individual cases. Rather, the trick is to analyze a large number of cases quickly to identify those that drive the results and focus more detailed analytical effort on them. (Frequently, that means topical cases are not the ones that turn out to be important. For example, Korea did not prove to be a stressing or unique case for bombers, although the defense community as a whole has been focusing large amounts of effort on Korea recently.)

Table 2 shows some of the cases that we considered in analyzing conventional bomber operations. To add richness, they included cases from both the old and the new worlds. Each represents a different kind of tactical problem to solve—armor in prewar Iraq; infantry in Iran as well as a generally growing military capability in all areas; a mature, balanced military with a spectrum of capabilities in North Korea; potential for weapons of mass destruction and ap-propriate delivery systems in a number of countries. Most have potentially threatening air defenses, although they vary in character among countries. What they all have in common, however, is their great distance from the United States. If the United States continues to reduce its military presence overseas, as it was certainly doing before Desert Shield, then a timely military response to crises is likely to be increasingly difficult.

Conflicts such as Bosnia and Somalia are new to the list. The air defense environments are relatively benign, with the possible exception of low-altitude flight in areas where simple short-range air defense systems exist in numbers. The more fundamental problem in those cases is determining what, if anything, bombers could successfully target that would either affect the outcome of the military conflict or persuade combatants to give up the struggle. Properly equipped bombers could easily destroy a lot of things—vehicles on the road, fixed installations of any sort, perhaps some sorts of troop concentrations. However, making the case that such attacks matter is problematical at best. Moreover, if the opportunity for meaningful use of bombers should arise, conducting these sorts of operations is less stressing for the bomber force than other generic classes of missions that should already be "on the list."

Potentially interesting targets in some conflicts remain elusive for bombers or anything else. The U.S. performance in finding and destroying Scud mobile missiles in Desert Storm was abysmal. As weapons of mass destruction and advanced delivery systems continue to spread, interest in destroying them is likely to increase. If technology eventually permits, bombers might be employed either to find and destroy mobile missiles on the ground or perhaps to attack missiles in flight. That sort of mission could provide yet another basis for structuring the bomber force, if bombers proved to be the solution of choice. The technological possibilities and potential operational concepts are too immature to be of much use in structuring the bomber force for the immediate future, however.

Table 2

Some Typical Conventional Cases Considered

Case	Distance from United States (nmi)	Potential Target Sets		Air Defense Environment
		Types	Number	
"Old world" cases:				
Europe: Post-CFE	3500–5000	Interdiction targets, air defenses	Very large	Severe
Iran	6500	Hard bridges, airfields	Small, repeated attacks required	Heavy
Pacific	6600	Airfields, ocean choke points	Small, repeated attacks required	Heavy
NATO Northern Flank	3000	Ships, ocean areas, loading sites, airfields	Moderate, re-peated attacks required	Heavy
Vietnam ("Linebacker III")	7200	Lines of com-munications, air-fields, storage areas	Moderate	Severe
"New world" cases:				
Iran	6500	Complete spec-trum of military and economic targets	Moderate-large	Heavy, but spotty
Iraq/Kuwait–Saudi Arabia (pre-Desert Storm)	6000	Armor, special weapons facilities, air defenses, command structure	Large	Heavy
North/South Korea	4800	Spectrum of military targets	Large	Moderate
Bekaa Valley	5400	Buildings, air defenses	Small	Severe
Libya	4800	Plants, buildings	Small	Modest
Bosnia	4500	?, artillery posi-tions?, "value targets"	Moderate	Light, except at low altitude
Somalia	7000	?, "road warriors?"	Small	Nonexistent, except at low altitude

Implications for Bomber Force Planning

In general, we employed this sort of "scenario screening" process to try to answer the following kinds of questions:

- What are interesting generic cases that provide a basis for structuring a future bomber force?
- Are there cases where bombers offer unique advantages over other types of forces?
- Should some cases be eliminated from consideration because they are either "too hard" or because bombers don't matter much one way or the other?

Eventually, a policymaker will have to make a value judgment about which of the cases where bombers might contribute matter enough to him to justify investing in a particular kind of bomber force.

STRUCTURING A BOMBER FORCE FOR THE "NEW WORLD"

Addressing these questions requires examining the potential roles of bombers and their effectiveness in those roles, how potential targets drive force structure, the importance of weapons, the survivability of bombers, and the necessary bomber force structures to support a spectrum of overall concepts for U.S. power projection abroad. Then the analysis must consider cost projections and cost-effectiveness comparisons among various bomber options and between using bombers and alternative approaches to reduce policymakers' choices to a set of value judgments. This section deals with the first set of issues. The final section of the paper discusses the analytical challenge for dealing with the cost-effectiveness issues.

Critical Roles for Long-Range Bombers

The Leading Edge Role. The potential use of long-range bombers to bring firepower to bear early in a distant conflict to buy time for other forces to arrive predated the end of the Cold War. Even during the Cold War, heavy bombers could have played an important role in major conventional campaigns against the Soviets and their allies if they were used properly. For example, B-52s could have been first on the scene in places such as the mountain passes of northern Iran in the old Cold War scenarios that worried about a possible Soviet thrust into Southwest Asia to capture oil fields vital to the West. RAND analysis in the 1980s showed that a modest-sized bomber force, if armed with the proper weapons, could have delayed the attackers long enough to give U.S. forces a chance to move into the theater and "get in the game" rather than face an outright defeat. Moreover, bombers with high-quality conventional weapons might have been the only practical alternative to using nuclear weapons. Similarly, long-range bombers might have been employed effectively in other regions, such as NATO's northern and southern flanks, where U.S. and allied forces were outgunned, and the rapid application of massive firepower against various kinds of enemy forces could have made a difference.

With the end of the Cold War and the apparent trend of withdrawing most U.S. troops from overseas bases, the potential value of using long-range bombers in the initial phases of a major campaign as well as for limited raids worldwide became much greater. Even before the Gulf War, RAND analysis highlighted the importance of this role for long-range bombers. Key objectives early in any such campaign typically include some combination of the following:

- Deter a potential enemy from acting, if possible.

- Deny the enemy an easy victory or opportunity to increase the "entry price" to the war drastically, particularly by stopping or at least seriously slowing a fast-moving offensive (i.e., a blitzkrieg-like invasion).

- Blunt a slow-moving offensive.

- Look committed and competent enough to persuade regional powers in particular to cast their lot with the United States and its allies rather than remaining neutral or supporting the other side.

- Earn and maintain the support of the American public and decisionmaking elites.

- Prevent the enemy from hampering the flow of U.S. and other supporting forces into the theater.

- Destroy any potentially valuable enemy assets that could be easily or quickly moved or hidden.

- Destroy any support facilities that could have an immediate impact on an enemy's ability to wage war.

The details will, of course, vary from campaign to campaign. The most demanding problems are those where the enemy controls the operational tempo of the campaign, and the United States and whatever allies it has must be able to counter the enemy action. The most obvious example is the need to counter an invasion, where failure means having to displace an entrenched enemy later at much greater cost. Similarly, the United States must preserve whatever bases it needs in the region to move forces into the theater. Typically, that means preventing an enemy from destroying critical airfields or ports or otherwise interfering with air or sea "bridges" into the theater. Finally, there may be a few select targets that are so important to the enemy's immediate war effort or have such critical long-term value and are "perishable" (i.e., could be moved or hidden quickly) that they warrant an early attack.

All this must be done in a very delicate political environment. Losses must be kept to an absolute minimum to keep the American public on board. The action must look effective and decisive to persuade jittery nations in the region that by siding with the United States, they will be backing a winner. On the other hand, the action should not look too heavy-handed to keep other allies on board. This could be a tall order.

With a limited U.S. presence on the ground in most parts of the world and weak indigenous forces in some critical areas, dealing with these problems could be quite challenging. Moving ground forces and land-based tactical air forces into a combat zone takes time and at least some safe local bases from which to operate. Naval forces can do some things if they are already on the scene. If not, ships could take days or even weeks to arrive, depending on where they are when the conflict erupts and what kind of military operations are needed. If massive and/or sustained firepower is needed, naval forces may not be adequate in any case.

By contrast, long-range bombers can bring massive firepower to bear virtually anywhere in the world in a matter of hours from relatively safe bases in the United States or elsewhere outside the immediate conflict area. Moreover, long-range bombers can sustain operations as long as the weapons, stockpiles, logistics support structure, and replacement crews at their operating bases hold out. This capability for long-distance, massive, sustained strike operations is what long-range bombers bring to the party.

The Gulf War Experience. What happened in the Gulf War—and what did *not* happen, but *could* have—crystalized both the problems that future conflicts could pose and the potential that heavy bombers offer in the early stages of major conflicts. Figure 8 shows the rate at which U.S. forces arrived in the theater. Recall the problem that was on everyone's mind at the time: What if Saddam Hussein doesn't stop with Kuwait but instead keeps on moving into Saudi Arabia? If he had, stopping the kind of armored invasion that he could have mounted would have required the United States and its coalition partners to be able to mount a major interdiction campaign against Iraqi armor. It was several weeks after Iraq's initial invasion of Kuwait before the United States had enough tactical aircraft in the theater to mount that level of interdiction campaign. Adequate ground forces would not have been available until much later. Even then, the weapons and command-and-control structure to sustain interdiction operations on a continuing basis were not yet in place, so the defensive interdiction campaign would have been sporadic at best.

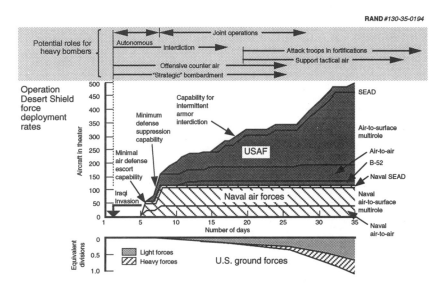

Figure 8—Potential Role of Long-Range Bombers in the Initial Phases of a Major
Theater Campaign

The problem could have been considerably worse. The first U.S. tactical aircraft on the scene came from two carriers that were in the region and were able to reach the theater within a few days. Ironically, one of those carriers was on its way out of the Arabian Sea when the crisis broke, and it was ordered to return to the Persian Gulf area. Had the crisis developed a few days later, the buildup of theater airpower would have been even slower. Since the U.S. carrier fleet is limited in size—and getting smaller—relying on carriers to cope with the initial phases of a major theater campaign tacitly assumes that the United States has at least a few days' notice that a serious crisis is brewing, to make sure that at least one carrier could reach the area. Getting enough carriers on station to provide massive firepower, if that were needed, could take anywhere from days to weeks, depending on the circumstances, and might even prove totally impractical.

By contrast, heavy bombers could have been there on the first day of the war and, assuming capabilities that they may obtain in the future, could have brought the kind of massive firepower to bear that could have halted an armored invasion as well as destroying any other key targets necessary to defeat the Iraqi thrust. However, such a task would be quite demanding for bombers:

• They would have to have good enough weapons to be effective against a variety of targets, particularly armored vehicles in this case.

- They would have to be able to operate relatively autonomously for a period of time in a hostile environment, which means they could not rely on fighter support to defeat air defenses, surveillance aircraft to help locate targets, or nearby bases to refuel and rearm.

As it happened, Saddam Hussein chose not to press his advantage and eventually suffered a crushing military defeat. A future Saddam Hussein, learning his own lessons from the Gulf War, might choose differently. If so, bombers could be the primary instrument in preventing a quick military victory and a political fait accompli. However, the demands on the bomber force will be considerable, as the rest of this paper will show.

How Effective Would Bombers Be in the Leading Edge Role? Figure 9 shows three approaches that the bombers could use in this role. The first relies on fighter escorts and air defense suppression assistance from other aircraft. This is the kind of thing that coalition forces did in Desert Storm in conjunction with massive defense suppression attacks and might be able to do again under similarly favorable conditions. The weakness is that it *requires theater bases for the fighters.* Thus, it may not be a practical option at the outset of a war.

The second possibility relies on using standoff aircraft that employ cruise missiles with sufficient range to keep the aircraft beyond the reach of the enemy's air defenses. This approach should be effective against known fixed targets, assuming that adequate intelligence support and mission planning capa

RAND#130-36-0194

Support requirements \\ Strike aircraft	Penetrating B-52s or B-1s	B-52s with cruise missiles	B-2s
Support aircraft			
– Air defense suppression	3 EF-111s 8 Wild Weasels	4 Wild Weasels	—
– Escorts	20 F-16s	10 F-15s	—
– Other • Target acquisition (mobile targets) • Air surveillance	1 JSTARS 1 AWACS	1 JSTARS 1 AWACS	None against massive movement (e.g., armor)
– Tankers[a]	3 tankers/bomber (CONUS basing) 0.67–1 tanker/bomber (Diego Garcia) 8 tankers (support aircraft)	3 tankers/bomber (CONUS basing) 0.5–0.67 tanker/bomber (Diego Garcia) 0–4 tankers (support aircraft)	1 tanker/bomber (CONUS)
Planning support	• Detailed current threat data • Target locations • Strike coordination • Weapons planning and interface	• Detailed intelligence data on targets • Extensive mission planning capability	• Target locations • High-quality navigation • Onboard software and wiring to weapons
Other support	• Theater bases • Munitions and loading facilities	• Theater bases	—

[a] Assumes a strike against Southwest Asia targets with bombers based either in CONUS or Diego Garcia and support aircraft based in theater (e.g., Saudi Arabia).

For attacks on moving targets only; protect JSTARS.

Figure 9—Alternative Operational Concepts for Bomber Forces

bility for the weapons exist. That is, of course, what B-52Hs did at the outset of Desert Storm. They flew from Barksdale AFB in the United States and launched long-range cruise missiles at power generation, transmission, and military communications facilities in Iraq. However, any need to attack movable targets—countering an armored invasion, for example—would introduce a whole new set of problems. Even assuming the cruise missiles themselves could be made effective (i.e., inflight target location updates of some sort to compensate for the long missile flight times), the bombers still need to be able to locate the targets. If they rely on JSTARS, for example, the JSTARS aircraft would probably be vulnerable to long-range SAMs or airborne interceptors if it got close enough to enemy armor to be effective. That means fighter protection for the JSTARS, which in turn means theater bases or possibly aircraft carriers on the scene. Thus, standoff cruise missile carriers could be effective operating autonomously against fixed targets, but not against movable targets like invading armies unless some sort of survivable target acquisition system could be provided.

The third approach would be to use B-2s, which, by contrast, could operate autonomously against a large spectrum of targets of interest, if they prove sufficiently stealthy. In particular, the B-2's radar has the potential capability to detect and locate large moving targets like armored divisions on the march, so it would not require the assistance of other aircraft like JSTARS. Unlike individual vehicles—mobile ballistic missile launchers or mobile command posts, for example—invading armies are hard to hide, are easy to identify well enough to attack, and must keep moving (i.e., invading) to be effective. Also, the B-2 should not need external assistance in suppressing defenses. As a result, the *B-2 is particularly well suited for use in the initial stages of a campaign, and that rationale, although controversial, was a more convincing argument for the B-2 than its nuclear role even during the Cold War.*

Another Role: Massing Firepower Against Tactical Forces. As a campaign progresses and more U.S. forces arrive in the theater, the role of heavy bombers can evolve in different ways. One possibility is releasing the heavy bombers for use elsewhere if near-simultaneous conflicts were to break out. A more standard use for heavy bombers is to continue to provide massive firepower when the situation demands. Supplying massive firepower is a fundamental advantage that heavy bombers offer even if other forces are present.

The United States has, of course, used bombers that way in the past, sometimes effectively, sometimes not.[5] However, deciding how best to apply that massive firepower has been a subject of continuing controversy since the days

---

[5]For recent analyses of the effectiveness of conventionally armed heavy bombers in Vietnam and elsewhere, see Johnson (forthcoming) and Clodfelter (1989).

of Giulio Douhet and Billy Mitchell. RAND analysis has, for a number of years, highlighted the potential value of using bombers against tactical forces.

For example, consider how heavy bombers could have been employed most effectively in NATO's central region during the Cold War days. The dominant problem that NATO faced in the central region was halting an armored invasion by a numerically superior Warsaw Pact force: failure meant defeat no matter what else happened in the theater; success meant victory. Recognizing this, NATO focused its attention for decades on trying to provide its tactical ground and air forces with suitable weapons to defeat armor. By contrast, SAC's doctrine at the time called for using B-52s to attack fixed targets deep in the Warsaw Pact's rear area. Not only would the B-52s not have survived repeated sorties into the Warsaw Pact's rear area if they had to penetrate Pact air defenses, but these attacks would also probably have had little effect on the outcome of the war. By contrast, arming the bombers with cruise missiles that NATO was planning to buy for its fighter forces and using those missiles for relatively shallow attacks to help concentrate massive firepower against armored columns and air defenses, along with selected attacks on key bridges and other chokepoints, would have had a much more direct effect on the war and would have freed fighter sorties for other missions.

RAND analysis showed that conventional B-52 forces of the size that the United States was considering at the time, if equipped with proper weapons and operating in conjunction with other NATO forces, could have halted a Warsaw Pact armored invasion. *Using bombers this way runs directly counter to the strategic bombing doctrine that has governed the employment concepts for long-range bombers since their inception.* However, more flexible thinking about the most effective way to use bombers is going to be even more important in developing a joint arms concept of military operations to deal with the exigencies of the emerging world.[6]

Other Potential Roles. Other roles might emerge for bombers that are difficult to plan for in advance. For example, the proliferation of weapons of mass destruction and theater ballistic missiles is receiving a considerable amount of attention these days. So far, nobody has come up with a satisfactory way to deal with this important problem, although all sorts of possibilities are being vigorously examined. Long-range bombers could possibly play a role in defeating mobile ballistic missiles. Ironically, this is a variant of the old strategic relocatable target (SRT) problem that didn't make much sense in the old strategic world but might in the new world where the missiles could become a

---

[6]For hints of the brewing doctrinal and tactical dispute, see Warden (1989) for a view that is popular in many parts of the U.S. Air Force. For a comparison from a naval perspective of Air Force and Navy approaches to using airpower in the Gulf War, see Friedman (1991:169–196).

centerpiece of an enemy's capability rather than merely a footnote. On the other hand, absent a viable operational concept, there is little basis for using this class of mission to structure the force.

How Potential Targets Drive Bomber Force Structure

Given these two major roles, what are the potential *targets* and how effective would bombers be against them?

Determining What Matters. The essence of analysis of conventional bomber effectiveness is determining what matters for a range of classes of conflicts and its meaning for bomber force structure. The analytical tools available range from elaborate campaign models to simpler models to common sense. The problem is much more complex than the old SIOP-style analysis, where the main measure of effectiveness was the number of targets of various sorts, perhaps weighted by value assessments, that could be destroyed. Here, making some estimate of the overall effect of destroying particular kinds of targets is an integral part of the analysis. Moreover, the need to reattack some classes of targets periodically affects force structure, and the timeliness issue is particularly important in structuring the overall bomber force.

What follows shows some of the flavor of our analysis. In general, we come to very different conclusions than, for example, Colonel John Warden did in his influential analysis of planning air campaigns (Warden, 1989) or the notions of "strategic paralysis" that are currently in vogue in some circles.[7] That in turn leads us to different views about structuring bomber forces than the conventional wisdom in the Air Force suggests. That conventional wisdom was shaped by old world attitudes, however, and this is an appropriate time to reexamine them.

Establishing Target Classes. Figure 10 shows how we categorized and divided potential bomber targets for the purposes of analysis. We defined three major categories of targets:

- *"Strategic" fixed targets:* Installations that are important to a nation's long-term military potential and its economic well-being, but do not, in general, have much short-term impact on its ability to make war. (National command centers are a potential exception.)

- *Fixed tactical targets:* The set of installations in fixed locations that might actually contribute to an ongoing war. Targeting priorities will obviously vary from case to case.

---

[7]For a discussion of "strategic paralysis" as an objective for the employment of airpower, see Barlow (1992). RAND is conducting research to assess strategic paralysis issues and options in some detail.

RAND#130-37-0194

"Strategic" fixed targets	Fixed tactical targets	Mobile tactical targets
National Command Centers	Airfields	Armored forces
Nuclear facilities	— Shelters	Infantry
Chemical/biological weapons facilities	— Parking areas and shelters	Ships
Missile and aircraft production facilities	— Runways	Mobile SAM sites
Other munitions production facilities	Command, control, and communications	Mobile offensive missiles
Power plants	EW/GCI	Mobile C^3
Chemical plants	Fixed SAM sites	
Refineries/POL	Fixed field fortifications	
Port facilities	Fixed offensive missile sites	
	Critical lines of communication (e.g., highway bridges)	

Figure 10—Potential Target Classes for Heavy Bomber Attack
in Conventional Operations

- *Mobile tactical targets:* The set of mobile or relocatable targets that could have an impact on an ongoing war. Again, some kinds of targets are going to be more valuable than others in particular situations.

The problem for structuring the bomber force is not to determine a rigid hierarchy of targets for bombers to attack. Rather, it is the opposite. In specific future situations, a theater commander on the scene (or, perhaps, a political leader if the issue is sensitive enough) will have to make the call about what is most important to attack at any particular moment in the conflict. The problem for force planners is to try to make sure that the commander has the right aircraft and weapons available to give him the flexibility to do whatever he needs to do. The challenge is doing that in a fiscally constrained world. The analytical problem is to identify what factors drive the size and/or the quality of the bomber force and its weapons. Of particular interest are:

- Target sets that could be "weapon sinks" and drive force requirements (tactical airfields and field fortifications are examples).

- Target sets where the kind of massive firepower that bombers can supply matters.

- Target sets that must be attacked at a particular time and perhaps in large numbers because of the operational tempo of the campaign (invading armored forces are an example).

- Targets that require high-quality or special weapons to destroy (various kinds of underground bunkers are typical examples).

- Small sets of targets that could dramatically affect the outcome of a campaign if destroyed at the right time. (Examples are very hard to define, the conventional wisdom to the contrary notwithstanding. Saddam Hussein is the usual example cited. Even in cases where this could be true, the effect on force structure, beyond assuring that it includes effective weapons, is generally nil.)

- Other targets that must be attacked at the right time to have an impact (weapon storage sites and nuclear facilities where critical nuclear materials could be removed quickly are examples).

Attacking Fixed Targets. In our analysis of some of the "old world" cases involving fighting Soviet forces on several fronts outside Central Europe simultaneously, fixed target sets were major factors in sizing the bomber force. The most demanding sort of air campaign against fixed targets we identified that had reasonably high military leverage was a sustained attack against moderately large numbers of airfields. If such an attack were comprehensive enough to include attacks on runways, support facilities, sheltered aircraft, and aircraft in the open, large quantities of high-quality, diverse weapons could be required to attack a number of bases, particularly if the enemy were able to repair damage to airfields rapidly enough to require periodic reattacks. *However, the need for this level of attack on enemy airfields is more typical of the old world than the new.* Even the former Warsaw Pact air forces might not have been formidable enough to justify an attack of this scale. Thus, only an emerging regional superpower that relied heavily on its air force would be likely to warrant a large bomber attack on air bases early in a campaign and, therefore, require a large number of bombers devoted to attacking fixed targets. We see no such threats on the horizon now.

In fact, a general characteristic of the sorts of countries that the United States is likely to collide with in the new world is that they *do not have large numbers of valuable fixed targets.* Granted, that could appear to be the case because the United States has never bothered to look hard for targets in most countries. We found a few cases where destroying a relatively small set of targets might offer considerable leverage (generally attacks against chokepoints in unfavorable terrain to delay an invading force), but when those unusual situations occurred, a small, properly equipped bomber force would have been sufficient for the task.

Simply on first principles, Third World countries in particular don't have large numbers of valuable "strategic" targets, and few of those that do exist need to be attacked in either a timely way or en masse. Thus, air campaigns against these sorts of fixed targets should never stress the size of a future bomber force as long as the bombers have suitable weapons.

The same general message applies to attacks against most kinds of fixed tactical targets, although there are a few wrinkles that are worth discussing briefly. We generally allocated some bomber attacks early in a major campaign to suppressing selected elements of enemy air defenses and attacking a few major command-and-control installations.   However, we usually found that only relatively limited defense suppression attacks were likely to be either necessary or particularly effective during the initial phases of the campaign when stealthy aircraft and cruise missiles were carrying the load before the bulk of U.S. forces reached the theater.

Command-and-control attacks are more problematical, even though the conventional wisdom says that they should have a very high priority. (One also needs to distinguish between a "command-and-control" attack used as a euphemism for trying to kill enemy leadership *per se* and a real command-and-control attack that is intended to degrade the enemy's military capability.) There are several general problems with designing command-and-control attacks:

- Defining an enemy's command-and-control network (and, therefore, understanding how to attack it) is an extremely difficult intelligence problem in any case and virtually impossible in the sort of future time frame that would be of use to force planners.

- Measuring the effects of command-and-control attacks is extremely difficult, except perhaps in very specific, structured situations.

- The size of potentially effective command-and-control attacks bifurcates. If a small number of critical nodes can really be identified, then the attacks should only require a modest number of appropriate weapons. If not, the necessary attacks could be massive.

As a practical matter, a battlefield commander is likely to try to attack at least a modest number of key command-and-control sites in hopes that such attacks *will* disrupt the enemy's warfighting capability, so force planners need to provide forces that allow him that option. On the other hand, planning forces on the assumption that such attacks would be adequate to defeat an enemy *in lieu of* direct attacks on its forces would be extremely risky. As a result, the possible need to attack critical command-control sites should have little effect on the overall size of future bomber forces, although it does reinforce the need for combinations of stealth and standoff weapons.

Attacking Mobile Forces. Mobile targets come in a variety of flavors, as Figure 10 shows. Of the possibilities, the class of targets that is probably most useful for structuring a portion of the future U.S. bomber force is advancing armor.[8] There are several reasons why:

- An armored invasion against an ill-prepared adversary gives the attacker control of the operational tempo of a campaign and must be countered effectively to avoid a decisive defeat that could be difficult and costly to reverse.

- In the early days of a campaign, the only option available might be long-range bombers for countering the armored advance because Army forces might not have arrived in necessary numbers and Navy forces, if present, would lack the firepower necessary to halt the advance.

- Invading armored forces in division strength are relatively easy targets for appropriate sensors to detect, unlike, say, mobile missiles.

- Large formations of armored vehicles make ideal targets for the kind of massive firepower that bombers can deliver.

Figure 11 shows why suitable armed bombers are an attractive option for countering an armored invasion.[9] The figure shows "before" and "after" computer simulation images of an Iraqi armored division in a tightly packed formation advancing into Saudi Arabia. The image on the right shows the results of an attack by three B-2s armed with inertially guided tactical munitions dispensers (TMDs) carrying Skeet submunitions.[10] Over half of the combat vehicles in the division were destroyed within seconds, which should not only be enough to stop that division, but also, according to standard rules of thumb, damage it so heavily that it could not be reconstituted. Each damaged vehicle

---

[8]For a more thorough unclassified treatment of the use of heavy bombers against armored forces, see Buchan et al. (1992).

[9]These particular simulation results were generated using the JANUS model. JANUS is a high-resolution, stochastic, two-sided, closed, interactive, computerized, ground combat simulation/wargame used for combat developments, doctrine analysis, tactics investigation, scenario development, field test simulation, and training. JANUS is used at more than 24 sites within the United States Army, and by RAND, the Institute for Defense Analyses, and Lawrence Livermore Laboratories, where JANUS was first developed.

Other models were also employed in the armor-interdiction analysis. These included GAMES, a model used widely in Army circles, and two simpler in-house models.

[10]Adding inertial guidance packages to gravity weapons like bombs and TMDs provides a cheap means for increasing their accuracy. It allows the bomber crew to control the pattern of their weapons, thereby employing them much more effectively against an area target such as an armored division. Skeet is a "smart" submunition that uses infrared sensors to detect hot spots on vehicles and home in on them. The Air Force's Air Combat Command proposes to begin procuring limited production quantities of Skeet submunitions this year.

RAND#130-38-0194

Armored division in road march   Combat vehicles destroyed by B-2 raid

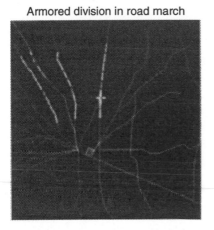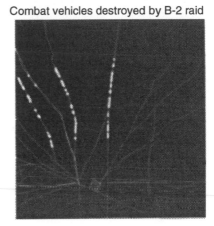

* 3 B-2s above the armored column
* Inertially guided TMD/Skeet submunitions

Figure 11—Potential B-2 Effectiveness in Armor Interdiction

was hit by several Skeet submunitions, typically about five, thereby effectively removing any ambiguity about damage levels to vehicles. Thus, heavy bombers are particularly effective against armor because they can concentrate massive precision firepower against a class of target that is both vulnerable to that kind of attack and important to destroy in a timely manner.

Effects on the Overall Campaign. We found that the level of interdiction capability described in Figure 11 would be sufficient to halt an armored invasion of Saudi Arabia by Iraq virtually in its tracks. In its absence, the sort of ground forces that Iraq possessed at the outset of the Gulf War could have captured key ports, airfields, and oil fields in Saudi Arabia in a matter of days *even if Saudi forces on the scene fought effectively and consistently against them.* If the Saudi resistance had collapsed as the Kuwaitis did, the situation could have been much worse. That is why the armor interdiction mission is so important and why it should be a high-priority mission for bombers if they are the only ones on the scene. *We could identify no other target set that bombers could attack that could solve this problem or have an equally dramatic effect on this class of campaign.*

Moreover, using a one-division/day interdiction rate for planning purposes is not a bad standard for major theater campaigns based on historical experience. Defeating armor at that rate *would have halted any armored invasion in history except the U.S. invasion of Iraq in Desert Storm.* Even there, however, the cost of the U.S. victory would have been much higher if the Iraqis had had this sort of interdiction capability, and the prospect of such losses might have given the United States pause in considering such an operation. Moreover, had the allies spread their offensive over more invasion corridors, they might even have been defeated by such an interdiction capability. In the emerging world, relatively few countries could mount this level of armored invasion against a relatively unprepared foe. Thus, having a bomber force that could, among its other capabilities, destroy an armored division per day should both provide a unique and important warfighting capability and act as a powerful deterrent in the new world.

The Importance of Weapons

Every RAND study of the effective use of airpower in the last decade has emphasized the importance of high-quality weapons. That is true for bombers as well as fighters. Figure 12 shows generically how the relative effectiveness of various kinds of weapons improves against various kinds of targets as weapon accuracy increases. It also shows what various kinds of guidance technologies can achieve. *In general, we found that the technical capability exists to allow conven-*

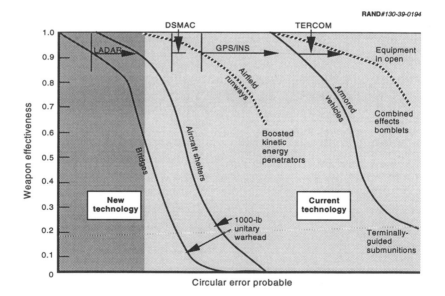

Figure 12—Conventional Munitions Effectiveness

tional weapons to destroy virtually any target of interest as long as its location and nature are known precisely. The issue is finding the most cost-effective weapons to procure. We found that bombers offer several advantages in this regard.

Matching bombers and weapons is one of the most critical issues in structuring a bomber force for the new world. Figure 13 emphasizes some of the key issues:

- Bomber payload capacity for various types of weapons.
- Weapon standoff range.
- Programmatic status of various weapons.

As the figure shows, there are substantial payload advantages for the bomber if it can penetrate to within a few miles of its target. If the bomber has to stand off more than a few miles, the volume and shape of existing and planned weapons as well as the carriage possibilities on the bombers severely limit the number of weapons that the bombers can carry.[11]   Once that threshold has been crossed, increasing the standoff range of the weapon has little or no effect on the bomber. Another advantage of employing gravity and very-short-range glide weapons is that cheap technological improvements can dramatically improve their effectiveness. We found, for example, that adding inertial guidance kits can make existing stockpile bombs and munitions dispensers very effective at a very low cost without the need to initiate entire new weapons programs.

Programmatic status is an important consideration as well, especially given current fiscal constraints that make beginning new programs particularly difficult. Recently, the Joint Standoff Weapon (JSOW) and the Joint Direct Attack Munition (JDAM) have been established to provide bombers and fighters with new short-range weapons. (Their characteristics are summarized in Table 3.) In addition, TSSAM and ALCM-C, medium- and long-range conventional cruise missiles, respectively, have emerged out of the "black" world.

---

[11]This has less to do with the laws of physics than with artifacts of the design of the various bombers—especially their bomb racks, rotary launchers, and bomb bays—and both existing and planned weapons. If the need were great enough, new weapons with modest (i.e., 50–60 nmi) standoff range could probably be designed that could be carried in larger numbers on the bombers. At some point, that might be justified. However, at the very least, new weapons programs would be needed, a difficult process in the current fiscal environment. Moreover, significant modifications to the bombers would probably be needed to permit them to use their payload capability more efficiently. Some of our current research addresses these issues and will analyze how major an effort would be required to modify the bombers.

RAND#130-40-0194

• Existing weapons • *Planned weapons* • **Possible new weapons**	Penetrating bombers			Standoff cruise missile carriers
	Very short range	Short range	Medium range	Long range
Nuclear weapons	Bombs		Short range attack missile (SRAM-A)?	Air launched cruise missile (ALCM)
			~~SRAM II~~	Advanced cruise missile (ACM)**
Conventional weapons	Bombs, submunitions dispensers —*Inertially guided weapons* • Bombs (JDAM-I) • **TMDs** —*Other precision-guided bombs (JDAM-III)**	*Have Nap* *Joint Standoff Weapon (JSOW)*	*Tri-Service Standoff Attack Missile (TSSAM)*	Tomahawk? ALCM-C **New conventional cruise missile**
Typical carriage capability	30–80 (≤1000 lb) 16–24 (2000 lb)	8–22		

* Joint Direct Attack Munition (JDAM)
** Buy limited to 528 (PAA), 640 (TAI)

Figure 13—Bomber Weapon Options

Table 3

JSOW and JDAM Weapon Systems

Weapon Name	General Description	Dimensions Length × Width (in)	Warhead Weight and Type	Performance Range (nmi)
JSOW[a]	Unpowered, GPS-aided standoff weapon	160 × 16.51	1000-lb class 24 Skeet submunitions	15–50 nmi
JDAM[b]	Inertial/GPS-aided bomb	154 × 18.1	~2000-lb high explosive	~18 nmi from high altitude
JDAM-II[c]	Inertial/GPS-aided bomb	90 × 10.6	502-lb high explosive	~18 nmi from high altitude
JDAM-PIP[d]	Inertial/GPS-aided bomb with terminal seeker	>154 × 18.1	~2000-lb high explosive	~18 nmi from high altitude

[a]Joint Standoff Weapon (JSOW).
[b]Joint Direct Attack Munition (JDAM). A 1000-lb warhead is planned for the F-22.
[c]For the U.S. Navy.
[d]JDAM Product Improvement Program (restructure of the former JDAM-III program).

ALCM-C was used successfully by B-52s in the early hours of Desert Storm. Key questions remain, including the following:

- Does a moderate-range cruise missile such as TSSAM have adequate range to allow current bombers to stand off beyond the range of future enemy air defenses?
- Will limiting the buy of ACMs to 640 allow enough ALCMs to be converted for conventional use (i.e., to ALCM-Cs) to eliminate the need to develop a new long-range conventional cruise missile?
- Is the current emphasis on large (e.g., 2000-lb) bombs warranted, or should more emphasis be placed on improving the capabilities of smaller (e.g., 500-lb) weapons?
- Are JSOW and JDAM the right weapons for all the bombers?

Figure 14 further illustrates the importance of high-quality weapons in attacking a spectrum of fixed targets effectively and efficiently. The figure shows the relative numbers of bomber sorties necessary to destroy a comprehensive set of "strategic" targets in a representative Third World nation. The comparisons are striking. The best bomber—the B-2—would need roughly three times as many sorties to destroy a particular set of fixed targets if it had to employ "dumb" 500-lb iron bombs than any appropriate combination of new or old bomber and high-quality weapons. Notice also that *there is very little difference*

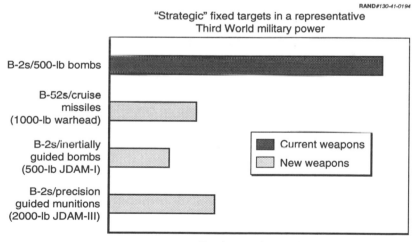

Figure 14—Bomber Weapon Effectiveness Against Fixed Targets

in sortie requirements among the high-quality weapon options. The slight differences include some interesting wrinkles, however:

- The most efficient combination shown is the B-2 armed with inertially guided 500-lb bombs, which are both smaller and less accurate (but much cheaper) than the cruise missiles or precision-guided weapons used in the other cases. The reason is that this target set, which is typical of many that we examined, contains a number of relatively large facilities that could be attacked very efficiently with controlled patterns of moderately accurate small weapons, *exactly the kind of payload that a penetrating heavy bomber can deliver!* This highlights the potential value of *cheap upgrades to small bombs* for bombers.

- There are no compelling reasons not to rely primarily on standoff cruise missiles to attack most fixed targets in the early phases of future wars, particularly in view of the small B-2 buy currently authorized. That would make effective use of current bombers.

These general findings are consistent with the experience of Desert Storm, where B-52s dropped nearly a third of all the bombs used in the war[12] but did much less measurable damage to particular targets than the F-117s did with many fewer laser-guided bombs. Effective in the normal sense or not, the B-52 raids apparently did scare the wits out of dug-in Iraqi troops, prompting many to surrender. Perhaps General Chuck Horner, the CENTAF commander in the Gulf War, was correct when he observed that this sort of massive terror bombing might harden the will of civilian populations, but it certainly seemed to break the will of military forces. With more accurate bombs (but not necessarily anything nearly as accurate as laser-guided bombs), the bombing might have proven physically as well as psychologically effective. Even with current accuracies, bombs delivered in large quantities can help open corridors for offensive ground forces.

Survivability of Bombers

Survivability of bombers is likely to become even more important than usual in the future:

- With a bomber force of limited size and, at most, one open production line (i.e., the B-2 line), losing bombers would have both immediate and long-term impact on U.S. military capability.

---

[12]Accounts of the Gulf War, including bombing statistics, abound. The "official version" is U.S. Department of Defense (1992). Hallion (1992), Coyne (1992), and Winnefeld, Niblack, and Johnson (1994) focus on the air war.

- Losing bombers in the early phases of a conventional war could have an immediate impact on the perceptions of all concerned about who was likely to win (and, therefore, which side to choose, whether to become involved, etc.), what the cost was likely to be, etc.

As a result, the United States is likely to be especially risk averse in using its bomber force, particularly in either the early stages of a conflict or in raids (e.g., Libya) where the primary objective is to send a political message. Since it is precisely those kinds of operations for which bombers are particularly well suited, those are the stressing cases on which bomber survivability analysis should focus. As noted earlier, bomber survivability is much less an issue in the later stages of a conflict when the enemy's air defenses have been beaten down and the bombers can expect considerable help in penetrating what defenses remain (e.g., escorts, jamming).

The details of bombers' capability to penetrate specific air defenses remain classified. However, Figure 15 shows the kinds of results one could expect from notional bombers facing generic classes of air defenses in two different kinds of countries that might "bound" the likely situations that the United States might have to deal with in the future. The details of the postulated air defenses vary considerably, but both have at least a small number of modern airborne interceptors and enough modern SAMs to provide terminal defenses for at least a few key installations.

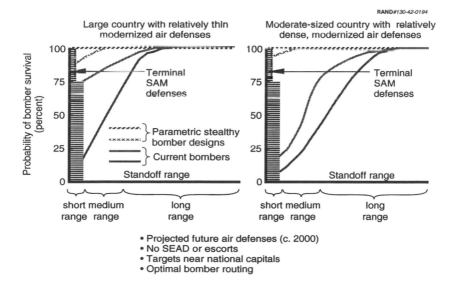

Figure 15—Notional Penetration Capability of Bombers Against Future Air Defenses

The key variable in Figure 15 is how close the bombers can get to their targets without running excessive risks. That equates to the amount of standoff range that their weapons need. Recall from Figure 13 that there are substantial payload advantages if the bombers can approach to within a few miles (i.e., 5–15 nmi) of their targets. Beyond that, there is a substantial payload penalty to pay. Moreover, the cost of the weapons generally increases substantially. Both the payload penalty and the weapon costs are relatively insensitive to the actual standoff range required once the initial threshold has been exceeded. However, there could be a major programmatic issue if bombers needed a new long-range cruise missile to stay out of harm's way.

There are several general messages from Figure 15. The first is the impact of stealth. The three notional stealth bomber designs shown permit the bombers to fly to within a short distance of targets deep in the homelands of the two countries shown. Even the least stealthy of the three bombers would have to rely on standoff weapons of only modest range to attack their targets directly or suppress critical defense sites near them. Thus, they could take maximum advantage of their potential payload capability and rely mainly on weapons that are currently in development.

The details of stealth technology remain highly classified. However, enough material has been presented in the open literature to help explain in general terms why these results come out the way they do.[13] Key elements of stealth include the following:

- Attention to all the ways that an aircraft could be detected (e.g., radar, infrared sensors, visual sighting, acoustic signature, etc.).

- Use of radar absorbing materials (RAM) to absorb as much incident radar energy as possible.

- Shaping the body to direct reflected radar energy in relatively harmless directions. (Bistatic radar systems could, in principle, be a problem, but constructing an effective defensive system based on bistatic radars would be extremely expensive and operationally difficult.)

- Locating the engine nozzles so that the aircraft appears "hot" only from a very limited range of viewing angles.

Despite some enthusiasts' unfortunate claims to the contrary, stealth technology does not represent anything like a "Romulan cloaking device" that renders aircraft invisible. Rather, it does two things:

---

[13]Sweetman (1989:37–63, 85–119) describes the evolution of stealth technology in general and its application to the B-2. More technical descriptions of stealth techniques appear in Knott et al. (1985:159–220, 239–272) and Lynch (1992).

- Stealth dramatically reduces the ranges at which sensors can detect a vehicle from a wide variety of viewing angles.

- Stealth allows long-range detection in only a few directions and hard presses any defenders that do detect the vehicles from these angles to do anything about it, by making it difficult to maintain a track and engage the stealthy vehicle.

The net effect of stealth is to *minimize the number of engagement opportunities that the defense gets* rather than allowing engagements to occur and focusing on defeating the defenses each time, which is how current bombers try to survive, by relying on electronic countermeasures to defeat enemy weapons, for example. Actually, stealth could reduce the effectiveness of some defensive weapons in any engagements that do occur by reducing the effectiveness of some kinds of fuses and seekers. However, that should be considered more a "bonus" effect than a fundamental aim of stealth.

That is why stealthy bombers do so well in situations such as those illustrated in Figure 15. They survive by:

- Avoiding the dominant area air defense threat, which in most countries is airborne interceptors.

- Routing around, or detecting and avoiding, modest numbers of high-quality SAMs that might be encountered on the way to targets.

- Flying above the coverage of antiaircraft artillery (AAA) and short-range SAMs that could be numerous and difficult to avoid at low altitude.

- Using short-range standoff weapons to attack targets defended by high-quality SAMs.

Nonstealthy bombers do not fare nearly as well, as Figure 15 shows, precisely because the defense gets too many chances to engage them. Even the modest numbers of modern airborne interceptors that most Third World countries are likely to have in the future could pose a formidable threat to non-stealthy bombers trying to penetrate deep into hostile territory without assistance. Differences in bomber characteristics (e.g., radar cross-section, speed) make some difference in the degree of risk, as Figure 15 indicates. However, if the risk of bomber attrition is to remain very low in the early stages of a conflict, *nonstealthy bombers need long-range cruise missiles* for deep attack regardless of the details of the defenses, the relative size of the country being attacked, or the exact characteristics of the bomber. Identifying that kind of "simple truth" is precisely the objective of this kind of analysis.

Implications for Bomber Force Structure and Operational Employment

Given the preceding considerations of roles, how targets determine force structure needs, and the importance of weapons and survivability, what are the necessary bomber force structures to support a spectrum of overall concepts for U.S. power projection abroad?

Planning for the "New World." Nuclear arms control could potentially have seriously restricted the bomber force structure options for conventional operations. However, neither the START I nor START II agreement appears to limit U.S. possibilities for maintaining an effective bomber force for either nuclear or conventional operations in the new world. Even before the old world finally died out, our analysis showed that conventional rather than nuclear mission requirements were dominating the calculus of structuring the bomber force. During the transition, we found four generic classes of situations that dominated bomber force structure considerations:

- *Limited raids.* Raids of the Libya variety require a small number of long-range bombers with high-quality weapons. For most scenarios, bombers with long-range cruise missiles would be adequate, probably even preferable. For operations demanding more flexibility, stealthy B-2s might be the system of choice. In either case, force size is not a driving factor but quality is, because of the risk to the aircraft and the need for effective weapons and targeting systems.

- *Selective attacks on a spectrum of key fixed targets.* Analyzing those relatively unusual situations where attacking a modest number of fixed targets could be militarily decisive early in a campaign suggested that about one wing of long-range cruise missile carriers or B-2s would probably be an adequate force. If this is the only way bombers were to be employed, such a force might be sufficient. Interestingly, the specific cases that led to this generic class of scenario were more typical of the old world than the new.

- *Major regional conflict with a major regional power.* This class of conflict typically places serious demands on most elements of U.S. military forces. A large-scale armored invasion might be part of such a conflict. If so, that is probably going to be the driving factor in determining bomber requirements and should certainly be the dominant factor in planning for generic levels of conflicts. This is the kind of situation to which most of the previous analysis of armor interdiction with bombers applies.

- *Major regional conflict with a regional/global superpower.* The difference between this level of conflict and the previous one is the quality of the opposition. It is more typical of the kind of threat that the Warsaw Pact used to pose to NATO, complicated by the fact that in the future, there might not be a comparable military force in place to face the initial assault. For the bomber force, this level of conflict basically requires the ability to deal simultaneously with an armored invasion and the need to attack a substantial number of fixed tactical targets. (Airfields make good planning surrogates and may actually be the most critical targets to attack early on in this sort of campaign.) *It is unclear whether this kind of threat will ever emerge again in the world, and how much weight U.S. planners ought to give to the possibility in making force structure decisions.*

Policymakers could then choose a bomber force based on the class of conflict they wanted to prepare for. Analysis can inform those choices to a degree, but ultimately, value judgments are required.

The new world is likely to prove quite different from the old one in ways that we can anticipate only imperfectly. Probably the key factor for the bomber force is developing the flexibility inherent in the aircraft to do a range of things so that they can cope with any situation, recognizing that bombers are not likely to be much help in solving some kinds of military problems. These include guerrilla conflicts or low-intensity conflicts of the Somalia and Bosnia variety, except for punitive attacks, which are basically subsets of the generic cases described above.

Similarly, in places such as Korea, there are other options available that might be better or at least adequate, although bombers could play a role as they have in the past. The point, from a force planner's perspective, is that *these are lesser included cases of more stressing generic scenarios* and, therefore, are not of much use in structuring the bomber force.

Structuring the Bomber Force. Figure 16 shows the numbers of bombers that recent RAND analysis found to be appropriate for dealing with various

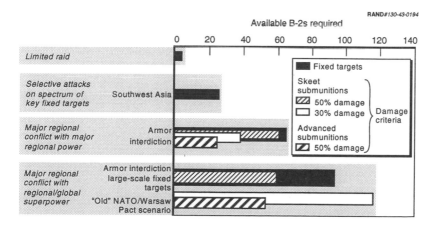

Figure 16—Number of B-2s Required for Conventional Operations

generic classes of scenarios if the bomber force were composed largely of B-2s. With a limited buy of B-2s, a more complex, integrated mix of bombers will be required.

Structuring the Bomber Force for Fixed Targets. In general, considering the spectrum of diverse kinds and levels of conflict, the variations in types of fixed targets to be attacked, the problems of operational tempo of a campaign, and the spectrum of related considerations, a maximum of about 50 properly armed bombers should be adequate for even the most demanding conflicts that are likely to arise in the new world. Moreover, cruise missiles should be able to handle the bulk of the most demanding missions against fixed targets in the initial phases of conflicts.

Structuring the Bomber Force for Armor Interdiction. The B-2 would be the bomber of choice for large-scale armor interdiction early in a conflict because its stealth allows it to get close enough to the targets to take maximum advantage of its payload capacity and its onboard sensors should be adequate to find the armored columns without compromising its location. Thus, the B-2s could be first on the scene and even sustain operations from U.S. bases if necessary, operating as shown in Figure 17.

However, getting three B-2s over the target at the right time (i.e., when the attacker chooses to advance) could be a considerable challenge, depending on the circumstances, and could require many more B-2s. Figure 18 shows the cascading effects of various factors that determine the overall size of the bomber force necessary to support the level of armor interdiction in the simulation. Simple counters by the enemy—spreading formations and interspersing

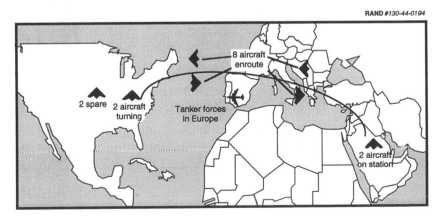

RAND #130-44-0194

Figure 17—Operational Concept for a B-2 Interdiction Campaign in Southwest Asia

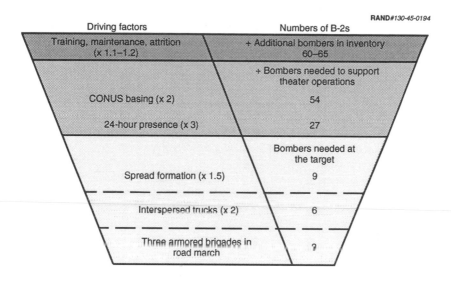

Figure 18—Conventional B-2 Antiarmor Operations—What Drives Force Levels

support vehicles with combat vehicles—could triple the number of B-2s needed over the target. To be able to strike any time the enemy chose to move could triple the number of bombers required to be available for the mission.[14] Having the capacity to conduct operations from bases in CONUS until bombers could move to forward bases could double it again. Adding another 10–20 percent to the overall bomber inventory to account for bombers that are in depot for long-term maintenance, are being used for training, have been lost over the years, or are otherwise unavailable for combat *could lead to a requirement to purchase 60 or more B-2s for the mission alone.*

Since the B-2 buy is currently capped at 20 (see Figure 19), the question is, How effective could those 20 be, and how can this mission be best accomplished? There are two possible paths to explore. The first is to use better technology to improve the capability of the limited number of B-2s in the planned force. The second is to use other forces to supplement their firepower.

---

[14]It is possible that the B-2 will prove not to be stealthy enough to operate safely in daylight; that remains to be proven one way or the other in the test program. However, halving the size of the B-2 force on the assumption that B-2s could operate only at night guarantees an enemy freedom of operations for half a day no matter how stealthy the B-2 turns out to be and *telegraphs that message in advance.* For example, the Iraqis would have had more than ample time to overrun Saudi Arabia before the United States could have responded with tactical forces even if they could only have operated safely during daylight hours.

RAND #130-46-0194

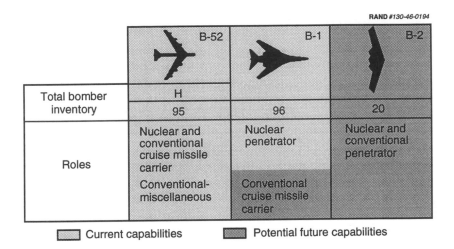

	B-52	B-1	B-2
Total bomber inventory	H 95	96	20
Roles	Nuclear and conventional cruise missile carrier / Conventional-miscellaneous	Nuclear penetrator / Conventional cruise missile carrier	Nuclear and conventional penetrator

Current capabilities   Potential future capabilities

Figure 19—The Largest Currently Proposed U.S. Long-Range Bomber Force

Improved technology might be able to reduce the growth of the bomber force shown in the lightly shaded area at the bottom of Figure 18. In essence, the bomber force is being forced to grow to compensate for the limitations of the Skeet submunitions and the targeting systems on the bomber. Basically the submunitions are being forced to search too large an area looking for suitable targets, and that triples the number of bombers required in this particular example.

Better technology might be able to increase the efficiency of the attack and reduce the number of bombers required. One possibility is using better submunitions. Our initial examination of the possibilities for "buying back" effectiveness suggests that an improvement of at least a factor of two could be achieved, thereby reducing the required B-2 force to about 30. More precise targeting of Skeets might achieve the same effect, but that would place additional demands on the sensors and targeting systems on board the bomber. At some point, however, the continuing competition between sensors and countermeasures is likely to become critical.

Whether using still-better technology could "buy back" the whole factor of three, thereby making a force of about 20 B-2s fully effective, remains to be determined. That is about the limit that better technology could achieve. The other factors shown in Figure 18 reflect operational constraints that are not really amenable to technological "fixes." Compromises there could seriously affect the overall operational effectiveness of the force.

Moreover, even under the best of circumstances, a force of only 20 B-2s would leave virtually no margin for error in performing even this single type of mission. In practice, it might be possible to maintain only two rather than three B-2s on station for armor interdiction. While that would be potentially very useful, it might not achieve the mass of firepower necessary to be really decisive. Moreover, it would give short shrift to other potentially important missions, such as selective defense suppression, that B-2s might be called on to perform.

The solution to this problem lies in finding ways to use the different bombers, and perhaps other early-arriving forces, together to help each other in an integrated operational framework. That approach also provides an overall framework for structuring the whole bomber force.

Operational Employment of a Mixed Bomber Force. Figure 20 shows a basic division of labor among the different bombers that would result in getting the maximum mileage from a constrained bomber force even in a very demanding scenario:

- B-52s armed with cruise missiles to attack time-critical fixed targets early on. (B-1s could be used instead if they were successfully modified to launch cruise missiles.) A maximum force of about 40 or so might be needed for a

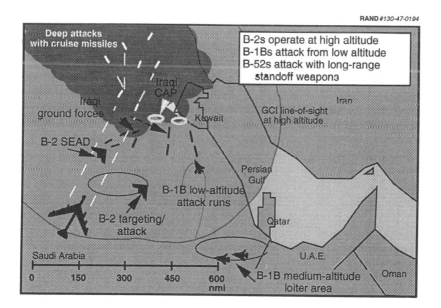

Figure 20—Possible Bomber Operational Concepts for Large-Scale
Conventional Conflicts

single very demanding theater, but fewer would be adequate for most "new world" situations that are likely to emerge. That sort of force could also inflict considerable punishment on a country, apart from any direct military impact, if it were employed against "strategic" targets.

- Twenty (or more) B-2s could be employed against armored forces if necessary to halt an armored blitzkrieg and selected defense sites. This force could also inflict serious damage on advancing infantry. (Ironically, a dispersed advancing infantry force can be more demanding to attack with bombers than armor because the area that needs to be attacked is so large and the "value" is so distributed. In general, we found that a very large bomber force could be needed to stop a large infantry force if usual measures of effectiveness were applied. On the other hand, the psychological shock value of constant bombing and dropping of antipersonnel mines could have a disproportionate impact on an infantry force.)

- B-1s could supplement the B-2s in the interdiction role *if they could be made effective and survivable.*

The first two points are relatively straightforward and were discussed earlier. The last point, however, is at the crux of the problem of how to "make do" with a limited B-2 force. The issues are:

- How to make the B-1 effective and survivable.

- How to use the B-2 to help the B-1.

Using the B-1 for Interdiction. There are several key ingredients to using the B-1 effectively in this role to supplement the B-2:

- Engaging the armored force beyond the reach of the invader's homeland air defenses.

- Targeting the armored force.

- Avoiding or defeating whatever organic air defenses accompany the armored force.

- Minimizing encounters with any airborne interceptors that are operating autonomously providing air cover for the invading force.

Solving the first problem basically requires suppressing any long-range radars or fixed, long-range SAM sites that are near enough to the invader's borders to support the invading force. That is relatively straightforward.

The second problem is much more complex because it requires both the B-2 and the B-1 to operate in new and different ways. The B-2 bears the burden of finding the targets not only for itself but for the B-1 as well. Then, the B-2 has to play a JSTARS-like role and guide the B-1s to their targets. That requires appropriate communication links aboard the aircraft and adds a new dimension to the duties of both aircrews.

Dealing with the organic air defenses of an invading armored force could be challenging as well, depending on the quality of those defenses. It is also the driving factor in determining the kinds of weapons that the bombers need to carry and ultimately, the size of the force required.

Figure 21 shows three generic levels of ground-based air defenses that the B-1s might have to face in engaging an armored division along with the consequences for the bombers. Virtually all armies have at least short-range, low-altitude, air defense systems—antiaircraft artillery (AAA), shoulder-launched infrared SAMs, and the like. As the first case in Figure 21 illustrates, the most effective counter to these kinds of defenses is simply to fly above them. That has the added advantage of allowing B-1s to carry a full load of gravity weapons instead of having to pay the payload penalty for using standoff weapons.

There is a more fundamental message as well in the low-altitude air defense portion of Figure 21. *Flying high may be preferable to flying low in a variety of situations in the new world.* Short-range, low altitude, air defense systems are already present virtually everywhere in the world, and higher-quality systems

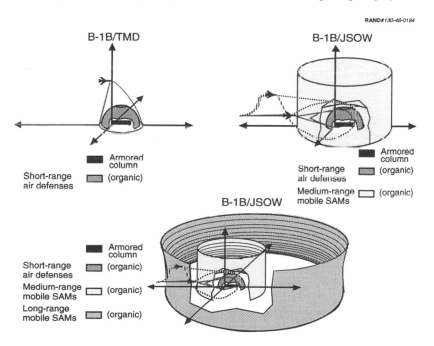

Figure 21—Potential B-1 Vulnerability to Generic Ground-Based Defenses

such as Stingers are proliferating rapidly.[15]   In general, these systems are less effective individually than their longer-range counterparts (although there are exceptions), and they are able to defend less territory.   On the other hand, if they are sufficiently numerous, these systems could collectively "get lucky" and bring down an occasional penetrating bomber, particularly since some of the defensive counters that aircraft typically employ might not be completely effective against some ground-based defenses in the close quarters of a low-altitude engagement.   In the old world of trying to penetrate the Soviet Union or the Warsaw Pact, the high- and medium-altitude air defenses were so good and so numerous in many key areas toward the end of the Cold War that flying low and taking a chance of a random encounter with a low-altitude tactical SAM or AAA system appeared to offer the best hope of surviving, particularly on a one-time-only SIOP mission.

In the new world, the calculus is frequently going to be different.   In some cases, countries may simply lack high-altitude air defenses.   In others, those defenses may be effectively suppressed.   For example, a situation could come up again as it did in Desert Storm, where the massive initial defense-suppression efforts and complete U.S. air supremacy allowed U.S. bombers relatively free rein flying at high altitude.   That is why arming all the bombers with inertially aided TMDs and bombs to give them weapons that are cheap and effective, even if dropped from high altitude, is an attractive option.

On the other hand, high-quality, mobile, medium-range SAMs such as the Russian SA-6 and the U.S. IHAWK are proliferating as well, and they could be used to defend armored divisions.   If they are, then as Figure 21 shows, non-stealthy bombers such as B-1s will no longer have the luxury of flying high and very close to targets with impunity.   Since minimizing risk to bombers is crucial to getting by with a modest-sized bomber force, the prudent course would be to rely on modest-range standoff weapons such as JSOW to stay outside the coverage of the medium-range SAMs.   However, that means reducing the effective payload capacity and increasing the overall number of bombers required by a factor of about three to six.   Also, if the standoff range increases too much, the effectiveness of the attack is going to decrease as Figure 22 shows, thus requiring either better submunitions, more bombers, or both.

As higher-quality, longer-range, mobile SAMs proliferate, the problem could get much worse.   The only practical option is to suppress the long-range SAMs, probably by launching defense-suppression weapons from the B-2, allowing the B-1s to attack the armored columns with JSOW-class antiarmor weapons.

---

[15]Lory Arghavan of RAND has analyzed proliferation of air defense systems of various sorts in a to-be-published study.

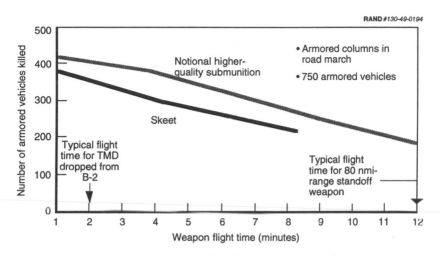

Figure 22—Sensitivity of the Attack's Effectiveness to Weapon Flight Time

Even if EW/GCI radars and ground-based air defense control centers near the border that could direct airborne interceptors can be destroyed, airborne interceptors operating autonomously near the invading armored columns could still pose a threat to the bombers, particularly to the B-1. The operational problem is actually quite complex, depending critically on the actual geometry of the engagement. The B-1 needs to be able to enforce the most favorable geometry in any engagement to give it the best chance of surviving any possible encounters with modern fighters.

Using the B-2 to Support the B-1. One possibility for doing that is using B-2s in the area to "direct traffic," managing the air battle with their stealthy radars in much the same way that an Airborne Warning and Control System (AWACS) does in a more conventional air battle. Basically, the B-2 scans the area for enemy fighters and locates and tracks any that it finds. When the coast is relatively clear, it calls the B-1s, which are orbiting at a safe distance, and directs them along the safest route to the target. Typically, the B-1s would fly low over relatively friendly territory, approach the targets from the safest azimuth, launch their weapons, and leave along a path selected by the B-2s that were orchestrating the engagement.

That is a tall order for both the B-1 and B-2. Different types of bombers have never before been used on combined operations. Moreover, the B-2 would have to play a JSTARS and AWACS-like role in addition to delivering weapons itself. That goes far beyond anything the B-2 was originally intended to do and would pose considerable challenges to both the bombers' human crews and their technical capability. Although the bombers probably have the potential capability to do these new kinds of missions, technical modifications would undoubtedly be required, and considerable practice would be necessary to demonstrate that the operational concepts were really practical. *This kind of innovative use of bombers is probably the key to success in the new world.* The operational complexity is also part of the price for buying only a small force of B-2 bombers.

Bombers and Other Forces: Competition and Cooperation. As the U.S. military shrinks in size, competition for resources is inevitable. One likely result is a sharpening of distinctions among appropriate roles and missions (i.e., who does what) both among and within the various services. Figure 23 illustrates the kind of trade that is going to be made more often. It compares the total potential killing capacity of B-2 bombers and a new stealthy medium-range attack aircraft, the AX, based on aircraft carriers, against armored vehicles in the early stages of a conflict when no other forces were available. The basic assumptions are the following:

- The bombers are based in CONUS, and the carriers on station are already in place at the start of the war and in range of their targets.
- The aircraft have comparable weapons (i.e., Skeet antiarmor submunitions).
- Each aircraft carrier carries one full wing of AX attack aircraft as part of its total complement of aircraft.
- Both can sustain operations as long as necessary.

The comparison considers the potential AX aircraft designs, all of which have much more range-payload capability than current A-6 and F/A-18 naval attack aircraft. The figure shows that 14 B-2s could produce about the same total firepower as three carriers worth of the largest AX aircraft considered, six carriers worth with the medium-sized AX, or nine carriers worth with the smallest of the AX designs. That means, in the latter case for example, it would take three-fourths of the currently planned carrier fleet using a new aircraft to deliver the same firepower as 70 percent of the currently planned (and largely paid for) B-2 fleet in this particular mission.

In the larger scheme of things, this suggests that heavy bombers are better suited for massive attacks against ground targets than carrier-based aircraft. A better role for carrier-based aircraft if the carriers were already on the scene would be extended air defense command-and-control in support of long-range bombers.

In a similar vein, B-1s could replace other tactical aircraft in some types of long-range interdiction and deep-strike missions, operating in conjunction with other aircraft in the area. We have only begun doing these trades, so we do not know how they will come out. However, retaining additional B-1s and putting them at risk along with other tactical aircraft could be a cost-effective option in the current fiscally austere environment.

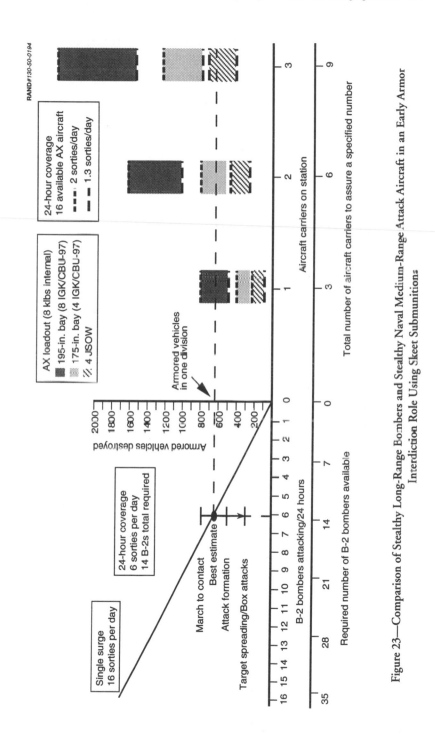

Figure 23—Comparison of Stealthy Long-Range Bombers and Stealthy Naval Medium-Range Attack Aircraft in an Early Armor Interdiction Role Using Skeet Submunitions

Other Considerations. There are a number of other factors important to bombers that this discussion has barely touched on. For example, tankers are critical to bomber operations and are going to be much in demand for any future crisis where U.S. forces have to deploy overseas. In general, we found the critical element to be *access to overseas bases for tankers.* If tankers can only use CONUS bases, the numbers required could quickly become prohibitive.

Logistics support, maintenance, spare parts, and predeployed or rapidly deployable weapons stockpiles are going to be important as well. That could be a particular problem for the B-1, since it was never really intended to fly sustained conventional missions.

CRITICAL DECISIONS FOR THE FUTURE BOMBER FORCE

An Integrated Approach to Bomber Modernization

Figure 24 shows a "mini-roadmap" charting the critical issues that the Air Force needs to address over the next few years in modernizing its bomber force to cope with problems that might emerge in the new world. The key for both conventional operations and nuclear war, if the danger were to reemerge, is

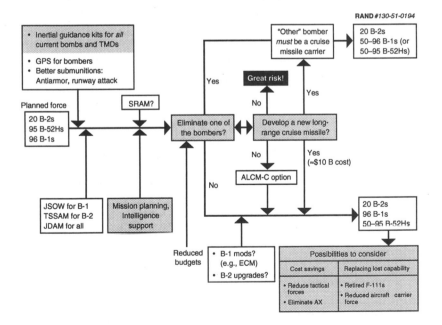

Figure 24—Possible Evolutionary Paths for the Bomber Force

providing appropriate weapons for the bombers along with whatever supporting systems are necessary to make them effective.

One particularly critical early decision is adding inertial guidance kits to *all* current bombs, particularly the 500-lb MK82, and TMDs. Adding inertial guidance kits only to 2000-lb bombs would miss an opportunity to use the force more effectively. Equipping all three bombers to carry these weapons would allow the United States to conduct another Desert Storm–type operation in which bombers operated in a relatively benign environment, but this time the improved weapons would make the bombers much more effective. Best of all, the cost of this improvement would be quite modest.

Mixing and matching the other bombers and weapons suggests the following critical pairings:

• A short-range, standoff weapon (e.g., JSOW) for the B-1.
• A longer-range defense suppression missile for the B-2.

Improved antiarmor submunitions (i.e., better than Skeet) and runway attack submunitions would greatly improve the effectiveness of the entire Air Force and other services as well. If nuclear use of bombers is to be retained as a serious future option, the penetrating bombers need a high-performance, short-range, standoff weapon such as the Short Range Attack Missile (SRAM) to defeat modern terminal defenses. Given the cancellation of SRAM II, either the safety problems with SRAM-A are going to have to be solved or a new missile is going to have to be developed. Since others covet the current SRAM boosters for other applications (e.g., tactical ballistic missile defense), "benign neglect" could be a risky approach to this issue.

A similar problem could exist in the nuclear cruise missile world because of the limited buy of ACMs. Converting more of the current ALCMs to conventional cruise missiles like the ones that B-52s launched in Desert Storm would reduce the stockpile of existing nuclear cruise missiles still further. Even preserving the nuclear certification of some of the bombers could become an issue as they are modified for more demanding conventional missions. *At some point, a conscious decision should be made about the future nuclear role of bombers* rather than allowing the capability to wither away implicitly.

However, the Air Force has to face two major decisions:

• Retire or not retire one of the three bombers.
• Develop a new long-range cruise missile.

The order and logic of the decisions are important. *The choices on these questions would be considerably easier if the Air Force also had the option of procuring a larger B-2 force.*

444 New Challenges for Defense Planning

If the Air Force chooses to eliminate either the B-1 or the B-52H and procures only 20 B-2s, then the bomber it retains *must* be a long-range cruise missile carrier to minimize the risk to the bomber force while still providing it with some capability to play a useful role in the critical early stages of a conflict. With a bomber force this small and with little hope for building more in a reasonable amount of time, minimizing the risk to the bombers is central to preserving the long-term military capability of the United States. That means, among other things, that *a sizable force of long-range conventional cruise missiles is particularly important.* As a practical matter, that means developing a new long-range cruise missile, because converting nuclear ALCMs to conventional ALCMs could produce a force of only a few hundred to a thousand or so conventional cruise missiles at most.

Over the long term, thousands of cruise missiles are likely to be necessary for conventional operations. For example, combinations of attacks against key time-urgent tactical fixed targets, particularly airfields, bridges, weapon-storage sites, and air defense installations, could quickly absorb hundreds of cruise missiles, even thousands in a prolonged campaign. Moreover, considering the time necessary to develop, produce, and field new weapons, either the cruise missile inventory needs to be large enough to deal with several wars, or production lines have to be open and have adequate capacity to build large numbers of cruise missiles quickly. Thus, ALCM-C is an interim solution at best.

Without long-range cruise missiles for nonstealthy bombers, there is a great risk that the United States could have a couple of bad days in a major conventional conflict and lose the bulk of its heavy bomber force with no timely way to rebuild that national capability. That is particularly true if the United States decided to use the bombers early on in the traditional way against "strategic" targets.

A force of 20 B-2s and a substantial number of cruise missile carriers would have considerable capability and should be considered the core of any future bomber force. It could attack most critical fixed targets as well as a modest number of mobile targets even in the early stages of a campaign. It could handle modest armored interdiction campaigns but probably could not entirely halt an armored attack of the scale that the Iraqis could have mounted against Saudi Arabia immediately after they overran Kuwait. Improved antiarmor submunitions would be particularly important to develop and procure.

The size of the cruise missile carrier force depends primarily on whether part of the force is to be preserved for nuclear operations alone, as planners during the Cold War would undoubtedly have preferred, or the nuclear cruise missile carriers are to be used to launch conventional cruise missiles as well. In the former case, all the remaining bombers (either B-52s or B-1s) should probably be retained. In the latter, about half the current force of either bomber would probably be adequate.

Using B-52s as cruise missile carriers and retaining B-1s for other duties opens up some new operational possibilities and avenues for analysis. Retaining all three bombers in appropriate numbers could provide capability, flexibility, and "breathing space." With the B-52s playing the role of cruise missile carriers and B-2s hitting key mobile and other high-leverage targets (as well as orchestrating the rest of the air battle), theater commanders have more options to put the B-1s at risk and take advantage of their large payload capacity.

There are two possibilities:

- Adding 20–50 B-1s equipped for armor interdiction could provide enough additional interdiction capability to give the bomber force enough firepower to handle even sizable armored invasions.

- Keeping additional B-1s might allow savings in other areas if the B-1s could replace other systems.

The second point is quite important and represents the kinds of trades that will increasingly be the coin of the realm as budgets continue to tighten, competition intensifies, and cooperation increases among the services.

If more B-2s (say, a total force of 40–50) were available, the need to retain B-1s and invest in a new long-range cruise missile would be greatly reduced. With JDAM-class weapons and TSSAM-like cruise missiles for special applications, a B-2 force of that size supplemented by a modest number of properly armed B-52s would be a more effective force in a broad spectrum of scenarios. Moreover, forgoing the new long-range cruise missile and retiring the B-1 (including eliminating the need for additional modifications to make it fully effective in conventional operations) would defray a substantial fraction of the cost for purchasing the additional B-2s. Still further savings might be possible if this bomber force could replace other types of forces for other missions.

The most pressing need is for a new way of thinking about how to employ bombers as flexible tactical aircraft. New operational concepts, some of which we have begun to explore, will be necessary. Joint operational concepts will need to be explored as well. Those, in turn, will raise new technical issues about the capabilities of bombers and improvements that might be needed. Examples include:

- B-2 sensor performance, computer hardware and software, cockpit displays, crew workload.

- Weapon system integration.

- B-1 electronic countermeasures.

- Mission planning.

Old, familiar issues like B-1 electronic countermeasures (ECM) will probably have to be revisited in a different context.[16] The B-2 needs to demonstrate that it can locate targets and deliver short-range weapons while still remaining stealthy enough to elude defenses. Beyond that, it will have to perform new types of missions (e.g., locating targets for other aircraft and helping them avoid defenses) if its potential capabilities are to be fully utilized. New, more fundamental questions, like what bomber crews need to do their jobs in a more demanding, less familiar role, will have to be addressed. We have just begun new research to try to get a better handle on these problems.

OBSERVATIONS ON THE ANALYSIS PROCESS

The process of doing bomber studies is going to have to change, too. Life was much simpler when all we had to worry about was determining the ability of bombers to avoid an initial attack, penetrate Soviet air defenses, and deliver nuclear weapons against targets in their SIOP mission. But, even proceeding with that relatively classical analysis, we discovered some potential dangers in the analytical process that the new emphasis on using large computer models tends to exacerbate. We don't consider these to be particularly cosmic revelations; rather, we regard them as refinements to the list of classical pitfalls in systems analysis.[17] For example:

- Reliance on large computer models can be as much of a curse as a boon. The effort and time required to collect the requisite information, run the models, and interpret the results can actually reduce the scope and usefulness of the analysis.

- Demands of the models will tend to overwhelm even the largest computers, both in terms of processing capacity and data storage. No matter how fast computation capability grows, demands of models will grow faster. (We used to make the lights in Santa Monica blink on and off routinely, not to mention infuriating colleagues who were competing for computer time, when we tried to run several large models—say, STRAPEM and ESAMs— at the same time.) Even the most capable computers cannot solve the combinatorial problems inherent in trying to analyze exhaustively all potential cases. And even if they could, just wading through the computer ouput

---

[16]The issue for B-1 ECM is no longer whether it is good enough to make penetrating B-1s as effective as stealthy bombers on the one hand or cruise missiles on the other. Now the question should be, Given that B-1s are going to be put at risk to some degree, can an effective ECM suite be devised, and is it worth the cost? That question is actually a harder one to answer.

[17]For discussions of the traditional pitfalls in systems analysis, see Quade (1968) and Kahn and Mann (1957). Insights based on more contemporary experience with military systems analysis are included in several chapters of Hughes (1984).

would be a daunting task. Thus, *choosing the right cases to run is still the essence of the systems analysis art.*

- Data-hungry models can seriously limit the number of cases that can be run and the range of sensitivities that can be tested. *Basing an analysis on a few very detailed cases can lead to seriously erroneous policy-level results.* It is far better to consider a much broader range of cases treated in varying levels of detail.

- *Third-order effects can swamp first-order effects.* A particular problem with relying heavily on large models is their very level of detail. Just the mechanics of setting up runs and getting correct results requires that all the details be correct. Even reaching agreement on what constitutes "correct" results can be an arduous (and onerous) task. That gives undue weight to resolving relatively trivial issues at the expense of focusing on more important parameters. (Unfortunately, the computer doesn't know that the clutter rejection capability of a SAM is much more important in policy-level studies than the coefficient of a third-order term in a guidance loop!) Moreover, the lack of transparency in many computer models can compound the difficulty of interpreting even correct results. As a result, *there is a great danger of missing the forest for the trees and risking really misleading policymakers.*

- *Developing the proper level of detail at the appropriate level in the modeling hierarchy is critical to effective analysis.* Although this sounds like a first principle, we found that many widely used models violated it routinely. For example, we generally found that one-on-one engagement models sometimes needed to be even more detailed and campaign-level models much less detailed than they are currently. One major campaign-level model that we employed extensively incorporated just the wrong amount of detail: it modeled engagements in so much detail we could only analyze a modest number of cases, but the engagement analysis was not detailed enough to avoid obvious errors. The result was a model that allowed us to consider too few cases and sometimes produced erroneous results on those cases. We had to modify the models extensively and use them with great care to avoid these problems.

- *Use of detailed models can lead to an excessive concentration on the present (or near-present) at the expense of the future.* Since detailed models usually require very precise information about weapon characteristics, defense locations, terrain, or similar very specific parameters to run, there is a strong tendency to rely heavily on data about current systems, defense deployments, etc. That is a potentially fatal flaw in analyses that are intended to inform decisions about future force structures, for example, since the future weapons characteristics and force deployments cannot be known with that degree of precision. Similarly, *no future force structure or policy choices should ever turn on "quirky" characteristics of weapon systems or assumptions about enemy force deployments.* Thus, unless great care is exercised, the very detail in the large models can be self-defeating in doing sensible policy analysis. Overall results should be explainable in terms of "simple truths."

Thus, even in analyzing the relatively well-behaved old world, we found that we had to use considerable care in doing useful analysis with a collage of high-fidelity models. Some of the specific approaches that we found useful included:

- *Decomposing even fairly integrated problems into manageable pieces, analyzing the pieces, and then reintegrating them.* This process allows using different models for different parts of the problem and permits extensive sensitivity analysis to address specific issues (e.g., saturation of local defenses). Obviously, doing the analysis this way requires great care in both the initial decomposition of the problem and the eventual reintegration of the pieces to make sure that nothing gets lost. However, proceeding this way proved to be considerably better than the alternative.

- The availability of straightforward but powerful tools like large-scale spreadsheets greatly facilitates "wiring together" the individual analyses of disparate parts of the problem.

- "Desensitizing" the analysis is as important as subsequent sensitivity analysis. For example, that means making sure bomber and cruise missile routes, placement of defenses, and offensive and defensive tactics are representative of interesting situations—that is, good but not necessarily optimal. In other words, both sides should be allowed to play the game well. Neither should succeed or fail based on either heroic efforts or gross incompetence.

- Even analyzing the old-world large-scale conventional wars, perhaps involving the use of long-range bombers, generally requires using different sets of models. In particular, one can use campaign-level penetration models such as STRAPEM, but these are not particularly well-tailored tools. On the other hand, land-combat models that permit measuring the effects of a bombing campaign on the course of a ground battle are frequently necessary to analyze how bombers should be employed and to determine what kind of force is appropriate.

Finally, our experiences underline the problems for analyzing cost-effectiveness in the new world:

- Evaluating equal-cost and equal-benefit solutions, while sometimes possible and always tidy from an analytical point of view, may be inadequate in the broader policy arena. Real alternatives may have neither equal costs nor equal benefits and don't lend themselves to a mechanistic approach. Then the task of analysis is to identify the respective costs and benefits of each real option as well as possible to inform policymakers' choices.

- In general, cost-benefit analysis will be less tidy than in the past. Options will have to be evaluated in more of an operational context. For example, bombers that arrive early in a conflict solve one set of problems and then would probably be available to play a role later in the campaign. Thus, a direct cost-effectiveness comparison between, say, early-arriving bombers and late-arriving army theater missile systems would miss critical elements of the capabilities of the systems. Similarly, comparisons involving multi-role systems (e.g., aircraft carriers), which will increasingly be the rule rather than the exception, must be conducted at a high enough level to capture all the disparate roles of different systems adequately.

In spite of all the advances in computers and modeling, bomber analysis remains an art, untidy at best. In the future, as bomber analysis becomes more integrated with overall tactical operational analysis it will become even more untidy. As the new world evolves, the key in the bomber world will be flexible machines and flexible thinkers.

BIBLIOGRAPHY

Barlow, Jason B. (1992), *Strategic Paralysis: An Airpower Strategy for the Present*, Air University, Maxwell AFB, Alabama.

Brown, Michael E. (1992), *Flying Blind: The Politics of the U.S. Strategic Bomber Program*, Cornell University Press, Ithaca, NY.

Buchan, Glenn, et al. (1992), *Use of Long-Range Bombers to Counter Armored Invasions*, RAND, Santa Monica, CA.

Clodfelter, Mark (1989), *The Limits of Air Power: The American Bombing of North Vietnam*, Free Press, New York.

Coyne, James P. (1992), *Airpower in the Gulf War*, Air Force Association, Arlington, Virginia.

Cunningham, John H. (1973), *Parameters Affecting SAM Coverage Versus Low-Altitude Targets*, RM-1740/1, General Research Corporation.

Davis, Paul K. (ed.) (1994), *New Challenges for Defense Planning: Rethinking How Much Is Enough*, RAND, Santa Monica, CA.

Dyson, Freeman J. (1979), *Disturbing the Universe*, Harper and Row, New York.

Friedman, Norman (1991), *Desert Victory: The War for Kuwait*, Naval Institute Press, Annapolis.

Hallion, Richard P. (1992), *Storm Over Iraq: Air Power and the Gulf War*, Smithsonian Institute Press, Washington, D.C.

Hughes, Wayne P., Jr. (ed.) (1984), *Military Modeling*, Military Operations Research Society, Alexandria, VA.

Jacobson, H. I. (1977), *Analytic Modeling of the Interaction Between Fighters and Bombers*, RM-2078, General Research Corporation.

Johnson, Dana J. (forthcoming), *Roles and Missions for Conventionally Armed Heavy Bombers—An Historical Perspective*, RAND, Santa Monica, CA.

Kahn, Herman, and I. Mann (1957), *Ten Common Pitfalls*, RAND, Santa Monica, CA.

Knott, Eugene F., et al. (1985), *Radar Cross Section*, Artech House, Norwood, MA.

Koopman, Bernard O. (1946), *Search and Screening*, OEG Report No. 56, Operations Evaluation Group, Office of the Chief of Naval Operations, Navy Department.

Lynch, David (1992), "Low Observable Stealth Radar," unpublished course notes, Hughes Advanced Technical Education Program, El Segundo, CA (forthcoming book).

Morse, Phillip M., and George E. Kimball (1987), *Methods of Operations Research*, Peninsula, Los Altos, CA (reprint of 1946 report).

Quade, E. S. (1968), "Pitfalls and Limitations," in E. S. Quade and W. I. Boucher (eds.), *Systems Analysis and Policy: Planning Applications in Defense*, American Elsevier, New York.

Schultis, William J. (1978), *A National-Level Analytic Model for Penetration of Various Combined Air Defense Deployments by Cruise Missiles or Bombers*, Institute for Defense Analyses.

———— (1979), *Penetration of Randomly Deployed SAM Systems—An Improved Model*, Institute for Defense Analyses.

Sherry, Michael S. (1987), *The Rise of American Air Power: The Creation of Armageddon*, Yale University Press, New Haven, CT.

Sweetman, Bill (1989), *Stealth Bombers*, Motorbooks International, Osceola, WI.

U.S. Department of Defense (1992), *Conduct of the Persian Gulf War: Final Report to Congress*, U.S. Government Printing Office, Washington, D.C.

Warden, John A., III (1989), *The Air Campaign*, Peragmon-Brassey's, New York.

Weapons Systems Evaluation Group (1950), *Report on Effectiveness of Strategic Air Operations*, Weapons Systems Evaluation Group Report No. 1, Office of the Secretary of Defense.

Wilson, Andrew (1968), *The Bomb and the Computer*, Delacorte Press, New York.

Winnefeld, James A., Preston Niblack, and Dana J. Johnson (1994), *A League of Airmen: U.S. Air Power in the Gulf War*, RAND, Santa Monica, CA.

Chapter 14

A FIRST LOOK AT OPTIONS FOR POLAND

Charles T. Kelley, Jr., Daniel B. Fox, and Barry A. Wilson

The Central European nations are now in the process of shaping their military strategy and forces for the future. The United States has an interest in promoting a stable military balance of power in the region, one that leaves these nations with enough military force to protect their borders, but with insufficient strength to threaten their neighbors. This paper examines the potential force requirements for one of those nations, Poland. It uses a scenario of a Russian attack to evaluate four widely different defense concepts. The defense concepts are adapted from previous RAND research on NATO's defense requirements.

INTRODUCTION

European security in the years ahead will be affected importantly by the defense agendas pursued by East European nations. This is especially the case for the northern tier countries of Poland, Hungary, and the former Czechoslovakia, but also for the Balkan nations. Formerly heavily armed members of the Warsaw Pact, most of these nations are fledgling free-market democracies with as yet no discernible military identity. Major force reductions in all cases are being compelled by economic circumstances and by the Conventional Forces in Europe (CFE) Treaty, but all of the nations will continue to field military forces of some sort. The forces that they will deploy, and the defense strategies that they embrace, will affect Europe's stability in what promises to be a tumultuous era ahead. If these nations disarm to the point of creating a power vacuum across Eastern Europe and the Balkans, the entire area will be left vulnerable to outside pressure and aggression. But if these nations choose to arm themselves too heavily, they will pose threats to each other, and stability will be threatened for entirely different reasons.

This research was conducted as part of a study on the future of East European defense policies and military forces and was sponsored by the Office of the Secretary of Defense. Results were briefed to senior Polish defense officials at a conference cosponsored by RAND at Warsaw in March 1993.

The United States and its NATO allies have an interest in promoting a stable military balance of power in this region, one that leaves these nations with enough military force to defend their borders, but insufficient strength to appear threatening to their neighbors. This interest is especially keen because some of these nations have expressed a desire to draw closer to NATO, perhaps even to become members of the alliance. That desire is no stronger anywhere than in Poland, the largest and, arguably, the most important of the East European nations from the viewpoint of NATO security interests.

When Poland was a member of the Warsaw Pact, its defense planning was conducted by the Soviets. The mission of Polish forces was clear: to support a Soviet attack into Western Europe. That was to be accomplished in western Poland by fitting Polish divisions into an overall attack scheme across the inter-German border and, in the east, by providing the transportation network to move troops and supplies from the Soviet Union to the forward combat areas. Likewise, Polish defense doctrine was forced to march in lockstep with that of the Soviet Union: the purpose of its forces was to conduct offensive operations using mass and shock to cause breakthroughs for exploitation by follow-on forces in order to encircle and destroy the opponent's forces quickly.

Now, of course, Poland's security environment has changed considerably. The Warsaw Pact, along with the Soviet Union, has ceased to exist. Poland is not a member of any security alliance, and although that status may change in the future, it must now decide—with its own interests in mind—what its defense policies are to be. These defense policies are no doubt going to have a decidedly defensive flavor compared to the policies that were followed by the Warsaw Pact. But restructuring the Polish military to give it a more defensive orientation will take resources that are in increasingly short supply as Poland devotes a larger share of its GDP to meet its domestic needs. Moreover, perhaps the most radical change that has occurred for Poland is the makeup of its neighbors. A few years ago, Poland was bordered by three nations, *none of which exists today.* Gone are the Soviet Union, Czechoslovakia, and the German Democratic Republic—replaced with Russia (Kaliningrad), Lithuania, Belarus, Ukraine, Slovakia, the Czech Republic, and the Federal Republic of Germany. To analyze Poland's defense needs for its new security environment, the following questions need to be answered:

- What threats to the security of Poland's borders need to be considered?
- Are there deficiencies in current Polish military capabilities in meeting those threats?
- If deficiencies exist, what defense concepts can correct them?
- Of the promising defense concepts, which are the most practical to implement?

The purpose of this paper is to provide preliminary answers to these questions.

ILLUSTRATIVE PLANNING SCENARIO

Poland is surrounded by countries of varying geographical size and population (see Figure 1). Although the likelihood of conflict between Poland and its neighbors is believed low for the foreseeable future, for defense *planning* purposes it is prudent to consider the possibility of conflict occurring with one or more neighboring states.

Poland's neighbors possess military forces of varying potential. Figure 2 displays two measures of ground and air force capabilities as depicted by the maximum allowable numbers of ground force equipment (tanks plus armored combat vehicles plus artillery pieces) and air force equipment (combat aircraft plus attack helicopters) according to the CFE Treaty (see IISS, 1992).

Figure 2 can be divided into three regions. The first region contains those countries—Lithuania,[1] Belarus, Czech Republic, and Slovakia—that do not

RAND #130-67-0194

Figure 1—Poland and Its Neighbors

---

[1]Lithuania is not a party to the CFE Treaty. However, its equipment levels are included in Figure 2 for completeness.

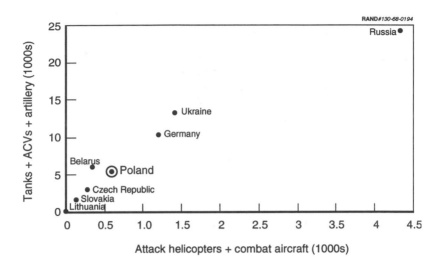

Figure 2—CFE Limits on Major Force Equipment

pose a threat to Poland's territorial integrity, and thus, for our purposes, can be ignored.[2]   The second region consists of two countries—Germany[3] and Ukraine—whose force levels are individually about twice the size of Poland's. That numerical superiority is somewhat misleading because it does not take into account certain disadvantages and advantages that the attacker and defender have, respectively.   For example, if Ukraine were to attack Poland, it would likely need to leave significant force levels behind to protect its own borders, greatly reducing the force size that it could employ in an attack.[4] Similarly, because it is generally believed that a defender would normally enjoy an advantage in exchange ratio over an attacker, the attacker might need an overall initial force advantage of greater than 1.5 to 1 (3 or 4 to 1 along the main axis of army level advance) in order to prosecute successfully a campaign (this assumes comparably capable forces and the absence of surprise).[5]

---

[2]This does not mean that special forces might not have to be configured to protect against minor border incursions by small groups of irregular troops from these or other countries, but these force requirements are apt to be minor in comparison to those that are needed to halt a major invasion.

[3]As long as Germany is firmly anchored to the West through NATO, Poland should have no fear of attack from that quarter.

[4]This assumes that Ukraine and Russia are not in a state of cooperation that would allow Ukraine to prudently employ all of its forces in an attack on Poland.

[5]The relationship between force-ratio requirements at theater, main-sector army, and tactical levels is discussed in Davis, Howe, Kugler, and Wild (1989).

Moreover, an attacker would have to assume that the population of the defender nation would participate actively and directly in the defense of its country, thereby resulting in the attacker expending more force than would be needed to prosecute an attack against regular military units. Consequently, an attack by either Germany or Ukraine on Poland might well not succeed.

The third part of the figure consists of the Russian data point. Overall, Russian strength is about five times that of Poland's in both the ground and air force categories. That strength is sufficient so that Russia could leave a strategic reserve behind, have enough force to ensure security of its lines of communication into the Polish theater, and have more than enough force left over to exceed the 1.5 to 1 attack criterion. Therefore, for illustrative *planning* purposes, we select a Polish-Russian scenario[6,7] for investigation.

Scenario Details

While we do not have operational details on how the Poles would defend against a major attack, a remarkable lead article in a respected Polish General Staff journal provides some insights (see Balcerowicz, 1992). The article describes a plan to form territorial forces and to integrate them with regular army units in an active defense, and to improve the defensive preparation of the territory. Figure 3 illustrates where major and secondary lines of defense might be located to counter an attack from the east or the west. The Poles have recently expanded their military districts from three to four in order to provide more balanced protection of the perimeter of their country. In the event of a major attack from, say, the east, the first strategic line of defense would be manned by forces from the two eastern districts, while forces from the western districts would move eastward and man the second strategic line of defense. It is this general scheme of operation that we employ in our analysis of Polish capabilities to defend against a Russian attack.[8] Figure 4 summarizes the attack and defense scheme for this illustrative planning scenario.[9]

---

[6]However, this is not a worst-case scenario from the Polish point of view. Russia could reach an agreement with Ukraine or Ukraine and Belarus to perform a joint attack against Poland.

[7]A scenario and analysis of a Ukrainian attack on Poland is currently under investigation at RAND.

[8]See Szayna (forthcoming) for an analysis of the journal article.

[9]A definitive analysis of Polish defense needs should examine a variety of scenarios that vary by the amount of mobilization time available, warning time available, location of the attack, and so on. Our purpose in using a single illustrative planning scenario was to provide an initial screening of quite diverse defense options. The more promising concepts, however, should be subjected to a more definitive analysis later.

SOURCE: Brig. Gen. Boreslaw Balcerowicz, Col. Jacek Pawlowski, Col. Jozef Marczak, "Koncepcja strategicznej obony Polski" (The Strategic Concept of the Defense of Poland), *Mysl Wojskowa*, No. 3, 1992, pp. 5–13.

Figure 3—Polish Strategic System of Defense

The Russian and Polish orders of battle are shown in Figure 5 for divisions, equivalent divisions,[10] combat aircraft, and attack helicopters. The force levels are CFE-constrained. All of the Polish forces are assumed to be available for the defense. About half of the 50 divisions the Russians are assumed to have at the turn of the century are assumed to participate in the attack, with the re-

_____

[10]An equivalent division is defined as combat power, measured in terms of numbers and types of equipment, using the 1990 U.S. 1st Armored Division as the standard.

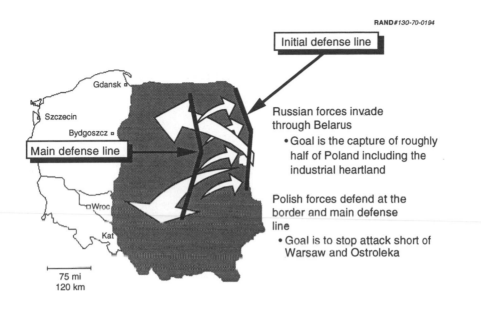

Figure 4—Illustrative Planning Scenario

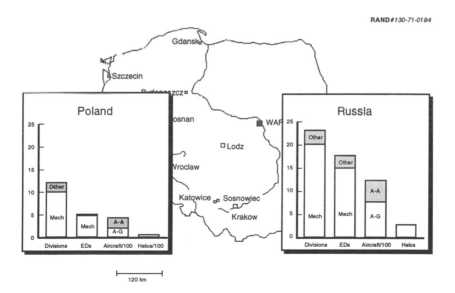

Figure 5—Static Force Balance

mainder withheld for a strategic reserve and to protect the lines of communication through Belarus.[11]

Figure 6 shows the array of Russian and Polish ground forces prior to the attack. Russian forces are divided between two main axes of attack. It is assumed that there is sufficient warning time that Polish forces are able to reach their wartime positions in time to construct deliberate prepared defenses to a depth of 10 km at the first defense line and to a depth of 15 km at the main defense line. Six of the ten Polish divisions man the forward defensive positions to delay and attrit the attacking forces with the remaining defenders situated at the main defense line that is protecting Warsaw and the Polish heartland. Polish territorial units[12] are situated between the two main defense lines. If Polish troops located in the forward defense line cannot hold against the attacking force, they would plan to fall back as best as they could to help man the main defense line. The main defense line is located approxi-

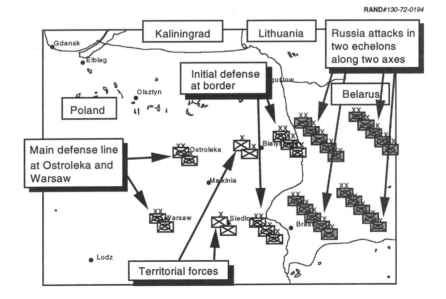

RAND#130-72-0194

Figure 6—Base Case Defense

---

[11]Belarus is assumed to be neutral and does not attempt to prohibit passage of Russian forces and supplies.

[12]An important innovation as part of the new Polish defense concept is the formation of regional territorial forces (see Szayna, forthcoming). The territorial units would cooperate closely with regular army units, would defend specific objects, and could engage in guerilla operations in areas seized by the aggressor.

mately 150 km behind the forward defense line. For the purposes of this analysis, we assume that a successful defense has been achieved if the main defense line is not breached.

The contribution of air forces plays an important role in the assessment of both sides' capabilities. Russian medium-range bombers escorted by fighter aircraft are employed for offensive counterair. Russian and Polish fighter-bombers are split about evenly between the close air support (CAS) and battlefield air interdiction (BAI) missions, while attack helicopters are used solely for CAS. Polish fighters are employed mainly on air defense, although some are also used as escorts for aircraft conducting the BAI mission.

Methodology

The principal methodological tool used to evaluate the base case outcome and to compare alternative improvement options was the Integrated Theater Model (ITM) that was developed as part of the RAND Strategy Assessment System (see Bennett, 1993). ITM, as its name implies, is an integrated air and ground theater-level combat model that operates at the operational level of warfare. Ground forces are followed at the level of divisions and independent brigades. ITM is designed specifically to examine the operational level of maneuver. The ITM commands allow the user to direct the maneuver of ground forces so that counterattacks, envelopments, and flank attacks can be explicitly modeled. ITM includes concepts of phases of battle (such as preparation, assault, breakthrough, and exploitation and pursuit). The model predicts breakthroughs and assesses increased losses to the defense under conditions where such breakthroughs traditionally have occurred. It assesses breakthroughs where the density of defending forces is too low, where a static defensive line is penetrated, or where an infantry force with limited mobility is overrun.

Combat adjudication is accomplished taking into account the type of contact between forces (e.g., front-to-front), the character of the battle (determined by the current activity of each side and the preparations that the defender has made), the nature of the environment (the type and width of terrain and any placement of mines on the battlefield), and the composition of forces (combined arms effects). The final stage of combat adjudication is the calculation of fire support effects coming from fixed-wing combat aircraft, attack helicopters, and artillery. ITM then simulates close combat and determines the kills achieved and the movement of the opposing forces.

Base Case Results

Tables 1 and 2 show some of the detailed results of the base case. Not surprisingly, given the preponderance of Russian forces, the simulation suggests

Table 1

Base Case Results—Ground Forces

	Polish Forces	Russian Forces
Initial EDs	4.4	16.0
Attrition by day 5[a]		
By ground	1.6	1.6
By combat aircraft	0.7	0.4
By attack helicopters	2.3	0.3
Repaired during conflict	0.6	0.4
Final EDs	0.4	14.1

[a]The main defense line was breached at D+5. At that time, the combat simulation was stopped.

Table 2

Base Case Results—Air Forces

	Polish Forces	Russian Forces
Initial aircraft		
Combat aircraft		
Air-to-air	163	301
Air-to-ground	185	701
Multipurpose	75	167
Total	423	1169
Attack helicopters	30	388
Attrition by day 5[a]		
By air-to-air	110	6
By ground-to-air	52	130
By air-to-ground	132	0[b]
Final aircraft		
Combat aircraft		
Air-to-air	38	299
Air-to-ground	74	685
Multipurpose	38	163
Total	150	1147
Attack helicopters	9	274

[a]The main defense line was breached at D+5. At that time, the combat simulation was stopped.

[b]Polish air forces did not attack Russian airbases.

that the main defense line could be breached in less than a week of combat. This occurs for two principal reasons:

- The Russians have an initial 3.6:1 advantage over the Poles in ground combat capability. Even though the Polish ground forces have an exchange ratio advantage over the Russians as they attempt to penetrate through the prepared defenses at the border (and later at the main defense line), it is not enough to offset the Russian advantages in numerical strength and firepower. The initial exchange ratio is 0.5:1 (Polish losses/Russian losses) in the forward defense line. Even with that favorable exchange ratio, the Russian force ratio grows in its favor. Moreover, that line is breached in one day, and from then until D+3, when the main defense line is reached, the exchange ratio rises to 3.4:1 in the Russians' favor. The Poles are pushed out of the main defense line in two days. The force ratio at the time that the main defense line is breached has grown to 35:1 in the Russians' favor with the virtual annihilation of the Polish ground forces.

- The Russians have about an overall 3.7:1 numerical advantage in air-to-ground aircraft, including attack helicopters. For attack helicopters alone, the ratio is greater than 10:1 in the Russians' favor. This means that even if the Poles could achieve a favorable exchange ratio for ground-to-ground operations while in prepared defense positions, the ratio would be reduced substantially over time due to the overwhelming superiority of the Russians in air-to-ground attack capability.

We now turn to a discussion of defense options for improving Poland's capability of successfully defending against an attack of this magnitude.

ALTERNATIVE DEFENSE IMPROVEMENTS

The defense planning problem facing Poland—attempting to halt an armored attack within a relatively short distance of the border while outnumbered—is reminiscent of the problem faced by NATO when the Warsaw Pact existed as a formidable alliance and posed a direct and immediate threat. Defense of NATO against a Warsaw Pact attack was studied seriously for nearly forty years, beginning with the establishment of force goals adopted by the North Atlantic Council in early 1952.[13] For our initial examination of possible ways to improve Poland's current defense posture, it is worthwhile to revisit some earlier RAND work.

During the 1970s and 1980s, RAND devoted a substantial portion of its national security research resources to topics related to the defense of NATO's

---

[13]For an excellent historical discussion of NATO's efforts to establish concepts for defense of the Alliance from the beginning to the end of the Cold War, see Kugler (1993).

Central Region. These topics ranged from studies of individual detailed force improvements, such as increasing the survivability of NATO's air bases to conventional and chemical attacks, to studies of broad theater-level defense concepts. It is the latter category that is most relevant for the subject of this paper. One of the RAND studies, conducted in the early 1980s (Levine, Connors, Weiner, and Wise, 1982), surveyed numerous proposals for defending NATO. From the results of that survey, a few defense options that captured the key features of many of the proposals were identified and analyzed (Weiner, 1986). It is these options that form the basis of four initiatives that we will apply to the Polish situation in an analogous way. The four options and their particular implementation scheme for this study are:

- Increase forces
  — Add more Polish divisions
- Reconfigure existing forces
  — Distributed area defense
- Significantly improve defensive capabilities
  — Barrier defense
- More reliance on airpower
  — Interdiction belt

Add More Polish Divisions

This option is probably the most straightforward way of dealing with the imbalance of Polish and Russian forces. Adding divisions (and supporting artillery units) could increase the size of the Polish force to such a level that it could defend successfully at the main defense line, at least as simulated by the ITM. Polish ground force strength was increased by an ED at a time until the attack on the main defense line stalled. The additional EDs were added to the main defense line in keeping with the original defense concept. The attack stalled when between 6 and 7 EDs (13 and 16 divisions) were added. Results are shown in Table 3.

There are two principal advantages to the option of adding more Polish divisions. First, standing forces are a visible deterrent. Unless the attacker can create conditions such that the defender's standing force cannot be brought to bear at the point of attack, e.g., by a surprise attack that allows the attacker to achieve its objectives before the bulk of the defender's force can engage in combat, the attacker is likely to be deterred by a simple comparison of relative force strengths. Second, standard force elements, such as mechanized and armored divisions, have been tested in actual combat. Their effectiveness in bat-

Table 3

Effectiveness Estimates

	Day Conflict Stopped	Main Defense Line Breached?	Ground Losses Russia (EDs)	Poland (EDs)	Final Force Ratio
Base case	D+5	Yes	2.0	4.0	35:1
Add divisions	D+10	No	14.0	10.5	1.6:1

tle is better known than that of units whose composition is experimental, i.e., whose effectiveness has been measured through computer simulation or through operational testing alone.

There are several disadvantages to this option. Standing force structure is expensive to organize, equip, and train. The simulation results suggest that Poland would need to more than double the size of its ground forces in order to mount a steadfast defense at the main defense line. Additionally, a more than doubling of Poland's standing army from 10 divisions to 23–26 divisions might appear quite threatening to Poland's neighbors, such as Belarus or the Czech Republic. Finally, an increase in force level of this magnitude would result in violations of the CFE Treaty both in terms of treaty-limited equipment and personnel-strength limits.

Distributed Area Defense

The distributed area defense force consists of numerous, small, semi-autonomous fire units operating in the northeastern portion of Poland opposite the main direction of the Russian attack. Figure 7 shows the area of operation of the fire units.[14] Each fire unit is committed to defend a specific sector. Their effectiveness is achieved by attacking enemy forces all along the axes of advance rather than positioning large forces directly ahead of the attacking formations. The fire units are backed up by mobile reserve divisions located immediately behind the area that the fire units occupy. In this case, the mobile reserves are located at the main defense line. The sole purpose of the fire units is to reduce the invading force by attrition to a level so that it can be repulsed by the mobile reserves. Regular Polish mechanized divisions are demobilized to provide the personnel to man the fire units.

---

[14]Although the illustrative planning scenario examined here is of a Russian attack through Belarus, the fire units might also protect simultaneously against a secondary attack from Kaliningrad.

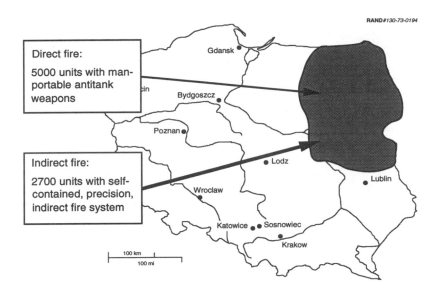

RAND#130-73-0194

Figure 7—Schematic Representation of Distributed Area Defense

Weiner (1986) examined this concept in detail. That study considered two kinds of complementary fire units: direct-fire and indirect-fire systems. The direct-fire units would be equipped with antitank weapons with limited antiair capability to counter suppression attacks by attack helicopters and would operate in and around urban and forest areas. The particular weapon system investigated was a man-portable laser beam rider missile system. The indirect-fire unit would possess a self-contained, precision, indirect-fire system. The system investigated in the prior study was an armed reconnaissance scout vehicle chassis equipped with a telescoping pole and two missile-launcher racks. The system operates from concealed positions in woods or urban areas.

The concept was evaluated (in an era before ubiquitous computer graphics) using human participants for command decisions, a three-dimensional terrain board with a scale of 1:10,000 (see Figure 8), and several computer programs. The terrain board represented a 20 km by 25 km area immediately to the west of the (then) inter-German border. For the Polish analysis (with an area of 300 km by 100 km), we used the same density of fire units as was used in the NATO–Warsaw Pact case.[15]

---

[15]The terrain in the part of Poland where Russian forces are attacking is less urbanized than the terrain board data. There is, however, substantial forest that should provide much the same channelization and opportunities for ambush.

Figure 8—Terrain Board

For Poland, this amounted to about 7700 fire units with 5000 direct-fire and 2700 indirect-fire units. About 4 2/3 Polish divisions need to be demobilized to provide the 50,000 troops to man the fire units. That would leave about 5 1/3 divisions or 2 2/3 EDs to provide the mobile reserve force. If we assume that the Poles can successfully defend at the main defense line if the theater-level force ratio is no greater than 1.5, then the fire units need to attrit 12 Russian EDs. The rule of thumb is that there are about 1000 armored vehicles in one ED, meaning that the fire units need to kill 12,000 vehicles for the distributed area defense concept to be successful.[16]

The rate of the number of vehicles required to be killed per day per unit depends upon how rapidly the attacker moves through the area defended by the fire units and the fraction of the fire units encountered by the attacker. Figure 9 shows the required rate of kills as a function of those two parameters. For example, if the attacker takes two days to traverse 100 km and if he concentrates his axes of attack such that only one-quarter of the fire units are able to engage, then each fire unit needs to be able to kill about 3.5 vehicles per day.

---

[16]All the combat vehicles in a unit do not have to be killed before the unit becomes ineffective. The fraction that do need to be killed for a unit to have to be withdrawn from combat depends upon the particular circumstances, but most analysts assume that when a unit has suffered around 30–60 percent casualties it will need to be withdrawn and reconstructed before it can fight again. Here, however, we take a more conservative approach and assume that the casualties are concentrated rather than being spread nearly uniformly across the attacking force.

The results from the prior study of a two-reinforced-regiment attack across the 20 km by 25 km area suggest that each engaged fire unit could kill 2.3 vehicles in a three-hour period.[17] Therefore, the kill rates shown in Figure 9 do not seem unreasonable to achieve. The results are summarized in Table 4.

The principal advantages of the distributed area concept are that (1) it makes use of the potential high leverage that can be provided by technology and (2) it is not a threatening force posture because it is inherently defensive in nature.

Its principal disadvantages are that (1) the concept of distributed defense for large-scale operations is unproven, (2) the units need to have access to secure supplies and hiding places in order to be effective over a considerable period of time (perhaps up to several days), and (3) the simultaneous autonomous operation inherent in the operation of thousands of small-sized units may lead to degradation of overall system performance because of uncoordinated fires. Additionally, a determined attacker with enough artillery and air-to-ground capability might be able to punch through faster than the calculation suggests. With regard to the latter topic, Russian air superiority could be particularly

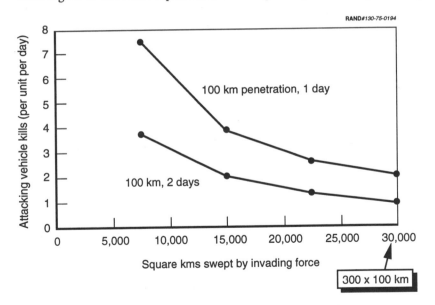

Figure 9—Effectiveness of Distributed Area Defense

---

[17]The contribution of attack helicopters in locating and destroying the five units was considered in deriving the results of the earlier study.

Table 4

Effectiveness Estimates

	Day Conflict Stopped	Main Defense Line Breached?	Ground Losses Russia (EDs)	Poland (EDs)	Final Force Ratio
Base case	D+5	Yes	2.0	4.0	35:1
Add divisions	D+10	No	14.0	10.1	1.5:1[a]
Distributed area	D+2	No	12.0	1.8[b]	1.5:1

[a]Combat was stopped when the force ratio fell to 1.5:1.

[b]EDs associated with personnel of divisions that were disbanded to obtain personnel to man *all* fire units.

worrisome for the defense. The fire units would need at least a limited organic air defense capability. Finally, the use of dismounted infantry as a way of "eating through" the distributed area defense needs to be analyzed. That tactic would involve much slower movement of the attacker but would require some anti-infantry capability in the fire units.

Barrier Defense

Weiner (1986) reviewed several proposals and studies of various types of barriers for improving NATO's defenses. As a result of his survey, he found that:

- Barriers require widths of several tens of kilometers, especially against modern, precision weapons.
- Barriers must be backed up by mobile reserve forces.
- Barriers should consist of interlocking rather than individual positions.
- Barriers should make extensive use of underground facilities including "pop-up" capabilities for sensors and weapons.

As a consequence of these findings, he concluded that the key characteristic of a successful barrier is that it should be a modern Maginot Line, i.e., reinforced concrete and steel interconnected fortifications in depth with major weapon systems, including advanced surveillance and precision fire weapons, throughout the length of the zone. That type of barrier applied to the Polish defense situation is illustrated in Figure 10.

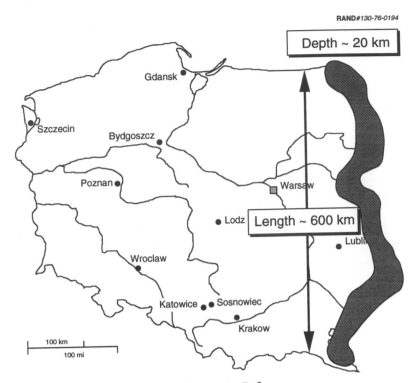

RAND#130-76-0194

Depth ~ 20 km

Length ~ 600 km

Figure 10—Barrier Defense

We assumed that the barrier would be manned by territorial forces organized for this purpose leaving the regular Polish army units as the mobile reserve. The air campaign for this situation was the same as described earlier except that one-half of the Russian CAS and BAI sorties and all of the attack helicopter sorties were assumed to be employed in the attempt to breach the barrier. Following Weiner, we investigated various exchange ratios that the barrier would have to achieve so that a successful defense could be mounted by regular Polish units at the main defense line. We found that an exchange ratio of between 6:1 and 7:1 would be sufficient. Results are shown in Table 5.

The principal advantage to the barrier defense is that it provides potential high leverage, i.e., a force multiplier, to an outnumbered and normally outgunned defense.

The potential disadvantages are several. First, a fortified barrier of the type described here will be expensive. Land will have to be acquired. Displaced persons will have to be relocated. Construction costs for a sophisticated barrier system will be high. Second, the type of barrier described here requires about

Table 5

Effectiveness Estimates

	Day Conflict Stopped	Main Defense Line Breached?	Ground Losses Russia (EDs)	Ground Losses Poland (EDs)	Final Force Ratio
Base case	D+5	Yes	2.0	4.0	35:1
Add divisions	D+10	No	14.0	10.1	1.5:1[a]
Distributed area	D+2	No	12.0	1.8[b]	1.5:1
Barrier defense (exchange ratio = 7)	D+8[c]	No	10.5	—[d]	1.2

[a]Combat was stopped when the force ratio fell to 1.5:1.

[b]EDs associated with personnel of divisions that were disbanded to obtain personnel to man *all* fire units.

[c]Barrier assumed breached at D+8.

[d]Casualties to barrier defenders (~60,000 troops) were not evaluated.

60,000 troops.[18] Third, a fortified barrier may be vulnerable to attack by airpower with precision weapons or vertical envelopment. Finally, ever since the Maginot Line fell, barriers—justifiably or not—have not enjoyed a good reputation.

Interdiction Belt

The final improvement option is the use of airpower to attrit, slow, and disrupt the attacking force so that the Polish ground forces are able to establish an effective defense at the main defense line. This concept—called the interdiction belt—would ideally employ airpower in two phases: (1) to create chokepoints along the lines of communication (LOCs) used by the attacking forces and (2) to proceed with follow-up attacks against enemy units as they attempted to transit the "belt." Figure 11 shows one possible location of the interdiction belt—just to the east of the Polish-Belarus border.[19]

Because it was beyond the scope of this study to conduct a LOC analysis, we only employed airpower in Phase Two operations, i.e., in direct attack of

---

[18]We did not demobilize active units in order to provide the personnel to man the barrier. To do so would have raised the required exchange ratio to about 8:1.

[19]The exact location would depend upon where it is most efficient to cut the LOCs.

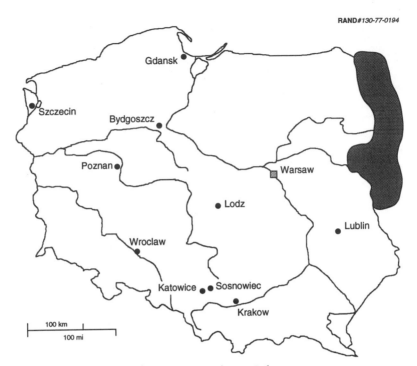

RAND#130-77-0194

Figure 11—Interdiction Belt

enemy units.[20] We also assumed that the airpower contribution would come from NATO countries.[21]   Specifically, we assumed that the interdiction aircraft were F-16Cs and F-15Es. F-16Cs were assumed to kill one armored target per sortie (Shlapak and Davis, 1991) and F-15Es four targets per sortie.[22] Aircraft were added in increments of 120 until a satisfactory result

----

[20]This assumption leads to an overestimation of the number of aircraft required to successfully interdict the enemy units, i.e., to inderdict them to the extent that Polish ground forces can mount a successful defense at the main defense line, because it does not take into account the bunching of targets behind chokepoints.

[21]NATO could also contribute ground forces for the defense of Poland in addition to or instead of air forces. However, NATO would have to overcome the malpositioning of ground forces for that option to be viable. The logistics lines to support NATO ground force operations in Poland for ground units normally based in Germany could be as long as 750–900 km (Fox and Bordeaux, 1993). Consequently, because of airpower's mobility we chose it as the more likely NATO contribution to Polish defense in the early stages of a Russian-Polish conflict should NATO choose to become involved.

[22]The difference between the effectiveness of the F-16 and F-15 is due to payload considerations.

occurred. We found a successful defense could be mounted when between 120 F-15s and 360 F-16s and 120 F-15s and 480 F-16s were available.[23] Results are shown in Table 6 for the case when a total of 600 aircraft were added.

One advantage of this option is that it focuses air attacks on a relatively small area. Thus, it should be possible in peacetime to preplan the use of airpower to create chokepoints on specific LOCs. Furthermore, because the attacks take place at a shallow penetration distance outside of Polish territory, air losses should be minimized.

A disadvantage is that the effectiveness of the concept may be sensitive to weather conditions. From the Polish point of view, another disadvantage is that the Poles must rely on the participation of outside forces for their defense. This is contrary to the Polish desire to possess a self-sufficient defense capability.[24]

OTHER CONSIDERATIONS

Each of the options described above was evaluated according to its effectiveness. For two of the options—added Polish divisions and the interdiction belt—achievement of a successful defense was measured in terms of the num-

Table 6

Effectiveness Estimates

	Day Conflict Stopped	Main Defense Line Breached?	Ground Losses		Final Force Ratio
			Russia (EDs)	Poland (EDs)	
Base case	D+5	Yes	2.0	4.0	35:1
Add divisions	D+10	No	14.0	10.1	1.5:1[a]
Distributed area	D+2	No	12.0	1.8[b]	1.5:1
Barrier defense (exchange ratio = 7)	D+8[c]	No	10.5	—[d]	1.2
Interdiction belt	D+9	No	12.8	3.0	1.3:1

[a]Combat was stopped when the force ratio fell to 1.5:1.

[b]EDs associated with personnel of divisions that were disbanded to obtain personnel to man *all* fire units.

[c]Barrier assumed breached at D+8.

[d]Casualties to barrier defenders (~60,000 troops) were not evaluated.

[23]F-15Es were used to a limit of 120 aircraft, which is the maximum number that could be available given the projected U.S. inventory.

[24]On the other hand, reliance on outside assistance means that the Poles do not have to rely solely on their own resources to mount a successful defense.

ber of additional divisions or combat aircraft required. For the other two options investigated—distributed area defense and barrier defense—achievement of a successful defense was measured in terms of the effectiveness of individual units, in the case of the distributed area defense, or of the unit as a whole, in the case of the barrier. Each defense option was constructed to be equally effective, i.e., each option was able to achieve a successful defense at the main defense line. Because the options are equally effective, we must use other criteria to aid in the selection of the most promising option or options.

Five factors seem particularly important for this analysis of Polish defense needs: (1) the compatibility of the option with the CFE Treaty, (2) the cost of implementing the option as measured by the number of needed personnel and levels of other resources, (3) the confidence level associated with the effectiveness of the option, (4) the flexibility or usefulness of the option for scenarios or situations not considered in the present analysis, and (5) whether the defense option requires assistance from another country for its implementation.

A qualitative evaluation of how the four defense options score for each of the five factors is shown in Figure 12 in a stoplight fashion.

Adding Polish divisions scores poorly on two counts. First, Poland would have to violate the CFE Treaty in terms of both treaty-limited equipment and personnel in order to equip and man the additional divisions. The additional large amounts of equipment and personnel would require very large additional

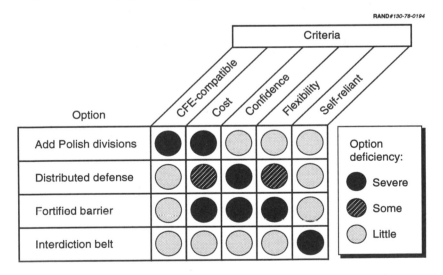

Figure 12—Evaluation of Options

defense outlays[25] not only to equip and man the units but also to train them. Otherwise, this defense option scores well with the other factors. The capabilities of standard divisions are well known, and their mobility means that they can be used to protect Poland's borders at any location.

Distributed area defense scores poorly on the confidence factor. The use of small autonomous units on the scale envisioned has never been tried before, and thus there will be considerable uncertainty about whether such units can stand up to an armored attack of the magnitude postulated here. Otherwise, the distributed area defense scores well with the other factors, although there may be some costs incurred as new weapons are procured that are suitable for the use of the fire units. However, those costs might be offset by no longer having to modernize the demobilized divisions that provided the personel to man the fire units. Moreover, because the fire units will train on specific terrain so that they will be familiar with hide locations, munitions resupply point locations, likely attack routes, and so on, they may not be able to be deployed to an unfamiliar area and still operate effectively if the attack should come from a different location and direction.

The barrier defense fails on several grounds. It will be prohibitively expensive to acquire the land and especially to construct the fortifications. A barrier has little flexibility unless it rings the country entirely. A barrier that protects only a portion of Poland's borders will have little or no utility to defend against an attack from a location and direction different from the one it was designed for. Finally, barriers have had a checkered history with regard to their effectiveness and do not instill confidence in many military minds. The Maginot Line is an example: although it was never penetrated by a direct assault, the ease with which it was circumvented is often pointed to, rightfully or not, as an example of the folly of overreliance on a fortified barrier.

The interdiction belt as implemented here with the use of NATO airpower scores high on all factors except self-sufficiency. With this concept the Poles must rely on outside assistance. Frankly, except for the untried concept of distributed area defense, it appears unfeasible for the Poles to defend themselves alone against a threat of the magnitude investigated here. So although the Poles would prefer to have the capability to defend themselves, the unfeasibility of achieving that goal makes the self-sufficiency factor less important and maybe even irrelevant in selecting a viable option for enhancing Poland's defense.

---

[25]Recall that this option would require more than double the number of existing Polish divisions.

OBSERVATIONS

This paper has described a first look at Poland's defense needs after the Cold War. It has examined a single illustrative planning scenario: a large-scale Russian armored attack. Other scenarios need to be examined to obtain a more complete understanding of Poland's defense needs. In particular, attention should be paid to scenarios that have a greater likelihood of occurring—most if not all of which would involve smaller force levels than were investigated here. These less-intensive combat situations would influence decisions about force structure. For example, the means for detecting border incursions by small groups of forces and for rapidly moving small, elite units to counter those incursions should prove especially valuable in those cases. However, for determining the overall shape of Polish defense needs, the situation analyzed here should be adequate, given the current political-military situation.

From the results of the analysis, we draw the following general observations:

- Currently, Poland is not well positioned to protect its borders against a serious attack by Russia. This follows from an inspection of the relative force strengths and compositions and is reinforced by the model results of a specific scenario.

- During the period of the NATO–Warsaw Pact confrontation, an enormous amount of time and intellectual effort was spent on examining different, and sometimes radical, defense concepts for successfully defending against a large armored attack in NATO's central region. With the dissolution of the Warsaw Pact and the breakup of the Soviet Union, that body of research has fallen into neglect owing to the simple fact that there is no military threat to those borders. However, that knowledge may be directly relevant to the defense problems of NATO's neighbors to the east.

- The analysis of the four improvement options showed that it will take a Herculean effort for the Poles to defend successfully on their own against an attack of the size examined here. Straightforward options to remedy the situation would violate the CFE Treaty, be too costly in terms of personnel and other resources, or a combination of both. The one attractive option examined that involved the use of only Polish forces was the reconfiguration of standard army units into numerous antitank teams. That option is consistent with the Polish desire to make more and better use of territorial forces. Additionally, such restructuring should not alarm Poland's neighbors because those units would have a strong defensive orientation. While the simulation shows that this restructuring can result theoretically in a self-sufficient capability, a great deal more analysis of possible countermeasures is needed in order to weigh the risks involved before wholesale restructuring takes place.

- The one option investigated that involved outside assistance was the contribution of NATO airpower. Ground force assistance from NATO, or a combination of air and ground force assistance could have been analyzed also. But because Poland is not a member of NATO, forces belonging to NATO member countries would not be based in Poland before the outbreak of hostilities. Once a crisis had occurred, or when it had been determined that combat was imminent, NATO would need to deploy forces into Poland if it agreed to assist Poland. Because of their mobility, air forces would be able to deploy faster, and because of their long combat radius, they would not have to move as far into Poland as ground forces in order to engage the attacker's forces. A significant but not unduly large number of NATO aircraft are required to assist Polish forces in defending against the magnitude of the attack examined here.

- The results of the analysis point to the direction of what might be an optimal mixed solution: a combination of restructuring a portion of Polish ground forces and the contribution of NATO airpower.

- Obviously, the longer Polish ground forces can delay the attacking force from reaching the main defense line, the longer NATO airpower will have to attrit, slow, and disrupt the attacking forces. If the Poles are concerned about the kind of attack analyzed here, they should give consideration to acquiring these capabilities. In this regard, the West German experience of the past few decades should be instructive.

- In order for NATO airpower to be effective, a wide range of measures from basing and protecting NATO aircraft at Polish bases to conducting air operations with NATO and Polish forces needs to be considered by both Poland and NATO so that the potential contribution of NATO airpower can be realized in possible future operations. An option not discussed here, but which would alleviate some of the need for access to Polish bases, is the use of long-range aircraft such as the B-2.

This analysis has only scratched the surface of the problems associated with configuring defenses to meet the new challenges that Poland is facing. Yet the general outlines of a possible solution are apparent.

BIBLIOGRAPHY

Balcerowicz, Brig. Gen. Boreslaw, et al. (1992), "The Strategic Concept of the Defense of Poland," *Mysl Wojkowa*, No. 3.

Bennett, Bruce W. (1993), *RSAS 5.2 Summary*, RAND, Santa Monica, CA.

Davis, Paul K. (ed.) (1994), *New Challenges for Defense Planning: Rethinking How Much Is Enough*, RAND, Santa Monica, CA.

Davis, Paul K., Robert D. Howe, Richard L. Kugler, and William G. Wild (1989), *Variables Affecting Central-Region Stability: The "Operational Minimum" and Other Issues at Low Force Levels*, RAND, Santa Monica, CA.

Fox, Daniel B., and John Bordeaux (1993), *Global 92 Analysis of Prospective Conflicts in Central Europe in 2002*, RAND, Santa Monica, CA.

International Institute for Stategic Studies (IISS) (1992), *The Military Balance 1992–1993*, Brassey's Ltd., London, England.

Kugler, Richard L. (1993), *Commitment to Purpose: How Alliance Partnership Won the Cold War*, RAND, Santa Monica, CA.

Levine, Robert, T. T. Connors, M. G. Weiner, and R. A. Wise (1982), *A Survey of NATO Defense Options*, RAND, Santa Monica, CA.

Shlapak, David A., and Paul K. Davis (1991), *Possible Postwar Force Requirements for the Persian Gulf: How Little Is Enough?* RAND, Santa Monica, CA.

Szayna, Thomas (forthcoming), *Changing Polish Defensive Plans: Implications for the United States*, RAND, Santa Monica, CA.

Weiner, Milton G. (1986), "Analyzing Concepts for the Defense of NATO," in Reiner K. Huber (ed.), *Modeling and Analysis of Conventional Defense in Europe: Assessment of Improvement Options*, Plenum Press, New York.

Chapter 15

NOT MERELY PLANNING FOR THE LAST WAR

Bruce W. Bennett, Sam Gardiner, and Daniel B. Fox

This paper describes insights from a lengthy series of game-structured exercises attempting to avoid the usual sin of preparing to fight the last war. In these exercises, Red teams were tasked to develop aggressive strategies to prepare for future regional conflicts involving the United States, strategies that would reflect lessons learned from the Persian Gulf War by U.S. adversaries. The teams began by identifying their military objectives and deciding how U.S. strengths might impede those objectives, then turned to defining approaches for countering those strengths. Blue teams (U.S. and allies) responded to these Red approaches, looking for appropriate countermeasures. Not surprisingly, the Red strategies sought to avoid the circumstances that made the dramatic U.S. victory against Iraq possible. These involved a broad mix of initiatives at the strategic, operational, and tactical levels of warfare. The paper argues, for example, that the United States should expect conflicts in which: the context makes it difficult for the United States to intervene or to enlist the support of regional allies; acts of aggression are deliberately quick and limited; operations involve infantry in cities, mountains, and forests rather than heavy forces on long road marches; and the weapons and tactics used make it difficult for the United States to engage without suffering significant casualties. The paper also argues that weapons of mass destruction in the hands of regional states will cast a long and unpleasant shadow over future contingencies, requiring major changes in U.S. operations and sometimes making intervention doubtful.

INTRODUCTION

Analysts, like generals, often spend much of their time planning for the last war. The imagery of Operations Desert Storm and Desert Shield is still strong in our minds, and it is hardly surprising that so much current effort is going into studies that contemplate something akin to a replay of the Gulf War.

In this paper, however, we describe an effort to deviate from that standard pattern. For several years, RAND has conducted an effort on the future of warfare.[1]   Initially, it focused on the implications of the current military-technical revolution, which was to a large extent demonstrated in the Gulf War.[2]   Subsequently, it has focused on the lessons presumably derived from that war by current and future U.S. adversaries.

This research has employed a mixture of human gaming and analysis (the overall results of this research are documented in Bennett, Gardiner, Fox, and Witney, 1994).   The gaming has usually involved a mixture of some civilian analysts and a large number of serving or retired military officers, typically at the rank of Lieutenant Colonel/Colonel (Army, Air Force, Marines) or Commander/Captain (Navy).   We conducted nine such games at RAND on major regional contingencies, and three on lesser regional contingencies.   Four dealt with the Persian Gulf (these games are described in some detail in Bennett, Cecchine, Fox, and Gardiner, 1993), three with Europe, one with Korea, and one with concurrent conflicts involving Korea, the Persian Gulf, and Cuba.   Within this series we have considered the use of disabling technologies,[3] future technologies, and some other special items.   The project team[4] was also heavily involved in several dozen other war games at the National War College and the other Senior Service Colleges, including games focused on the problems of regional nuclear powers, and the Global Series of war games played at the U.S. Naval War College each summer.

The most important contribution of the games we have played is that we have forced ourselves to look at the other side.   We have looked at how other militaries might react to U.S. forces and doctrine.   We have focused on the two-sided character of war.

In this paper we focus largely on the future of warfare games and the insights gained from them.   Having learned in other games that players representing the United States and its allies (a Blue team) had difficulty, in the af-

---

[1]This work has been sponsored by Andrew Marshall, OSD's Director of Net Assessment, who has long been interested in ways to encourage thinking about non-standard scenarios and "soft" factors in warfare.

[2]However, even in this focus, we considered a broader range of issues such as strategy and doctrine, as suggested in Gardiner (1992c,d).

[3]Disabling weapons are intended to prevent the employment of military forces, rather than to destroy them; as a result they are sometimes referred to as nonlethal weapons.   For example, a chemical that causes fuel to turn to jelly would be a disabling weapon because it would prevent movement of opposing vehicles.   While transforming fuel to jelly should not kill opposing forces directly, it could lead to their death because they become isolated from supplies or because they face other threats.   Thus such a technology is only nonlethal in terms of direct effects.   See Gardiner (1993a,c).

[4]Besides the authors, the project team has included John Bordeaux, Arthur Bullock, Margaret Harrell, Robert Howe, Mark Hoyer, Carl Jones, Bruce Pirnie, John Schrader, Barry Wilson, and Nicholas Witney, all of RAND.

termath of the Gulf War, recognizing any serious opposition threat, we organized most games so that a single team played both the Blue and Red roles (Red representing the appropriate U.S. adversaries). The team began by assuming the role of the Red military; they were instructed to prepare for a future war with the United States. In the various games, the Red team was often briefed on the outcome of strategies that played to the U.S. strengths, as had Saddam Hussein in the Gulf War. The Red team was then asked to formulate creative approaches that did not cater to those strengths. To do so, they could consider the range of strategies and operational art that might be applied and could develop force structure and acquire new technologies (within constraints) that might occur over a number of years. The players then assumed the role of a Blue team and developed responses to the various threats postulated for Red.

To describe the insights gained from this work, we first review some key features of the Gulf War and then describe the broad lessons that potential future adversaries of the United States presumably learned from that war. We then provide a survey of the project team's observations, each discussed in a separate section: (1) warfare will be highly uncertain and variable (even more than conventional wisdom already recognizes); (2) adversaries will seek new patterns of warfare to oppose the United States; (3) these patterns will involve highly asymmetric strategies in which the adversaries avoid confronting U.S. strengths, instead playing on U.S. weaknesses; and (4) weapons of mass destruction will cast a shadow over almost all future contingencies.

THE GULF WAR AND ITS IMPLICATIONS

The Gulf War was the paradigm of what U.S. forces, as currently equipped, trained, and structured, do best. It provided the perfect showcase for the U.S. ability to bring to bear overwhelming conventional power in a coordinated, combined-arms fashion, with a precision made possible by advanced guidance technologies and superior surveillance and target-acquisition capabilities (Department of Defense, 1992). It was the ultimate demonstration of the doctrine of overwhelming force in action and of the invincibility of U.S. power in a conflict of this type.

Yet there are many reasons to believe that the results of Operation Desert Storm were unique to the warfare environment in which it was waged: The national command authority was willing to approve the use of overwhelming force. The United States was at the absolute top of the Cold War buildup. Every combat arm had significant technological advantages. There were no major distractions of U.S. attention and plenty of time to prepare. Allies were willing to defray U.S. costs. Also, a highly developed infrastructure was well supported by theater allies. The initiative was entirely with the coalition after

Iraq had seized Kuwait. In addition, the terrain was favorable, being mostly flat with dry soil.   Moreover, we faced a nearly friendless opponent whose forces proved to be highly unbalanced and whose personnel proved to be dispirited and demoralized even before the fighting began. Also, Iraq pursued a passive and entirely conventional operation. While Iraq had a number of chemical weapons, it had no nuclear warheads.

Moreover, it is important to remember that even if this warfare environment were duplicated, the dynamics of warfare imply that what succeeds once may not be equally successful again:

> As in any game from football to chess, each contestant is possessed of an independent will and can only be controlled by the other to a very limited extent. With each side seeking to achieve his objectives while preventing the other from doing the same, war consists in large part of an interplay of double-crosses. The underlying logic of war is, therefore, not linear but paradoxical. The same action will not always lead to the same result. The opposite, indeed, is closer to the truth. Given an opponent capable of learning, a very real danger exists that an action will not succeed twice because it has succeeded once (van Creveld, 1989: 319).

Sun Tzu also recognized the folly of trying to repeat previous successes when he stated, in *The Art of War:*

> Do not repeat tactics that have gained you one victory, but let your methods be regulated by the infinite variety of circumstances.

HOW, THEN, SHOULD WE THINK OF THE FUTURE?

Much of U.S. thinking about the future of warfare seems fixed on developing capabilities and how they will allow the United States to be even more decisive in future conflicts than we were in Operation Desert Storm. Many of the new technologies being pursued are impressive and will give the United States revolutionary capabilities in areas such as global surveillance and communications, precision strike, air superiority and defense, sea control and undersea superiority, advanced land combat, and nonlethal weapons (five of the science and technology thrusts introduced in Director of Defense Research and Engineering, 1992).

At the same time, any prospective opponent could gauge U.S. strengths from Operation Desert Storm. Prospective opponents appear to be adjusting their approaches to warfare in ways that the United States is likely to find challenging. Indeed, whoever next decides to embark on behavior that could lead to conflict with the United States (by threatening either our vital interests or the peace) is likely to have as a prime objective avoiding any repeat of the Gulf War scenario. He will no more seek to confront U.S. power on U.S. terms than David would have gone out against Goliath with a sword and shield.

As we look to the future, we need to weigh the impact of U.S. military advances against the likely actions that opponents could take to counter U.S. strengths. We are forced to contemplate what opponents *could do* to counter U.S. strengths, since we may not be able to predict with any precision what they *will do*. We need to paint as negative a picture as possible to cover the range of possible opposition actions, recognizing that in most cases we will not face that full range because neither the planning nor the implementation of plans by prospective opponents is likely to be flawless. We also must recognize that we could miss key themes, especially starting from U.S. mind-sets; thus we should expect some substantial surprises in future conflicts—e.g., the surprise of threats we had not expected and threats we had expected that did not materialize. Thus, we are forced into an era of managing uncertainties and developing approaches for handling especially the most dangerous ones.

Much of our work to date has focused on major regional contingencies (MRCs), such as might occur in Korea, the Persian Gulf, or Europe. We have only recently extended our thinking to lesser regional contingencies (LRCs) such as Somalia and Bosnia. Figure 1 illustrates the range of scenarios we have considered. As shown, we divided the possible contingencies into three categories:

1. MRCs in which the United States would be likely to sense a vital interest (with Korea and the Persian Gulf having primacy in current defense planning).
2. Other MRCs in which the United States would be more likely to play a peace-enforcing role.
3. LRCs in which the United States would probably also play a peace-enforcing role.

UNCERTAINTY AND VARIABILITY OF WARS

The range of potential contingencies in Figure 1 suggests that future threats are highly uncertain with respect to the identity of the opponent, his objectives and strategy, the qualities of the technologies available to him, his force

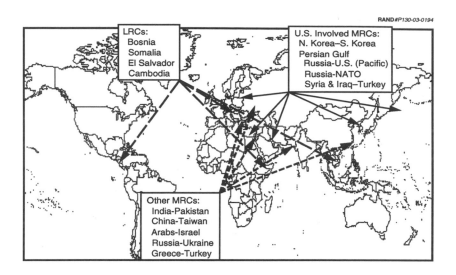

Figure 1—Classifying Future Contingencies

structure, and the skill with which he will apply his forces.[5]   By comparison, although the certainties were greatly exaggerated, the historical Soviet threat was nonetheless *relatively* certain in many dimensions—primarily with respect to the order of battle, weapon holdings, weapon quality, and operational style. While much of historical defense planning and analysis focused on "expected" conditions, the recent course of contingencies suggests that ignoring what will often be vast uncertainties is a serious peril.

Conditions encountered in future contingencies can be expected to vary enormously from possible theater to possible theater; the variables include weather, terrain, infrastructure, the degree of possible allied involvement on either side of the conflict, and the coherence and motivation of the adversary's forces. These conditions define the warfare environment that we would experience in a given contingency. To better clarify the kinds of differences that might be expected, Table 1 contrasts conditions in the historical Central European environment and the Korean theater, where U.S. forces would fight as part of the Combined Forces Command (CFC).

During the Cold War, the United States focused considerable effort on understanding the Soviet Union, its objectives, its technologies, its force

---

[5]This is not to say that some key aspects of these contingencies cannot be foreseen. For example, the two MRCs of principal interest still involve Korea and the Persian Gulf.

Table 1

Differences in Warfare Environment (An Example)

Major Issue (Example)	Historical Central Europe	Korean Theater
Context of conflict	Adversary aggression	Adversary aggression, adversary civil war, or ally initiative?
Objectives (U.S.)	Survival and freedom of NATO countries	Aid regional ally
Strategy (Adversary)	Defeat U.S./NATO forces in the field (selectively defeat weak partners)	Deter U.S./Japan involvement by creating "strategic events"
Operations (Offensive ground concept)	Penetration and envelopment of defending forces to destroy them; secure terrain objectives	Suppression and rapid penetration of defending units to secure terrain objectives
(Offensive air attack concept)	Use offensive counterair to suppress NATO air forces; establish local air control where possible	Suppression of CFC air forces with special operations forces and missiles; threaten Seoul and support ground forces when possible; use of ambush tactics defensive
(Chemical use)	Low chance, moderate preparations	High chance, low preparations
Resources (Assault forces)	Heavy forces with artillery support	Infantry with artillery and special operations forces support
Performance (Adversary's training)	Not as good as NATO in air or ground training	Highly inferior in air training, although tactics appropriate; superior to South Korea in ground training?
Allied cooperation (Defensive alliance)	Large group of allies who clearly perceive a mutual threat	ROK firm, U.S. likely firm, other regional actors may delay in participation
Other factors (Ability of terrain to support armor)	Good—extensive road network and many good off-road options	Poor—mountains channel terrain, few roads, rice paddies deny most off-road options except when ground freezes

structure, and its doctrine. It was argued that Soviet doctrine and weapons would be used by almost any adversary the United States might face and, therefore, could be the focus of U.S. defense thinking. In the future, prospective opponents will be more diverse, and the United States must generally confront them with reduced intelligence resources because of budget constraints. As a result, at least some of the Blue players in our games anticipated surprise and sought a C^3I system sufficiently robust to respond appropriately. Not only should the United States anticipate surprise in the form of inadequate or ambiguous warning, it may also be surprised about important details of the opposition's force structure, military technologies, and operational characteristics. For example, Stingers or SA-16s appearing by surprise could be devastating to helicopter-intensive operations or the airlift. A covert, last-minute emplacement of mines could wreak havoc in any amphibious operation expected to be straightforward, or new kinds of missiles or tactics might seriously reduce our efforts to suppress enemy air defenses. Such surprises could cause significant reversals in the conflict and undermine U.S. will. Many Blue players feared that the United States would not be prepared to adapt to such new conditions. For example, as opposition lethality increased, the Blue players felt uncomfortable adjusting to low-density, nonlinear combat environments.

NEW PATTERNS OF WARFARE[6]

In the wake of Operation Desert Storm, and with the dissolution of the Soviet Union and the sharp subsequent reductions in the militaries of the new states that the Soviet Union used to comprise, the United States has become the world's predominant conventional (and nuclear) military power. While a number of countries still field more ground force divisions, the United States has major advantages in force quality, combined arms capabilities, alliances and strategic mobility.[7] Despite planned reductions in U.S. military forces, it appears that technological innovation will help the United States sustain these advantages well into the next decade.

Potential adversaries can recognize this edge. Thus, in our games, the adversary typically does whatever he can to avoid a conflict of the Persian Gulf type. Based on these games, we expect that the prime aim of an adversary will be to ensure that U.S. conventional forces cannot be brought decisively to bear. He will be acutely aware both of U.S. strengths and of the fact that the preferred U.S. *pattern of warfare* would involve several weeks of unopposed deployment, followed by the establishment of operational dominance (via air su-

---

[6]By a pattern of warfare we mean the objectives to be pursued, the sequence of actions planned, and the general strategy and operational art that a side proposes to follow.

[7]Unfortunately, some current and prospective U.S. adversaries appear determined to pursue irregular (guerrilla) warfare, a form of warfare in which the United States is not predominant. RAND is working on characterizing U.S. peace-enforcing efforts to better understand the differences that irregular warfare makes to U.S. power projection.

periority, sea control, and attack of strategic targets), setting the scene for counteroffensive and decisive war termination (Figure 2 illustrates this preferred U.S. pattern of warfare).[8] He will realize that the pattern for the successful application of U.S. force requires time, cooperative allies in the region, and an enemy willing to present and identify himself. The intelligent adversary will seek to deny all these factors to the United States, and he may be able to do so because normally he will have the initiative. He will be aware of the possibilities open to him to counter U.S. capabilities in asymmetrical fashion at the operational level; for example, in trying to counter U.S. airpower, he might follow the logic shown in Figure 3, working backward from his objective to the campaigns, battles, and engagements that might be expected to accomplish it. This "threat menu" defines a number of ways an opponent might attempt to overcome U.S. airpower, such as campaigns that focus on limiting the number of U.S. aircraft in a theater area, reducing the number of sorties that the aircraft can fly, and/or limiting the effectiveness of sorties against targets. In turn, the adversary could limit the number of sorties by attacking airfields or national logistics (for example, destroying petroleum distribution and refining capabilities) or by timing a battle to occur in bad weather. Attacks on our air bases are a particular concern, since U.S. air forces will likely be concentrated on a small number of bases.

We refer to this as a threat menu because we believe that most opponents would choose multiple battle and engagement approaches, hoping to increase the potential of countering the U.S. capability. For example, an adversary

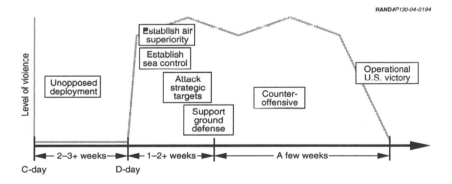

Figure 2—Assumed Pattern of Warfare by the United States

---

[8]C-day is the day in a crisis when U.S. force deployments begin into a theater, and D-day is the day when combat begins in a theater.

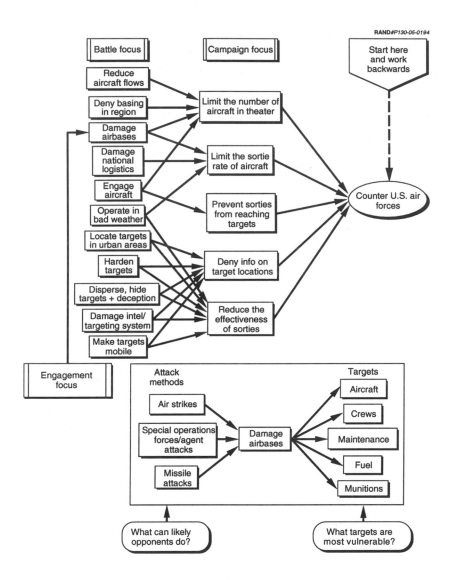

RAND#P130-05-0194

Figure 3—A Threat Menu

might target U.S. airfields while interdicting the regional fuel supply and field-ing a range of surface-to-air missiles with which to defend his forces and infra-structure. He might also attempt to prevent naval forces from coming within aircraft range of theater targets by sea-denial efforts including mines, antiship missiles, and other threats to interdict U.S. naval forces or at least deny sea control for some period of time. In our gaming, we use the threat menu to show the range of possible threats that could be posed against U.S. forces, then temper the list by considering what specific adversaries might be able to do and how the United States might respond, as discussed in the upcoming section on asymmetrical battles.

While such operational-level reactions to U.S. warfare patterns are important, most adversaries will realize that *their most effective responses will be made at the strategic level.* The adversary will likely adopt a strategy to deter U.S. intervention, to reverse it if it occurs, or, over a longer period, to wear out U.S. resolve and interest.

The United States is vulnerable to such actions because it no longer perceives a threat to its survival, as it did during the Cold War. Such a threat simplifies strategy: survival is an absolute imperative. The lack of such a threat implies that the objectives of U.S. military operations will be limited in the future. (For example, in Desert Storm the U.S. objective was to restore Kuwaiti independence, the flow of Gulf oil, and the regional balance of power; the United States did not perceive a threat to its national survival.) In turn, limited objectives imply that the United States will have to address basic tradeoffs when becoming involved in future conflicts: Are the losses and risks it will incur justified by the gains it may achieve? How many American lives and how much cost is the United States willing to trade, over what period of time, to ensure the security of any specific foreign power or to bring stability back to a given region? Limited U.S. objectives thus set a framework against which opponents can operate to deter U.S. involvement or cause a decision to terminate involvement. Ultimately, only the U.S. President and Congress will make this decision, which will be heavily influenced by how they personally feel about such tradeoffs and by how they react to the judgments of the media and public opinion. Thus, even who these leaders *are* makes a difference.

In our games, the perceived strength of the United States meant that prospective opponents in MRCs could not plan to win in conventional regular combat that lasted long enough for the United States to effectively project forces (i.e., beyond about one month). Thus, U.S. military power was seen as conveying a high level of deterrence against prospective opponents. (This perception was extremely strong among most of the senior officers who have been involved in our games. It was undoubtedly affected by the Desert Storm experience and was perhaps stronger than warranted.)

The potential military approaches that each side might employ include such options as[9]

---

[9]See Gardiner (1993d). Another military approach would be to punish the opposing country, perhaps through strategic attacks. While such an approach seems to have worked in the context of crisis coercion (e.g., the attack a few years ago against Libya), it

- Destroying or neutralizing the opposition army (along the lines recommended by Clausewitz), which could apply for U.S. actions in a few MRCs when U.S. interests are high and the opponent has significant but attackable forces (e.g., Desert Storm).

- Seizing complete control of the opposing country, when its forces are small and easily overcome (e.g., Grenada or Panama). Even small local forces may be difficult to overcome if they assume guerrilla tactics; thus, this option probably will not be readily available to the United States.

- Attacking the opposition strategy (as recommended by Sun Tzu), when the opposition's forces are either superior or not very vulnerable and/or his national interests are low (e.g., U.S. participation in Bosnia or Somalia). This approach seeks "strategic events" that will cause the opponent to change strategy.

Each option involves a different pattern of conflict.

Because of U.S. military strength, most opponents will find only the third approach feasible; thus, the United States will normally find itself defending against "strategic events." Such strategic events will capitalize on U.S. limited objectives and thus will be aimed at causing the United States to appraise intervention in terms of the balance between the costs and benefits. The battle in Mogadishu on October 3, 1993, was a case in point, when elite U.S. rangers suffered scores of casualties. The political aftermath even included calls for the Secretary of Defense to resign.

As this example from Somalia illustrates, a major change has occurred in public expectations that casualties will be very low (e.g., tens or hundreds), in part because they will be avoided by use of precision weapons. U.S. casualties could thus become a major focus for the opposition in creating strategic events: The U.S. will to participate in a nonvital conflict may be seriously affected if casualties do not conform to these expectations. Yet casualties could be significantly higher in future contingencies because of enhanced weapon lethality, increased requirements for infantry (as opposed to mechanized) operations, nonlinear or urban battlefields and operations against the U.S. rear areas, irregular (guerrilla) combat operations by opposing forces, and the potential use of weapons of mass destruction.

Against this background, our gaming and analysis have suggested a range of methods by which the adversary who foresees or engages in conflict with the United States could (and probably will) try to improve his chances of success. It is convenient to consider these methods under six headings:

---

is less clear that such an approach would stop, let alone reverse, the hostile actions of an aggressor (indeed, the strategic bombing of Desert Storm apparently did not have such an effect). We have, therefore, not yet pursued this approach in any detail.

1. Preparation for conflict with the United States.
2. Disruption of U.S. abilities to form coalitions.
3. Formation of anti-U.S. coalitions.
4. Manipulation of the strategic context.
5. Manipulation of the strategic environment of the military campaign.
6. Manipulation of the operational environment of the military campaign.

The adversary will be able to mold contingencies using these methods because he will have the initiative in the conflict, at least at first.

Preparation for Conflict with the United States

Potential future adversaries might seek to reduce U.S. military power and influence in two ways:

- By affecting U.S. interest in military affairs (long time scale) with the intent of reducing the size and capabilities of U.S. military forces.
- By disrupting U.S. strengths (political, economic, and military).

The results of these two methods would often be at odds. For example, if the world oil market faced a constant terrorist threat against oil shipments, U.S. attention and resources would probably be diverted to deal with such threats and thus be less available for major regional contingencies, but U.S. interest in military affairs would be heightened. The challenge for the opponents would thus be to find the proper mix of efforts.

Our Red players generally concluded that an apparently benign world environment would be most advantageous to their interests, because the United States would then tend to focus inward. The U.S. domestic budget would tend to rise at the cost of further military cuts apparently warranted by the lack of international threats. To the extent that U.S. economic recovery did not occur or was slow, the resulting military cuts could become large and generally irreversible (at least within a few years), reducing the ability of the United States to intervene in future conflicts.

In some of our games, the players found that the many international frictions faced by the United States appear to be fertile ground on which to disrupt U.S. strengths. For example, the disagreements between the United States and its major trading partners on trade practices could be aggravated by appropriately timed revelations of "unfair" behavior (from a U.S. perspective) and perhaps amplified into trade warfare by the natural forces developing around the world. Such developments would have serious implications for the U.S.

economy but would generally not heighten U.S. interest in military affairs. U.S. willingness to become involved in foreign conflicts could also be reduced if it were to become entangled in some difficult and unresolvable lesser regional conflicts around the world. U.S. involvement in trade and military conflicts might then be turned to incite anti-American feeling among the populations of U.S. allies, putting stress on U.S. forward presence and its ability to form coalitions.

Some Red players also considered becoming involved in U.S. domestic politics. For example, cases could occur in which commitments of funds through third parties would affect American political campaigns. While such actions are risky, they could also bring significant returns because of the importance of who the U.S. decisionmakers are at the time of the conflict, and because the decisionmakers will also determine the size and character of the U.S. forces as they evolve during the preparation period. Indeed, for opponents who can afford to wait, the election of specific U.S. decisionmakers might be a more important condition for war initiation than any given force structure or technology change.

Disruption of U.S. Abilities to Form Coalitions

One key element of Desert Storm was the U.S. ability to form an international coalition. The political reasons for coalitions are likely to be compelling in many future MRCs—the benefits being greater international legitimacy ascribed to a collective action and the improved chances of maintaining domestic support if allies are seen to be bearing their share of the burden. The military arguments for acting as part of a coalition will also remain and may intensify. While in Desert Storm the major fraction of the military power came from U.S. forces, the United States is likely to find itself more dependent on coalition partners in future conflicts because of the reductions planned in U.S. forces and because those forces may continue to lack specialized resources to deal with some key threats. For example, the United States may still have to rely at least in part on coalition partners to support any kind of broad-scale naval mine-clearing operation. Regional allies will also be depended on for support infrastructure (including ports, airfields, and elements of resupply).

While not anxious to deal with this subject, the Blue players in our games usually came to recognize that they needed cooperation from regional countries to support their operations in any given theater, especially if the United States must deploy into a hostile environment. For example, if North Korea were able to heavily interdict South Korean airfields, airfields in Japan, Russia, and/or China would be critical to U.S. operations in Korea. The failure to form an appropriate coalition could completely undermine U.S. willingness or capability to intervene.

The warfare preparations of Red players therefore included efforts to undermine or delay U.S. coalitions. Clearly, the United States needs to be proactive in forming and maintaining relations with key allies essential to resolving prospective future conflicts. To the extent that U.S. attention turns increasingly toward internal issues or toward more divisive economic and human-rights issues, maintaining such relations will become more difficult. Tradeoffs will be necessary, as well as keeping issues in different spheres separate. The United States cannot afford to treat nations as either with us or against us, good or bad.

The United States also needs to prepare for combined operations in future coalitions. U.S. coordination and preparation with prospective coalition partners are needed in peacetime to be effective in wartime.[10] Without a sense for a threat in a given region, such preparations may not be made; thus, by maintaining a benign appearance as suggested above, prospective opponents can reduce the likelihood that we make such key preparations.

Formation of Anti-U.S. Coalitions and Coordinating Crises

Many prospective U.S. opponents around the world share common concerns and interests (in particular, a serious dislike of the United States) and thus have some basis for coalition formation. These common interests have appeared as part of weapon technology trades in the recent past, such as North Korean technological support of ballistic-missile and other weapon developments in Syria and Iran.[11] The Red players in our games did not feel that

---

[10]In Desert Storm the United States resolved combined-operations problems in part by placing coalition ground forces with which U.S. forces were less well integrated into a single area of operations; the ongoing reductions in U.S. force levels may not allow such a luxury in the future. Clearly, the United States needs to better understand the forces of its prospective coalition partners: how they operate, what their strengths and weaknesses are, and how they differ from U.S. forces. Investments of this sort, supported by joint and combined exercises and training, can significantly improve the effectiveness of future coalitions and in some cases perhaps help the United States make intervention decisions (for example, if it becomes clear that the U.S. forces available are insufficient to meet limited U.S. objectives). A tremendous tension is evident in making such evaluations: If the United States properly evaluates the forces of a prospective ally, it will undoubtedly identify many deficiencies (even U.S. forces have deficiencies), but if these deficiencies become publicly known, confidence in the ally may be undermined to such a point that the United States is unwilling to support it.

[11]"Western intelligence sources report . . . a series of secret deals between the Stalinists of North Korea and the ayatollahs of Iran. Under the arrangement, Tehran is giving the Pyongyang government $500 million to help it develop a ballistic missile sys-

sufficient commonality of interests existed among prospective U.S. opponents for them to form a close alliance; they did, however, recognize the value of facing the United States with simultaneous contingencies and agreed that if (and only if) each party had reason to independently confront the United States, they would have every reason to do so simultaneously.[12]

While the United States has the ability to pursue a major regional conflict in many regions around the world, it has only limited ability to do so in two or more MRCs simultaneously. This situation is implicitly recognized in the Administration's recent "Bottom-Up Review" of U.S. forces for the post–Cold War world (Aspin, 1993), which sets as a goal the fielding of forces sufficient to fight and win two "nearly simultaneous" MRCs and notes that in consequence "our plans call for substantial enhancements to our strategic mobility," including sealift and airlift. The review also notes that "certain specialized high-leverage units or unique assets might be 'dual tasked,' that is, used in both MRCs." The implication is that the near-simultaneous eruption of two MRCs would pose some very severe problems. The United States might have to dilute its effectiveness in each theater area or allow the opponent in one theater to achieve its objectives while the United States attempted to resolve the conflicts sequentially.[13] Such conditions raise the intervention risks for the United States and may undermine U.S. will (internal political resolve) to intervene.

Manipulation of the Strategic Context

For any regional power contemplating an aggression that risks a U.S. response, the first lesson from Saddam Hussein's debacle must be to take pains with the political stage-management. In the force-structuring component of our games, we purposefully pressed Red players to acquire a range of sophisti-

---

tem that could deliver nuclear and chemical warheads to targets in Japan. In return, North Korea has agreed to sell an unspecified number of nuclear bombs to the Iranians and to provide them with designs for nuclear-weapons-reprocessing plants. According to one estimate, by 1995 the North Koreans could possess sufficient weapons-grade plutonium to manufacture as many as seven bombs." "Washington Whispers," *U.S. News and World Report*, March 29, 1993, p. 18.

[12]See, for example, Silverberg (1993:18). Much of the discussion on this subject, however, neglects the fact that most countries would have to be fairly desperate to begin a war in which they anticipate U.S. intervention against them. Such desperation might compel them to take actions (such as coordinating efforts with another "renegade" country) beyond those we might otherwise normally expect.

[13]The "win-win" or "win-hold-win" strategies assume that the United States can indeed handle these kinds of circumstances. The players in our games were less optimistic, assuming that the opponents would fight the United States on an asymmetrical basis, as discussed below.

cated weapon technologies before conflict initiation. When the players were then directed to engage the United States and its coalition, they concluded that weapon acquisition took third place in importance behind the strategic context and the concept of operations.

Events must be handled so as to provide the United States with the best possible excuses and reasons *not* to intervene and strategic events that challenge any decision to intervene. The strategic "target" of adversary action is the U.S. will to intervene. While U.S. opponents might have some difficulty achieving these effects, some of the political strategies they might attempt to employ are the following:

- The situation should be presented as one in which U.S. intervention is demanded neither by national interest nor by considerations of principle. A requirement would be to broadcast assurances relating to the well-being of U.S. nationals or the continuing availability of important raw materials (such as oil). It would also require an effort (possibly over many months in advance) to convince U.S. public opinion that the victim of the aggression did not deserve the spilling of any U.S. blood in his defense. This effect might be achieved if the target country's government were perceived as totalitarian, oppressive, and/or in a state of anarchy (so that invasion could be represented as a necessary restoration of law and order).[14]

- Bearing in mind the time required by the United States to deploy into any theater, the aggressor might be well advised to pursue a short war. He would create the desired end state on the ground before the United States could respond.[15] This would probably require a strategy of surprise, giving the United States minimal response time[16] (at the expense to the aggressor

---

[14]Most U.S. adversaries cannot directly cause such perceptions in the United States, but they may be able to contribute to them. For example, North Korea might attempt again to destabilize South Korea, inciting riots to cause a harsh reaction by the South Korean government that would project an image of anarchy and oppression.

[15]Reduced U.S. forward deployments exacerbate the problem of short warning. Short warning limits ability to *deny* opposition objectives, instead driving the United States to either a strategy of *punishment* or a large-scale *counteroffensive*. Since a counteroffensive restoring the status quo ante would require far more U.S. force than a defensive operation, inadequate forward-deployed forces would raise the cost of U.S. intervention and might tip the balance in favor of not intervening at all.

[16]For example, in the Gulf War the United States did not respond militarily until after Kuwait had been captured. Historically, many analysts assumed longer U.S. preparation times, in part to allow ground forces to deploy and participate in the conflict. Moreover, much of the military analysis community argued against assuming the need for short response times because of (1) the need for opponents to mobilize and prepare and (2) the quality of U.S. intelligence and warning capabilities. However, with limited objectives, an opponent might forgo some preparations, if by so doing he delayed the U.S. response. The United States needs not only the ability to perceive military preparations, but also a more general understanding of the opposition's intent

of less-than-perfect preparedness and more limited objectives).[17] (An example might be the North Koreans seeking to move the DMZ toward the Han River and to transform Seoul into an "international city.") In addition, the U.S. President might have to pause at the beginning of a conflict to build a consensus within the United States and internationally; such a pause might give opposition forces time to achieve their objectives unless regional allies could defend forward. As Hitler demonstrated in the 1930s, successful attainment of a series of limited objectives can in due course add up to the attainment of some very large ones. If a new situation favorable to the aggressor could be rapidly stabilized, U.S. intervention might be not only militarily more difficult but also politically more objectionable: "restarting the bloodshed."

- The aggressor would be best served by creating termination conditions that would be preferred to military intervention by at least some within the United States. These conditions should be achieved before significant U.S. intervention. Creating them might involve crushing the local military opposition, providing some form of legitimate political government for the captured territory, guaranteeing and demonstrating ready access to the captured resources (e.g., maintaining the flow of oil), and establishing prepared positions for forward-deployed forces from which to defend the captured territory.[18]

- Ideally, aggression would be timed to take place when the United States was distracted by some significant crisis elsewhere.

The interesting question is, "What does it take to deter U.S. intervention?" Historically, our analyses of deterrence have focused on deterring opponent (especially Soviet) action; in the future, we need to be able to address deterrence of the United States in order to prepare for, or perhaps forestall, contingencies that capitalize on such deterrence.

(the problem faced by both the United States in the Gulf War and the Soviet Union in 1940), and the will to respond given the various uncertainties. Short response times appear to have become the base assumption in recent Defense Department analyses. See, for example, Aspin (1993), especially pp. 5–6.

[17]However, in some of our Persian Gulf games, U.S. strength caused the Red players to *expand* their objectives. They concluded that they could win only by "securing the entire Saudi peninsula," so as to make even a medium-term U.S. intervention very difficult. This usually meant occupying parts of the peninsula that they could reach quickly, and then heavily damaging other areas' airfields and seaports to deny their use to the United States.

[18]Saddam Hussein clearly attempted to achieve some of these conditions in the wake of his attack on Kuwait. Still, he failed to prevent U.S. intervention, in part by being unable to achieve more fully acceptable terminating conditions (e.g., the lack of a legitimate successor Kuwaiti government) and in part because of the resolution of the U.S. President.

Manipulation of the Strategic Environment

In future conflicts, the United States will want a quick, decisive campaign, with relatively few casualties. Based on our Red team behavior, it seems likely that the adversary will seek to demonstrate that this U.S. game plan will not be achievable. Some skill will be required in the modulation of the level of violence. A strategic event involving some spectacularly heavy loss of U.S. forces at the outset of the conflict could lead to a U.S. withdrawal, similar to that following the truck-bomb attack on the Marine barracks in Beirut several years ago; on the other hand, it could precipitate a firm U.S. commitment similar to that following the Japanese attack on Pearl Harbor.[19]   To create the proper kind of strategic event, a smart adversary might follow a progressive approach, along the lines set out below.

The immediate imperative would be simply to demonstrate that "blood will flow" in consequence of U.S. intervention; this approach would be particularly effective if the initial aggression were carried out with relatively high casualties. For this purpose, losses by the regional participants, including the aggressor, would be as good or better than U.S. losses and perhaps even more effective if the United States caused some of the losses. Consider for example the shock felt in Britain at the sinking of the Argentinean cruiser *Belgrano*, with heavy loss of life, in the opening stages of the Falklands conflict. Civilian casualties would be particularly effective; perhaps the United States could be manipulated into shooting down another commercial airliner. Civilian casualties could also be maximized during the anticipated U.S. strategic air campaign by careful collocation of targets: every bunker should be beneath a Sheraton, every SAM battery on the roof of a mosque, and every chemical warfare factory beside an elementary school.[20]   The probability of creating a strategic event could be maximized by granting full access to the U.S. and international media. Even if American will were not significantly shaken, the support of any coalition would surely be complicated.

---

[19]Some analysts have argued that a large part of the difference between these two cases is a clear U.S. sense of national interests and objectives in the Pearl Harbor case (the solution to stopping the Japanese was clear though difficult) versus a poor sense of the same issues in Beirut. The clarity of solution in future major regional contingencies will be muddled by perceptions of the Gulf War outcome (and despite the U.S. limited objectives): Did the United States really solve the Iraqi threat in Desert Storm, or did it simply provide a temporary resolution that will fester (while Saddam Hussein continues to control Iraq)?

[20]A major uncertainty is the extent to which U.S. public opinion, and perhaps more importantly international public opinion, would allow collateral damage. The experiences of both the Gulf War and Somalia suggest that some collateral damage would be tolerated, but large numbers (hundreds?) of particularly innocent casualties might become a heavy burden.

The United States, too, might suffer casualties. In the early stages before the United States is fully committed, it would be better for the opponent to inflict casualties by "indirect" means, avoiding an incontrovertible "signature" and, therefore, not providing a clear justification, or target, for retaliation. Examples might be the use of naval mines or of third-party terrorist and/or special forces attack. As in the case of the attack on the American Marines in Beirut noted above, the lack of an obvious target against which to retaliate could deepen the sense of unease in the United States about just what its forces are getting into, more than it would inflame U.S. national desire for revenge.

If, despite such tactics, a significant U.S. intervention were to proceed, the adversary might need to create a strategic event with sufficient military or psychological impact to stop the intervention in its tracks and cause a reassessment by the United States (and/or its partners) of the wisdom of the course on which they had embarked. A really devastating series of terrorist attacks, perhaps even on the U.S. homeland, might achieve this purpose. The sinking of a major naval ship would be such a strategic event, if it could be done. An appropriate strategic event might be caused by the use of nuclear, biological, or chemical (NBC) weapons against U.S. or coalition forces in the field, concentrations of relatively less well protected coalition forces in rear areas, the homelands of regional coalition partners, or even, as ballistic and cruise-missile technologies proliferate, against the U.S. homeland itself. Any such strategic event would clearly be high risk—it might very well cause a "Pearl Harbor" reaction, leading to an ultimate "Hiroshima" and drive for unconditional surrender.[21] At the very least, it would achieve an "operational event" involving a significant time-out in a campaign that was developing badly.

In our games, the players normally felt that opponents would not attack targets within the United States even if they could (because such attacks would be likely to strengthen the U.S. will to respond). They also thought that opponents should consider only targets within the theater and en route to the theater. Few Red players in our games were willing to attack U.S. air forces in the United States (where the aircraft tend to be most vulnerable) because they anticipated that such attacks would solidify U.S. public opinion against the opposing power(s) and increase the likelihood and persistence of U.S. involvement in the regional conflict. We are less certain that opponents with different cultural norms and attitudes toward revenge would refrain from such attacks,

---

[21]The U.S. response to casualties is also likely to be a function of the way in which the attrition occurs (e.g., the sinking of a cruiser by a mine may have a different impact than opposition forces shooting U.S. soldiers), the potential for recurrence (e.g., if one cruiser has been sunk by a mine, other ships could be as well), and who has suffered (e.g., U.S. servicemen being shot may be different from U.S. civilians being shot).

especially once the United States had pressed strategic attacks against their homelands.

Manipulation of the Operational Environment

At the operational level, opponents might be able to manipulate many aspects of future warfare. For example:

- The aggressor could force the United States to deploy into a hostile environment. In Desert Storm the United States could deploy into secure ports and airfields and enjoy the advantages of substantial host nation support. In future wars, prospective opponents will have significant incentives to threaten U.S. entry into the theater. At the lower end, such a threat might imply that the United States must deploy security and area defensive forces (such as Patriot missiles) early and face the increased risk of significant losses early in the campaign. Such changes could significantly lengthen the time required to put a complete defensive force into a theater, especially if the United States were also forced to operate through damaged facilities and to bring all of its own supplies (e.g., fuel). Moreover, the opposition players felt that airfields and port facilities were very high-density target areas that invited attack. At the high end of such threats, the United States might have to add several campaign phases in which it secured the required lines of communication and entry points before it could even deploy into the theater. If, for example, the Strait of Hormuz were closed by a combined threat of mines, land-based antiship missiles, aircraft, and submarines, it might take some time to neutralize these threats and even enter the Persian Gulf (let alone put substantial forces ashore).

- If the campaign developed into ground engagements, the adversary would be guided by the need to maximize U.S. casualties. He would aim for a nonlinear battlefield with intermining of the sides' forces and close contact with U.S. forces. This would make the targeting of his forces more difficult and U.S. fratricide more likely. The adversary might be willing to accept very adverse loss ratios to cause high U.S. losses (as in Vietnam). In addition, the cultures of at least some prospective U.S. opponents view revenge as acceptable and expected, which might prompt them to attempt to impose some direct losses on the U.S. citizens (recall Saddam's use of hostages).

- Adversaries are likely to prefer fighting in urban terrain where, because of concerns about collateral casualties, the United States might have to limit its use of advanced munitions, especially area-effects weapons.

- An opponent would be conscious of the "seams" in the C^3 of coalition forces; he might even seek to create conditions in which coalition forces erroneously attack each other (or appear to have done so).

- More generally, opponents are likely to seek infantry as opposed to armored engagements (in part by seeking enclosed terrain) beccause they reduce the advantages of U.S. armor and expose U.S. personnel more to attrition.

- If an adversary felt he could not win the conventional battle, he might resort to classical guerrilla tactics. He would deny battle to U.S. forces when he did not possess an advantage and press battle selectively when he felt there was an advantage to be gained. In Somalia, General Aideed has shown himself the most recent exponent of this approach.

In essence, the opponent would attempt to create a battlefield environment more like Vietnam than the Persian Gulf. He would be seeking "operational events" in which U.S. failures to achieve objectives or the costs it paid led to a change in the operational approach. For example, some limitations the United States might have to face include the following:

- The abandonment of air bases, ports, or other facilities struck with persistent chemical weapons, since decontamination uncertainties might imply too great a risk against the requirement to minimize casualties.

- The abandonment of parts of the operating environment because of opposition threats. For example, U.S. air forces might choose not to operate below 10,000–15,000 feet because of air defense artillery and shoulder-fired SAM threats.

- The abandonment of many kinds of operations. For example, the United States might conclude that an amphibious assault could be too risky if the opposition was likely to possess nuclear weapons or even chemical or biological weapons. In our war gaming experience, amphibious assaults against enemy territory (e.g., against Pyongyang or Wonsan in Korea) were often staged as part of a U.S. coalition counteroffensive, in which a military threat was placed against the survival of the opposition regime. In our games, a nuclear response (or at very least a chemical response) was often employed (the opposition attempting to break the back of the U.S. threat and U.S. will before it could mature), especially since that response can be executed on the opponent's own territory or in its coastal waters (very different from striking coalition territory). This limitation complicated likely U.S. responses. Indeed, in some cases, Red players considered weapons prepared in the form of a nuclear land mine, which would be detonated by the incursion of U.S. forces.

From the opposition perspective, it would clearly be ideal if operational events could be created that also became strategic events. Thus, if North Korea could induce the United States to abandon its air bases in South Korea and, by so doing, cause a crisis of U.S. will to intervene in a Korean war, the operational development would serve overall North Korean objectives well. The opposition will recognize, however, that the outcome of such a strategic event could be a renewed and expanded U.S. intervention (especially if many Americans were killed by chemical weapons or a nuclear attack).

In preparing to fight against the United States, potential aggressors are likely to recognize that if their operations are successful, they would have to trade their expected gains for the losses they might suffer. In particular, the U.S. emphasis on targeting strategic C^3 suggests that it would attempt to threaten the survival of opposition regimes.[22] In our games, most Red players viewed regime survival as ultimately their most important objective and thus found such a U.S. interest (and capability) very deterring; however, they were prepared in some cases to take extreme measures in response to such U.S. actions (see the discussion of third-party nuclear weapons below), hoping to dissuade the United States from pressing such threats. Such campaigns would create a mismatch in objectives, with the United States still having limited objectives but potentially having pushed its opponents into unlimited objectives. We must also consider alternative criteria for decisionmaking by future foes, such as cases in which U.S. opponents attack as a last desperate attempt to survive.[23]

ASYMMETRICAL BATTLES WILL CHARACTERIZE WAR[24]

Recent military discussions have described several alternative future battle-fields. Russian writings have focused on a high-tech, symmetrical development along the lines of what the United States achieved in Desert Storm and is seeking with further developments of military technologies. Since few if any future U.S. opponents are likely to be able to respond symmetrically, we antic-ipate that future battlefields will develop asymmetrically. The extremes in

---

[22]The United States might also threaten the survival of the opposing regime by destroying its economic infrastructure. Indeed, almost any form of strategic attack is likely to escalate U.S. objectives to theater strategic from theater operational, though the United States may lack an overall approach to a theater strategic conflict resolution—which may become a problem, especially in maintaining domestic and coalition support, in future conflicts.

[23]One might argue that North Korea may be approaching such a point, as its economy seems headed for failure; a similar perspective contributed to the Japanese initiation of their involvement in World War II. We have found that it is difficult for U.S. players to take this view, because they do not find themselves in desperate circumstances.

[24]The importance of the asymmetrical battle first came to our attention in the work done by Lieutenant General Phil Shutler, USMC (ret.). General Shutler applied the framework of asymmetrical battle to describe the success of U.S. operations in the Pacific during World War II. He uses this idea of asymmetrical battle in a course he teaches at the National Defense University.

asymmetry may occur if a high-tech U.S. force is countered by a guerrilla force practicing irregular warfare. These alternatives have substantially different implications from each other and require differing analytic approaches, e.g., as outlined below.

The High-Tech, Regular Combat Battlefield

Recent Russian writings on the future of war focus on the developing high-tech, regular combat battlefield (see, for example, Dick, 1993). They believe that

> future war will be dominated by precision weaponry, "information support" (i.e., reconnaissance and C3) and electronic warfare (EW), the three being integrated with synergistic effect into a combat system which will again fundamentally change the nature of warfare.

> Long-range battle is not merely enjoying an increasing role but will become the dominant, and often an independent, form of combat in future war. Employing EW, fixed and rotary wing aviation, cruise and ballistic missiles and long range tube and rocket artillery with ACMs, key elements of the enemy's tactical and operational groupings will be engaged throughout the depth of their deployment very soon after their detection by multifarious air and space based reconnaissance means. Effective strikes may be exploited rapidly by air and air-ground echelons—air assault, forward, raiding and enveloping detachments—to defeat or destroy the crippled and disrupted enemy and gain a tempo. What used to be thought of as the "main forces," the bulk of the tank and mechanized troops, will essentially be reduced to the role of exploitation elements (as, indeed, they were regarded in the nuclear period). For safety, they may be held far from contact with the enemy "main forces" during the decisive "electronic-fire engagement," and may, even on commital, engage in close combat for far briefer periods than hitherto (Dick, 1993:2).

Maneuver takes on a new role at two levels. Tactically, "units move frequently to increase their chances of ducking out from under an upcoming strike" (Dick, 1993:6). Operationally, the combination of air power (including helicopters), missiles, and long-range raiding and vertical envelopment has fundamentally changed the character of battles. For example,

> raiding forces in the enemy's depth may not so much aid and support the advance of the main forces as be their cutting edge. After all, the main combat power of either side will reside in its long range weaponry and associated "information support" and command and control, which are deployed in the depth, and the destruction or disruption of these will confer a major, perhaps decisive advantage to the more successful side.

Defensively,

> even if the defender were able to deploy huge numbers, it would not be possible to create an insurmountable defence. No matter how well prepared in the engineering sense, no matter how dense or deep, precision and ACM strikes will blast breaches as assuredly as their nuclear predecessors (albeit without the latter's collateral damage and contamination which hindered exploitation). Moreover, vertical envelopment will also be used to erode the cohesion of the defence. Rather, operational defence will have to deploy half or even more of available forces in the second echelon and rely on maneuver for success. After prolonged debate, the Russian theorists are now coming to accept that only manoeuvre defence is viable on the future battlefield. This will comprise firstly the manoeuvre of fire, obstacles (remote mining) and electronic strikes to inflict attrition and disruption on the attacker while he is approaching the forward edge. When penetration—accepted as inevitable—occurs, the defender will conduct delaying actions, withdrawal to depth positions or counter-penetration where the attacker is strong, and counter-thrusts where he is vulnerable. The aim will be to affect such a change in the correlation of forces that the defender can seize the initiative and, exploiting successful counter-strikes, go onto the counter-offensive (Dick, 1993:7).

A Reactive Approach

Dick (1993:13) concludes his description with some interesting comments:

> It is, however, unlikely to say the least that Russia will be able to make the technological or the economic progress in the foreseeable future that will be required to keep the country in the first rank of powers able to conduct high-tech, high intensity conflict. Once again, as in the twenties and thirties, theory is marching well ahead of practical ability. More disturbing still for Russia, however, is the fact that her military thinkers seem to be devoting their talents to the study of the sort of war Russia is perhaps least likely, as well as least able, to fight. Little work appears to be done on the mid and, particularly, low intensity conflict that is certain to trouble the country.

If the Russians are unlikely to be able to pursue the high-tech approach, we can expect few others will have that ability, although the Swedish approach to the high-technology battlefield is an interesting complement and counterpoint, as described in Gardiner (1993b).

An alternative way of addressing U.S. military power can be referred to as the "reactive" approach. The foregoing analysis assumed a smart adversary might try to manage American responses by avoiding U.S. strengths and exploiting U.S. weaknesses. Similar considerations could inform his approach to military planning. For example, the adversary would be likely to avoid air combat with the United States (a symmetrical response) and instead seek to destroy U.S. aircraft on the ground or apply passive defenses to his targets to make them difficult to destroy using aircraft. His exploitation of U.S. weaknesses would create asymmetrical battles. A similar approach might be expected to exert some influence on the force structure he adopts and the military technologies he pursues, over time.

This argument should not be overstated: no regional power will be guided in these matters solely or even primarily by the prospect of conflict with the United States.[25] Regional powers are influenced in their military decisions primarily by regional considerations. Desert Storm may have demonstrated that a conventional air force will be of little use to a regional power up against the United States, but it does not follow that a country such as Iran will not wish to maintain such an air force to assist in dealing with its regional opponents. Also, it should not be assumed that if a regional power chooses to pursue NBC weapons or ballistic or cruise-missile technology, it will be doing so primarily to confront the United States; such proliferation is likely to continue to be fueled, as in the past, by regional rivalries and ambitions and by the imperative of regime survival.

Countering U.S. Strengths

Nevertheless, aggressive regional powers can be expected to concentrate on developing capabilities that advanced military powers will find hard to deal with. They should not be expected to do so by matching U.S. capabilities, in large part because many U.S. capabilities are highly advanced (they cannot be matched in the short term) and are also cultural in many cases. For example, U.S. airpower is as much as anything a function of issues such as training approaches, the responsiveness of personnel to training, the willingness and ability to delegate authority and support independent operations, and the ability to assimilate a complex situation rapidly and determine an appropriate course of action. Thus, even if U.S. opponents acquired Flanker or Fulcrum aircraft, they would not be likely to pose a major air threat against U.S. air forces (at least in the short term).

Other ways do exist to counter U.S. strengths.[26] Opponents can often find a wide range of counters, many of which do not require high levels of skill. Opposition acquisition of key weapon technologies and the fielding of appropriate weapon systems could significantly impact both opposition and U.S.

---

[25]However, countries like North Korea that face established U.S. alliances or declared interests might be strongly influenced by the likely requirement to deal with the United States if they were to attack a neighbor.

[26]The counter capability logic is developed in more detail in Gardiner (1992a), Bennett (1993c), and Fox (1993b).

doctrine and, by implication, U.S. force structure. For example, how would the United States respond to an opponent with a large cruise missile force equipped with sensor-fuzed weapons designed to defeat current armored/ mechanized forces and doctrine (a capability postulated by several of our Red teams)?[27] Because these counters are not symmetrical with U.S. capabilities, U.S. analysts have tended to discount them in their analyses (if the United States has chosen not to pursue these approaches, how important could they be?), even though the capabilities they target (such as U.S. intelligence dominance) are often highly concentrated target systems that are relatively fragile and susceptible to damage.[28] But some intelligence indicates that efforts by prospective opponents to acquire a range of key weapon technologies are already underway. Goliath must expect David to choose his own weapons and must be ready to engage in asymmetrical battles.

The threat menu illustrated in Figure 3 assists us in this process. It provides a framework for us to focus on the kinds of potential threats and to decide which are significant and serious enough that they need to be considered in formulating potential threat environments (which make up a part of the warfare environment discussed above) and in developing intelligence-collection requirements for a given theater.

Technologies Can Also Work Against the United States

As this analysis shows, the reactive approach may involve more or less high-tech capabilities; that is, technology does not uniformly favor the United States and in some ways can be selectively used to effectively counter its capabilities.

The implication is that the future holds a different kind of military competition. Rather than the historical pattern of competition in largely symmetrical areas (e.g., tanks versus tanks or fighters versus fighters), analysts should expect opponents to pursue a few different technologies in a combined-arms approach to deal with U.S. strengths (and not just for a single "silver bullet" to defeat U.S. forces). This complicates analysis because it largely invalidates simple symmetrical capability comparisons (such as the traditional tank-versus-tank

---

[27]Sensor-fuzed weapons are large packages carrying many submunitions that can each acquire a vehicle and attack it independently. Other examples might include the FOG-M wire-guided antitank/antiaircraft missile, exploitation of U.S. assets such as the GPS system to perform highly accurate long-range bombardment, or the use of nuclear explosions in the outer atmosphere to threaten the U.S. C^3I.

[28]The intelligence community representative to the RSAS Working Group has consistently pointed out that while U.S. intelligence collection platforms and communications systems tend to be relatively secure, the command and intelligence facilities in the theater are often relatively vulnerable, especially to well-orchestrated agent, special operations forces, or ballistic missile attacks.

measures) and requires a battle or campaign orientation in order to make meaningful comparisons.

For example, Red players in our games examined the various antiarmor weapons they might develop, ranging from sensor-fuzed weapons to ATACMs to infantry weapons such as the FOG-M.[29] They believed that if these technologies could be acquired in sufficient numbers, they might be able to neutralize the strengths of U.S. armored forces, including their mobility and ability to maneuver.[30] They recognized that such capabilities might force the United States to reconsider the Army force structure (which is now projected to consist primarily of heavy armored and mechanized units) and Army doctrine and force employment concepts, although they hoped that the United States would be slow to recognize their new capabilities and not begin to adjust until problems developed on the battlefield.

The Red players recognized that the Iraqi use of ballistic missiles in Desert Storm showed how the possession of some weapon technologies by an opponent could force the United States to rethink its capabilities and operations. But they viewed such impacts as almost purely strategic and sought weapons that would cause combined operational and strategic impacts. The Russian Scud-D could be such a weapon. It reportedly has a 45-meter CEP (the radius of a circle within which half the missiles will land), a runway-penetration, submunition warhead with a 125-meter radius of effects, and an antipersonnel submunition warhead with a 250-meter radius of effects.[31] Similarly, they wanted to acquire sophisticated, deep-water mines; even if they could scatter only a few of these throughout the waters within 500 or so miles of the theater, the belief was that such weapons could cause a strategic disaster to U.S. forces or cause the United States to stand off for a protracted period while deep-water mine hunting proceeded.

As a general proposition, Red players sought to acquire weapons that were relatively simple to employ (e.g., cruise missiles as opposed to manned aircraft) and yet would challenge the United States with significantly increased lethality. They anticipated slow or no U.S. reaction to such developments. Even if the

---

[29]Fiber Optic Guided Missile, which has both antiarmor and air defense capabilities.

[30]While the Red players attempted to disperse these weapons to make them less vulnerable, they did not systematically examine the relative vulnerability of their projected forces compared to U.S. forces. That effort must still be pursued.

[31]These Scud parameters are described in *Jane's Strategic Weapon Systems.* Runway cratering would not be the only desired effect against airfields; rather, such submunitions could also be effective in damaging unsheltered aircraft, maintenance facilities, petroleum pipelines and storage, and crew facilities.

United States responded to a more lethal battlefield by reducing force density, they might achieve their objective of preventing the United States from bringing to bear a force of critical mass sufficient to rapidly defeat their forces.

The Low-Tech, Irregular Combat Battlefield

Another approach, more correctly an extreme of the reactive approach, would involve the U.S. opponent pursuing the kind of low-tech, irregular combat battlefield that the United States experienced in Vietnam or more recently in Somalia. This kind of battlefield could occur in environments where U.S. opponents have little or no armor, having instead a predominantly infantry force structure.

Recognizing that the United States can operate on the high-tech plane, less capable adversaries would avoid direct U.S. power, taking the initiative only in circumstances where they perceived some advantage or were required to defend some vital asset. We refer to this characteristic of irregular warfare as the "ability to deny battle" (Gardiner, 1993d). This approach would allow opponents to manage attrition and maintain more satisfactory loss exchange ratios, where otherwise U.S. firepower would be devastating. Here opponents could focus on creating engagements when U.S. and/or coalition forces were particularly vulnerable, engagements that might become operational or strategic events if U.S. and/or coalition forces sustained relatively high losses. As a result of this mode of operation, long periods of low/no intensity combat operations might occur, even if U.S. forces were attempting to perform active offensive roles, and then a sudden surprise of a major engagement could happen in which U.S. forces might sustain significant losses. Only high concentrations of force in an area might be sufficient to prevent such attacks, and even then an opposition sniper or the detonation of a truck bomb might negate U.S. efforts to maintain control of the situation.

In contrast to the high-tech battlefield described above, the low-tech battlefield is one in which the United States cannot be expected to maintain information dominance. Many of the U.S. intelligence systems are excellent at determining the locations of large weapons like tanks and armored personnel carriers, but have much more difficulty locating infantry, especially infantry that may often not wear uniforms and may appear from cover suddenly, only to disappear almost as suddenly. While the United States has had some luck historically in following key personnel through their use of communications systems, the news reports from Somalia suggest that General Aideed, who eluded U.S. capture for months, did so because of his avoidance of phones and other systems we could monitor, instead choosing to communicate by messenger and low-power radio transmissions.[32]

The opponent who pursued irregular warfare would generally have the initiative in combat operations against the United States.[33] This case might be even more true in peace-enforcing situations where the rules of engagement might often constrain U.S. forces to fire only when fired upon. Moreover, such an opponent might be able to largely negate the effectiveness of advanced U.S. weaponry by denying targeting information or by putting targets in areas the United States was reluctant to strike (because of concerns about collateral damage). The more options the opponent had for hiding forces, the more difficult would be U.S. combat operations, making the availability of reasonable hiding places a key characteristic of such warfare (thus a desert would be a less ideal terrain for irregular operations than a heavily forested or urbanized area). In this context, irregular warfare would clearly be a stronger defense: opposition forces would be able to intermix with friendly populations and employ known hiding locations.

The Combined Battlefields of the Future

We anticipate that the future battlefield experienced by U.S. forces will evolve as some combination of these approaches. In part, the combination will be a function of the force structure of U.S. opponents and of the terrain in which they operate. Few U.S. opponents will be able to field forces capable of the high-tech operations described above. However, since the United States will certainly have such capabilities, consideration of the high-tech battlefield does provide a framework for contemplating prospective U.S. strengths and weaknesses.

If many prospective U.S. opponents fall closer to the low-tech image, then the United States can expect significant irregular combat confrontations, since in such confrontations it appears to have the least relative advantage. This situation will be particularly true when U.S. forces play a peace-enforcing role,

---

[32]A recent report indicated that the relatively rapid response of Somali guerrillas to U.S. ranger operations occurred because Aideed followers near the Mogadishu airport used oil drums (following the ancient African tradition) to communicate that ranger teams had taken off and appeared to be heading for guerrilla targets. "Inside Mogadishu," *Time*, November 8, 1993, p. 17.

[33]The United States may be able to gain the initiative by identifying and striking targets with high value to the opposition (for example, locating the opposition leadership and attacking it). However, such operations are likely to confer the initiative only transiently and, to the extent that U.S. forces must expose themselves in an area of heavy opposition presence to perform such actions, may quickly yield the initiative to the opponent in some cases.

giving the opponents the advantage of carrying out largely defensive actions against the U.S. forces. To the extent that U.S. forces are introduced to stop an aggressor, that aggressor is less likely to be able to base his operations on irregular warfare because of the difficulties of power projection in this kind of warfare. Therefore, in such circumstances, the United States may be able to gain much better control of the battlefield (against a low-tech opponent forced to fight predominantly regular warfare to achieve his objectives).[34]

Whether dealing with a high-tech or a low-tech battlefield, in some ways the outcomes will be the same. In both cases, the battlefield will be nonlinear, with lower densities of forces than historically anticipated. In both, opposing forces will need to hide to survive, making rapid target acquisition and delivery of fires necessary for the United States to destroy them. And in both, the key U.S. forces will often be long-range weaponry, which the opponent will want to attack directly. This situation will be facilitated by the likelihood that such weaponry may be relatively concentrated in a few locations (such as airfields, artillery, and attack helicopter bases).

Across the types of battlefields, the command-and-control system of the future battlefield must be highly robust and adaptive. If the United States is to fight at low densities in nonlinear combat, it must be prepared for significant devolution of authority necessary to pursue what could be very complex conditions when viewed in the aggregate. The United States must also be prepared to somehow integrate the complex situation into a coherent picture and apply supporting fires and other assistance in a meaningful manner. Poor C^3 may mean that fratricide will increase to an intolerable level or that the United States will continue fighting the enemy of the last battle even after he has evolved and has begun to fight differently.

NUCLEAR, BIOLOGICAL, AND CHEMICAL WEAPONS[35]

Nowhere will the asymmetries in approaches be more pronounced than in the respective readiness of the United States and potential regional adversaries to introduce the shadow of NBC weapons, and even their use, into a crisis. It is argued above that regional proliferators will not set out to acquire nuclear

---

[34]The example of Vietnam may raise a question about this statement, and yet the difficulties faced by the United States in Vietnam were caused in large part by the combined internal/international character of the conflict, in which Viet Cong forces in particular could operate largely based on the "defensive" dimension of irregular warfare discussed above.

[35]The results of some of our games in this area are reported in Gardiner (1993e) and Fox (1993a). Some of RAND's other work in this area is found in Millot, Molander, and Wilson (1993); Molander and Wilson (1993); and Bennett (1993d).

weapons specifically for confrontation with the United States. But many may conclude that it would be foolish to get into such a confrontation unless so equipped. This argument applies with equal force to chemical and biological weapons, which are too often forgotten in the analysis of regional contingencies and may more than compensate for their lesser effectiveness by their relative ease of acquisition.

Historically, the United States viewed its strategic nuclear weapons as the ultimate deterrent force in the world, extending at least some degree of protection to any country coming under the U.S. nuclear "umbrella." However, the Red players in our games paid scant attention to U.S. strategic nuclear weapons; they doubted whether the United States would use such weapons in any of the conditions considered (even after the Red players' own use of nuclear weapons) and thus felt largely undeterred by them. This issue clearly needs further study, and real-world adversaries might well behave differently.

Viewing NBC from the Adversary's Perspective

The attraction of nuclear weapons for many actual or aspirant proliferators may extend beyond the potential they offer for regional domination and become the ultimate means for ensuring regime survival. Nuclear weapons provide the regime with a deterrent to attacks against it or a counter to those attacks should they occur (again, with the focus on attacks from regional powers more often than on attacks from the United States). In some cases, the intimidation and deterrent motives may be hard to disentangle; possession of nuclear weapons may provide a secure basis for expansionist policies, putting a ceiling on any losses should adventurism miscarry.[36] Either way, whether the dominant impulse toward acquisition is aggressive or defensive, proliferators will rightly feel that their new status has an impact on the regional balance of power.

They may also believe that, balance of power and insurance considerations apart, nuclear weapons will furnish them with the *means* to decisively affect the course of any conflict in which they find themselves actually engaged, whether

---

[36]In the games, Red players contemplated using nuclear weapons (and perhaps other weapons of mass destruction) to threaten their neighbors (either explicitly or in a veiled manner) if a U.S. lodgment or U.S. basing were allowed; they also considered directly threatening a U.S. lodgment or other initial deployment with nuclear weapon use. The Red players felt particularly aggressive in these areas when they had a dozen or more nuclear weapons and could thus expend some in such efforts and still retain a capability for guaranteeing regime survival. They generally concluded that having a dozen or more nuclear weapons was a significantly different condition from having only two or three.

with the United States or a regional power—that is, the ability to create strategic events.

U.S. Responses to the Nuclear Shadow

It is perhaps more likely than not that any future regional contingency in which the United States finds itself involved will be overshadowed by an explicit or implicit NBC threat. The threat might be more in terms of potential than actual use, bearing on the crisis in the following ways:

- The possession by the adversary of an NBC arsenal might be a strong disincentive for the United States to become militarily involved in the first place—especially if use, whether by terrorist or missile means, is credibly threatened against the U.S. homeland.

- Potential coalition partners, especially those geographically closest to the adversary, might be more difficult to enlist, fearing nuclear strikes from the aggressor.

- The possibility of tactical use might seriously inhibit U.S. deployments and might cause major changes in operational planning. In general, the United States would have to avoid concentrations of forces that could become a target for weapons of mass destruction. Concentrated deployments through a limited number of debarkation ports might have to be avoided; intense air operations from a small number of in-theater bases might have to be replaced by more dispersed and/or longer-range operations; amphibious landings might have to be ruled out as presenting too concentrated and attractive a target.[37]

- The United States might have to reconsider its doctrine of conventional theater/strategic attack, since it threatens the existence of the aggressor's regime, and the aggressor is likely to look to nuclear weapons to assure that survival. That is, serious attacks against the aggressor's leadership might trigger a nuclear response intended to change the U.S. strategy and remove the threat to the aggressor's regime. The United States would, therefore, need to consider other alternatives, to include abandoning conventional theater/strategic attacks in such a situation, limiting such attacks to non-leadership targets, or preparing to preemptively destroy the aggressor's nuclear weapons before starting its attacks on the aggressor's leadership.

- Even after a successful conventional campaign, coalition war aims might have to be circumscribed to avoid threatening the adversary's ultimate survival and thus potentially triggering a Samson response (the opponent self-destructing and attempting to take U.S. forces with him).

---

[37]Many players in our games have referred to such U.S. amphibious landings as "nuclear magnets."

When facing an adversary armed (or possibly armed) with nuclear weapons, the United States will be likely to focus a significant portion of its strategic attack effort on preemptively destroying the opposing nuclear weapons conventionally. This effort could divert a nontrivial fraction of the total attack away from other valuable targets.[38]

U.S. Responses to Attacks by Regional Nuclear Powers

As suggested above, the actual use of NBC weapons would be a high-risk strategy for the adversary. It should not, therefore, be regarded as excluded. As a major "strategic event," it might disrupt the whole political momentum of the U.S. response. It could certainly be expected to induce a pause on the battlefield, while Washington and other coalition capitals digested the implications. It might sow discord among coalition partners, as arguments ensued as to the appropriate response. An adversary might calculate that it would, in effect, be a "no-added-cost" option: given an increasingly advertised U.S. tendency to view nuclear weapons, as much as chemical and biological weapons, as lacking both utility and legitimacy, the adversary could hope that the U.S. response to his own NBC use would merely be continued prosecution of the war against him by conventional means. The United States needs to consider whether it should take action to strengthen the perception of regional nuclear powers that their use of nuclear weapons will prompt a U.S. nuclear response.

The war games provided some interesting insights into this issue. In most cases, the Blue players concluded that a response with nuclear weapons would not inflict much more damage on the opponent than continued conventional operations because of the lethality of U.S. conventional munitions. Moreover, in the common case where opposition use of nuclear weapons is a desperation move, the Blue teams did not perceive the need to respond with nuclear weapons in order to achieve their operational objectives. Some Blue players contemplating a nuclear response feared that the U.S. public might react negatively to a U.S. nuclear attack in the context of a limited war that the United States appears to be otherwise winning. Therefore, in an attempt to maintain U.S. coalitions and in trying to preserve the international consensus against the opponent that has used nuclear weapons, *many Blue teams did not respond with nuclear weapon use.* In part, Blue teams had difficulty identifying appropriate targets for nuclear weapon use (often because of the conventional damage already done). Moreover, the fact that it might take several dozen tactical nu-

---

[38]In Desert Storm, about 10 percent of the total air-to-ground sorties were directed against NBC targets and the associated Scud launchers; in retrospect, a number of NBC targets were missed (mainly because of inadequate intelligence), and few Scuds were destroyed.

clear weapons to neutralize an opposing army division surprised many players. Often, the Blue players threatened a heavy nuclear response to further nuclear weapon use by the opponent and increased the conventional campaign against opposition strategic targets (especially remaining nuclear weapons and associated C^3I).

In the cases where the Blue teams did use a nuclear response, they tended to escalate the level of nuclear violence. Thus, in one exercise played by 12 teams in which the Red team used one or two nuclear weapons against U.S. forces or theater infrastructure, the seven Blue teams that responded with nuclear weapons used an average of 16 weapons, and the numbers ranged from 4 to 50. Some Blue teams have used a nuclear response to serve as a deterrent against other Third World nuclear powers, or have been anxious to respond to the perceived outrage of the U.S. public. Interestingly, Blue players who had dealt with nuclear weapon use in recent games appeared considerably more prone to respond with nuclear weapons when the problem was posed in a second game.

In this specific context, we should note that games may be an inadequate framework for addressing some issues associated with weapons of mass destruction. Just as the media and public response to the use of Scud missiles in Desert Storm far overwhelmed any expectations, so might use of "strategic" weapons of a future war, forcing the United States to take different actions. It is difficult to infuse game players with the emotionalism of threatened nuclear weapon use, or the carnage of actual nuclear weapon use, in order to properly capture the reactions that might actually occur.

Delivering Weapons of Mass Destruction

While various delivery means may be employed with nuclear weapons, most regional powers working on nuclear weapons seem to have chosen ballistic missiles.[39] However, we also see some evidence of interest in cruise missile technology in many countries and suspect that cruise missiles may become an alternative delivery means during the next decade.[40] The choices here are important; much effort has gone into controlling ballistic missile proliferation because of its clear tie to nuclear weapons, while much less emphasis has been placed on cruise missile proliferation. Cruise missiles appear to be the preferred delivery means for chemical or biological weapons and for some newer

[39]This choice is in part due to a lack of confidence of these countries in their air forces and the fact that they have not yet mastered cruise-missile technology.

[40]A "Pentagon study said Syria, Iran and China are aggressively developing cruise missiles—the first ones are expected operational by the year 2000." "News Highlights," DoD's *Early Bird*, February 1, 1993, p. 16.

munitions such as fuel air explosives, because such missiles make it much easier to disperse these munitions in appropriate patterns around targets. Thus, we would expect substantial efforts to develop and deploy cruise missiles that could carry weapons of mass destruction.

CONCLUSIONS

Despite its military power, the United States may face severe challenges in future major regional contingencies. If the reactions of our Red players are reliable, the old deterrent effect of strategic nuclear weapons appears to have little effect on prospective regional adversaries. Instead, they may perceive that they can achieve their objectives by proper exercise of operational initiative, by making the cost of U.S. intervention high, and by otherwise appropriately setting the political context and parrying U.S. military strengths for at least some period of time. If so, we may see a repeat of the conditions surrounding World War I, in which to wait was to fail (see Tuchman, 1962). At the very least, the context for deterrence has changed, and the United States must seriously reconsider how it may or may not play a role in future major regional contingencies.

War appears to be evolving and perhaps evolving quite rapidly. The battlefield of the future could well be quite different from the battlefield of the Gulf War or a battlefield that we might expect to see today. Military analysis must begin to comprehend these potential changes.

BIBLIOGRAPHY

Aspin, Les (1993), *The Bottom-Up Review*, Department of Defense, September.

Bennett, Bruce W. (1993a), "Flexible Combat Modeling," *Simulation & Gaming*, June, (also available as a RAND reprint, RP-220).

———— (1993b), *Global 92 Analysis of Prospective Conflicts in Korea in the Next Ten Years*, RAND, Santa Monica, CA.

Bennett, Bruce W., Margaret Cecchine, Daniel B. Fox, and Sam Gardiner (1993), *Technology and Innovations in Future Warfare: Wargaming the Persian Gulf Case*, RAND, Santa Monica, CA.

Bennett, Bruce W., Sam Gardiner, Daniel B. Fox, and Nicholas K. J. Witney (1994), *Theater Analysis and Modeling in an Era of Uncertainty: The Present and Future of Warfare*, RAND, Santa Monica, CA.

Department of Defense (1992), *Conduct of the Persian Gulf War: Final Report to Congress*, April (three volumes).

Dick, C. J. (1993), *Russian Views on Future War*, Conflict Studies Research Centre, The Royal Military Academy Sandhurst, June.

Director of Defense Research and Engineering (1992), *Defense Science and Technology Strategy*, July.

Fox, Daniel B., and John Bordeaux (1993), *Global 92 Analysis of Prospective Conflicts in Central Europe in 2002*, RAND, Santa Monica, CA.

Millot, Marc Dean, Roger Molander, and Peter Wilson (1993), "*The Day After...*": *Nuclear Proliferation in the Post–Cold War World—Volume 1: Summary Report*, RAND, Santa Monica, CA.

Molander, Roger C., and Peter A. Wilson (1993), *The Nuclear Asymptote: On Containing Nuclear Proliferation*, RAND, Santa Monica, CA.

Pirnie, Bruce (1993), *Global 92 Analysis of Prospective Conflicts in the Persian Gulf in 2002*, RAND, Santa Monica, CA.

Schrader, John Y. (1993), *Global 92 Analysis of Prospective Conflicts in the Tigris-Euphrates Watershed in 2002*, RAND, Santa Monica, CA.

Silverberg, David (1993), "Bottom-Up Review: The Big Bet's No Bad Bet," *Armed Forces Journal International*, October.

Tuchman, Barbara W. (1962), *The Guns of August*, Macmillan, New York.

van Creveld, Martin (1989), *Technology and War: From 2000 B.C. to the Present*, The Free Press, New York.

Many of the insights from the future of warfare games have been discussed in a RAND newsletter, originally called the *RSAS Newsletter*, later renamed *Military Science & Modeling*. In particular, see:

Bennett, Bruce (1993c), "A Counter-Capability Framework for Evaluating Military Capabilities," RAND, *RSAS Newsletter*, February.

————— (1993d), "Countering North Korean Nuclear Proliferation," RAND, *Military Science & Modeling*, August.

Fox, Dan (1993a), "Atoms for Peace," RAND, *Military Science & Modeling*, August.

————— (1993b), "Counter-Capability Air Campaigns," RAND, *RSAS Newsletter*, February.

Fox, Dan, and Bruce Bennett (1992), "The Future Military Environment and Military Modeling," RAND, *RSAS Newsletter*, November.

Gardiner, Sam (1992a), "It Isn't Clear Ahead, But I Think I Can See the Edges of the Road: The Character of Future Warfare," RAND, *RSAS Newsletter*, November.

————— (1992b), "The Lineage of the Nonlinear Battle," RAND, *RSAS Newsletter*, January.

————— (1992c), "The Military-Technical Revolution: More Than Military and More Than Technical," RAND, *RSAS Newsletter*, January.

————— (1992d), "Overwhelming Force: A Guide for Policy or a Strategic Principle for Historians?" RAND, *RSAS Newsletter*, January.

——— (1993a), "Even Nonlethal Weapons Might Kill the Notion of Peacemaking," RAND, *Military Science & Modeling*, August.

——— (1993b), "High Tech Commandos: The Swedish Version of the Fragmented Battlefield," RAND, *Military Science & Modeling*, August.

——— (1993c), "The Nonlethal Revolution in Warfare: Maybe Not Such a Revolution," RAND, *Military Science & Modeling*, May.

——— (1993d), "Playing With Mush: Gaming Lesser Contingencies," RAND, *Military Science & Modeling*, November.

——— (1993e), "Playing With Nuclear Weapons," RAND, *RSAS Newsletter*, February.

Chapter 16

EXTENDED-COUNTERFORCE OPTIONS FOR COPING WITH TACTICAL BALLISTIC MISSILES

Richard Mesic

This paper describes recent RAND work on concepts for attacking theater ballistic missile (TBM) systems—either before launch or shortly thereafter ("extended-counterforce options"). It describes how RAND assessed the performance of the Desert Storm "Scud hunt" in 1991, developed analysis tools such as simple computer simulations, and applied these tools in a systems analysis of options for coping with a wide variety of possible future TBM threats. Finally, the paper presents observations from that analysis and suggests directions for exploring operational concepts and systems initiatives that could enhance the country's counter-TBM capabilities over the years ahead.

INTRODUCTION

Tactical ballistic missiles (TBMs) became a pressing military issue in the Gulf War when Saddam Hussein mounted his Scud attacks against Israel and Saudi Arabia. He had threatened to use missiles and had hinted that they might be armed with chemical warheads. Before the actual attacks, however, U.S. military planners had largely discounted their significance because of the Scud's low accuracy. As a result, when dealing with Scuds became a political imperative as Saddam Hussein used them as a terror weapon to bring Israel into the war (Atkinson, 1993), the U.S. response was largely ad hoc. It was also largely ineffective, even though the Patriot part of the response seemed very effective at the time.[1]

While Iraqi use of TBMs in 1991 presented only a marginal military threat, the attacks demonstrated that TBMs constitute a plausible and potentially severe future military threat—especially if we remain as unprepared for countering them as we were in the Gulf War.[2] If Saddam Hussein had armed his

---

[1] Shaver (1994) discusses ballistic missile defense.

[2] For a very interesting historical perspective on the beginnings of the TBM problem, see Irving (1964), which describes England's World War II struggle with the German V-1 and V-2 threats. There are amazing parallels between the problems England faced

Scuds with chemical or nuclear warheads, the course of the Gulf War, if not its outcome, would have been quite different. Future adversaries might be more reckless and lethal. Indeed, planners are increasingly realizing that in the very near future, U.S. ability to forge effective political and military coalitions and to project power in major regional conflicts (MRCs) could be critically impaired by the presence of TBMs—especially if armed with chemical, biological, or nuclear weapons of mass destruction (WMD) (Millot, Molander, and Wilson, 1993).

RAND began studying this issue in 1991, when it was asked by OSD's Deputy Director for Tactical Warfare Programs (TWP) to review and analyze the Desert Storm performance of U.S. forces in several mission areas, including what had become known as the Scud hunt in Iraq. Following this initial Desert Storm "lessons learned" study, concluded in the fall of 1991, RAND was asked by the Air Force and OSD to extend the research to consider future threats and responses.[3]

The purpose of this paper is to describe our work on these matters and to explain key issues and options. It describes how we assessed the Desert Storm experience, developed computer simulations, and applied systems analysis to explore future threats and possible counters. This exercise was a necessary first step in addressing the appropriate investment balance among various elements or "pillars" of an overall theater missile defense (TMD) architecture (Mesic, 1994). One consequence of our work was the development of the concept of "extended counterforce," which includes attacking TBMs and their support systems on the ground and TBMs in their boost or postboost ascent phase, primarily with aircraft weapons.[4]

When RAND undertook this work, TMD research and development was primarily focused on terminal and midcourse defense with systems such as improved Patriot and the Theater High Altitude Area Defense (THAAD). Counterforce and attack of missiles in boost phase and later in the ascent phase

---

in the 1940s and the problems the coalition faced in the Gulf War fifty years later. The counterforce tactics in both wars were similar, with similar lack of success.

[3]Giles Smith led the overall team of the initial Desert Storm research. I was the principal investigator for the Scud-hunting work, with support from Jerry Stiles and Kurt Rogers. Our subsequent work has been in a project led by David Vaughan. He, I, and Joel Kvitky have collaborated on most of what this paper discusses, hence, my frequent use of "we" throughout.

[4]Classical "counterforce attacks" focus on striking weapon systems before they are launched or on destroying launchers to prevent reloads. Attacks on the missiles in flight have been considered "defense." However, since some of the same manned-aircraft systems can be used for counterforce and attack of missiles early in flight, this paper uses the concept "extended counterforce" to include both.

was largely neglected.[5] Counterforce itself was considered to be a "straight-forward" byproduct of established air interdiction tactics and systems, and ascent-phase intercept was seldom considered. Our research demonstrated that effective extended-counterforce operations, to the extent that improvements are feasible, will require substantial focused development effort. Such operations share many critical elements with air-interdiction missions, but they also involve many new and stressing requirements. They may also be critical to overall counter-TBM effectiveness, because systems like Patriot and THAAD have distinct limitations (Larsen and Kent, 1994, Mesic, 1994, and Shaver 1994).

THE SCUD HUNT OF DESERT STORM

Study Approach

RAND was charged with evaluating the effectiveness of the 10,000 or so Desert Storm aircraft sorties (10 percent of the total) that were specifically directed at finding and destroying Scud systems on the ground—the so-called Scud hunt. The assessment was to help OSD respond to a series of specific congressional questions on the performance of U.S. weapon systems in the Gulf War.

At the time, there were no published reports or other readily accessible materials to help us understand what was attempted in the Scud hunt, assess how effective those actions were, or, most important, analyze the reasons for the successes and failures. Furthermore, there was no accepted precedent, because the Desert Storm Scud campaign was truly an extemporaneous affair. We decided to adopt a two-track approach that involved both empirical work and modeling. The empirical work included interviewing the air crews and reviewing standard wartime documents such as logs and mission reports. The modeling work amounted to building simple computer simulation models. These efforts were complementary and interactive. The interviews helped us build the simple models, and exercising the simple models helped us focus interview questions and the search for data. We developed a story based on anecdotal evidence, mostly pilot first-person reports, and used the quantitative models to help fill in the gaps and resolve the conflicts in the anecdotal and record data. Table 1 lists our primary data sources, which represented a broad cross-section of organizations involved in Scud operations and related systems and technology development.

---

[5]The one notable exception to this was the ARPA Warbreaker initiative, which was focused on advanced technologies for finding and killing TBMs in deep hides.

Table 1

Background/Information Gathering

Organization	Points of Contact	Topics
AF HQ TAC	Col Miller et al.	MNS, integration of AFTMD, A-Team, historian
AF 405th TTW	LTC Mullins	F-15E Scud CAP ops in Desert Storm
AF 16th Special Ops Sq, Hurlbert Field	LTC Spencer	AC-130 in Desert Storm
AF HQ SAC	LTC Johnston	TMD architecture, ASARS
AFSPACECOM	Capt Rhodes, Mr. Darrah	TMD priorities, role of space systems
ESD/MITRE	LTC Toole	BM/C^{3}I, missile defense coordination
ASD	LTC Bostleman	Boeing flight demo
FTD	Mr. Boyd, Mr. Nelson	TBM threat, signature modeling
PWW	Mr. Merrick	TBM threat, Desert Storm Scud campaign
Air Staff	XPF	Desert Storm targeting
JCS	LTC Attichson (J-2)	Touted Gleam
CENTCOM	Capt Deluke, Mr. Rubright	Scud campaign, future needs
SDIO	Amb. Cooper, Mr. Gerry	Perspective on TMD
TMD	Mr. Israel	Counterforce, emplaced sensors
POET	Mr. Grayson et al.	Counterforce study
Grumman	Dr. McNiff	JSTARS in Desert Storm
Boeing	Mr. Blaylock et al.	CMT workshop
DARPA	Dr. Murphy, Dr. Heber	DARPA CMT initiatives
OSD(DDR&E)/TWP	Dr. Head, Mr. Kendall	Desert Storm Scud hunting
OUSD(Policy)	Mr. Schulte	Desert Storm
OSD(P&E)	Dr. Chu	Desert Storm

Operations in the Scud Hunt

Let me now review briefly the operations used against Scuds. *Fixed* Scud-related targets were included in the attack plans developed before the strategic air campaign started. However, *mobile* Scud systems (TELs and the missiles they carry) were not.[6] The Scud hunt against the field-deployed TELs was planned and started several days into the war as the importance of the Scud threat became apparent.

---

[6]I use the term TEL to stand for both the Russian-made transporter-erector-launchers and the Iraqi-built tractor-trailer missile-erector-launchers usually called MELs.

The Scud hunts proceeded as follows (Atkinson, 1993; DoD, 1992:225ff). Many types of aircraft (B-52s, . . . A-10s; F/A-18s, . : . S-3s) were involved, but the bulk of the effort was carried out by F-16s and F-15Es in the southeast and western areas of Iraq, respectively.   Because of their APG-70 multimode radar and LANTIRN pods (low-altitude navigation and targeting infrared for night) the F-15Es were the most capable system for attacking TELs.

Except for daylight reconnaissance missions flown by A-10s along roads, the Scud hunts were conducted at night.   Over 80 percent of the Scud launches occurred at night, no doubt because the Iraqis felt more secure operating under cover of darkness.   The Scud-hunting tactics combined (1) hunter-killer operations in geographic "Scud boxes" and (2) combat air patrol (CAP) operations with targeting cues furnished by external assets such as special operations forces (SOF) and launch detection satellites (DSP) (DoD, 1992, app. K).   The attack aircraft generally operated at medium altitudes (15,000 to 20,000 feet) to avoid the unsuppressed antiaircraft artillery (AAA) and shoulder-fired infrared surface-to-air missile (IR SAM) threats.

In the cued operations, the aircraft were given target locations, typically by voice, and the pilots would fly to the target area, attempt to find the target believed to be a TEL, and then attack it with the most appropriate munitions on board.

Analysis issues surfaced immediately in our interviews with the flight crews. The most apparent was the obvious discrepancy between the pilots reporting *hundreds* of TELs killed and intelligence information strongly indicating that the Iraqis had an order of magnitude fewer TELs altogether.   How could this difference be reconciled?   The air crews were highly professional, but in this war as in earlier ones, their perceptions were highly optimistic.   Unfortunately, hard data on these matters were unavailable during the course of the study, so we had to explain the inconsistencies and estimate what really happened by relying heavily on analytic models in the form of computer simulations.[7]

Modeling and Analyzing the Campaign

After our project team understood generally how the Scud hunts were conducted and had analyzed characteristics of the relevant sensors and weapons, we began to develop the simulation models.   At this point, the work could literally have been performed with a pencil on the back of a small envelope, but we adopted a modular building-block approach that allowed us to add complexity and fidelity as we gained knowledge about threat operations, tactics,

---

[7]Subsequently, UN teams in Iraq to destroy residual weapons have been able to proved a more complete picture of Iraqi Scud operations. Their reports confirmed the conclusions of our work, to the effect that Scud hunting had been ineffective.

and systems.   Figure 1 shows a schematic diagram of the model, which was implemented as a BASIC program on a Macintosh IIci.   The model was event driven, with extensive parameterization and Monte Carlo processes.   The model included detection, discrimination, and attack of TELs amidst clutter.

The most basic "notable event" for the Scud hunt was the generation (through a Monte Carlo process) of a targeting cue.   These cues might come from an offboard sensor system or from a sensor on board the search aircraft. These cue events had a few basic parameters in common, even though the processes through which they were generated and the parameter values were different from case to case.   The common parameters were (1) probability P_d that a threat activity (e.g., launch, movement to a launch site, preparation to launch) would be detected; (2) false alarm probability P_{fa} (or, more precisely, temporal and spatial density of false reports over the search area); and (3) probability of target kill P_k based on several factors, including the probability that the cue got from the source to the attack aircraft, cue time delays from the detected event, distance of the CAP aircraft from the cue, uncertainty area associated with the cue, and finally, the reliability and lethality of the munitions.

Detection events were based on a search process that was simulated as a Poisson process.   For a Poisson process, the probability distribution of the waiting time t between "detection events" is $P_d(t)$, where:

$$P_d\left(t\right) = 1 - e^{-RDt}$$

and where R is the search rate (in square kilometers per hour) and D is the density (number per square kilometer) of both real and apparent targets (i.e., Scud TELs and "clutter" targets).

Given a random detection, the probability P_{Scud} that the object was a Scud TEL is then:

$$P_{scud} = D_S\big/\left(D_S + D_C\right)$$

where D_S is the density of Scuds and D_C is the clutter-object density.

Given a detection, we assigned baseline parameter values for the discrimination-decision probabilities as follows (based on the limited experimental data available to us at the time).   If the notation $P(S/C)$, for example, stands for the probability of declaring the detection to be a Scud given that it is actually is a clutter object, then:

$$P\left(S/S\right) = 0.25; \; P\left(C/C\right) = 0.1; \; P\left(S/C\right) = 0.9; \; P\left(C/S\right) = 0.75$$

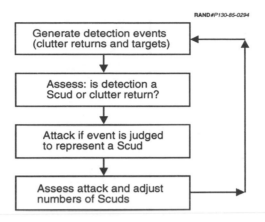

RAND#P130-85-0294

Figure 1—Schematic of Scud-Hunting Model Operation

As a baseline, we assumed that the probability of a kill given an attack decision was 0.9.

Other events the code recorded and assessed were (1) aircraft attacks (on both real TELs and false targets such as natural or cultural clutter, including commercial tractor-trailer trucks); (2) weapons used; (3) time (the sortie ended after the aircraft on-station fuel was gone—approximately 1.5 hours—or the weapons were all expended); and (4) kills of both false targets and TELs.

As mentioned earlier, we built placeholder modules for all processes known *a priori* to be relevant, even if our initial modules consisted of nothing more than parameter values (e.g., the discrimination probabilities above). For example, there was a "target detection module," even though we were not able initially to model the detection process, which involved unavailable data (e.g., TEL signatures in the various relevant spectral bands, sensor characteristics and modes, and background clutter). Later, these modules were refined as data became available.

Finally, we used Monte Carlo methods to assess the performance of the systems given random processes and uncertainties in scenario dynamics and systems operations. We typically ran a scenario 1000 times, which was about all the Macintosh IIci could handle in a few minutes. Statistics were recorded as these scenario replications were run, so that we could see quantitatively how effective the simulated systems worked. The measure of effectiveness (MOE) was Scud TELs killed per aircraft sortie. The code would generate an average value for this number and a measure of its variability (standard deviation) over the given number of trials.

As the model was developed, we checked it by running cases that we could evaluate by hand. As the code grew, its modular nature let us check each extension rather simply, even though the code as a whole was becoming much more complex. This ability to incorporate new information and adapt tactics was a key feature of the simulation approach. The underlying math was quite simple.

Initial Results

When we ran the simulations initially, using our baseline assumptions about parameter values, the results indicated that the typical Scud hunt sortie was probably unsuccessful. In fact, we estimated that the chance was less than 1 percent that an F-15E sortie would detect and kill a Scud TEL if it were exposed in the search area while the F-15E was searching for it. Of course, these first quantitative estimates depended on highly uncertain data, so the results were heavily caveated. For example, we had to estimate the probability that the F-15E's multimode air-air and air-ground APG-70 radar operating in the ground-imaging synthetic aperture radar (SAR) mode would detect an exposed TEL if it was in the radar's field of view. Similarly, we had to estimate the associated false alarm rate based on past data-collection experience with SAR systems similar to the F-15E's. The false alarm rate proved to be the most important and uncertain parameter in the simulation.

Given the large uncertainties, we focused on sensitivity analysis. We often plotted results in a "spider chart" as shown notionally (due to security classification of the actual results) in Figure 2. A spider chart plots the MOE (e.g., Scud kills) versus changes in various parameters P1, P2, . . . The baseline case is the spider's body, with each parametric excursion forming a pair of legs. If these legs were nearly horizontal over a reasonable range, as with P2 in the figure, then the results were insensitive to that parameter. On the other hand, if the legs showed considerable positive or negative slope (e.g., P1, P3, and P4), then that underlying uncertainty was critical. If a parameter was critical and the uncertainty was large, the study team focused parallel project activities on resolving those uncertainties.[8]

Given the quick-reaction nature of RAND's initial Scud hunt study, it was impossible to resolve many of the critical uncertainties, but the results supported the heavily caveated "best guess" that the hunts were likely unsuccessful, together with the reasons behind that judgment. The problem areas iden-

---

[8]In some cases a more complex approach is needed, as when the parameters are potentially correlated or their combined effects are nonlinearly dependent on the individual parameter values.

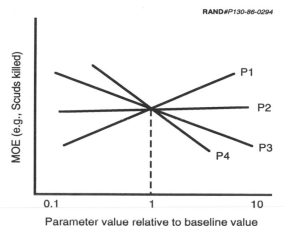

RAND#P130-86-0294

Figure 2—Spider Charts Show Sensitivity to Parametric Excursions

tified implied priorities for both near-term measures and longer-term RDT&E initiatives. The improvements we suggested were evolutionary. That is, we did not seek or discover promising new systems concepts or technologies that could confidently solve the problems we identified, but we did find several affordable modifications to deployed systems that would improve their capabilities in future scenarios similar to Desert Storm.

Details remain classified, but the Scud hunts were unsuccessful because the systems had inherent limitations (for Scud hunting) that were not well understood during the war. Tactics were ad hoc, but they were not the limiting factor. The limitations were intelligence shortfalls and operational and technical performance limitations of the surveillance sensors, attack-aircraft sensors, and processing systems. We know TELs were detectable for a time before and after a missile was launched, but those periods were brief and the TELs were often outside the coverage of systems such as the airborne Joint Surveillance, Targeting, and Reconnaissance System (JSTARS). So the first shortfall was surveillance *coverage* deep inside Iraq. If a TEL was detected, the sensors typically could not recognize it as such—sensor resolution limits were inconsistent with target *discrimination*. Therefore, the TELs (a very small fraction of all large vehicles in the area) were lost in the background traffic, and other vehicles (including decoys) were often mistaken for TELs and attacked. Finally, when cues were generated (e.g., by DSP), the responsiveness of the battle management/command, control, communications, computer, and intelligence systems (BM/C^{4}I) and CAP aircraft was inconsistent with effective attack prosecution. The aggressive and innovative crews did their best with what they had, but what they had was designed for other missions and was not up to the mission of finding and destroying Scud TELs.

SYSTEMS ANALYSIS ON COUNTERING TBMs

The Desert Storm analysis was a historical problem: How well did the coalition do, and what were the lessons learned? After that analysis was completed, RAND was asked by the Air Force and OSD to think about the TBM problem more generically. How might the threats evolve, and how should the country best prepare to counter them? The approach we used was a classic systems analysis that built on the insights developed from Desert Storm, but that examined a wide variety of future threats, scenarios, operational concepts, and costs.

Threat Operations

For analysis purposes, we assumed that the system to be countered incorporated a stressful mix of modes as follows:

1. Ground mobile TELs, logistics support, and C^3 systems.
2. Garrisons to accommodate peacetime operations.
3. A series of crisis and wartime technical support/resupply bases, hides/shelters, and presurveyed launch positions.

Although other basing possibilities exist, including such options as very hard underground silos or ship-launched ballistic missiles, they will not be discussed further in this paper for the following reasons. First, fixed targets such as silos are potentially vulnerable to very accurate conventional weapons and probably would not be attractive to our future adversaries (although Desert Storm attacks on soft fixed launchers were much less effective than originally believed). Also, fixing the missiles in silos would, coupled with their limited range/payloads, reduce flexibility. Second, we judged it less likely that our adversaries will develop TBMs based on aircraft, ships, or submarines, and we noted that even if such threats develop, attacking them will be special cases of U.S. counterair and naval operations. In what follows, then, we discuss only the mobile-missile threat.

The threat's TBM concept of operations (CONOPS) would depend on the mission and scenario context. If the TBM mission were peacetime or crisis coercion, then the threat CONOPS would emphasize measures to protect the missile systems from preemptive strikes. If the mission were warfighting, then the CONOPS would include measures to assure timely and effective missile salvos. The threat operations would have three distinct phases: peacetime, crisis, and war.

The **peacetime** CONOPS would accommodate training, security, survivability, and readiness needs. It would be designed to assure a smooth transition to crisis and wartime modes (if they differed). Day to day, some fraction of the TELs might be deployed to field sites for training or survivability. Additionally, the process of preparing additional wartime sites and "hides" (i.e., hiding places) could continue. From time to time, there would be field exercises to test the systems and crews. Occasionally, operational tests would include missile launches (perhaps with flight data telemetry).

Although some hides and launch positions would be used in peacetime exercises, wartime operations would probably not be limited to these sites. New launch sites could be covertly surveyed as required, and ad hoc shelter potential could be exploited (e.g., wartime use of hides in urban areas might be planned but not exercised).

The TBM CONOPS in a **crisis** would be the transition to a wartime posture for survivability and effectiveness. TELs and support vehicles would leave their garrisons and deploy to wartime technical support field sites or hides within range of their targets. The command authorities would, no doubt, be careful about maintaining positive control.

During the war, the CONOPS would be to launch strikes as ordered, while avoiding detection and attack. Launches would probably occur in salvos to maximize shock value, while saturating defenses such as Patriot. These launches could be preplanned, minimizing the need for communications between leadership and the missile batteries, or they could be in response to battlefield dynamics, in which case a more responsive BM/C⁴I system would be required.

TELs and crews would remain in the hides or technical support field sites to which they were dispersed until ordered to launch. Since the launch of a missile presents a strong signal, the launch site would be considered unsafe immediately after launch. Consequently, the crews would "shoot and scoot" to a hide. Still, the TELs and support vehicles would be exposed and in motion for some time before and after launch. If, for example, they shot from very near the hide they had been occupying, they might wish to abandon that hide and travel to a new one some distance away after launching. Or if they wanted to continue to use the hide they occupied before launch (because it contained reload missiles and other support assets, for example), they would drive a safe distance away before launching the missile, dashing back to the same hide afterwards. (It is possible that the Iraqis used a variation on this theme, using "temporary hides" between the launch sites and their main hides/resupply sites.) If possible, these launches would be scheduled to minimize detection potential (e.g., at night, in bad weather, or during predictable gaps in satellite or airborne surveillance coverage).

While this characterizes the general CONOPS, the details are more difficult to pin down and would be important to counterforce operations. These include the following:

- Hide characteristics (number, location, type, vulnerability, detectability).

- Launch timelines (transit to launch area, prelaunch preparations, launch, takedown, transit to hide). The total timeline might be between 15 and 45 minutes, with 30 minutes as a nominal figure.

- Missile range and likely targets (hence possible deployment areas).

- Reloads. If there were a TEL for each missile, the TELs would be expendable after launch, meaning that only the crews and necessary support systems would have to escape to a hide. If there were more missiles than TELs, the TELs would be reloaded by some sort of resupply vehicle or from hidden stores of missiles.

- C^3 systems (centralized or decentralized using land lines, including fiber optics, radio at diverse frequencies, couriers).

- Other radio frequency emissions (e.g., weather radars).

- Stealth, camoflage, cover, and deception (CCD), and decoys (hides, TELs, . . .).

- Defenses (soldiers, AAA, shoulder-fired IR SAMs, radar SAMs . . .).

- Special weapons (e.g., nuclear) and handling procedures.

It should be recognized that the actual wartime TBM CONOPS might not be very well known to U.S. planners. The simple reason is that the TBM missions and systems have a lot of operational flexibility that can be invoked without compromising effectiveness. For example, other than short wartime moves for survivability against counterbattery threats, TBM systems can remain hidden well in the rear. The equipment is relatively indistinguishable from normal background-clutter objects such as large commercial or military trucks and other vehicles. TELs do not have to engage enemy forces or occupy and hold territory as do tanks and armored personnel carriers. They do not have to be in relatively predictable locations (other than as dictated by range limitations) as do, for example, mobile SAMs, which are typically deployed near the assets they are defending.

A System Structure for Studying the Problem

The threat model we used was not a "validated" threat in the formal sense, but rather something we synthesized to capture the essence (and uncertainties) of describing the future land-mobile TBM threat. We thought first in terms of the Scud-like systems of Desert Storm, but we considered many variations and uncertainties to capture critical issues that should affect planning for future threats.

The key to the analysis was the description of a set of candidate extended-counterforce CONOPS. "Counterforce" includes systems and tactics aimed at significantly reducing or eliminating the enemy's ability to conduct threatening offensive operations with TBMs by attacking:

- The *fixed* TBM support infrastructure (industry, transportation systems, supply depots, garrisons, fixed launchers, shelters, and command, control, communications, and intelligence/targeting centers [C^3I]).

- The *mobile/transportable* systems elements in the field (TELs, missiles and warheads, missile resupply and maintenance vehicles, crew vehicles, C^3I vans, and security/air defense forces).

In addition (hence the phrase "extended counterforce"), we considered Air Force operations against the TBMs in flight (boost and, possibly, early mid-course or "ascent phase")[9] and other "forward area" Air Force operations that might enhance the effectiveness of non–Air Force "rear area" active defenses (e.g., warning and sensor cueing).

In the analysis, we assumed the following: The **peacetime extended-counterforce CONOPS** would be intelligence operations in preparation for possible crisis/wartime missions. The specific intelligence operations would be tailored to the threat area, but certain general features would be common.

- Overhead imagery and electronic intelligence (ELINT) would identify fixed TBM infrastructure assets such as fabrication sites, test ranges, fixed launchers, supply storage, garrisons, training areas, field launch sites, road networks, and some C^3I facilities.

- Terrestrial radars, airborne imaging, and ELINT would monitor missile tests and exercises, giving U.S. planners an understanding of the threat CONOPS and technical capabilities.

---

[9]It is common in the defense community to use "ascent phase" to mean the period after boost phase but before apogee. However, the boost phase is also a period of ascent, so we have deviated from that common but unfortunate jargon. The distinction between the boost and postboost portions of ascent phase are important. Boost-phase intercepts occur while the rocket is thrusting when lethality is very high and it is obvious whether the missile, if hit, has been killed. Later ascent-phase intercepts would occur exoatmospherically. They may be less stressing technically and economically than boost-phase intercepts (e.g., more engagement time and easier end-game homing outside the atmosphere), but lethality is uncertain, damage assessment may be difficult, and some debris (including warheads) might still follow a ballistic path to friendly areas, confusing the defenses and causing damage.

- Human sources (HUMINT) would monitor the flow of critical technologies and equipment, watch and exploit the international flow of TBM technical and military specialists, infiltrate TBM operational commands, and recruit in-country agents.

- These diverse types of information would be fused into a useful intelligence product describing:

  — Numbers and disposition of weapons of mass destruction.

  — Missile system technical features (reaction time, range/payload, range flexibility, missile-boost intensity profiles, CEP, TEL mobility, reliability).

  — Order-of-battle data.

  — Multispectral signatures of dispersible assets (e.g., TELs and decoys).

  — Location and vulnerability of critical facilities (e.g., storage bunkers, fixed launchers, command posts, communications facilities, etc.).

  — Wartime threat CONOPS (C^3, dispersal plans and deployment areas, potential hide sites, lines of communication, numbers of vehicles in a battery, CCD, air defenses, security forces, etc.).

In a **crisis**, the TBM intelligence focus would need to be sharpened and surveillance intensified. If possible, sources should monitor TBM deployment areas to detect and track dispersing TELs, warheads (particularly weapons of mass destruction), and other equipment to their field hides. The intelligence systems would also monitor C^3 sources to build a threat picture and provide strategic and tactical warning. Preemptive strikes might be necessary. Obviously, the potential for success would be strongly dependent on the quality of the intelligence picture.

The wartime CONOPS would include missions against fixed TBM assets, mobile systems in the field (before and after launch), and in-flight missiles. The general structure of the operational concepts that we explored is illustrated in Figures 3 and 4. This logical decomposition helped us identify possible counterforce paths, with their unique systems and operational requirements, and helped us perform an overall "completeness check" on the counterforce concepts.

Arrayed along the top are bubbles representing the possible states of the TBM threat. Arrayed in the left column are bubbles representing the critical generic extended-counterforce processes to be accomplished. The rectangular cells then indicate the specific processes applicable to each state of the threat. For example, MTI stands for "moving-target indicator," a system such as JSTARS that can detect and track moving vehicles in a clutter background using Doppler processing. Similarly, MTID stands for "moving-target identification," a notional system that can both detect and discriminate between TELs

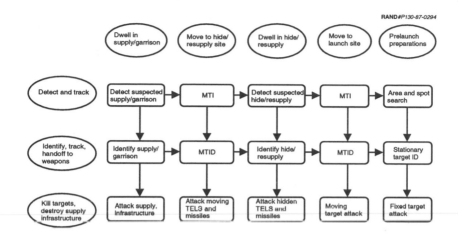

Figure 3—TBM Extended-Counterforce Event Structure (Prelaunch)

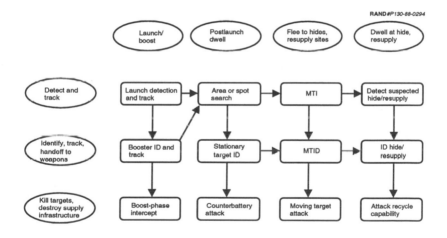

Figure 4—TBM Extended-Counterforce Event Structure (Postlaunch)

and other moving vehicles. Extended-counterforce CONOPS must have a feasible path following the arrows from the top row to the bottom row. Figure 3 covers prelaunch phases of TBM operations; Figure 4 covers postlaunch phases.

Assessing the potential ability of current and programmed systems to effect these CONOPS was, then, the study's objective. The systems and issues shown in Figure 5 constituted a baseline that stimulated consideration of up-

RAND#P130-89-0294

	Detect and track	Identify and handoff	Kill

Prelaunch operations:
• Fixed infrastructure
• Dispersed/mobile elements
  – Support
  – Missiles/TELs
	• Intell (NTM,...)
	• *Battlefield surveillance*
	  - JSTARS
	  - ASARS
	  - Other
	• *SOFs*
	• *Implants/mines (LOCs)*
	• *Aircraft platforms*
	  (manned, RPVs, UAVs)
		• Intell
		• *Battlefield surveillance*
		  - JSTARS (upgraded)
		  - ASARS
		  - Other
		• *SOFs*
		• *Implants/mines (LOCs)*
		• *Attack platforms*
		  - A-10, F-15E,...
			• *SOFs*
			• *Mines*
			• *Attack platforms*
			  - A-10, F-15E,...
			  - Cruise missiles
			• TBMs
			  - ATACMS

Boost and postlaunch operations
• In-flight missiles (boost)
• TELS (counterbattery)
	• DSP,...
	• Battlefield surveillance
	  - AWACS?
	  - TPS-59 or 75
	  - CB
	• SOFs
	• Implants/mines
	• Attack platforms
		• DSP,...
		• Battlefield surveillance
		  - AWACS?
		  - TPS-59 or 75
		  - CB
		• SOFs
		• Implants/mines
		• Attack platforms
			• SOFs
			• Mines
			• *Attack platforms*
			  - Missile
			  - Airborne laser

Study focus on items in italics.

Figure 5—Architectural Elements for Countering Mobile TBMs

graded systems (and some new systems). By and large, we focused on evolutionary extension of existing platforms because of fiscal realities: The services may be forced to do the best they can with what they have. In any event, this was a good place to start. The discussions in the next section provide a general overview of the structures and the systems and issues as they figure in prelaunch, postlaunch, and boost-phase or ascent-phase intercept operations.

Prospects for Prelaunch Counterforce Operations

The requirements and means for attacking fixed targets are not unique to the TBM threat. Since many of the TBM-related targets would be hardened and proliferated (e.g., weapon storage bunkers), the most efficient means of attack is likely to be air-delivered precision-guided munitions (PGMs) such as laser-guided bombs. An important precursor to the TBM CONOPS would therefore be operations against C^3I systems to blind or paralyze the air defense systems, followed by offensive counterair (OCA) and suppression of enemy air defenses (SEAD) missions to achieve air supremacy, so that the interdiction missions against fixed TBM facilities could be carried out at acceptable attrition levels.

The extent to which attacks on the fixed infrastructure could meet U.S. overall counterforce objectives will vary from theater to theater and scenario to scenario. The prognosis in general, however, is not very hopeful, for the following reasons. First and most important, it is very likely that the TBM mission-critical systems would be dispersed to wartime hides before the war starts. Second, killing these fixed targets might not be easy. They would likely be hardened and distributed and have built-in redundancy (particularly C^3I). Finally, intelligence might be poor, causing U.S. planners to focus on the wrong subset of fixed targets.

Once dispersed and in a "warfighting" posture, mobile TBM systems are a formidable challenge. Prewar intelligence might identify likely dispersal areas and constraints, finding suspected hides and presurveyed launch positions, identifying road networks and travel patterns, and so on, but currently conceivable counterforce CONOPS would still have to commit significant assets to *finding the targets*. This would involve detection and identification in the face of CCD countermeasures and air defenses. Once found, mobile systems would need to be tracked or killed promptly or they would be lost, so attack *timeliness* is an issue. Finally, all of this must be done with expensive systems that might be in short supply (e.g., surveillance aircraft) and which, therefore, could not tolerate much defensive attrition by airborne interceptors, SAMs, and AAA.[10]

Attack Operations on Fixed Targets. Various weapons might be used to attack fixed targets. If the targets were localized accurately (in a common coordinate system so that mapping and other localization errors were reasonable), indirect fires from MLRS or tube artillery might be used. Air-delivered weapons might be used for deeper targets. The weapon choice and effectiveness would depend on scenario-dependent factors (range, P_k, availability, survivability, and an assessment of the likelihood that the target does, in fact, consist of important TBM assets).

If there were too many potential targets to attack them all, then the CONOPS should include some sort of "occupancy check" or target verification prior to attack. This could be done in a variety of ways. However, assuming that none of the surveillance and intelligence assets that were used to develop the candidate targets can help (for example, the target planner cannot have an SOF soldier take a look), the best near-term approach would be to have an aircraft such as the F-15E fly near the target and image it using its APG-70 radar in the SAR mode or image it with LANTIRN. Unfortunately, due to the resolution limit of the F-15E's SAR, target discrimination capability will be limited, but it might be good enough, given other indicators. If a more

---

[10]Army systems such as ATACMS may also be able to play a role in TBM counterforce missions, but range limitations vis-à-vis 600-km Scuds, reaction time lags, and long missile time-of-flight currently limit effectiveness potential. The Army is addressing these issues, but at the time of our study it was our judgment that only airborne systems had significant extended-counterforce potential.

positive target ID is required, the F-15E would have to approach closer (say to within a mile or less from a 10,000-foot altitude) to image it with LANTIRN.[11]

Attack Operations on Mobile Targets. A variety of sensors might detect a TEL in motion. Possibilities include:

- Covertly implanted sensors at key road junctions or in suspected deployment areas. These could be unmanned seismic/acoustic, chemical or radiation detectors, or IR/visible imaging systems, or they could be manned lookouts with long-range passive imaging systems. If unattended ground sensors could detect and discriminate TELs, it might be just a small additional effort to turn these sensors into lethal mines. Other possibilities would be to attach tags covertly to the TELs so that U.S. systems could follow the vehicles to their hides to wipe out their "nests," or detections could be communicated to a central commander who would order other systems such as tactical aircraft to respond.

- Aircraft-based moving-target indicator (MTI) radars (on manned aircraft such as the TR-1 and JSTARS or on unmanned UAVs and RPVs). As JSTARS demonstrated in Desert Storm, MTI systems can be very effective. The problem is that the current MTI systems have limited discrimination potential (an exception might be wheeled versus tracked vehicles, due to the unique 2X doppler from the tracks).

It is conceivable that technology will support an effective moving-target identification (MTID) capability in the future,[12] but for now, how might our limited (nondiscriminating) MTI systems be used?

One approach is a form of gatekeeping. Suspected hides that, for whatever reason, target planners could not or did not want to destroy, could be surveilled by airborne MTI systems. Any traffic that was spotted would be, by association, a TBM system. Another approach would be to watch possible deployment areas and track vehicles suspected of being TBM-related—either because of the distinctive number of vehicles in the group or because the vehicles were in an area where non-TBM systems would not be expected to be seen. However, depending on the quality of U.S. intelligence, this area surveillance mode might filter out anywhere from most to almost no "possibles."

Given a possible TEL track, the CONOPS would be to track it until it stopped, at which point the spot would be imaged by other onboard sensors or by another platform and sensor cued by the MTI aircraft. The imager might be a SAR or millimeter wave (MMW) radar system with good all-weather,

---

[11]Second-generation FLIRs may improve effective ranges by a factor of two or more.

[12]The Navy's S-3 patrol aircraft currently has an "imaging MTI" system that exploits the known target motion (e.g., the pitch and roll of a ship at sea) to create low-resolution images.

day/night capability or an electro/optical (E/O) system for which weather might be an issue. To be of value, the image would need to have adequate resolution to identify the target. In theory, SAR images of this quality could be obtained from various sources. A variety of other imaging systems could be imagined, but the baseline CONOPS would use platforms such as either JSTARS or the TR-1, due to availability and responsiveness limits on other conceivable platform options (including all satellite systems).

The analysis issues here all relate to the detection characteristics of the MTI (P_d / P_{fa}), search rate, processing capacity, coverage areas (standoff [for survivability] and range limited), and data fusion potential (in the MTI platform and offboard in a central BM/C^{4}I system). The same issues must be addressed for the necessary spot imaging of targets once they stop.

Since the JSTARS/TR-1 cannot attack the targets they detect, they must pass cues through a BM/C^{4}I system to other systems that can prosecute an attack. If confidence in the track were high or traffic were light, an aircraft such as the F-15E might be vectored to the contact before it stopped (i.e., before it could be positively identified). More likely, however, the attack aircraft would be cued only after the TEL stopped and was fairly confidently identified. As with the attacks on fixed targets described earlier, the F-15E could acquire the target with its SAR or LANTIRN and, depending on the surface-to-air threat, might stand off as far as possible and drop weapons or first approach for target ID confirmation using LANTIRN.

Clearly, as in earlier cases, given a target's coordinates, a variety of weapons might be used to kill it. In this case, however, we assumed that the TEL might have been spotted on the way to a launch position. This implies that there would be a very short time to get to it before its missile was launched (a few minutes for advanced threats, up to 30 minutes for a current Scud).

An alternative prelaunch-kill CONOPS would be to use the strike aircraft as both detection systems and kill systems (recce-strike). For example, as was attempted in Desert Storm, F-15Es could fly over suspected launch areas and search for exposed TELs using their SAR and/or LANTIRN. They would attack contacts that satisfied their attack criteria. (In Desert Storm the criterion seemed to be "if it is a blip in the suspected Scud area, kill it." Target discrimination was not attempted, partly because AAA and IR SAM concerns kept the aircraft high (above 15,000–20,000 feet) and as far from the targets as possible.) The analysis issues center around sensor search rates, P_d / P_{fa}, and probability of recognition, P_r. These will be influenced by rules of engagement (minimum altitude, for example) and the scenario-dependent clutter.[13] Clutter includes "cultural" objects (e.g., commercial tractor-trailer trucks) and natural

---

[13]There is a possibility that the unique, potentially very large signature from the TEL with the missile erected vertically might be exploitable.

features that might fool the sensor operator (the assumption is that in the near term the only "automatic" target cueing/recognition [ATC/ATR] would be done visually by the pilot or weapons system officer [WSO]; in the future, data-processing technology may improve this capability, making it truly "automatic").

Prospects for Postlaunch Counterbattery Operations

Ballistic missile launches are difficult to hide from launch-detection satellites. So if in the future the United States fails to some extent in its prelaunch counterforce operations (as seems very likely), the fallback might have to be postlaunch counterbattery operations, using the very observable launches to localize the launch point.

Counterbattery attacks might be important from several perspectives. First, the enemy might intend to reload the TELs and use them again. This makes sense if the TELs are relatively complex and expensive. Unfortunately, as missile technology improves, the TELs could become less complex and costly, so that in the extreme, they might become "throwaways." Even if that happened, however, a counterbattery capability would have a negative effect on the crews, who might be less inclined to launch missiles if they knew they would be unlikely to survive.

The counterbattery CONOPS would start with a launch detection and resultant launch point estimate derived from backtracking the booster to the ground. This could be done with DSP by fitting the observed hits (spacing and intensity) to boost templates. Alternatively, the missile might be detected and backtracked by a radar on an aircraft or, less likely due to range limits, by a ground system such as the Air Force TPS-75 and the Marine TPS-59, or by the ship-based Aegis Spy radar. This initial TBM launch-point prediction (LPP) cue could be characterized by the launch-point uncertainty in CEP terms and its timeliness (time from launch to cue receipt).

If the LPP uncertainty were very small (say, a few hundred meters), this CONOPS would degenerate to the previous case, in which attacks were generated against prelaunch contacts. The LPP could be attacked with various indirect-fire weapons or aircraft. The only difference might be the timeline. The time from launch to movement away from the launch point might be very short, e.g., less than five minutes. When data-processing and cue-dissemination times are subtracted, the TEL might be running before the cue got to a shooter. Because of this, it probably would be necessary to use the initial cue to localize the TEL for detection and track by other area-surveillance systems such as JSTARS and/or to vector CAP aircraft such as F-15Es to the area where they would search for the TEL.

If the LPP were passed promptly to, for example, JSTARS, the CONOPS might be as follows. JSTARS would image the LPP uncertainty area at the highest possible SAR resolution in hopes of detecting the stationary TEL and support vehicles. The area to be imaged might be fairly large for current DSP capabilities, but great improvements are possible. A radar such as the TPS-75 with the "expert missile tracker" hardware and software modifications could reduce this area still further.

The location of possible TELs identified in these images would be compared with historical and real-time MTI data. The JSTARS operators would review their recorded MTI data in the LPP area to see if any candidate TEL hits corresponded to traffic patterns consistent with TBM operations. If the historical MTI data eliminated some of the imaged targets, then the next step in the CONOPS would be more effective. That step would be to focus the real-time MTI system on the suspected TELs to watch for movement. Here again, the operators would be looking for telltale patterns. Those contacts that passed these "reasonableness" filters would be tracked with the MTI system until they stopped.[14] The stopped vehicles would again be imaged in the hopes of identifying the targets.

In the meantime, an attack aircraft such as the F-15E would have been vectored to the LLP area. When it arrived it would get the best data JSTARS had at that time. As JSTARS data were refined, this would be passed to the F-15E (either directly or through a command center such as an airborne command, control, and communications system [ABCCC]). This means that there might be possible TELs at a number of fixed coordinates and there might be possible TELs in motion. The F-15E would begin trying to sort these out, attacking targets that met the attack criteria.

How the F-15E could best operate, given these data, needs to be analyzed more carefully. For example, it may be that the F-15E SAR could not improve on the target ID capability that JSTARS provides (the two SARs currently have about the same resolution limits). This suggests that the F-15E might use the SAR for initial "target" acquisition. Once acquired, these targets would be attacked, probably using LANTIRN. In this case, the objective would probably be to attack targets from the maximum possible altitude and standoff range for survivability against AAA and IR SAM threats that might be colocated with the

---

[14]Of course, the feasibility of tracking small clusters of vehicles from JSTARS-like standoff distances depends on the nature of the terrain and other obstacles (e.g., cities). For example, the Naval Weapons Center's "Line-of-Sight Handbook" shows that for a platform at 30,000 feet, the distance at which, on average, 50 percent of the ground targets would be visible is 250 km in flat terrain but only 50 km in "rough" terrain. If the criterion were 97.5 percent area visibility, these ranges would drop to 125 km and 25 km, respectively.

TELs. Therefore, it is unlikely that LANTIRN could contribute much to an improved target ID.

If the target locations of the fixed contacts and the tracks on moving contacts could be passed to the F-15E accurately enough (and there were no significant navigation, mapping, or reference system biases), the best target-acquisition mode for the F-15E might be to rely only on LANTIRN. The "target" the F-15E might find could be the exposed TEL or a suspected hide. Depending on altitude and standoff constraints that would be defense driven, the F-15E might be able to get close enough to the target to identify it. "Close enough" is probably a slant range of a few kilometers. If the only search/target acquisition system were LANTIRN, issues of the SAR performance against moving targets and the need for an MTI mode to find movers become moot.

Of course, if the F-15E had to search the LPP on its own (because it was outside JSTARS coverage, for example), then crews might find that the LANTIRN field of view/sweep rate was too small to be effective, so the F-15E might search primarily with the SAR, using the radar to cue LANTIRN for target "confirmation" and attack. In this case, an MTI mode might be desirable, particularly if the SAR and MTI modes can be interleaved.

As time goes on, the initial LPP would grow in size as the TELs fled. The search would end when the aircraft had expended its fuel or munitions (on possible TELs and hides such as buildings) or the TELs had probably reached their hides undetected (as little as five to fifteen minutes after launch).

The options here are many and complex, and most of them would require extensive efforts. The only near-term option we identified involved autonomous F-15E operations as described briefly in the summary section below. First, however, let us consider prospects for postlaunch kills.

Prospects for Boost-Phase or Postboost Ascent-Phase Intercepts

Both the prelaunch and postlaunch counterbattery CONOPS are very challenging and may prove to be too expensive to implement and too sensitive to responsive threat countermeasures. The sensors supporting these CONOPS need to have near-continuous availability and high search rates. The system must also be able to cull out false targets (a significant current deficiency). Finally, target contacts must be prosecuted within minutes. If these CONOPS prove to be unattractive, the shortfalls may suggest alternative CONOPS that might prove to be relatively attractive—in particular, boost or later ascent-phase TBM intercept.

The *a priori* logic behind shifting the focus to boost-phase or ascent-phase (BPI-API) intercept CONOPS (sometimes also referred to as "inflight") is as follows:

- The enemy might be able to hide his TBM systems before launch, but it is unlikely that he could do much about masking the actual missile launches. When missiles were launched, U.S. sensors would no doubt see them.

- Tight timeline requirements against the TELs postlaunch based on launch detections might drive the United States to new hypersonic air-launched standoff missiles. These missiles would need some sort of terminal homing or area coverage with smart submunitions, which are technically risky and, therefore, expensive.

- Compared with the difficulty of the counterbattery system sketched out above, an inflight intercept might be more attractive. The target signature of the inflight missile is huge, the background clutter and decoy potential are nil, and the interceptor performance required for inflight intercept is comparable to the missile performance required to attack the ground assets before they escape (3000–5000 ft/sec to ranges of 50–100 km).

With an in-flight intercept CONOPS that has intercept missiles (hopefully SRAM-sized or smaller) carried on CAP aircraft, a goal would be to minimize the number of aircraft needed to cover the likely launch areas. Thus, the issue is: How far out could the interception take place? The answer will depend on details that are still to be determined, but it is clear that boost-phase intercepts would not be possible if the intercept aircraft were cued by DSP. So the most likely solution would be to have modified air-air radars or simple IR sensors on board the patrol aircraft that could detect the missiles and target the interceptors.

SUMMARY AND CONCLUSIONS

Clearly, extended-counterforce options involve major technical and operational challenges. Nonetheless, they could prove exceedingly important. Attacks on *fixed* TBM infrastructure targets involve no special challenges. Our capability for such attacks will grow naturally as precision-strike capabilities improve (toward all-weather, high accuracy, long standoff, and high lethality). Attacks on time-critical *mobile* TBM systems are another matter and, as the paper has indicated, are likely to require a broad range of extended-counterforce measures for success.

Finding discrete mobile targets such as TELs in an uncertain clutter background is very challenging. Based on prior intelligence, counterforce operators would focus their search on the most likely deployment areas, but these could still be quite large and dispersed. The large search areas and brief exposure times of TELs imply that search rates will have to be very large. Furthermore, success will probably require a sequential, multilevel search-and-detection operation, followed by effective target-discrimination and recognition processes based on sensors operating on multiple platforms in diverse parts of the spectrum and using computationally intense automatic target cueing and recognition (ATC/ATR) to achieve a high probability of detection and a suitably low false-alarm rate. Relevant technologies and systems are being investigated in R&D efforts at ARPA and elsewhere, but are generally not yet mature.

The one bright spot is the ability to exploit the TBM's launch and boost signatures. A single IR sensor on a synchronous satellite can detect and track multiple ballistic missile exhaust plumes over the entire threat region in near real time. A radar, either on the ground or on an aircraft, can track the missile in flight at long range, as could an airborne IR sensor and laser ranger/tracker. The bottom line is that if TBMs are used, the launches should be visible. When the launch is seen, it is obviously too late to kill that missile on the ground, but several options still exist if the launch point can be localized quickly and the information passed to appropriate systems:

- Target the launch point, killing the TEL if it is still there. If there are multiple reload missiles per TEL (as there were in Desert Storm), this would be militarily important.

- Cue surveillance assets to the launch area so that they can find and trail the TEL to its hide site or resupply area. The hides can then be monitored or attacked by standard interdiction systems.

- Cue assets based on the launch signature and estimated trajectory data. Kill the TBM in its boost phase (high lethality and minimal problems of damage assessment) or later in its ascent (more dubious lethality and greater damage-assessment difficulties, but more time for the attack and little difficulty with atmospheric effects).

In considering the first two options, the study team concluded that the best, and perhaps only, near-term option would be to use F-15E aircraft on combat air patrol (CAP), as illustrated in Figure 6. The F-15Es would use their APG-70 air-air radar (with rather straightforward and inexpensive software modifications to detect and backtrack TBMs in flight). The range at which an F-15E might be able to detect the missile is, in fact, nicely balanced with the range at which the F-15E could subsequently fly to the estimated launch point and attack the TEL before it could escape. Alternatively, the F-15E could fly to the launch area and find the TEL using the radar in the SAR mode (if the TEL were still stationary) or find it with LANTIRN, even if it were moving. It could then be trailed, using either LANTIRN or the radar in the MTI mode. The running TEL or the hide/resupply site could then be attacked, or this in-

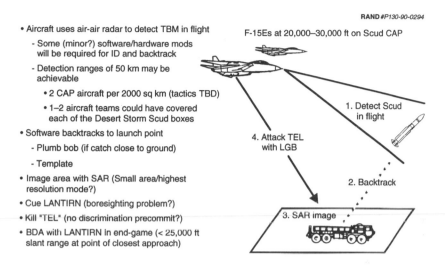

Figure 6—Possible Near-Term Autonomous F-15E Counterbattery Concept

formation could be handed off to another system for continuing monitoring and subsequent attack.

We performed a first-order force sizing assessment and investment strategy for this concept and found that it is feasible if it is possible to achieve "modest" intelligence successes in order to limit the potential launch areas that would need to be covered by these CAP aircraft. Although the next war is unlikely to look exactly like Desert Storm, it is nevertheless relevant to note that if this concept had been available, the same resources used in the unsuccessful Scud hunt could have been quite effective in counterbattery attacks. Instead of about 90 missiles launched, there might have been less than one or two dozen launched over the course of the war.

If the launch areas were larger next time, more dedicated aircraft would be needed for a high level of counterbattery effectiveness, but even if it was not possible to cover all launch areas, the counterforce operations could have *some* success, which would limit the enemy's operational flexibility and effectiveness. As a side benefit, this concept could be extended to a modest boost-phase intercept system, with the development of an intercept missile.

The options for attacking the TBM in flight all involve advanced capabilities that are not currently in hand. They have great potential value, however. Further, some of the critical elements of these options are the same as those required for the counterforce options described above.

Implications

Our quick-look study of extended-counterforce options had several implications for policy, programs, and operations:

- TBM extended-counterforce missions are not a lesser included case of current and projected airborne interdiction missions. Special programs are needed.[15]
- While robust capabilities would require breakthroughs and major investments, nontrivial improvement of capability could be achieved with modest expenditures and minor modifications to deployed forces (as suggested in the discussion attending Figure 6).
- Investments in counterforce R&D and acquisition should be brought more "in balance" with other TMD initiatives within BMDO, under BMDO leadership and direction, and with BMDO funding. In parallel, the U.S. intelligence community should give these problems much greater emphasis.
- TBMs, particularly if armed with weapons of mass destruction, will have a dramatic effect on U.S. coalition building and power projection. U.S. leaders need to realize that prospects for extended-counterforce capabilities are inherently uncertain. Further, military leaders in a future MRC will likely not be able to predict confidently the success of counterforce operations (either preemptive in a crisis or in response to wartime threats). This means that we may have to accept greater risks or stay home.

BIBLIOGRAPHY

Atkinson, Rick (1993), *Crusade: The Untold Story of the Persian Gulf War*, Houghton Mifflin, Boston, MA.

Davis, Paul K. (ed.) (1994), *New Challenges for Defense Planning: Rethinking How Much Is Enough*, RAND, Santa Monica, CA.

Department of Defense (1992), *Final Report to Congress on the Conduct of the Persian Gulf War*, April, U.S. Government Printing Office, Washington, D.C.

Irving, David (1964), *The Mare's Nest*, Little, Brown and Company, Boston, MA.

Larsen, Eric, and Glenn Kent (1994), *A New Methodology for Assessing Multi-Layer Missile Defense Options*, RAND, Santa Monica, CA.

Mesic, Richard (1994), "Defining a Balanced Investment Program for Coping with Tactical Ballistic Missiles," in Davis (1994).

---

[15]In the two years since Desert Storm, U.S. counterforce capabilities have not improved.

Millot, Marc Dean, Roger Molander, and Peter Wilson (1993), *"The Day After..."*: *Nuclear Proliferation in the Post-Cold War World*, 3 vols., RAND, Santa Monica, CA.

Shaver, Russ (1994), "Priorities for Ballistic Missile Defense," in Davis (1994).

Chapter 17

MILITARY ISSUES IN MULTINATIONAL OPERATIONS

Margaret Cecchine Harrell and Robert Howe

Given the increasing likelihood of U.S. military involvement in future multinational operations, there is a need to rethink the general preparation and employment of U.S. forces for such operations, including how the forces should be selected, organized, trained, equipped, deployed, sustained, and controlled. From assessing results of recent operations and from comparing current Army procedures and preparations with those of other nations, we conclude that there are important changes in doctrine and training that should be made. These changes do not require large-scale or fundamental changes in Army structure, but they will not occur unless given high priority and sustained attention.

INTRODUCTION

Recent years have seen an increasing willingness from the international community to intervene in what used to be considered purely internal matters. The 1990s have even seen a willingness to intervene with force. The examples in Iraq, Somalia, and the former Yugoslavia are breaking new ground and, if they indicate a trend, hold some profound implications for the United Nations, regional international organizations, the United States, and the U.S. Army. This paper describes some of the changes the Army may need to make if it is to be better prepared for and more effective in a wide range of multinational military operations.

There is a limited experience base for learning lessons relevant to the current era. Prior to World War II, one or more of the "great powers" would intervene when it felt that its interests were threatened, but the interventions were usually of a different character than the ones of interest today. Since World War II, the United Nations has conducted numerous peacekeeping operations, but although these have typically involved military forces, their purpose has almost

---

This paper was presented at a Naval War College conference, "Beyond Traditional Peacekeeping," 23–24 February 1994. The proceedings will be published in Donald C. F. Daniel and Bradd C. Hayes (eds.), *Beyond Traditional Peacekeeping*, London: The Macmillan Press, forthcoming.

always been to monitor compliance with a truce or a cease-fire agreed to between the parties before the commitment of forces. It was not anticipated that
military action would be necessary to enforce or impose the agreement.
Indeed, the UN force could be withdrawn if one or both parties revoked the
agreement (this occurred in the Sinai in 1967). The situation is seldom so
straightforward today.

UN interventions have often been long term and relatively open ended.
The operation in Cyprus is approaching its 30th anniversary, and the observer
group in Kashmir is approaching its 45th. The mandates that establish or extend such operations usually do not even address the subject of termination.
The presence of the UN force sometimes appears to reduce the parties' incentive to negotiate a solution, since the situation remains reasonably stable and
the costs of the force are borne by others (e.g., in Cyprus and Kashmir). These
loosely defined missions are tolerable when the cost is low. The United
Nations Military Observer Group in India and Pakistan (UNMOGIP) is estimated to cost about $7 million per year, and there have been only six fatalities
in its 45 years. The United Nations Protection Force (UNPROFOR) in the
former Yugoslavia, on the other hand, is costing the UN over $900 million per
year (plus unreimbursed costs by the participants), and there have been 59 fatalities in less than two years. The second United Nations Operation in
Somalia (UNOSOM II) has had even higher costs in money and lives. Costs
such as these in recent operations make open-ended commitments much more
worrisome.

For the United States, the cost of most UN peacekeeping operations has
been mainly financial, since the Cold War kept the military forces of the
United States and the Soviet Union on the sidelines. While continuing to bear
the ever-increasing financial costs, the United States is now under growing internal and external pressure to commit forces to a variety of operations.
Whether and how to become more involved and whether and how to effect
changes in the United Nations to make it more effective in these operations are
very pressing issues but are beyond the scope of this paper. Our concern is
with the implications of these peacekeeping/peacemaking operations for the
United States military, and particularly the Army, if we *do* become involved.

In the next section we discuss multinational operations, the issues they raise,
and the lessons available from other countries. We address these issues in the
context of military activities that take place in preparing for and conducting
any military operation, and we assess the impact of multinational, particularly
peacekeeping, operations on them. The activities we address are selecting,
equipping, training, deploying, organizing, controlling, and sustaining the
force. In the final section we present some conclusions about those implications and the changes required for U.S. forces to participate most effectively in
future multinational peace operations.

MILITARY ISSUES

For any military operation, there are certain classes of activities that must be conducted to accomplish the mission. The individuals or units to carry out the operation must be selected and trained, organized, and equipped. They must be deployed to the area of operations and sustained while deployed. They must be subject to good command and control while carrying out the mission and eventually being withdrawn. However, the emerging class of commitments for multinational peace operations appear to require some modification of current U.S. military notions of how to prepare for and execute missions.

Some activities, such as training, will require adjustments or additions for those units likely to participate in multinational operations. Other activities may vary enough to conflict with conventional experience and maximum military effectiveness. For example, at one point during the UN operation in Cyprus, the local population developed a particular animosity toward the British soldiers and were inclined to attack British patrols. To counter this, the operation commander integrated the patrols so that each nationality participating in the operation was represented on each patrol. The differing national doctrines and training standards probably would have reduced the military effectiveness and limited the response capability of the patrols. However, the multinational patrols had the desired effect of deterring attacks, so the potential reduction in effectiveness never was tested or became a problem.

If military operations exist as a continuum with conventional operations at one extreme and pure observer missions at the other, it is clear that the tension with conventional doctrine occurs around the middle of the continuum. This is evident in the control and organization of missions. When conventional combat is certain, the units should always operate as national entities at as high a level as possible for maximum effectiveness. For observer missions, combat is not part of their mission, and multinational participants can be integrated at a much lower level.[1] In the middle, however, the situation will generally be unclear and hard decisions will be necessary.

In the next few pages we will discuss military activities as they pertain to multinational peace operations. As appropriate, we give examples from previous commitments under UN or other international auspices and present solutions that appear to have been successful. The purpose of this section is to provide the basis on which to draw lessons for the U.S. Army, which we will discuss in the concluding section.

---

[1]M. Harrell recently visited a MINURSO (the United Nations Mission for the Referendum in Western Sahara) observer site in the Western Sahara that was staffed by sixteen officers representing a total of eleven countries and five continents.

Selection

Selection of individuals or units to participate in multinational operations is, arguably, the most critical step in the mission. There are significant variations among nations in the approach to this step. Even within the same nation the process and criteria have changed between operations. The process ranges from complete volunteerism by individuals to the involuntary assignment of existing units.

Prior to about 1990, virtually all multinational operations were classic peacekeeping or observer operations under the auspices of the United Nations. The staffing of these operations was characterized by the more or less complete exclusion of the United States, the Soviet Union, Japan, and China. Those who did staff the missions can be loosely divided into two categories: relatively well-to-do nations from Europe and the Americas who provided forces at considerable expense to themselves out of a sense of obligation, and Third World nations that, whatever their sense of obligation, found that the United Nations payments more than adequately compensated their expenses. The former tended to use volunteers, whereas the latter would more commonly send existing units, although there are many exceptions.

The Nordic nations provide a classic example of the use of volunteers. Those nations all have universal military service, so virtually the entire adult male population has basic military training. Each nation periodically asks for volunteers for UN missions and selects the proper mix of individuals for known or anticipated missions. These individuals are then formed into units as appropriate and trained prior to their deployment. Upon return from the mission the volunteers return to their civilian or military occupations, and other volunteers are sought for subsequent missions. This process is facilitated by common training procedures among the countries and by specialization in the conduct of certain training, such as that of military observers.

The volunteer process has worked quite adequately for low-intensity missions such as that of the UN Force in Cyprus. The forces involved are relatively small, operations are at the small-unit level, and the units are expected to avoid conflict under all but the most extreme circumstances, such as when they come under attack. The 1990s, however, have ushered in new types of multinational operation. Operation Provide Comfort, in the aftermath of Operation Desert Storm, for the first time found the international community imposing itself to provide humanitarian relief without the acquiescence of the country involved. The various operations in Somalia similarly found the United Nations entering more or less uninvited, with quite large force requirements. And in Cambodia, the UN Transition Authority was invited to supervise the transition, but the forces required to do so were far larger than for previous operations. Thus, some of the new missions have been large and nontraditional. At the same time, however, the UN has continued to carry out more-traditional peacekeeping missions in Pakistan, the Middle East, Africa, and Central America. Thus there is now a broader range of missions.

This broader range of missions is causing a rethinking of the nature of the forces and operations needed. Norway and Denmark, which have traditionally relied on individual volunteers for individual missions, have recognized that this process is inappropriate for some of the emerging missions (i.e., those that go beyond classic "monitoring"), and thus they plan to form a standing force for missions in which hostilities can be expected and for which obtaining volunteers at the time might be difficult. At the same time, the United States is experimenting with individual volunteers from the Reserve Components to staff part of the Multinational Force and Observers in the Sinai, which, although not a United Nations force, has many of the characteristics of a UN peacekeeping force. Other nations, such as Finland and Sweden, plan to stay with their traditional process but recognize that they can do so only by restricting the missions for which they will provide forces. More generally, then, it seems that there is no single approach to selecting and preparing personnel for UN missions. In some cases, missions can be performed by individual volunteers, but in other cases standing units with appropriate training will be necessary.

Unit selection varies by country. The Nordic countries have traditionally formed standby units designed explicitly for UN missions. They continue to do this when the forces deployed leave them sufficient room under their legislated ceiling. The standing brigades being formed in Norway and Denmark would be in addition to these standby units. Canada predesignates the unit likely to deploy for the next peace operation. Interestingly, this unit is rarely deployed; generally there is sufficient preparation time to deploy other units. The U.S. selection process is complicated both by the wide variety of force types available and by the political implications of any warning or deployment order. Thus, the political tendency is not to designate a unit until employment of U.S. force is certain.

Discussions during this research indicated some limitations in the Army personnel records system. A number of cases were described in which individuals were identified serendipitously as having an ideal background for particular missions, after personnel-record screening had failed to identify them. The Army has an extensive system of personnel records that include, in principle, information on language skills and ethnic background. It was beyond the scope of our research to study whether the problem was in the completeness of the records or the technique used to search them. However, the rather exotic locales of some missions, and the rapidity with which they are sometimes mounted, establish the need for the Army personnel records system to identify rapidly and reliably, for example, someone who grew up in Haiti and is presently serving in the United States Army.

Equipping

Equipping a force is a separate issue regardless of the selection process. Aside from activities such as Operation Desert Storm, more properly described as a war, multinational operations tend to have requirements for which almost no normal military unit is properly equipped. Truce-supervision or election-monitoring missions require little or no weaponry but may require proportionately enormous mobility assets, since the distances involved are usually very large in relation to the size of the monitoring force involved. Other, less benign, environments such as Somalia place different demands.

A unit required to perform convoy escort and protection, as well as security of relief workers and supplies, needs to be able to defend itself and its charges. Since it is trying to avoid open conflict, it should be able to rely on non-provocative passive protection as much as possible, so that not every incident requires response with firepower to protect the force. However, most armies of the world tend to have either light infantry or heavy mechanized forces. Neither is appropriate for the average peacekeeping or humanitarian relief mission.

In many scenarios, mechanized forces have weapons and vehicles that are more powerful than required for the threats they are likely to face. They place enormous demands on lift forces, are difficult to sustain, and lack the capability to see and be seen without excess risk to themselves or the adversary. Infantry forces, on the other hand, are useful for urban patrolling but lack the mobility to operate effectively outside of urban or other close environments. So, regardless of the type of unit selected for a mission, it will likely need to be reequipped to perform it. One of the better equipment decisions to date seems to be the armored HMMWV recently acquired by the U.S. Army for operations in Somalia. This vehicle combines occupant protection with all-around visibility and retains the option to deliver fire if necessary. It also overcomes a major flaw pointed out to us by some Nordic officers that their armored wheeled vehicles place the driver directly over the front wheels, where he is at much greater risk if the vehicle hits a mine. The armed vehicles with side gun ports used by the Botswana forces are also well suited.

Other less-expensive equipment is also needed by U.S. troops in preparation for multinational peace operations. U.S. forces in Somalia needed face shields and batons to passively protect themselves and provide crowd control and passive force protection; hand-held metal detectors for weapons searches; shorter-barreled weapons for urban operations; and more communications equipment to accommodate the vast territory of Somalia.[2]

Equipment issues have some serious implications for the United States and the United Nations. Many of the countries likely to provide forces for the United Nations lack the resources to provide themselves with the equipment to be effective in more demanding environments, and the UN procurement system is not designed to acquire and store equipment for future operations. Thus, the United States and its better-equipped allies are likely to find themselves under increasing pressure to provide equipment for large contingents from other nations. These demands could range from chemical protective masks and communications equipment to helicopters and other mobility assets. Although it is fairly simple to provide boots or guns to other contingents, even chemical protective masks require training for proper use. Further, although the lack of equipment will compromise a contingent's effectiveness, some shortages are likely to limit the capability of U.S. forces serving in the same mission. For example, the United States was unable to use tear gas in Somalia as a defensive or crowd-control measure until the other UN contingents were supplied with chemical protective masks.

Training

Training military personnel for multinational operations has many dimensions, but the underlying requirement is a solid foundation of basic military training and the discipline derived from such training. With such a foundation, the additional requirements for multinational operations can be learned quite readily. Experience has shown, however, that contingents without such basic skills and discipline can become part of the problem rather than part of the solution in multinational, and particularly peacekeeping, operations.[3]

Training requirements vary considerably by the type of mission. The closer the mission is to conventional combat, the less unusual training is required for U.S. forces. Lower-intensity operations such as observer missions and extended protection of humanitarian relief (for example, Iraq and Somalia) place

---

[2]The lack of proper equipment can also create morale problems, especially when other national contingents have equipment seemingly better that that available to U.S. forces. Some 10th Mountain Division soldiers resented the fact that the Tunisians had later models of the M-16 than they did, and that some contingents had bulletproof vests, whereas the Americans had standard flak jackets.

[3]The *Washington Monthly* (1994) cites an example of the Bulgarian contingent in Cambodia, some members of which had been released from prison for the mission. Reportedly, some members of the contingent threatened the life of LTG Sanderson over pay issues, and on the flight home they wrecked the inside of their aircraft.

requirements on military personnel that differ from normal operations and hence require a degree of specialized training. In some cases the force must "unlearn" some skills and habits. For example, in active combat, military units on patrol attempt to avoid being seen while observing as much as possible. But in many peace operations, being seen is as important and perhaps more important than what the patrol sees.

There are a number of approaches used by different countries to train for United Nations or other multinational operations. Of these, the training conducted by the Nordic countries is the most formal and established. Each country conducts one specialized training course for the benefit of all and, increasingly, for personnel of other nations. Thus, the courses for observers, staff officers, military police, and logisticians are conducted by combined faculty so that common standards prevail. In addition, the four countries have formed a common committee for the development of training standards, which publishes a common training manual for troop training for United Nations operations. Unit training is generally conducted by the officers of the unit, with support from the specialized centers. The officers receive extensive orientation that usually includes a visit by the commander and key staff to the area to which the unit is being deployed.

Some other nations have developed various forms of specialized training facilities, in many cases patterned after those of the Nordic countries or the one developed by Great Britain to train units being sent to Northern Ireland. The United States has only recently begun to participate extensively in multinational operations with the United Nations and has developed no specialized UN training facility, although there are discussions about the desirability of doing so. However, the curriculum at both the JRTC[4] at Fort Polk and the CMTC[5] in Europe has been modified to give units a basic familiarity with such operations during their regular training cycle.

Given a general familiarity with the issues, and conventional combat skills, there are two kinds of specialized training that U.S. units or individuals deployed will require. The first includes the skills generic to these kinds of missions, such as negotiation and increased combined operations experience.[6] This requirement is most likely to affect officers and noncommissioned officers. The second addresses mission-specific issues, including culture, rules of engagement applied to likely tasks such as cordon and search, and the humani-

---

[4]Joint Readiness Training Center.

[5]Combat Maneuver Training Center.

[6]Experience has shown that junior officers require more combined operations experience in the new multinational operations that may conduct combined tactical operations. In conventional operations, only the more senior officers required combined operations expertise.

tarian relief organizations (HROs) and other organizations in the mission area. In addition, the projected organization of the multinational force must be considered, to provide as broad as possible ability to work with the other national contingents. This training should be provided to deploying units, and it would also benefit significantly from the example of similar programs currently being conducted.

Deploying

In most past multinational operations, the force deployed either to a friendly country or to a situation in which the parties wanted their presence. Hence, the force went into a benign environment, and no special attention to deployment was required. Chartered civilian aircraft were usually quite adequate.

There is an increasing tendency for operations to involve environments that, if not openly hostile, carry at least a risk of immediate conflict upon entry. This has been demonstrated in the U.S. concern about security upon initial entry into Somalia and the more recent example of opposition to entry into Haiti. Given the risk of armed opposition, more and more attention will inevitably be paid to forced entry capability.

There are very few countries in the world with even a minimal capability for forced entry, and no other country approaches the United States in this regard. Hence, future operations are likely to see calls for the United States, and a few Western European countries such as France and England, to perform the initial entry and then to establish a secure environment for the deployment of other national contingents. Such an approach could involve acute sensitivities, however, since many of the likely sites for future operations are in areas with a history of European colonialism or U.S. interference. Further, such a policy would be counter to an important objective in multinational operations—spreading the burden and risk while demonstrating that the world is united behind the operation.

Organizing

Organizing can be separated into two different sets of issues: the organization of multinational missions, and unit organization. Organization of the mission headquarters staff and the geo-military division of tasks and territory is vital to the success of multinational missions, and it is loaded with very visible political obstacles. The force commander should be a good choice militarily and should also not appear to have political bias; staff elements must represent the variety of countries and continents involved without compromising headquarters capability. For example, staffing the headquarters intelligence element will be more important in the missions that resemble peace enforcement or conventional warfare, such as Somalia or Bosnia, than it is in traditional peace-keeping or observer missions, such as Cyprus and the Sinai. Because the United Nations does not have an intelligence capability, intelligence-critical missions such as Somalia must rely largely on the intelligence assets of the contingent countries, especially the home country of the intelligence staff officer. The UNOSOM II French U2[7] was supported by an American Deputy U2. This arrangement provided sufficient intelligence input to the planning staff, but still only limited intelligence was releasable to some of the contingents involved in the mission.

Despite the international concern for political impartiality perceived vital to the success of many UN missions, there remains considerable U.S. concern about the command of its forces by foreign commanders. The belief that some foreign military leaders with limited military experience are politically appointed, as well as fears of different degrees of concern for troop safety, have produced a public reserve about U.S. soldiers operating under a non-U.S. commander. The UNOSOM II organization was designed to counter these reservations as much as possible. Although the force commander, General Cevik Bir, was Turkish, the American Major General Montgomery was the deputy force commander as well as commander of U.S. forces in Somalia. The U.S. combat troops in Somalia reported to Montgomery but not to Bir. Such a compromise may be useful in future missions also. The problems with the command situation in Somalia appear to have resulted not from the in-country command organization but from issues of control and command organization for U.S. soldiers that bypassed the established UNOSOM II and USFORSOM[8] commands.

Unit organization will become increasingly important if small units—e.g., brigades or battalions—continue to be deployed without their superior division or corps. These units will require increased self-sufficiency in areas such as maintenance, transportation, and civil-military relations, and they may require some revision in the U.S. Army approach to organizing for combat. The organization and control of the logistics elements may become increasingly important.

If the current experiment with using volunteers for the Multinational Force and Observers (MFO) in the Sinai is successful and the Army chooses to continue the approach of forming voluntary, ad hoc units for sustained missions, then organizing the force will become a greater issue. A type Table of Organization and Equipment (TO&E) must be developed and volunteers

---

[7]The U2 is the intelligence staff officer for a United Nations command element.
[8]U.S. Forces Somalia.

sought for the specific skills involved. These personnel must then be assembled, organized, equipped, and trained for the mission. This may well call for increased U.S. participation in the programs of other countries or, more likely, the creation of an element similar to the United Nations Training Centers in the Nordic countries.

Controlling

There are many special control issues in multinational operations. Some, involving differences of command-and-control procedure, intelligence sharing, language, and cultural differences, are due to the multinational nature of the operations. Others are due to the particular constraints under which UN forces must often operate, and they show up in such matters as rules of engagement.

Despite the established command structure of any UN mission, the actual control of any forces in a multinational mission will continue to be problematic. While countries agree to the established UN mission organization, most retain their option to "call home." Although all contingents formally report through their contingent commander to the UN force commander, most also report unofficially to their own national command. This arrangement is usually not problematic in traditional and stable missions. But those missions that experience creeping objectives or increasing threat will have a greater degree of problems with contingents that refuse the force commander's orders, or refer to their national command for approval. Ironically, it is in just these circumstances, such as seen in Mogadishu, that force commanders need to rely upon the contingents' response to directions.

Despite the established command structure of any UN mission, the actual control of U.S. forces will vary. Concern about the command of U.S. forces is reflected in the following statement by President Clinton:

> My experiences in Somalia would make me more cautious about having any Americans in a peacekeeping role where there was any ambiguity at all about what the range of decisions were, which could be made by a command other than an American command with direct accountability to the United States.[9]

Some of the complexity of command issues can be seen in the Somalia experience, in which the U.S. Logistics Support Command and UNOSOM II staff were under the operational command of the UN, while the initial U.S. combat forces were under the tactical command of USFORSOM (with Major General Montgomery acting as the commander of U.S. forces in Somalia and also the deputy UN force commander under General Bir). The arrangements

---

[9] *Los Angeles Times*, October 13, 1993, p. A1.

were apparently not entirely satisfactory, since the issue of clear control of U.S. forces was addressed again as a new Joint Task Force to be commanded by Brigadier General Carl Ernst was contemplated in October 1993:

> Key Pentagon officials said the decision was aimed at establishing clear U.S. control over U.S. forces . . . Montgomery's role has at times been clouded by his parallel title of deputy commander for UN operations in Somalia . . . the new structure would effectively strip Montgomery of his hands-on responsibility for U.S. warfighting in Somalia.[10]

These variations in control complicate planning, especially contingency planning. Furthermore, Generals Bir and Montgomery had some difficulty during UNOSOM II ascertaining whether certain contingents would participate in a response operation. For example, the Italian contingent declined participation in some operations and required coordination through political channels, the Pakistanis expressed reluctance,[11] the French have been cited as "unable or unwilling,"[12] and the Moroccans needed frequent approval from their home command.

Intelligence capabilities also complicate planning and the control of forces. U.S. units will receive intelligence from U.S. national assets with various levels of restriction placed on its dissemination. It can be expected that at least some other participants may have equally constrained information. Thus, some contingents may be expected to conduct activities without being told why. The strange bedfellows resulting from the process of obtaining participation in multinational operations are unlikely to produce a high level of trust and respect among the participants. Since the UN is unlikely to create a true intelligence capability, the problem of information sharing is a long-term issue, and procedures must be developed to limit the problems resulting from restrictions.

Some of the control problems in multinational operations can be alleviated by having liaison officers with local civilian agencies and HROs as well as among the militaries. However, the effectiveness of any mission liaison officer is restricted both by the intelligence issue mentioned above and by language and culture. These difficulties are alleviated somewhat because UN operations commonly use English as the *lingua franca*. However, while officers assigned to observer missions are usually fluent in English, the troops assigned to larger missions are likely not to be. The U.S. military has trained many personnel in language, and the Army in particular has a Foreign Area Officer (FAO) program involving not only language but extensive training in the appropriate culture. But the FAO program was never very large, and it has concentrated dis-

---

[10]*Inside the Pentagon,* October 14, 1993, p. 1.
[11]*The New York Times,* October 25, 1993, p. 1.
[12]Elliot (1993:34).

proportionately upon Europe and the Far East, as has most of the non-FAO language training. Army Special Forces also contain many individuals with language and cultural skills, and unlike the FAOs, these skills are likely to be oriented more toward Third World nations in which peace operations are more likely. Like the FAO program, however, the Special Forces are not a large organization, and they have many missions.

The problems that can result from the limited availability of linguists are illustrated by the difficulty in locating Somali/English interpreters. It has been reported that only seven individuals in the entire U.S. military establishment were fluent in Somali in 1992. The Army used headquarters staff with foreign language skills as liaisons to the various contingents, but some liaisons depended completely upon the other contingent's English skills. Hence the liaison to the Moroccan contingent in Somalia once found himself under fire without any English-speaking noncasualties among the Moroccans.

Liaison is further complicated by the fact that many of the people with whom the military will have to deal will have little understanding of the military and may be actively antimilitary. This will likely be especially true of the volunteer nongovernment organizations, many of which were formed largely due to mistrust of or dissatisfaction with government agencies, including the military. In Somalia, the relationship between the humanitarian relief organizations and the United Nations command was based on coordination rather than an established chain of command. Some, including Admiral Howe, have suggested that there needs to be a clearer sense of who is in charge. Because the operations of the two are fundamentally different, despite increasingly similar objectives, coordinative relationships are frustratingly ineffective. However, HRO control of the military is obviously unlikely, and military control of the HROs would be equally unattractive to the HROs and in direct violation of some HRO charters. Hence, expanded participation in multinational operations will generate increasing pressure on the Army to expand its linguistic and cultural capability at a time when budget and manpower pressures make it organizationally difficult to expand *anything*, even if the number of personnel involved is small.

Rules of engagement (ROE) are a key aspect of controlling forces. In peace operations these tend to be quite elaborate and restrictive. The vast territory over which many peace operations extend, variations in communications equipment, varying national styles of operations, and different degrees of training among the contingents further complicate the application of ROE. Newly evolving missions such as the Somalia operations will include even more complicated ROE. Further, interpretation of the ROE will vary because of differences in training, and possibly different cultural biases about the people of the host nation.

In Somalia, the ROE depended upon perceived threat and proportional response. While the contingents responded within the ROE, there was a great deal of variation in interpretation. Anecdotally at least (with all the shortcomings of such information), the Pakistani forces were notorious for their more brutal responses; the Belgians believed in "smacking the people and then feeding them;"[13] the Malaysians sometimes fired indiscriminately;[14] and the Italians were the source of ill will amongst the UN forces for their soft treatment of the Somali people. Although there was considerable public concern that the U.S. forces might resort to the application of major force for which they are superbly trained, training vignettes and individual anecdotes indicated possibly excessive restraint by the U.S. forces—more than that required by the ROE or recommended for personal safety by the high command. In our discussions, we also found that even within the U.S. forces there were often considerable differences in the way the ROE were perceived at the various levels of command, with the lower echelons frequently interpreting them in a manner more restrictive than intended.

The control problems associated with multinational peace operations are not new, and are not likely to be resolved easily. The political issues of whether U.S. forces should be commanded by other than a U.S. officer have received considerable attention. The final decision is, to a large degree, external to military control. Regardless of the decision, the U.S. military must prepare for missions where the control of some contingents is uncertain, where language problems are likely, where intelligence resources are not communally available, and where contingency plans are both vital and uncertain.

Sustaining

Traditional peacekeeping/observer missions have not had elaborate logistical requirements. Because these missions rarely involve combat and are often small, the ammunition and other requirements are limited. Countries generally are expected to provide deploying contingents with 60 days of equipment and supplies, and then the UN is to provide most support while the countries continue to provide specialty and cultural items such as certain foods. But because of administrative problems, the transition to UN logistical support is frequently problematic even when costs are low and the environment benign. For example, reimbursement for items purchased by the countries is extremely slow and often depends upon local contractor support.

---

[13]Anecdote by U.S. Army officers who had interacted with the Belgian forces in Kismayu.

[14]Discussion of the October 3 operation in *The New York Times*, October 25, 1993, p. 1.

Moreover, sustaining the newly evolving UN missions will be a substantially more difficult task than it was in the peacekeeping and observing missions of the past. Forces may be larger and heavier than before, and there may be more countries involved, with uncertain support from local governments and contractors. All of this suggests increased sustainment demands and difficulties, as well as substantial interoperability and distribution problems. Even if the contingents involved are self-sustaining for the first 60 days of the mission, it is doubtful that the UN system could manage the daily food, water, petroleum products, and maintenance support necessary during the balance of an extended mission. If, as in Somalia and as is more likely in future missions, many contingents deploy without initial support from their own country, the logistical problems will begin at the start of the mission.

Combined operations are likely to place heavy demands on a logistics structure that is staffed and stocked to sustain only the U.S. force. If accommodation is not made for these demands in advance, the quality of sustainment of U.S. units is likely to decrease. When contingents show up poorly prepared, the United States, or other lead countries, can be expected to provide for them. Regardless of past attempts to insist that contingents come well prepared for the mission, duties, and theater location, some countries continue to send poorly equipped and prepared contingents with little or no materiel, inadequate personal gear such as boots or coats, and limited or no rations. Regardless of any policy to do otherwise, it is likely that the United States will have to provide, at least initially, support for these other nations.

In contrast, when countries plan to sustain themselves, the United States will have to share airfield and port access. Many of the decisions on access are politically determined before deployment. Thus, countries may obtain airfield or port access disproportionate to their actual or planned troop involvement. Because future missions are likely to take place in less-developed areas, these agreements could stress already meager port and airfield facilities.

The United States may also expect to provide some support to the local people. Although there have always been civilian victims of military conflicts, the newer breed of mission that assumes or requires some degree of consent from the hosting people will increase the level of local assistance for several reasons. First, the goodwill of the people is important to the mission, and people are more receptive to militaries that bear clothing, other comfort items, and food. Secondly, the lack of a true rear area will increase the U.S. military exposure to such victims. Ironically, the U.S. military will likely have less difficulty if the mission objectives include such support, as provisions are likely to be provided by sources other than the U.S. military. If, however, humanitarian support is not a stated objective, it is likely that the U.S. military will find some of its own sustainment going to the local population.

The United States may expect some sustainment from the UN or some other regional organization sponsoring a mission. However, this sustainment is likely to be limited by bureaucratic delays and obstacles. The UN is unaccustomed to supporting missions with dozens of countries and thousands of personnel. The UN is also limited by the deficit of UN payments by member countries and by strict purchasing restrictions imposed by member countries. The UN requirement to select the lowest bidder[15] resulted in such inadequate items in Somalia as fire trucks without hoses, spotlights without bulbs, and barbed wire lacking barbs.[16] Further, the geographic restrictions[17] for new suppliers resulted in multiple-month delays for equipment that could have been purchased and shipped within the week from the United States.[18]

When the United States contributed the Logistics Support Command to UNOSOM II, many believed it was both a unique capability and vital contribution to the mission. However, the French contingent in Somalia depended on the UN only for water and fuel; it received weekly food and mail flights and 70 sealift containers monthly. Likewise, the Canadians received three C-130 logistics flights daily. While the U.S. logistic support is an excellent capability and a well-valued contribution to UNOSOM, many UNOSOM II staff acknowledged that other countries could provide similar support, and it seems apparent that a combined logistics effort of involved countries could also support the mission. While many attribute the impending failure of the Somalia mission to the scheduled U.S. departure, this is more because of the resulting political message than the withdrawal of logistical support. Even Admiral Howe acknowledges that the U.S. logistical support will be missed less than the U.S. communications capability.[19] While sufficient sustainment is unlikely to result solely from UN logistical support of future missions, U.S. logistical support is not the only solution; other Western countries involved in the mission can provide mission sustainment. Regardless of the contributing countries, however, the interoperability issues and the involvement of less-prepared countries will continue to complicate any large-scale mission.

---

[15]This is, to a large degree, a U.S.-imposed restriction.

[16]From an interview with Major General Montgomery.

[17]Determined as a function of the site of the operation.

[18]From an interview with Douglas Manson, Director of Administration, UNOSOM II.

[19]From an interview with Admiral Jonathan Howe, Special Representative to the Secretary General, UNOSOM II.

CONCLUSIONS

It seems clear that there are a number of important measures, including procedural changes, that should be taken to improve the effectiveness of the U.S. Army in preparing for and conducting multinational operations. These should be a high priority. On the other hand, it is interesting to note that the measures needed would not require large-scale or fundamental changes in Army structure and training. The existing base is a good deal more appropriate than is sometimes realized. We may continue to have problems, however, since even though many of the measures we suggest don't require fundamental change, that does not mean they will be easy.

With very few exceptions, the overriding concern in the performance of the tasks involved in such operations is either personnel selection or control of operations. Good leadership and disciplined troops are the key factors. Although multinational peace operations differ considerably from the conventional operations that the United States has most of its experience in, the U.S. Army can adapt for the opposite end of the conflict continuum. This is not to say that trained conventional forces are automatically prepared for peace operations, but rather that there are straightforward measures and means to accomplish the adaptation. It is interesting to note that some other countries have concluded that conventionally prepared forces can adapt to peace operations somewhat more readily than they adapt back.

The increase in the variety of likely U.S. military missions continues to add to military training and preparation requirements. Given these competing priorities, preparation for peace operations must entail minimum effort and maximum effect to still accommodate conventional readiness and strength. However, the adjustments required are relatively small and manageable, and many of the issues have already been addressed by other countries.

The United States has capabilities in several fields that far exceed those of any individual country and in some cases, such as strategic airlift, probably exceed the capability of the rest of the world combined. On the other hand, it does not have large numbers of infantry units and is likely to have even fewer in the future, while the armies of most countries are primarily infantry. Hence, it would behoove the United States to avoid commitment of significant-size infantry units that can be supplied by others and to expect to supply specialized forces in which it has a comparative advantage, such as aviation, intelligence, communications, and airlift. In some circumstances the ability to operate at night, which is present in most U.S. Army units, may also prove to be a capability that should be supplied to multinational peace operations.

One difficulty encountered when the decision was made to take part in the humanitarian effort in Somalia was the absence of detailed planning for such things as obtaining linguists. It appears that the limited amount of planning resulted from the concern that beginning to plan openly would indicate a decision to intervene and might in essence produce a political imperative. Since good planning would have entailed many actions which by their nature could not be kept secret, some essential planning was deferred until after the decision. However, it appears that the services and the Joint Staff could alleviate some of this problem by announcing openly which forces would be called upon *if* a decision were made to commit to a multinational operation in a particular region or in a particular time frame.[20] The units on the list could then take such actions as necessary to prepare for potential deployment without co-opting the political process in doing so.

Even if such designation were made, however, it can be expected that at the time of commitment there would be changes in the troop list. Hence, all or at least many Army units need a broad familiarity with multinational operations.

The level of peace operations is increasing at the same time that the size of the active army is shrinking rapidly. There is, however, a large pool of prior-service personnel serving actively in the reserve components. Reservists have demonstrated in the past a willingness to be activated voluntarily when they can contribute. The Army has begun to explore ways to include these personnel in supporting long-term operations. It is unlikely that mobilization authority will be available for routine operations, and units can hardly be expected to volunteer en masse, given pressures of job and family. But for many support functions and for relatively low-intensity situations, units formed specifically for a particular deployment and then disbanded upon return might work for the United States as they have for the Nordic countries and others. Obviously, the role of such units would be limited, but if they can be used effectively it will reduce the burden on the active component that is heading toward being overcommitted. It will be necessary to create a support structure to recruit, train, and support such units, but indications are that this structure could be considerably smaller than the portion of the Army that would be relieved of the deployments. One caution, however, is in order. If the experiment is successful and expands to missions beyond the MFO, then individuals who volunteer for such units should volunteer for deployment as necessary rather than for specific missions or localities. The experience of the Nordic countries illustrates the difficulties that mission-specific contracts can cause.

---

[20]We recognize that there are objections within the Army to such a unit designation. However, we do not mean to imply that the unit so designated would have peacekeeping as its primary mission, but rather that it would serve in a similar capacity to the ready brigade of the 82nd Airborne Division and could plan accordingly.

There is a need for an organization responsible for determining doctrine, training, and equipment needs for units deployed in situations in which a unit's normal structure and equipment are inappropriate and for acquiring and storing special items of equipment. The need for such an organization was highlighted by the experience of the 10th Mountain Division in Somalia cited earlier. The light infantry was not designed for some missions and situations that it encountered, and it needed augmentation of vehicles and communications equipment to be effective in its area of operations. Such augmentation had not been predicted, and there was need for hasty training and doctrinal modification.

The suggested organization should not be one that simply collects after-action reports, but should be capable of ensuring that someone has the responsibility and authority to do something about deficiencies and to plan ahead. It should be a high-level organization because, in addition to monitoring doctrine and training, it should develop, procure, and store certain equipment packages that would be available equally to any deploying Army unit, be it the 10th Mountain Division, the 25th Infantry Division, or the 1st Cavalry Division.

The U.S. military, and the Army in particular, can expect to become increasingly enmeshed in multinational operations of various types. It is to be hoped that the ability of the United Nations, or perhaps regional organizations operating on its behalf, to plan and sustain such operations will improve. But this cannot be assumed, and the United States must be prepared to provide not only for itself but for other participants in the operation.

BIBLIOGRAPHY

Elliot, Michael (1993), "The Making of a Fiasco," *Newsweek*, October 18.

Gordon, Michael R., and Thomas L. Friedman (1993), "Disastrous U.S. Raid in Somalia Nearly Succeeded, Review Finds," *The New York Times*, October 25.

Howe, Jonathan, Admiral, USN (ret.) (1993), Special Representative to the Secretary General, UNOSOM II, interview by M. Harrell, November 8, Mogadishu, Somalia.

Lauter, David, and Paul Richter (1993), "Clinton to Insist on U.S. Control of GIs in UN Roles," *Los Angeles Times*, October 13.

Manson, Douglas (1993), Director of Administration, UNOSOM II, interview by M. Harrell, November 8, Mogadishu, Somalia.

Montgomery, Thomas M., Major General, USA, Commander USFORSOM and Deputy Commander UNOSOM II, interview by M. Harrell, November 8, Mogadishu, Somalia.

Part Five

Building the Defense Program

Chapter 18

ASSESSING THE AFFORDABILITY OF FIGHTER AIRCRAFT FORCE MODERNIZATION

William L. Stanley

Fighter aircraft are a critical component of U.S. military force projection capabilities and represent a large expenditure item in the defense budget. As defense budgets decline, affordability becomes an increasingly important consideration in fighter aircraft force modernization decisions. This paper describes and applies two complementary approaches for assessing the affordability of alternative mixes and force sizes of fighter aircraft under a broad range of assumptions treated parametrically to reflect uncertainty and highlight tradeoffs.

INTRODUCTION

In the wake of the Cold War, the Bush administration initiated substantial reductions in military forces exemplified by the so-called Base Force of 1990. This policy decision set the United States Air Force on a path to 26.5 equivalent fighter wings, a 30 percent reduction in its fighter aircraft forces. After these initial cuts, discussion of further cuts became an exceedingly sensitive matter for Defense Department officials and the military services. Nonetheless, as the economy slipped into recession, budget deficits grew, and defense budgets continued to decline, serious questions remained about the affordability of the Base Force.

In late 1990, with the approval of the Air Force, RAND began a fighter modernization study that examined the affordability of the 26.5-wing fighter Base Force and alternative force postures. Periodic briefings over several years by the author to the Air Force addressed a number of key dimensions of fighter force affordability. Findings about what fighter forces the Air Force could afford were often at odds with the publicly stated force objectives of the Defense Department and the Air Force. However unwelcome those findings were, the Air Force, a sophisticated client, reviewed them with interest.

RAND colleague Gary Liberson made important contributions to the affordability assessments described in this paper.

At this writing, the Base Force has become a way point on a path to the substantially smaller 20-wing fighter force outlined in the Defense Department's Bottom-Up Review of 1993 (Aspin, 1993; Powell, 1993). That force size is similar to the range of affordable forces identified in earlier RAND analysis. This paper describes some of the generic methodology and results from that RAND assessment of fighter force affordability.

The Department of Defense continually faces modernization decisions involving many different kinds of military equipment. With some tailoring, the generic features of the methodology applied in this paper to assess the affordability of fighter force modernization should be applicable to assessing the affordability of other defense systems as well.

FRAMEWORK FOR MODERNIZATION

Operation Desert Storm illustrated the critical and decisive role that fighter aircraft forces play in the United States' power projection capabilities. These aircraft, embodying the latest in U.S. aircraft technology, cost tens of billions of dollars to develop, procure, and operate, and they represent one of the single most costly categories of equipment expenditures in the defense budget. In the post–Cold War era, power projection remains an important instrument of U.S. policy. The military services strive to keep the power projection capabilities of their fighter aircraft modern and effective despite declining defense budgets and contracting force structures. Few question the value of fighter aircraft for force projection, but the affordability of those forces has become a major subject of debate. Affordability has assumed increasing importance as a design consideration for new fighter aircraft.

The question of fighter force affordability is wrapped in uncertainty. How much will defense budgets fall and at what level will they stabilize? What fraction of those defense budgets will be devoted to fighter modernization in the competition for scarce resources? How much will fighter force structures contract? What will next-generation aircraft cost, and what kinds of aircraft might be developed and procured? The challenge for the analyst is to illustrate the range of uncertainties, identify which uncertainties make a difference and which answers to policy questions are largely invariant to the uncertainties, show decisionmakers the implications if various futures become a reality, and lay out the consequences of alternative choices about fighter modernization.

Why Modernize?

A legitimate question in the post–Cold War era is, Why modernize at all? The mix of U.S. fighter/attack aircraft used during the Gulf War clearly demonstrated their superiority. The design lineage of some of these aircraft, such as the A-6 and F-4, is traceable to the 1950s. Others, such as the F-111, were developed during the 1960s. The most numerous aircraft in the force were largely developed during the 1970s, including the F-14, F-15, F-16, and A-10. Even the F-117 stealth fighter had begun full-scale development by 1979. Absent the superpower competition of the Cold War that was the principal impetus for developing such aircraft for more than four decades, what factors remain that drive the need to upgrade or replace the aforementioned aircraft?

Despite the demonstrated dominance of U.S. and allied airpower in the Gulf War, modernization remains necessary. The U.S. military cannot be confident that it will have the same extended time for deployment or as favorable circumstances for force employment in future conflicts. Even in the post–Cold War era, new aircraft and their associated weapons, as well as increasingly lethal surface-to-air missile defense systems, continue to be developed and enter the world arms market. These weapons threaten the superiority of U.S. systems and provide an impetus to improve the capabilities of those systems, albeit at a more measured pace than during the Cold War. Public intolerance for casualties in military operations and the fact that the U.S. military will have to operate with much smaller force structures are two other important factors that provide impetus for wanting qualitatively superior systems.

The improving capabilities of potential adversaries is not the only reason for modernization. The military services must replace aircraft when they reach the end of their structural service lives or simply become technologically obsolescent. Also, new technologies emerge that present opportunities to develop completely new military capabilities (stealth is a good example). Modernization can take many forms: upgrades to existing aircraft, development of derivative designs or completely new aircraft, and nonaircraft solutions to remedy mission needs (e.g., the use of cruise missiles for attacking fixed targets).

A desire to maintain the design and production capabilities of the defense industrial base can also provide impetus for modernization efforts. The Defense Department at times may make sustaining purchases of aircraft, submarines, land-combat vehicles, and surface ships even when there is no compelling need to replace existing equipment. Such purchases are designed to keep the industrial base "warm" and avoid costly and lengthy reconstitution efforts at a later date or in a national emergency when the Defense Department needs new equipment quickly. Industrial base considerations are growing in importance in the post–Cold War era as the pace of threat-driven modernization diminishes.

Modernizing airpower assets will not be cheap, particularly as RDT&E and procurement costs for aircraft are rising at the same time DoD budgets are falling. A central question is how best to modernize the smaller force structures of the future. Uncertainties about the size of future defense budgets and DoD's acquisition priorities over time make it difficult to answer this question definitively. One can, however, define the setting for acquisition and the constraints on modernizing fighter forces, define some of the key choices facing the services, and illustrate what may be fiscally possible.

These assessments of fighter force affordability involve two special considerations. One is always present, whereas the other is the product of the end of the Cold War and hence is more unique.

Long Acquisition Cycles

The analyst of today must look much further into the future than his predecessors when assessing fighter force modernization plans. The U.S. Army Air Force gave the Lockheed Aircraft Company the go-ahead to build a new jet-propelled airplane using the British DeHavilland-built Halford engine in June 1943. The XP-80 aircraft flew six months later, on schedule. Lockheed delivered the first production P-80A 21 months from the go-ahead decision. The aircraft entered operational service less than three years from the go-ahead decision (Knaack, 1985:1–4). Uncertainty involving the course of World War II made defense planning in this era difficult, but the shorter cycles of development and production were generally more amenable to analysis and planning than the extended fighter aircraft acquisition cycles of today.

It now typically takes from 10 to 15 years to develop and field a new fighter (Drezner and Smith, 1990). When considering the phasing of two or more new aircraft, the analyst may have to look 20 years or more into the future to have some assurance that he is recommending an affordable acquisition plan. Dealing with these extended timescales shapes the analysis approach to assessing the affordability of fighter modernization. In the long view of fighter modernization, long-term averages of budgets and expenditures assume more importance than what happens in the next year or two.

Post–Cold War Force Contractions

Beside taking a long view of fighter modernization, the analyst of today must also recognize certain unique opportunities available in the post–Cold War era as the military transitions to a smaller fighter force structure. In the decidedly non-steady-state situation of the 1990s, as forces contract, temporary opportunities will exist to use excess aircraft from the Cold War era to buy time for the orderly development and introduction of new fighter weapon systems. Complementary analysis approaches can deal with long-term, steady-state modernization issues and the more dynamic transitory environment of the 1990s.

Assessing Affordability

Assessing the affordability of fighter aircraft modernization involves comparing the prospective level of funding available for modernization to the cost of developing and buying desired forces.

Funds for the defense budget are derived from the domestic economy, with the amount of funding for defense bearing at least some relationship to the health and size of the domestic economy, the latter measured in terms of gross domestic product or GDP. The legislative branch in concert with the executive branch negotiates the level of defense spending. Each service gets, or perhaps more accurately, fights for, its share of that budget. Part of the Air Force and Navy/Marine Corps budgets are devoted to aircraft modernization in general and fighter modernization more specifically. Because of changing priorities, funding allocations in the defense budget change from year to year, although each service tries to protect or increase its share.

Figure 1 illustrates some of the more important degrees of freedom the services have in designing fighter acquisition strategies. It provides a somewhat

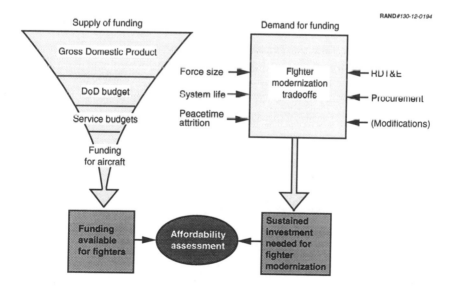

Figure 1—Assessing Affordability

idealized picture of the supply of funding for fighter modernization, since actors in the funding process do not make decisions about each service's fighter acquisition in isolation. The analyst needs to be cognizant of this so he can express his results in terms that are meaningful to the various actors in the process. For example, in recent years, the debate about funding for fighter modernization has been expressed in terms of the total funding available for the Air Force and the Navy to force the DoD and the services to come to grips with fighter aircraft tradeoffs across service lines.

The amount of funding required for fighter modernization depends on the number of aircraft that the services must replace each year and the cost of the replacement aircraft. Replacement requirements depend on the size of the force (normally expressed in terms of fighter wing equivalents), how long aircraft are retained before they need to be replaced (system life), and the level of attrition experienced during normal peacetime training operations. Fortunately, wartime losses are not a regular occurrence; hence, these replacement requirements are normally dealt with on a case-by-case basis. The military planner does, however, try to size his forces so he has adequate aircraft to operate despite anticipated losses in wartime.

Decisions about the quality of the aircraft purchased heavily influence the magnitude of development (research, development, test, and evaluation—RDT&E), and procurement expenses. In addition, acquisition planners often weigh spending funds to modify existing aircraft against buying new aircraft.

Traditionally, the terms of debate about modernization costs have prominently featured consideration of development and procurement costs. Operations and support (O&S) costs—the costs required to operate aircraft and provide their logistical support for 20 to 30 years—have not received comparable attention. Depending on the aircraft concept, undiscounted O&S costs for 20 years of operations can approach or exceed original procurement costs.[1]

Decisionmakers trying to find room in tight budgets for aircraft development and procurement expenditures in the near term have been reluctant to attach an equal weight to O&S cost savings promised by proponents of new design concepts—savings that are difficult to measure and that may or may not be realized 10 to 20 years in the future. At the same time, the services have appropriately placed increasing emphasis on achieving those O&S characteristics that will ensure that future aircraft can perform their missions. Life cycle costs that include development, procurement, and operations and support costs have become one decision criterion in many design competitions.

---

[1]When expenditures or savings occur over an extended period of time, the time value of money becomes increasingly important. For a discussion about the appropriateness of discounting in defense analysis, see Fisher (1970).

It has become a "given" that future aircraft must have better O&S characteristics than current aircraft. Aircraft designers believe future "clean-sheet" designs can, in principle, achieve 20 percent savings in O&S costs over aircraft performing similar missions today. This magnitude of cost saving, while not inconsequential, does not dominate the overall costs of developing and buying new aircraft.

In deciding the importance of O&S costs in particular affordability analyses, the analyst should examine the differences in these costs among competing alternatives. O&S costs can assume potentially more importance when very different approaches to satisfy similar missions are compared, such as comparing the costs of keeping manned strategic bombers on alert for nuclear deterrence with the cost of performing the same function using intercontinental ballistic missiles. In this decision, O&S costs became a very important consideration. The value of including O&S costs in affordability analysis becomes less clear cut when comparing two similar types of fighter aircraft having more subtle differences in O&S costs.

BUDGET REALITIES AND FIGHTER AIRCRAFT COSTS

Falling Budgets

No one can confidently predict the size of future defense budgets, but a parametric treatment of defense funding shaped by projections made inside and outside the government establishes a broad range of possibilities for assessing fighter aircraft affordability. These projections assume that defense budgets continue to decline until the late 1990s and perhaps stabilize thereafter (see Figure 2). Unless a compelling new threat materializes, structural budget deficit problems facing the nation will likely temper efforts to increase defense spending in real terms after the major drawdown of the 1990s runs its course. If this assumption proves to be erroneous, policymakers will have the far easier task of developing modernization strategies in an expanding rather than declining budget environment. The middle budget estimate shown in Figure 2 has proven to closely resemble the evolving budget picture as the Clinton administration has defined its plans; however, the full range of estimates are carried through the analysis.[2]

---

[2]The administration expects a 40 percent or more real decline in the size of the DoD budget by 1997 measured relative to budget levels of 1986, which would put the budget at $213 billion (FY93 dollars) by 1997. To maintain readiness accounts, the administration expects that modernization accounts will shoulder a disproportionate share of the cuts (perhaps falling by 50 percent or more relative to 1986 levels) (Morrocco, 1993b:42–43).

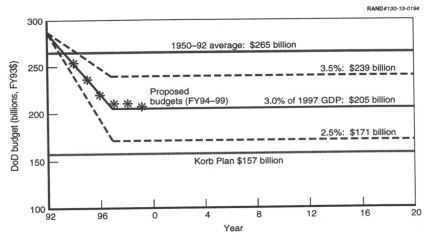

SOURCE: Aspin (1993); parametric estimates.

Figure 2—Range of Projections for DoD Budget

Budget Shares

The average fraction of the DoD budget historically allocated to fighter modernization may not be a good guide for the future. Disproportionate reductions in modernization accounts could reduce the overall level of funding available. Conversely, the end of the Cold War and recognition of the value of airpower growing out of the Gulf War experience could alter the historical allocation of defense resources between strategic and general purpose accounts to the advantage of fighter modernization.

Figure 3 illustrates a range of annual RDT&E and procurement funding possibilities for Air Force and Navy aircraft modernization as a whole ($10–20 billion in FY93 dollars) and fighter modernization specifically ($6–12 billion). It shows both historically based average shares of DoD budgets (the lines that split the two shaded areas from left to right) *and* larger and smaller budget shares[3] (the lines defining the tops and bottoms of the shaded areas) that represent the cyclic variations in modernization priorities during the 1970s and 1980s. All of these funding estimates (even those assuming higher-than-average shares of higher-than-expected DoD budgets) lie below average expenditure levels for modernization in past decades.

---

[3]One standard deviation above and below the average share.

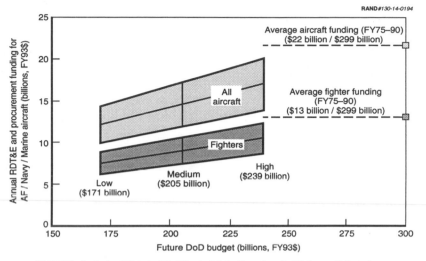

RAND#130-14-0194

SOURCE: Analysis of historical DoD budget data; Department of Defense, *Selected Acquisition Reports* (various systems and years).

Figure 3—Possible Future Funding for Aviation Modernization

Through the years, some give-and-take generally occurs within aircraft modernization accounts between funding fighter aircraft and other aircraft types. As planned buys of several key Air Force transport and bomber programs (e.g., C-17, B-2) are completed around the turn of the century, there may be some opportunities to shift more aircraft modernization funding to fighter programs. Wholesale funding shifts from other parts of the budget to fighter modernization are less certain. Funding for operations and maintenance, space, tactical missile defense systems, environmental cleanup of DoD facilities, and a host of other programs will compete for scarce dollars.

Substantial modernization requirements for nonfighter aircraft needs will compete with Navy fighter programs for funding. Moreover, it will take decades to modernize the full complement of Navy aircraft, and costly shipbuilding needs cannot be neglected for that long.

Rising Aircraft Costs

Increases in fighter aircraft RDT&E and procurement costs, illustrated in Figure 4, are expected to largely offset the savings from buying fewer replacement aircraft because of force structure reductions. Growth in RDT&E expenditures, driven by development of the Air Force's F-22 program in the 1990s, underscores the importance of leveraging RDT&E investments across

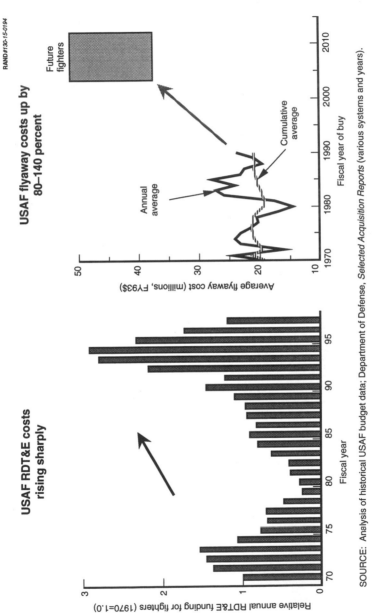

Figure 4—USAF Fighter RDT&E and Procurement Costs Are Increasing

multiple Air Force and Navy programs to moderate that component of modernization spending.

During the 1970s and 1980s, the Air Force procured large quantities of A-7s, A-10s, and F-16s whose relatively lower costs counterbalanced the greater costs of the F-15, such that the cumulative average flyaway cost remained remarkably constant, although the average cost in any given year fluctuated depending on the mix of aircraft procured. That trend is expected to change as the Air Force prepares to purchase its next generation of fighter aircraft.

The expected rise in average fighter procurement costs facing the Air Force is at least as dramatic as growth in RDT&E costs and even more important, because over the long run, procurement costs account for the majority of fighter modernization costs.[4] The services influence these aircraft cost trends by their choices with respect to the quality and mix of aircraft they acquire.[5] To some degree, they can trade quantity for fewer more capable and costly aircraft.

Understanding the reasons behind the growth in RDT&E and procurement costs of new fighter aircraft is an area ripe for further research. Lower production rates and quantities expected in future aircraft programs do not fully explain the 80 to 140 percent intergenerational procurement cost increases shown in Figure 4. Historically, cumulative average unit procurement costs have tended to increase on the order of 10 percent with a halving of produc

---

[4]During the 1970s and 1980s, procurement, including procurement for modifications, accounted for 86 percent and RDT&E for 14 percent of modernization costs for Air Force fighter aircraft. Findings derived from analysis of historical Air Force budget data.

[5]Since the 1970s, the Air Force has followed a "high-low mix" philosophy, in which it bought more costly, specialized aircraft in smaller quantities (F-15s, F-111s, F-117s), and bought less costly multirole or close air support–capable aircraft (F-16s, A-10s) to fill out the force structure. A typical breakdown might be two-thirds multirole and close air support (CAS) aircraft, 20 percent air superiority aircraft, and 13 percent interdiction aircraft. The greater quantities of the less costly multirole and CAS aircraft tend to partially compensate for the typically more costly but numerically fewer air superiority and interdiction aircraft. For a historical perspective on the rationale of the high-low force mix concept, see Schlesinger (1975).

The range of future fighter costs shown in Figure 4 reflects a 2:1 weighting of less-costly to more-costly aircraft. The $63-million-plus (FY93 dollars) F-22 air superiority fighter is assumed to be the high-cost aircraft and $25 to $45 million multirole fighters the low-cost aircraft. Costs could easily exceed the range of values shown in Figure 4 if the F-22 experiences typical procurement cost growth. Moreover, interdiction aircraft, another of the high-end specialized aircraft, have tended to have higher costs in the past than air superiority aircraft.

tion quantities or production rates.[6] Measured relative to acquisition programs of the past two decades, future acquisition programs could experience changes in production rates or quantities of this magnitude. A declining defense business base over which to spread fixed costs might increase these historical norms.

The quest for greater combat capability undoubtedly contributes to cost increases in RDT&E and procurement. Stealth, for example, has emerged as a whole new design consideration that permeates the development and production process. A better understanding of the contributors to growth in aircraft costs can lead to the formulation of more informed acquisition policies.

TWO VIEWS OF AFFORDABILITY

In assessing affordability, the analyst has at least two distinct choices of approach for comparing prospective levels of funding available for modernization to the cost of developing and buying forces. The analyst can adopt a steady-state perspective that takes a long-term view of affordability or can adopt a more dynamic perspective that considers year-to-year fluctuations in the funding requirements for individual programs. Both approaches have advantages and are complementary. This paper focuses on the former approach but illustrates some of the advantages of the latter as well.

Steady-State Affordability

In a steady-state approach, the analyst uses long-term averages of budgets and expenditures to assess the enduring affordability of alternative force modernization concepts. The long lead times required to develop and put into production new weapon systems, and the inevitable uncertainties they will introduce, make the steady-state approach a desirable component of any affordability assessment that must look decades into the future. The steady-state approach lends itself to an exploration of the basic relationships between important modernization parameters such as modernization funding, aircraft cost, useful life, and force structure size that can lead to a better understanding of what factors really influence affordability. It can help to narrow the range of force sizes and mixes that are potentially affordable and worthy of further analysis. While it cannot eliminate the uncertainty associated with looking decades ahead, it provides a convenient framework for accomplishing parametric analy-

---

[6]This cost behavior is for complete fighter aircraft weapon systems following a 90 percent production quantity or rate learning curve. (Department of Defense, *Selected Acquisition Reports*.)

sis to identify the uncertainties that really can make a difference in policy decisions about modernization.

Dynamic Assessments of Affordability

For all its strengths, the steady-state analysis approach cannot capture certain temporal dimensions of force modernization. When weapon systems are not acquired or retired in a steady-state manner or when there may be substantial give-and-take in the availability of modernization funding for particular equipment types over time, the analyst must employ a more dynamic assessment approach. He must assess the impact of specific changes in equipment replacement requirements over time and their consequent influence on year-to-year funding needs for modernization. Comparing annual funding requirements against probable funding levels provides a means to identify funding peaks caused by concurrent aircraft development or production requirements, illustrates the temporal competition for funds from nonfighter aircraft programs, identifies potential opportunities for collaboration, and can help in evaluating policy options for alleviating funding problems.

In the particular case of the 1990s, two transient effects influence modernization funding needs. A dynamic assessment approach can incorporate consideration of the post–Cold War surplus of aircraft whose availability may moderate the pace of aircraft replacements in the immediate future. It can also assess the upturn in fighter funding requirements that may occur after the turn of the century, brought about by the comparative hiatus in fighter procurement of the 1990s.

ASSESSING STEADY-STATE AFFORDABILITY

Establishing Key Relationships

An assessment of steady-state affordability begins by establishing aircraft replacement requirements and RDT&E and procurement costs, illustrated below for Air Force aircraft. One would follow a similar approach differing in some of the details to calculate Navy requirements.

The Air Force's Air Combat Command expresses average annual aircraft replacement requirements as

$$N_{ac} = N_w * \left\{ \left(W_{ac} / L \right) + A_w \right\} \tag{1}$$

where

N_{ac} =   annual number of replacement aircraft needed

$$N_w = \text{number of equivalent fighter wings}$$
$$W_{ac} = \text{number of aircraft needed per wing (100)}$$
$$L = \text{useful life of aircraft (years)}$$
$$A_w = \text{peacetime aircraft attrition per wing per year}$$
$$(1 \text{ to } 1.3).$$

The number of inventory aircraft needed per fighter wing is generally assumed to be 100, including 72 combat-ready aircraft plus 28 other aircraft for fulfilling training, testing, and depot maintenance and modification needs.[7]   The useful life denotes how long the aircraft stays in the force.   Additional aircraft are also needed to compensate for aircraft attrition that occurs during normal peacetime operations.[8]

Annual RDT&E and procurement costs for modernization are given by

$$C_T = C_{RDTE} + N_{ac} * C_{fly} * F \qquad (2)$$

where

$$C_T = \text{total annual modernization cost}$$
$$C_{RDTE} = \text{annual research, development, test, and evaluation cost}$$
$$C_{fly} = \text{average flyaway cost of mix of aircraft purchased}$$
$$F = \text{scale factor to obtain unit procurement cost.}$$

RDT&E costs would normally be estimated using historical budget data and future estimates of annual development costs for fighter aircraft programs as a whole.[9]   Flyaway costs are obtained from a variety of sources (*Selected Acquisition Reports* published by the Department of Defense, contractor or service briefings, etc.).   Flyaway costs do not generally include allowances for initial spares, peculiar support equipment, training items, etc.; hence, a scale factor is included to arrive at a unit procurement cost.   This scale factor can vary from program to program but might typically range from 1.2 to 1.25,

---

[7] Air Combat Command (various years).

[8] Useful life can be driven by the period of time over which an aircraft type can remain viable against adversary systems, by the fatigue life of its airframe, or by the technological obsolescence of its other systems.   The attrition factor can vary for different aircraft.   A factor of 1 to 1.3 aircraft losses per wing per year is often used for planning purposes. (Air Combat Command, various years.)

[9] During the 1970s and 1980s, Air Force fighter development costs fluctuated over a wide range, but averaged on the order of $1 billion per year expressed in FY93 dollars. The Advanced Tactical Fighter, now the F-22 program, has raised RDT&E expenditures to higher levels; see Figure 4.   Based on analysis of historical budget data and Department of Defense, *Selected Acquisition Reports* (various years).

increasing costs by 20 to 25 percent over flyaway costs (often more for Navy aircraft).[10]

These relationships and supporting data provide a means to measure how steady-state modernization funding requirements are influenced by key parameters such as the cost of the aircraft the military services buy and the force structure size they want to maintain.

Assessing Affordability of Air Force Force Structures

During 1991 and 1992 there was much debate about the affordability of a 26.5-wing post–Cold War Air Force fighter force structure. Uncertainties about the availability of funding for fighter modernization and about the relative numbers and costs of the aircraft that would make up future fighter forces clouded that debate. The elements of the steady-state assessment approach just described, including application of equations 1 and 2, provided a means to illustrate the sensitivity of conclusions about affordability to those uncertainties. For most reasonable assumptions, the conclusions about affordability were robust to the uncertainties in several key factors. Annual RDT&E and procurement costs to modernize a 26.5-wing fighter force could easily exceed the funding associated with even a higher-than-average budget share for Air Force fighter modernization of a higher than expected DoD budget.

Figure 5 illustrates the relationship between annual costs for modernization and fighter aircraft flyaway costs for two assumptions about aircraft useful lives. The vertical axis measures annual RDT&E and procurement modernization costs for a 26.5-wing fighter force. The horizontal axis is the average flyaway cost of the mix of aircraft purchased to modernize that 26.5 wing force structure. For this steady-state analysis, an average annual Air Force expenditure of $1.4 billion for fighter aircraft RDT&E is assumed (see equation 2), representing a compromise between historically lower RDT&E costs from 1975 to 1990 and the higher costs of funding fighter RDT&E during the 1990s. An analyst might adjust assumptions about RDT&E expenditures depending on expectations about cooperative RDT&E programs and the future mix of new and derivative design activity that could influence RDT&E expenditures.

---

[10]Flyaway costs are a function of the cumulative quantity of aircraft produced and the rate at which they are produced. Calculations using equation 2 can be as specific as the analyst desires, if one chooses to reflect specific assumptions about production quantity and rate effects. The author has typically used a flyaway cost representative of current procurement plans, and has reserved more detailed calculations of production rate and quantity effects for the dynamic affordability analysis technique that is described subsequently.

The shaded band between roughly $3 billion and $7 billion on the vertical axis of Figure 5 defines a range of possible annual modernization funding levels. The range is defined by a lower-than-average share for Air Force fighter modernization of a lower-than-expected future DoD budget (the $171 billion DoD budget noted in Figure 3) and a higher-than-average share of a higher-than-expected DoD budget (the $239 billion budget noted in Figure 3).[11]

With RDT&E costs assumed constant, changes in assumptions about average procurement costs account for the changes in annual modernization funding requirements shown in Figure 5. Note that for a wide range of assumptions about the costs of a mix of next-generation aircraft as well as for both assumptions about aircraft useful life, annual modernization costs for a 26.5-wing force would exceed probable funding levels.[12] They would exceed even

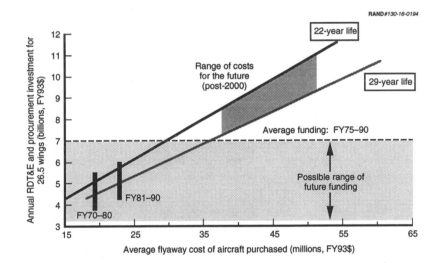

Figure 5—Affordability Assessment for 26.5-Wing Fighter Force

---

[11]Figure 3 provides a collective look at funding possibilities for Air Force and Navy aircraft modernization and fighter aircraft modernization specifically. Figure 5 illustrates funding possibilities for Air Force fighter aircraft specifically.

[12]For illustration, it was assumed that two $25 million or alternatively $45 million multirole fighter aircraft or MRFs were purchased for every specialized aircraft costing $63 million. The 2:1 buy ratio yields the cost band shown in Figure 5. The multirole costs span options ranging from modest changes to the existing F-16 multirole aircraft design that is currently the single most numerous aircraft in the Air Force fighter inventory to the costs of completely new aircraft designs. The $63 million estimate is representative of an F-22-class aircraft, before applying any typical cost-growth factor, so the affordability situation could look considerably worse than that shown in Figure 5.

the average funding for 1975 through 1990 (horizontal dashed line) when the Air Force had a much larger fighter force structure and defense budgets were much larger. These analysis results, questioning the affordability of the fighter Base Force, prompted probing questions to the author about methodology and assumptions and promoted discussion among Air Force leaders about the leverage they had to make the fighter Base Force more affordable through their policy actions.

As a byproduct, the affordability assessment quantitatively illustrated that retaining aircraft longer, with a corresponding reduction in annual replacement requirements, is one avenue to containing modernization costs. During the Cold War, the Air Force tried to renew its fighter force every 22 years to counter threat advancements. With the superpower competition abating, the Air Force should be able to retain its aircraft longer. Retaining aircraft for 29 years (the structural life of a typical airframe in an active unit) could reduce acquisition costs for modernizing a 26-wing force by more than $1 billion annually (in some circumstances higher maintenance and modification costs for older aircraft might offset some of these savings).[13] Savings from retaining aircraft longer are not, however, large enough to bring modernization costs for a 26.5-wing fighter force into line with probable funding levels. That conclusion, in turn, raises the issue of what size force is affordable.

The size of the force the Air Force can afford depends on the quality of the mix of airplanes it buys (reflected in their costs) and the funding available for modernization. Figure 6 illustrates the tradeoffs between force size and annual modernization funding for a range of average aircraft flyaway costs associated with alternative mixes of aircraft.

There are some clear choices. If the Air Force forgoes the next generation of fighter modernization and instead buys modestly upgraded models of existing F-15 and F-16 aircraft—reflected by the mix of $25 and $50 million aircraft to the left in the figure—it could probably retain a fighter force structure on the order of 26 wings.

---

[13]Questions about the relative desirability of upgrading or life extension versus buying new equipment can only be answered in the context of specific systems. Frequently the question involves operational capability considerations as well as economic considerations. It may often be cheaper to maintain and/or upgrade an older aircraft in lieu of buying a new system, but at some point the compromises in capability may simply be unacceptable. On the other hand, some investments can enhance capability and pay for the cost of the upgrade by reducing maintenance and logistics costs that would otherwise have been incurred without the upgrade.

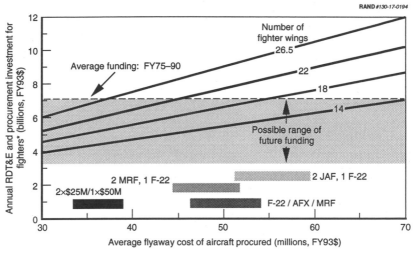

Figure 6—Steady-State Air Force Fighter Funding Needs

Modernization with more costly next-generation aircraft appears possible only at much smaller force structure levels.[14] The F-22 fighter now in development is expected to assure air superiority for decades to come, but its $63-million-plus flyaway cost means that in developing a replacement for the F-16, the Air Force will have to keep a tight cap on future multirole fighter (MRF) costs to sustain a force structure of a viable size. During 1991 to 1993, and particularly during the Defense Department's Bottom-Up Review, several options for joint Air Force and Navy fighter development programs were proposed with varying degrees of commitment and definition, ranging from $45 million for a multirole Joint Attack Fighter (JAF) to $80 million for an at-

---

[14]The horizontal bars in Figure 6 represent the range of costs with and without typical procurement cost growth (16.6 percent) for aircraft bought in the proportions noted. The F-22/AFX/MRF mix is assumed to be bought in proportions of 21/12/67 percent. The historical cost growth factor includes the normal increases in cost as new models of a production series are issued. For illustration, without cost growth, MRFs are assumed to cost $35 million (FY93 dollars), F-22s $63 million, high-end AFXs $80 million, and multirole JAFs $45 million. The $50 million and $25 million costs are meant to be broadly representative of what modestly improved F-15s and F-16s might cost if bought in quantity. (Unpublished RAND database of weapon system cost growth derived from Department of Defense, *Selected Acquisition Reports* (various years); United States Air Force (1992); Morrocco (1993a:21–22).)

tack/fighter aircraft (AFX).[15] Even a $45 million aircraft may simply be too expensive to make up the backbone of the Air Force fighter force.[16]

Figure 7 shows the force structure impact as Air Force multirole aircraft increase in cost, assuming they comprise two-thirds of the force and that the remainder of the force would have costs comparable to F-22s.

For a given level of modernization funding, each $10 million increase in the flyaway cost of the multirole aircraft subtracts three to four wings of force structure. As it buys more costly aircraft, the Air Force must weigh the presumably greater capability of each individual aircraft against the desirability of having a larger force. Acquisition of a $45 million multirole fighter does not appear consistent with maintaining a force of 20 wings or more, particularly

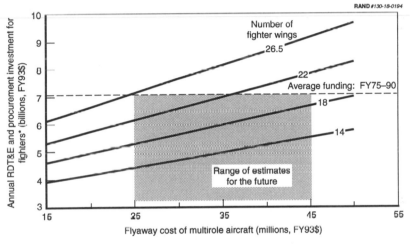

*Assumes 29-year fighter life, 2/3 multirole aircraft, 1/3 F-22-cost fighters

Figure 7—How Cost of Multirole Aircraft Influences Affordability of Force Structure

---

[15]United States Air Force (1992); "CBO Analysis" (1993).

[16]The definition of a JAF, including its cost, was always quite fluid. Some officials suggested a flyaway cost target in the range of $40–45 million. For illustration, a cost of $45 million is assumed in Figure 6. The DoD's Bottom-Up Review subsequently retreated from proposing a particular joint service aircraft solution and instead called for the initiation of a $2–2.5 billion five-year Joint Advanced Strike Technology (JAST) program to study how the Air Force and Navy could build aircraft using common component technologies to meet their individual operational needs. ("USAF, Navy Plan" (1993); see also Aspin (1993).)

since even typical procurement cost growth in the F-22 program would subtract about two additional wings from each force structure line shown in Figure 7.[17]

Assessing Affordability Across Service Lines

The debate about fighter modernization has increasingly been framed in terms of the design solutions and funding needed to satisfy both Air Force and Navy needs. A desire to avoid duplicative RDT&E expenditures and to gain economic benefits from common procurements at higher production rates and in larger quantities have prompted this modernization perspective.

By combining the previously described analysis approach for assessing the affordability of Air Force fighter force structures with a similar approach for analyzing Navy and Marine aircraft, one can assess the collective affordability of Air Force and Navy fighter force structures for various levels of modernization funding.

After making allowances for funding the modernization of other aircraft types, cuts of 50 percent in modernization accounts suggested by DoD officials when measured relative to 1986 levels might leave somewhat less than $11 billion per year for Air Force and Navy fighter modernization by 1997.[18] Figure 8 shows that this funding falls short of that needed to simultaneously support modernization of a force of 20 to 24 fighter wings and fighters for 10 to 12 carriers, even with Navy actions that will, at least temporarily, reduce its aircraft replacement requirements.[19] Both services face probable further

---

[17]Defense officials have suggested that 20 wings is the minimum fighter force structure with which the Air Force can contribute to the national military objective of being able to fight two major regional contingencies near-simultaneously in Southwest Asia and Northeast Asia (Aspin, 1993).

[18]Morrocco (1993:42–43) and internal RAND estimates of the cost of nonfighter programs for the future. An alternative computation technique yields a lower projected funding estimate for fighter modernization. Between 1975 and 1990, the Air Force and the Navy collectively received on average 4.4 percent of the DoD budget for fighter RDT&E and procurement. This would be $9.4 billion (FY93 dollars) of the $213 billion budget projected for later in the 1990s, less than the $10.8 billion depicted in Figure 8. The $10.8 billion estimate reflects an expectation of some diminution in the Air Force's funding needs after the turn of the century for aircraft other than fighters.

[19]The Navy plans to temporarily allow the complement of fighter/attack aircraft to drop below the normal 60 aircraft per carrier and will integrate some Marine Corps F/A-18 units with its carriers. Figure 8 shows an extreme case assuming the Navy drops to 50 fighter/attack aircraft per carrier and integrates all Marine F/A-18s onto carriers. For illustration, the figure also assumes the force structure of Marine Corps F/A-18s (but not VSTOL aircraft) is scaled down as the carrier force is parametrically reduced.

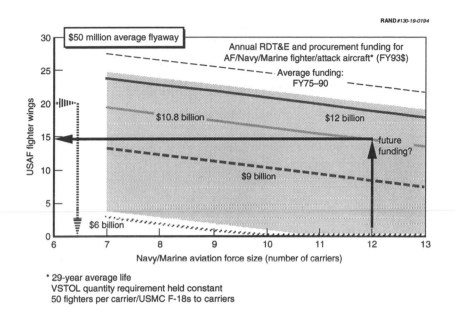

Figure 8—Acquisition Tradeoff Between Carrier- and Land-Based Fighter Aircraft

compromises on force structure and/or aircraft developments. In all cases, of course, affordability considerations must be weighed against national security objectives that tend to set minimum acceptable force levels.

Several policy actions could influence the tradeoff space shown above. All involve some degree of compromise or tradeoff. At the highest level, a national debate can take place about the size of defense budget needed to meet national policy objectives. Apart from that, if the services attach a high enough priority to fighter modernization, they might shift more resources to the task at the expense of other service accounts. They could decide to retain aircraft longer than the 29 years assumed in Figure 8 through programs of upgrades and service life extensions. They could buy less costly aircraft to bring down the average cost of their mix of aircraft or try to collaborate on fighter acquisition programs in efforts to reduce total development and procurement costs. All of these options are amenable to assessment in a general sense by the methodology just described. Assessing fighter modernization across service lines underscores the need to view fighter modernization from a national perspective to arrive at equitable tradeoffs.

DYNAMIC CONSIDERATIONS IN ASSESSING AFFORDABILITY

Uneven Procurement Patterns

The need for dynamic assessments of affordability becomes apparent when one examines historical procurement patterns for fighter/attack aircraft. During the past several decades, such aircraft have not been procured at steady rates but rather in bunches—often at high rates (see the Air Force pattern in Figure 9). Note that while procurements vary widely from year to year, the average of those procurements (211 aircraft per year) is within about 5 percent of the computed steady-state value (~200 aircraft per year) required to sustain the size force structure that existed in any given year.

As these aircraft retire in large numbers after 20 to 30 years of service, it will be fiscally impossible to buy replacement aircraft at the same rates because of declining defense budgets. Force structure reductions and longer aircraft retention will substantially reduce the number of replacement aircraft required annually (perhaps to less than half the levels of the 1970s and 1980s), but increasing RDT&E and procurement costs will erode much of the prospective savings from buying fewer aircraft. While many of the aircraft currently in the

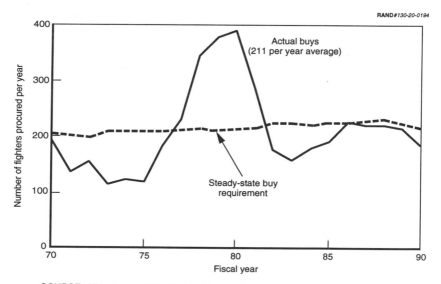

SOURCE: Historical Air Force budget data.

Figure 9—Uneven Air Force Fighter Procurement Patterns

force will not be retired until after the turn of the century, acquisition cycles of 15 years or more to develop and field new systems require that planning for the phasing and funding of replacement systems begin in the 1990s.

Developing Replacement Programs

To develop funding profiles for the replacement systems, one must assess when and at what rate they will be needed, and the stream of development and procurement costs to deliver them. When a new system is needed can depend on one or more factors, including technical obsolescence of the old system, ser-vice-life limits, attrition of inventories below required numbers, erosion of ca-pability margins relative to threats, etc. The rate of introduction of a new sys-tem depends on the rate of retirement of the old system and on force structure objectives.

Figure 10 illustrates notionally the process of scheduling a replacement pro-gram to fill 11 wings of the fighter force structure with a particular aircraft type. In this case, one early block of airplanes reaches its service-life limit first and is retired to meet a new reduced force structure objective of 11 wings. Subsequently, normal peacetime attrition occurs and in fact reduces the inven-tory to a level below that required for the desired 11-wing force structure. Finally, the remaining aircraft reach their service-life limit and are retired at a fairly rapid rate. A replacement program starts in 1994 in order to begin deliv-ering production aircraft 13 years later.

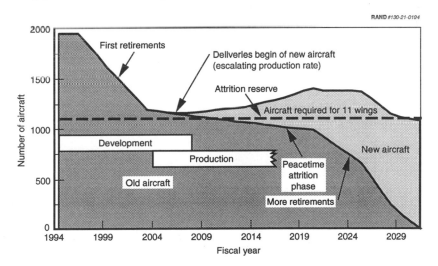

Figure 10—Notional Aircraft Replacement Program

Assessing Funding Requirements over Time

Using historical experience from other programs, contractor or Air Force cost estimates, cost-estimating relationships, or otherwise informed estimates, the analyst develops a time stream of funding requirements consistent with a selected development and production delivery profile. Often several iterations are required to arrive at affordable plans that deliver aircraft when needed, if in fact an affordable solution exists.

The analyst repeats this process for each element of the fighter force and merges those estimates of funding requirements with similar estimates for satisfying other aircraft needs. This provides a picture of the affordability of a particular acquisition strategy involving a particular force structure objective and mix of aircraft. A funding profile for Air Force systems is shown in Figure 11 for a 19–fighter wing force structure as well as associated modernization programs for other aircraft systems.[20]

These profiles include typical RDT&E and procurement cost growth factors for fighter and nonfighter programs. In comparing the funding requirements against typical Air Force shares for aircraft modernization of a $205 billion DoD budget, this force size and mix of aircraft appears affordable, although the Air Force would have to manage some funding peaks. However, this strategy assumes that the Navy pays the predominant share of development funding for a specialized attack aircraft, the AFX, which the Air Force in turn buys as its interdiction fighter. When one considers the costs of Navy aircraft modernization in a manner analogous to the Air Force, the conclusion is that such modernization would only be affordable at very low production rates and at a force level of around 8 carriers of aviation, well below the 12-carrier force size the Navy deems necessary to satisfy national military commitments.[21]

---

[20]Figure 11 includes estimates of future fighter program funding requirements and, to anticipate possible competition for funding from other aircraft modernization programs, notional estimates of funding for other aircraft programs as well. These programs, which have not officially begun, include follow-ons to the AWACS and Joint STARS radar platforms, a replacement for the EF-111 electronic warfare aircraft, and additional procurement of C-17s beyond currently programmed quantities to meet mobility requirements as older airlift aircraft retire. The particular course of action the Air Force chooses in replacing these systems will obviously influence funding requirements. The estimates shown in the figure were developed based on past acquisition history and experience with intergenerational cost increases of military aircraft. (Department of Defense, *Selected Acquisition Reports,* (various years and systems); historical Air Force budget data.)

[21]Defense officials have suggested that a 12-carrier Navy force (actually 11 active and 1 reserve/training carrier) is needed to meet the national military objective of being able to fight two major regional contingencies near-simultaneously in Southwest Asia

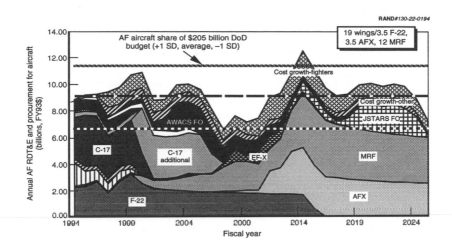

Figure 11—Air Force Funding Profile

From a joint service perspective, this strategy does not appear to simultaneously satisfy both affordability and force structure constraints; not enough funds are available to adequately support the number of new aircraft programs in this strategy. Although differing in some details and providing a richer temporal view of modernization funding requirements, the dynamic picture of affordability yields results that are quite similar to those of the steady-state affordability assessment approach illustrated earlier.

Further iterations on force size and aircraft mix, like those already illustrated, led to the conclusion that in the immediate future, the services could afford perhaps one new fighter program in addition to the Air Force's F-22 and the Navy's F/A-18EF. Since both services will need additional replacement aircraft during the first decade of the next century, the question of whether some form of joint acquisition program can satisfy both services' needs has to be answered by development efforts by the end of the decade. As information about various aircraft development options is developed, the dynamic affordability assessment technique can help in evaluating the affordability consequences of separate programs and those employing varying degrees of collaboration across services.

---

and Northeast Asia while also fulfilling other required commitments such as force presence and peacekeeping (Aspin, 1993).

POSTSCRIPT ON ASSESSMENT APPROACHES

The two approaches for assessing affordability bring different and complementary perspectives to the issue of fighter affordability. The steady-state assessment approach structures the debate about modernization by establishing the basic relationships between important modernization parameters—many of which decisionmakers can influence through their policy choices—and quantifying the consequences of particular policy actions. It provides a means for assessing the importance of uncertainty in those parameters, and for developing an enduring view of affordability. In practice, it has reduced the task of building modernization strategies and assessing their affordability from year to year by defining the domain of affordable force sizes and aircraft mixes that should undergo further analysis. The author has observed that the steady-state assessment approach tends to provide more enduring answers because of its use of the underlying factors influencing affordability.

The dynamic approach adds the temporal dimension to affordability assessment by identifying changes in funding needs over time, phasing problems, and potential opportunities for collaboration. Its results are expressed in the language of decisionmakers who must build programs and submit budgets; hence it has direct relevance to their function.

Defense planners can productively apply both affordability assessment approaches in the coming years as they address difficult decisions about developing new systems and structuring forces in an era of declining budgets.

BIBLIOGRAPHY

Air Combat Command, *Fighter Roadmap*, various years.

Aspin, Les (1993), *The Bottom-Up Review*, Department of Defense, Washington, D.C.

"CBO Analysis Questions Cost Savings of Joint Attack Fighter" (1993), *Inside the Air Force*, May 14.

Department of Defense, *Selected Acquisition Reports*, various years and systems.

Department of Defense and United States Air Force, miscellaneous budget data, various years.

Drezner, J. A., and G. K. Smith (1990), *An Analysis of Weapon System Acquisition Schedules*, RAND, Santa Monica, CA.

Fisher, Gene H. (1970), *Cost Considerations in Systems Analysis*, RAND, Santa Monica, CA.

Knaack, Marcelle Size (1985), *Post–World War II Fighters*, U.S. Government Printing Office, Washington, D.C.

Morrocco, John D. (1993a), "Joint Attack Fighter Eyed to Replace A/F-X, MRF, and F-22," *Aviation Week & Space Technology*, May 3.

——— (1993b), "Modernization Funds to Bear Brunt of Pentagon Cutbacks," *Aviation Week & Space Technology*, June 7.

——— (1993c), "Pentagon Faces $88 Billion Cut," *Aviation Week & Space Technology*, February 22.

Powell, Colin (1993), statement by Chairman of the Joint Chiefs of Staff at a September 2 press briefing describing results of the DoD Bottom-Up Review.

Schlesinger, James (1974 and 1975), *Annual Report of the Secretary of Defense to the Congress of the United States, FY75 and FY76/77*.

United States Air Force (1992), *Advanced Medium Range Interdiction Aircraft*, briefing.

"USAF, Navy Plan $2–2.5 Billion for Joint Strike Aircraft Program in FYDP" (1993), *Inside the Air Force*, September 10.

Chapter 19

MODERNIZING AIRPOWER PROJECTION CAPABILITIES: LOOKING TO GET MORE OUT OF LESS

Edward R. Harshberger and Russ Shaver

In light of the resounding allied victory in the Gulf War and strong pressures to reduce DoD spending, this paper explores the question, "Why modernize?" In response, the authors attempt to define the military rationale for both the nature and the timing of specific modernization options for air superiority and air-to-ground assets. In summary, they support the following recommendations: (1) procure the F-22 at a cost-efficient pace, (2) fully fund and integrate an array of modern air-to-ground weapons into bombers and fighters, (3) fully fund the bomber roadmap and examine additional measures to improve conventional bomber capabilities, (4) cancel the A/F-X interdiction fighter, increasing reliance on bombers and long-range fighters (e.g., the F-15E) for the interdiction role, and (5) defer a decision on a multirole fighter until the range of multiservice needs and options has been more fully explored. These recommendations are structured to be affordable, even at sharply reduced budget levels, assuming reduced force levels (consistent with recommendations from the Bottom-Up Review), suitable acquisition phasing of programs, and a systematic effort to reduce unnecessary cross-service duplication of effort.

INTRODUCTION

Perhaps the most striking lesson of the Gulf War was that airpower could dominate forces deployed on the ground and to a large degree dictate the outcome of the war. The extent of this dominance went well beyond expectations. Its implications for how the U.S. military should plan for and prepare to fight future major regional conflicts are profound.

Although a major war between superpowers is—for now and hopefully forever—a thing of the past, regional and local conflicts are as plentiful as ever.[1] The unpredictable locations and timing of these conflicts place a premium on future forces that can be *rapidly deployed* over great distances *on short*

---

[1] It is often argued that the superpower conflict deterred these regional conflicts out of fear that regional wars might escalate into dangerous global confrontations.

notice and that can inflict *potent damage* on the enemy's forces without unduly risking American lives—a necessity for current U.S. national security policy.[2] These force capabilities do not generally exist today, i.e., there are plausible conflict scenarios where U.S. force capabilities would be found wanting. Fortunately, the means to obtain the needed capabilities are at hand. This paper describes what we believe needs to be done to bring a major element of these capabilities into the force posture, i.e., the modernization of airpower.

While there is little debate about the importance of airpower today, there is considerable debate about the importance and required timing of its modernization. In light of the resounding allied victory in the Gulf War and the changed geopolitical environment, the question is often asked whether we need to modernize at all, and if so, whether the nation can afford it at this time.

Given dramatically smaller defense budgets, the central question for DoD planners is what investment strategy in this area would provide the greatest leverage to U.S. national security. Airpower modernization is but one potential place to invest scarce funds. Naval forces, ground forces, special operations forces, space, training, and so forth, are all seeking their share of the shrinking DoD budget pie. Uncertainties abound, making the establishment of priorities a difficult challenge.

This paper argues that airpower has emerged as a central instrument of U.S. national security strategy and that certain systems need to be modernized if the nation is to be able to carry out that strategy successfully in the future. Our focus is on major regional conflicts, more or less patterned after the Gulf War and a potential war in Korea, where we believe airpower's role can be dominant. Nevertheless, the application of airpower to lesser conflicts (e.g., Bosnia or Somalia) can also be highly valuable, albeit of a somewhat different character.[3]

This paper also describes briefly how modernization can be made affordable under reduced DoD budget levels[4] through force reductions, sequential acqui-

---

[2]As military budgets decline, an ever larger fraction of U.S. forces will be stationed within the United States. In addition, the size of the active force will be significantly smaller, placing an ever greater burden on force quality and readiness.

[3]Airpower assets like AC-130 gunships and attack helicopters are playing an important role in Somalia, while fighters are performing air sweeps over Bosnia and airborne surveillance platforms are providing valuable intelligence.

[4]Because of the plethora of important budget priorities facing DoD over the next decade and beyond, we have defined affordable as being consistent with airpower assets receiving a share of the overall DoD budget that is consistent with the past. Recognizing that budget shares have gone through substantial variations over time, our analysis assumes that the averages of the past (in terms of percent of the total budget) will still be reflected the future.

sition, shared developments across the services, and avoidance of expensive duplication. A broader view of affordability can be found in Stanley (1994).

AIRPOWER'S CHANGING ROLE

Although airpower played an important role in both Korea and Vietnam, it did not dominate the ground war or strategically dictate the outcome. But times have changed. There is little dispute that airpower, applied through coordinated actions of the three services and their coalition partners, paved the way for the rapid and overwhelming ground victory in the Gulf War, a victory achieved with remarkably few casualties against an enemy force that was, on paper, among the most formidable in the Third World.

Changes in the global geopolitical environment make it likely that airpower's importance will continue to grow. It is reasonable for U.S. planners to expect that future conflicts will offer little actionable warning, that the country being attacked will be badly overmatched in terms of military capabilities, and that peacetime basing of U.S. forces in any theater or region will be unlikely. Planners will also have to consider the possibility of an opponent armed with weapons of mass destruction and with the means to deliver them (e.g., by ballistic or cruise missiles).[5]

If vital U.S. interests are at stake, we will be faced with the challenge of deploying forces a long distance, into a hostile environment against ground forces that initially outnumber ours and those of our allies, where ports and bases are threatened by attack, even by weapons of mass destruction, and where rapidity of force projection will be critical to stop advancing ground forces. Should a regional conflict start before U.S. deployments are far along, Air Force and Navy airpower will be the primary option to halt the invasion and stabilize the situation.

Airpower can achieve this ambitious goal and become a central instrument of U.S. national security strategy in the future through the synergistic combination of several evolutionary developments: (1) ubiquitous surveillance using modern sensors, (2) highly survivable weapon platforms aided by stealth technology, (3) lethal munitions with accurate endgame guidance units, and (4) a

---

[5]The growing likelihood that future opponents will possess weapons of mass destruction is a serious issue that goes well beyond the capabilities of airpower modernization. Airpower assets can and should play an important role in both denying the use of these weapons and in shooting them down once launched (see Mesic, 1994a,b and Shaver, 1994).

responsive and flexible command-and-control system (battle management) that permits their effective use.[6]

Desert Storm was an important testing ground for many of these developments.[7] The Gulf War showed the importance of the following:

- *Rapid control of the air.* Control of the air in the Gulf War was achieved through overwhelmingly successful air-air engagements, suppression of critical enemy ground-based air defense assets, and lethal attacks against critical air defense command-and-control facilities, air bases, and enemy aircraft on the ground (sheltered or not). Allied air forces flew unopposed over Iraq for much of the war. This freedom of the skies enabled the other capabilities of airpower to be exploited.

- *Effective mobility interdiction.* As CNN showed vividly to the nation, allied air was capable of lethal attacks against enemy forces moving along the highways. Not shown by CNN, but still of critical importance, was that the threat of attack from the air was omnipresent, pinning forward-deployed forces in their defensive locations. Unable or unwilling to move and lacking intelligence about U.S. ground force movements—a consequence of airpower's ability to cripple Iraq's C^3I system in addition to controlling the sky—enemy ground forces were isolated, surrounded, and quickly defeated by allied ground forces. Allied air forces also successfully located, attacked, and destroyed stationary armored vehicles and trucks. It was reported that Iraqi soldiers abandoned their equipment on numerous occasions whenever they thought they were under air attack, so conditioned were they to the thought that the most dangerous place to be in the war was inside their armored vehicles.[8]

- *Effective supply interdiction.* Relentless airpower attacks along Iraq's lines of communication (including bridge attacks) greatly diminished the supplies that reached the troops in the front lines. Postwar interviews showed that major elements of these troops deserted and those who didn't were suffering from starvation, lack of clean water, and a general shortage of materials. Rather than simply reducing ammunition and other warfighting consumables, supply interdiction sharply lowered the fighting morale of the troops and is believed to have been a major contributor toward the lightly contested advances that the allied ground forces experienced.

---

[6]High-quality people, realistic training, innovative tactics, and responsive strategies are equally vital for transforming advanced technology into an effective military capability.

[7]While evolutionary developments exist in all these areas, few were available for deployment and employment at the time of the Gulf War.

[8]It was suggested at the end of the Gulf War that, in the face of enemy control of the sky, the day of the tank as an effective fighting instrument was past.

- *Denial of effective enemy command, control, communications and intelligence.*
While this denial was widely credited with limiting Saddam Hussein's
ability to control his forces, it also effectively blinded the military field
commanders, thereby permitting allied air and ground deployments and
employments to go largely undetected, assuring the success of the war-
terminating "left hook" of the ground campaign. It is widely asserted that
this was the first information-driven war, and the U.S.-led coalition won it.

This successful air campaign allowed the allied ground forces to maneuver
freely; they controlled both the tempo and tactical conditions of fights on the
ground, gaining a great strategic advantage. While the Army used superior tactics and equipment, it is doubtful that the rapid and overwhelming success of
the ground armies would have been possible without the prior conditioning
from the air forces.

WHY MODERNIZE?

Of course, Iraq and its surrounds were a near-perfect place for the effective
application of airpower. Open deserts, limited road networks, and generally
excellent flying weather greatly helped the allied air forces achieve their various
missions. No prudent planner would assume that the conditions of a future
conflict will be so favorable to airpower's application. In addition, Iraq was
unprepared to deal with allied airpower, posing an ineffective air defense and
an army that relied on heavy tanks that, as it turned out, simply provided
excellent targets for aircraft attack operations. And it seems unlikely that a
future enemy will patiently allow the United States and its allies to
uncontestedly build up their forces over a period of six months. To replicate
with confidence the kinds of outcomes achieved in Desert Storm will require
additional modernization of selective assets.

There are at least four additional reasons for investing in airpower modernization. First, many of our first-line aircraft are aging and require replacement
within the next 10–20 years. This problem is particularly urgent for Navy aircraft, but it applies to Air Force and Army airpower assets as well. Second, new
threat technologies will almost certainly emerge to challenge existing U.S. and
allied airpower assets. Despite the demise of the former Soviet Union and the
economic difficulties being faced by most of the industrial nations, advanced
airpower systems and technologies are under development in various countries.
Inevitably, these developments will lead to modernized threats in Third World
countries. Third, the full potential of airpower cannot be attained without
selected modernization. The importance of modern weapons is an especially
good case in point (we will discuss this later). Fourth, the smaller size of the
U.S. future force posture, already reflected in Secretary Aspin's Bottom-Up

Review, will place a higher premium on the quality of individual systems. The United States will simply have to do more with less.

SOME UNDERLYING ASSUMPTIONS

This paper operates under several assertions and assumptions. First, while airpower assets can play an important military role in almost all conflicts, they will make their greatest contribution in major conflicts in regions of the world far from the United States. Much of the modernization suggested here deals with providing capabilities to deter and, if necessary, defeat hostile aggression in major regional conflicts with minimal casualties.

Second, while airpower assets consist of many systems (e.g., aircraft, weapons, C^3I systems, etc.), this paper focuses on aircraft because it is the most costly portion of the modernization effort. Furthermore, we focus on modernization alternatives and suggest desired approaches for air superiority and air-to-ground power projection assets. We do not discuss the various specialized assets and capabilities possessed by the United States, such as defense suppression aircraft, jammer platforms, and information-gathering platforms. These assets provide capabilities unmatched anywhere in the world, are a relatively small portion of our force in terms of numbers and cost, and are obvious and necessary candidates for continued modernization.

Finally, it is clear that U.S. force postures will shrink well below current levels. Our aircraft modernization options assume an Air Force force posture of roughly 20 fighter wings (made up roughly of 4 wings of air superiority fighters, 11 wings of multirole fighters, and 5 wings of other, e.g., recce or SEAD, aircraft) and 10–12 Navy aircraft carriers with a roughly equal number of carrier fighter wings (whose composition remains to be determined).

This final assumption is, perhaps, the area where this paper can best be accused of "oldthink." The force structure noted above, while smaller, is directly related to the airpower force that existed at the close of the Cold War, in both the types of individual force elements and their rough ratios in the force. We have chosen to build this paper around such a force for reasons of relevance; we frankly believe it to be the most likely course for the nation over the next few years—and perhaps the best course.

Nonetheless, other, very different force structures can be postulated. Instead of a "high-low mix" of forces,[9] such as those proposed above, one

---

[9]High-low mix refers to buying some aircraft that are highly capable and highly expensive (the high side of the mix) and some that have lesser capability and are of low cost (the low end of the mix). It is generally recognized that not all aircraft in a total fighter force posture need to have comparable capabilities. Because, for reasons of total cost, it is expected that the majority of the force will consist of "low-end" aircraft, these

might construct a much smaller force of highly specialized and capable aircraft and weapons. Such a strategy is implied by some recent statements from the current administration. A force constructed on these lines would have wide-ranging effects on the employment and costs of our airpower forces and the infrastructure that supports them; to our knowledge, these effects have not been analyzed to date. Investigation of such revolutionary alternatives should continue and, if fruitful, might constitute the strongest arguments against the conclusions expressed here.[10]

MODERNIZING AIR SUPERIORITY FIGHTER FORCES

The cornerstone of U.S. airpower strategies is the capability to gain and maintain control of the skies rapidly and with high confidence. The key asset the military services have to accomplish this objective is the *air superiority fighter*. Although Navy and Air Force air superiority fighter aircraft have performed well against opponents, both services are actively pursuing options for modernizing their respective air superiority aircraft.

The F-14, the Navy's air superiority fighter, was mainly acquired in the 1970s and, with life extension programs, will reach its structural lifetime limits around 2010. Unfortunately, the Navy's F-18C multirole aircraft will begin to age out even earlier, and the A-6 will be out of the force by the year 2000. For this reason, the Navy's decision on a replacement for the F-14 is highly constrained by the budget realities of meeting nearer-term fighter modernization needs. At present, the multirole F/A-18EF is the planned replacement for both the F-18C and the F-14.[11] Multirole force issues are discussed below, but given the constraints on Navy decisions, we will focus here on the Air Force's air superiority modernization decision.

Although, with life extension programs, the current Air Force air superiority fighter, the F-15C, will not reach its structural lifetime limits until 2010 or later, the Air Force plans to begin replacing these aircraft early in the next

---

aircraft are designed to be "general purpose" in character. Buying a force consisting only of specialized "high-end" aircraft would reduce the total force size significantly, although individual aircraft would be much more capable in their designated roles than the "low-end" alternative.

[10]See "Silver Bullet Option Eyed For F-22, SSF," *Aviation Week & Space Technology*, May 31, 1993.

[11]This is the decision of DoD's Bottom-Up Review. Still to be decided is whether the Navy will in the future need an air superiority aircraft with capabilities comparable to those being designed into the Air Force's F-22, or whether the F-18's capabilities (comparable to those of the F-15C) will suffice for Navy missions.

decade with the F-22.[12]   This timing is driven by the manner in which the United States procured its current forces in the past. The United States procured a large number of aircraft in the late 1970s and early 1980s (the F-15 and F-16 forces), all of which will begin to wear out toward the end of the first decade of the next century. To maintain reasonable force levels (even the lower levels we foresee), avoid unmanageable budget spikes, stay within general budget ceilings, and provide some industrial stability, the United States must phase its tactical aircraft modernization programs over time. The air superiority portion of the force is the portion slated for early replacement—hence the timing of F-22 procurements; the replacement for the F-16 will follow.

Why Not Buy More F-15Cs?

Before we can begin to argue the benefits and costs of the F-22 and other alternatives, we need to answer a more basic question: Why can't the United States buy more F-15C aircraft? The recent overwhelming success of the F-15C in Operation Desert Storm reinforces this question. Why modernize a force that so totally dominated recent opponents?

The answers to these questions lie not in the past but in the present and future. Present U.S. dominance of the skies rests on three key factors: (1) the capabilities of U.S. aircraft platforms, (2) the capability of U.S. air-to-air weapons and avionics, and (3) the level of training and skill of U.S. pilots. When we examine the potential capabilities of future adversaries, we see the reasonable possibility of substantial threats to this dominance emerging over the next 10–20 years. The magnitude of these threats (in terms of numbers of aircraft deployed, etc.) is likely to be quite limited,[13] but even limited numbers of advanced aircraft, armed with modern weapons and avionics and flown by well-trained pilots, would be cause for serious concern.

It is undoubtedly true that the pace of tactical aircraft modernization has been slowed by the collapse of the U.S.-Soviet competition. U.S. intelligence agencies have recently downgraded their estimates of the technical sophistication of future air threats, based on slowed Russian development with the end of the Cold War. However, development of aircraft and weapon systems is still underway around the world and will continue, albeit at a slower pace, in the

---

[12]An initial operational capability (IOC) of 2003 was spelled out in the Bottom-Up Review.

[13]Other RAND analysis suggests that, outside of Russia and perhaps China, no other country in the Third World will have the technical and financial resources to build or buy an air force to match that of the United States.

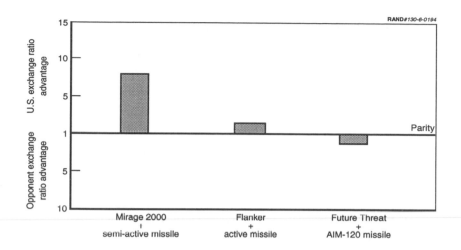

Figure 1—F-15C with AIM-120 Versus Future Threats

future. Figure 1 indicates the extent to which likely threat upgrades can erode current U.S. advantages.[14]   U.S. strategy for major wars calls for rapid victory with minimal casualties.   Parity or near-parity with an opponent is simply unacceptable; it leads to extended air battles with heavy losses to both sides.

The erosion of U.S. technical advantage evident here is largely driven by the combination of missile technologies and the radar and avionics required to effectively operate them.   Application of straightforward radar cross-section (RCS) reduction techniques by the opponent could actually result in an adverse exchange ratio for the U.S. F-15C.   Importantly, the technologies that underwrite the results of Figure 1 are well within the reach of our technical competition and are being actively pursued around the world.   Active missile programs are underway in France (the MICA), Britain (the Active Skyflash), and Russia (the AA-12).   Advanced radar and avionics are planned for the French Rafale, the European EFA fighter, and the Japanese FX and are currently being exported on the U.S. F-15E, F-16, and F-18 aircraft.   Both the

---

[14]The results shown are from computer modeling of four-versus-four aircraft engagements assuming equal pilot ability.   "Exchange ratio" refers to the ratio of expected losses of aircraft in these engagements.   The "Mirage 2000 + semi-active missile" threat represents assets that U.S. pilots would face today.   The "Flanker + active missile" threat represents assets that Russia is currently marketing.   The "Future Threat + AIM-120 missile" consists of straightforward RCS reduction techniques, a better radar, and an AMRAAM-like missile.

French Rafale and the Russian MiG prototypes employ RCS-reduction techniques.[15]

Figure 2 shows some of the problems raised by loss of superiority in aircraft engagements. It shows a straightforward projection of the results of Figure 1 to a multiday campaign. Plotted are two metrics—days to air superiority and U.S. attrition suffered while achieving air superiority.[16] In the figure, attrition is defined to be U.S. aircraft lost, divided by the original inventory of 72.

Two current U.S. advantages are not incorporated in the technical analysis shown above: pilot training and numbers. The United States has consistently invested in well-trained pilots. Others, especially Third World countries, have so far lacked the ability to pursue realistic operational training. Perhaps this trend will continue in the future, virtually guaranteeing U.S. superiority in the air. Nevertheless, it is a mistake to assume that the task is insuperable. For instance, the Israeli air force maintains a highly skilled pilot force with an economy a small fraction of that of the United States. More than money, training a pilot force requires consistent and purposeful action over time. The United

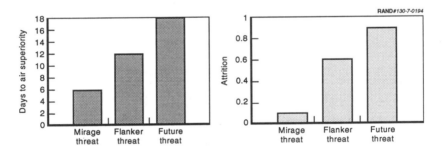

Figure 2—Campaign Implications of Threat Improvements

---

[15]The limited RCS reduction assumed in the Future Threat will almost certainly appear on future foreign aircraft. However, we do not expect to see current advanced U.S. stealth capabilities matched by foreign aircraft designers in this time frame.

[16]The campaign involved the following conditions: 100 threat aircraft facing 72 U.S. aircraft deployed over three days, with one engagement per aircraft per day. After the third day, additional U.S. fighters are deployed as attrition fillers. No additional enemy aircraft are assumed available; i.e., once they lose their 100 aircraft, their air force is gone. "Air superiority" is defined as destroying 80 percent of the opposing force. Note that against the Future Threat, the opponent would meet this criterion before the United States.

States cannot afford to assume that all potential opponents will lack long-term competence and direction.[17]

In the same vein, advanced U.S. air forces vastly outnumber all others (China and Russia excepted); perhaps overwhelming numbers of F-15Cs will solve the problems noted above. This notion, while appealing, considers neither our shrinking force structure nor U.S. deployment constraints, which will limit the early numbers of U.S. aircraft available to fight in any given theater. U.S. opponents will continue to enjoy a home-field advantage. During this phase, a few squadrons of quality aircraft could seriously contest U.S. air superiority.

Given the critical importance that our current and future strategies place on air superiority, the clear and reasonable path of threat evolution, and the uncertainties surrounding the relative quality and quantity of future opposition, it becomes clear that the United States, as it replaces aging aircraft, must move beyond the capabilities of the F-15C.

Air Superiority Modernization Options

Modernization can take the form of a new aircraft design, the F-22, or modification and upgrade of an existing design, an option we are calling the "F-15I."

The F-22 is currently in the engineering and manufacturing phase of development. It is an all-aspect, stealthy fighter, outfitted with advanced avionics, including an electronically steerable array (ESA) radar and advanced countermeasures. Although designed primarily as an air-to-air fighter, the F-22 can carry two 1000-lb-class Joint Direct Attack Munition (JDAM) air-to-ground weapons with minimal modification. Our analysis indicates that the F-22 will maintain extremely high capability (exchange ratios of 20–30:1) against all conceivable threats, through a combination of stealth, avionics, and weaponry.

Alternatives to the F-22 have been suggested, however. The most viable would take advantage of the fact that as a result of Saudi F-15E production, the F-15 production line remains available, allowing an upgraded variant, the "F-15I," to be developed and procured on roughly the same schedule as the F-22. ESA radar technology must be used to enhance radar capability as well as allow some RCS reduction, and avionics and countermeasure devices could be added to further enhance survivability. Current missile capabilities could

---

[17]In addition, longer-range active missile and enabling avionics technology may simplify the task of pilot training by lowering the relative importance of close-in, high-g dogfighting.

also be enhanced with addition of a longer-range variant of the AIM-120 missile.[18]

The major reason the United States might wish to pursue such an alternative is, quite simply, cost. An F-15I with an improved weapon would almost certainly cost less to develop and procure than the F-22; after all, the F-15 is an existing airframe with a long production history and an operating production line. While speculative, cost savings might reach 20 percent of the F-22's remaining acquisition cost.

What the United States would purchase at this lower price would be a capable air superiority weapon system, albeit lacking both the F-22's level of effectiveness and its robustness to threat evolution. Our analysis indicates that the F-15I with an AIM-120X would maintain its effectiveness against the future threats examined above, at least until the opponent deploys long-range missiles.[19]

Given a choice between these two approaches, we believe that the F-22 is the preferred air superiority modernization option for a number of reasons:

- The F-22 will maintain a dominant, enduring air-to-air capability against all threats over the next 20 to 30 years.

- All-aspect signature reduction on the F-22 will allow it to deal effectively with surface-to-air defenses, a critical factor in assuring air superiority over enemy territory if opponents pursue heavy surface-based defenses.

- Emphasis in the F-22 design on reliability, maintainability, and deployability should provide significant operational and support advantages.

- The F-22 builds on and augments our investment and current advantage in stealth technologies—an ongoing area of military technological competition.

- Design and procurement of a new aircraft such as the F-22 would help maintain our shrinking defense aerospace industrial base.

- A new design will provide flexibility in the far future. Since the United States rarely uses its aircraft solely for the original design purpose (witness the F-15), this flexibility could be a critical factor.

We have reached our conclusions on the F-22 through both analysis and subjective balancing of benefits and costs; these conclusions might change if F-22 costs increase significantly. Cost should remain a key item of scrutiny for the F-22 program.

---

[18]Improved kinematic performance is a preplanned product improvement program for the AMRAAM.

[19]The technologies that enable longer-range, active missiles are being actively pursued in several nations. Active seeker programs are noted above, and France, for example, is currently pursuing ducted rocket technology development.

MODERNIZING AIR-TO-GROUND ASSETS

Freedom of the skies during Desert Storm allowed the United States and its allies to bring to bear a staggering array of air-to-ground capabilities, from precision strikes against bunkers, aircraft shelters, and individual tanks to wide-area attacks against troops and supply areas. Many platforms were used with a wide variety of weapons.

Despite the impressive performance in Desert Storm, the United States faces a range of modernization issues with respect to its air-to-ground forces. We discuss three especially critical areas here: (1) air-to-ground weapons and sensors, (2) deep attack and interdiction forces, and (3) multirole fighter forces.

Advanced Weapons for Bombers and Fighters

Weapon procurements are expected to remain a very small portion of service budgets. Nevertheless and quite noteworthy, our current ground target attack capabilities can be improved by almost an order of magnitude (through improved weapon lethality) within these very modest planned investments. This advance, when coupled with the scale of projected threats, brings within reach the ability to destroy most fixed targets and many mobile targets early in a conflict. With technologies under development today, weapon effectiveness is likely to be limited more by near-real-time target location and identification problems than by weapon (or munitions) lethality considerations.

But the United States must buy the weapons and integrate them into its weapon systems, and weapons have historically been given short shrift when budgets tighten.[20] The classes of weapons now in development could provide a quantum leap in U.S. capabilities to accomplish rapidly most conceivable targeting objectives with minimal collateral damage, regardless of time of day or weather. Aside from defeat in the budget wars, the greatest risk is the urge to add "nice-to-have" attributes to those required. Remarkable performance is available, but each increment of added performance also adds cost and risk, delaying the realization of needed capabilities.

A number of weapon and munitions initiatives, most of which should be vigorously pursued, are now in various stages of procurement or development. Among the most important are *the JDAM family of weapons*, which will provide fighters and bombers with a near-all-weather, day or night, precision-strike capability at relatively modest cost; *the family of sensor-fused antiarmor submunitions*, including SKEET and BAT, which provide a multiple armor

---

[20]There is an understandable tendency to preserve basic assets (e.g., aircraft) and slow modernization activities. There is no shortage of weaponry to hang on aircraft, so if a war occurs, aircraft can still fly and fight.

kills per sortie capability to fighters and bombers;[21] and *suitable standoff weapons*, including JSOW (short-range), TSSAM (medium-range), and TLAM (long-range), each of which provides high-confidence kill capabilities against heavily defended targets.[22]   Figure 3 shows some of the key capability improvements possible with some of these weapons. Plotted is the fraction of the Desert Storm Master Target List that could be attacked with a greater than 80 percent chance of hitting the target (single-shot probability of hit greater than 0.8) versus the accuracy of the attacking weapon. The most accurate weapons are generally those with terminal seekers. JDAM-1 weapons, with GPS-aided inertial guidance, vary in accuracy depending on weapon/aircraft integration and targeting methods.[23]

Procurement of these modern weapons continues to represent the single most cost-effective step that could be taken to improve our air-to-ground capability. A conservative estimate of the costs for all these programs is 15 to 20 billion dollars of RDT&E and procurement, spread over 15 to 20 years, with no significant rise in manning requirements. Moreover, as discussed below, successful development of these weapons and integration with fighter and bomber forces may enable the United States to avoid replacement costs for interdiction fighters.

Deep Attack Forces

U.S. planners face important decisions about deep-attack aircraft. In the near term, several steps are necessary if the United States is to reorient its bomber force toward conventional warfighting. In the farther term, the United States faces the need to replace the aging elements of the interdiction fighter force.

Near-Term: The Bomber Force. Recent RAND analysis has shown that bomber forces equipped with modernized weapons (i.e., those discussed above) can have a dramatic impact on the outcome of large regional conflicts. The bomber's inherent range-payload attributes provide the potential, through their

---

[21]An inertially aided tactical munitions dispenser, currently planned, should enable effective employment of sensor-fused weapons from medium-to-high altitude in the near term.

[22]Past RAND analyses have shown the need for a TSSAM-like air-launched cruise missile with increased range (roughly 400 miles versus TSSAM's 150 miles). If added to the force, it would allow the United States to employ B-52G bombers effectively before full establishment of air superiority. Additional conversion of ALCM missiles to ALCM-C variants could serve this purpose at very low cost.

[23]The ability to hit the target (as plotted) is only one component of lethality. Some targets (a small fraction) will require explosive charges larger than planned for JDAM, TSSAM, JSOW, and TLAM.

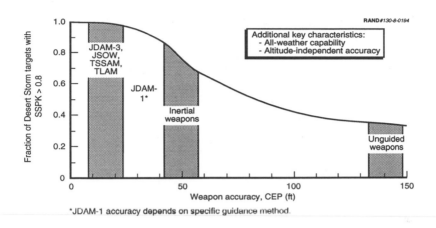

*JDAM-1 accuracy depends on specific guidance method.

Figure 3—Target Coverage Versus Weapon Accuracy

ability to initiate near-immediate operations from CONUS and nontheater overseas bases, to deny an enemy quick victory. As fighter forces arrive, the bomber forces can add to the weight of the attack against virtually all enemy target types, hastening the pace of victory. Given its stealthy characteristics, the B-2 is particularly attractive for employment against enemy targets before establishment of air superiority. Figure 4 illustrates, in tons of bombs dropped, the contribution that bombers can provide in the first two weeks of a war in a far-flung theater.[24]

Some bomber force modernization measures, such as survivability improvements to the bombers and integration of the modernized weapons addressed earlier, have been spelled out in the Air Force's bomber roadmap. While the roadmap will result in a more effective conventional bomber force, additional actions are needed to reach the full potential of these bomber/weapon systems. The focus of additional efforts should be on creating a more flexible bomber force, with rapid access to targeting and threat information and the ability to respond more swiftly to changing conditions and to flexibly employ a variety of munitions through weapons carriage modifications.[25]

---

[24]For a complete set of assumptions on sortie rates and weapon loadouts, see Ochmanek and Bordeaux (1993). Bombers are assumed to fly from Guam, Diego Garcia, and Fairford. Sortie rates for bombers therefore range from 0.5 to 0.25.

[25]Sometime during the next two decades the question of a next-generation bomber will arise. B-1Bs will not last forever; twenty B-2s by themselves are limited in what they can provide. The answer to the question rests on how the Air Force deals with the need for a fighter to replace the F-16.

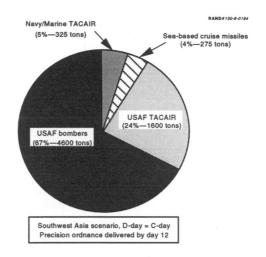

Figure 4—Bomber Contribution to Early Fixed-Target Attacks

Current bomber roadmap costs are 3 to 4 billion dollars over several years; this modernization would be cost-effective at twice the price.

Far-Term: The Interdiction Fighter Force. Two of the Air Force's interdiction fighters, the F-111 and F-117, are aging and may have to be retired in the first decade of the next century. Navy A-6 aircraft will be retired by the end of this decade. The two realistic options for replacing the capabilities of these aircraft are as follows:

1. Do not replace these aircraft. Place the responsibility for deep attack on a combination of the F-15E force, modified F-14 aircraft,[26] the bomber force, long-range cruise missiles, and the F-22 modified to carry JDAM internally.[27]

2. Replace all current deep-attack aircraft with a high-end, joint aircraft (such as the A/F-X) specifically designed as a deep, stealthy, precision attack aircraft capable of carrier and land employment. This approach is the current plan.

---

[26]Initial plans call for adding a laser-guided bomb (LGB) delivery capability to the F-14 as well as compatible bomb racks. Additional modifications to enable JDAM, TSSAM, and JSOW would be required.

[27]The F-22 can carry two 1000-lb-class JDAM-1 weapons with minimal modification.

It is in the area of interdiction fighter forces that the United States can reap the benefits of the modernization measures we have proposed earlier. *At this time, we believe that option 1 is preferred and, specifically, that the modernization measures discussed previously eliminate the near-term need to develop the A/F-X.* This approach assumes that the Navy will not replace its deep-attack aircraft with a new aircraft and will focus on cruise missiles as the sole, future naval deep-strike option, a direction that appears consistent with the Navy's recently adopted littoral strategy.

We base our argument on three fundamental assumptions: (1) new and more effective weapons will be successfully developed, (2) bombers will be successfully "conventionalized," and (3) the F-22 will be procured and evolve à la the F-15.

The weapons discussed above would allow a wide range of aircraft, both bombers and fighters, to conduct accurate attacks under nearly all weather conditions without the need to carry and integrate laser designator equipment. With standoff, such attacks could be carried out at ranges sufficient to ensure the survivability of delivery aircraft and naval forces.

The bomber force, with suitable modification and weapons, greatly expands deep-attack capability. B-52 aircraft served as area attack systems and cruise missile carriers in Desert Storm and could continue this role in the future. In addition, the B-2 bomber has the potential to add unique capabilities, namely rapid, long-range, high-payload, accurate, stealth attack capabilities. Finally, and in spite of the many problems associated with the B-1B,[28] we believe that a combination of the standoff capabilities of weapons such as JSOW and TSSAM and an emphasis on integrated conventional operations with tactical aircraft will result in effective B-1B conventional employment, effectively filling the F-111 strike role.

Finally, if procured, a modestly modified F-22 force (capable of launching two JDAM-1 weapons as discussed above) could be turned to several uses after air superiority is achieved, including ground attack and suppresion of enemy air defenses (SEAD) operations. In the ground attack role, our analysis indicates that the amount of accurate ordnance delivered by the F-22 force could in fact be substantially higher than that of the current F-117 force. The F-15E and F-14 supplement the capabilities above and maintain the capability to employ laser-guided bombs where appropriate.[29]

---

[28]Problems with the B-1B have been chronicled by many, including RAND. Most of the analysis of the B-1 has been conducted in the context of strategic nuclear attack, and the major, expensive problems have generally centered on defensive avionics.

[29]In addition, the F-22 could act as a hedge to the renewed need for a future land-based interdiction fighter if other elements of the modernization effort fail. A ground

Option 1 is consistent with our previous modernization arguments: it builds upon investments in bomber and weapon modernization and capitalizes on the stealth capabilities of the F-22. It is also in line with fiscal reality, a reality made harsher by the relatively near-term need to address the multirole fighter force.

The Multirole Fighter Force

The relatively inexpensive and numerous F-16 is currently the Air Force's multirole fighter (MRF) and constitutes the bulk of its force structure. Given current uncertainties about the service life of the various F-16 variant airframes and the ultimate number of land-based multirole wings in our future forces, the procurement start for F-16 replacement probably begins after the year 2005 and possibly later. This was, in fact, the timeline for Air Force MRF procurement until very recently.

As noted previously, the Navy faces a much nearer-term fighter modernization problem than the Air Force. Current plans call for the Navy to replace its F-18C force with F/A-18EFs. The Navy has argued that the F/A-18EF is a straightforward upgrade to previous F-18 variants. In essence, the F/A-18EF can be procured in the relatively near term, as early as 1999.[30]

Figure 5 paints a stark picture of the expected lifetime of the Navy and the Air Force multirole force structure over time (the F-16 drawdown is consistent with the planned reduction in the total number of fighter wings in the Air Force; the naval aircraft drawdown leaves carrier decks without aircraft).[31] Many potential solutions to this dilemma have been floated recently, and many new aircraft combinations have been discussed, including new concepts like the Joint Attack Fighter (JAF).

In this debate, three options have received considerable scrutiny over recent months; together they capture the range of possibilities for future multirole forces:

1. The Navy replaces its entire force with F/A-18EF aircraft in the near term. The Air Force delays procurement of a non-joint MRF until roughly 2010

---

attack version of the F-22 could conceivably be created, involving significant R&D to ensure continued stealth and range/payload performance.

[30]Numerous observers have noted that the F/A-18EF differs significantly from previous F-18 variants. It is possible that F/A-18EF development may slow if concerns over technical risk are valid. See Franklin Spinney, "Fly Off F/A-18E vs. 18C," U.S. Naval Institute *Proceedings,* September 1992.

[31]The F-16 estimates are based on a 4000-hour lifetime for F-16 blocks 10–30 and 8000 hours for later blocks and include the latest decision to procure the aircraft in 1993. F/A-18EF lifetimes assume a 3500-hour life for the F/A-18AB variants.

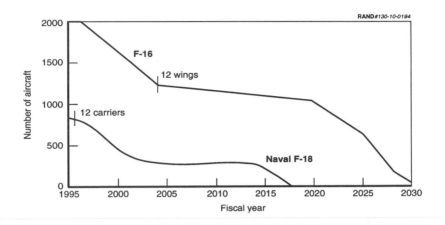

Figure 5—Relative Multirole Forces over Time

by a combination of near-term procurements, F-16 (SLEP) efforts, and force reductions. This approach is similar to current plans.

2. The Navy and Air Force both procure the F/A-18EF as their (now joint) multirole aircraft. This option requires that only one multirole aircraft be procured and, because of shared costs, could mean a larger Air Force multirole force than could be expected if the Air Force pursued multirole development on its own.

3. The United States delays the onset of both Navy and Air Force retirements and develops a new joint multirole aircraft, the JAF. Options to delay the onset of force retirements would include life extension programs for current assets and some new, near-term procurement. Naval near-term procurement could include the F-18C. Air Force near-term procurement could include the F-16 or F-15E.

Option 1 addresses the split between the Air Force and the Navy in terms of the timing and relative cost of their multirole fighters. It satisfies the Navy's nearer-term need while deferring the Air Force's decision until MRF development can be afforded. However, given the similarity in the Air Force and Navy multirole mission, option 1 seems unsatisfying. The F-18EF is only a modest improvement over the F-18C, and future budget constraints may force the Air Force to acquire either a low-cost MRF or fewer aircraft. The combination of two aircraft development programs and smaller aircraft buys for each would seem to create unnecessary costs for the nation.

Option 2 better addresses this cost concern. Given R&D savings, the larger buys associated with a joint program, and reasonable programmatic timing, option 2 is likely to be affordable to both services and to cost less overall than separate programs. While the F/A-18EF will cost more per unit than either the F-18C or the F-16, it is also somewhat more capable than either aircraft. But option 2 results in a multirole force (the bulk of our fighter forces) that consists largely of 1970s technology for the next 30-plus years. This prospect should be disturbing, especially when one contemplates the potential for radical change that the world has so recently demonstrated. At the very least, this decision would place a very high premium on the air superiority and ground defense suppression elements of our force, perhaps leading to other, indirect costs.

Option 3 addresses the weaknesses of options 1 and 2. It has the cost benefits associated with a single, jointly purchased aircraft and could avoid potential technical obsolescence. However, option 3 has its own set of serious difficulties. The poor record of past Navy/Air Force joint aircraft developments is testimony to the problems of the joint approach—many difficult technical tradeoffs are involved in creating aircraft that meet the needs of both services. Moreover, the disparity between the Navy and Air Force cost and schedule requirements may be too great to bridge with a single, new, joint program.

So we appear to be back where we started. The arguments have come full circle. Although the budgetary and timing requirements of the multirole fighter debate are well understood (and more flexible than many would imply), we believe that the desired characteristics of a future multirole fighter are not at all clear. For instance, in the context of our total force structure, should the future multirole aircraft be more heavily weighted toward ground attack than current aircraft? Should they be equipped for defense suppression? How do new weapons (air-to-air and air-to-ground) affect the avionics needed on the aircraft? How stealthy should future multirole aircraft be? No persuasive answers to such questions currently exist.

Therefore, we propose a fourth course—"delay and decide"—which is in many respects a hybrid of all three above.[32] Moderate near-term procurement and life extension efforts can gain the United States both time and budget leeway—two years is easily feasible. The time gained should be used to conduct a thorough analysis of the above three options in terms of their likely budgetary impact and the adequacy of capability they would provide the nation over time. Building on this base of knowledge, the budget leeway gained should enable the United States to pursue a more considered multirole force

---

[32]Although the publication from which this paper was taken was completed before the Bottom-Up Review was released, it appears that we and DoD came to essentially the same decision. Their "delay" is accompanied by a serious technology exploration effort aimed at providing the essential data for the "decide" decision, an approach that has real merit.

modernization strategy. Our haste in dealing with present budget extremities should not risk the future effectiveness of the bulk of our air forces.

AFFORDING AIRPOWER MODERNIZATION

Modernizing airpower assets will not be cheap. Finding the budgets needed will require an examination of overall DoD acquisition priorities and budgets. The recent history of the acquisition budget is not promising. The budgets available for force modernization (and for that portion of the acquisition devoted to aircraft) have dropped dramatically during the past decade and will continue to decline for at least several more years. The overall drop in aircraft procurement exceeds 60 percent, suggesting that the sum of aircraft acquisition funds spent in the 1980s will not be replicated over the next 25 years.

The budgets specifically targeted for fighter and weapon modernization are only a fraction of the total aircraft acquisition. Using historical shares (both average and maximum percentages) to bound estimates of future fighter acquisition budgets, the resulting arithmetic suggests that throughout the next two decades the total budget available for future fighter modernization programs will be capped in the neighborhood of $9 billion to $12 billion (constant FY93 dollars).[33] These levels are well below the averages spent on fighter modernization over the past several decades. Recognizing that future fighters will cost more to acquire (even in constant dollars) than their predecessors, either the budget share for fighter modernization must increase sharply, or the number of new aircraft bought in the future will be much smaller than in the past.

How then is airpower modernization to occur? At least five approaches need to be considered.

Reducing the Total Size of the Fighter Forces. Driven by near-term budgets, the Air Force and the Navy are already reducing their fighter force to levels well below those specified in General Powell's Base Force.[34] It is still unclear how much further these forces can be reduced before national security is affected. Support for a two-MRC (major regional contigency) strategy suggests a floor of about 18–20 wings.

Trading Quality Versus Quantity. Figure 6, drawn from previous RAND analysis,[35] shows an Air Force–specific example of the connection between

---

[33]This cap assumes a total DoD budget of around $200–210 billion per year (constant FY93 dollars) after 1997. The spread is based on historical budget allocations.

[34]Secretary Aspin's Bottom-Up Review has recently announced plans to reduce the number of Air Force tactical fighter wing equivalents to around 20. The review also recommends a reduction in Navy carrier air wings to about 11, consistent with operating 12 carriers, assuming Marine air wings will be periodically assigned to carrier duty.

[35]See Project AIR FORCE Annual Report, fiscal year 1992, AR-3800-AF, RAND.

number of tactical fighter wings and average aircraft unit replacement cost for a new multirole fighter. The upper bound of the range of estimates for annual expenditures approximates the rate of spending during from FY75 to FY90, a period of historically high investments in fighter aircraft. A calculation more representative of past average percentage expenditures on aircraft modernization would place the yearly average just above about $5 billion. For a variety of reasons, we expect that a realistic estimate for Air Force spending falls between these two, perhaps around $6 billion. At this rate, and seeking to retain 20 fighter wings, the MRF unit cost must come in at less than $30 million per aircraft. This number is not significantly different from the cost of simply buying more F-16s off the existing line, suggesting that a new MRF will necessarily be limited in its performance improvements.

By jointly funding a multirole fighter with the Navy, the development cost savings and the lower unit cost per aircraft (due to the larger total buy size) would allow this unit price to increase, perhaps to more than $40 million. Obviously, more money per airplane implies a plane with better range/payload, better stealth characteristics, and better offensive and defensive avionics.

This begs the question of what aircraft attributes are really needed and how much quantity the Air Force could reasonably give up (below 20 wings) to increase the quality of the resultant force. The desired attributes of a new MRF rest in part on the new weapons and the successful modernization of the bomber fleet. The improved capability of the bombers and weapons will affect the fighter's employment and, hence, its needed performance. Similarly, the

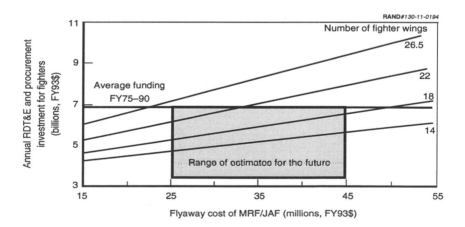

Figure 6—Relative Multirole Forces over Time

more robust the enemy defenses (air and ground based), the greater will be the need for stealth. Given the inherent uncertainty in some of these factors, it is wise to hedge toward better aircraft.

Space and time considerations suggest that there is a minimum-sized (in terms of numbers) Air Force below which significant capabilities will be lost. Where is this minimum? We cannot offer a number with any confidence. But if the Air Force must simultaneously (1) engage in a MRC, (2) preserve a reserve so that it can intervene in a second concurrent MRC, (3) still fulfill other overseas commitments, (4) retain a rotation base, and (5) leave some room for training and the like, a force sized much below 20 wings is likely to be too small.

Acquisition Phasing. Even acquiring less-expensive fighters, the Air Force and the Navy will have to carefully space their acquisition of new fighters. The problems associated with this phasing would be lessened if the new multirole fighter were acquired by both services, but given the current development of the F-22 and the F-18E/F, it will be difficult to start a new fighter program within this decade.

Reducing Redundancies. Much of what has been written about service redundancies is misplaced (e.g., four air forces versus one). And not all redundancies are bad or should be eliminated (most provide useful hedges against inherent uncertainties in system performance, scenario details, etc.). Nevertheless, serious review is needed to determine where additional unwanted redundancies and overlaps lie. As all services have or are obtaining advanced airpower systems, all should be included in the review.[36]

Exploiting Complementary Assets. Still another way to save money is to discourage individual services from operating independently and to promote the employment of complementary assets. There is evidence that this is happening, through joint developments (e.g., the JDAM weapon family), joint planning (e.g., the prepositioning of ships loaded with Air Force munitions and aviation fuel), and joint operations (e.g., the coordinated use of Air Force and Navy electronic combat aircraft in suppressing enemy air defenses). It should also be considered for modernization programs.

Theater missile defense is one example of the need for cooperation of the services in modernizing airpower assets. Each service has an important role to play in this critical area: the Army and Navy in providing terminal defenses against tactical ballistic misssiles (TBMs), the Air Force in counterforce and boost-phase defensive operations against TBMs, and all three in defense against cruise missiles. No single service activity is likely to provide the desired level of

---

[36]The Bottom-Up Review presumably took these overlaps into consideration when it derived force requirements.

defense on its own.   A balanced approach, currently missing, is needed for success.

CONCLUSIONS

Given the downsizing of the U.S. military, the likelihood that future conflicts will be fought in locales where U.S. troops are not deployed in peacetime, and the prospect that these wars will start with little "actionable" warning for U.S. political leaders, the possession of overwhelming airpower is the most important option available to the United States to underwrite its national interests.   Technology has afforded us the opportunity to obtain this capability. While budgets will constrain the pace of modernization, the military leverage provided by the promised enhancements compensates, to some degree, for anticipated force reductions.

To possess overwhelming airpower throughout the next several decades, we recommend the following DoD actions:

* Develop and acquire the F-22 in suitable numbers (roughly four wings).
* Vigorously pursue weapon and munitions modernization, including the acquisition of JDAM-class weapons, TSSAM, JSOW, intertially-guided TMDs, antiarmor munitions (SKEET, BAT), etc.
* Modernize the bomber force for conventional operations.
* Cancel the joint A/F-X interdiction fighter program.
* Actively investigate the range of options available for multirole forces.
* Reduce duplicative efforts where appropriate.
* Identify and exploit complementary capabilities among different weapon systems to achieve warfighting objectives at lower cost.

Shifting reliance to airpower has important implications for how the total U.S. military is structured.   This paper suggests a shift in priorities toward modernizing airpower assets, be they Air Force, Navy, or Army.   It further urges careful consideration of complements and overlaps, to ensure that what needs to be funded will be funded.   It is time to recognize the critical importance of airpower in our future military strategies, and to act accordingly. Airpower is not by itself sufficient, but it constitutes the most cost-effective approach we have toward deterring conflict and (if necessary) creating an environment conducive to decisive victory in future large-scale regional conflicts.

BIBLIOGRAPHY

Davis, Paul K. (ed.) (1994), *New Challenges for Defense Planning: Rethinking How Much Is Enough*, RAND, Santa Monica, CA.

Mesic, Richard (1994a), "Defining a Balanced Investment Program for Coping with Tactical Ballistic Missiles," in Davis (1994).

——— (1994b), "Extended-Counterforce Options for Coping with Tactical Ballistic Missiles," in Davis (1994).

Ochmanek, David, and John Bordeaux (1993), "The Lion's Share of Power Projection," *Air Force Magazine*, June.

Shaver, Russ (1994), "Priorities for Ballistic Missile Defense," in Davis (1994).

Stanley, William (1994), "Assessing the Affordability of Fighter Aircraft Force Modernization," in Davis (1994).

NOTE: This paper is a modestly revised version of *Modernizing Airpower Projection Capabilities*, RAND Issue Paper 126, by Russ Shaver, Edward R. Harshberger, and Natalie Crawford, distributed widely within the government in September 1993.

Chapter 20

ASSESSING THE STRUCTURE AND MIX OF FUTURE ACTIVE AND RESERVE ARMY FORCES: A CLASSIC PROBLEM IN DEFENSE ANALYSIS REVISITED

Bernard D. Rostker, Bruce W. Don, and Kenneth Watman

This paper describes a detailed 1992 study of options for adjusting the mix of active and reserve army forces. The options consider "roundup" and "roundout" concepts, special training units, approaches that call for training and rounding out units with battalions or companies rather than brigades (i.e., integrating at a lower level), and different peacetime readiness levels for reserve-component units. The analysis takes a systems approach and is keyed to the national military strategy and the illustrative planning scenarios associated with that strategy, although the study also examined the sensitivity of conclusions to scenario assumptions and various types of uncertainty. Having described the study and its conclusions, the paper discusses the "Base Force" of the Bush administration and the "BUR force" of the Clinton administration. Many of the study's proposed changes in the active/reserve mix have been included in the BUR force (e.g., special training units), but others have not, notably the proposal to plan on integration of battalions rather than brigades. There is also a significant apparent inconsistency between the BUR's requirement for national-guard divisions to be deployable within 90 days and the lift capability that will be available for that task. The enhanced readiness requirement for these divisions should probably be reexamined. Issues and options on the active/reserve mix will need to be reexamined more generally as the United States refines its national military strategy for the post–Cold War era, changing further details of the planning scenarios and adjusting the means used to accomplish peacekeeping and peacemaking missions.

INTRODUCTION

The question of how active and reserve forces should be combined into a coherent force structure is a classic problem in defense analysis, both as a recurring issue and as an illustration of the application of systems analysis to defense decisionmaking. This paper considers both aspects. It uses the continuing debate over the proper mix of active and reserve forces in the post–Cold War period to show how *time-phased* requirements-based planning can be used to develop and assess alternative force-structure options. After reviewing the historical context, the paper

- Presents a conceptual framework for considering alternative structures and mixes of active and reserve forces.

- Discusses demand for and supply of military forces in illustrative planning scenarios.

- Describes our 1992 assessment of several force-structure alternatives in light of military requirements for two major regional contingencies (MRCs).

- Comments briefly on the Clinton administration's treatment of active/reserve mixes in its Bottom-Up Review (BUR) study (Aspin, 1993).

Although the paper draws heavily on a particular study, most of the issues and options it discusses will continue to be among the most important in any study of the active/reserve mix.

THE HISTORICAL CONTEXT

The structure and appropriate mix of active and reserve forces has been debated ever since the founding of the Republic. When the framers of the Constitution allowed for both a federal military and a state militia to "provide for the common defense,"[1] they effectively pitted the executive branch against the Congress (the members of which have constituencies with strong sympathies for the "militia" in the form of reserve-component forces). They also set the stage for an enduring rivalry between professional and citizen soldiers. In fact, the relationship between the regular and militia components has been debated, defined, and redefined after every major war since the Revolution in light of wartime experiences, changes in federal and state roles, shifts in national priorities, and the evolution of America as a world power.

The modern debate on the matter dates from 1970, when, with the end of the Vietnam War in sight, the end of conscription at home, and in order to reduce expenditures, Secretary of Defense Melvin Laird ordered "reductions in overall strengths and capabilities of the active forces, and increased reliance on the combat and combat support units of the Guard and Reserves" (Laird, 1970). He proposed that a new "Total Force Concept" be applied in "all aspects of planning, programming, manning, equipping and employment of Guard and Reserve Forces." In 1973, Secretary of Defense James Schlesinger told the military departments, "The Total Force is no longer a 'concept.' It is

---

[1]Article 1, Section 8, of the U.S. Constitution gives Congress the power to "raise and support armies . . . to provide and maintain a navy . . . [and] to provide for organizing, arming and disciplining the militia."

now the Total Force Policy which *integrates* the Active, Guard and Reserve forces into a homogenous whole" (Schlesinger, 1973).

The issue was raised again at the end of the Cold War, when Congress, in the Defense Authorization Act of 1990, directed the Department of Defense (DoD) to undertake a study of "total force policy, force mix and military force structure." The resulting report (Department of Defense, 1990) focused on what it called the "Base Force," a particular force structure the DoD considered appropriate for the new era and which it used as the basis for the FY 1992 defense program. Congress, sensitive to arguments from the reserve components, rejected the Bush administration's plan and mandated a reserve manning level substantially greater than the one President Bush had requested.

Congress also required the Secretary of Defense to undertake a new study that would provide the "comprehensive analytic information" needed to evaluate the mix of reserve and active forces considered acceptable to carry out expected future military operations. The legislation required an emphasis on land-force missions and directed an examination of the time required to prepare forces for combat and the costs associated with alternative force mixes and structures. The legislation also provided that the study be conducted by a federally funded research and development center (FFRDC) that was independent of the military departments.

RAND's National Defense Research Institute (NDRI) was selected to conduct the assessment. NDRI was supported in this study by other FFRDCs, namely RAND's Army-sponsored Arroyo Center and its Project AIR FORCE, the Logistics Management Institute (LMI), the Center for Naval Analyses (CNA), and the Institute for Defense Analyses (IDA). The RAND study (NDRI, 1992) was delivered to the Bush administration in December 1992. The study was forwarded to Congress, but with the change in administrations in January 1993, the Secretary of Defense and the Chairman of the Joint Chiefs of Staff did not provide their written comments to Congress as called for in the Defense Authorization Act of 1990. In September 1993, the Clinton administration proposed a new mix of active and reserve forces based upon its "Bottom-Up Review" (BUR) of defense concepts, plans, and programs (Aspin, 1993). In what follows we first describe the original study and reactions to it. We then discuss briefly the relationship between its conclusions and the programs emerging from the BUR.

DESIGNING ALTERNATIVE FORCE STRUCTURES: A FRAMEWORK FOR ANALYSIS

The RAND study team started building an analytic framework by identifying the factors that are most important in defining different active/reserve force structures and mixes. Although existing and proposed active/reserve force structures can be described in a great many ways,[2] we found that four factors are especially important:

- Purpose of the force.
- The National Military Strategy (and related planning assumptions).
- Criteria for structuring forces.
- The type and level of integration of active and reserve forces.

Purpose is the reason a military force exists. Military forces have two broad classes of roles: conflict and nonconflict. The conflict role is usually thought of as the principal purpose of military forces and the role for which forces are generally structured (i.e., sized, equipped, and configured).[3] We follow that approach here also. However, the U.S. military historically has had such nonconflict roles as civil engineering, the maintenance of civil order, disaster relief, and forest-fire fighting. Responsibility for these nonconflict missions cuts across all the components: active, National Guard, and federal reserve forces. But despite the evident importance of such nonconflict missions as drug interdiction and disaster relief, and of nonfederal missions for the states,[4] requirements for active *and* reserve forces have traditionally been *structured* to support only conflict missions (see, e.g., Congressional Budget Office, 1992:13). That is, the nonconflict missions have been performed using the force structure decided upon by focusing on conflict missions.

The **National Military Strategy** establishes a broad philosophy about the missions of U.S. military forces and the particular challenges that are to drive planning (Powell, 1992). Its primary implementing documents, the Defense

---

[2]The practices of foreign military services provided a number of active and reserve paradigms for us to consider. We also found diverse approaches within the U.S. military. Individual experts, other research organizations, and military-affiliate organizations such as the National Guard Association of the United States (NGAUS) and the Reserve Officer Association (ROA) made specific proposals that emphasized different principles for organizing active and reserve forces. Still other suggestions came out of interviews with senior leaders in all the services, and their active and reserve components, as well as interviews with senior staff in the Office of the Secretary of Defense and the Joint Staff.

[3]The Army does have an organization—The Army Corps of Engineers—structured for nonconflict missions. Its emphasis is civil works, including flood control and maintaining and regulating inland waterways.

[4]To illustrate some of these, consider that during FY 1989, the National Guard was called upon to assist state governors in four civil disturbances and 53 natural disasters. Also, acting under Title 32 (state) status, in FY 1991 it provided 875,000 man-days in support of marijuana eradication operations, container searches, aerial and ground transportation, and other counterdrug activities. See Duncan (1992).

Planning Guidance (DPG) and the Illustrative Planning Scenarios (IPS), provide the specific time-phased requirements for structuring the force, and they help to identify the role of each service and component in peacetime and conflict. For the purpose of the study, we assumed the validity of the strategy, although we examined scenario variations.

Criteria for structuring forces lie at the heart of different interpretations of Total Force Policy—i.e., the policy determining the totality and mix of active and reserve forces. Currently, there are two competing views. DoD policy has long held that in meeting the National Military Strategy, cost-effectiveness should be the major consideration when making choices about the active/ reserve mix. A second view argues that some reserve *combat* forces must participate in any conflict to ensure that the commitment of forces truly represents the political will of the American people. This view stresses the "value of the citizen-soldier concept to American support for our military and national will in crisis situations" (see U.S. House of Representatives, 1993) and is seen as requiring a President "to seek, or feel assured of, popular support for a major conflict, by requiring them to mobilize citizen-soldiers" (Sorley, 1991). As put by Les Aspin, then chairman of the House Armed Services Committee,[5]

> [I]n some contingencies . . . the decision to go to war and risk large numbers of American lives must be shared with, and supported by, the American people and Congress. [The late Army Chief of Staff, General Creighton] Abrams and Laird set us on the right path for dealing with this issue, by insisting that it involve a decision to send America's citizen soldiers into war. If we stick to that path, we'll make the right decisions (Aspin, 1992b).

Finally, **the type and level of integration** dictate the form that alternative force structures take and, most important, the time it takes to prepare units for combat. By "type" of integration we mean the relationship between active and reserve units. This includes the way forces are organized, manned, equipped, and trained, particularly the kind of pre- and postmobilization training support that active units provide reserve units.[6] By "level" of integration, we mean the point in the chain of command where active commanders become responsible for reserve units. Typically, army reserve forces can be integrated into active

---

[5]The former president of the Adjutants General Association of the United States, Major General Robert F. Ensslin, Jr., has also argued that "for larger scale operations, the Guard and Reserve—*to include major combat units*, should have to be called. The reasoning is threefold; first, the importance of involving the Congress and the people; second, to allow the diplomatic and political processes to be as fruitful as possible; and third, the Guard and Reserve's proven ability to perform the mission and the attendant peacetime cost savings" (Ensslin, 1992:9, emphasis added).

[6]Several of the current models are roundout and roundup, integrated active and reserve units, associate units, augmentation, fillers and cadres, and active leadership of reserve units.

formations as companies, battalions, brigades, or divisions. If, for example, a reserve brigade joins two active brigades to fill out a division, this is called "roundout." If instead the reserve brigade is added to a full three-brigade division, it is augmenting the nominal capability, which is called "roundup." This distinction will be critical in some of what follows.

The type and level of integration, particularly the pre- and postmobilization training relationship between active and reserve forces, considerably affect the training requirements of reserve forces. The *rate* at which reserve forces can train up and deploy in contingencies is determined by training requirements dictated by the particular level and type of integration used.

These defining factors provided the conceptual framework for designing forces. In our study, which we shall refer to as the "Force Mix Study," we developed and analyzed a number of force structures that included combinations of various types and levels of integration. We also considered explicitly whether the resources necessary to conduct the training were available. To assess the alternatives, we needed to make reasonable assumptions about specifically what U.S. military forces were expected to accomplish over time—i.e., about the *time-phased demand* for the forces. We also had to make reasonable assessments of the availability of forces over time—i.e., about the *time-phased supply* of forces. In the next two sections we describe how we did this in the Force Mix Study.

UNDERSTANDING THE TIME-PHASED DEMAND FOR MILITARY FORCE

The Bush administration and Congress defined the purpose of both active and reserve forces in terms of meeting "expected future *military* missions." We took the Defense Planning Guidance (DPG) and its supporting Illustrative Planning Scenarios (IPS) as authoritative statements of military requirements, thereby focusing on a particular set of warfighting challenges.[7] However, given our congressional mandate, it was incumbent upon us to perform our own

---

[7]There are proposals for expanding the nonconflict roles of the military into new mission areas. Senator Nunn, for example, described some of these new areas in a floor speech: they would include military-based training to improve the basic skills of high-school dropouts, rehabilitation and renewal of community facilities, and other activities. However, we found no written disagreements with the force-*structuring* strategy we used in the study, even from those arguing for expanded or new nonconflict missions. For example, in his proposal for civil-military cooperation, Senator Nunn said, "Any such project must be undertaken in a manner that is consistent with the military mission of the unit in question. . . . The attention of DoD's civilian and military leadership must remain focused on training the Armed Forces for their primary mission, which is the military mission." See Nunn (1992:S8602).

independent analysis, *using assumptions different from those incorporated in the IPS* (as shown later) to understand how robust the alternative active/reserve force structures and mixes were to changes in scenario and other factors.[8]

DPG Military Requirements

The three key elements of the Bush administration's DPG with respect to conventional forces were "Forward Presence," "Crisis Response," and "Reconstitution." We accepted the DPG's requirements for both forward presence and reconstitution as stated. For the Crisis Response requirements, we focused on what the DPG and IPS call Major Regional Contingency (MRC)-East (the Persian Gulf), MRC-West (Korea), and MRC-Concurrent Contingencies. The analysis of each MRC, including the concurrent contingencies, was constructed in the same way. The United States first deploys an "Initial Response Force" for the defensive phase of the crisis. Under favorable circumstances, this force may also be adequate for early counteroffensive operations. The range of force deployments also includes a larger "Decisive Force," capable of conducting a massive counteroffensive, even under less favorable conditions. The basic U.S. concept of operations provides for the deployment of the Decisive Force *as quickly as lift will permit.* However, deployment of this force would be dependent on the absence of threats elsewhere at the time. Obviously, the prospect of a second concurrent contingency could affect the timing of force deployments.

Alternative Scenarios

Our analysis of the MRC requirements used the RAND Strategy Assessment System (RSAS), a global-conflict simulation that includes the capability to examine combat in multiple theaters, national- and theater-level decisionmaking, and strategic mobility. For MRC-East, we considered three levels of *force effectiveness*[9] and two excursions varying how quickly the United States and the Gulf Cooperation Council (GCC) states respond to an unfolding crisis. Table 1 shows the resulting six analytic cells.

---

[8]Senator Nunn expressed his view of just how important such excursions were: "If you let me write the scenarios, I can tell you before you do your study how it is going to turn out" (Nunn, 1992:80).

[9]We are referring here to the qualitative fighting effectiveness of a force, which may be a good deal less than one might expect from its size and equipment. Some armies fight better than others because of differences in officers, training, motivation, doctrine, and culture. Accounting for this is now crucial in defense analysis (Davis and Finch, 1993:24).

Table 1

Matrix of MRC-East Cases (RSAS Analysis)

	Relative Force Effectiveness		
	High	Medium	Low
Base-response case (C = S = D − 17; M = D)	GCC forces nominal	GCC forces nominal	GCC forces ineffective
	Iraqi forces ineffective	Iraqi forces nominal	Iraqi forces less effective
	USAF highly effective	USAF nominally effective	USAF less effective
Slow-response case (C = S = D + 5; M = D + 60)	GCC forces nominal	GCC forces nominal	GCC forces ineffective
	Iraqi forces ineffective	Iraqi forces nominal	Iraqi forces effective
	USAF highly effective	USAF nominally effective	USAF less effective

NOTE: S = day of initial call-up of reserve units; C = deployment day; D = hostilities day; M = day of partial mobilization allowing extended use of reserve forces.

The medium-effectiveness case assumes that GCC and Iraqi forces are roughly equal in fighting ability and that airpower has about the same impact on the ground war as it did in Operation Desert Storm. The case of low allied force effectiveness assumes virtual collapse of the GCC forces, which in turn reduces air effectiveness, due to command-and-control problems. The case of high allied force effectiveness assumes staunch performance by the GCC, poor performance by the enemy, and air-to-ground effectiveness greater than that achieved in Desert Storm.

Understanding Military Requirements Using Computer Simulations

Figures 1 and 2 display the results of the force-on-force RSAS simulations for the base-response case and slow-response case, respectively. The vertical axis denotes U.S. Army units required in the theater. The horizontal axis denotes time. The specifics of C-, S-, M-, and D-day decision times appear below the horizontal axis.

There is a degree of uncertainty about when future forces can arrive in theater; it depends on the amount of strategic lift that has been provided for them. This is represented in the figures by a shaded cone that is bounded by our high and low estimates of lift availability. While deployment is an uneven process,

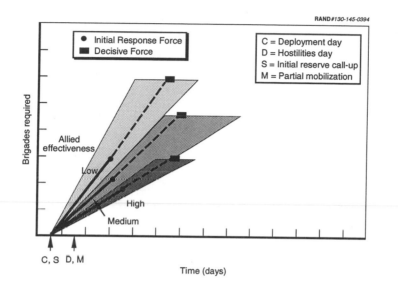

Figure 1—Force-Level and Timing Requirements: Base-Response Cases,
MRC-East

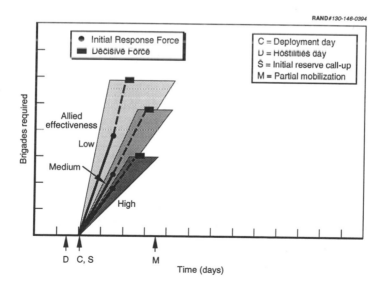

Figure 2—Force-Level and Timing Requirements: Slow-Response Cases,
MRC-East

the details of the process are not important here, and so we have used straight-line approximations for the lift curves.

The solid line on these charts connecting C-day to the Initial Reaction Force requirement is a straight-line approximation of a deployment curve needed to reach the required force levels by the required time. The requirement for the size and timing of the Initial Reaction Force is driven in each case by the assumed pace and size of the enemy's mobilization and attack. In MRC-East, our simulations established the size and arrival requirement for the Initial Reaction Force so that the ports in northern Saudi Arabia remain in allied hands and are usable. Once that attack is controlled by the Initial Reaction Force, the size of the Decisive Force was determined as that force required to drive the enemy out of Saudi Arabia and Kuwait with minimal U.S. casualties. The dashed line extending from the Initial Reaction Force point indicates when the Decisive Force would arrive if the forces continued to arrive at the same rate at which the Initial Reaction Force was deployed. Its arrival time in theater, however, is a function of lift capacity rather than a specific requirement determined by the application of an analytic model. As a result, the Decisive Force could arrive at any point along the top of the cone, depending on the lift available, and still achieve its mission.

Figures 1 and 2 illustrate some significant features of the cases assessed for MRC-East. Figure 1 indicates that in situations where the United States responded quickly (in this case $C = D - 7$, meaning that deployment began seven days before D-day), force requirements were relatively insensitive to allied capabilities. This was because (not shown on chart; see full study for details) by D-day or very shortly thereafter the United States had all of the Air Force IRF and significant quantities of Army and Marine forces in the theater. By contrast, in the slow-response case illustrated in Figure 2, there were no U.S. ground forces in theater on D-day, and only limited Air Force and Navy air forces. As a result, success in the scenario required a very rapid deployment rate (compare the slopes of the lines in Figures 1 and 2) and was quite sensitive to the assumed effectiveness of GCC and Iraqi forces.

Understanding Military Requirements from Interviews and a War Game

As mentioned above, there was no clear-cut way to decide how quickly the Decisive Force had to be deployed. Nor could computer simulations resolve the issue. To better understand the implications of being able to conduct a major counteroffensive earlier rather than later, we had extensive interviews and discussions with theater commanders and their staffs in the contingency theaters. Second, we organized a political/military game at which very senior retired general officers from all four services were asked to evaluate these kinds of costs and risks.

Our initial hypothesis was that once the battle was stabilized with no further enemy advances, a significant delay could be tolerated before the arrival of the forces needed to comprise the Decisive Force. That is, they could be delayed as necessary for training to a high level of combat proficiency. What difference would it make if the delay were, e.g., three or four months rather than one or two? Without exception, the theater commanders (CINCs), their staffs, and participants in the game held the contrary view: They argued that it was absolutely unacceptable to delay the delivery of the Decisive Force. During that delay, friendly casualties would inevitably be suffered, and there would be an increased risk that the basic conditions of the contingency might change. For example, the friendly coalition might break down, or the adversary might use weapons of mass destruction. As one player observed, "people are dying" while commanders wait for trained reserve combat units to deploy. There is no way to quantify this risk. It is possible that none of these negative effects of delay would, in fact, be suffered. However, the question was why the United States should run the risks at all if the lift is available. Therefore, in our force employment analysis, we required the Decisive Force for each scenario to close as quickly as projected strategic lift permitted. The shaded cones shown in Figure 1 reflect differing assumptions about how much strategic lift the United States would have in the years ahead.

Conclusions Concerning Required Military Forces

By and large, our assessment of force requirements in the contingencies studied confirmed the earlier conclusions of the Joint Staff, which had been incorporated in the Bush administration's DPG. We concluded that a force of four to five Army divisions plus about two divisions of Marines would indeed be adequate to execute the strategy for a single MRC and, importantly, that the need for this level of force was consistent with prudently conservative assumptions about allied fighting effectiveness and airpower's effectiveness, rather than worst-case assumptions.[10] Indeed, the assumptions were *optimistic* in assuming reasonably prompt national decisions to mobilize and deploy the force. That is, while confirming the DoD's previous analysis in the large, we also found that outcomes of the planning scenarios were *very* sensitive to changes in the times at which U.S. forces were mobilized and deployed. Although we cannot elaborate here (details of the analysis were classified), even small changes in

---

[10]The Clinton administration reached similar conclusions a year later (Aspin, 1993:19).

C-day, S-day, and M-day assumptions exercised a powerful effect on the size and timing requirements for the Initial Response Force and on the ultimate size of the Decisive Force.[11] Thus, the "requirement" for four to five Army and about two Marine divisions is "resonable," but by no means precise.

UNDERSTANDING THE SUPPLY OF MILITARY FORCES IN THE POST–COLD WAR ERA

Given the lift-specific, time-phased requirements for military forces discussed above, the time it takes to prepare forces for combat is the critical factor in determining if a specific unit can be active or reserve. All units, active and reserve, must go through a similar generic process: They must be notified, assemble their personnel and physical assets, complete any necessary training, and prepare administratively and physically for deployment overseas. However, American active-duty units are generally expected to maintain high levels of readiness so they can deploy for contingency operations on extremely short notice; deployment simply is not delayed to allow time for them to improve their preparedness. Reserve units go through a much more deliberate process, starting with a political decision to exercise presidential authority to call up selected reserve units, the timing of which is of great concern to military planners. Other things being equal, the quicker reserve units can be made ready, the more of the overall force structure can be in the reserves.

The critical and time-consuming period of postmobilization reserve-unit training depends on the type and level of integration, as discussed above, and, more particularly, on the following:

- *Missions.* The range and difficulty of tasks the unit will perform in wartime. The broader and tougher the missions, the more extensive the preparation time needed.
- *Performance objectives.* The level of proficiency required in the missions and constituent tasks. The higher the level of proficiency required, the greater the preparation needed.
- *Peacetime activities and resources.* The types and amounts of training the units conduct. The more and better the peacetime training, the shorter the preparation needed upon mobilization.

---

[11]Because of such sensitivities, one can argue that it is more appropriate to base planning on the objective of increasing the size of the "scenario space" over which favorable outcomes can be achieved. See Davis and Finch (1993:43ff) and Davis (1994a).

- *Postmobilization training capacity.* The availability of active-duty personnel to concurrently train reserve units. The greater the capacity, the faster reserve units can be deployed.

Since nearly all the combat elements of the Army reserves are in the National Guard rather than the Army Reserve, we shall now focus on National Guard units.

Preparation Times for a Single National Guard Combat Brigade

There is considerable uncertainty about the time it would take to prepare a *single* representative National Guard maneuver brigade for combat today, and even more uncertainty about how long it would take in the future, depending on what reforms are enacted, what resources are budgeted, and how new initiatives are implemented. We chose to be conservative, to minimize risk to the country and individual reservists themselves. In this we followed the lead of then-Congressman Les Aspin: "Where inadequate training and preparation would cost lives, any error should be on the side of safety" (Aspin, 1992a). Moreover, we noted a number of promising procedural reforms and argued that they should be further developed, but until their effectiveness were proved we believed it would be imprudent to reduce our postmobilization training estimates. We did, however, provide new estimates for organizational reforms that directly reduced pre- and postmobilization training requirements.

Our estimate of unit preparation times for Army brigades was based on research by RAND's Army-sponsored Arroyo Center (Lippiatt, Polich, and Sorton, 1992) that focused on the postmobilization requirements to train troops to perform required combat skills, and on interviews with senior active and retired Army and National Guard officers familiar with the challenge of mastering the difficult battle management tasks required of higher-level commanders. We concluded that the figure of 128 days (albeit overly precise) was a prudently conservative estimate of the time it would take to prepare combat brigades for battle, i.e., to accomplish the 12 tasks outlined in Table 2, assuming an effort to implement the Army's Bold Shift initiative to improve readiness with insights based on the Desert Shield and Desert Storm experiences.[12] In this case, "nominal" assumptions seemed too optimistic after our analysis.

---

[12]See also NDRI (1992:149) for Center for Naval Analyses estimates of Marine Corps training-time requirements based on Sims (1992). See also Tilson, Horowitz, and Roberson (1992) for work by the Institute for Defense Analyses.

Table 2

Estimates for Army Reserve Component Combat Brigade Preparation Time

	Assumptions about Success of Bold Shift Initiative		
	Optimistic	Nominal	Prudently Conservative
Initial mobilization activities			
1. Mobilization order, home station to mobilization station move	3	4	4
2. Mobilization station to collective training site move	6	7	8
3. POM and individual training	2	2	3
Crew and platoon training			
4. Maintenance, gunnery preparation, COFT, tank/Bradley crew gunnery skills test	4	7	10
5. Gunnery Tables IV–VIII	14	17	22
6. Gunnery Tables XI–XII	5	6	7
7. Squad drills, platoon lanes, STXs	4	8	11
Training while task-organized			
8. Company team lanes and STXs	14	18	22
9. Company/battalion combined-arms live-fire exercise	6	7	8
10. Battalion task force operations	4	6	7
11. Brigade and battalion task force operations (could be at National Training Center)	10	12	12
Training recovery and preparation to move			
12. Maintenance, recovery, and preparation for loading	7	10	14
Total number of days	79	104	128

SOURCE: Lippiatt, Polich, and Sortor (1992). The Army's Bold Shift initiative is a series of measures to improve readiness and reduce training time.

Options for Reducing Combat-Unit Preparation Time

There have been many proposals to improve reserve combat unit readiness. The most recent were enacted into law in October 1992 as part of Title XI. However, virtually all of these have focused on incremental procedural changes. We examined a number of ways to save *substantial* amounts of post-mobilization time and, at the same time, decrease the risk of inadequate peacetime readiness among reserve troops and leaders. The methods identified included: using computer simulations for training; reforming the underlying conditions that constrain reserve peacetime readiness; using two sets of equipment to prepare early-deploying reserve combat units, thus permitting parallel training and shipping of equipment; and integrating active and reserve units at lower echelons, to cut training tasks and increase confidence in leadership skills. We assessed the last option in greatest detail.

Integration at Lower Echelons

During the Gulf War the Marine Corps sent reserve combat units to the theater, and its ability to do that is often attributed to the fact that it integrated its units at echelons lower than brigades (or, in this case, regiments). In order to better understand and analyze the possibilities of integrating Army units at lower levels, we developed specific battalion and company "roundout" designs and discussed these designs with numerous experts in the active Army and National Guard. Table 3 shows some of the key characteristics of Army heavy-maneuver units at the various echelons.

During the time allowed for the study, it was not possible to definitively evaluate the organizational effectiveness of battalion and company roundout. However, based upon discussions with active and retired leaders in the active Army and the Army National Guard, we identified a number of evaluative factors. As Table 4 indicates, there are arguments for rounding out at the brigade, battalion, and company levels. The brigade-level roundout is familiar, while U.S. Army active- and reserve-component officers are less familiar with and more suspicious about integration at lower levels (although Marines integrate reserves at company and battalion levels). The brigade-level roundout system also provides more command opportunities and may result in the reserve units having higher prestige. Costs are slightly higher (by a few percentage points) for company- and battalion-level integration, but the lower-level integration allows quicker employment—after about 60 to 80 days of training, compared to the baseline of 120 days.

Postmobilization Training Capacity

The above discussion focused on the time it takes to prepare a *single* National Guard maneuver brigade for combat. The force contains more than one unit, however, and the Army's ability to conduct postmobilization training at multiple sites will determine the total number of units that can deployed at any time. The critical constraint in the future is likely to be the number of active-duty personnel and training sites available to train reserve units. The Army's Inspector General estimated that during the Persian Gulf War as many as 2800 active-duty soldiers were supporting the training of a *single* reserve

Table 3

Characteristics of Army Heavy-Maneuver Units by Echelon

	Brigade	Echelon Battalion	Company
Key features	Combined arms: maneuver, fire support, close air support, Army aviation and combat service support	Combined arms: primarily maneuver with integrated direct and indirect fires	Single tactical function: direct fire and maneuver
	Mix of weapon systems	Mix of weapon systems	Single primary weapon system
	Variable organization	Fixed organization	Fixed organization
	Fights task-organized	Fights task-organized	Fights as integral unit
	Indirect troop control	Less direct troop control	Direct troop control
	Improved sustainment, executes all combat service support functions	Limited sustainment, organic maintenance, and transportation	(Requires external) support for maintenance and sustainment
Control area of responsibility	<300 square km	<50 square km	<10 square km
Planning horizon	24–48 hours	12–24 hours	12–24 hours
Personnel	3000–5000 people	500–850 people	65–200 people
Primary skills	75+	30+	3–4
Major combat vehicles	200–300	50–70	10–12

Table 3—continued

	Echelon		
	Brigade	Battalion	Company
Combat	Simultaneous integrated close and rear operations	Integrated close operations	Close operations
	Execute and plan current and future operations; think in time and space	Execute current operations	Execute current operations
	Prioritize, assign and allocate missions and assets	Fight the maneuver battle	Shoot and maneuver
	Integrate and synchronize all seven battlefield operating systems and significant complex coordination	Integrate various battlefield operating systems and perform direct coordination	No integration and only simple coordination

Table 4

Assessment of Roundout Options

Assessment Factors	Roundout Echelon		
	Brigade	Battalion	Company
Command authority and accountability	3 command echelons between crew/platoon training and active command	2 command echelons between crew/platoon training and active command	1 command echelon between crew/platoon training and active command
Complexity of postmobilization training	Very complex: requires extensive postmobilization combined arms training	Less complex, but requires significant postmobilization combined arms training	Least complex: most consistent with crew/platoon peacetime training
Equipment maintenance	Maintained by civilian reserve technicians	Maintained by civilian reserve technicians	Maintained by active-duty gaining battalion
Availability of postmobilization training areas	Only 3 to 5 areas with sufficient size to support brigade operations	Sufficient areas generally available	Numerous areas available
Peacetime active-unit training	Full functional training for all active units, including cross-battalion combined arms	Full functional training for 2 battalions out of 3; brigade training more difficult	Full functional training for 2 companies out of 4 or 1 out of 3; battalion training more difficult

Table 4—continued

Assessment Factors	Roundout Echelon		
	Brigade	Battalion	Company
Mobilization flexibility for active parent division	Very flexible: can easily deploy active brigades without roundout brigades	Most flexible: maintains battalion unity; can easily deploy more active battalions without roundout units	Least flexible: deployment must await company training or companies must extensively reorganize to deploy active portion
Estimated postmobilization training time	128 days or more	70–90 days	60 days
Personnel/career development	Command opportunity through brigade (normally O-6)	Command opportunity through battalion (normally O-5)	Command opportunity through company (normally O-3)
Acceptance	High acceptance: maintains status quo and provides largest number of senior reserve billets	Acceptance in doubt: both active and reserve components express reservations	Significant resistance: likely to be resisted by both active and reserve components
Resources	Current budget	Additional steady-state cost of $24 million per roundout division per year	Additional steady-state cost of $68 million per roundout division per year

NOTE: Brigade-level roundout means that a reserve brigade fills out a division with two active brigades.

roundout brigade. The size and low efficiency of this training approach (a ratio of nearly 1:1 for active forces and reserve forces in the trainer/trainee relationship) suggests that *dedicated* training assets must be provided for postmobilization training of reserve combat brigades, rather than depending on the ad hoc approach used in the Gulf War. These assets may be the same as those used in peacetime to perform other training functions. Many discussions with active and retired senior Army leaders also indicate that these training assets must be active organizations competent in training methods and current doctrine.

ASSESSING FORCE-MIX OPTIONS TO MEET TWO MAJOR REGIONAL CONTINGENCIES

Against this background, the RAND 1992 Force Mix Study assessed the Base Force and a number of other *equal-cost alternative* force options against the general military requirements presented in the DoD Defense Planning Guidance. According to the DPG, active components should "supply combat and support forces for the initial response to contingencies that arise on short notice." Reserve forces should "contribute mobility assets in short notice crisis, support and sustain active combat forces *and provide combat forces* in especially large and protracted contingencies" (emphasis added). It also stated that "mobilization of some Reserve Component combat forces can provide the force expansion needed to enhance the U.S. capability to respond to another contingency."

The Base Force

The Base Force was designed by the Bush administration to meet a National Military Strategy that focused on regional defense. Sometimes described as the 12/6/2 force, it contained 12 active divisions, 6 reserve divisions, and 2 reserve cadre divisions. It is presented in detail in Figure 3,[13] which illustrates a way of depicting alternative structures that we found exceptionally useful—despite its apparent complexity.

---

[13]Detailed unit-level "troop lists" were developed for all options using LMI's Forces, Readiness and Manpower Information System (FORMIS) and computer files provided by the Army.

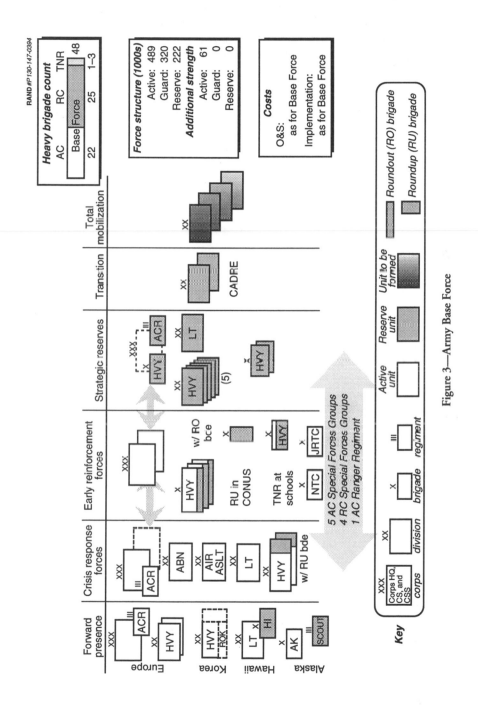

Figure 3—Army Base Force

Description. In Figure 3, the major combat units of the Army component of the Base Force are arrayed along the lines of their nominal responsiveness to contingency needs (crisis response, strategic reserves, etc.).[14] The forward-presence forces provide a peacetime deterrence capability and are the most readily available forces to any given theater. In Europe, they consist of a corps with two divisions, an Armored Cavalry Regiment (ACR), and the corps' associated combat support and combat service support. In Korea, these forces are two brigades of a heavy division, which relies on a brigade from South Korea (ROK) for the third brigade of maneuver forces that normally completes a division. This division is "rounded up" with a reserve-component brigade that is stationed in CONUS but has a primary mission to deploy to the Korean theater to augment its parent division in war. An active-component light division is stationed in Hawaii and is complemented by a reserve brigade of light infantry. In Alaska, the active-component forward-presence force consists of a light brigade, and the reserve force consists of a highly specialized Arctic Scout Regiment.

The crisis response forces stand ready to respond to regional contingencies. They include a corps consisting of three specialized divisions (airborne, air assault, and light infantry); two heavy divisions with reserve roundup brigades (indicated by the shaded vertical rectangles), which add a fourth brigade to a division; an Armored Cavalry Regiment; and the corps' associated combat support and combat service support. As indicated by the dashed corps symbol and light double-headed arrows, a second corps (headquarters, support and nondivisional combat assets) may be created to act as part of the crisis response forces, depending on circumstances.

The early reinforcement forces provide the capability to build a decisive force in theater and consist of a corps (or possibly two) with associated nondivision combat and support units and three heavy divisions, each of which includes a roundout reserve brigade (shown by the horizontal shaded rectangle).

The force structure of Figure 3 (the Base Force) contains four corps in all; we have depicted the fourth as part of the early reinforcement forces, though it may form part of the crisis response force as indicated above or provide the corps-level leadership and assets for the strategic reserve. We have also depicted the reserve roundup brigade, which augments the two U.S. brigades of the division in Korea, in the early reinforcement column to stress that it is not located overseas.

The strategic reserves provide strategic depth. In the Base Force, they consisted of six reserve divisions (five heavy and one light) as well as four brigade-

---

[14]This categorization is not definitive: The light division in Hawaii can perform the crisis response mission, for example.

sized reserve units (three independent heavy brigades and an Armored Cavalry Regiment).

The ability to transition from full mobilization of existing units to total mobilization, which would create entirely new divisions, was provided in the Base Force by two specialized "cadre" divisions. These are reserve units and would provide the leadership and training necessary to create new combat units. These newly formed units are depicted in a conceptual manner by the division symbols with variable shading shown in the total mobilization column; there may be more or fewer than the four shown.

In addition to these forces, the Base Force also included five active-component and four reserve-component Special Forces Groups and one active-component Ranger Regiment. As indicated by the large double-headed arrow in the figure (bottom of third column), these forces may play a role over a wide range of responsiveness, depending on the situation.

The figure also shows the specialized trainer units included in the Base Force. Some of these, such as the mixed active/reserve unit shown as a trainer unit at the Army's branch schools, might be assigned a wartime mission in the theater of conflict (in the past this has been as part of a theater's operational reserves). Others, such as the brigade located at the National Training Center (NTC), would typically continue their training mission during wartime.

The three panels to the right of the figure show additional measures of the Base Force. Because many of the divisions in this and our other alternatives are mixed active/reserve units, we have found brigade counts to provide a clearer picture of the active/reserve mix of any given force. The panel at the upper right shows the number of active and reserve heavy brigades in this force structure, as well as the number of brigade-sized units specialized for heavy force training. The trainer units that would typically deploy to theater and those that would most likely continue their training mission during a conflict are reported separately.[15] The total number of deployable heavy brigades is annotated at the end of the bar.

The combat units depicted in the figure accounted for only about 46 percent of a force that totaled over one million. This is because combat support and combat service support units are not shown in the figure, nor is the supporting infrastructure base of the Army, known as the "TDA Army." We have fully specified these critical parts of the Army for each of the alternatives presented in this paper and showed the resulting personnel totals in the middle panel to the right of the figure. The panel also shows the additional manning

---

[15]The Base Force contained one of the former, the mixed active/reserve unit discussed above, and three of the latter, the brigade at the NTC and the "cadre" divisions. If "deployable" trainer units are moved to theater early in a crisis, it is not clear how reserve combat unit train-up could be conducted.

provided to enable combat units to remain at full strength, even though many of the Army's personnel are in transit or full-time training at any given time. As indicated in the panel, additional manning was not provided for the reserve component, resulting in the undermanning of reserve combat units whose personnel are in training.

A cost categorization is shown in the lower panel. This panel classifies the alternatives as to whether they have costs associated with the current budget level (the same long-term recurring costs as the Base Force), or a budget level that is about 10 percent lower.

Analysis. The capability of the Base Force to generate fully trained combat (maneuver) units is illustrated in Figure 4. The left-hand panel shows the DoD's initial expectations; the right-hand panel shows the results of our assessment.

The panels of Figure 4 show a generalized training plan using the graphic symbols to represent the number of trainer and trainee units and the time it would take to accomplish the training. The two panels contrast the implicit expectations of Army planners (left panel) with our assessment of how quickly the Base Force could prepare reserve maneuver units for combat (right panel). The vertical axis of each panel identifies the units available to provide training to the reserves; e.g., the top row shows the parent divisions training their three round-out brigades. The horizontal axis shows the number of months after mobilization. Units to be trained are located on this trainer-time grid according to when they would be ready to deploy. For example, the top row shows the three roundout brigades being fully trained approximately three months after initial mobilization.

As illustrated in the left panel, the *implicit assumption* of the Base Force was that the three roundout brigades slated for "early reinforcement" (normally thought of as available in about three months) could indeed be available on that schedule. The Base Force was assumed capable of training the equivalent of a division (three heavy brigades) every three months thereafter to rebuild nondeployed Army capability in CONUS. This would restock nondeployed combat capability at a very slow rate, and it raised questions of both the deterrent value of the reserves and the immediate capability to respond to a second contingency.

The Base Force Capabilities. Our independent estimates of postmobilization training requirements suggested (right panel of Figure 4) that *reserve combat brigades would not be ready for combat in less than about 120 days—a month longer than the 90 days assumed in the original Base Force work by DoD.* We could match DoD's result only with optimistic assumptions (e.g., left column of Table 2). Under the system associated with the Base Force, the units would have needed more time to hone their combat skills and the combat leaders more time to master the difficult tasks of synchronization and coordination.

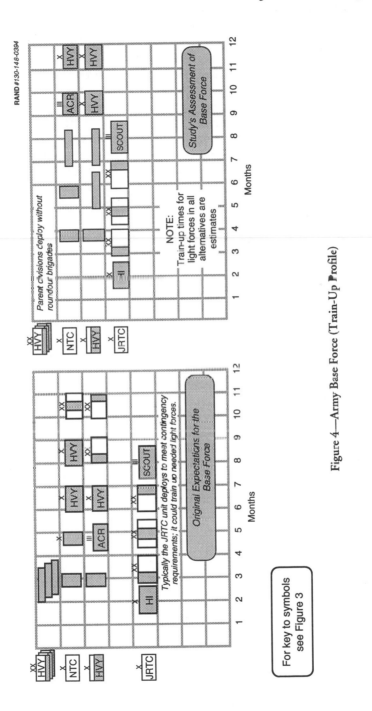

Figure 4—Army Base Force (Train-Up Profile)

Six active brigades could have been deployed as two active three-brigade divisions instead of waiting to train their reserve units, or as three full divisions, by replacing the reserve brigades with active brigades from Europe, as was done during the Gulf War. However, this would have deprived the reserve brigades of their anticipated postmobilization trainers, and it is not clear how these units would have completed their preparation for combat. In contrast to the force during the Gulf War, the Base Force did not have sufficient additional active units available to train the roundout brigades.

Our assessment of the postmobilization training capability of the Base Force was that five months into a contingency, only two reserve heavy brigades (less than a division's combat power) would be ready to deploy, instead of the five to seven heavy brigades that were expected. This was very much slower than the rate that we judged above to be excessively long.

In sum, we found that the Base Force faced two problems in meeting the total force needs of the National Military Strategy: having fully trained reserve combat brigades to complete the forces needed for an initial contingency, and quickly rebuilding the Army's rapid response capability to respond to another contingency—as a deterrent or as a fighting force.

The Enhanced Active Army Force (Roundup-Only Alternative)

Given the problem of having fully trained National Guard roundout brigades ready for early deployment during an initial contingency, senior Army leaders suggested this alternative: a force structure with enough active combat brigades to provide the Decisive Force required for the most demanding MRC by eliminating the roundout divisions and replacing them with fully structured active divisions. Existing reserve brigades would *round up* active divisions when they became available after the required postmobilization training, or their personnel could be assigned, as needed, as fillers or to replace combat losses. In order to make this option cost the same as the Base Force, the larger active force required reductions in the overall number of National Guard divisions. The cost tradeoff was roughly one active division for three National Guard divisions. The details of this force are presented in Figure 5.

Description. In this option, forward-presence and crisis-response forces were similar to those of the Base Force, with the exception that there is no reserve augmentation for the two-brigade division in Korea. Early reinforcement forces were substantially different in that they include an active-component Armored Cavalry Regiment and three additional active brigades. These brigades provide the three early reinforcement divisions with a three-brigade active-component nucleus that is capable of deploying without a postmobilization training delay. These three brigades and their nondivisional combat and

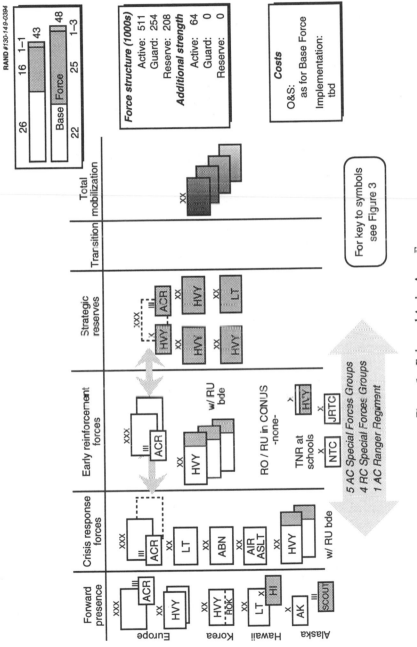

RAND #130-149-0394

Force structure (1000s)
Active: 511
Guard: 254
Reserve: 208
Additional strength
Active: 64
Guard: 0
Reserve: 0

Costs

O&S: as for Base Force
Implementation: tbd

For key to symbols see Figure 3

5 AC Special Forces Groups
4 RC Special Forces Groups
1 AC Ranger Regiment

RO / RU in CONUS
-none-

TNR at schools

w/ RU bde

w/ RU bde

Forward presence | Crisis response forces | Early reinforcement forces | Strategic reserves | Transition | Total mobilization

Europe | Korea | Hawaii | Alaska

Figure 5—Enhanced Active Army Force

support forces had a somewhat higher proportion of active-component units because of their envisioned earlier deployment. These divisions were augmented by reserve roundup brigades, such divisions thus forming "rectangular," or four-brigade, divisions. Once augmented, they might be able to sustain 24-hour operations for a longer period. The strategic reserves were reduced in this alternative to three heavy divisions, two independent, heavy brigade–sized units, and a light division.

As shown in the upper right panel of the figure, the overall force was smaller than the Base Force by some five heavy brigades, but there were four more active heavy brigades.

Analysis. The Enhanced Active Army Force alternative is more able than the Base Force to meet the initial contingency requirements. However, it suffers from very nearly the same limitations as the Base Force: the inability to rapidly prepare follow-on reserve forces to ensure that the United States has a ready force as deterrence against a second contingency, or to meet the requirements of that conflict should it occur. As shown in Figure 6, only three reserve brigades could be trained at a time; thus, very few reserve combat divisions could be rapidly brought up to standards. Finally, on a nonanalytic level, this force sharply reduced the overall size of the Army reserve components. During our political/military game, the players judged this force to be politically unacceptable to Congress because of the substantial reduction of politically popular reserve forces.

RAND/LMI Alternative Force

RAND and LMI worked to develop a force option that corrected the problems observed in the Base Force and the Enhanced Active Army Force. This option enabled reserve combat units to fight in the first MRC and provide for a rapid buildup of fully trained units that could "respond to another contingency." The key features of this option were as follows:

- The integration of selected reserve units into active formations of lower-level (battalion- or company-roundout) to ensure that the early reinforcing divisions could deploy, when required, with a fully trained reserve complement.

- Reliance on four-brigade, "rectangular" divisions built with reserve roundup brigades to provide reserve forces that could deter or respond to contingencies.

- Provision for reserve-unit additional manning that would allow reserve units to be fully manned by trained personnel so they could quickly deploy.

RAND #130-150-0394

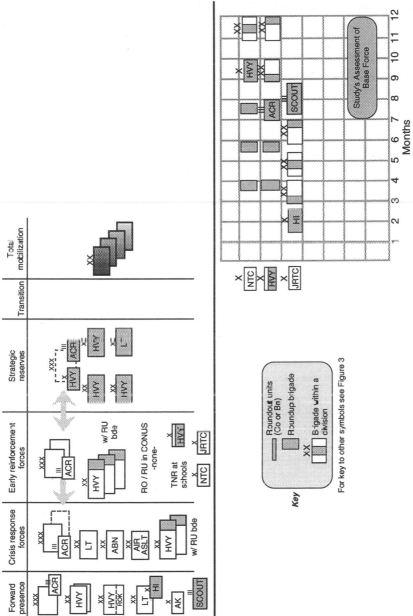

Figure 6—Enhanced Active Army Force (Train-Up Profile)

- The creation of specialized active-component trainer commands to provide effective and timely postmobilization training. During peacetime, these commands would also support ongoing proficiency training of the reserves.

- A shift of selected portions of combat support and combat service support (CS and CSS) missions to the reserve component to offset the cost of the above initiatives.

- The adoption of the associate-unit concept[16] to provide extra crews, operators, and maintenance personnel for select Army units, such as attack helicopters, Multiple Launch Rocket System (MLRS) artillery units, and select support units to enable 24-hour operations, and provide a robust support capability for early-deploying units.

Description. The key features incorporated in the RAND/LMI Alternative Force are illustrated in Figure 7.[17] The forward presence forces in Europe consisted of two divisions modeled after our current forward presence in Korea. These divisions consisted of two U.S. heavy brigades each. Each relied on a third allied brigade to complete its readily available combat forces in an extension of the current move within NATO toward more reliance on multinational units. These divisions were also augmented with a roundup brigade of U.S. reserve forces, stationed in CONUS, which would be available to augment the divisions in Europe once they had been trained up. (These are depicted as part of the early reinforcement forces along with the roundup brigade for the division in Korea.)

The crisis response forces also incorporated additional reserve forces in the form of roundup brigades of light infantry to augment the specialized divisions. These reserve units were designed to provide fundamental light infantry capabilities for these specialized forces. The purpose is to ensure that the specialized capabilities were not tied down by necessary combat and security duties that precluded their availability for missions that could be performed only with specially trained and equipped forces.

The early reinforcement forces are larger and more responsive in this alternative than in any of the force structures previously discussed. The increased responsiveness is due to the reliance on lower-level roundout (denoted with the dotted pattern in the figure) in each of the heavy early reinforcement divisions.

---

[16]Developed by the Air Force, the associate unit is a hybrid that combines active and reserve personnel into a single unit upon mobilization. In this approach, an Air Force Reserve "associate" unit trains on its affiliated active unit's equipment. The associate unit's air crew personnel commonly are mixed with active personnel for peacetime training, and associate unit maintenance personnel participate in the maintenance of the active unit's equipment.

[17]In the study, what we are calling here the "RAND" alternative was called the "NDRI" alternative because the study was conducted by NDRI, a RAND division.

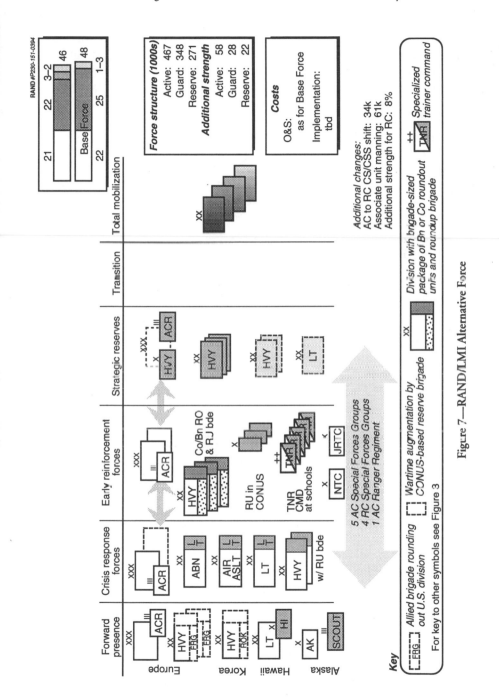

Figure 7—RAND/LMI Alternative Force

In our illustration of this concept, a brigade-sized package of combat forces was integrated into the three active brigades in battalion- or company-sized units. This allowed the parent units to deploy as three-brigade divisions with a fully trained reserve complement, and also allowed them to meet contingency requirements.[18] The larger early reinforcement forces were due to an additional fourth brigade in each division (a reserve roundup brigade). These augmented the deployed forces after completing postmobilization brigade-level training. The early reinforcement forces also included an active Armored Cavalry Regiment.

Strategic-reserve divisions in this alternative were of two different types: The first were fully constituted and had a primary mission as a division. (There are three heavy divisions of this type; they are shown with darker shading in the figure.) The second were those units whose maneuver brigades have been "pushed forward" in the mobilization sequence to provide roundout brigades for earlier-deploying forces (the two heavy divisions and one light division shown with lighter shading and a dashed outline in the figure). The reserve divisions in this category consisted of the division headquarters and division troops. They had a primary mission of providing roundup units for the crisis response and early reinforcement forces, as well as the responsibility for managing the mobilization, training, and deployment of their reserve forces during a crisis.[19] Each of the two heavy reserve divisions in this category would be associated with four roundup brigades; the reserve light division would be associated with the three light roundup brigades.

One of the most significant innovations in this alternative was the establishment of specialized trainer commands. These five commands (depicted with the diagonal in the figure) would provide postmobilization training for reserve brigade-sized units. They could simultaneously train five roundup brigades in most major scenarios. Three of those commands would also form an active cadre for the three fully structured strategic reserve divisions once their postmobilization training mission was complete. The remaining two trainer commands would continue their training mission after full mobilization. Together with the training units at the National Training Center (NTC) and the Joint Readiness Training Center (JRTC), they would provide a core capability to develop new units during total mobilization.

---

[18]Each division is afforded a brigade-sized package of reserve combat power which is organized and integrated in company-level or battalion-level building-block units.

[19]This dual relationship is similar to that practiced today in the Air Force Associate Program, in which reserve crews are organized in associate squadrons to facilitate the management of reserve-component matters but augment active-component squadrons for operational employment.

The force structure for the RAND/LMI alternative also included several other initiatives:

- A shift of 34,000 combat support and combat service support spaces from the active component to the reserve component.[20]

- An additional 8 percent strength for reserve units to insure that these units are more fully manned by trained personnel.

- 60,000 additional reserve personnel in associate units that provide extra operators and maintainers to leverage existing equipment such as attack helicopters and MLRS rocket launchers This would also allow more dedicated, around-the-clock support operations.

Analysis. The RAND/LMI Alternative Force was designed to better meet contingency requirements (1) by integrating reserve units at a lower level to ensure that the roundout unit can be made ready and deploy with its parent unit and (2) by explicitly providing for the rapid training of reserve brigades to insure a capability for a second contingency. These postmobilization training profiles are shown in Figure 8.

These changes substantially decreased the elapsed postmobilization training period required to provide a force that could be rapidly deployed to handle a second contingency. The strategic reserve in this force was available and fully trained months earlier than in any of the alternatives previously examined. After they had completed their postmobilization training mission, these units could become an active-component cadre around which new divisions could be formed.

Comparison and Assessment of Alternatives

Table 5 summarizes the major features of the *equal cost* Army alternatives, and Figure 9 shows the ability of each alternative to build up combat power, as measured in the number of heavy maneuver brigades that are "combat ready" and have completed the required postmobilization training. In these alternatives, only the RAND/LMI Alternative Force increased the likelihood that roundout units would have able leadership, complete their postmobilization training, and be ready to deploy with their parent units. Most important, the

---

[20]In light of the high level of peacetime demands made on our armed forces that we have seen in the past two years (such as peacekeeping/peacemaking operations), assessments of peacetime requirements in addition to warfighting requirements need to be made to insure that this many support troops could be moved to the reserve components. In the absence of reserve call-up/mobilization (often the case in peacetime operations), these reserve support troops are only available in limited numbers to meet the requirements of peacetime operations.

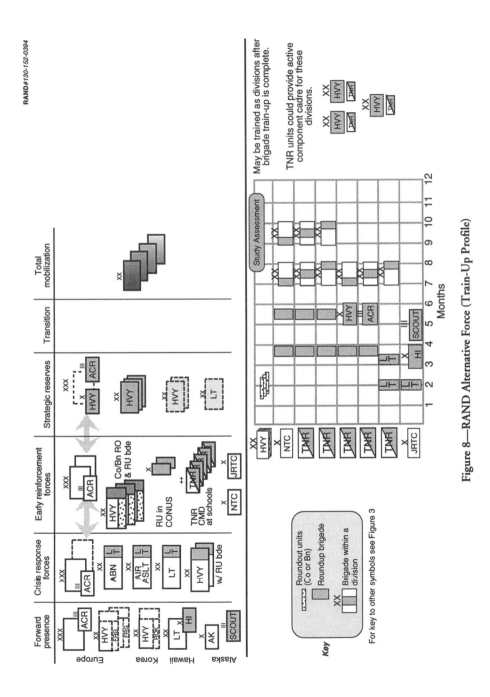

Figure 8—RAND Alternative Force (Train-Up Profile)

Table 5

Summary of Army Force Alternatives

	Army Force Structure Alternatives		
	Base Force	Enhanced Active Army	RAND/ LMI
Cost:	Base Force	Same as Base Force	Same as Base Force
Divisions AC/RC/Cadre	12/6/2	12/4/0	12/6/0
Heavy brigades AC/RC	22/25	26/16	21/22
Light brigades AC/RC	13/5	13/5	13/5
End-strength AC/RC	536/542	575/463	525/679
Level of integration	Brigade	None	Company or battalion
RC-CSS/ CS shift	0	0	34,000
RC associate unit manning	0	0	61,000
RC: additional unit strength	0	0	50,000
AC: training commands	0	0	5

RAND/LMI alternative rounded out at the company or battalion level and created dedicated active training units to ensure that the reserve combat units could be trained even if a major regional contingency were underway. In terms of effectiveness (as measured by the number of fully trained heavy brigades a force structure provides to the strategic lift system for deployment to theater) the RAND/LMI option provides 20 percent fewer brigades than the Enhanced Active Army option initially; by the three-month point both force structures provide an equal number of brigades, and at the end of eight months the RAND/LMI alternative provides 25 percent more force. During the first three months, this comparison is likely to be biased in favor of the Enhanced Active Army option, as strategic lift may not be available to move the trained brigades it can provide during this time frame.

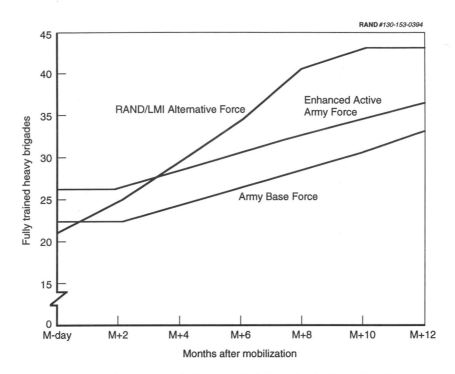

Figure 9—Comparison of Alternatives' Ability to Train Heavy Combat
Brigades over Time

UPDATE: OBSERVATIONS ON THE CLINTON ACTIVE/RESERVE-MIX DECISIONS

Our study was concluded in 1992. It received significant praise from members of Congress and was widely read by senior military personnel and civilians. Shortly thereafter, President Clinton was elected, and the new administration began its own major review of defense programs, called the Bottom-Up Review (BUR) (Aspin, 1993). Its results were released in the fall of 1993. Although we cannot assess its conclusions in detail, because many of the details are not yet publicly available, we can nonetheless make a number of observations based on our 1992 study.

In many ways, the BUR incorporates and extends the analytic structure discussed above, e.g., the use of scenarios as a planning tool (Aspin, 1993:14). In some ways it is a logical continuation of U.S. military policy, but in others it departs from prior concepts in very significant ways.

Changing Roles and Missions

Starting with the defining purpose of active and reserve forces, the BUR breaks with the past by formally recognizing the nonconflict missions of the National Guard. Specifically, it apparently commits the Clinton administration to "provide [the Army National Guard and other Army reserve components with the] added capability to respond to external conflicts *and to support civil authorities at home*" (Aspin, 1993:94, emphasis added); e.g., "Substantial numbers of reserves must be available during both peacetime and wartime to support civil authorities in responding to domestic crises."

While the BUR confirms the importance of maintaining a forward, overseas presence and planning for two MRCs, the Clinton administration now includes "peacekeeping, peace enforcement and other intervention operations" and has dropped reconstitution from what were the elements of regional defense strategy. Similarly, the BUR reinforces and extends the notion of initial and decisive response forces into "four phases of U.S. combat operations," which now include providing forces for a postwar stability phase (Aspin, 1993:16–17). Continuing the basic framework of the analysis is important because, as our simulation analysis showed, the timing of the decisive (now third) phase of combat is critical in determining if Army reserve *combat* forces can be made ready in time to participate in the battle to "decisively defeat the enemy."

Particularly noteworthy is that the BUR also seems to initiate an important change in the respective roles of active and reserve forces. The BUR contemplates ten *all-active* Army divisions and seems to have deemphasized the role of the reserves in providing combat forces for, at least, the first MRC. For example, according to the BUR, the programmed ten all-active Army divisions would be sufficient to

> allow us to carry forward with confidence our strategy of being able to fight and win two major regional conflicts nearly simultaneously. However, it leaves little other active force structure to provide other overseas presence or to conduct peacekeeping or other lower-intensity operations if we have to fight two MRCs at once. If such tasks become necessary or if either MRC did not evolve as we anticipated, *then we might be required to activate significant numbers of reserve component forces* (Aspin, 1993:30, emphasis added).

The BUR argues that reserve combat units can "provide forces to supplement active divisions, should more ground combat power be needed to deter or fight a second MRC. . . . [i.e.,] If mobilized early during a conflict, brigade-sized units could provide extra security and flexibility if a second contingency arose while the first was still going on." [21]

---

[21]See Aspin (1993:22). At the National Guard Association Meeting Secretary Aspin said that the 37 National Guard brigades would "augment and reinforce the 10 active

This change seems to reject the second criterion for structuring forces—i.e., that some reserve combat forces should participate in any conflict to ensure that the commitment of forces truly represents the political will of the American people. This change is made explicit in the BUR's discussion of Defense Foundations: Reserve Component Forces.

> One of the most important tasks is to define explicitly the roles and missions we expect the reserve components to perform in the new security environment. During regional contingencies, Guard and reserve forces will continue to pro- vide—as they have in the past—significant support forces, many of which would deploy in the early days of a conflict. Reserve component combat forces will both augment and reinforce deployed active forces and backfill for active forces deployed to a contingency from other critical regions.[22]

A Further Look at Reserve-Component Forces in the BUR

In many ways, the BUR Army structure is a hybrid of several alternatives reviewed by the RAND Force Mix Study. The BUR incorporates the all- roundup feature of the Enhanced Active Army alternative and many of the re- forms incorporated into the RAND/LMI alternative. Specifically, the BUR report acknowledges that during the Gulf War, the National Guard combat brigades needed more postmobilization training than expected. It recognizes the need for readiness divisions—called Training Commands in the Force Mix Study—"to assist with the training of reserve component units during peace- time and crisis" (Aspin, 1993:95), but it makes no mention of the number of these that would be available and whether this number could train reserve units at the rate required by the deployment goals. The BUR also introduces a new concept for the premobilization preparations of units during a period of strate- gic warning. The BUR continues the Title XI reforms, but does not pick up on lower-echelon integration as a means to reduce postmobilization training requirements and reduce train-up times.

One unique feature of the BUR is the commitment to 15 enhanced-readi- ness Army National Guard brigades that will be "organized and resourced so that they can be mobilized, trained and deployed more quickly . . . to be able to reinforce active component units in a crisis. The goal is to have these brigades ready to begin deployment in 90 days" (Aspin, 1993:94). While this

---

Army divisions we plan, and supply support forces needed to sustain them in crisis and war." (Les Aspin, "Prepared Remarks at the National Guard Association Conference," Biloxi, Mississippi, October 11, 1993, p. 4.)

[22]See Aspin (1993:91). The BUR does, however, see a new mission for the Army National Guard and Reserve forces to "share the burden" of conducting peace opera- tions and rotational forces during an extended crisis.

is stated as a goal, in many ways it seems inconsistent with (1) the ability of a relatively small number of CONUS-based active Army divisions to provide enhanced training during peacetime, e.g., training on the order of that provided the pilot units of the Army's Bold Shift initiative,[23] (2) programmed post-mobilization training resources,[24] and (3) projected lift availability in the "90-day period" to transport these units overseas. Accordingly, if fully implemented, the BUR's 45 "ready" brigade-size units—30 active and 15 reserve—that would be ready within 90 days after initial mobilization would far exceed the U.S. ability to lift them and their support. Given these limitations and the high cost of making National Guard combat brigades available so quickly, a more phased approach to a smaller number of reserve combat units may be appropriate.

The BUR and Other Force Mix Options

While many of the details of the BUR are not yet available, the RAND/LMI team did consider how it would spend a budget of about the same size as the BUR's—approximately 10 percent lower than the Bush defense program that was planned for the latter part of the decade.[25] This Reduced-Budget Alternative provides for ten active divisions, the same number as the BUR, but three of the divisions are rounded out with National Guard companies or battalions. It provides a total of 25 National Guard brigades, compared with "about 37 brigades" in the BUR force structure. In peacetime it has six National Guard division headquarters. It has five "training commands" to provide for simultaneous training of a like number of brigades. It shifts 34,000 combat service support and combat support troops from the

---

[23]An Army-sponsored RAND study of Bold Shift 1992 found that active-component support of National Guard brigades ranged from 15,000 man-days to 25,000 man-days per brigade. Moreover, this demand was not evenly spaced over a year and represented a significant peak load problem for the Army. The BUR does note the need for "readiness divisions" to "provide the peacetime and post-mobilization training assistance needed by reserve component combat and support divisions" (Aspin, 1993:95). These "divisions" have not yet been programmed.

[24]The Force Mix Study estimated that it would take 5000 personnel, equally split between active and reserve personnel, to train two National Guard combat brigades in peace and after mobilization. The BUR sees a requirement for 15 enhanced brigades *ready to begin deployment in 90 days*. See Appendix E, "Concept for Trainer Commands to Train Reserve Roundout Brigades," in NDRI (1992:316–321).

[25]One area *not* analyzed by the Force Mix Study was the implications of "peacekeeping, peace enforcement and other intervention operations" on the structure and mix of active and reserve forces. Therefore, the following discussion considers *only* the requirements to win two nearly simultaneous MRCs.

active Army to Army reserve components. This change, in particular, might not be possible if the Army is engaged in large-scale or frequent peacekeeping, peace enforcement, or other intervention operations. In total, this alternative provides for an active Army of 475,000 people, (20,000 less than the Clinton administration's FY 1995 budget) with 635,000 Army reserve-component personnel (60,000 more than the Clinton administration's FY 1995 budget).[26]

As shown in Figure 10, in this alternative, forward presence forces in Europe consist of one division (two active-component heavy brigades stationed in Europe, an allied brigade, and a U.S. reserve-component brigade stationed in CONUS). The crisis response forces contain only two specialized divisions (airborne and air assault). We maintained the roundout structure with integration at the company or battalion level. Only two heavy reserve roundup brigades are depicted under the early reinforcement forces, to reflect the smaller force stationed in Europe and associated lower requirement for roundup brigades.

One heavy and one light reserve division in the strategic reserves are annotated with a (–) to indicate the absence of one of the roundup brigades associated with each of these formations. Support forces associated with these units have been sized as if the divisions had a full complement of brigades to provide a slightly more robust support structure in this alternative than would otherwise be the case.

This alternative, as illustrated in Figure 11, is potentially better matched to available training-base capacity and is more consistent with available lift than the BUR is.

THE UTILITY OF TIME-PHASED, REQUIREMENTS-BASED PLANNING

In this paper we have shown the utility of time-phased, requirements-based planning for developing and assessing alternative force structures.[27] As the example of the Force Mix Study demonstrated, the process begins with identification of those factors that are most important in defining the alternatives. In this case, the initial requirements were defined by the Bush administration in the Defense Planning Guidance and redefined by the Clinton administration in the Bottom-Up Review. The BUR added requirements for peacekeeping and domestic missions to the requirement of two major regional contingencies

---

[26]However, 47,000 of the 60,000 are in a reserve-component personnel account rather than in units.

[27]In the study, however, we treated strategic lift as a constraint. A broader study could have considered trading off increases or decreases in lift and various active/reserve options.

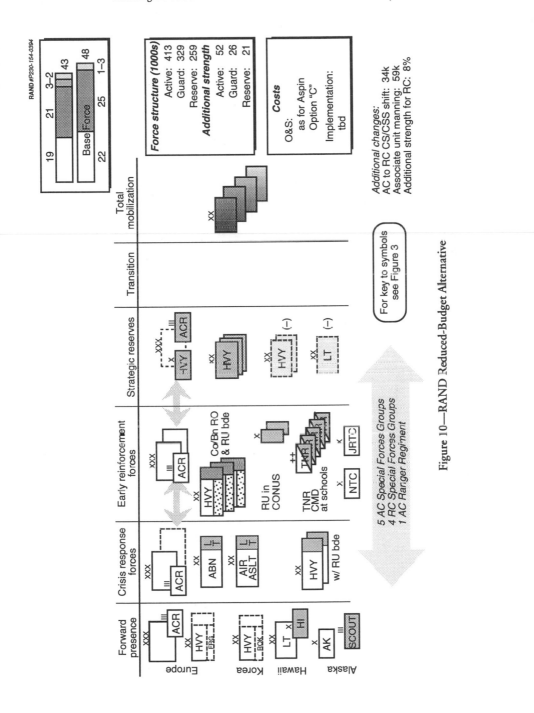

Figure 10—RAND Reduced-Budget Alternative

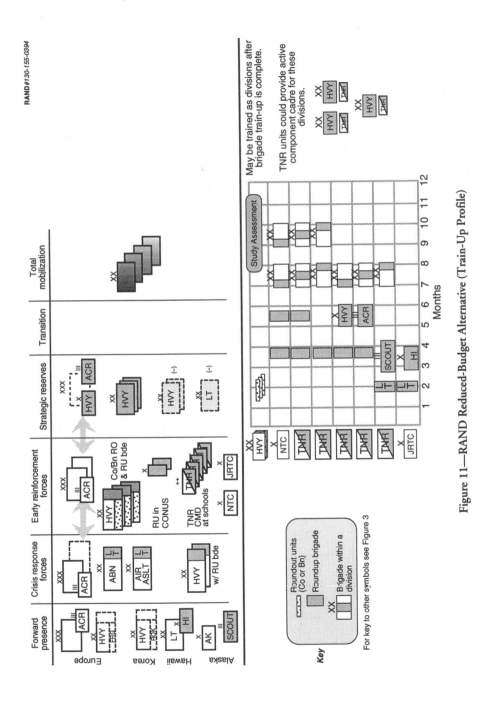

Figure 11—RAND Reduced-Budget Alternative (Train-Up Profile)

first developed in the DPG. While these new requirements will be the subject of future study, the MRC requirement is reasonably well understood and lends itself to time-phased scenario analysis and computer simulations. These computer simulations provide the basis (assuming extensive sensitivity analysis) for defining the demand for future military forces. There are, however, many alternative ways that the demand can be met. We have shown how the critical and time-consuming period of postmobilization training depends on the type and level of integration and how these factors structure the options that were presented to decisionmakers at the end of the Force Mix Study.

As our discussion of the BUR indicates, many elements of the basic framework described in this paper are being used today to fashion the Clinton administration's force structure. We expect that they will continue to be highly relevant to future discussions of the active/reserve mix.

BIBLIOGRAPHY

Aspin, Les (1992a), *Alternatives, Supplemental Material,* U.S. House of Representatives, Armed Services Committee, March 24.

——— (1992b), "Combat Power from the Reserve Component," memorandum to members of the House Armed Services Committee, May 7.

——— (1993), *The Bottom-Up Review,* Department of Defense, Washington, D.C.

Congressional Budget Office (1992), *Structuring U.S. Forces After the Cold War: Cost and Effects of Increased Reliance on the Reserves,* Washington, D.C.

Davis, Paul K. (1994a), "Institutionalizing Planning for Adaptiveness," in Davis (1994b).

——— (ed.) (1994b), *New Challenges for Defense Planning: Rethinking How Much Is Enough,* RAND, Santa Monica, CA.

Davis, Paul K., and Lou Finch (1993), *Defense Planning for the Post–Cold War Era: Giving Meaning to Flexibility, Adaptiveness, and Robustness of Capability,* RAND, Santa Monica, CA.

Department of Defense (1990), *Total Force Policy Report to the Congress,* December.

Duncan, Stephen M. (1992), *Statement of the Department of Defense Coordinator for Drug Enforcement Policy and Support,* Hearing before the Subcommittee on Investigations, House Armed Services Committee, April 29.

Ensslin, Major General Robert F. (1992), *Public Policy Dimensions of Base Force and Reconstitution Strategy for the National Guard,* Adjutants General Association of the United States, February 1.

Laird, Melvin (1970), *Support for Guard and Reserve Forces,* Department of Defense Memorandum, August 21.

Lippiatt, Thomas F., J. Michael Polich, and Ronald Sortor (1992), *Post-Mobilization Training of Army Reserve Component Combat Units,* RAND, Santa Monica, CA.

National Defense Research Institute (NDRI) (1992), *Assessing the Structure and Mix of Future Active and Reserve Forces: Final Report for the Secretary of Defense,* RAND, Santa Monica, CA.

Nunn, Sam (1992), "Forging Civil-Military Cooperation for Community Regeneration," floor speech, *Congressional Record,* June 23.

Powell, General Colin L. (1992), *The National Military Strategy 1992,* Joint Staff, Department of Defense, Washington, D.C.

Schlesinger, James (1973), Department of Defense Memorandum, August 23.

Sims, W. H. (1992), *USMC Active and Reserve Force Structure and Mix Study, Vol. III,* CNA Research Memorandum 92-185, Center for Naval Analyses, Alexandria, VA.

Sorley, Lewis (1991), "Creighton Abrams and the Active-Reserve Integration in Wartime," *Parameters,* Summer.

Tilson, John, Stan Horowitz, and Merle Roberson (1992), *Alternative Approaches to Organizing, Training and Assessing Army and Marine Corps Units,* Institute for Defense Analyses, Alexandria, VA, November.

U.S. House of Representatives (1991), National Defense Authorization Act for Fiscal Years 1992 and 1993; *Conference Report,* Report 102-311, Sec. 402.

Chapter 21

STRATEGIC MOBILITY IN THE POST–COLD WAR ERA

David Kassing

Strategic mobility is taking on increasing importance in national security planning. DoD has major programs underway to remedy the most glaring deficiencies revealed during recent deployments. Analysis supports the acquisition of air and sealift to improve early force closures. Analysis also shows that programs to acquire lift should be accompanied by management actions to ensure that all lift can be used effectively. In particular, DoD needs mechanisms to better match planned lift with the size and structure of the forces to be deployed. DoD should also allocate resources to maintain access to civilian-owned ships and aircraft that are useful to DoD. Finally, DoD needs to improve information and command-and-control systems so that all lift resources can be put to the best use in deployment operations.

INTRODUCTION

The United States is the only nation with the capability to move large forces quickly and support them in distant contingencies. This capability to deploy rapidly and sustain forces at long distances is a key attribute of U.S. "superpower" status.

In the post–Cold War world, mobility is taking on greater importance. Emerging military plans are increasing reliance on forces based in the United States to respond to regional contingencies. Strategic mobility forces allow the United States to deploy military power to distant crises that cannot be resolved by diplomacy alone. They enable the United States to contribute to peacekeeping and peace enforcement, carry out humanitarian assistance, and provide relief in natural disasters. Mobility forces enable the United States to support international coalitions or to act unilaterally if conditions require.

Recognizing the fundamental importance of mobility, the Department of Defense is giving increased attention and funding to programs that enhance the ability to deploy and sustain U.S. forces in distant contingencies. This paper analyzes issues that DoD must face in transforming mobility forces from a Cold War posture to one shaped to meet the needs of uncertain future regional contingencies, peacekeeping operations, and humanitarian missions.

At the most general level, the conclusion is that appropriate ship and aircraft procurement programs are underway. These actions remedy the most obvious shortfalls and satisfy the most vocal constituencies. But to realize the full benefit of expensive lift programs, further, less obvious changes are needed. DoD must adapt its mobility planning and management procedures to reflect a total mobility-systems perspective for post–Cold War operations. Many in DoD believe it already has, and changes are indeed being made in many mobility organizations and processes. However, these changes generally reflect local concerns and initiatives rather than the necessary end-to-end, top-down perspective that would be consistent with the new priority being given to mobility. This paper addresses some additional needed changes: management actions to match force readiness and lift capacity, new incentives for civilian participants, and improvements to information, intelligence, and command-and-control systems. Such improvements can make mobility more responsive and more efficient, but they cannot provide answers to the difficult question of "how much mobility is enough" to provide U.S. leaders with military options for an uncertain post–Cold War world.

This paper begins with a review of mobility forces and their employment in recent operations. Then it examines four of the most important planning and management issues that emerge from this review.

MOBILITY FORCES AND OPERATIONS

The Mobility Force Structure

Strategic mobility forces, like most U.S. military capabilities, are planned to meet the demanding requirements of major regional contingencies. In such contingencies, ground forces, and particularly the Army, provide the bulk of the equipment and personnel (70 to 80 percent) for the mobility forces to deliver. Though smaller in cargo volume, Air Force wings and squadrons have special requirements for timely deployment, including aerial refueling and other enroute support. Battle groups and other U.S. Navy operations impose a small demand for the services of strategic mobility forces.

U.S. mobility operations employ a well-established set of coordinated actions. In normal times, most U.S. forces are based in the continental United States. When called to deploy, most Army force equipment is sent to the area of the contingency on sealift, and the soldiers are flown over later to "marry up" with the equipment as it arrives. If equipment has been appropriately prepositioned in the contingency area, only the troops and some specialized equipment must be flown to the theater. Since the mid-1980s, the Marine Corps has had three brigades' worth of unit equipment and supplies prepositioned on ships—the Maritime Prepositioning Ship (MPS) program.

Personnel are flown to contingencies to use equipment on the MPS. The Marines can also deploy a full division on amphibious assault shipping, although it takes several weeks to assemble the shipping for a division-sized Marine Expeditionary Force (MEF). Air Force units generally fly their own aircraft to the crisis area—an operation that often involves substantial aerial refueling operations. Aircraft squadrons also require airlift to move supply, maintenance, and other logistic support personnel and equipment to the theater.

This style of mobility operations has focused planners' attention on three main parts of the mobility force structure: airlift, sealift, and prepositioning. Airlift programs include specialized military aircraft (C-17s, C-5s, C-141s, C-130s, and KC-10s) designed to accomplish unique military tasks that civilian air transports cannot be expected to do. DoD airlift programs also envision using civilian transports where they can do the job. Sealift programs are similarly structured; they include specialized sealift ships operated by the government (Fast Sealift Ships (FSS) and the Ready Reserve Force (RRF)) and plans for tapping civilian shipping when it may be needed. Earlier prepositioning programs (POMCUS programs, standing for Prepositioning of Materiel Configured in Unit Sets) emphasized storing military equipment on the ground in areas where crucial national interests were threatened (such as Western Europe). During the 1980s, these land-based prepositioning activities were supplemented by new programs to store equipment and supplies aboard ships that could be stationed near likely trouble spots. Taken together, airlift, sealift, and prepositioning programs consume the lion's share of the funds DoD allocates to mobility.

The advantages and problems of each of the three elements of the mobility force structure have become well recognized. Airlift programs can provide rapid response, but their great expense limits their total capacity. Sealift programs are less expensive and can deliver large volumes of heavy forces, but they are relatively slow in making initial deliveries. Prepositioning allows the United States to get large and heavy forces into action quickly, but only if the warehouse (land-based or floating) is located close to the combat zone.[1]

This traditional focus on the "mobility triad" highlights the expensive intercontinental or "over-the-oceans" portion of deployment operations. More comprehensive planning views mobility as a total system using an "end-to-end"

---

[1]Advancing technology may, eventually and at great expense, alter these fundamental relationships. High-speed surface craft, such as Wing-in-Ground-Effect vehicles or surface-effects ships, could shorten the time it takes to deliver large volumes of heavy military materiel. Currently, these vehicles are severely handicapped by technological risks and affordability problems. In any event, they would never match the speed of initial response that aircraft will continue to provide.

or "fort-and-factory-to-foxhole" perspective. From this perspective, mobility includes moving units and supplies from bases, warehouses, and factories to the seaports and airfields where equipment and supplies are loaded on ships and airplanes. It calls attention to trucking and rail capabilities (including facilities at DoD installations for outloading units, specialized rail cars for hauling tanks, and unique materiel-handling equipment), staging areas and berthing spaces at U.S. seaports, and facilities for DoD to use in handling containerized cargo.

Equally important, an end-to-end perspective calls attention to the mobility operations needed to receive forces in the theater, move them forward to operational areas, and keep them resupplied with fuel, ammunition, food, water, spare parts, and many other types of supplies. Much of this capability must itself be deployable on a schedule that gets it to the theater before large forces begin to arrive. Reception and forward-movement operations employ specialized materiel-handling equipment, considerable trucking, and trained personnel. In-theater operations also need to be linked reliably to deployment command-and-control systems.

Making such complex end-to-end mobility operations work efficiently and responsively requires extensive management or "command and control," in military parlance. The command-and-control system must coordinate the moves of the deploying forces with the availability of the needed transportation. It must be able to plan deployments as well as time allows, monitor the status of ongoing deployment operations, and communicate changes to all affected participants. DoD employs the Joint Operation Planning and Execution System (JOPES) operating through the Worldwide Military Command and Control System (WWMCCS) for these management functions. The services and the transportation operating commands have developed dozens of their own command-and-control systems for meeting their more specialized needs and responsibilities.

The deploying forces themselves are obviously an integral part of strategic mobility activities. The readiness of the forces must be balanced with both the needs of the theater commanders and the availability of airlift and sealift. Information on size, composition, and capabilities of deploying forces is a critical input to mobility planning.

Recent Experience in Deploying U.S. Forces

U.S. forces have been successfully deployed several times in the last five years. Operation Just Cause, in December 1989, began with an airdrop of paratroopers into several areas in Panama. Their operations, and those of other U.S. forces already in Panama, were supported by airlift from the United

States. The massive force deployments to the Gulf region for Operations Desert Shield and Desert Storm (ODS) drew on almost every element of U.S. mobility capabilities (as well as chartered U.S. and foreign-flag shipping) and taught many valuable lessons. Since the Gulf War, mobility forces have supported humanitarian operations in northern Iraq, Bangladesh, the former Soviet republics, and, most prominently, Somalia. They have also assisted communities stricken by natural disasters in Guam, Florida, Hawaii, and India. Mobility planners have worked through the details of deploying peace-keeping forces to Bosnia.

Although each of these efforts has taught valuable lessons to the strategic mobility community, the scale and scope of deployments to Saudi Arabia provide the clearest evidence on mobility performance and problems.[2] Mobility systems eventually got the job done; the investments and organizational changes made during the 1980s clearly paid off.[3]

In spite of those improvements, airlift and sealift performance was significantly less than had been expected. Figure 1 compares actual sealift performance with planned deliveries. It shows sealift deliveries during the first 80 days of Desert Shield deployments and compares them with the performance anticipated in a detailed joint deployment plan prepared and validated by the U.S. Central Command in mid-September 1990 (five weeks after deployments started). Such plans changed frequently and dramatically earlier in ODS, but by mid-September the operators had developed a fairly good appreciation of their needs, and the magnitude of the changes had diminished. As Figure 1 shows, sealift deliveries lagged the plan by two to three weeks.

---

[2] *Getting Military Power to the Desert* (Kassing, 1992) provides an overview of deployment operations during the Gulf crisis and highlights some of the key lessons learned. The historian of the U.S. Transportation Command has prepared a comprehensive report on Desert Shield/Desert Storm transportation operations (Mathews and Holt, forthcoming). The *Strategic Deployment Review Study* (Vance, 1992) analyzes Army deployment operations and compares them with prewar assumptions. A careful assessment of airlift performance during Desert Shield/Storm is provided in *An Assessment of Strategic Airlift Operational Efficiency* (Lund, Berg, and Replogle, 1993). Kassing (1993) provides an description and analysis of initial (December 1992–January 1993) Army deployments to Somalia for Operation Restore Hope.

[3] In particular, the success of the ODS mobility operations was the legacy of earlier decisions to create the U.S. Central Command (CENTCOM) and the U.S. Transportation Command (USTRANSCOM), to increase strategic air and sealift, and to establish afloat and maritime prepositioning programs. Airlift provided under the Civil Reserve Air Fleet (CRAF) program delivered some 500,000 passengers without serious problems. Also, creative and productive innovations were made during the operation. The Special Mid-East Shipping Agreement and Desert Express are two prominent examples.

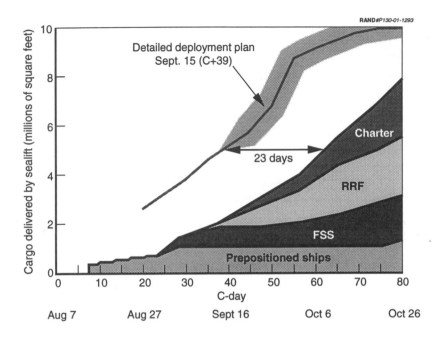

Figure 1—During Desert Shield, Sealift Performance Lagged Plans

Figure 2, drawn from RAND work (Hura, Matsumura, and Robinson, 1993) compares the performance of airlift with expectations based on the sorts of planning factors used in airlift studies before Desert Shield.[4]   The initial projection was that airlift could deliver nearly 6000 tons a day to Saudi Arabia in an all-out effort.   Studies of deployment capabilities yielded similar estimates.   In Desert Shield, however, only a portion of the Civil Reserve Air Fleet (CRAF) was used initially, and only volunteer reservists could be used for the first few weeks.   Thus, the estimate was cut to about 2800 tons per day.   In actuality, airlift delivered an average of only 2300 tons per day during the first 54 days of operations.   Performance was lower because airfield capacity for airlift activities was limited, aircraft payloads were less than planned, and aircraft utilization rates fell short of expectations.   Later, when more airfield capacity was available, reserves were activated, more CRAF aircraft were called into service, and some cargo was carried from Europe (a shorter distance), airlift deliveries rose to 3600 tons a day, which was still well below the originally expected delivery rate.

---

[4]See Hura (1993:17–22) for additional analysis of airlift performance in Desert Shield.

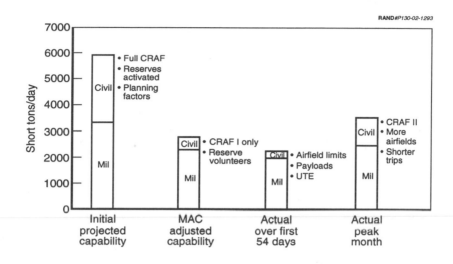

Figure 2—During Desert Shield/Storm, Airlift Performance Was Below Expectations

A second important observation on Desert Shield was that civilian transportation resources contributed significantly to the successful deployment and resupply operations. "Volunteer" civilian aircraft began operations on August 7th, well before CRAF was activated. By the end of the deployment, civilian aircraft had delivered 27 percent of air cargo and 64 percent of personnel closed in the theater. Contracted civilian-owned shipping—both U.S. flag and foreign flag—carried about 40 percent of the unit equipment delivered by ship, a similar proportion of ammunition deliveries, and essentially all resupply cargo sent by sea. Operations of some civilian aircraft and ships created minor, transient difficulties when air combat began in mid-January, but these were quickly overcome. Overall, civilian ships and aircraft performed well; their contributions were clearly vital to the success of Desert Shield/Desert Storm mobility operations.

A third key observation from Desert Shield/Desert Storm is that information and command-and-control systems contributed to deployment difficulties. The deployments were begun without a fully developed, "transportation feasible" deployment plan. Planners and operators quickly learned that elaborate command-and-control systems without the right information were not very useful. The construction of the first plan took several days longer than advertised. Priorities changed as CENTCOM's appreciation of the situation improved. Units often arrived for loading aboard ships and aircraft with different cargo, and generally more cargo, than planning data led transportation operators to expect. Many service and transportation command, control, and information systems could not be readily linked to each other or to JOPES, the key element of DoD's command-and-control system. Deployment databases were found to be unreliable. The resulting coordination problems between transportation operators and deploying units sometimes resulted in inefficient use of resources. Not enough trained JOPES operators were available; also, some installations lacked the equipment needed to use the system. The command system was unable to notify logisticians in the theater about the cargo and personnel aboard aircraft before they touched down in Saudi Arabia. While it is impossible to estimate a specific number to describe the cumulative impact of these problems, they certainly contributed to the lower-than-expected performance depicted in Figure 1.

Close students of deployment operations took away many, many more detailed lessons about such diverse topics as database accuracy, ship loading procedures, air base constraints, reserve force activation processes, expediting resupply actions, the use of containers, and the performance of maritime prepositioning ships. Movements within the United States had few problems. In contrast, reception operations were initially hampered by lack of deployed U.S. logistics services.[5] Distribution of resupply cargo was a continuing problem.

Since the Gulf War, U.S. mobility forces have been employed in support of many humanitarian and disaster relief activities in addition to routine military activities such as training and logistics operations. The most prominent of these, the deployments to Somalia for Operation Restore Hope, taught lessons about the problems of getting U.S. forces into regions where local facilities were poor or nonexistent. Though individually small—Restore Hope amounted to only about 5 percent of the Desert Shield/Storm deployment workload—the cumulative effect of multiple operations taxed the available active DoD capabilities, particularly airlift. The main lesson of the recent past is that relatively small but unpredictable demands have become a near-continuous "fact of life" for mobility planners and operators.

Facing the Future

Experience is a good teacher, but it is not, by itself, sufficient to provide the nation's leadership with the options needed in future contingencies. Operation Just Cause did not prepare deployment planners for Operation Desert Shield; and neither of those taught many of the lessons that would be

---

[5]Initial force reception operations relied on hired buses, local food supplies, contracted facilities and host nation labor, all "managed" by a few U.S. logisticians. Pagonis (1992: 82–83).

learned during Operation Restore Hope. Solving all the problems that emerged during these three operations would not necessarily prepare deployment capabilities for "near-simultaneous" contingencies in Southwest Asia and Korea. Planning carefully for that eventuality may not meet the needs of the next crisis requiring deployments of U.S. military power.

Determining how much mobility is enough cannot be derived from analysis alone. Because of the many fundamental uncertainties they face, mobility planners cannot prescribe the "right amount" of mobility for DoD to acquire. The uncertainties fall into three broad classes. First, there are uncertainties about the nature of future contingencies (the enemy forces, the availability and capability of facilities in the area, distances to the area and enroute bases, host nation capabilities, coalition forces and capabilities, and many more). A second class of uncertainties relates to the U.S. forces to be sent to the contingency (the size and composition of the forces, their readiness, their locations, etc.) Taken together, these two create uncertainties about the nature of the transportation capabilities the United States will need. Uncertainties about availability, readiness, and performance for both military and civilian transportation systems create the third class of uncertainties.

Although, in theory, sufficient mobility could be provided to hedge against all these eventualities, in practice that mobility posture would not be affordable. Drawing the line, deciding which specific risks to accept, determining how much lift is enough (and what to spend to acquire it) is ultimately a judgment call for top DoD leadership. The rest of this paper draws on recent research in RAND and elsewhere that casts light on major mobility planning issues.

Summary: Lessons for Post–Cold War Mobility Planning

Several issues emerge from this review of mobility forces and their performance in recent operations. First, the experience of Desert Shield/Desert Storm suggests that U.S. capabilities for early deliveries need to be increased so that commanders can get the forces they need, when they need them. Second, the relationship between the size, capability, and readiness of the forces being deployed must be related to the structure and readiness of the mobility forces. Third, participation by civilian ships and aircraft contributes significantly to total deployment and sustainment capability. Fourth, mobility information and command-and-control systems must be improved to enable them to handle unpredicted and fast-breaking contingencies and humanitarian operations. Finally, although analysis can help inform decisions about required mobility capabilities, it cannot provide final answers. Each of these issues is examined below.

INCREASING LIFT CAPACITY

Estimating Lift Needs

Although Desert Shield deployments were successful, it has been widely recognized that future contingencies could be more demanding, particularly in the early stages. The three main sources of concern are:

1. Future opponents might not provide the United States with the luxury of several months to complete deployments.

2. The modern airfields and seaports in Saudi Arabia were better than might be available in other regions.[6]

3. Future opponents might be expected to develop new capabilities to oppose U.S. deployments.

The Clinton administration recognizes these problems and is strongly supporting major enhancement efforts that build on the efforts of the last decade. As a result, DoD has significant airlift, sealift, and maritime prepositioning programs in motion. These programs appear to be "roughly right" in addressing future DoD needs for strategic transportation capabilities.[7] The resulting mix of mobility forces will be responsive, flexible, and reasonably economical.

Several particular items are worth special mention. The Army has developed an "Army Strategic Mobility Plan" (ASMP) with a goal of having "three divisions 7500 nautical miles from the United States within 30 days" (Sullivan, 1993). This time is about half that needed to close the first three Army divisions in Desert Shield. The Army "Contingency Response Force" has been identified and is being trained, equipped, and supported to meet the stringent readiness requirements of the ASMP.

DoD plans also call for the acquisition of additional sealift and airlift. Plans include the acquisition of 19 large, medium-speed roll-on/roll-off ships for surge sealift and afloat prepositioning costing as much as $5 to $6 billion. Contracts have been let for some of these ships. Airlift programs have had another careful review. Procurement of the C-17 airlifter will be continued, although for a smaller force than the Bush administration planned (perhaps as

---

[6]The experience in deploying through the very limited infrastructure in Somalia during Operation Restore Hope added considerable weight to this concern.

[7]This does not mean that issues such as the number, speed, and employment of the planned ships or the capabilities and comparative advantage of the C-17 relative to alternative airlifters cannot be debated further. For example, the technical and management problems of the C-17 have been discussed for years, and this debate is likely to continue until the problems are clearly resolved or the program killed. Some such issues are discussed below. But the present DoD ship and aircraft acquisition programs address the main needs and appear to provide generally efficient and effective capabilities.

few as 40 rather than 120). In addition, a "nondevelopmental" aircraft may be acquired to meet accepted requirements for both operational flexibility and total airlift capacity. The total cost of the Clinton airlift program will be at least $12 billion for procurement. Taken together, these lift programs should enable DoD to realize the aims of the Army plan while also deploying substantial Marine and tactical air forces in a range of potential contingencies.

For the most part, these programs are based on the work of the Mobility Requirements Study (MRS), a DoD study led by the Joint Staff, which was largely completed in 1991.[8] Drawing on many of the lessons learned from Desert Shield/Storm, the study examined mobility force needs for major regional contingencies. The work began by using wargaming analyses to examine the effects of different force deliveries on the success U.S. forces had in achieving their objectives. The results showed that early closure of heavy ground forces and greater rapid reinforcement from the United States significantly enhanced mission performance. The study assessed several sorts of risk and recommended that DoD 20 acquire more large, medium-speed roll-on/roll-off sealift ships for use in prepositioning and surge deliveries. It also recommended expansion of the RRF and increasing the readiness of RRF ships. Another key insight from the MRS study was that reception constraints and airfield availability (both enroute and in the theater) limited U.S. force closures in some regions and that the C-17 significantly improved prospects for success in contingencies in those regions. This study has set the direction for most DoD mobility planning; its results have generally been adopted by the Clinton administration. Though the Bottom-Up Review did not directly examine airlift program issues, the MRS is being updated to reflect changes in planning assumptions, force structure, and lift system availabilities.

Developing CONUS Facilities

Mobility operations in the continental United States (CONUS) are less affected by shifting post–Cold War planning to regional contingencies than are the other links in strategic mobility. Moreover, deployments to Desert Shield/Storm did not reveal any major problems in CONUS lift. DoD downsizing, base closures and consolidations, and force drawdowns do create some new planning conditions. In general, though, there is little uncertainty about where Army, Navy, Marine Corps, and Air Force units will be based and which will be kept ready for early deployment. Similarly, there is little uncertainty

---

[8]The full study is classified, but see *Defense 92*, Rathbun (1992), Blair (1992), and, for a critical discussion, GAO (1993). The MRS built on a lengthy series of earlier studies that strengthened understanding of mobility tradeoffs, refined mobility models, and created extensive mobility databases.

about which seaports and airfields will be used to support force movements and sustainment operations.

The problem, then, is to ensure that CONUS facilities are brought into balance with other deployment capabilities. Resource planning to support deployment operations within CONUS is a service responsibility. Alhough this leg of mobility operations has received little public attention, the services have recognized the need to prepare their facilities to allow faster deployment operations in the future. The Army, in particular, has identified needs for additional rail cars, loading facilities, container facilities, port staging areas, and other deployment "infrastructure" items; it has funded initial improvements in these capabilities.

Adding Surge Sealift Capacity

Sealift ship acquisition began to gain momentum in 1993. Congress previously had appropriated $2.5 billion for sealift ship procurement, and DoD has recently moved ahead toward the MRS-recommended sealift posture.

The Navy has contracted for the conversion of five ships to better enable them to carry DoD cargoes. Contracts have also been let for the construction of two new large, medium-speed roll-on/roll-off ships (LMSRs); these contracts give the Navy options to procure an additional ten ships. If present plans to acquire a total of 19 ships are fulfilled, DoD should have them operational in the year 2001: 5 conversions and 14 newly built ships. As discussed below, 9 of the ships will be assigned to prepositioning the equipment of a heavy brigade and support force equipment at sea. The cost of acquiring the 11 ships for the surge sealift role should be in the neighborhood of $2.5 to $3.0 billion. These 11, combined with the existing 8 Fast Sealift Ships (FSS), provide sufficient capacity to enable the Army to meet the requirements for the early closure of two heavy divisions. These ships will be partially manned and kept in a high state of readiness.

The Maritime Administration (MARAD) has acquired 12 used roll-on/roll-off ships with the intent of adding them to the RRF and building it toward a goal of 140 ships. Another $15 million was appropriated for additional ship acquisitions in 1994 and MARAD expects $161 million in 1995. The RRF provides a low-cost surge capability for larger contingencies. Since much of this capability would be used only in the (rare) largest contingencies, it is sensible to acquire used rather than new ships.[9] It is also important that MARAD

---

[9]Minor contingencies and humanitarian operations may employ a small number of RRF ships on occasion. Because of cost considerations, however, other shipping (available charters and FSSs) are the preferred sealift for such operations.

funds RRF maintenance to ensure the fleet's readiness. As with the LSMRs and FSSs, the RRF roll-on/roll-off ships will be kept ready for deployment operations with partial crews aboard at all times.[10]

Adding Airlift Capabilities

The Clinton administration has worked through difficult, costly, and arguable decision issues about the C-17 program and its alternatives. The issues arose because the C-17 has been encountering technical, cost, and management problems. The ultimate capability of the program came into question, and Congress slowed its funding. Alternatives considered in the Pentagon included an extensive program to extend the useful life of the C-141, renewed production of C-5s, and acquisition of civilian aircraft (747s or DC-10s) modified for DoD purposes. Technical review indicated that the C-17's engineering problems could be corrected and that extending the service life of the C-141 was problematic.

The decision apparently is to accept at least 40 C-17s and to begin a program for a "nondevelopmental" aircraft.[11] A mix of the two would provide the nation with a limited "direct delivery" capability and meet total airlift goals at a smaller cost than a pure C-17 program. Moreover, the approach adopted provides strong incentives for the C-17 contractor to remedy promptly the program's management, cost, and technical problems. Although a buy of only 40 C-17s is what has been announced, the possibility of additional C-17 procurement is held open, provided that the contractor can overcome the program's several problems. The drawback of this approach is the initial handicap of high unit costs associated with low rate production and small total buys.

---

[10]The need to "round out" the manning of LSMR, FSS, and RRF roll-on/roll-off ships poses some manning issues, as does the need to provide crews for the other ships of the RRF. The projected decline in U.S.-flag shipping implies that manning a larger reserve fleet from a smaller U.S. mariner pool could become a real constraint on large-scale deployment operations such as those required by near-simultaneous regional contingencies. However, the experience of ODS (when foreign-flag ships with foreign crews performed well) suggests that foreign mariners can be employed with little risk, at least in the absence of enemy opposition. Nonetheless, DoD is, appropriately, considering reserve mariner program options as a preferred solution for manning any RRF ships activated.

[11]The nondevelopmental airlift aircraft might be either a "derivative" of an available commercial wide-body aircraft design or renewed procurement of the existing C-5 Galaxy airlifter. DoD expects to complete a competition examining the costs and capabilities of the nondevelopmental designs in 1995. The ability to meet military airlift requirements should be an important standard.

Analysis shows that the preferred airlift aircraft depends on scenario conditions—airfield constraints, in particular.[12] As a recent RAND study put it, "Airlift capacity is highly sensitive to basing constraints."[13] The C-17 is designed for short runways and to allow efficient ground operations. As a result, the C-17 has the potential of using more airfields and making deliveries nearer the battlefield, i.e., direct deliveries. The C-17 is smaller, has a shorter turn radius, can back up, and can unload faster. As a result, it can also make more efficient use of available parking area.

Another RAND analysis (Gebman, Batchelder, and Poehlmann, forthcoming) focuses directly on the desired airlift mix. This work highlights the differing abilities of airlift aircraft to use the world's airfields. The ability to use airfields depends on the strength or weight-bearing capacity of the runways as well as on their length. The C-17 has an apparent advantage because it can land at much shorter airfields than the C-5 or large civilian aircraft. Much of that advantage disappears, however, when the strength of runways is considered; many shorter runways are not strong enough to bear the C-17's weight in repeated operations.

The same analysis considered the performance of different mixes in a single major contingency. The results showed that if runway length and ramp space (but not runway strength) are the effective constraints on airlift operations, the C-17 is the cost-effective choice for increasing U.S. airlift capability—if it performs as planned. Thus, the fully capable C-17 provides airlift operators greater flexibility than the alternatives to cope with many airfield constraints. On the other hand, the same analysis shows that if airfield constraints are not limiting in future contingencies (as in developed economies such as Saudi Arabia, Korea, and Europe), a military version of commercial aircraft, not the C-17, provides the least-cost way of adding to the tonnage airlift delivers.

Since neither the location of future contingencies calling for airlift nor the airfield capacities available for airlift operations can be confidently predicted, a mixed program of C-17s and modified commercial aircraft yields a robust capability. The cost to complete the mixed program such as DoD is reportedly aiming at should be in the range of $12 to $15 billion in acquisition costs.

---

[12]Airfield constraints may be encountered anywhere that U.S. forces may be deployed. They arise from three different causes: (1) physical limitations such as runway length, parking space, refueling facilities, materiel-handling equipment, etc.; (2) competition from other users of scarce airfield resources, in particular, the operations of tactical aircraft; and (3) limitations imposed by local political authorities (both at the destination and enroute).

[13]Bowie, Frostic, Lewis, Lund, Ochmanek, and Propper (1993:35).

As amply demonstrated in Somalia, the C-130 allows access to airfields where other aircraft (including the C-17) cannot go. A set of upgrades to engines and landing gear can increase this advantage. It would be imprudent to halt C-130 production on the assumption that the C-17 will provide sufficient tactical lift.

Enhancing Prepositioning

Maritime prepositioning for Army unit equipment (a brigade of armor and transportation, communication, engineering, intelligence, and military police units) is a new element in the mobility posture. This program responds directly to the MRS finding that early closure of heavy forces, when added to light Army forces, Marine Corps expeditionary forces, and tactical air, significantly reduces the risk of an enemy breakthrough on the ground.

DoD is planning to use nine of the new roll-on/roll-off ships (LMSRs) to preposition a brigade of armor and support equipment at sea so that it could be sent to either the Persian Gulf or an Asian contingency. The procurement cost of these ships will be between $2.0 and $2.5 billion. The equipment to be stored on the ships will be drawn from existing Army inventories. DoD is also implementing an interim program to preposition Army equipment—drawn from war reserve stocks in Europe—in chartered ships. Ship loading began in late 1993. The cargoes will be transferred to the new LMSRs as they are delivered in the late 1990s.

Maritime prepositioning issues go beyond ship procurement. Ship loading plans, operating patterns, and maintenance cycles must be shaped to ensure high readiness for varied contingencies. Maritime prepositioning capabilities need to be melded into Army training and exercise plans. It is also important to note that there are airlift requirements associated with maritime prepositioned Army units, for both personnel and cargo that cannot be stored at sea.

Finally, plans and operations for Army, Air Force, and Marine Corps prepositioning must be fully coordinated. Either airfield, airlift, or seaport constraints could prevent the simultaneous closure of all DoD prepositioned forces. In that case, the theater commander must decide which force he wants delivered first and provide guidance to the mobility forces.

The Clinton administration is also planning to increase and adapt prepositioning on land. The Bottom-Up Review (Aspin, 1993) aims at prepositioning two brigade sets of equipment in Southwest Asia: one would be placed in Kuwait; the location of the second is being negotiated. Consideration is also being given to prepositioning more equipment in South Korea.

Planning Force Reception Capabilities

Mobility operations cannot be considered complete until the arriving units are reassembled and ready for the theater commander. Whether delivered by prepositioning or from the United States, arriving forces must be unloaded, organized into operating units, armed, fueled, and readied to perform their missions. Their personnel must also be housed, fed, and otherwise provided for while their units are being reassembled.

Force reception is arguably the most difficult mobility operation and the one most affected by uncertainties about future contingencies. Operational planning for reception depends on the missions to be undertaken, the expected enemy course of action, local geography and environment, available host nation support, and the time available to accomplish the deployments.[14] Resource planning for reception is largely in the hands (and budgets) of the services; their resource planners must provide capabilities that hedge against a wide range of potential circumstances.

Planned prepositioning helps with this problem. U.S. Marine Corps MPSs carry a balanced mix of combat and force service support equipment as well as sufficient consumable materiel (including water production capabilities) to sustain the force for at least 30 days. Moreover, the Marines have organized and trained specialized units to deploy early and accomplish the reception operation.

Having learned from recent operations, Army prepositioning plans envision similar operations. Prepositioned equipment will be kept ready and periodically exercised. Army prepositioning ships will carry the transportation and materiel-handling equipment and supplies needed early in force reception operations. The Army's plans include prepositioning watercraft and other Logistics-Over-the-Shore (LOTS) programs in the expectation that some future contingencies will not enjoy sufficient seaport capacity. Planning for the Army's Contingency Response Force includes a broad and balanced range of support units.

The Air Force reception problem is different only in degree. Although most Air Force units can fly directly to their intended operating bases, the units still require housing, engineering, medical, supply, and other logistics support as they arrive and prepare for combat. Much of this support can be flown in as well, but planned sortie rates imply high rates of consumption for ammunition and fuel. The Air Force has been able to preposition munitions and some support equipment ashore in some theaters (and more at sea). However, there is

---

[14]Consider, for example, the contrast between conditions in Somalia and those in Saudi Arabia. Each of the factors mentioned differed significantly between these two recent deployments.

generally a requirement to transport these supplies from the prepositioning sites to the operating airfields that depends on the same uncertain scenario factors as affect the other services.

Joint coordination in resource planning for force reception is particularly difficult. Each service naturally gives first priority to supporting its own force deployments, although attempts are made to ensure that cross-service support is also prepared. Continued progress toward joint logistics planning is vital to assuring coordinated procurement and readiness for force reception capabilities. This is an important challenge to the joint community.

Summary

DoD is taking major steps to improve capabilities for rapid deployments. Prepositioning will be increased, new ships have been ordered, and new airlift is being procured. These programs address one of the main lessons learned from the Desert Shield/Storm experience. Although it is likely that some will quibble about the size and speed of the new ships, the mix and cost of the airlift program, and the appropriate mix and siting of prepositioned forces, the central thrust of these programs is on the mark. The main issue is affordability: how to balance the budgets for mobility with the budgets needed for improvements in other important DoD capabilities.

MATCHING LIFT PROGRAMS WITH DEPLOYING UNITS

Efficiency in mobility operations requires matching transportation to the forces and supplies to be sent. This problem occurs when deployment operations are being executed, as well as when future mobility forces are being planned and procured. Failure to achieve the proper balance in either process results in unfortunate surprises and disappointing performance.

Matching Lift and Units During Deployments

Deploying units tend to treat lift as a "free good" available in whatever quantity they need. Earlier it was noted that units shipping out to Desert Shield/Storm often arrived for transportation with more cargo than the lift system expected. The result had to be a change in someone's plans. The units either had to leave something behind or, more often, had to accept delayed closure into Saudi Arabia. Alternatively, the transportation forces had to change assignments of lift (at some cost in lift system performance) and thereby disappoint another user waiting somewhere else for scheduled lift. In any case, performance suffered.

What can be done to improve processes for balancing cargo and lift when deployment operations are being executed? Better communication, more liaison, and improved databases lead toward the needed convergence of expectations. But stronger steps are called for. One promising approach would be to set and enforce deployment cargo constraints or lift budgets. All potential deploying units would be assigned cargo weight, footprint, and volume limits for contingencies. Assignments of airlift and sealift in contingencies would be consistent with the assigned limits. Deploying unit commanders would be allowed latitude in selecting specific equipment to ship within their allowance so they can make last-minute adjustments ("tailoring") to the needs of the specific contingency. To make good choices, the commander would need a good understanding of his mission and the conditions he will encounter.

Deployment constraints should be regularly reviewed and revised as necessary by joint actions of area commanders in chief (CINCs), USTRANSCOM, and the services. Revisions would reflect changes in missions, threats, and technology. The process of negotiating revisions would stress that lift is not a "free good." The same process would help identify the case for longer-run solutions such as procuring additional ships or aircraft.

Such a system of lift budgets has several benefits beyond improved coordination in executing deployments. Faced with a constraint on their deployment, operational planners would be induced to make intelligent use of the lift provided by the planning and programming system. The process of changing allocation (within a fixed overall total) would help identify the contributions provided by the additional lift.

Matching Lift and Units When Planning

Planning lift procurement entails a similar problem. Tactical air wings and Army units can be expected to change as time passes. Their size and composition change as the threats to be faced change and as technology makes new capabilities available. In particular, the weight and "footprint" of major Army units have tended to grow monotonically.

Table 1 provides evidence on recent growth in the weight and footprint of Army divisions.[15] The entries in the table are annual growth rates for either the weight or footprint in the "Table of Organization and Equipment" (TOE) of standard Army divisions. Though there is considerable variation, the weight of all units grew at least a rate of 4 percent a year. At that rate, total weight

---

[15]Individual entries in Table 1 were calculated by comparing data from Military Traffic Management Command (1991) with the 1989 edition of the same publication.

Table 1

Recent Growth in the Size of Army Divisions

Type of Division	Average Annual Growth Rate 1987–1990	
	In Weight	In Footprint
Air Assault	8.8%	5.2%
Armored	8.4	2.6
Infantry	4.6	0.4
Light Infantry	4.5	3.1
Mechanized	9.0	1.6

would double in 18 years. The variation in footprint growth rates is even greater, but the average annual rates of increase were at least 2.5 percent. The trends in growth of unit weight can be traced back as far as 1969.[16]

Unless lift system planners accurately anticipate the changes in the size of the units, future lift systems will be asked to carry, commanders will be surprised and disappointed in the event of future deployments. But the effects of shortsighted planning will also be felt at higher levels as long-planned lift capabilities turn out to be inadequate. Growth in the footprint of Army cargo for 10 years at a 2 percent annual rate would require four more LSMRs to deliver the Army's Contingency Response Force on the schedule the Army's strategic mobility plan envisions. This increase is 20 percent over the planned buy of 20 ships. If growth continues at the higher rates recently experienced, even more shipping would be needed. The procurement cost of these added ships would be at least $1 billion, if Army unit growth were anticipated and the added lift programmed.

Some would argue, however, that technology will soon allow us to reverse the trend of the last 20 years and reduce the amount of materiel the U.S. must deploy to prevail on the battlefield for major contingencies. New vehicles may be smaller and individually more lethal. Thus, the number of systems to be deployed to overcome particular threats can be reduced, and each one would

---

[16]There are several explanations for the steady growth. For one, the need to counter increasingly sophisticated enemy forces led to increases in armor, sensors, and firepower in weapon systems. M1 tanks, Bradley fighting vehicles, and high-mobility multipurpose wheeled vehicles (HMMWVs) are all larger and heavier than the systems they replace. For another, Army force development processes have not considered deployment constraints. For a third, Army decisions on division structure are seldom challenged by outsiders, although Army support force needs have been. Under this circumstance, some capabilities might migrate from the support to the divisional structure.

use less transportation capacity. Higher lethality from precision-guided weapons implies smaller needs for munitions resupply, so logistics deployments can be cut. Modern communications and reliable transportation can permit "support from afar" so other rear-area force deployments can be reduced as well.[17] Advances in microelectronics and materials technologies add to the potential for reductions in the size and weight of military capabilities. Proponents of such technologies envision dramatic reductions in the requirements for lift. Other assessments see more limited reductions in the materiel that will have to be shipped to future contingencies. A reduction of 20 percent in military cargo to be sent would be both a real surprise and a real boon.[18]

Planning future lift for the long term calls for the simultaneous consideration of these complex factors. Because procurement program lead times are long (generally five to ten years), none of these factors are known when procurement decisions must be made. Deployment planners must aim to balance future lift capabilities with expected needs for moving forces. They do not want to have future operations caught short of true lift requirements. Nor do they want to spend scarce funds on capabilities that will no longer be needed soon after they become available.

The proper match of lift capacity and demand depends on the range of contingencies anticipated, the projected capabilities of potential enemies, and the combat power of future U.S. forces. The latter depends, in turn, on the effectiveness of the weapon systems new technologies may make available for future forces. Each depends on the availability of future funding.

As far as can be told, DoD mobility planners have been neutral on these issues. When examining future movement requirements, the Mobility Requirements Study used the amounts of cargo Army units had in the early 1990s. Thus, the study anticipated neither growth nor reductions in the amount of cargo future systems would have to carry to major contingencies. The implication is that current DoD mobility programs assume a neat balance between two opposing trends. Future mobility planning studies should give explicit attention to estimating future workloads so that planned lift capability is matched with planned unit composition.

---

[17]The Army study of the Gulf War noted, "Technology, in fact, will allow a fighting CINC to build and sustain a theater while carrying with him to the theater significantly less of the logistics needed to support the campaign" (Scales et al., 1993:377).

[18]This analysis has focused on the potential impact of technology on ground force deployments. Another, related analysis suggests that new technology (advanced air delivered weapons and C^3 systems) may enable aircraft to play a larger, even a "dominant," role in the initial stages of major contingencies when opposing forces present lucrative targets. By this analysis, ground force deployments could be reduced or slowed because of airpower's enhanced lethality. (See Bowie, Frostic, et al., 1993.)

Summary

Matching the supply of lift with the needs of units is vital when deployments are being executed. It is equally important when plans for future lift programs are being made. DoD should consider adopting an evolving system of "lift budgets" to coordinate the expectations of transportation agencies and deploying units. Future mobility planning studies should make the effort to assess trends in unit sizes and the potential of new warfighting technologies before they conduct analyses to find the preferred mobility posture.

MAINTAINING ACCESS TO CIVILIAN TRANSPORTATION

The record is clear: lift that is owned and operated in the civilian sector can make significant contributions to U.S. post–Cold War mobility. Should DoD aim to maintain or enhance this contribution for future mobility operations?

Analysis shows that it is less costly to employ civilian capabilities than for DoD to own and operate some kinds of general purpose transportation. For example, chartering commercial roll-on/roll-off (Ro-Ro) ships for Desert Shield/Desert Storm cost an average of $30,000 per day for 100,000 square feet of shipping space. Government-owned ships from the RRF cost nearly $40,000 per day for the same capability just to operate. The advantage of the charter option is strengthened by noting that this comparison omits several categories of cost the government option incurs: the original cost to buy and maintain the ship, break-out and mobilization costs, and the expenses of returning the ship to the RRF after an operation is over. Comparisons of airlift costs show similar differences. For the government to acquire, train, and operate the airlift capacity provided by CRAF would have cost the taxpayers several tens of billions of dollars over the past 30 years. This analysis suggests that DoD should strive to maintain access to civilian transportation services for use in contingency operations.

This is, in fact, DoD policy. DoD transportation policy recognizes the advantages offered by employing commercial operations and calls on DoD components to maximize the use of transportation from the civilian sector.[19] Moreover, transportation capabilities in the civilian economy grow in response to economic development and demographic change.

---

[19]This policy has been endorsed by the Clinton administration. According to the Director, Program Analysis and Evaluation, in the Office of the Secretary of Defense: "It is long standing national policy to rely on the maritime industry to meet DoD requirements, to the extent that industry can do so, and we intend to continue that policy" (Lynn, 1993).

The relevant question is what policies may be needed to maintain access to civilian transportation. This problem must be addressed in the context of developments that appear to be acting to limit the availability of civilian resources to DoD:

- Increasing divergence of DoD needs and civil capabilities.
- Declining incentives for civilian transportation operators to support DoD.
- Increasing concern by some operators about the potential loss of competitive positions when called to national service.

Some trends in the economy are leading civilian operators to acquire and operate ships and aircraft that will be less useful to DoD than those they currently own. Commercial shippers are increasingly using container ships for most types of shipments. As a consequence, shipping lines are steadily acquiring container ships and retiring Ro-Ro ships. In the long run, fewer Ro-Ros will be available for charter. Although the future civilian shipping pool may have a larger total capacity, it will contain less of the shipping capacity DoD prefers.[20]

In the military, other trends are reducing the peacetime cargo the DoD has to transport. Access to contracts for carrying DoD cargo is one of the main incentives that draws airlines into the Civil Reserve Air Fleet (CRAF). As U.S. forces overseas are drawn down, the cargo incentive is reduced. Some analysts expect that DoD shipments to Europe may be cut as much as 50 percent.

Finally, commercial operators are concerned that diverting their resources to serve DoD needs in crises, even short ones, would allow competitors to gain a foothold with their regular customers. As they see it, the result could be a permanent loss of hard-won business. During Desert Shield/Storm, CRAF operators used this argument to forestall activation of the full CRAF fleet. At the same time, U.S.-flag ship operators used similar arguments to successfully oppose activation of the Sealift Readiness Program.[21]

These concerns are real. Nonetheless, the magnitude of the cost advantages DoD gets from using commercial ships and aircraft suggests that it can pay higher incentives and still benefit by using privately owned transportation in

---

[20]Similar concerns exist about airlift. Some argue that developments in air transportation—particularly hub and spoke operating patterns—are leading airlines to shift their new aircraft purchases to smaller, shorter-range aircraft. Thus, the future U.S. commercial fleet will have fewer large, long-range airplanes, the sort needed for intercontinental mobility operations. (See Bowie, Frostic, Lewis, Lund, Ochmanek, and Propper, 1993:35.)

[21]U.S.-flag ship operators did employ many of the same ships to carry containerized resupply cargoes to Saudi Arabia. Under a contractual arrangement, called the Special Mid-East Shipping Agreement, some 700,000 tons of food and other supplies were delivered.

large deployments. DoD needs to systematically investigate the costs and benefits of alternative incentives for civilian operators to support it in major contingencies. The potential payoff is high, particularly if DoD can maintain access to a constant share of growing civilian cargo airlift capacity.

It seems clear that DoD should consider new incentive programs to maintain or increase access to civilian airlift and sealift. Several such programs can be suggested:

- Retainer programs in which the government would pay operators a fixed fee in return for a contractual commitment to support DoD in contingencies.

- Tax and regulatory relief for commercial operators who make firm commitments to support DoD contingency operations.

- Increased preferential access to government peacetime business in return for long-term commitment to support DoD.

- Premium payments for commercial resources only when used in contingencies.

The Clinton administration has taken one such initiative, though in the Maritime Administration rather than DoD. The President's budget for fiscal year 1995 requests $1 billion to fund a "Maritime Security Program." The funds would be raised by increasing taxes on all ships entering U.S. ports. This program, if enacted and funded, would make annual payments for as many as 52 U.S.-flag ships operating in U.S. foreign trade. The billion dollars would be disbursed in payments of $2 and $2.5 million per ship over a ten-year period. In return, ship operators are to be required to make the funded ships available to the Secretary of Defense "in times of emergency." Thus, the Maritime Security Program can be viewed as a retainer program.[22]

Though it is premature to estimate how well this program will work to replace or supplement organic DoD shipping, several questions can be asked: What types of cargo ships will be nominated by their owners? How much will they add to DoD's lift resources for dry cargo and petroleum products? In an emergency, how soon will the ships be available to load DoD cargo? Experience suggests that only a few of the covered ships would be available promptly to meet DoD "surge" demands for sealift. Unless there are signifi-

---

[22]Something like this type of arrangement is included in the Maritime Security and Competitiveness Act of 1993 passed by the House of Representatives in November 1993. The act provided annual payments of about $2 million per ship to shipowners who meet certain conditions and agree to make the ships available "as soon as practicable" when called by the Secretary of Transportation. The final form of any such legislation must await Senate action.

cant increases to DoD capability, the Maritime Security Program is best viewed as an effort to keep U.S.-flag ships operating in international trade.

As is often the case, it is easier to suggest options than to identify the preferred one at the preferred level of risk.   However, the lift incentive issue is ready-made for economic analysis and quantitative modeling.   The options sketched above differ significantly in several respects: how they affect DoD-owned transportation, what they may cost DoD and the government, when the costs are incurred, and the size of the potential response from commercial transportation operators.   Their relative desirability depends on careful economic modeling and projection of commercial air and sea cargo markets.   It also depends on the costs of DoD organic capabilities that depend on how much they are operated in peacetime.   Experimentation with different incentives may be necessary to determine how much DoD would have to offer and how far (and under what conditions) the costs of the alternative incentives would offset the potential benefits.   The problem is complex, and the solutions for airlift and sealift may well differ.   It needs to be attacked from a "top down" perspective.

Summary

Maintaining access to civilian-owned airlift and sealift provides real advantages for DoD.   Civilian transportation provides extra capabilities at relatively low cost.   Changing circumstances, however, are altering the balance, and DoD needs to reconsider what it is willing to pay to maintain access to civilian ships and aircraft.   The authoritative study of post–Cold War requirements, contributions, and costs of civilian transportation capabilities has yet to be done.

IMPROVING PLANNING AND COORDINATION FOR MOBILITY

Acquiring sealift ships and new airlifters will not, alone, provide DoD with responsive mobility.   Most present day DoD command-and-control procedures were put in place a decade ago and designed to meet the needs of that time. Taking the initiatives that are needed now to attract civilian transportation, to adopt an end-to-end perspective, to integrate force design considerations and make other such initiatives will require strong and dedicated leadership. Although implementation will add somewhat to costs, institutional inertia will also be a barrier.   To move ahead, DoD must make three comprehensive changes in command and control: identify and centralize responsibility for mobility management, improve planning processes (including the acquisition of relevant information), and overcome problems of coordination in transportation operations.

Identifying Responsibility

Command and control implies that there is some organization in charge, a place where "the buck stops" when hard choices must be made. When military forces are being deployed, this organization is the supported CINC, the command charged with responsibility for conducting the operation. Although "human nature" sometimes takes over in crises and subordinate commanders take well-meant but unapproved initiatives, the primacy of the supported CINC (subject to the directions of the Chairman of the Joint Chiefs of Staff) has been clarified by the Goldwater-Nichols Defense Reorganization Act.[23] The supported CINC "validates" deployment plans and so simultaneously informs the USTRANSCOM of his priorities, identifies the required units, and states when they are needed. For forces within the United States, the newly established U.S. Atlantic Command (USACOM) is taking on the responsibility for training and providing the units or "force packages" (from any or all of the four services) to meet the supported CINC's needs. USTRANSCOM is responsible for scheduling and operating all "common user" transportation resources on behalf of the supported CINC.

For peacetime planning, and particularly for resource planning, the situation is less clear. An end-to-end perspective calls for high-level leadership, especially if it is concerned with balancing planned forces with planned lift. Finding such a perspective in the present DoD organization is not easy. No "single manager" is responsible for mobility resource planning. In the Office of the Secretary of Defense (OSD), the Program Analysis and Evaluation office plays an important and comprehensive advisory role on most mobility issues. However, the Assistant Secretary for Command, Control, Communications, and Intelligence oversees the design and development of the information and communications systems that support mobility; resource-allocation and procurement decisions are ultimately made by the Comptroller and Acquisition authorities in OSD.

The dispersion of responsibility is even greater in the military organizations. Of course, the Chairman of the Joint Chiefs of Staff (CJCS) has the overall responsibility. On his staff, mobility is addressed by a division of the Deputy Director of the Logistics Directorate for Plans, Analysis, and Resources. Each regional Unified Command is tasked to prepare operation plans for potential

---

[23]In Operation Desert Shield/Desert Storm, the supported CINC was the U.S. Central Command, under the leadership of General Norman Schwarzkopf. The phrase "human nature" is his.

contingencies in his area of responsibility. USACOM will certainly have a role in resource planning as it becomes established. The CJCS also looks to USTRANSCOM for planning deployments and executing transportation operations and for policy, guidance, and standards on transportation issues across the board. The services are responsible for organizing, training, and equipping their forces and for logistics support, as well.

DoD lacks a high-level focal point for mobility planning and resource allocation. Rather, coordination in mobility has been achieved by a series of study efforts such as the Mobility Requirements Study. In effect, DoD mobility planning proceeds by a committee process, with all the well-recognized advantages and drawbacks of such processes. Study projects, like committees, draw diverse organizations together and focus their attention on important questions. But there is a price. Committees tend toward consensus decisions that provide something for all participants. Study groups, like committees, are intermittent, so follow-up is chancy at best. The process focuses on ship and aircraft programs and leaves the planning, programming, and budgeting for mobility command and control, infrastructure, and training to the many separate DoD agencies and service organizations involved.

Mobility programs and issues have clearly risen on the agenda of top defense managers. High priority has been given to funding ship procurement, much top management attention has gone into resolving airlift issues, the Army is restructuring itself to provide a trained and ready contingency force, and readiness is being stressed throughout DoD.

Planning and managing mobility as an end-to-end process and coordinating it across the services, defense agencies, and unified commands call for high-level, full-time leadership. Established organizations need to be shaken up and energy focused on employing the latest management technologies to solving mobility planning and coordination problems. The several tasks for high-level leadership include:

- Planning resource acquisition programs and monitoring their progress.
- Coordinating command-and-control system developments and assuring effective interfaces.
- Coordinating and standardizing databases and other sources of information.
- Arbitrating lift budgets and other disputes over the allocation of common lift resources.
- Assessing lift system capabilities.
- Planning and arranging joint lift exercises.

Although the need for top-level leadership is clear, the precise organizational location is not easy to identify. Among civilian leadership, the Assistant

Secretary of Defense for Special Operations and Low Intensity Conflict provides a prototype for the kind of organization needed. Within his domain, he is responsible for policy, missions, forces, and resources (including any specialized mobility assets). But mobility is a quintessential joint military operation, and leadership for executing joint deployments is squarely placed in the unified command system. The solution, as for Special Operations, may be shared responsibilities between a high-level civilian staff and the Joint Staff.

Centralization of leadership has costs as well as benefits.[24] The question is whether the benefits of improved coordination in planning outweigh the added costs. These costs include the direct costs of management organizations and the information and the command-and-control systems they require. In addition, less visible indirect costs arising from reduced competition among DoD organizations and the layering of management must be considered. Both kinds of costs can be controlled by careful implementation. Any new organization to provide top-level mobility leadership should not simply be added to the existing structure. It should also reflect the necessity of decentralizing the execution of mobility operations and provide the proper goals and incentives to coordinate mobility activities to best serve the supported commanders.

Making Mobility Plans

Mobility planning must, of course, be adapted to the general approach used for planning forces and systems. Prescriptions for defense planning under the uncertainties of the post–Cold War world have been discussed by Davis.[25] For the most part, they can be applied directly in mobility planning. However, three issues unique to mobility planning need to be considered: criteria, data, and models.

Establishing Criteria for Mobility Planning. Judging "how much is enough" is never an easy task, particularly in planning military capabilities. There are many serious uncertainties and an understandable desire to minimize risks. Yet resources are scarce, and hard choices must be made.

The dilemma is readily apparent in mobility planning. For any particular contingency, the responsible commander will always want more forces, faster. Fifteen tactical air squadrons are better than twelve. Twelve squadrons fully operational in five days are preferred to the same capability three days later. Fifteen squadrons in five days are good; sixteen are better yet; seventeen are still better. Where should the line be drawn?

---

[24]Brauner and Gebman (1993) examine issues arising from industry and DoD experience with consolidation of supply, maintenance, and manufacturing activities.

[25]See Davis and Finch (1993) for a comprehensive "vision" of post–Cold War planning.

The answer is certainly in terms that describe the performance of the contingency mission and relate performance to mobility system cost. The best method is to use a two-step process. As described in the Mobility Requirements Study, mobility planning work should begin with analysis that identifies the military benefits from putting ground and air forces into the theater faster. Several measures of effectiveness should be examined: the extent of the enemy advances, casualties to U.S. and any coalition forces, enemy forces destroyed, time to restore borders, etc. This step establishes the incremental benefits of differing speed of deployments. Note that it deals with combat outcomes, not traditional mobility goals of the amounts of cargo delivered. Note also that this approach, like that for planning combat forces, requires many more assumptions and introduces additional uncertainties.

The second step should look directly at the mobility forces needed to put the forces into the field faster. Here, analytical tools are required to find the most efficient mix of sealift, airlift, and prepositioning for delivering the forces deployed on the schedules examined during the first step. This step establishes the incremental costs of deployments of differing speeds.

How fast U.S. military forces should be closed, and by implication the level and mix of mobility systems, can be decided by comparing the incremental benefits and costs of speed in delivering forces to the theater. This should not be thought of as a simple mechanical comparison. There are many uncertainties, and reasonable people may differ in their evaluations of future conditions. Moreover, some important variables will never be captured in quantitative analyses. Improved data and advanced models can help by facilitating sensitivity tests, rapid evaluations of multiple options, and consideration of multiple scenarios.

The need for robustness applies with equal emphasis to the mobility force posture. A robust force (or capability) performs well under a wide variety of scenarios. Put another way, a robust mobility capability degrades gracefully even if the conditions assumed when it was planned fail to occur in practice.

The poorer the ability to predict future contingencies, the greater the desirability of robust capabilities. However, robustness will fail as a decision criterion unless two fundamental improvements in analysis can be made. First, there is always a cost associated with achieving a robust mobility capability, whether measured in dollars or forgone capability under some conditions. Analyses should estimate and report these costs. Second, all forces possess a degree of robustness, but the analytical community lacks measures to compare the amount or degree of robustness among alternative mobility postures. Unless mobility analysts come up with such a measure, robustness—like beauty—will remain in the eye of the beholder.

Improving Data for Mobility Planning. Post–Cold War mobility operations present far greater demands for information and intelligence support than did well-structured Cold War deployment plans. Since mobility planners face a wider array of potential contingencies, they need additional information of every kind. Planning factors of all sorts should be reviewed and updated in light of diverse potential regional contingencies.

Two types of new information needs, however, merit special attention. First, intelligence support must include assessments of potential opposition to U.S. strategic mobility operations. Second, the intelligence community must provide more detailed appreciations of the capabilities of ports, airfields, and roads in areas where the United States may deploy. When used in mobility force planning, both types must focus on projected future capabilities, allowing for the effects of economic development, technology, and growth.[26]

Saddam Hussein allowed the United States almost seven months of unopposed deployments and paid the price. Future opponents have probably observed that U.S. deployment operations may offer large and vulnerable targets. They may well conclude that one of the best ways to defeat the United States is to impose early losses on its deploying forces and prevent it from entering. Developing conventional capabilities to attack deployment operations should not pose insuperable economic or technical issues for emerging regional powers.

Several types of threats may be anticipated. An opponent with the substantial armored forces should recognize that U.S. airpower presents the greatest early threat to early success. He may, therefore, decide to take actions to slow the deployment of U.S. tactical air capabilities. Direct action against the "air bridge" may result in the loss of a small number of aircraft, but ultimately such losses would not have much effect on deliveries. A perceptive opponent may choose to attack the airfields that U.S. tactical air is using. Several kinds of potential opposition should be considered: ballistic and cruise missile attacks, air attacks, and guerrilla and special forces operations. The possibility of chemical and biological attacks should be considered. Opposition to airlift need not be confined to the area of the contingency. Some potential opponents may attempt to disrupt enroute airlift operations or support. Mobility planners need to be able to track such developments and incorporate potential threats into their planning studies.

Prepositioned shipping would also provide attractive targets for an aggressive regional power. Maritime prepositioning enables the United States to deliver heavy forces early, as well as to land the support needed to support forces arriving from CONUS. Potential threats include minefields and anti-ship missiles as well as missile attacks on seaports. Since successful prepositioning

---

[26]The Joint Intelligence Center at the U.S. Transportation Command is the logical organization to produce both types of planning estimates.

operations blend airlift and sealift capabilities, both air and sea ports provide targets for potential opposition to attack.

The objective of estimating the capabilities potential that enemies may develop for these types of opposition to deployment operations is not to suggest that U.S. deployments will be unsuccessful. It is the starting point for developing countermeasures that will enable the United States to deploy successfully when opposed.[27]

Viewing deployment capabilities in an end-to-end or "fort-and-factory-to-foxhole" perspective emphasizes the requirements for facilities—seaports, airfields, and other infrastructure—to enable deployments to proceed smoothly. In the United States, such facilities can be selected and configured to support anticipated operations. In some other important regions, the U.S. military is quite familiar with seaports and airports. Intelligence information on the capabilities of facilities available in many other contingency areas, however, is sketchy at best. The contrast between U.S. knowledge of seaports such as Rotterdam, Antwerp, or Pusan and its prior understanding of conditions at Mogadishu is striking. Deployment planners did not have reliable information on water depths there until U.S. forces measured them in the early days of Operation Restore Hope.

Operational planners need better information on current capabilities in all potential contingency areas. Much of this is readily available, although it needs to be collated and assessed for mobility planning. In most places, facilities can be visited and their equipment and performance observed. Commercial ship and airline operations are supported by publicly available databases. Moreover, many port authorities regularly advertise their capabilities.

Program planning necessarily looks five to ten years ahead. The ships and aircraft in DoD's acquisition programs will not be fully in place for that long. Therefore, planners considering future ship and aircraft programs must assess the capabilities of foreign ports and airfields five to ten years hence. Generally this has not been done in earlier deployment studies. Rather, most studies examine future airlift and sealift capabilities to deliver, using current facilities.

Estimates of future capabilities can be derived from several sources. Construction of new facilities is usually a long-term effort; many authorities publicize their development plans. Other estimates can be based on general economic trends in seaborne trade, air travel activity, and air cargo operations.

Enhancing Mobility Planning Models. Mobility planners use models to assess the capabilities of current and future transportation systems.[28] A recent

---

[27]As, for example, is the case for U.S. theater air defense initiatives, which are giving major consideration to defending early U.S. contingency operations, including deployment operations.

[28]See Schank, Mattock, Sumner, Greenberg, Rothenberg, and Stucker (1991).

RAND review of the models used in the deployment community identified several problems. Available models generally work only in one direction—from individual systems to deployment capabilities—although many important planning problems call for the opposite approach—finding the systems needed to meet deployment requirements. There are many mobility models, but no single model can be used for end-to-end mobility planning. The models have not been validated, and few individuals fully understand how they work. Since the models do not recognize the many uncertainties that characterize crisis and wartime mobility operations, sensitivity testing is hampered. Finally, their results do not serve the needs of analysts addressing post–Cold War mobility resource planning issues.

Many of these problems can be reduced if new modeling technologies are employed. The RAND review suggested that DoD examine the two formal modeling techniques: mathematical programming and knowledge-based models. Mathematical programming models made possible by advances in hardware and algorithm development can directly yield the "optimal" mix of deployment systems for meeting given requirements, or they can be used to identify the best way to employ a given mix of mobility forces to maximize deliveries. Knowledge-based models can apply decision logic and expert rules. The rules express causal relationships among events in mobility operations. Thus, knowledge-based modeling permits analysis of management decisions and policies that affect the performance systems. Both approaches, when compared to the large-scale mobility simulations widely used, promise more understandable, more flexible, and faster modeling operations.[29]

Summary. Mobility planners need a new suite of tools to confront the multifaceted problems of post–Cold War regional contingencies, peacekeeping operations, and humanitarian activities: relevant criteria, new kinds of data, and improved models. The total cost of a set of improved planning tools, perhaps as little as $20 to $40 million, is likely to soon be repaid from program savings.

Coordinating Mobility Operations

Desert Shield/Storm revealed many kinds of coordination problems in executing deployment operation. This conclusion is not surprising, given that the operation began on short notice and without a fully developed plan for forces and transportation. The problems were overcome by the efforts of mobility leaders, planners, and operators using telephones, faxes, and "stubby pencils"

---

[29]Two current RAND reports illustrate the two approaches, provide prototype models, and demonstrate their advantages. See Rothenberg, Stucker, Mattock, and Schank (1993) and Mattock, Schank, Rothenberg, and Stucker (1993), respectively, for analyses of knowledge-based and mathematical programming mobility modeling.

rather than the JOPES/WWMCCS system. As time passed and experience accumulated, workable plans were developed, JOPES shortfalls were overcome, and the system began to function. Although many coordination lessons were learned and many fixes suggested, Restore Hope deployments to Somalia encountered most of the same coordination problems.[30]

Analysis of Army deployments during Desert Shield/Desert Storm suggests three classes of improvements to deployment planning and coordination procedures and systems.[31]

Part of the problem stemmed from a mind-set developed from decades of deliberate planning for Cold War deployments. Procedures developed for the relatively predictable deployments of a global war with the Soviet Union need to be reexamined and adapted to post–Cold War circumstances. DoD needs command-and-control practices that recognize the new reality: political sensitivities, initially poorly defined missions, ad hoc coalition partners requiring unpredictable support, major operational uncertainties, and fast-breaking contingencies. A better approach to planning and training for coordinating future mobility operations would emphasize flexibility and adaptability, i.e., training personnel, building systems, and adapting practices to reflect the realities of post–Cold War contingencies.

For example, DoD needs readily available and reliable information and a trusted tool for providing rapid (a few minutes) and authoritative "top-down" estimates of total deployment requirements so that mobilization of mobility systems can be coordinated with planned force and support deployments. A top-level tool, using aggregate data, is needed because initial planning is likely to be done on a "close-hold" basis. Yet the highest-level planners can be expected to ask many "what if" questions to help them reach crucial decisions.

A second set of problems with JOPES can be traced to outdated information science and computing systems. The problem has technical and bureaucratic roots, although the technical problems have their own sources in the DoD bureaucratic procurement regulations. JOPES development was begun in the mid-1970s with great expectations for the application of the information technology of the time to speed deployment planning and coordinate deployment operations. The program was laid out in increments, and the first incre-

---

[30]In October 1992, funding for the WWMCCS ADP Modernization (WAM) program was terminated. However, development of JOPES ADP "prototypes" is continuing with the aim of providing information technology that will allow JOPES users to access a variety of modeling and analysis tools. The aim is to allow mobility planners to use several new planning tools including DART (a database management program to allow rapid analysis of deployment data), JFAST (a tool for determining transportation feasibility), LOGSAFE (tools for estimating sustainment requirements), and scheduling and movement tools to improve in-transit visibility.

[31]See Stucker and Kameny (1993). This section draws heavily on their work.

ment envisioned a modest goal: integrating two existing deployment information systems. Nonetheless, almost two decades later DoD was still calling JOPES "a developmental system." Meanwhile information systems technologies (hardware, software, decision aids, displays, etc.) had advanced in leaps and bounds. Many units with access to the JOPES considered it "user hostile," and many other units still lacked access. Most users knew that better information technology was easily obtainable in the private sector.

A complete reengineering of the JOPES/WWMMCS is desirable. Outmoded and unnecessary procedures need to be cut away and up-to-date information technology applied. As a RAND analysis puts it, "How the systems and databases are interconnected is an open issue," but whether to do it is not.[32]

Adapting and improving personnel skills are the third type of improvement needed to better coordinate future deployments. Changing the ingrained habits and mind-sets from Cold War activities is one goal. Increasing the pool of trained, capable personnel is another. The first requires greatly increased emphasis on realistic, "no-plan" exercises to both learn and teach lessons about procedures for coordinating fast-breaking contingencies. The second requires recognition and rewards for those who gain superior skills and use them in positions calling for outstanding planning and coordinating performance. Mobility planning and coordination must become more than secondary skills in the post–Cold War U.S. military.

SUMMARY

Changes in the military planning environment are increasing the importance of strategic mobility forces in U.S. military planning. DoD's new leadership recognizes this importance and has approved programs that will enhance the responsiveness of U.S. deployments by increasing maritime prepositioning, adding to "surge" sealift capabilities, and acquiring new airlifters. These are essential steps in posturing U.S. military force to meet the demands of uncertain future contingencies.

Buying more sealift and airlift will not necessarily result in faster deployments. Other constraints may come into effect, other processes may slow reactions and degrade deployments. Management improvements must be taken to hone investment programs and ensure that DoD gets the most out of all available lift capabilities. New procedures are needed to match the capacity of lift

---

[32]Many obvious questions must be addressed. For example, what organizations need access to the system and when? This translates into where workstations and communications need to be installed. How can databases be kept more timely and accurate? Who should control changes to databases used in coordinating deployment operations?

with the amounts of cargo to be moved, both when actual deployments are unfolding and when planning future lift programs. DoD needs to adapt its plans for using civilian-owned transportation to present and future realities. Although this policy will probably cost more, the benefits of planning for civilian support will continue to outweigh the costs. Effectively employing new mobility capabilities in post–Cold War contingencies also calls for comprehensive changes in mobility information and command-and-control organizations, systems, and processes.

Taken together, these investments and improvements should give the nation a responsive, flexible, and highly capable strategic mobility force. Thus future presidents will have dependable options for using DoD's diverse capabilities across the full range of future contingencies.

BIBLIOGRAPHY

Aspin, Les (1993), *The Bottom-Up Review*, Department of Defense, Washington, D.C.

———— (1994), *Annual Report to the President and the Congress.*

Berman, Mort, and Grace Carter (1993), *The Independent European Force: Costs of Independence*, RAND, Santa Monica, CA.

Blair, Rear Admiral Dennis (1992), *Presentation to the Committee on Appropriations, Subcommittee on Defense*, 102nd Congress, Second Session, May 5.

Bowie, Christopher, Fred Frostic, Kevin Lewis, John Lund, David Ochmanek, and Philip Propper (1993), *The New Calculus: Analyzing Airpower's Changing Role in Joint Theater Campaigns*, RAND, Santa Monica, CA.

Brauner, Marygail, and Jean Gebman (1993), *Is Consolidation Being Overemphasized for Military Logistics?* RAND, Santa Monica, CA.

Davis, Paul K., and Lou Finch (1993), *Defense Planning for the Post–Cold War Era: Giving Meaning to Flexibility, Adaptiveness, and Robustness of Capability*, RAND, Santa Monica, CA.

Gebman, Jean, Lois Batchelder, and Katherine Poehlmann (forthcoming), *Finding the Right Mix of Military and Civil Aircraft: Vol. I, Executive Summary*, RAND, Santa Monica, CA.

Hura, Myron, John Matsumura, and Richard Robinson (1993), *An Assessment of Alternative Transports for Future Mobility Planning*, RAND, Santa Monica, CA.

Kassing, David (1992), *Getting Military Power to the Desert: An Annotated Briefing*, RAND, Santa Monica, CA.

———— (1993), *Transporting the Army for Operation Restore Hope*, RAND, Santa Monica, CA.

Lund, John, Ruth Berg, and Corinne Replogle (1993), *An Assessment of Strategic Airlift Operational Efficiency,* RAND, Santa Monica, CA.

Lynn, William (1993), Statement before the Merchant Marine Subcommittee of the Senate Committee on Commerce, Science, and Transportation, August 5.

Mathews, James, and Cora Holt (forthcoming), *So Many, So Much, So Far, So Fast: The U.S. Transportation Command and Strategic Deployment for Operation Desert Shield/Desert Storm,* U.S. Government Printing Office, Washington, D.C.

Mattock, Michael, John Schank, Jeff Rothenberg, and James Stucker (1993), *New Capabilities for Strategic Mobility Analysis Using Mathematical Programming,* RAND, Santa Monica, CA.

"Mobility: Force Projection," *Defense 92,* March/April.

Pagonis, Lieutenant General William (with Jeffrey Cruikshank) (1992), *Moving Mountains: Lessons in Leadership and Logistics from the Gulf War,* Harvard Business School Press, Cambridge, MA.

Rathbun, Lieutenant Commander Robin (1992), "Strategic Mobility for the 1990s: The Mobility Requirements Study, *Strategic Review,* Summer.

Rothenberg, Jeff, James Stucker, Michael Mattock, and John Schank (1993), *Knowledge-Based Modeling for Strategic Mobility Analysis,* RAND, Santa Monica, CA.

Scales, Brigadier General Robert H., Jr., et al. (1993), *Certain Victory: The US Army in the Gulf War,* Office of the Chief of Staff, United States Army.

Schank, John, Michael Mattock, G. Sumner, I. Greenberg, Jeff Rothenberg, and James Stucker (1991), *A Review of Strategic Mobility Models and Analysis,* RAND, Santa Monica, CA.

Stucker, James, and Iris Kameny (1993), *Army Experience with Deployment Planning in Operation Desert Shield,* RAND, Santa Monica, CA.

Sullivan, General Gordon (1993), Hearings before the Subcommittee on Department of Defense, Committee on Appropriations, House of Representatives, 103rd Congress, First Session, April 22.

U.S. Army, Military Traffic Management Command, Transportation Engineering Agency (MTMC) (1991), *Deployment Planning Guide,* Report OA 90-4f-22.

U.S. General Accounting Office (1993), *DoD's Mobility Requirements: Alternative Assumptions Could Affect Recommended Acquisition Plan,* GAO/NSIAD-93-103.

Vance, Captain Elizabeth (1992), *Strategic Deployment Analysis Review, a briefing,* U.S. Army Concepts Analysis Agency, Bethesda, MD.

Chapter 22

REINVENTING THE DoD LOGISTICS SYSTEM TO SUPPORT MILITARY OPERATIONS IN THE POST–COLD WAR ERA

Rick Eden, John Dumond, John Folkeson, John Halliday, and Nancy Moore

The current DoD logistics system was designed primarily to meet the threat of this century's third great European land war. The system assumed the need for massive amounts of logistics resources, much of them prepositioned in Western Europe, the presumed theater of operations. Today that threat is substantially reduced, defense budgets have fallen precipitously, and U.S. military power, including logistics support, must be projected from the continental United States (CONUS). The logistics system designed for the Cold War is too costly, slow, and inefficient for the post–Cold War era. To match today's changed needs and reduced resources, the DoD must make the military logistics system much leaner, more robust, and more flexible. In the parlance of the commercial world, the system must be "reinvented." This paper advocates three broad strategies for doing so, drawing on the highly effective business improvement practices of the best commercial firms. The first strategy is to focus the entire system on meeting the needs of the customer, the operational commander. The second strategy is to design and manage logistics processes to make them more efficient and effective. The third strategy is to design and redesign weapon systems to make them more readily supportable. Each strategy is illustrated with analyses from RAND logistics research conducted for the Army, the Air Force, and the Office of the Secretary of Defense. These analyses suggest that the DoD logistics system may be able to achieve near order-of-magnitude improvements in its efficiency and effectiveness.

INTRODUCTION

This paper advocates three broad management strategies to guide the DoD as it strives to significantly improve military logistics systems. Each of the strategies reflects well over a decade of logistics research conducted by RAND for the Army, the Air Force, and the Office of the Secretary of Defense. This research has been devoted primarily to logistical innovations in the DoD; in recent years, it has included investigations of the best commercial practices, under the general hypothesis that these might be applicable to military logistics. The paper does not survey this body of research but draws on it selectively to illustrate the three strategies.

The strategies can also be viewed as a framework for guiding the development of a research agenda to provide analytic support for changes in DoD logistics policy and practice. This is an exciting period for military logistical analysis for two reasons: The first is the challenge of adapting a revolutionary new set of logistics concepts to the military sector—in effect, bringing the decades-old DoD logistics system up to date with the best commercial practice. The second is the prospect of achieving improvements in the system's effectiveness and efficiency that are nearly an order of magnitude in scale.

We provide a vision of a DoD logistics system that is fundamentally different from the current system and much more suited to the support requirements of the post–Cold War era. However, much work remains to be done to apply new ideas to the existing system, given the risks associated with military operations. There are military purposes that have no analog in the civilian sector, and thus arguments by analogy may seriously understate the difficulty of implementing innovative business practices in the military logistics system.

The Current DoD Logistics System

The current DoD logistics system was designed at a time when military materiel was relatively inexpensive and transportation was relatively expensive—the opposite of the situation today. Agility and efficiency do not characterize the system; rather, it is best described as massive. It was designed primarily to move very large amounts of materiel to Europe, and its performance presumes a great mass of logistics resources—stock, personnel, and facilities—positioned throughout the system. It consists of several echelons of support, each heavily endowed and all linked by a massive supply system. The forward operational units have their own set of repair capability and stocks; another set of stocks and repair capability resides within the theater; and a third set is in CONUS.

A few numbers will help establish the truly enormous scale of this current system. As of the end of 1992, the DoD had over $150 billion in inventory of principal and secondary items.[1] Approximately $80 billion was in inventory of

---

[1] *Department of Defense Supply System Inventory Report, September 30, 1992.* Principal parts are weapon systems that are not platforms, i.e., not aircraft, vehicles, ships, or missiles. Secondary items are consumable and repairable items that are not principal items. Some of these, such as spare parts, support principal parts; others, such as food and medicine, do not.

The value of current inventories within each of the services is now significantly less than it was just a few years ago, for two primary reasons: First, the services have revalued their inventories downward several times. Second, some inventory has been shifted out of the services as a result of the consolidation of supply depots within the DoD. However, within the Defense Logistics Agency (DLA), inventory levels have grown correspondingly.

spare parts. If the Army were a private firm, it would have been number seven in the *Fortune* 500; the Air Force would have ranked in the top five.[2] Annually, the Army alone performs almost a half million repairs and overhauls at its depots. The Army logistics system has $40 billion in inventory, and one-third of that ($14 billion) is in spare parts. Such volume is not handled expeditiously. Frequently, repairs take from three weeks to nine months to complete. Requests by Army battalions for parts generally take days to weeks to reach a source of wholesale supply; it may take months for an operational unit to have its requisition filled.

Desired Characteristics of the Post–Cold War Logistics System

With the end of the Cold War, a new approach to providing and managing logistics support is clearly needed. The post–Cold War national security environment calls for much smaller forces to be projected from CONUS to conduct a variety of lesser operations throughout the world. The logistics structure must be redesigned to support the new environment. It cannot be focused on a European scenario or any other single dominating scenario; it cannot presume host nation support; and its successful performance cannot depend on expensive logistical mass. It should presume that deployed forces may need to be supported in large part from afar because a fully developed logistics base in the theater of operations is unlikely. It must also presume that the multiple echelons of support that have been doctrinal for major operations, such as the scenario of a major European land war, may be eliminated. In their place, a much leaner structure designed to provide support more rapidly and accurately will be needed. The intermediate echelons of support may be tailored to specific mission needs with an eye to minimizing the deployment burden. To meet the support requirements and budgetary constraints of the post–Cold War era, DoD must seek radical, almost order-of-magnitude improvements in the performance of its logistics system. The DoD logistics structure must become much leaner, more flexible, and more responsive.

Strategies for Reinventing the DoD Logistics System

When the terms "leaner," "flexible," and "responsive" are used with regard to the military logistics system, comparisons to commercial industry immediately come to mind. It is widely recognized that a new management paradigm has emerged in the business world. This paradigm has several elements. It is based on satisfying the final customer, so that the customer is the focus of all

---

[2] *Air Force Magazine*, May 1992.

the efforts of the serving organization. Measurable performance goals are established in support of that customer. Products and services are evolved to meet the customer's needs and/or add value for that customer. Old processes are reengineered—that is, major changes are made to the way business is being done, not marginal changes or short-term emphasis (see Hammer and Champy, 1993; Davenport, 1993). These major changes seek to eliminate non–value-adding activities and improve value-adding activities. The latter can often be accomplished through management and technological innovations, including the incorporation of new information and communication systems.

Using this new paradigm, the best commercial firms have successfully been pursuing near order-of-magnitude improvements to meet the challenges of their increasingly competitive environment. For example, we see such improvement with regard to reductions of inventory. The service parts division of Cummins Engine Company reduced its average inventory on the floor at a given time from a value of $173 million to $22 million, even though the number of items supported by the inventory increased.[3] Detroit Diesel Remanufacturing has been able to reduce its safety stock from 30 days to 5 days by reengineering its operations. On-time delivery performance can be greatly improved also. Titeflex, a small firm that manufactures high-pressure hoses and connectors, had at one time secured a supplier niche within the U.S. government (Blaxhill and Hout, 1991). In the late 1980s, competition for that market developed and Titeflex needed to make changes. Within two years, the company moved from 15 percent on-time delivery performance to better than 80 percent and reduced production lead time from weeks to days.[4] U.S. automakers have risen to the challenge of significantly improving the quality of their product. These examples demonstrate that near order-of-magnitude improvements in business performance are feasible today.

We hypothesize that DoD can reinvent its logistics system by applying similar concepts. This paper proposes three broad management strategies to guide DoD as it revolutionizes the way it performs its logistics function:

1. Managers throughout the logistics system should focus on meeting the needs of the system's ultimate customers—theater commanders and commanders of operational units.

---

[3] Discussion with managers of service parts distribution center at Cummins, March 1993.

[4] American Production and Inventory Control Society meeting, Salt Lake City, September 1992.

2. Managers should design and manage all logistics processes to make them more responsive and efficient—in commercial terms, reengineer them and then seek continuous process improvements.

3. Weapon systems should be designed and redesigned to be more supportable.[5] In terms of the commercial paradigm, this means evolving the product to meet the customer's needs.

This paper will address each of these management strategies in turn.

STRATEGY 1: FOCUS THE LOGISTICS SYSTEM ON THE CUSTOMER'S NEEDS

Shortcomings of Local Goals and Measures of System Performance

Currently the performance of many logistics activities is not linked to the needs of the system's final customer, the operational commander. The logistics system is composed of many processes, each of which in turn is composed of activities that span organizations and even services. These processes and activities rely on local goals and measures of effectiveness and efficiency. Logistics managers at the unit level, where the operational forces reside, may be close enough to observe the logistics needs of those forces and act to support the commander. But at echelons more distant from the units and installations, in the theater and within CONUS, the ability to see the support requirements of operational forces declines. While these more distant organizations want to "do the right thing" in terms of contributing to operational capability, their aim has been to improve the efficiency of each of their activities and processes, and local performance measures are developed and used for this purpose.

One example of a local measure is "fill rate," which is used within the supply community. On the surface, this measure may appear to be an appropriate choice; however, its use in the absence of more global measures leads to suboptimal performance of the logistics system as a whole. For example, the Defense Logistics Agency (DLA) rates its centers on how well they provide support in terms of the number of requisitions they fill upon receipt. Over time, the supply managers have learned that if they keep high-volume items (which also tend to be low-cost items) in stock, their fill rate will look better. Unfortunately, many items that hold down the availability of a weapon system are high-cost, low-demand items. So although the supply manager has an ex-

---

[5]A more general form of this strategy, which extends beyond logistics, is to design operational units to be more readily supportable—i.e., lighter, more survivable, and more lethal—and more deployable. On improving the deployability of our military forces for the post–Cold War era, see Kassing (1994).

cellent fill rate, weapon system availability may suffer. Moreover, when the fill rate goal has been met, there is no incentive to improve performance.

Another local measure is full-truckload shipments. Transporters now reduce the frequency of pickups and dropoffs because they get rated on how fully the trucks are loaded, not on the effectiveness of the logistics system as a whole. A $30 million aircraft may wait days for a part to save a few transportation dollars. Similarly, repair organizations tend to be rated on the utilization of their repair capacity, not necessarily on which items they repair or on how well they fix items that will, in fact, contribute to a weapon system's availability. Thus, they may devote resources to fixing items for the stock pool rather than items that a customer is waiting for.

In short, local measures often help meet only local goals for effectiveness and efficiency; they do not take into account the consequences on the effectiveness and efficiency of the logistics system as a whole.

The Need for a Common Goal Throughout the System

Rather than relying on local measures, the most successful commercial firms teach the importance of focusing on the customer and meeting the customer's needs. We believe that the logistics system should learn from what is done by those firms, recognizing that adaptations of commercial practices may not be straightforward. The customer of the logistics system is the operational commander. The operational commander needs his weapon systems to be available throughout a given mission scenario. A great deal of experience and research have shown sustained weapon system availability to be an excellent proxy for operational capability.[6]   We advocate the efficient provision of *sustained weapon system availability* as the key goal of the military logistics system.[7]

---

[6]On weapon system availability and weapon system management, see Dumond, Eden, and Folkeson (1993). Other relevant RAND publications include Tsai, Tripp, and Berman (1992); Moore, Stockfisch, Goldberg, Holroyd, and Hildebrandt (1991); Robbins, Berman, McIver, Mooz, and Schank (1991); Berman, McIver, Robbins, and Schank (1988); Crawford (1988); and Berman, Halliday, Kirkwood, Mooz, Phillips, Kaplan, and Batten (1985).

[7]We recognize that the DoD logistics system has other goals, many of which are important to achieving operational success. Nevertheless, we advocate the provision of sustained weapon system availability as the key goal because of the U.S. military's reliance on major frontline weapon systems to achieve its operational goals in most missions. For some military forces, including those of the United States itself before this century, sustained weapon system availability would probably not be considered the key goal of the logistics system. In the goal stated here, "weapon system" can be understood in a broader sense to include "soldier."

Let us examine more fully what the customer of the logistics system needs, focusing on the support of a frontline advanced weapon system. Consider a hypothetical situation in which an operational commander has 46 Comanche helicopters assigned to him and requires a minimum of 35 Comanches to be available to execute a planned scenario (i.e., a minimum 75 percent availability requirement). The scenario to be supported will last at least 70 days. On about day 40 of this scenario, operations are planned that will require each of 35 helicopters to fly about three hours a day. For the 20 days preceding that period of operation, the force will conduct some preparatory training. During the training period, the commander plans an hour and a half of flying per day per Comanche. Prior to the training, normal peacetime operation will continue, during which the Comanches fly about three-quarters of an hour per day. The logistics managers need to be able to sustain weapon system availability at those planned levels through the full scenario.

Figure 1 displays the logistician's task schematically. It shows the logistics system as a collection of inputs and processes that must be combined to provide the output. The logistics manager is concerned with controlling the use of his inputs and processes in such a way as to meet the customer's needs. To do that he must continually assess the performance of his inputs and processes and then make adjustments as necessary.[8]

Assessment Systems That Can Link Logisticians' Actions to System Performance

Logistics managers need information systems—data systems and analytic capabilities (i.e., decision support tools)—that will help them assess their ability to meet the logistics needs of operational commanders. These systems can help them understand how their local actions contribute to the goal of meeting the customer's needs. The logistics manager in our example is concerned with sustaining the required level of Comanches throughout the scenario. Let us suppose that, using an assessment tool, the manager finds that with a given set of logistics policies, he is projected to be able to meet the combat commander's needs until four days into the most demanding portion of the scenario.

---

[8]This single example of a logistician meeting the customer's needs is not meant to imply that logistics managers will optimize to support a single commander in a single scenario. Policies and practices must be flexible and robust across a wide range of potential scenarios.

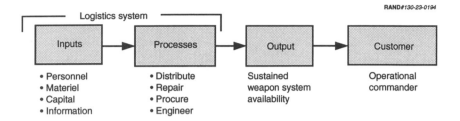

Figure 1—DoD Logistics from a Systems Perspective

At this point, an assessment tool should also enable the logistics manager to assess how alternative policies would affect his ability to meet the operational commander's needs.[9]

Assessment tools can also be used to support the planning, programming, and budget execution system. For example, assessments of the capability (and therefore the shortfalls) of the current logistics system to meet the operational requirements of the services can guide the execution of the current budget, as well as the planning and programming for future resources.[10]

STRATEGY 2: REENGINEER LOGISTICS PROCESSES TO MAKE THEM MORE RESPONSIVE AND EFFICIENT

The first management strategy is to focus the entire system on the customer, the operational commander. Now we turn to the second strategy—to design and manage the DoD logistics processes as a whole to make them more responsive and more efficient in meeting the customer's needs.

---

[9]When the logistics manager identifies a preferred alternative policy—in this example, such a policy might be to use prioritized repair and prioritized distribution of spares—he can take both short- and long-term implementation actions. His short-term goal is to support the operational commander's imminent mission. To accomplish this goal, the logistics manager may direct that "top priority" be given to this particular commander's needs. More formal policy implementation for long-term changes over the set of all possible forces and scenarios would likely require changes to current policies and information systems to support their implementation. One such system, a decision aid called DRIVE, is discussed later in this paper.

[10]RAND has been developing, prototyping, and testing assessment tools to help logistics managers understand their sustainment capability. Early in the 1980s, RAND started work with the Air Force on an assessment tool called Dyna-METRIC, which is now being used by the Air Force Materiel Command. RAND is currently working with the Army to develop a version adapted to meet the distinctive needs of that service.

Inadequacies of the Current Logistics System

The current logistics system is much too costly, slow, and inaccurate. Tens of billions of dollars of stock are tied up in DoD inventory of spare parts to support service needs. These stocks accumulate in warehouses, transit, and repair activities. The DoD has relied on such stockpiles to buffer against uncertainty—both in demand and in the performance of the logistics system itself in meeting that demand.

Operation Desert Shield and Operation Desert Storm (ODS) demonstrated clearly that the system can do what it was fundamentally designed to do, namely, push a massive amount of materiel forward. But yesterday's processes are no longer adequate for today's challenges and budgets. Long queues and delays continue. Moreover, having stock everywhere does not necessarily mean that the operational units are going to possess or receive the right stock at the right place at the right time. It is too expensive and logistically impossible to have everything everywhere. Although some logistics managers thought that the logistics system performed very well in ODS—and by some measures, it can be argued that it did—many operational commanders would criticize the performance of logistics support.[11] For example, the Army had units that for months did not receive the correct repair parts to return out-of-commission tanks to mission-ready status.

The DLA reported a fill rate of 96 percent, indicating to them (using their local measure) that they did an excellent job. But parts did not get to the commanders when and where they were needed. For example, the military had 25,000 40-foot containers of materiel[12] delivered to the theater that had to be opened to determine their contents. Many were not opened until months after the war was over. Thus, having massive amounts of stock—even in the theater—does not necessarily provide the availability required by operational commanders.

The Need for Increased Efficiency with Reduced Resources

As an additional challenge, the new environment calls for more effective use of the reduced resources. The DoD can no longer afford great logistics mass, even if it were willing to accept processes that, by the standards of today's best commercial practice, are expensive, unresponsive, and unreliable. In this new environment, resources (personnel, materiel, and capital) are being drawn down. This means that the logistics mass that allowed the military to circumvent distribution problems will decrease greatly. Traditionally, the military has

---

[11]Many others, including members of Congress, have criticized its cost.

[12]25,000 of about 40,000 total containers of sustainment materiel.

been able to bring massive logistics resources to bear on an operation because it had substantial forces that were not committed to the current conflict. These uncommitted forces provided a pool of people and materiel to fill long pipelines, to overfill authorized stocks, to track down scarce materiel and missing orders, and to work around the standard distribution system. Tomorrow's forces will be much smaller. For example, the Army will decline from its Cold War level of 18 active divisions to 10 or fewer. Fewer resources such as end items, stock, and manpower will be available to compensate for shortfalls in the performance of the distribution system. Moreover, the logistics mass will often be considered a liability rather than an asset for a CONUS-based power projection force, because it costs too much, is troublesome to deploy, and increases the number of relatively soft, vulnerable targets. Especially in the early stages of a deployment, logistics mass is competing with operational forces for airlift and sealift whose availability is constrained both physically and budgetarily.

Two important actions are needed to compensate for reduced resources: (1) reengineering logistics processes to make them more efficient and more effective, and (2) making better use of technology (particularly information and communication technology) to support those reengineered processes. It is important to note that we are not advocating merely new information systems, but new information systems in support of radically improved processes. Experience has shown that attempts to achieve a "technological fix" by automating existing ways of doing business do not lead to radical improvements in performance or cost reduction (Tapscott and Caston, 1993).

Commercial firms have achieved the greatest gains in productivity and efficiency from a combination of reorganization, technology, and process reengineering that takes maximum advantage of the available technology. For example, Bell Atlantic analyzed one process and found it to consist of 13 different steps that together required an average of 15 days to complete, although they involved only 10 hours of actual work (Hammer, 1993). Table 1 compares the

Table 1

Gains from Automating Existing Processes Compared with
Automating Redesigned Processes (% saved)

Savings	Automating Existing Process	Automating Redesigned Process
Time	~ 10	97
Cost	~ 10	89
Labor	20	75

estimated benefits of automating an existing process (the sort of automating that DoD, as well as some commercial firms, has tended toward) with the actual gain achieved by reengineering the process to take full advantage of automation (Hammer, 1990; Davenport and Short, 1990). Automation alone yields time and labor reductions and cost savings of only about 10 to 20 percent, while a combination of automation and process redesign yields reductions and savings of 75 to 97 percent. Improvements of these latter magnitudes are what DoD needs, given recent and forthcoming budget reductions.

Some specific case studies illustrate the point. General Motors invested heavily in automation in response to the challenge of the Japanese automakers, but it simply automated the old mass-production process. It achieved only small gains in productivity, cost savings, and quality. By contrast, Portland General Electric implemented complementary technological, organizational, and engineering changes. It achieved impressive results. Processing time dropped from 15 days to only a half day. The company estimates that one aspect of automation, electronic data improvements, would have produced only 10 percent of the time savings by itself. Costs declined from $90 per transaction to $10 (Davenport and Short, 1990). Similarly, Ford Motor Company redesigned and automated its accounts payable operation and achieved a 75 percent personnel reduction (Hammer, 1990). It estimates that automation alone would have produced savings on the order of 20 percent. The remainder of the savings resulted from a total redesign of the processes. Automating cumbersome procedures does not make them less cumbersome. The greatest gains occur when the procedures are redesigned to take full advantage of technological capabilities.

Companies that have taken advantage of automation to radically change their processes have increased the quality and reliability of their products and service while increasing the speed of that service and the ease of interaction between customers and suppliers. At the same time, these companies have lowered their costs of materiel, management, and labor. But these changes have not occurred without transition costs. New information systems, retraining staff, and consensus building consume considerable resources and time and require a strong commitment from both management and subordinate staff.

Substituting Speed and Accuracy for Logistics Mass

We have seen that the speed and accuracy of processes can be dramatically improved in the commercial sector. We have some evidence to suggest that DoD logistics processes can be reengineered to achieve similar improvements in speed and accuracy by eliminating non–value-adding activities and focusing on improving value-adding activities. Collectively, these techniques for substituting velocity and accuracy for mass in the defense logistics system comprise a management approach that we term "velocity management." Adopting this approach will require a radical change in mindset and philosophy.

Consider the implications that a velocity management approach would have for one component of the DoD logistics system, the distribution system. Figure 2 shows the performance of the Army distribution system during ODS. It compares both the Uniform Materiel Movement and Issue Priority System (UMMIPS) time standards and Persian Gulf experience in average days to the Port of Embarkation (POE)—the easiest part of the process—for high-, medium-, and low-priority orders as reported by the Army's Logistics Control Agency (LCA).[13] These data show that the system did not meet its own standards for performance at any priority level during this operation. For example, high-priority items took more than three times as long to reach the POE as the UMMIPS standard for receipt by the customer.

The first steps in reengineering such a poorly performing system are to distinguish value-adding from non–value-adding activities in the process and to remove the latter. Figure 2 also shows how the time it took an order to reach the POE was divided between movement (a value-adding activity in distribution) and processing and hold (non–value-adding).[14] Clearly, the bulk of the

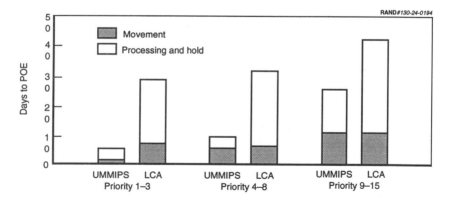

Figure 2—Amounts by Which Actual Distribution Times During ODS Exceeded the Standard

[13]Accurate actual times are available only through the POE. After the POE, the data become sparse because documentation took a back seat to attempted delivery.

[14]Processing and hold time is that period spent at any of the following locations: in theater, National Inventory Control Point, depot, Container and Consolidation Point (CCP), or POE. The assignment of times to movement versus processing and hold is not perfect because we were limited by the coarseness of the actual data.

time is spent in processing and hold, which alone exceeds the UMMIPS standards. An analysis of high-priority requisitions during ODS indicates that processing and hold times averaged 22.2 days for the highest-priority items (priority 1–3) and accounted for 74 percent of the time from requisition to receipt at POE.[15] Such delays in distribution should be unacceptable even for low-priority items.

Even shortening the movement time to zero (which is impossible) will not solve the current distribution problem. Any strategy to improve distribution times must drastically reduce these lengthy processing and hold times. In the best commercial practice, many of these steps have been eliminated and others have been automated.

In addition to slow average times, the current distribution system suffers from highly variable performance. Unaccountably, some requisitioned items move fairly quickly, while others lag for almost unbelievably long times, even if they are in stock and not on backorder. Figure 3 shows how long it took requisitions to reach the CONUS POE during ODS, assuming that the items were in stock (i.e., there were no backorders). These results are based on an analysis of raw data collected over 18 months, obtained from the Army's

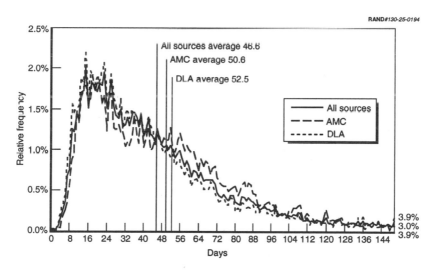

Figure 3—Times for Requisitioned Items to Reach the CONUS POE During ODS

---

[15]This analysis is limited to requisitions that were captured by the standard data system.

Logistics Intelligence File (LIF), which includes much of the ordering done for ODS. Figure 3 also indicates the average time to POE and the organization that managed the item (the Army Materiel Command or the DLA).

What is most striking are the long tails to the right associated with the relative frequency of days from the time an item was requisitioned until it reached the POE.[16] (We truncated the tails here for plotting purposes.) The Army cus-tomers do not experience the average times reported by DoD's performance measures. Rather they observe a highly variable and unpredictable process. In addition to the obvious costs associated with these long pipeline times, there are other costs such as loss of customer confidence in the system and a resulting range of coping behaviors associated with the high variability of the order fulfillment times. Unreliable and slow performance affects customer behavior. Poor performance leads to distrust of the system, which can lead to rational but counterproductive coping behavior that often exacerbates poor performance—for example, flooding the system with multiple requisitions or deploying with higher-than-authorized levels of stock. In contrast, good performance builds customer trust, particularly in peacetime, which can even further improve performance, as when customers are willing to share spare supplies because they know the system will replace them quickly.

Lessons in Distribution from a Top-Performing Commercial Firm

Now let us compare the highly variable and generally very slow performance of DoD in distributing spare parts to the performance of one of the best commercial firms, Caterpillar. Caterpillar parts available in both the DoD and commercial inventories are delivered from Caterpillar's distribution facilities much faster than by DoD from its depots. If we consider the effect of local stock, we find that Caterpillar delivers 99.8 percent of its high-priority parts orders within 48 hours. And suppliers deliver over half of the 0.2 percent of the parts on backorder in 5 days or less. Table 2 compares Caterpillar commercial parts distribution with distribution by DoD before, during, and after ODS. The Army data reflect a subset of Caterpillar parts in the Army supply system.

---

[16]It is tempting to attribute these long tails to the large surge and the resultant backlogs that occurred at CCPs and the aerial ports in CONUS. However, similar analyses of raw data from the Somalia operation and from normal peacetime operations showed that although the mean times from document date to POE decreased because backlogs were no longer a problem, long tails still occurred in the relative frequency distribution of process times for overall time from document date to POE, as well as for each of the segments.

Table 2

Comparison of Caterpillar and DoD Delivery Times (No Backorders)

	Delivery Time (days)	
	CONUS	Outside of CONUS
Caterpillar	1–2	2–4
DoD		
Pre–ODS	13–23	21–66
ODS	21–36	47–48
Post–ODS	14–26	50–68

Caterpillar achieves superior performance not only by eliminating non–value-adding activities but also by improving the speed and accuracy of its value-adding activities. When we compare Caterpillar's distribution system with that of DoD, two aspects stand out: First, the Caterpillar system has far fewer nodes (i.e., points where information and/or materiel is handed off). Second, and perhaps more important, those nodes are linked by a uniform data system and a primary performance measure—meeting the customers' needs for parts in a reliable and timely manner. Caterpillar obtains high performance by electronically linking its worldwide network of 256 independent dealers and 25 distribution centers, by setting high standards, and by demanding high performance.

Applying Velocity Management to DoD Logistics Processes

We are aware that Caterpillar's distribution system does not compare with every aspect of DoD logistics system. Caterpillar's system resupplies a large number of spare part types (470,000) through a geographically dispersed system. Moreover, it obviously does not have to move a large volume of commodities such as food, fuel, and ammunition. The equipment requiring parts has a well-established demand history (unlike much DoD equipment that only rarely operates in the environment for which it was designed), so the company knows which parts to stock in the field and which to store centrally. Caterpillar obviously does not face the same challenges that DoD faces, but in certain dimensions, Caterpillar's operation resembles that of the DoD, which also must resupply a relatively low volume of spare parts. And along those comparable dimensions, Caterpillar has achieved great success by applying certain techniques, including a simplified distribution structure and a linked data system.

The services have already experimented successfully with applications of a velocity management approach to their logistics processes. For example, RAND has been working with the Air Force as it makes some radical improvements to processes associated with repair of high-technology components. Figure 4 indicates the magnitude of those improvements.

During two recent exercises, the Air Force focused on reducing the repair cycle of 32 high-cost components of the F-16 radar. The original repair system being reengineered had two categories of high-value components: components that were of "very high" value, and components that were of "high" (though substantially less) value.[17]   Under the original system, both types of components took about 32 days from the time they were removed from the aircraft to the time they were repaired at the depot and ready for reissuance. RAND and the Air Force tested a way to move the components through the system more rapidly that would enable the Air Force to reduce expensive inventory further. By reengineering the processes, the Air Force eliminated many of those non–value-adding activities that occur from the point at which the component fails to the point when it is received at the depot. By applying differential management and special handling throughout the process to the seven very-high-cost components, the Air Force managers reduced their repair cycle times by more than half, to 15 days. They then took additional actions to remove 10 days from the repair cycle of the high-value components and an additional 3 days from that of the very-high-value components through further improvements in material handling. These improvements saved the Air Force approximately $10 million per year in operating and support costs, while sustaining the same levels of availability that existed with the old processes.

The Air Force then went further to streamline the handling of the components at the depot. It was able to remove another 14 days of non–value-adding activities from the high-cost cycle and 6 days from the very-high-cost cycle. This amounted to a total improvement of 75 percent in the time to repair for high-value components and an 81 percent improvement in the time to repair for very-high-value components. The reduction in cycle time it achieved by reengineering its processes provides the Air Force greater flexibility and responsiveness and is of the near order-of-magnitude scale needed in these changing times.

Reducing cycle times—the amount of time it takes to get things through the system—provides other benefits as well, including the reduction in inventory needed to support the shorter pipelines. RAND analysis of some Martin

---

[17]The "value" of components was established by multiplying unit cost by demand rate by flying hours per day. Seven of the 32 components were valued at more than $300,000 per day. These are the "very-high-value" components. The "high-value" components were valued at up to $75,000 per day.

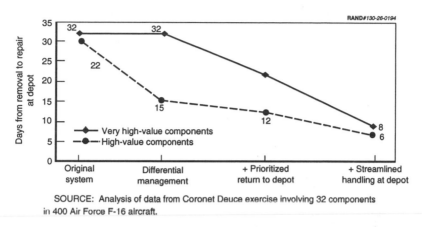

SOURCE: Analysis of data from Coronet Deuce exercise involving 32 components in 400 Air Force F-16 aircraft.

Figure 4—Radical Improvements Resulting from Reengineered Processes

Marietta data associated with one high-technology element of the Apache helicopter provides an example.[18] About $60 million in stock of Target Acquisition Designation Sight/Pilot Night Vision Sensor (TADS/PNVS) components is needed to keep a 90-day repair pipeline filled. If the Army could move these components through the repair process faster and achieve 15-day repair cycles, it could reduce the necessary stock to about $10 million, more than offsetting the increase in transportation costs. In this case, transit times as well as inventory processing and repair processing times are reduced. Transit time can be reduced by using a priority distribution system. Non–value-adding administrative delays can also be eliminated to improve velocity through the repair process.

Reengineering the Army Munitions Distribution System

These examples have emphasized one aspect of reengineering, the elimination of non–value-adding activities to improve the velocity of logistics processes. An example that emphasizes the improvement of value-adding activities is provided by a recent analysis of the Army munitions distribution system.[19]

The current Army munitions distribution system, which relies on break bulk operations, provides supply at a velocity that, at least initially, is too slow to support many contingencies. In ODS, the first break bulk munitions ship from CONUS arrived in the theater more than 20 days after the first sealifted combat forces, primarily because of the long time required for loading and un-

---

[18]Related analyses appear in Robbins et al. (1991).

[19]Unpublished study by K. Girardini et al., RAND, 1993.

loading of break bulk cargo (upon arrival, unloading took an additional 15 days). Furthermore, break bulk operations require munitions to be handled at each change of mode, from outload at the depot to final delivery to the soldier in the field. While value-adding, these activities result in a cumbersome process that takes excessive time to surge capacity.

Commercial firms long ago moved from break bulk operations to containerization, in order to reduce intermediate handling at changes in transport mode (e.g., ship to rail, rail to truck). With the fielding of the palletized loading system (PLS), it will be possible for the Army to use containerization to achieve such benefits in munitions distribution. While many such benefits are inherent in the use of containerization, the extent of those benefits is a strong function of modifying doctrine and practices that are carryovers from a distribution system that evolved for break bulk cargo.

Containerization and intermodal operations represent the introduction of a new technology in ammunition distribution, just as computers and information technology have been inserted into numerous business and logistics processes. It is clear from the literature that to derive maximum benefit from a new technology, it is necessary to critically review current doctrine and practices. A prime example of carryover of a current practice to containerization would be continued exclusive reliance on dedicated munitions ships. Containerization provides the opportunity to shift from the large, infrequent deliveries associated with dedicated munitions ships to smaller, more frequent deliveries. This shift could be achieved by putting a limited number of ammunition containers on the decks of ships delivering unit equipment. Such a practice would provide several advantages: The velocity of supply would be increased, since the most ready and fastest ships are used for unit equipment; munitions delivery would be better synchronized with the arrival of units; vulnerabilities to disruption and interdiction would be reduced; and workload for the in-theater distribution system would be more balanced.

A second example of shifting from current practices would be to pre-stuff a limited quantity of munitions stored at depots in containers. This would enable the depots to rapidly deliver initial sustainment, increasing the velocity of supply. Also, the munitions for some high-tonnage rounds, such as artillery (which can represent 50 percent or more of the total munitions tonnage for a deployment), can be stuffed in depots in combat-configured loads (e.g., mixed loads of projectiles and propellant), thereby dramatically reducing the tonnage requiring intermediate handling in the theater.

A new management scheme will have to be established for the positioning and employment of different container types, including commercial 20-foot containers, MILVANs, original-design PLS flatracks (not Internal Standards Organization (ISO)-compatible), and enhanced-design PLS flatracks. For example, original-design flatracks could be stored with units or on afloat prepositioned shipping (APS) ships, thereby minimizing the negative impact of the non–ISO-compatible design (unit trucks deploy on roll-on/roll-off ships (Ro/Ros), and the current APS fleet is composed entirely of break bulk ships whose loads will have to be containerized for distribution in the theater). Enhanced flatracks, which are ISO-compatible, could be stored, some prestuffed, at depots for initial sustainment. Finally, in a very large contingency, depots could shift to MILVANs and commercial 20-foot containers when the theater distribution system is more developed. Munitions-handling equipment such as cranes and trucks that are compatible with these platforms must be acquired for both CONUS depots and deploying units.[20]

Although implementing such a system would require investments, the result would be much more efficient, flexible, and responsive than the current Army munitions distribution system. But, as the above examples suggest, it is necessary to review doctrine and practices from the CONUS depots to theater distribution to derive maximum benefit from the shift to containerization and to create a "seamless" munitions distribution system.

Decision Tools to Control the Use of Scarce Resources

The application of velocity management will improve the speed, accuracy, and reliability of logistics processes and will decrease reliance on logistics mass, particularly stocks. The result will be a much leaner system. We recognize the need to use resources much more effectively with this leaner system. No longer will it be possible to rely on massive resources to cover uncertainty and risk (frequently a failed attempt, as in the case of the 25,000 containers of unknown contents in ODS). Decision support tools are needed to help control these lean resources. As an example, consider a logistics manager who must support several operational units simultaneously. Each of these operational units is about to engage in an activity that will consume logistics resources. The logistics manager is concerned with providing the right material to the units, in a prioritized fashion, so that each unit will meet its requirements. In the case of repairable items, he is concerned not only with distributing stocks but also with repairing assets that are broken, so that they will be available to distribute in the near future. And he is also concerned with determining what he needs to acquire from the echelon above. His focus is on using the whole set of logistics resources to sustain the operations.

RAND has been working on resource control tools to help the manager respond to the customer's needs, by providing sustained weapon system availabil-

---

[20]The Army is procuring the PLS truck, which provides a deployable container-handling capability; it is scheduled for fielding in early 1994. However, the planned number to be procured has recently been reduced.

ity. RAND's work with the Air Force in the early 1980s on a model called DRIVE (Distribution and Repair in Variable Environments) serves as the basis for tools that have been implemented within the Air Force (Abell et al., 1992). DRIVE can support the prioritization of repair for components and subcomponents to ensure that constrained resources are used to best advantage in keeping weapon systems available. The DRIVE model has been revised to support the Army's needs, and testing has been completed at the U.S. Army Missile Command (*Readiness-Based Maintenance Economic Analysis Final Report,* 1992). Another version of that model that addresses more of the issues associated with the unit level, including budget constraints, has also been developed and is currently being tested at the 4th Infantry Division at Fort Carson.

STRATEGY 3: DESIGN AND REDESIGN WEAPON SYSTEMS TO BE MORE SUPPORTABLE

We now turn to the third strategy for reinventing the DoD logistics system: designing and redesigning weapon systems to be more supportable. Weapon systems create a burden on the logistics system that can be reduced by design. If weapon systems were made more fuel-efficient or more accurate, for example, the demands for fuel and munitions would be less. Advanced weapon systems provide a margin of technological superiority over potential adversaries, but they can create an extra maintenance burden on the logistics structure because of their complexity. The complex components of these weapon systems are fundamentally different from the mechanical components that were typical of older systems in ways that make them much more difficult and expensive to maintain.

When components fail, it is expected that they will be identified, removed, replaced, and in the case of repairable components, repaired, and then made available as a replacement stock for another faulty component. Unfortunately, fault isolation and removal is not always straightforward with high-technology components. As Figure 5 indicates, these components present two types of problem: (1) a design problem that shows up in all the weapon system components of a certain type and configuration, and (2) a few high-technology "lemons," i.e., individual components that exhibit chronic performance degradations.[21]

---

[21]The problem of lemons among weapon systems and weapon system components was first investigated by RAND in the early 1960s. (See McGlothlin and Donaldson, 1964, and Donaldson and Sweetland, 1966.) The chief concern with lemons during that period was their effect on the availability of fully mission-capable weapon systems.

RAND#130-27-0194

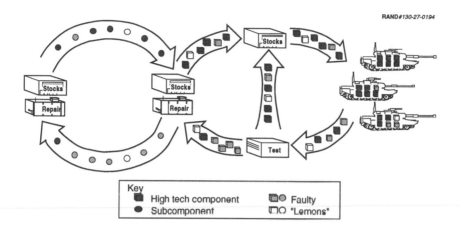

Figure 5—Repair Systems for High Technology Components Flooded by False
Negatives and False Positives

As the icons in the figure suggest, these design problems and lemons flood
the current system with false negatives—components that are thought to be
broken but are not—and false positives—components that are thought to be
fixed or "good" but are not. Current DoD acquisition and maintenance processes lack a strong capability to isolate and remove design problems and
lemons.

Scope and Consequence of Poor R&M Performance

Examples of these two problems are provided by RAND's analysis of the
reliability and maintainability of high-technology components of the F-16
(Gebman et al., 1989). (Similar problems exist with other frontline weapon
systems that RAND has analyzed, including the F-15, the M1A1 tank, and the
Apache attack helicopter.[22]) Frequently, the high-technology components of
the F-16 radar will encounter a fault, necessitating some troubleshooting.
Using a data sample of more than 16,000 flight hours, the study determined
that maintenance technicians find nothing wrong about one time in two.
When they do find something wrong, they may isolate the wrong item to replace. Thus they often replace two or three parts to fix a single problem.

More recently, the concern has shifted to the disproportionate cost burden associated
with a few components that contribute little to operational capability.

[22]For the F-15, see Gebman et al. (1989); for the M1A1, see Berman et al. (1988);
for the Apache, see Robbins et al. (1991).

Some of the removed components are, in fact, good, but they are placed into the repair system. When these good components are tested, they should test good and be returned to stock. However, sometimes they test bad, and a repair action is taken. Unfortunately, some faulty components pass the diagnostic test when they are not good and are sent back to stock. These faulty components are then reinstalled in weapon systems, where they again prove faulty during the operational mission. These fault isolation and removal problems were evident at each echelon of the maintenance system (see Table 3). At the unit level, half of the maintenance actions to correct a malfunction resulted in no repair; at the intermediate level, one-third of the maintenance actions resulted in no repair; and at the depot level, one-fifth.

There are two important inferences to be drawn from these data. The first is that many maintenance hours are expended without benefit. The second is that many weapon systems, components, and subcomponents are considered fully operational when they are not. In other words, these design problems generate excessive support costs and result in overestimating the capability of a fielded weapon system.

Lemons represent a different problem, though they lead to the same general consequences. They are very difficult to identify and even more difficult (sometimes even impossible) to fix. They frequently circulate through the logistics system, moving from one weapon system and unit to others. Lemons cause about 20 times the number of unnecessary replacements of subcomponents at the intermediate echelons—remarkably, high-technology lemons were found to create about half the workload at the depot repair shops. And of course the presence of these lemons in weapon systems cause commanders to overestimate the number of available systems that are truly fully mission-capable.[23]

Table 3

Fault Isolation and Removal Problems at Each Echelon of F-16
Support (in percent)

Maintenance Actions	Depot	Intermediate	Unit
With repair	80	67	50
Without repair	20	33	50

[23]The keys to identifying lemons and breaking this cycle of waste are serial number tracking of high-technology components, data collection of component activity, and an aggressive analysis program to identify problems.

Maturing Weapon Systems for Greater Availability at Lower Costs

The current acquisition process was designed to serve the needs of the Cold War. When the United States faced a very strong Soviet threat, weapon systems were designed, developed, and fielded because superior capability was needed to counter that threat. There were good reasons—of both cost and risk—for fielding weapon systems that were not fully mature in terms of their reliability or maintainability. As a result, these weapon systems typically did not achieve the full level of availability that they might have if the design had been matured through a longer development cycle.

Now that the United States is in an environment in which it is not necessary to rush to a high rate of production—and some programs will never achieve a high rate of production—DoD can change the acquisition process to permit the maturation of high-technology systems before fielding. RAND has developed an approach, called "maturation development," to improve the current process for developing and maintaining weapon systems. The approach addresses both of the maintainability problems identified above, design problems and lemons. Maturation development is anticipated to result in increased weapon system availability rates at lower life-cycle costs.[24]

The goal of maturation development is to make high-technology component designs more reliable and maintainable upon full fielding.[25] The key el-

---

[24]Maturation development has not yet been field tested as a complete concept. Elements of the approach have been applied in the Minuteman, Hawk missile, F-15, and F-16 programs. The maturation approach was developed in RAND research on the F-15/F-16 in the mid-1980s. That experience informed a large RAND study in support of the proposed Light Helicopter Experimental (LHX)—now called the Comanche—helicopter. (See Berman et al., 1989.) In the late 1980s, RAND estimated that without a successful maturation development program, the high-technology components of the LHX would likely account for 80 percent of the cost of the spares and 80 percent of the repair cost, and would result in 70 percent of the downtime. Now that acquisition of the Comanche has been delayed, RAND is working with the Army to test this maturation approach during the upgrade of the Apache fleet. For further discussion of maturation development, see Dumond, Eden, McIver, and Shulman (1993).

[25]There are a number of analogs to maturation development in commercial industries. One is the practice of software firms in distributing "beta" versions of new products to a limited set of users. These users test the new product in what could be described as its "normal, operational environment" and uncover bugs and design deficiencies that the firm can choose to correct before distributing the full market version. Another analog is the use of pilot plants in the processing industries. Rather than building a full-scale factory employing a new process, a firm builds a small but fully functional plant to test the new concept operationally. These practices have in common the recognition that complex mechanisms cannot be fully matured until information is available regarding how they perform while operating normally in a real-world environment.

ement of this approach is an intensive data collection and analysis period prior to full-rate production. The approach calls for the manager to freeze the weapon system design during the low-rate production phase of the acquisition process, operate a small number of the weapon systems intensely, and collect and analyze a great deal of detailed data. On the basis of the analysis, the service using the system would modify the design to produce a more mature weapon system, one that will provide required performance at lower life-cycle cost. This data collection period could take months, perhaps even a few years.

To support this phase of intensive operation, data collection, and analysis, an integrated database should be established during the earliest phases of development. After the logistics design problems are identified and the weapon system is modified, the effects of the changes should be monitored. This verification of the corrections occurs during the late stages of low-rate production and after the modified weapon system is fielded.

Through the fielded phase, the analysis system should be used to detect and isolate the lemons—by tracking components by serial number—as well as any new design problems that emerge because of changing missions or aging effects. This approach is applicable not only to the development of new weapon systems but also to system upgrades and mission modifications.[26]

DIRECTIONS FOR FUTURE ANALYSIS

To review, we have advocated three strategies for reinventing the DoD logistics system: (1) focusing all the logistics actions on the customer's needs, (2) redesigning the processes themselves to be more efficient, and (3) designing and redesigning the weapon systems to meet the customer's needs and to reduce the burden on the logistics structure. The aim is to provide a much leaner, more flexible logistics system that will meet the nation's needs for support of its military operations in the post–Cold War era.

Taken together, these strategies offer a very positive view of the potential for major, even radical, improvements in effectiveness and efficiency. However, two major caveats are in order.

First, even if we can accept these general strategies as valid, much more effort is needed to establish that specific commercial innovations are appropriate for or can be adapted successfully for use by the DoD military system. This needed effort is broad in scope, in terms not only of its exploration areas, but also of its methodologies. In addition to examinations of current commercial and DoD practices, it is necessary to undertake experiments, tests, demonstra-

---

[26]This discussion is not meant to imply that maturation development obviates the need for improvements to engineering or manufacturing processes.

tions, and simulations of the proposed alternatives. A strong base of facts is needed to demonstrate clearly to policymakers the cost and operational effects of proposed reforms of the DoD logistics system. The investigations may reveal that DoD will not be able to achieve the same scope of change or scale of cost savings and performance improvements that some commercial firms have achieved.

Second, even for those commercial innovations that appear applicable or adaptable to military logistics use, implementation may prove difficult or even impossible. Certainly, implementation within DoD is likely to be more difficult than it is in any commercial firm, and the track record of commercial firms in making radical changes successfully is not strong (by one estimate, less than half of the attempts at reengineering succeed). One reason is structural: The experience of commercial firms suggests that a prerequisite for successful implementation is strong, sustained leadership that can provide a compelling vision of change, powerful agents of change, and sufficient resources for change. The DoD logistics system is, of course, composed of many processes and activities organized across multiple agencies and services. Thus, for most logistics processes and activities, there is no single person or ogranization responsible for systemwide performance. For this and other reasons, the implementation models used by commercial firms may also not be applicable to or adaptable for the DoD logistics system, and much of the implementation experience of those firms may be of limited utility to DoD policymakers.

To conclude, we must remember that the stakes are high. Even partial failure to reinvent DoD logistics system could be immensely damaging and dangerous. For one thing, although naive talk of a "peace dividend" has disappeared, it remains true that the nation is committed to shifting more of its resources away from national defense, and many policymakers, including some within DoD itself, have expressed the expectation that a greatly improved logistics system will help realize substantial savings.

In addition, and more important, the nation will not tolerate any increased risk to the safety and effectiveness of its deployed forces. A reinvented logistics system must be a superior logistics system, improved not only in its efficiency but also in its effectiveness. This requirement applies to the system during transitional periods as well, even when they involve major, systemic change. The need for the logistics system to operate with full effectiveness through all reforms is an additional implementation challenge.

BIBLIOGRAPHY

Abell, J. B., et al. (1992), *DRIVE (Distribution and Repair in Variable Environments): Enhancing the Responsiveness of Depot Repair*, RAND, Santa Monica, CA.

Berman, M., J. Halliday, T. F. Kirkwood, W. E. Mooz, E. D. Phillips, R. J. Kaplan, and C. L. Batten (1985), *Integrating Basing, Support, and Air Vehicle Requirements: An Approach for Increasing the Effectiveness of Future Fighter Weapon Systems*, RAND, Santa Monica, CA.

Berman, M., D. W. McIver, M. L. Robbins, and J. Schank (1988), *Evaluating the Combat Payoff of Alternative Logistics Structures for High-Technology Subsystems*, RAND, Santa Monica, CA.

Berman, M., et al. (1989), *Reducing Risks Associated with Developing the LHX Mission Equipment Package*, RAND, Santa Monica, CA.

Blaxill, Mark F., and Thomas M. Hout (1991), "The Fallacy of the Overhead Quick Fix," *Harvard Business Review*, July-August.

Crawford, G. B. (1988), *Variability in the Demands for Aircraft Spare Parts: Its Magnitude and Implications*, RAND, Santa Monica, CA.

Davenport, Thomas H. (1993), *Process Innovation: Reengineering Work Through Information Technology*, Harvard Business School Press, Boston, MA.

Davenport, Thomas H., and James E. Short (1990), "The New Industrial Engineering: Information Technology and Business Process Redesign," *Sloan Management Review*, Vol. 13, No. 4.

Davis, Paul K. (ed.) (1994), *New Challenges for Defense Planning: Rethinking How Much Is Enough*, RAND, Santa Monica, CA.

Department of Defense Supply System Inventory Report, September 30, 1992 (1992).

Donaldson, T. S., and A. F. Sweetland (1966), *Trends in Aircraft Maintenance Requirements*, RAND, Santa Monica, CA.

Dumond, J., R. Eden, and J. Folkeson (1993), *Weapon System Sustainment Management*, RAND, Santa Monica, CA.

Dumond, J., et al. (1994), *Measuring Weapon Systems for Increased Availability at Lower Costs*, RAND, Santa Monica, CA.

Gebman, J. R., et al. (1989), *A New View of Weapon System Reliability and Maintainability*, RAND, Santa Monica, CA.

Hammer, Michael (1990), "Reengineering Work: Don't Automate, Obliterate," *Harvard Business Review*, July-August.

Hammer, M., and J. Champy (1993), *Re-engineering the Corporation*, Harper Business, New York.

Hillestad, R. J. (1982), *Dyna-METRIC: Dynamic Multi-Echelon Technique for Recoverable Item Control*, RAND, Santa Monica, CA.

Kassing, David (1994), "Strategic Mobility in the Post–Cold War Era," in Davis (1994).

McGlothlin, W. H., and T. S. Donaldson (1964), *Trends in Aircraft Maintenance Requirements*, RAND, Santa Monica, CA.

Moore, S. C., J. Stockfisch, M. S. Goldberg, S. M. Holroyd, and G. Hildebrandt (1991), *Measuring Military Readiness and Sustainabilities,* RAND, Santa Monica, CA.

"The New Eagles: Command in Transition," 1992 USAF Almanac (1992), *Air Force Magazine,* May.

Readiness-Based Maintenance Economic Analysis Final Report (1992), Management Analysis, Inc.

Robbins, M. L., M. B. Berman, D. W. McIver, W. E. Mooz, and J. Schank (1991), *Developing Robust Support Structures for High Technology Subsystems: The AH-64 Apache Helicopter,* RAND, Santa Monica, CA.

Tapscott, Don, and Art Caston (1993), *Paradigm Shift: The New Promise of Information Technology,* McGraw-Hill, New York.

Tsai, C. L., R. Tripp, and M. B. Berman (1992), *The VISION Assessment System: Class IX Sustainment Planning,* RAND, Santa Monica, CA.

Washington Headquarters Services, Directorate for Information Operations and Reports (1992), *Department of Defense Supply System Inventory Report,* September 30.

Chapter 23

DEFINING A BALANCED INVESTMENT PROGRAM
FOR COPING WITH TACTICAL BALLISTIC MISSILES

Richard Mesic

As the United States contemplates theater missile defenses (TMD) it will be considering how best to balance its investments among different defense layers in an overall architectural context. Many of the possible defense components are still purely conceptual, but illuminate some of the central issues. One conclusion is that in a two-layer defense, at least one of the layers should have a very low leakage. Since only terminal/midcourse defenses are advanced enough to justify confidence (and since their effectiveness is less scenario dependent), it makes sense for DoD to set a priority on perfecting a terminal/midcourse system. That said, the long-run usefulness of TMD may depend critically on having two or more layers, especially if future adversaries have fractionated payloads (e.g., early release of multiple canisters with chemical weapons). Thus, if the United States were to begin deploying a one-layer terminal/midcourse system, it might at some point become cost-effective to introduce one or more additional layers, at constant overall cost, by forgoing some of the expansion of the first layer that would otherwise take place. Adding layers is much more attractive when one focuses on incremental rather than sunk costs, or when one considers problems associated with deliberate threat fractionation, debris from initial intercepts, and identifying which targets have already been "killed." Surprisingly, analysis suggests that the cost to maintain constant effectiveness in a multilayer system scales only linearly with the size of the threat, which means that there is some reason to hope that robust TMD is at least feasible. This depends, however, on success in developing "forward-layer" systems for counterforce, boost-phase intercept, or postboost ascent-phase intercept—systems that can destroy missiles before fractionation occurs and, in some instances, with minimum ambiguity about results.

This paper reflects many discussions and ideas from collaboration with David Vaughan, Glenn Kent, and Russ Shaver in an Air Force–sponsored project led by Vaughan.

INTRODUCTION

An overall architecture for theater missile defense (TMD) can be conceived as an appropriate mix of four types of system, or four "pillars":

- Active defense, with several distinctly different types:
    - — Terminal defense (e.g., Patriot or THAAD, located near the targets to be defended).
    - — Midcourse defense (e.g., THAAD, located near the targets and capable of midcourse intercept).
    - — Boost-phase or postboost ascent-phase defense (BPI-API) (e.g., a system of forward-operating aircraft with high-energy lasers or capable of launching hypersonic interceptors at a missile during its boost phase or postboost ascent phase before apogee).
- Counterforce (e.g., a system using F-15Es to attack the transporter-erector-launchers (TELs) before, during, or after the launch of missiles).
- Passive defense (e.g., hardened aircraft shelters and revetments, suits and masks to protect against chemicals, and CCD—camouflage, concealment and deception).
- Battle management/command, control, communications, computers, and intelligence (BM/C^{4}I).

As the United States contemplates TMD it will be considering how best to balance its investments in the different types of systems. In this paper I consider tradeoffs among the various types of active defenses that can be imagined, some of which overlap with counterforce systems in that they depend on forward-operating aircraft that must search mobile-missile deployment areas.[1]   I will attempt to explain in simple analytic terms some of the tentative insights gained from a very short RAND study on the subject requested by the Air Force. While the models and assumptions used here are quite simple, they illustrate what appear to be fairly general truths. The discussion is methodological and parametric, because it will be some years before enough data become

---

[1]One can consider BM/C^{4}I to be more of a foundation than a pillar, and assume that the necessary and appropriate investments will be made in this foundation when the time comes. This is not borne out by history, since battle management C^{4}I has often been underfunded, but the issues involved are beyond the scope of this paper and quite different in kind than those treated. Passive defenses are also rather different in kind. Further, investments in passive defense are in practice almost independent of investments in the other pillars. They may become quite important in the context of defense against chemical, biological, and nuclear weapons, but there is not much of a "mix" issue.

available on costs and weapon-system effectiveness to make definitive judgments. Indeed, at this point, the discussion is forward-looking and analytically structured speculation about a subject that may become increasingly important in the years ahead if R&D efforts to improve TMD begin to pay off.

The paper proceeds as follows. First, I discuss a two-layer defense system with layer 1 being an unspecified "early kill" system (e.g., a forward-operating ascent-phase and/or boost-phase intercept (BPI-API) and/or a counterforce system [prelaunch missile kill]) and layer 2 being a "late kill" terminal and/or midcourse defense system. I shall examine how effectiveness varies as a function of the size and quality of those layers. Then I discuss the cost-effectiveness of different mixes under a variety of different assumptions. The next step is to reconsider the way in which one thinks about the problem: Are we designing the ultimate system from the outset, or do we anticipate building a one-layer system first and then considering whether to add another layer or expand the first? The perspective here makes a big difference, as do the "requirements" one levies on the system.

I next consider architecture issues associated with three-layer systems with costs that all depend primarily on numbers and effectiveness of interceptor missiles. I discuss how "optimal" system architectures minimizing cost vary with assumptions about defense interceptor performance—and, importantly, with assumptions about perfect information and command-control capabilities for real-time adaptation of firing doctrine.

I will then turn briefly to the issue of architectural impact of killing TELs after they launch a TBM—this is sometimes referred to as postlaunch or "counterbattery" counterforce operations. Postlaunch operations are of special interest for two reasons. First, unlike the prelaunch counterforce operations, there are feasible and affordable systems (e.g., the F-15E concept presented in Mesic, 1994) for postlaunch operations that could be fielded in the near term. Second, postlaunch operations have so far been relatively neglected in TMD architectural studies, possibly because the potential impact, as simple as I believe it is, has been misunderstood.

Finally, I shall discuss a number of qualitative considerations that should be important in determining future architectures. I end, then, with a speculative but partly integrated description of key considerations and a number of tentative conclusions about the types of system likely to be attractive and what kind of an investment strategy will make sense in the years ahead—a strategy that balances near-term conservatism against the need to invest in R&D with very high potential leverage in the long term.

TRADEOFFS BETWEEN TERMINAL/MIDCOURSE AND COUNTERFORCE/BOOST-ASCENT-PHASE LAYERS

Measures of Effectiveness

There are many measures of effectiveness (MOEs) for anti-TBM systems, but in this discussion the focus will be on the following:

- Leakage L (the percent or fraction of attacking weapons that are expected to penetrate the defenses, with L_1, L_2, . . . representing leakages of successive defense layers and Pk_1, Pk_2, . . . the kill probabilities).

- Confidence or probability $P(L_{max}; M)$ of achieving a specified low leakage L_{max} (typically zero) against a nominal threat of M missiles.

Another important measure is the cost of achieving a specified value of L or $P(L_{max}; M)$. Thus, we can consider both equal-cost and equal-effectiveness comparisons.

Effectiveness of a Two-Layer System

Equal-Effectiveness Comparisons. Consider now a two-layer defense architecture. The first involves unspecified counterforce (e.g., attacking TELs) and/or API-BPI systems. For this example the details are unimportant—all that matters is that this layer "kills" threat missiles with probability Pk_1 before they are exposed to the defenses in the second layer.[2] The second involves terminal and/or midcourse intercept. These active defense systems are described by the number of defense interceptors used to engage each threat object and by the single-shot kill probability ($SSPk_2$) of each interceptor. Suppose, for illustrative purposes, that we require a 10 percent overall leakage ($L = 0.1$) from this two-layer TMD system. There are different combinations of the two layers that would accomplish this, as shown in Table 1. The first layer is characterized by a simple Pk_1, without specifying what the kill mechanisms are. The second layer is characterized by the number of interceptors, N, available per initial threat missile (before attrition by the first layer) and by the $SSPk_2$ of each interceptor. The leakages (per threat missile) of the two layers are then:

$$L_1 = 1 - Pk_1$$

---

[2]This Pk_1 should be interpreted as the result of *all* counterforce operations, which might involve multiple "shots" at the missiles.

$$L = L_1 \times L_2 = \left(1 - Pk_1\right) \times f \times \left(1 - SSPk_2\right)^n.$$

The total number of inventory terminal (and/or midcourse) interceptors per threat missile, N, shown in Figure 1, is related to n simply as:

$$N = f \times L_1 \times n.$$

That is, because the first layer kills a portion of the original missiles, the second layer's targets are only those that remain, multiplied by the fractionation f (assume $f = 1$ in this example) that occurs between layers.[3]

As Figure 1 indicates, there are many combinations that achieve the overall goal of 10 percent leakage ($L = 0.1$). For example, if there is no first layer at all, then the system succeeds with only one interceptor per target if $SSPk_2 = 0.90$, or if it has two interceptors per target with $SSPk_2 = 0.68$, and so on. Later I shall consider how assumptions about costs allow us to assess which combination is most cost-effective.

Another observation from Table 1 is that increasing the effectiveness of the first layer doesn't reduce the required effectiveness of the second as much as one might think (it does, however, reduce the acquisition costs of the second

Table 1

Equal-Effectiveness Two-Layer Systems with 10 Percent Leakage

Effectiveness of First Layer (Extended Counterforce): Pk_1	Second-Layer Interceptors per Threat Missile : N	$SSPk_2$ Required of Interceptors to Achieve 10% Overall Leakage
0	1	0.9
	2	0.68
	3	0.54
0.5	0.5	0.8
	1	0.55
	1.5	0.42
0.9	0	—

[3]This is not strictly true, in that debris from the first-layer intercepts may also appear as targets to the second layer. Also, it may or may not be possible to identify which of the targets were destroyed by the first layer; they may still appear to be important targets. I shall discuss such complications later in the paper.

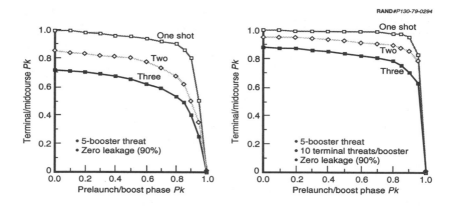

RAND#P130-79-0294

Figure 1—Tradeoffs Between Pillar Effectiveness for Zero Leakage Against Small Threats

layer, since the interceptor inventories per threat missile can be reduced as shown in Table 1). For example, as Table 1 shows, even if the first layer were 50 percent effective in destroying ballistic missiles, each interceptor in the second layer would still have to achieve a *SSPk* of 0.8 to reach the desired level of overall effectiveness if only a single interceptor were launched at each missile that survived the first layer. (Note that this case is the "0.5" entry in the second column in Table 1 since only half of the threat missiles reach the second layer of the defense.)

As a second example of equal-effectiveness comparisons, consider the same generic two-layer system, but now require a 90 percent nominal probability of zero leakage against a total threat of *M* missiles; i.e., $P(0; M) = 0.9$.[4] Here the probability calculations are a bit more complex, because the probability of zero leakage depends on the total threat, *M*:

$$P\left(0; M\right) = \left[1 - \left(1 - Pk_1\right) \times \left(1 - SSPk_2\right)^n\right]^M$$

---

[4]I use the phrase "nominal probability" here because the "real" probability depends on factors outside the simple mathematics assumed. For example, a system with an interceptor *SSPk* of 0.9 as measured in test programs may in fact have some deeply hidden fatal flaw when used operationally. The probability of that is not included in the assessment of *SSPk*. One historical example of this involved deployed nuclear weapons with very high nominal reliabilities that were eventually discovered to have defective firing mechanisms.

In this expression n is the number of interceptors per salvo in layer 2. Figure 1 illustrates tradeoffs in effectiveness between the layers of this notional two-layer system if the requirement is 90 percent probability of zero leakage. The three curves in each graph correspond to cases in which the second-layer active defenses make one, two, or three shots per engagement (n = 1, 2, or 3).[5] The graph on the left is for a five-missile threat (M = 5) with no fractionation (f = 0); the graph on the right is for the same five-missile threat, but in this case it is assumed that those missiles that survive the first layer fractionate into ten objects each (f = 10), all of which the second layer must intercept (e.g., with midcourse or terminal defenses).

The first insight here is that the required value of $SSPk_2$, i.e., the required kill probability of the second layer's interceptors, is only a very weak function of the first layer's effectiveness (Pk_1) over a wide range of possible effectiveness levels, and vice versa. For example, in the single-warhead threat case (left graph), assuming two shots per target, the required $SSPk_2$ varies from only 0.85 to 0.8 as the effectiveness Pk_1 of the first layer varies from 0 to 0.5. It follows that

- To achieve a high probability of zero leakage in a two-layer system, at least one of the layers has to be very good with high confidence.

- If both are very good, so much the better—there is room for some unexpected performance degradation.

This is just mathematics, so far. If we speculate a bit about real-world implications, note that from Desert Storm experience it seems that achieving a *reliably* high-effectiveness prelaunch counterforce system may be impossible, or at least very difficult, if it depends on searching the deployment area quickly and repeatedly. This is not to say that prelaunch kills won't occur or that defense planners should not work on systems to achieve them; it does suggest that in thinking about two-layer systems, the first of which depends on counterforce operations, we have no basis for believing that we will ever be able to achieve reliably high performance for the first layer (Mesic, 1994). This, coupled with the conclusion above, implies that

- A high priority should be placed on perfecting systems to engage the missiles after launch, whether terminal and midcourse defenses, which are relatively well understood, or the more embryonic BPI-API defenses.

---

[5]These shots can be in a single salvo or sequential (shoot [S], shoot-look-shoot [S-L-S], or shoot-look-shoot-look-shoot [S-L-S-L-S]). There is no difference from the perspective of this example between salvo launches and sequential launches with kill assessments between launches, but there is a significant difference if the issue is required interceptor inventory.

- Working to improve the effectiveness of truly synergistic multilayer defense architectures (e.g., counterforce, terminal and midcourse defenses, and BPI-API defenses) makes sense, but more in the sense of pursuing advanced R&D with high *potential.* If initial efforts prove successful, the multiple layers could prove to be an extremely valuable hedge against performance shortfalls in BMDO's (previously SDIO's) midcourse and terminal intercept systems focus (that may have common or correlated failure modes).

Later, as considerations not modeled in these simple initial analyses are introduced, I will qualify these implications, particularly as they pertain to the relative significance of BPI-API systems in the overall TMD architecture.

Cost-Effectiveness Comparisons.   The preceding discussion, which suggested a first priority on perfecting midcourse and terminal defenses, did not depend on costs.   Implicitly, we were assuming that such a strategy was affordable.   Would the conclusion about focusing on the active-defense layer change if we considered costs?   Unfortunately, we lack reliable cost data (and will continue to for some years), but we can make some simple and parametric estimates that are in themselves revealing.

Let us assume a very simple two-layer defense cost model in which total system cost C is given by:

$$C = C_1 + C_2 = \left(B_1 + I_1 \right) + \left(B_2 + I_2 \right)$$

where B_i are the fixed, "buy-in" costs for layer i (i.e., the cost of RDT&E and setting up initial production capabilities), and I_i are the incremental costs of acquiring more capability in layer i (e.g., additional interceptors for a terminal defense or additional aircraft for a counterforce capability).

For the second layer of terminal and midcourse defense, let us assume that I_2 is merely proportional to the number of interceptors.   For an extended-counterforce system, such as one using search aircraft to find and kill TELs, let us assume that I_1 is proportional to the number of search aircraft. We can relate cost to effectiveness as measured by first-layer leakage L_1 as follows:[6]

$$L_1 = 1 - K \times \left(1 - \exp\left[-q \times I_1 \right] \right)$$

---

[6]This expression can be derived from search effectiveness models in which the search rate is assumed to scale directly with the investment I_1 and the search process is Poisson, with the resultant negative exponential form shown here for expected leakage after a specified search time.

where both K and q are parameters; q is a scale parameter that relates search effectiveness to marginal costs (i.e., the cost of one more search aircraft).

For the sake of illustration, let us now make some specific assumptions about these cost-effectiveness parameters. These are strictly notional, since no credible search concepts have yet been demonstrated, much less costed realistically. The illustration assumes that $B_1 = B_2 = 100$ in some cost units, that I_1 and I_2 are variables (in the same cost units) where $I_2 = 1 \times$ number of defense interceptors, $I_1 = C - C_2 - B_1$, and that the constant q is about 0.01 and $K = 0.9$.

The idea explored in Figures 2 and 3 is that for a given (fixed) total investment in the two layers (or "pillars"), there is a preferred allocation to each. If overall leakage L is plotted versus the percent of the total budget dedicated to the first pillar, then as resources are increased in the first pillar and decreased in the second (to keep the total investment constant), the minimum point in that curve represents the optimal allocation. If the minimum occurs somewhere in the middle, such curves are sometimes called "bucket" curves.

Using this simple cost model, Figure 2 shows the number of leaking weapons as a function of the percent of budget allocated to layer 1 (counterforce or boost-phase defense). It assumes a threat of 100 missiles. Each curve in Figure 2 shows results for a different total budget. This particular set of calculations assumes that the second-layer interceptor $SSPk_2 = 0.5$ and that at most two interceptors can be salvoed against each missile.

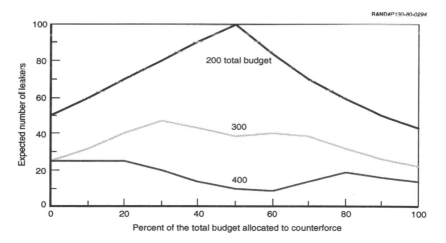

RAND#P130-80-0294

Figure 2—Effectiveness of Equal-Cost Systems
(Assumes 100 missiles with one warhead each and terminal $SSPk_2 = 0.5$)

Although the curves are notional because the cost model (and parameter values) are invented, they illustrate points that seem likely to be valid with more realistic figures. Obviously, as the top two curves show, if the buy-in costs for each system (prior to fielding any capability) are 100 units, then if the United States has only 200–300 units total for the integrated system (this is for each region to be defended in this way), it cannot afford to invest anything in more than one pillar—the preferred solution is to spend everything on one or the other. The top two curves would suggest that the best approach would be to buy a layer-1 system (the minimum is at the right side), but this is an artifact of the model, which is probably overly optimistic regarding the counterforce layer. Only when the budget is assumed to be 400 units (the bottom curve) is the optimal solution a mix of layers 1 and 2 (about 60 percent–40 percent).

In Figure 3 I have used the same assumptions, with one exception: I have assumed that the fixed costs associated with the second layer are "sunk"; i.e., B_2 = 0. Now, the three curves in Figure 3 represent *additional* investment levels of 200, 300, or 400 units. For the 300- and 400-unit investment curves there is now a pronounced "bucket," with the bias toward counterforce. Note, not surprisingly, that the leakage for the optimal mix in Figure 3 at a total additional budget of 300 (with 100 buy-in for layer 2 assumed sunk) is about the same as the 400-unit optimal from Figure 2, and that an additional 100-unit investment in Figure 3 reduces the leakage only slightly (from 9 to 4).

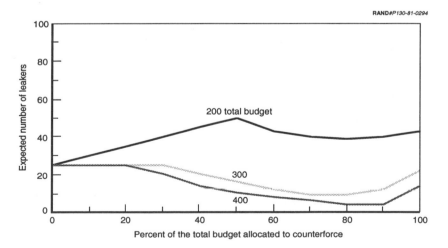

Figure 3—Mixed Solutions Are Possible If Buy-In Costs Do Not Dominate

Finally, in Figure 4 we look at the potential impact of threat fractionation on optimal two-layer solutions. All the parameters have the values used in Figure 2, but now I have assumed that any missile not killed by the counterforce system presents the midcourse and terminal defenses with five warheads rather than one. The dashed curve on the bottom is the same as the 400-unit cost curve from Figure 2 for comparison (i.e., this dashed curve corresponds to the case of no fractionation). Notice that if the 400-unit budget were maintained, then the optimal solution would be to invest everything in counterforce, but even then, leakage would be about eight times higher than in the optimal (mixed) nonfractionated threat case. The good news is that leakage can be reduced to the nonfractionated threat case by doubling the total budget to 800 units and fielding a two-layer defense.

In summary, the points that can be made from these notional examples that are probably independent of the (fictional) details are the following:

• Assuming large fixed or buy-in costs, only at high budget levels or very high fractionations is there a "bucket" in the curves, indicating that a mix of systems looks attractive.

• The effectiveness of a two-layer system will, at lower budget levels, be substantially lower than for an equal-cost one-layer system for unfractionated threats. That is, "the bucket may be upside down," contrary to conventional wisdom.

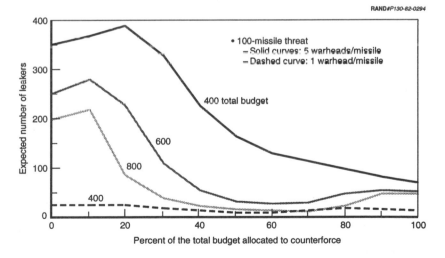

Figure 4—Threat Fractionation Increases Defense Costs and Shifts Emphasis to Counterforce Solutions

These conclusions reinforce the earlier conclusions in arguing that in developing an investment program, the priority should be on making *one* layer highly reliable first. Since we do not even know yet how to build an effective extended-counterforce layer, the priority should go to terminal and midcourse defenses. On the other hand, it should be evident that eventual success against larger and more troublesome threats than the simple Scuds used in Desert Storm depends very much on developing successful extended-counterforce capabilities.

Cost-Effectiveness Revisited When a First Layer Is Partly Deployed

As stated above, we do not currently know how to build an effective layer for boost-phase/ascent-phase (or counterforce). If we could, however, it might have high leverage. An investment strategy, then, should take the view that we begin with the terminal/midcourse systems, but at some point in their deployment, we should consider in the light of then-existing capabilities whether it would be wise to begin diverting some of the planned program funds into a new layer of defense, rather than merely expanding the number of terminal/midcourse interceptors. How effective the additional layer would need to be before the diversion would be justified would depend, of course, on all the cost and effectiveness parameters of the overall problem, but those calculations could be done from time to time as new information became available. Moreover, other considerations might play a pivotal role in determining when additional layers should be added, as subsequent sections of this paper will suggest.

COST-EFFECTIVENSS RELATIONSHIPS FOR MULTILAYER ACTIVE DEFENSES

Optimal (Cost-Minimizing) System Architectures

So far, discussion has focused on architectural tradeoffs between terminal-or-midcourse-intercept systems and forward-operating defense systems. Now let us turn our attention to tradeoffs among different layers of a multilayer active-defense system, all of which depend fundamentally on interceptor effectiveness. In particular, consider a three-layer system attempting to deal with a 100-missile threat. Each layer has interceptors with *SSPks* of P_1, P_2, P_3 and a doctrine calling for shooting n_1, n_2, n_3 interceptors at each target, respectively. For simplicity here, I shall ignore fixed costs of each layer and assume that the variable costs of the layers are proportional to the interceptor costs, which are the same for each layer.

We will seek the minimum cost to achieve the requirement of zero leakage with high probability (e.g., $P(0; M) = 0.9$) against the specified threat (e.g., $M = 100$ missiles). The mathematics is too complex to be presented here, but Table 2 shows the optimal (minimum-cost) allocation of resources among layers.[7] The table assumes $SSPk$s of 0.5 for each layer.

In viewing Table 2 we can see that the optimal allocation of fire across layers is highly skewed (1, 2, and 7 shots per target in layers 1, 2, and 3, respectively). By contrast, the number of interceptors in the various layers is roughly constant. A simple two-layer example will help explain these results.

What is happening between layers is a "shoot-look-shoot" phenomenon. For example, if the defense allocates one 0.5 $SSPk$ interceptor per threat missile in the first layer, then we would expect 50 missiles (half of the assumed total of 100) to leak through to the second layer. If the defense shoots a salvo of two interceptors at each of these leakers in the second layer, we would expect 12.5 leakers through the two-layer system ($100 \times 0.5 \times 0.25$). The defense's total interceptor buy (cost) would be 200 ($100 + 2 \times 50$). Notice that if the defense used these 200 interceptors in a one-layer defense, the leakage would have been

Table 2

Optimum (Minimum-Cost) Three-Layer System for Achieving 90 Percent Probability of Zero Leakage Versus 100 Unfractionated Missiles

Objective: Minimum cost deployment (# interceptors) for specified performance (P (no leakage) > 0.9) against known threat (e.g., 100 missiles)

Layer 1	Layer 2	Layer 3	Total
$SSPk$ = 0.5	$SSPk$ = 0.5	$SSPk$ = 0.5	
Shots/object = 1[*]	Shots/object = 2	Shots/object = 7	Max 10 shots/object
100 deployed	100 deployed	88 deployed	288 int deployed
Leakage = 50	Leakage = 12.5	Leakage = 0.1	P (no leakage) > 0.9

[*]Other solutions in addition to 1 – 2 – 7 are: 1 – 3 – 6, 2 – 2 – 6, and 1 – 2 – 7.

---

[7]Three different groups at RAND derived the minimum-cost solutions using three different methods. Glenn Kent (Larson and Kent, 1994) worked the problem analytically, using reasonable approximations to simplify the mathematics; David Vaughan solved the recursive equations involved exactly; and the author used an exhaustive-search approach with a personal computer (a Macintosh IIci, using a BASIC program). Although the results are consistent, different insights emerged from the different approaches to the problem.

higher (25 versus 12.5). That is the kind of leverage that is behind the allocation shown here.[8]

Table 3 now shows an important qualitative insight that emerged from the several RAND studies of "optimal" system design. Using the same assumptions about *SSPks* and costs, but varying threat size, we see that, contrary to the initial intuition of most people (including the author),

- System cost, for achieving a 90 percent likelihood of zero leakage, grows only linearly with the size of the threat (less than linearly if one includes fixed costs).

- It appears plausible that a high-confidence defense system could be developed for a threat of tens or even hundreds of missiles—even with some degree of fractionation (remember that the effective threat size is the number of objects that must be attacked, which may be a factor many times larger than the number of missiles).[9]

The Need to Hedge Against Uncertainty

The problem with "optimal" solutions is that they are sometimes very sensitive to parameters about which there is considerable uncertainty. As a result,

Table 3

Costs of Optimum (Minimum-Cost) Three-Layer Systems Scale Almost Linearly with the Size of the Threat

Threat Size	Shots per Object	Cost (Interceptors)	Relative Cost
50	1 – 2 – 6	138	X
100	1 – 2 – 7	288	2.1 X
200	2 – 2 – 7	588	4.3 X
400	2 – 3 – 7	1188	8.6 X
800	2 – 3 – 8	2400	17.4 X
1600	2 – 3 – 9	4850	35.1 X

---

[8]Note that when an object is "killed" in one layer, it is assumed in this simplistic model that it is "gone" in the next. This implies that there is a perfect kill assessment or discrimination capability. RAND has also investigated cases in which this does not hold, but these results will not be presented here (see Larson and Kent, 1994).

[9]The plausibility of this *mathematical* argument rests on the assumption that the underlying technical performance of the systems is as specified—clearly, "real world" concerns about performance shortfalls or risks should temper this optimism.

the defense planner needs to understand this sensitivity and consider building a nominally suboptimal system that will hedge better against uncertainty than would the fully "optimal" one.

Table 4 shows what will result from a system designed with the nominally optimal allocation of interceptors and fire doctrine if one layer does not live up to expectations (table on the left) or if the threat is larger than expected (table on the right). There are two leakage columns, each corresponding to a different but equivalent optimal allocation. The numbers in the leakage columns show the expected leakage for two cases. The first number shows the result if the fixed ("optimal") firing doctrine is used, while the second number (in parentheses) shows the result if the firing doctrine is reoptimized in real time (within the inventory deployment constraints driven by the optimization) so as to make the best of a bad thing when it is observed that there has been a failure in an earlier layer. The results show several sensitivity phenomena. First, *the failure of a single layer can be very serious*. Second, *the earlier the failure, the more serious*. Finally, if we can reoptimize the firing doctrine in real time, it can be very beneficial. (This final point could be used in developing the investment rationale for "balanced" investments in BM/C⁴I systems!)

To this point in this section I have optimized in order to meet the assumed "requirement" of achieving zero leakage with high probability (i.e., $P(0; M) = 0.9$). Furthermore, I allowed arbitrarily large salvo sizes in each layer, which is

Table 4

Optimum (Minimum-Cost) Three-Layer Systems Are Sensitive to Unanticipated Failures but BM/C⁴I Can Increase Robustness

System	Performance	Leakage[*] $1-2-7$	Leakage[*] $2-2-6$	Threat	Leakage[*] $1-2-7$	Leakage[*] $2-2-6$
Baseline	.5, .5, .5	0.1 (0.1)	0.1 (0.1)	Baseline (100)	0.1 (0.1)	0.1 (0.1)
1st layer failure	.1, .5, .5	40 (10)	56 (37)	150	50 (16)	50 (19)
2nd layer failure	.5, .1, .5	28 (9)	14 (6)	200	100 (56)	100 (56)
3rd layer failure	.5, .5, .1	6 (6)	3 (3)			

[*]First leakage number assumes fixed firing doctrine; number in parentheses assumes real-time optimization (within constraints of total inventory deployed prewar).

not realistic.[10] In Figure 5 I have plotted the probability of zero leakage versus cost of the optimal firing doctrine solution if the salvo size in each of the three layers (denoted by the three integers to the right of the points on the curve with the number in parentheses showing the expected leakage) is limited to three. (For reference, I have also indicated the unconstrained optimal solution point: $P(0; 100) = 0.9$ at a cost of 288 units.) The decisionmaker must decide if it is worth an additional 70 cost units (i.e., 25 percent more) to increase the likelihood of zero leakage from 0.7 to 0.8. Notice that the three-interceptor constraint did not let us achieve the 90 percent confidence goal. If this were a hard requirement, the solution would require a higher $SSPk$ than the 0.5 used in this example.

THE POTENTIAL ROLE OF POSTLAUNCH ("COUNTERBATTERY") COUNTERFORCE SYSTEMS

We now turn briefly to the issue of the architectural impact of killing TELs after they launch a TBM—sometimes referred to as postlaunch or "counterbattery" counterforce operations. Postlaunch operations are of special interest for two reasons. First, unlike prelaunch counterforce operations, there

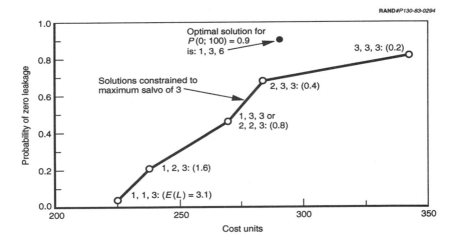

Figure 5—Confidence in Zero Leakage Is Expensive

---

[10]The probability of kill in a salvo of size n is modeled as $1 - (1 - SSPk)^n$ in these analyses. This assumes that each shot in the salvo is an "independent event" in the strict probabilistic sense. But in the real world, certain failure modes in each defense layer are likely to be correlated from interceptor to interceptor, in which case kill probabilities will not compound as this model suggests.

are feasible and affordable systems for postlaunch operations that could be fielded in the near term.   Second, postlaunch operations have so far been relatively neglected in TMD architectural studies, possibly because the potential impact, as simple as we believe it is, has been misunderstood.

If the probability of killing a TEL immediately postlaunch is Pk_0, then the probability that a given TEL will launch exactly m missiles before it is killed is:

$$P\left(m \text{ successful launches}\right) = Pk_0\left(1 - Pk_0\right)^{m-1} \quad \text{for } m = 1, 2, 3, \ldots$$

The expected number of launches is just $1/Pk_0$. So if $Pk_0 = 1$, there would be one launch; if $Pk_0 = 0.5$ there would be, on average, 2; and so on.

If, instead of the simplifying assumption we made above that there are an infinite number of reloads, we assume that there are at most T_{max} TBMs that each TEL can launch, then:

$$
\begin{aligned}
P\left(m \text{ launches}\right) &= Pk_0\left(1 - Pk_0\right)^{m-1} && \text{for } m = 1, 2, \ldots, T_{max} - 1 \\
&= \left(1 - Pk_0\right)^{m-1} && \text{for } m = T_{max} \\
&= 0 && \text{otherwise.}
\end{aligned}
$$

The expected value in this case is $(1 - (1 - Pk_0)^{T_{max}})/Pk_0$. If T_{max} is large and/or Pk_0 is small, this is approximately $1/Pk_0$.

The impact of killing TELs postlaunch is shown in Figure 6 in terms of the number of expected launches over the course of the war versus the probability that a TEL is killed each time it launches a TBM. Each curve represents a different TEL inventory, with the implicit assumption that there are unlimited reload missiles per TEL.[11]   For example, if the enemy had 100 TELs and we were able to, on average, kill a TEL postlaunch half the time, then we would expect only 200 successful launches before the enemy's entire launch capability was destroyed.   If his inventory of reload missiles were larger than this, those additional missiles would be "grounded," i.e., they would not have to be countered by other pillars of the TMD architecture.[12]

---

[11]This assumption was certainly reasonable in Desert Storm, since Saddam had only a handful of complex, expensive, Russian-supplied MAZ 543 TELs but hundreds of Scud missiles. Of course, in the future the number of reloads per TEL may be smaller (even zero), in which case the value of postlaunch kills would be proportionately smaller.

[12]For a more extensive development of these ideas, see Naff (1992).

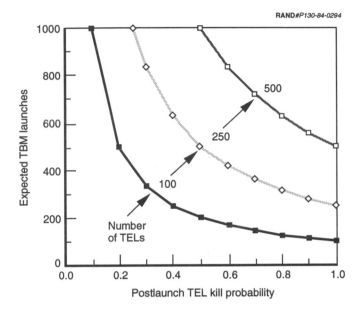

RAND#P130-84-0294

Figure 6—Postlaunch Kills Can Reduce the Threat Other
Defense Pillars Must Be Sized to Accommodate

Another way of looking at the potential utility of postlaunch kills is to think of them as "delayed effect" *prelaunch kills* in the sense that once all the TELs have been killed any unfired missiles have been "killed prelaunch." For example, with an initial threat of 100 TBMs and 10 TELs, a 0.5 postlaunch kill probability would imply that only 20 missiles of the total of 100 will be launched—a "delayed effect" prelaunch kill probability of 0.8. Given the difficulties and uncertainties in more conventional prelaunch kill systems and operations and the relative simplicity of postlaunch operations, this perspective on postlaunch kill operations may be particularly significant.

Obviously, if the costs to achieve a given level of postlaunch TEL kill capability were "small enough," there could be an overall TMD architectural cost savings due to the reduced threat the other pillars would have to be designed and fielded to counter. It is as simple as that. Of course, the actual cost implications are yet to be developed by the defense community, but these simplistic calculations suggest that postlaunch counterforce options should be taken more seriously than they have been to date.

OTHER ISSUES IN CONSIDERING FUTURE TMD ARCHITECTURES

Other Factors

The treatment of the pillar balance problem in this paper is far from complete. There are other dimensions to the problem that RAND has not yet attempted to analyze in which further quantitative analysis is possible:

- Warning and cueing of terminal/midcourse defenses from boost detection and IPP:
  - Reduce false alarms.
  - Allow earlier intercepts (less leakage and collateral damage).
- Less traffic for terminal/midcourse defenses (saturation thresholds).
- Deployment (to the theater) time-lines and area coverage effects.

The first set of analytic issues relates to the interaction between cueing systems (that might play a role in counterbattery operations or boost-phase intercept) and terminal defenses. Although we don't believe that DSP cueing was used by Patriot to engage the threat earlier, in theory there is some potential for expanding the terminal defense's battle space. The second issue relates to terminal defense saturation levels and suggests that prelaunch/boost kill could offer some relief. Finally, the third effect noted here relates to the scenario-specific deployment dynamics and coverage requirements. Target-area and forward-area defenses may have different response and effectiveness characteristics in different scenarios.

There are also less easily quantified counterforce issues, such as:

- Stress the enemy BM/C^{4}I so that attacks structured to counter defenses are less likely to succeed.
- Force the enemy to adopt a wider range of threat responses (cost and time):
  - Mobility and standoff.
  - Booster technology (solids, fast burn, . . .).

The less easily quantified aspects include disruption of enemy launch operations that might reduce his salvo potential, for example, which could have a beneficial effect on the terminal defenses. Finally, it is clear that we're faced with an action-reaction threat-countermeasure cycle. The more our defense pillars stress the enemy, the harder he'll have to work to attempt to counter the defenses. Hopefully, we are in a position that gives us an advantage in this process, and maybe our RDT&E and initial deployments can in fact even have a deterrent effect.

Qualitative Comparisons

In addition to these quantitative analyses, a balanced architecture must reflect informed judgments about qualitative features that may be as important as (if not more than) the quantitative analyses but which are not amenable to precise mathematical treatment. Good qualitative analyses require as much discipline and rigor as good quantitative methods do. The products of the qualitative analyses can be considered as "qualifiers" to the quantitative results. The products range from lists of unresolved (or even unresolvable) cost-performance issues and their explanations so that decisionmakers can mull them over, to qualitative comparison analyses (if the issue is X, then solution A is better than B—if the issue X is "important enough," then A might be selected even if it is less cost-effective than B in the quantitative analysis framework). The issue, of course, is completeness. Have the analysts overlooked any significant issues? The qualitative analyses approach, therefore, is an iterative (and unending) process of development and review, which requires a logical framework and clear documentation.

The issues of pillar balancing must be considered in some scenario context. Table 5 is an attempt to introduce a range of threats, scenarios, and defense implications (low, medium, and high sensitivity to missile leakage). The main point to be drawn from this matrix is that there are at least two distinct scenarios, each of which places unique stresses on the TMD systems. These scenarios involve conventional munitions on the one hand and weapons of mass destruction (WMD) on the other.

Table 5

Leakage Sensitivity Matrix: Where Should We Focus Our TMD Efforts?

Targets	TBM Weapon Type			
	Conventional Weapons		WMD	
	Unitary HE	Submunitions	Chemical	Bio/Nuclear
Cities	Low/Medium	Low/Medium	Medium	High
Ports	Low	Low	Medium	High
Airfields	Low	Medium	Medium	High
Battlefield	Low	Medium	Medium	High
Ships at sea	Very low	Very low	Medium	High

Defense issues:	Defense issues:
• Cost-effectiveness	• Very low leakage
• "Pillar" balance	• Lethality
• Integration	• Collateral damage

In the conventional weapons case, individual missiles are a limited military or political threat. In fact, for the rather primitive Scud missiles used by Iraq, the military significance was near zero, but the political significance was moderate to high because of the uncertainty about chemical warheads and the possibility that Israel might react to even limited conventional attacks in a way that would threaten the coalition. Clearly, for these conventional weapons scenarios, issues of defense cost-effectiveness, attrition rates, pillar balance, and integration are relatively straightforward. Everything is relative and subject to tradeoff analyses.

If WMD are introduced, however, the game changes. Even a single leaker has the potential for causing unprecedented damage. Therefore, the TMD issues are more likely to focus on *zero leakage, robustness to countermeasures, and high confidence to the point of "overkill."* Cost may be a secondary consideration. In this case, redundancy may be good even if, as seems likely, costs escalate. Clearly, a system that gives a high confidence of near-zero leakage will cost much more than twice as much as a 50 percent leakage system. Defense planners may need to face up to the fact that in these weapon-of-mass-destruction scenarios a "good" TMD system may not be good enough. The United States will probably have to invest a large amount in TMD in *all pillars.*[13]

Table 6 lists qualitative pros and cons associated with two generic pillars: the terminal and midcourse column is an aggregate of active-defense systems *deployed near the targets to be defended;* the prelaunch, counterbattery and BPI/API column represents a mix of systems from the counterforce and active-defense pillars described above that have the common characteristic of being *deployed in forward areas near the enemy's missile launchers.*

Each of the Table 6 items could be the topic of a ministudy of its own. The point to get from these lists of effectiveness pros and cons is that each column has its unique qualities and that neither is a complete solution to the TMD problem. For example, terminal defenses are deployed near the assets to be defended. This is a pro because it allows the defense to focus its resources where they are most needed. It is also a con because the areas to be defended could be large, forcing the defense to dilute its coverage. On the other hand, forward-area defenses, such as F-15Es searching for TELs, must operate over enemy territory, which is a con (usually, counterforce operations start with the assumption that air superiority or supremacy has been achieved). This can be a pro, however, if the threat area (e.g., Scud boxes in Iraq) is small relative to the

---

[13]But how much can we afford? The answer will hopefully emerge within the broader context of "counterproliferation." TMD is but one of the possible U.S. responses to the proliferation of WMD and delivery systems. As this is written, a responsive national counterproliferation policy and posture does not exist but is the subject of intense study.

Table 6

Pillar Qualities

Terminal and Midcourse	Prelaunch, Counterbattery, and BPI-API
1. Deployed near assets to be defended (pros and cons)	1. Deployed over enemy territory (pros and cons)
2. Predeployable (pro) or deployment delays (con)	2. Airborne systems may be quickly deployed (pro)
3. Potential for tailored or preferential defenses (pro)	3. Maximal expansion of defense battle space (pro)
4. Lethality issues (cons)	4. Lethality issues (pros and cons)
5. Countermeasure robustness (?) — Saturation (salvo, decoys, . . .) — MRV/MIRV/submunitions — Salvage fusing	5. Countermeasure robustness (?) — CCD, ECM, . . . — Active defenses — Booster technology (e.g., fast burn)
6. Relatively mature concepts and technologies (pro, but some risk)	6. Immature concepts and technologies (con)
7. Limited defended areas (con)	7. Large defended areas (pro)
8. Cost-effectiveness (TBD)	8. Cost-effectiveness difficult to predict (con)

area to be defended and adequate resources can be applied to the problem either in dedicated missions or assigned responsively to TBM targets of opportunity. Target area defenses can be deployed with the assets to be defended (e.g., ships, aircraft) and may be deployed prior to hostilities, but they may be airlift intensive, leading to serious delays in establishing "adequate" capabilities. Forward-area defenses may be deployable to the theater prewar, but obviously counterforce operations are only conducted during the war (except, importantly, some intelligence gathering and processing in support of anticipated attack operations). On the other hand, these systems may be self-deployable and, therefore, more responsive than the target-area defenses.

Similar arguments, pro and con, could be made for the other areas listed in Table 6. The last point in the right column deserves further comment. The issue centers on the scenario-dependent nature of counterforce operations and on the inherent uncertainties and the difficulty in measuring success. The community is still trying to sort out what happened in the Desert Storm "Scud hunt." Counterforce operations are a cat-and-mouse game. Balancing calculations must, therefore, accommodate the likely broad range of uncertainty in such operations.

There are significant uncertainties in all of these balancing analyses. Table 7 attempts to list some of the more apparent issues that may not be under the defense's direct control and shows how the two pillars (with boost phase separated here as a third or subpillar) are affected. A "−" means the pillar is adversely affected, a "+" means that the pillar is not significantly adversely affected, and a "+/−" means that it could go either way depending on the details.

What Table 7 shows is that there is a type of synergism possible through a mixture of pillar capabilities. Each pillar tends to be sensitive to different aspects of the threat or systematic failures. In some ways, this observation is similar to the strategic nuclear Triad rationale that has formed the basis for our deterrent posture for decades. While inherently difficult to quantify, this type of hedging analysis is an important consideration in pillar balancing.

IMPLICATIONS

Quantitative analyses can be useful in highlighting the architectural issues and identifying performance goals and breakpoints, but optimal "balanced" TMD architectural solutions depend very much on constraints, judgments, and uncertainties that may be impossible to quantify. Key issues are often glossed over in such analyses as presented in this paper due to the difficulties in identifying, characterizing, and modeling them. Unresolved issues include:

- Battle management, surveillance, command, control and communications linkages, and implications (e.g., "real" shoot-look-shoot potential between or within defense layers).

- Confidence in actual defense system technical performance in uncertain wartime environments and against responsive enemy countermeasures.

Table 7

Hedging and Pillar Synergy

	Target-Area Active Defense	Boost-Phase Intercept	Attack Operations
Widely dispersed targets	−	+	+
No time to deploy terminal defenses	−	+	+
Systemic terminal defense failure	−	+	+
Early deployment	−	+	+
Decoys	−	+	+
Fast burn (or jinking)	+	−	+
Systemic boost intercept failure	+	−	+
Widely dispersed launchers	+	−	−
Prelaunch CCD	+	+/−	−
Prelaunch intelligence failures	+	+/−	−

- Requirements uncertainties relating to the deployability, timeliness, defended areas, leakage goals, and other "operational factors."

In the first uncertainty area, it may be, for example, that Patriot and THAAD in effect form a single active-defense tier instead of the two commonly assumed in analyses such as presented here. The central issues are threat surveillance, object discrimination, lethality, kill assessment, and hand-over from one defense system to another. In fact, two tiers could, for certain reasonable assumptions about these factors, actually be *worse* than the best single layer. Suppose, for example, that THAAD's lethality is poor, resulting in a cloud of debris that may contain a live warhead. Patriot, which may have had a relatively high P_k against the undamaged threat missile, may now have a tough discrimination problem *and* an intercept kinematics problem (e.g., unpredictable reentry dynamics from the damaged warheads). On the other hand, a single tier or system such as an airborne BPI-API system might provide a more confident and effective shoot-look-shoot capability (e.g., a shot during boost, followed, if necessary, by a shot postboost, possibly even prefractionation).

How well will we be able to predict TMD system performance given the wide range of uncertainties in the threats and scenarios? Can these factors be explored adequately in simulations and/or tested in the field? Optimal architectures are built upon assumptions or assessments about the interrelationships between the systems or "pillars." Will the uncertainties require so much architectural hedging that each pillar will have to be designed to, in effect, "go it alone"?

Finally, there are unresolved (unresolvable?) uncertainties about just what a TMD system might be asked to do in the future and under what circumstances it might have to perform its mission. The general issues of "requirements," constraints, and architectural measures-of-effectiveness must all be explored much further than I have done in this paper.

For now, BMDO has focused on terminal active defenses, tilting the investment decisions heavily in that direction. To some extent, this has already stacked the deck. This means that less mature concepts, such as BPI-API and counterforce, will have to be better developed before a significant architectural balance shift might be justified based on cost considerations. But the uncertainties discussed above (and others doubtless overlooked) argue for exploration of complementary systems or performance hedges such as BPI-API and counterforce.[14]

BIBLIOGRAPHY

Davis, Paul K. (ed.) (1994), *New Challenges for Defense Planning: Rethinking How Much Is Enough*, RAND, Santa Monica, CA.

Larsen, Eric, and Glenn Kent (1994), *A New Methodology for Assessing Multi-Layer Missile Defense Options*, RAND, Santa Monica, CA.

Mesic, Richard (1994), "Extended Counterforce Options for Coping with Tactical Ballistic Missiles," in Davis (1994).

Naff, Tim (1992), *TMD Attack Operations and Active Defense Functional/Quantitative Relationships*, Strategic Defense Command briefing.

Vaughan, David, and Richard Mesic (1994), *Investment Strategy for Theater Missile Defense*, RAND, Santa Monica, CA.

---

[14]These important issues on TMD investment strategy and rationale are the focus of ongoing work at RAND (see Vaughan and Mesic, 1994). In this work we have concluded that threat and scenario variations and TMD systems performance limitations and uncertainties have two principal effects:

(1) Multilayer defenses will probably have to be deployed to *hedge* against uncertainties in the performance and/or availability of specific systems. The issues then center on the uncertainties and risks and how to best design and balance our *hedged* architectures—as opposed to the focus in this paper on how to compound effectiveness with synergistic multilayer architectures using "nominal" (possible, later proven to be overly optimistic) performance estimates.

(2) To achieve significant TMD capabilities in the face of WMD threats in future major regional contingencies, *all* conceivable options should be explored. Even then, however, we may find that the best effectiveness we can project is not judged to be "good enough" for protection against WMD. This then leads to issues of "requirements" and "value." If we can't meet a perceived *a priori* "requirement," we need to revisit the requirements process to see if there are useful fallback positions. Similarly, given a range of potential capabilities that may fall short of our hopes, how do we measure their "value" to us and, in turn, assess "cost-effectiveness"? The answers could be quite complex because they involve the perceptions and possible responses of adversaries to any path the United States chooses. For example, proceeding with one or more less-than-perfect TMD systems might be sufficient to deter other countries from investing heavily in ballistic missile systems in the first place, and might ultimately prove to be the most "cost-effective" approach for the United States to take.

ABOUT THE AUTHORS

BRUCE W. BENNETT is an associate director of RAND's International Security and Defense Strategy Program. Dr. Bennett graduated from the RAND Graduate School and has a Ph.D. in public policy analysis. He has also worked at Science Applications International Corporation, and has taught in the Department of Military Strategy and Operations at the National War College, and in the School of Public Health at the University of California at Los Angeles. Dr. Bennett's current research is in the future of warfare, the military balance in Korea, military science and modeling, force structure requirements for peace operations, and military health care.

CHRISTOPHER J. BOWIE is a member of the senior staff at RAND. A historian by training, he holds a bachelor's degree from the University of Minnesota and a doctorate from the University of Oxford. Dr. Bowie has worked at RAND since 1981 on a wide variety of strategy and airpower issues. He also served from 1989 to 1991 on the Secretary of the Air Force's personal staff.

GLENN C. BUCHAN is currently associate program director for C^{3}I/Space in RAND's Project AIR FORCE. Before that he led a series of RAND studies on the use of long-range bombers. Dr. Buchan holds Ph.D. and B.S. degrees in mechanical engineering from the University of Texas and an M.S.M.E. from Purdue University. He has also worked for the Central Intelligence Agency, the Institute for Defense Analyses, and Los Alamos National Laboratory. His current research interests run the gamut from nuclear strategy to special operations.

PAUL K. DAVIS is RAND's corporate research manager for Defense and Technology Planning. He is also on the faculty of the RAND Graduate School of Policy Studies and chairs its program in national security studies. Dr. Davis graduated from the University of Michigan and has a Ph.D. in chemical physics from the Massachusetts Institute of Technology. He has also worked at the Institute for Defense Analyses, the U.S. Arms Control and Disarmament Agency, and, as a senior executive, the Office of the Assistant Secretary of Defense for Program Analysis and Evaluation. Dr. Davis' current research is in defense planning, political-military strategy, crisis decisionmaking, and advanced modeling and simulation.

BRUCE DON is a senior analyst at RAND, researching national defense issues and critical civilian technologies. He previously served as a program director for the Army's Arroyo Center at RAND, managing the Force Development and Employment research program, and as the associate program director in Project AIR FORCE's Theater Force Employment Program. Dr. Don received a B.S. in astronautics from the U.S. Air Force Academy and a Ph.D. in public policy analysis from the RAND Graduate School. His current work focuses on the national information infrastructure and initiatives to revitalize the American automobile industry. His most recently completed defense research assesses the best mix of reserve and active-duty forces for the armed services in a study mandated by the Congress and reported to the Secretary of Defense.

JOHN DUMOND is a senior policy analyst in RAND's Resource Management Department. He is currently studying the effects of alternative logistics practices and structures on the ability to support military forces. Dr. Dumond graduated from Indiana University with a Ph.D. and an MBA in operations management. Before coming to RAND, he was head of the Department of System Acquisition Management at the Air Force Institute of Technology. He has also had Air Force assignments in the areas of military operations, logistics, and acquisition.

RICK A. EDEN is a writer/analyst at RAND. He graduated from the University of California at Riverside and earned his Ph.D. in English language and literature from UCLA. Before coming to RAND he was an assistant professor of English at the University of New Mexico in Albuquerque, where he conducted research on prose style, text structure, and reading strategies. He has also taught at UCLA, the University of Southern California, California State University at Los Angeles, and the RAND Graduate School. For several years he has concentrated his efforts at RAND on military logistics.

JOHN R. FOLKESON, JR., is a senior analyst with the Resource Management Department at RAND. Dr. Folkeson graduated from Pennsylvania State University and received an MBA from the University of Missouri, and a Ph.D. in production and logistics management from the University of Houston. He is retired from the U.S. Air Force, where he served as a logistics analyst with the Air Force Center for Studies and Analyses and on the faculty of the Air Force Institute of Technology. His current research is in workload planning, force projection sustainment, logistics process improvement, information system modernization, and managing the implementation of change.

DANIEL B. FOX is a senior operations research analyst. Dr. Fox graduated from the University of Illinois with a B.S. in engineering physics and a Ph.D. in mechanical engineering, and from Oklahoma State University with a M.S. in industrial engineering. He served in the U.S. Air Force, with his last duty assignment at the Air University Center for Aerospace Doctrine, Research, and

Education, where he headed the Operations Analysis Division at the Air Force Wargaming Center. Dr. Fox's current research is in defense planning, military assessment, wargaming, and simulation.

FRED L. FROSTIC is a senior defense analyst and the associate program director for Force Structure in RAND's Project AIR FORCE Division. He is a graduate of the Air Force Academy, the Army Command and General Staff College, and the National War College. He has an M.S. in engineering from the University of Michigan. Prior to joining RAND, he served in the U.S. Air Force in a variety of assignments with fighter wings, in the Air Staff, and on the faculty of the Air Force Academy. At RAND, he has led a series of studies on force structure needs for the post–Cold War era that examine the strategies and performance of joint forces through simulation and analysis.

SAM GARDINER is a consultant with RAND. His most recent projects have focused on nuclear proliferation campaign planning and the character of future warfare. He teaches courses in theater warfare at the National Defense University. His final assignment before retiring from the Air Force was as Chairman of the Department of Joint and Combined Operations at the National War College.

JOHN M. HALLIDAY is the director of the Military Logistics Program for RAND's Army Arroyo Center. He came to RAND after a career in the U.S. Air Force in war planning, operational logistics, test and acquisition, and graduate academics. Dr. Halliday holds a Ph.D. in public policy analysis from the RAND Graduate School, an M.S. in operations management from UCLA, and a B.S. in economics from the U.S. Air Force Academy. Dr. Halliday's current research is in military and commercial distribution systems, strategic logistics process improvements, and force basing issues.

MARGARET CECCHINE HARRELL is an operations research analyst with RAND. She graduated from the University of Virginia and has a M.S. in systems analysis from George Washington University. Her recent RAND work has concentrated upon peace operations, ranging from traditional United Nations peacekeeping missions to the recent missions in Somalia, and their implications for U.S. forces.

EDWARD R. HARSHBERGER, a member of the Defense and Technology Planning Department at RAND, is currently serving as a special assistant to the Air Staff, Headquarters Air Force. He graduated from Williams College and earned his Ph.D. at the RAND Graduate School. He has worked in RAND's National Defense Research Institute and formerly led the Force Employment Project for RAND's Project AIR FORCE. Dr. Harshberger's most recent research is focused on force employment issues and the use of simulation for analysis and training.

BRUCE HOFFMAN is presently director of the Strategy and Doctrine Program in RAND's Army Research Division and a member of RAND's senior research staff. He was formerly associate director of both that program and the International Security and Defense Strategy Program in RAND's National Security Research Division. Before coming to RAND, Dr. Hoffman taught at Oxford University (from which he received his doctorate) and the University College at Buckingham in England. Dr. Hoffman holds degrees in government, history, and international relations. In August 1994 he will take up the post of Senior Lecturer in International Relations at St. Andrews University, Scotland.

ROBERT D. HOWE is a senior operations research analyst. He graduated from South Dakota School of Mines and Technology and has an M.S. in operations research from Rensselaer Polytechnic Institute. During a 27-year Army career, he served on both the Army Staff and the Joint Staff and was Professor of Military Science at Colorado School of Mines. Mr. Howe's current research is in Army organization and planning with focus on multinational and interservice issues.

DAVID KASSING is associate corporate research manager for Defense and Technology Planning and teaches public budgeting in the RAND Graduate School. He earned an MBA at Cornell and studied economics at the University of Chicago. Before joining RAND, he worked as an associate director of the Arroyo Center at the Jet Propulsion Lab, was president of the Center for Naval Analyses, and served as director of the naval forces division in the Office of the Assistant Secretary of Defense for Systems Analysis. His present research area is strategic mobility programs and operations. Most recently he has been analyzing the risks to mission success when all "required" forces cannot be deployed.

CHARLES T. KELLEY directs the National Security Research Division's program on international security and defense strategy issues. Previously he has been director of both the Resource Management Program, Project AIR FORCE Division, and the Ground Warfare Program, National Security Research Division, and associate director of the Force Employment Program of Project AIR FORCE. Dr. Kelley graduated from the University of Notre Dame, and has a Ph.D. in nuclear physics from Indiana University. His current research is in international security systems, force employment options, and weapon system analysis.

LT. GENERAL GLENN KENT (USAF, retired) received his B.A. in mathematics from Western State College and his M.S. in meteorology from the California Institute of Technology. After serving in World War II, he attended the Naval Postgraduate School and the University of California, receiving an M.S. in radiological engineering. He has served as Assistant to the Chief of Staff, U.S. Air Force, for Studies and Analysis, and as Director of the

Weapons Systems Evaluation Group, Office of the Secretary of Defense. His current research involves a range of national-security subjects, particularly in the areas of strategies, concepts, and allocation of resources.

RICHARD L. KUGLER is a senior social scientist at RAND, where he specializes in European security affairs and U.S. defense planning. He received his Ph.D. in political science from the Massachusetts Institute of Technology. Dr. Kugler has served in the U.S. Air Force and the Office of the Secretary of Defense, and has taught at the National Defense University and George Washington University. He has been associate head of RAND's Political Science Department and a member of the RAND Graduate School faculty. His current research activities include U.S. global military strategy, NATO out-of-area operations, the future of the western alliance, defense cooperation with Russia and Ukraine, Northeast Asian security affairs, strategic planning, and dynamic simulation analysis.

KEVIN N. LEWIS is a senior member of RAND's professional staff specializing in defense planning and budgeting issues. He has been a consultant to the Office of Technology Assessment, and a faculty member at Johns Hopkins University, the University of Southern California, and the RAND Graduate School. Dr. Lewis received a B.S. from Yale University in operations research, and M.S. and Ph.D. degrees in political science from the Massachusetts Institute of Technology. He is presently completing a book on the historical evolution of the U.S. defense posture and budget.

RICHARD F. MESIC is a senior researcher at RAND. He is a graduate of Knox College and Michigan State University with degrees in mathematics, probability, and statistics. The majority of Mr. Mesic's professional employment was at R&D Associates. He also worked with Defense Group, Incorporated (DGI) before coming to RAND. Mr. Mesic's focus over the years has been on strategic nuclear matters, including rationale and requirements, threat and operational analyses, and systems modernization trade studies. His current research emphasis is on counter-proliferation.

NANCY YOUNG MOORE is a senior member of RAND's Resource Management Department, where she works on military logistics and water policy. Dr. Moore has a Ph.D. in water resources systems engineering from UCLA, where she also earned a B.S. and an M.S. in engineering. She is a registered civil engineer with the state of California. Her current research is in adapting best commercial business practices to DoD logistics, particularly in materiel procurement and distribution.

BERNARD ROSTKER is the director of RAND's Defense Manpower Research Center. Recently, he led the congressionally mandated study, "Assessment of the Structure and Mix of Active and Reserve Forces," and the special study for Secretary of Defense Aspin on "Sexual Orientation and U.S. Military Personnel Policy." Dr. Rostker has been the Principal Deputy Assistant Secretary of the Navy (Manpower and Reserve Affairs) and the Director of Selective Service. In the latter capacity, he reorganized the Selective Service System and initiated the current registration program. At RAND, he has served as associate director of the Army Research Division and director of the Army Force Development and Employment program. Dr. Rostker received his B.A. from New York University and his Ph.D. from Syracuse University.

RUSS SHAVER is associate director (research) for Project AIR FORCE, and is currently acting as program director for its Aerospace and Strategic Technology Program. At RAND, Dr. Shaver has directed programs in both Project AIR FORCE and the National Security Research Division, served as an associate department head in the Washington Office, and has been a Corporate Fellow for defense analysis. He has led such diverse studies as Cost/Benefits of the Space Shuttle and The Air Force in the 21st Century. Dr. Shaver received a B.E. in mechanical engineering from Yale University and an M.S. and Ph.D. in applied mechanics from the University of California at Berkeley.

WILLIAM E. SIMONS, currently a RAND consultant, retired from the U.S. Air Force with the rank of colonel. His active military service included two tours of duty at Headquarters USAF and two years in the Office of Assistant Secretary of Defense for International Security Affairs. A former member of the senior staff at both RAND and the BDM Corporation, he is a graduate of the U.S. Naval Academy and holds an Ed.D. degree from Columbia University. Dr. Simons is co-editor (with Alexander L. George) of *The Limits of Coercive Diplomacy*, 2d Edition (1994), which includes his own case study, "American Coercive Pressure on North Vietnam —Early 1965."

WILLIAM STANLEY is a senior engineer in RAND's Defense and Technology Planning Department. Mr. Stanley received a B.S. in aerospace engineering from the University of Texas at Austin and an M.S. in engineering from UCLA. Before joining RAND, Mr. Stanley was employed by McDonnell Douglas. He is currently leading two projects at RAND, one examining strategies for modernizing tactical fighter aircraft forces, and one assessing approaches for sustaining the U.S. industrial base for expendable space launch vehicles. Mr. Stanley has done research in weapon system acquisition policy, aircraft technology assessment, and military systems effectiveness analysis.

JENNIFER MORRISON TAW is a political scientist in RAND's International Policy Department. Ms. Taw received a master's degree in political science from UCLA, where she continues to work towards her doctorate. Ms. Taw has also worked at the Stifting Wissenschaft und Politik in Ebenhausen, Germany. Her current research is on the operational, policy, and doctrinal issues related to low-intensity conflict, peace operations, and operations other than war.

KENNETH H. WATMAN is a senior researcher in RAND's International Policy Department. He graduated from Kenyon College and has a J.D. from

Case Western Reserve University School of Law. He is presently a doctoral candidate in political science at Ohio State University. Mr. Watman's current research is on defense planning, political-military strategy, and arms control.

DEAN WILKENING is a senior researcher in the International Policy Department at RAND. After receiving his Ph.D. in physics from Harvard University, he spent two years studying U.S. defense policy on a Ford Foundation fellowship at Harvard's Kennedy School of Government. His most recent work at RAND involves a fundamental reexamination of U.S. conventional and nuclear deterrence strategies as applied to potential regional adversaries, and analyses of the impact of deep reductions in the U.S. nuclear force structure on post–Cold War U.S. national security strategy.

BARRY A. WILSON is a senior programmer analyst. He graduated from California State University at Fullerton with an M.S. in computer science. At RAND he develops and supports analysis with combat models.